RINITATIS

TRINITY

*Frontispiece*: Portrait of Sir Thomas Pope, Kt, Founder of Trinity College, Attributed to William Stretes.

# Trinity

## 450 Years of an Oxford College Community

CLARE HOPKINS

OXFORD
UNIVERSITY PRESS

OXFORD
UNIVERSITY PRESS

Great Clarendon Street, Oxford OX2 6DP

Oxford University Press is a department of the University of Oxford.
It furthers the University's objective of excellence in research, scholarship, and education by publishing worldwide in

Oxford New York

Auckland Cape Town Dar es Salaam Hong Kong Karachi
Kuala Lumpur Madrid Melbourne Mexico City Nairobi
New Delhi Shanghai Taipei Toronto

With offices in

Argentina Austria Brazil Chile Czech Republic France Greece
Guatemala Hungary Italy Japan South Korea Poland Portugal
Singapore Switzerland Thailand Turkey Ukraine Vietnam

Oxford is a registered trademark of Oxford University Press in the UK and in certain other countries

Published in the United States
by Oxford University Press Inc., New York



First published 2005



British Library Cataloguing in Publication Data
Data available

Library of Congress Cataloging in Publication Data
Data available

ISBN 0-19-951896-3 978-0-19-951896-8

1 3 5 7 9 10 8 6 4 2

Typeset by SNP Best-set Typesetter Ltd., Hong Kong
Printed in Great Britain
on acid-free paper by
Biddles Ltd.,
King's Lynn, Norfolk

# *Foreword*

*The Honourable Michael J. Beloff, QC, President of Trinity College*

The modern appetite for anniversaries causes commemorative events to take place after ever decreasing temporal cycles; but on any view a 450th birthday qualifies for celebration both because nine successive unbroken half-centuries is a substantial period of time and because half a century itself has a resonance denied to, say, a mere decade.

The portrait of Sir Thomas Pope, Founder, which hangs in Hall actually identifies the date of Trinity's Foundation as AD 1554. But before 1752 the new year began on 25 March and the grant of letters patent to Sir Thomas to found a college was dated 8 March, so 2005 is the appropriate year to give thanks for the College's foundation, to reflect on its distinguished past, and to look forward in a spirit of hope and dedication to an equally distinguished future.

In the second of those exercises Clare Hopkins's excellent new history of the College will provide a pronounced stimulus. Trinity has been fortunate in its historians. H. E. D. Blakiston, then Fellow and Tutor, later a notable President, published his own work in 1898, as part of the Robinson series, taking the story up to the end of the nineteenth century. Michael Maclagan, then Senior Tutor, wrote what is in effect an extended, but characteristically elegant, essay in 1955, with a bare two pages devoted to the twentieth century, of which only just over a half had elapsed. Clare has been able to record and evaluate the significant changes which took place in the balance of that mobile era, as well as placing the age of Blakiston himself in its appropriate context. But unlike her predecessors she has eschewed the Durham prologue: she prefers to begin at the beginning.

It is something of a surprise to learn that in terms of age Trinity ranks only fourteenth among the Oxford colleges. However, in consequence it enjoys the luxury of space denied to older foundations within the walls of the city, not least the gardens which together with Hall and Chapel are a trio which has shaped Trinity from its origins until now. And there are other significant features of continuity. The

Foundation itself was marked by a magnificent feast; 'twas ever thus, and, it is to be devoutly wished, ever more shall be so. Philosophy has from first to last been present in the curriculum, though what constitutes Philosophy has changed over the centuries. The tradition of Fellows and Scholars standing until the President enters Hall at dinner has, dare I say, sensibly endured. 'The inherent expense of college life was another deterrent to poorer families' is a quotation from the chapter on the eighteenth century, but equally apposite to the twenty-first.

But other elements have changed. The tranquillity of the College's infant years was disturbed when two of the fellows breached the rule in the Statutes forbidding entry over the College wall; now every member of College has a key and can come and go as he or she pleases. The statutes themselves, seen in the new millennium chiefly as a source of ritual and protocol, were in earlier times a constant legal clog on college progress. In an age of competitive admissions, when selection is made on the basis of perceived academic potential, Founder's Kin is an all but forgotten footnote in history. In the eighteenth century, to hold a College office, nowadays regarded as a duty and a distraction from academic pursuits, was regarded as a privilege, no doubt because of the emoluments attached to it. Women, whose presence in College was once proscribed, now constitute up to half of the junior members.

Clare admirably conveys the extent (often forgotten) to which religion dominated college life until the end of the nineteenth century. We live in a more secular age, where neither President nor Fellows need to be in holy orders or even aspire to holiness, and the Chaplain's functions, if not his duties, are as much pastoral as spiritual. But any decline in faith has not been accompanied by a diminution of morality and high ideals, and the misogyny and racism—for the author's portrayal is warts and all—no longer reflect the College attitude at any level.

I am only the twenty-sixth President of Trinity. And Clare's text will properly remind the reader that the College has been shaped by some significant and long-serving predecessors: Yeldard; Kettell, who built Kettell Hall, Bathurst, who built the Garden Quadrangle and the Chapel, Blakiston, who built the new library, all of whom, except the first, have and merit their own chapter headings: *si monumenta requiris circumspice*. Only one Fellow, Tommy Short, who held a fellowship from 1816 to 1879, qualifies for such a dignity—a prize for longevity if nothing else. Percival, who served as President for only nine years between 1878 and 1887, also has a chapter to himself and so does Norrington, President from 1954 to 1969, but then Percival was responsible for the Front Quadrangle (the Jackson Building), the new President's Lodgings, and Trinity's own scientific revolution, while Norrington presided over the postwar boom years of rapid change and expansion.

Trinity has also been caught up in the ebb and flow of the nation's history; the religious struggles of the sixteenth century; the Civil War and the Restoration. And Trinity has contributed to that history too. Only Christ Church has produced more Prime Ministers—though by some margin—thirteen to Trinity's eighteenth-century three (Wilmington, Chatham, North). Balliol also has three, all in the twentieth century; Brasenose one, like University, Jesus, Somerville, and St John's. Trinity has also produced two Archbishops of Canterbury, one Archbishop of York, a Lord Chancellor, a Chief Justice, a Lord Chief Justice, a Cardinal, a Foreign Secretary, editors of *The Times* and the *Guardian*, a Chairman of the BBC, three Nobel Prize winners, an Olympic 400-metre gold medallist, two VCs, and numerous other statesmen and scholars, heads of houses and headteachers, bishops and judges, novelists and playwrights, actors and composers, poets and scientists.

While Blakiston meticulously listed famous men up to the end of the Victorian age (and praised the College that begat them) Clare Hopkins's concern is with lives at Trinity and not after it. Her interest, as her title makes clear, is in the College as a community which has looked after its members well, and, in return, has generally earned their love and respect.

Newman's appearance owes less to his later distinction as an educationalist and theologian than to his undergraduate letters to his mother. Pitt the Elder does not feature as the Prime Minister who defeated France, the old enemy, but as a father who declined to send his son to his Alma Mater, alas—since a brace of Pitts on the College Register would certainly elevate still higher the College's claim to be a nursery of the great as well as the good.

Clare Hopkins writes learnedly and eclectically of people and places, landscapes and learning, of architecture and accounts, of Grinling Gibbons and Christopher Wren, of Gryphons and Gordouli. Fellows, students, and staff, all elements of a single entity, are equally grist to her author's mill. For those with a taste for the extracurricular, she traces both the origins and the proud history of the Boat Club, head of the river for a quadrennium in the nineteenth century and for longer in the twentieth (and few colleges have enjoyed such riparian triumph), the Claret Club, now complemented by the Zuleika, the one socially select, the other selecting by merit—each no doubt reflecting the *Zeitgeist* of its birthday—and the Gryphon which chameleon-like has been sometimes an essay, sometimes a debating society, as the mood of its Master takes it. She has a fondness for revealing charts, and possibly an over-fondness for collegiate light verse—a perishable commodity from all but the most skilful hands.

A Magdalensis myself, until I took up office I had not appreciated that Trinity's size (in terms of the number of members) was in inverse proportion to its reputation. While always distinctively self-sufficient and at ease with itself, nonetheless it has always, when it has chosen to do so, punched above its weight, both within and beyond Oxford.

We may dare hope that Thomas Pope, looking down at his creation, would, once he had adjusted to a Trinity which is new—lawns where there were once trees, buildings where there were once gardens, women where there were once only men—would recognize that his heirs and successors are seeking to fulfil his original mission in a challenging environment. May Trinity live another 450 years; and may it then find—if books still exist—a chronicler of the intervening period as dedicated, as astute, and as humane as Clare.

# *Preface*

This is the first full-length history of Trinity since H. E. D. Blakiston's *Trinity College* (1898). My introduction to the early history of the college was through reading Blakiston, and I am indebted to his wealth of meticulous research and to his nose for a good story. I also follow gratefully in the footsteps of Michael Maclagan, whose 1955 *History of Trinity College* has ever been a useful resource.

When I first came to Trinity my focus was its archives, their administrative structure and content. But as I met present and past members, I began to appreciate that a college is not an institution, it is a community. As I have written this book, my main focus has been the people of the College: the presidents, fellows, scholars, and servitors; the undergraduates; and the at times almost invisible servants. Their daily lives and changing needs and aspirations have built buildings, laid out gardens, filled libraries, and created Trinity as it exists today.

In case any one should be disappointed, I must explain at the outset that the lives of the great and the good of Trinity's alumni are *not* chronicled in this book. But it is unusual to be famous as an undergraduate, or even for being a fellow. William Pitt, later Earl of Chatham, is here—notable for his excessive battels bills; John Henry Newman, later a Cardinal, is too—because he had one of the greatest exam crises of all time. For the study of Trinity's famous sons, the excellent *Oxford Dictionary of National Biography* is now available, and Appendix IV shows the impressive array of Trinity names that it contains.

Another explanation is due to those who may be dismayed by my decision to modernize the spelling and punctuation of early sources that are quoted in this book. I myself was dismayed when drafts of my early chapters elicited the response, 'how difficult the Founder's letters are to read.' Now, I hope, readers will catch the pace, the immediacy, and the humour of Thomas Pope's correspondence, just as his recipients did in the sixteenth century. And having modernized the Founder, it seemed illogical not to accord the same service to others in Trinity's early years; so I did.

There are many people for whose help I am deeply grateful. My greatest thanks are due to Bryan Ward-Perkins, Trinity's fellow archivist, for his unfailing interest and encouragement. This book would never have been written without his constant support, and a great deal of his time, given sacrificially but never complainingly over several years. He has suggested many important features of this book, and saved me from many serious errors. I am grateful to the President, Michael Beloff, and the Governing Body of Trinity, for allowing me to write this book to mark Trinity's 450th anniversary. My particular thanks to: Peter Brown for his regular advice and assistance on obscure (to me) Latin and Greek; to David Mills and Trudy Watt for insights into the complexities of running a modern college; to Justin Wark, Trinity's estates bursar, for his perspective on the identity of Trinity today. I must also acknowledge a great debt to the late John F. Wright, Trinity's estates bursar and tutor in economics 1955–95, without whose support of the college archive this book would never have been possible, and his untimely death so soon after his retirement deprived me of a kind and expert reader whose advice I have greatly missed. John had a deep understanding of the history of the college's administration, and an uncanny knack of asking the seemingly simple question that invariably led to useful lines of research. One such was 'how many rooms were there in the original President's Lodgings?'; readers will find the answer in Chapter 4.

My thanks are due to Lesley Smith, both Trinity old member and personal friend, who has read my drafts and made numerous useful suggestions and corrections with astonishing speed and insight. And to Alan Coates, old member, old and good friend, and expert on Trinity's old library, who has been of invaluable assistance with the history of the library, its books, and its users. Jan Martin, the librarian, always a supportive colleague and friend, has been of tremendous help in tracking down impossible books, incomprehensible references, and invisible libraries, and how patiently she has listened to me going on about the history of Trinity over the years! I am proud to count myself a member of the Trinity College staff, and I am grateful to all my colleagues who have encouraged and assisted me in my research; in particular to Yvonne Cavanagh, and to both David Goddard and Paul Lawrence, whose expert knowledge has elucidated various aspects of the buildings and gardens.

Trinity College is very fortunate in its archive, for the wealth of documents, photographs, and ephemera that old members have donated during the past two decades. Many of these items I have used in the later chapters of this history; all have provided valuable background information. I know of no other college with such rich and varied sources for the study of undergraduate life. It is always a pleasure to meet old members of Trinity at gaudies and Trinity Society functions, and I am grateful to all those who have talked to me about the College. One Trinity member deserving of special thanks is John Fraser (1952): no press-cutting agency could do a better job.

My thanks also to Andrew Hegarty, who has given generously of his time in reading a large part of this book in draft, and put his considerable knowledge of university history at my service. His advice has improved my text considerably, and pointed me towards some invaluable sources. Another college archivist and historian, Robin Darwall-Smith, has been liberal in his assistance on many areas of my research; and I am particularly grateful for the most cordial over-the-wall advice of John Jones, the archivist and historian of Balliol College.

I used to think that prefaces were formulaic, particularly where authors' families were concerned. But now I know the tremendous sacrifices made by their partners and children. My husband Tony Hopkins has been fantastic in his support, reading, rereading, and proof-reading with untiring cheerfulness and optimism. My children, David, John, and Grace (I have been working on this book since before she was born) have been wonderfully loving and forgiving when they have not had the time and attention that they deserve. My father, Geoff Hands, made an invaluable contribution in the shape of a programme (called 'lsd.exe') which can do arithmetic in 'old money'; I couldn't have written the Foundation Budget without it. Many friends have been a great source of strength and encouragement over the past few years: I thank you all.

My thanks to the following for help or information provided: Robert Beddard; Mr A. Fiddes (yeoman warder at the Tower of London); Penny Hatfield (Archivist, Eton College); Peter Cunich (formerly of Magdelene College, Cambridge); Hugo Brunner; John Maddison (Librarian, Exeter College); Judith Curthoys (Archivist, Christ Church); Alan Tadiello (Assistant Librarian, Balliol College); Giles Hudson (Museum of the History of Science, Oxford); Rob Petre (Archivist, Oriel College); Martha S. Vogeler; Simon Bailey (Oxford University Archives); Barton R. William Powlett. The following institutions and individuals have granted permission for the reproduction of manuscript material: the Bodleian Library, Oxford University (MS Rawl. 1386; MS Rawl. poet. 152, f.40; MS Rawl. Q. f. 5, f.21; MS Aubrey 12/35, 13/162–3; MS Ballard 49, f.172; MS add. D. 114, ff. 17, 20, 28, 75, 122; MS North D. 23, ff. 111, 116; MS North adds. C. 4, ff. 179–82; MS Top e. 41, ff. 53, 57, 265, 267; GA Oxon C 287; MS Eng. d 2606–8.); the National Archives, Kew (PROB11/21 7 Bodefelde; PROB11/42b 10 Chaynay; PROB 11/83 Dixy; SC11/548; E322/190; SP12/161 no. 13); Lambeth Palace Library, London (MS 1835; Davidson Papers vols 2 and 523); the Oxford University Archives (Hyp/B/11, f. 178, /15, ff. 18–19, /18, ff. 123–4, /28 ff.71–4); the Master and Fellows of Balliol College (Jowett Papers III N/208, 229, 234, 256, 261; Conroy Papers I B 20); the Provost and Fellows of Oriel College (Gov 4 B1/2/2; DL 1.6; DELR 7); the Rector and Fellows of Exeter College (Bray MSS, letter of R. Blacow to T. Bray, 1754, 3 Dec.); the Folger Shakespeare Library, Washington (Folger MS lb 558); the Houghton Library, Harvard University (bMS Eng. 1148 (1641 item 13)); Mr Hugh Legge (diary of his grandfather, Hugh Legge); Kathryn Baird (D. Phil. thesis); Nick Salaman ('bread-throwing' notice); Mr Len B. Walker (diary of his grandfather, James Walker); Mr Guy Symondson (correspondence of Sir Arthur and Bevil Quiller-Couch); Mr David Christie-Miller (correspondence and papers of Geoffrey Christie-Miller); Mr Alan Tyser (quotation from recorded interview); Mrs Pauline Cooper (correspondence and diary of Mr Stephen D. Cooper); William Orr (illustration 10.3); Mr Christopher Eve (correspondence and papers of Denis Eve); Professor Dinah Birch (TCA DD 375); William Whyte (D. Phil. thesis). Finally, my sincere thanks to all at the OUP who have played a part in the production of this book, in particular to Anne Ashby, my editor; and to Sandra Raphael for her expert contribution and advice.

C. H.

# *Contents*

# *Plates*

# *Figures*

# *Tables*

# Abbreviations

| | |
|---|---|
| Aubrey, *Brief Lives* | John Aubrey, *Brief Lives*, ed. John Buchanan-Brown (Penguin Classic, 2000) |
| BCO | Oxford, Balliol College |
| BCO Jowett | Oxford, Balliol College, Papers of Benjamin Jowett |
| Blakiston, *Trinity* | H. E. D. Blakiston, *Trinity College* (London, 1898) |
| Bod. Lib. | Oxford, Bodleian Library |
| Bod. Lib. Legge | Oxford, Bodleian Library, MS Eng. d. 2606, 2607, 2608, undergraduate diaries of Hugh Legge |
| *Breviarum* | '*Breviarum* or Short-notes', a collection of anecdotes told by Thomas Short (Fellow 1806–79), TCA OF 10/3a. |
| D | DORSO |
| *DNB* | *Dictionary of National Biography* |
| Durham, *Harris* | William Durham, *The Life and Death of Robert Harris* (London, 1660) |
| Edwards, *Oxford Tutor* | C. E. H. Edwards *An Oxford Tutor: The Life of the Rev Thomas Short BD* (London, 1909) |
| *End of an Era* | *End of an Era: Letters and Journals of Sir Alan Lascelles 1887–1920*, ed. Duff Hart-Davis (London, 1986) |
| Engel, *Clergyman to Don* | A. J. Engel, *From Clergyman to Don* (Oxford, 1983) |
| f. (ff.) | folio (folios) |
| gn. (gns.) | guinea (guineas). A coin worth £1 1*s*. |
| Hatcher, *Binyon* | John Hatcher, *Laurence Binyon: Poet, Scholar of East and West* (Oxford, 1995) |
| *Hearne* I | *Remarks and Collections of Thomas Hearne*, I, ed. C. E. Doble (OHS, 1884) |
| *Hearne* II | *Remarks and Collections of Thomas Hearne*, II, ed. C. E. Doble (OHS, 1884) |
| *Hearne* IV | *Remarks and Collections of Thomas Hearne*, IV, ed. D. W. Rannie (OHS, 1898) |

| | |
|---|---|
| *Hearne* VII | *Remarks and Collections of Thomas Hearne*, VII, ed. under the superintendence of the committee of the OHS (OHS, 1906) |
| HEDB | Herbert Edward Douglas Blakiston |
| Higham, *Dr Blakiston* | T. F. Higham, *Dr Blakiston Recalled* (Oxford, 1967) |
| Hillary, *Last Enemy* | Richard Hillary, *The Last Enemy* (London, 1942) |
| *HUO* | T. H. Aston, general ed., *The History of the University of Oxford*, 8 vols (Oxford, 1984–2000) |
| *HUO* 3 | James McConica, ed. *The Collegiate University*, volume III of *The History of the University of Oxford* (Oxford, 1986) |
| *HUO* 4 | Nicholas Tyacke, ed., *Seventeenth-Century Oxford*, volume IV of *The History of the University of Oxford* (Oxford, 1997) |
| *HUO* 5 | L. S. Sutherland and L. G. Mitchell, eds, *The Eighteenth Century*, volume V of *The History of the University of Oxford* (Oxford, 1986) |
| *HUO* 6 | M. G. Brock and M. C. Curthoys, eds, *Nineteenth-Century Oxford, Part* 1, volume VI of *The History of the University of Oxford* (Oxford, 1997) |
| *HUO* 7 | M. G. Brock and M. C. Curthoys, eds, *Nineteenth-Century Oxford, Part* 2, volume VII of *The History of the University of Oxford* (Oxford, 2000) |
| *HUO* 8 | Brian Harrison, ed., *Twentieth-Century Oxford*, volume 8 of *The History of the University of Oxford* (Oxford, 1994) |
| JFW | John Farnsworth Wright |
| JP | John Percival |
| Larminie, 'Account Book' | Vivienne Larminie, 'The undergraduate account book of John and Richard Newdigate 1618–1621', *Camden Miscellany XXX*, (1990) |
| LPL | Lambeth Palace Library |
| LPL Davidson | Lambeth Palace Library, Papers of Randall Thomas Davidson |
| l.(£) *s. d.* | Pounds (*libri*), shillings (*solidi*), pence |

| | |
|---|---|
| | (*denarii*). British currency before decimalization in 1972. There were 12 (old) pence in a shilling and 20 shillings in a pound. |
| Maclagan, *Trinity College* | M. Maclagan, *Trinity College 1555–1955* (Oxford, 1955) |
| MS | Manuscript |
| n. | note |
| n.d. | No date |
| *Newman Letters & Diaries* | *The Letters and Diaries of John Henry Newman*, ed. Ian Ker and Thomas Gornall, SJ, I (Oxford, 1978) |
| no. | number |
| OHS | Oxford Historical Society |
| ORS | Oxford Record Society |
| OUA | Oxford University Archives, Bodleian Library. |
| p.a. | per annum (each year) |
| Potter, *Headmaster* | Jeremy Potter, *Headmaster: The Life of John Percival, Radical Autocrat* (London, 1998) |
| Pycroft, *Memories* | James Pycroft, *Oxford Memories After Fifty Years*, 2 vols (London, 1886) |
| RB | Ralph Bathurst |
| *Report* | *Trinity College, Oxford, Report* (published annually) |
| SDC | Stephen D. Cooper (Trinity 1943) |
| Skinner 'Letters' | John Skinner, 'Letters from Oxford', Bod. Lib. MS Top. e.41 |
| Stone, 'Oxford Student Body' | Laurence Stone, 'The Size and composition of the Oxford Student Body 1580–1909', in *The University in Society*, ed. Laurence Stone, 2 vols (Princeton, 1975), i, 3–110. |
| TCA | Trinity College, Oxford, Archives |
| TCA Blakiston | TCA OF 20. Papers of Herbert Edward Douglas Blakiston |
| TCA Eve | TCA DD 308. Papers of Denis Eve |
| TCA Higham | TCA OF 22. Papers of Thomas Farrant Higham |
| TCA Lambert | TCA DD 20. Papers of James Lambert |
| TCA Maclagan | TCA DD 231 add. Papers of Michael Maclagan |

| | |
|---|---|
| TCA Memo Book 1–3 | TCA College Governement III, C/1–3. President's Memoranda of College Meetings |
| TCA Walker | TCA 156. Copy diary of James Leonard Walker |
| TCA Wayte | TCA OF 12.1. 'Samuel William Wayte', a collection of memoirs of Samuel Wayte |
| Temple, *Percival* | William Temple, *The Life of Bishop Percival* (London, 1921) |
| TNA | The National Archives (formerly the Public Record Office), Kew, London |
| v. | verso |
| *VCH Oxford, iii* | *The Victoria County History of Oxfordshire* III (Oxford, 1954) |
| vol. | volume |
| *Warton*, ed. Fairer | *The Correspondence of Thomas Warton*, ed. David Fairer (Athens, Georgia, and London, 1995) |
| Warton, *Bathurst* | Thomas Warton, *The Life and Literary Remains of Ralph Bathurst* (London, 1761) |
| Warton, *Pope* | Thomas Warton, *The Life of Sir Thomas Pope*, 2nd edn. (London, 1780) |
| Wood, *History* | *The History and Antiquities of the University of Oxford, by Anthony Wood*, ed. John Gutch, 2 vols (Oxford, 1796) |
| Wood, *Life* | *The Life and Times of Anthony Wood 1632–1695, described by himself*, ed. Andrew Clark, 4 vols (OHS 19, 21, 26, 30, 1891–5) |

# I

# *Thomas Pope, Our Founder*

*On saint Swithin's day, being the fifteenth of July* [1556], *the founder paid a visit to his college. He was accompanied by the bishops of Winchester and Ely, and other eminent personages. He dismounted from his horse at the college gate, where he was received by the president, who stood at his stirrup. At entering the gates he was saluted in a long and dutiful oration by the vice-president: after which the bursars offered him a present of embroidered gloves. From thence he was conducted with the rest of the company into the president's great chamber: the fellows and scholars standing on either side, as he passed along the court. Having viewed the library and grove, they proceeded to dinner in the hall, where a sumptuous entertainment was provided. The president sat on the left hand of the founder, yet at some distance, and the rest of the guests, and the society, were placed according to their rank, and in their proper order. There were twelve minstrels present in the hall; and among other articles of provision on this occasion, four fat does, and six gallons of Muscadel are mentioned. The whole expense of the feast amounting to £12 13s 9d. After dinner they went to evening mass in the chapel, where the president celebrated the service, habited in the richest cope; and the founder offered at the altar a purse full of angels. They then retired to the Bursary; where the founder paid into the hands of the bursars all the costs incurred by this visit: and gave them besides, at the same time, a silver goblet gilt, which being filled with hippocras, he drank to the bursars, and to all the company present. He then departed towards Windsor: but before he left the college, gave with his own hands, to each of the scholars, one mark.*[1]

So Thomas Warton, eighteenth-century fellow of Trinity, professor, poet laureate, and biographer of Sir Thomas Pope, quoted a contemporary description of the Founder's only visit to his new college. It is, sadly, a fantasy.[2] Warton is covering up for the fact that Thomas

[1] Warton, *Pope*, 122–3.

[2] For Warton's provenance of this description, see Warton, *Pope*, appendix XXIX, note a. For a study of Warton's fabrications in the *Life of Sir Thomas*, see H. E. D. Blakiston, 'Thomas Warton and Machyn's Diary', *English Historical Review*, 11 (April 1896).

Pope, although clearly delighted with Trinity, simply did not find it necessary to make the journey from London to Oxford even once, between his formal delivery of the premises to the first President in March 1555, and his death in January 1559. Warton is also providing detail, so manifestly lacking in the surviving records, of some of Pope's great wealth and status, symbolized here by extravagant dining, sumptuous outfits, and elaborate ceremonials, actually trickling down to the President, twelve fellows, and eight scholars. This is the way Trinity College's history should have begun, but did not.

## *The Life and Career of Thomas Pope*

Thomas Pope was not a university-educated man. His father William was a respectable yeoman farmer of Deddington, north Oxfordshire. The family home, Leadenporch House, was one of the largest buildings in the village.[3] William's estate comprised two homesteads, six virgates of land (about 180 acres), ten acres of meadow, twenty of pasture, and two of woodland, held from the Crown at Whithill within the Hundred of Wootton, and a similarly sized property held from the Duke of Suffolk in Hooknorton.[4] Thomas's mother, Margaret Yates of Standlake, near Witney, was William's second wife, and besides Thomas there were three daughters, Alice, Elizabeth, and Julian, and a much younger son, John. Thomas was probably born in 1507, his birthday perhaps on 7 August, or Jesus Day, which was the date he chose for Trinity to celebrate masses for his soul.[5] The Popes were a close-knit family, and Thomas was surely inculcated at a young age with the sense of family duty and loyalty that was so evident in his adult life. He was sent to Banbury Grammar School and Eton.[6]

William Pope's will, which remembered the extended family in its final bequest of 'to every godchild a sheep', implies a natural expectation that his heir would continue in the family farm, which on his death in 1523 was valued at £6 a year, while the capital bequests totalled £220.[7] But Thomas Pope was 16 when his father died, and he

[3] H. M. Colvin, *A History of Deddington* (London, 1963), 5.

[4] Inquisition post mortem of William Pope, Bod. Lib., MS Rawl. 1386.

[5] TCA Statutes, *Additamentum*.

[6] *'Ex scholis Etonensi vel Banburiensi, in quibus ipse olim in grammaticae rudimentis educatus eram'* ('from the schools of Eton or Banbury, in which I was myself once educated in the rudiments of grammar'), TCA Statutes, chapter 8.

[7] Will of William Pope, TNA PROB11/21 7 Bodefelde.

could see a horizon beyond the grass, sheep, and trees of his father. A professional career in the burgeoning Tudor civil service was a very realistic and possible option for a literate young man in the 1520s, and Thomas entered the law. He was first articled to Richard Croke, comptroller of the Hanaper, the chancery department which received fees for the sealing of charters and other documents. Pope retained a lifelong affection for the Croke family, and 'my old master's son Mr Croke' was included with a number of personal friends in Pope's will. He inherited the 'gown of black satin faced with lucern spots [lynx fur]' which is so familiar to all members of Trinity College in the Founder's portrait.[8]

By 1532 Pope was working in the Court of Chancery, and in the following decade he secured a series of increasingly lucrative and important posts. In October 1533 he was appointed Clerk of the Briefs in the Star Chamber, and the same month he received a reversionary grant of the Clerkship of the Crown in the Star Chamber (the position became his when next vacant, which occurred in 1537). His rapid advancement was in part owing to his genuine aptitude for government administrative service, and in part to good relationships with influential patrons, not least his first Lord Chancellor and 'singular good friend', Sir Thomas More.[9] The antiquarian Thomas Fuller quoted Claudius to describe Pope as '*fortunae suae fabrum*: the smith (who by God's blessing) hammered out his own fortune without any patrimonial advantage'.[10] In 1534 Pope became Keeper of the Change and Money in the Tower of London, where, very early on 6 July 1535, he broke the news to the imprisoned More that, before nine o'clock that morning, he was to be executed.

It was surely not lost on Pope that this was a significant date for More, the eve of the feast of St Thomas, and the octave of that of St Peter, origi-nator of the papal supremacy for which he was dying. The scene was described by More's son-in-law, William Roper, who related that More heard the news cheerfully, and expressed gratitude to the King, contentment with the passage of his final days, and a great willingness to 'rid me of this wretched world'. 'The King's pleasure is farther,' said Pope, 'that at your execution you shall not

[8] Will of Sir Thomas Pope, TNA PROB11/42b 10 Chaynay (Codicil).

[9] J. Lewis (ed.), *The Mirrour of Vertue in Worldly Greatnes, or the Life of Sir Thomas More Knight by William Roper* (1733), 98.

[10] Sallust, *Ad Caesarem Senem de Re Publica Oratio*, ch. 1, sect. 2; Thomas Fuller, *The History of the Worthies of England* (London, 1662), 223.

use many words.' More replied that he had intended a long speech, but would readily comply, 'and I beseech you, good Master Pope, to be a means to his highness, that my daughter Margaret may be at my burial.' 'The King is contented already,' said Pope. He was now in tears, and to comfort him, More declared, 'I trust that we shall once in heaven see each other full merrily, where we shall be sure to live and love together in joyful bliss eternally.'[11] By all accounts, More approached his execution, and the scaffold, in sparkling spirits. A final droll exchange with Pope, although not given by Roper, has perhaps the ring of truth. More struck the pose of a medical practitioner and 'further to put him out of his melancholy . . . took his urinal in his hand, and casting his water said merrily: I see no danger but that this man might live longer, if it had pleased the King.'[12]

On which wisecracking note, they parted. There are few other records of Thomas Pope's emotions. Sufficient evidence exists to suggest that, although he was not himself willing to stand against the monarch, he did share More's religious beliefs. In 1558 a Protestant ballad-writer observed of Pope, 'He is a perfect Catholic,'[13] and the foundation of Trinity College revealed a strong religious motivation and enthusiasm for the rites and ceremonial trappings of the Roman Catholic Church. Pope was at his most comfortable during the Catholic reign of Queen Mary, but although he held no office under her devoutly Protestant predecessor, Edward VI, he continued to receive grants of land from the Crown.[14] And it had been during the reign of Henry VIII, the first head of the Anglican Church, that Pope's rise in influence, in station, and in wealth was at its most rapid. In this, he paralleled his next patron, Sir Thomas Audley, the compliant Speaker of the House of Commons who facilitated the legalization of Henry VIII's divorce from Catherine of Aragon, and who, as the 'universally reprobated' Lord Chancellor, sentenced Thomas More to death.[15] Thomas Pope was living in Audley's household in 1535,[16] and the following year was described as his 'servant'.[17]

On 26 June 1535, Pope had been granted a patent for a coat of arms. He chose, '*per pale or* and *azure* on a chevron between three griffins'

[11] Lewis, *Mirrour of Vertue*, 98.

[12] J. H. Gent, *The History of the Life and Death of Sir Thomas More* (1662), 171.

[13] Washington, Folger Shakespeare Library, Folger MS Lb 558.

[14] For example, the Manor of Tyttenhanger was confirmed to Pope by Letters Patent of Edward VI.

[15] James Gairdner, *DNB*.

[16] Blakiston, *Trinity*, 31.

[17] *Letters and Papers Foreign and Domestic of Henry VIII* (1887), x, 573.

heads erased four fleurs-de-lys all countercharged'. This is the coat of arms that Pope gave to Trinity College, although there is no corroborative evidence for Warton's assertion that he ordered it to be 'placed in painted glass, twice in the Hall and twice in the President's Lodging'. Thomas Pope's crest also came to be used by the College, albeit 'improperly': 'two dragons' heads endorsed erased, a coronet about their necks countercharged *or and azure*, set on a wreath *or and vert'*. His motto was very much in character: *Quod tacitum velis nemini dixeris* (what you wish kept secret, tell no one). On 18 October in the same year Thomas Pope was knighted by Henry VIII.[18]

By now he was a married man. The antiquarian Francis Wise noted that Pope was 'divorced' from one Elizabeth Gunston, the marriage being annulled by the Dean of the Court of Arches on 11 July 1536.[19] Pope himself recorded in his breviary his marriage in London on 17 July 1536 to Margaret Dodmer.[20] She was the widow of Ralph Dodmer, a brewer and mercer who had served as Lord Mayor of London in 1529. By his marriage Pope acquired four stepchildren, Ralph, John, Ann, and Mary, and seems to have entered a period of great domestic happiness. In his will he recalled Margaret's 'womanly behaviour, truth, and honesty used towards me', and urged, for her sake, that the friends appointed to be overseers of his will should 'help to set forward' all her children, 'which be friendless'. He bequeathed to John Dodmer a picture of Margaret and 'the first token that ever his mother gave me': a gold bracelet, plus the gold ring attached to it, which 'I wear about my arm'.[21]

On Sunday 15 April 1537, at three o'clock in the afternoon, Thomas's only child was born, a daughter christened Alice. In his breviary Pope listed her godparents, John Ouley, Alice Hill, Joan Baltezer, and Katherine Dyer, but he did not record her early death.[22] On 16 January 1539 Margaret also died.[23] Her grieving husband buried her in a tomb in the north aisle of the choir of St Stephen's Church, Walbrook, in the City of London. He intended it to hold his own body

[18] 'Trinity College', *The University of Oxford*, vol. 3 of *The Victoria County History of Oxfordshire* (1954), 251; Warton, *Life of Sir Thomas Pope*, 16 note x; William A. Shaw, *The Knights of England* (London, 1906), ii, 51.

[19] TCA Misc. Vol. 1, f. 17. Wise was scholar of Trinity 1711, fellow 1718–46. There is no corroborative evidence for this assertion. The records of the Court of Arches were destroyed in the Great Fire of London in 1666.

[20] Bod. Lib., MS Aubrey 31, f. 11d.

[21] Will of Thomas Pope.

[22] Bod. Lib., MS Aubrey 31, f. 8v.

[23] Ibid.

also, and the inscription began *'Hic iacet Thomas Pope . . .'* (Here lies Thomas Pope . . .).[24]

In December 1536, Pope had secured the position that was to make his fortune, the treasurership of the newly established Court of Augmentations. He received an annual stipend of £120 and in addition considerable fees and perks.[25] The Court of Augmentations had the task of valuing and either receiving into the hands of the Crown or selling the lands and properties of the recently dissolved monasteries; it took its name from the increase in royal property that it generated. Pope was the second officer, under the Chancellor, with a solicitor, ten auditors, seventeen receivers, and a chaplain. It was the receivers, or visitors, who generally took possession of the surrendered estates and abbeys, but on one occasion only Thomas Pope was involved in person. On 5 December 1539 he went with the receivers to St Alban's Abbey. Two centuries later the Abbey's historian suggested 'it is highly probable he now first became acquainted with those ample manors and estates which he afterwards procured.'[26] In fact Pope had already been taking advantage of the wealth of church land and buildings suddenly available: earlier that year, after the surrender of the Cluniac abbey of Bermondsey in Southwark, he had ordered the demolition of the eleventh-century abbey church and built 'a goodly house . . . of stone and timber', where he was to reside for the next eight years.[27]

In the nineteen years of its existence the Court of Augmentations was the most important organ of Crown finance in England. Between 1536 and 1540, some 800 monasteries, friaries, and 'regular institutions' passed through the hands of the Court; and between 1545 and 1548 over 2,400 perpetual chanceries. The Dissolution of the Monasteries saw the land revenue collected by the Crown increase by approximately 200 per cent.[28] The Court's Treasurer was well positioned to increase his own estate, especially if, as John Aubrey tartly observed, he 'bought church lands without money'.[29] Aubrey's implication is this: land purchased from the Crown could be immediately

[24] John Stow, *The Survey of London* (London, 1633), 245. Pope's will states that Anne 'wife to my unfortunate brother John' was also buried in this tomb.

[25] *Letters and Papers*, xiii, pt 1, 572.

[26] Peter Newcome, *The History of the Ancient and Royal Foundation called the Abbey of St Alban* (London, 1795), 494 note b.

[27] Stow, *London*, 460.

[28] I am indebted to Dr Peter Cunich for this information.

[29] *Brief Lives, Chiefly of Contemporaries*, set down by John Aubrey between the years 1669 and 1696, ed. Andrew Clerk (Oxford, 1898), ii, 157.

leased to a tenant or tenants at a low rent but on payment of a large entry fine, which would then be available to meet the purchase cost.

The irony of a sincere Catholic getting so rich from the Dissolution of the Monasteries is matched by the further irony that a fortune made under a Protestant king was to be so devoutly bestowed on the establishment of a Catholic college. Pope may, like many, have been bowing to the inevitable in a changing world; he may have been already planning a future act of restitution of some of his wealth to the Church. But Pope's contemporaries had no doubt that it was money alone that motivated him. In 1550 Richard Goodrich wrote despairingly to William Cecil, for whom he was trying to conclude a purchase deal with Pope, 'He is such a money man, and has daily such adventures of gain, as I can do nothing with him.'[30] John Husee, agent to Arthur Plantagenet, Viscount Lisle, Henry VIII's Lord Deputy in Calais, deplored the ungentlemanly way in which Pope disdained bribes in the form of gifts, but would 'rather have ready money than wine, yea and does look for the same.'[31]

Pope's land holdings in 1555 were listed in the Letters Patent that granted him permission to found Trinity College. In Oxfordshire alone he was lord of eighteen manors; he owned property in the parishes of Wroxton, Balscote, Shutford, Dunthorp, Bruern, Showell, Swalcliffe, Swerford, Little Tew, Holcombe, Northleigh, Cogges, Wylcote, Wiggington, Tadmarton, Hook Norton, Sibford Gower, Sibford Ferris, Broughton Pogis, Bradwell, Kencot, Alvescot, Filkins, Clanfield, Holloway, Enstone, Woolaston, Mixbury, Ardley, Fewcott, and Tusmore, and had in addition the rectory of Bradwell, a pension from the rectory of Tadmarton, and the advowsons (the right of presentation to a vacant benefice) of Wylcote, Swerford, Wigginton, Tadmarton, Broughton Pogis, Bradwell, Kencot, Enstone, and Ardley. He owned manors, advowsons, and land besides in the counties of Surrey, Gloucestershire, Warwickshire, Bedfordshire, Derbyshire, and Hertfordshire.[32] Shortly after Trinity's foundation, Pope wrote up detailed notes in 'a book declaring what manors, lands, and tenements' he had had 'of the King's majesty, by purchase, and exchange,' and noting which properties had been sold and exchanged, which had

30 *Calendar of State Papers Domestic of Edward VI* (1992), 175.

31 Lawrence Stone, 'Terrible Times', *The New Republic* (5 May 1982), published in *The Reception of the Lisle Letters 1981–2* (University of Chicago Press, 1982), 45. I am grateful to Hugo Brunner for this reference.

32 TCA Charters A/2.

been given to the College, and which remained in his hands. Twenty-nine Letters Patent from Henry VIII, Edward VI, and Mary are cited, in addition to a range of other transactions. Amid his frenzied buying and selling, it is hardly surprising that Pope sometimes became confused. In his will he bequeathed to the descendants of his brother John the rectory estate in Bradwell, which he had already given to the College.[33]

Pope's earliest acquisition was by Letters Patent of Henry VIII, issued on 6 February 1537.[34] He was granted the manor house and demesne of Wroxton, in north Oxfordshire, five manors (Wollaston, Dunthorp, Dodington, Clyfton, and Hempton), three granges (Holcombe, Holwaye, and Churchill) and land in Thombley and Wardington. Of these, three of the manors, two of the granges, and the land was sold on or exchanged with the Crown. On 1 March he received by Letters Patent the manors and advowsons of Wroxton and Balscote, although the advowsons (excepting the tithes of the demesne land) were also quickly exchanged with the Crown. The manor and its seat, called simply Wroxton Abbey, were leased to Thomas Pope's brother John on 1 August 1551, and these, his first purchases, were to be the largest part of the estate given to Trinity College.[35] Trinity's endowment, which also included Holcombe Grange, may indeed have been marked 'by a touch of sentiment', but there is no evidence for the romantic tradition that the chalice and paten, sent by Pope for use in the College chapel, had ever belonged to St Alban's Abbey.[36]

Thomas Pope's second (or third) wife, 'The Lady Elizabeth' as she is familiarly known to all members of Trinity, married him on 1 January 1541. She was the daughter of Walter Blount, Esquire, of Blount's Hall, Staffordshire, and was a widow. By her first husband, Anthony Basford (or Beresford), Esquire, of Bentley, Derbyshire, she had a son, John. He and Elizabeth's two younger brothers, Walter and William, were also welcomed into Thomas's family circle. In 1547 Thomas and Elizabeth acquired a country residence at Tyttenhanger in the parish of Ridge in Hertfordshire. The house was a former grange of St Alban's Abbey, built by the thirty-first Abbot, John Moot, in 1405, as 'a fair mansion . . . where he and his successors might retire for their ease and pleasure and recreate themselves with their friends and relations'. It was completed by Moot's successor, John de Wheathampstead, who

[33] TCA Charters A/3. [34] TCA Founder A/1. [35] TCA Charters B/1.32.
[36] Blakiston, *Trinity*, 54; H. C. Moffatt, *Old Oxford Plate* (London, 1906), 155.

added a chapel decorated with images of 'all the saints of his own Christian name of John . . . painted on the walls'.[37] The property was granted to Thomas by Henry VIII, and confirmed by Edward VI on 23 July 1547.[38] In London, Thomas and Elizabeth benefited still further from the Dissolution of the Monasteries when they moved into the former Benedictine convent at Clerkenwell, conveyed to Thomas by Letters Patent of Queen Mary in February 1557.[39]

How soon did Thomas and Elizabeth Pope begin to consider the possibility of founding a college in Oxford? In the years following their marriage Thomas was actively involved in the foundation of a Cambridge college, as an executor of Sir Thomas Audley.[40] In 1542, while Lord Chancellor, Audley had refounded the former Buckingham College (a Benedictine house) as 'Magdalene'. The new name not only conferred a note of respectability, echoing as it did the dedication of an established Oxford college, but (pronounced 'maudlin') it was also a clever pun on his own surname. Magdalene College, however, was woefully under-endowed, and no statutes had been drawn up by the time of Audley's death on 30 April 1544. Of the five executors, Thomas Pope seems to have played the greatest part in shaping the new foundation, advising on statutes that 'demonstrate[d] the commonsense touch', and he finally signed the Statutes on 16 February 1554.[41]

## *Durham College*

Around the time of Audley's death a significant document arrived in the Augmentation Office: a detailed survey of the premises of Durham College and St Bernard's College in Oxford.[42] Durham College was a Benedictine foundation which functioned as a cell of the Abbey of St Cuthbert in Durham, from where monks would be sent to study within the University.[43] Durham College's earliest begin-

[37] Henry Chauncy, *The Historical Antiquities of Hertfordshire* (London, 1700), 502.
[38] TCA Founder A/1.
[39] Warton, *Pope*, 169 note u; TNA Add Patent Rolls (Phil. Mar. an.3.5. Feb 1 Par.4).
[40] Peter Cunich, David Hoyle, Eamon Duffy, and Ronald Hyam, *A New History of Magdalene College, Cambridge* (Cambridge, 1994), 55–6. [41] Ibid., 59.
[42] 'The Situation and View of Durham College and Bernard College', TNA SC 11/548. This document is undated, but catalogued as 1544.
[43] For a detailed history of Durham College, see Blakiston, *Trinity College*, chapter 1, on which this account is based.

nings were in 1286, when the abbess and convent of Godstow granted 'arable lands . . . in the suburbs of Oxford . . . and whatsoever right they had in void grounds beside Perilous Hall in Horsemonger Street' to the 'Prior and convent of Durham'. In 1381 Thomas Hatfield, Bishop of Durham, had endowed the College generously, to provide an annual income of 200 marks for the maintenance of a community of eight monks—one selected by the Prior to be Warden—and eight secular scholars. In the following decades a quadrangle was built, with chapel, refectory, library, and chambers, and fifteenth-century accounts of the College suggest a studious and comfortable mode of life for the monks. Durham College was twice surrendered to the Crown: on 31 December 1540 and (after a respite as a cell of the newly reconstituted Cathedral Chapter of Durham) again on 20 March 1545.[44]

St Bernard's, lying to the north of the Durham College precinct, was a Cistercian college, founded by Henry Chichele, Archbishop of Canterbury, in 1437, the same year in which he founded All Souls.[45] The college statutes were issued in 1446. England's Cistercian houses supported the monks studying there, and the buildings were generously endowed in the succeeding century. St Bernard's College was surrendered to the Crown in 1540.[46]

The description of the two neighbouring colleges, possibly drawn up for the office of the Treasury of the Receipts of the Exchequer, allowed for easy comparisons between the two sets of redundant collegiate buildings.[47] Durham stood 'plain north without the walls of Oxford', St Bernard's 'by the street . . . leading towards Woodstock'. The way in to Durham College lay via a long and narrow 'entry' from which a 'gate broad for a cart' gave access to the grove, and to a stable with 'slatted' roof. St Bernard's College boasted 'a fair gate' and over it, two 'storeys in a tower'. It also had a Great Window in its Chapel, an extensive kitchen, and an exit into the fields of St Giles' parish.[48]

In 1546 St Bernard's College and half of the grove of Durham College, which the St Bernard's community had been leasing, were

[44] TNA E322/190.

[45] C. E. Mallett, *A History of the University of Oxford* (London, 1924), i, 406.

[46] *The Victoria History of the County of Oxford*, iii, ed. H. E. Salter and Mary D. Lobel (London, 1954), 258.

[47] Mallett, *History of the University*, i, 136.

[48] 'Situation and View'.

*1.1* Trinity's 'Ancient Entrance', drawn by Francis Wise in 1733.

granted to Christ Church. Later, they were to form the core of St John's College. The Founder of St John's, Thomas White, was a prominent London merchant, who served as Lord Mayor in the year ending November 1554. He and Thomas Pope were well acquainted, although there is no evidence of any detailed collaboration or discussion of their neighbouring colleges.[49]

Durham College lay empty for almost eight years, until on 4 February 1553 the buildings and the remainder of the grove were granted to Dr George Owen of Godstow, the court physician, and William Martyn of Oxford. On 20 February 1555, Owen and Martyn reconveyed the premises to Thomas Pope, who, sixteen days later, was granted the right to establish his College by Letters Patent from Queen Mary and King Philip.

The buildings described by the Court of Augmentations' surveyor were well suited to the plain and religious college that Thomas Pope was to found. One came first to 'a proper fair chapel', which measured 60 feet by 26, and entered through a door in the east end into an antechapel with small altars to left and right. This Chapel had been built in 1406–8 (at a cost of £135 18*s*), and was dedicated in 1409 and licensed for burials in 1412. The altars were dedicated in 1414 and 1417. John Aubrey described them as he saw them in 1642: 'on the back side of the screen had been two altars (of painting well enough for those times, and the colours were admirably fresh and lively). That on the right hand as you enter the chapel was dedicated to St Katharine, that on the left was the taking of our Saviour off from the cross.' Beyond the screen was the choir, which had a high altar and 'fair seats on every side', accommodating fifty. Useful facilities included a 'little pair of organs and a vestry'. The surveyor made no mention of the windows, but Aubrey commented on the 'northern coats' in the east window, and noted 'in every column a figure, e.g. St Cuthbert, St Leonard, St Oswald. I have forgot the rest.' [50]

A door opposite the chapel entrance led to two first-floor chambers; or one turned right into the College's single quadrangle, where, 'out of the quadrangle there [was] a door going in to a low chamber.' This room, known today as the Old Bursary, and the room above it (one of the two chambers reached via the door opposite the chapel in 1544) were—and are—the oldest surviving part of Durham College.

[49] *VCH Oxford*, iii, 258.

[50] 'Situation and View'; Aubrey, *Brief Lives* (Ralph Kettell), 181.

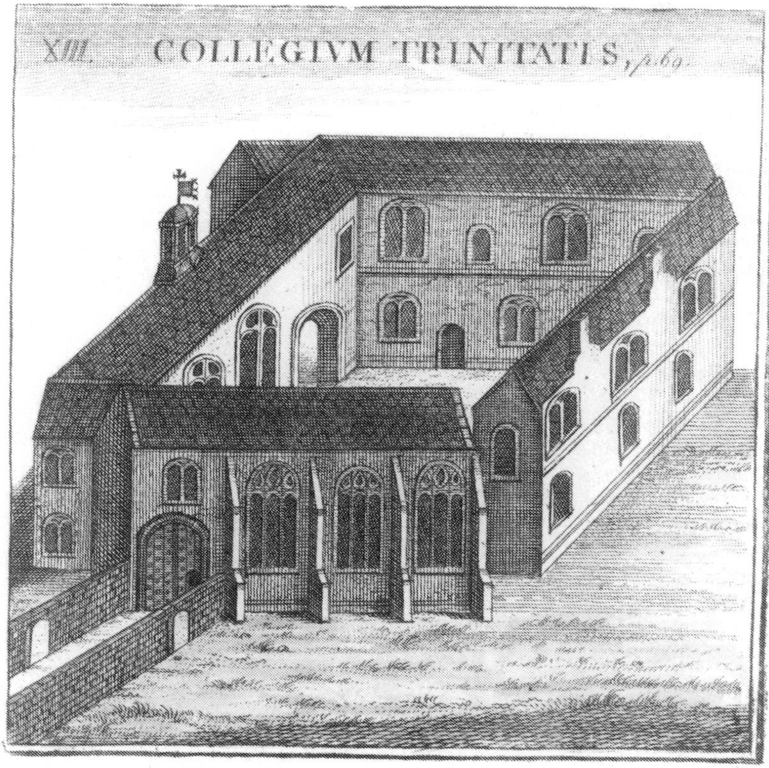


*1.2* Trinity in 1566, as drawn by John Bereblock.

They may have been built in 1326 when the Bishop of Lincoln gave the Prior licence to build an Oratory.

The hall, on one's left, was also 'fair'. It was heated by a fire in the centre of the floor, and the smoke escaped through louvres in the roof, which can be seen in Bereblock's 1566 drawing of the quadrangle (Plate 1.2). The hall measured 60 feet by 30, and provisions could be stored in two butteries to the north of the entry passage. The outer buttery measured 40 feet by 12, the inner 18 by 8. More chambers lay above. Durham College had fourteen chambers altogether and, partitioned off within them, sixteen studies. Most of the chambers were well proportioned; the largest, a first-floor room with its own fireplace and used by the warden, was 40 feet by 18, while the ground

*Table 1.1* Durham College chambers in 1544.

| *Chamber* | *21st-century equivalent [italics indicate original rooms still in existence]* | *Size (in feet)* | *Studies* | *Size of studies (in feet)* |
|---|---|---|---|---|
| Over chapel entry | SCR 'Tower Room' | 20 × 18 | 1 | |
| To W of this | *SCR 'Common Room'* | 36 × 18 | 2 | Each 6 × 8 |
| Low chamber at SE corner of Quad | *Old Bursary* | 36 × 16 | 2 | |
| Above the buttery | Staircase 11, rooms 1 and 7 | 30 × 18 | 2 | |
| Above kitchen passage | | 15 × 12 | 1 | 12 × 12 |
| First floor parlour, N range of quad | Above Pig and Whistle | 21 × 18 | 1 | 'little' |
| 2 low chambers | Staircase 17, ground floor | 40 × 18 | | |
| Warden's chamber | Staircase 17, first floor | 40 × 18 | 2 | |
| NE corner of quad, ground floor | *Staircase 10, Domestic Bursar's room* | 27 × 18 | 2 | |
| NE corner, first floor | *Staircase 10, room 3* | 7 × 18 | 1 | |
| A fair chamber | *Bursary office* | 27 × 18 | 2 | |
| A fair chamber above | *Danson Library* | 27 × 18 | | |
| SE corner of quad, adjoining vestry | *Staircase 9, Accountant's office* | 18 × 15 | | |

*Source*: TNA SC11/548.

floor beneath was divided into two. The smallest chambers were over the kitchen passage, just 15 feet by 12, and in the south-east corner of the quad, 18 feet by 15. The accommodation was ample for the monastic community, and indeed, some rooms were rented out to other members of the University.[51]

A library for study and a grove and gardens for recreation completed the College facilities. The first-floor library was entered from a small landing, to which stairs led up from an entry in the quad below. It measured 27 feet by 18, and was 'well desked and well floored'. The Library had been built in 1417–18. Canon Streeter considered its floor to be 'remarkable'. Medieval libraries, although not usually built on the ground floor, were often tiled. But the Durham College Library had a double timber floor, with a longitudinal central beam giving additional support to strong transverse joists, on top

[51] For example, Gilbert Kymer, physician to Duke Humfrey and Chancellor of the University 1446–53, dated his Acts from Durham College. H. E. D. Blakiston, 'Some Durham College Rolls,' pt 1, *Collectanea III*, ed. Montagu Burrows (OHS 1896), 17.

of which were laid planks that ran longitudinally. Above these was a second floor of very wide oak boards which ran lengthways on the west side of the Library and crossways on the east. The surveyor also observed that the library had 'a timber floor over it'; he meant the timber boarding of the arched ceiling, the barrel shape of which can still be seen today in some of the attic rooms above.[52] The library windows, although not mentioned in the survey, were glazed and painted. Aubrey remembered seeing figures and inscriptions, including 'an image of John of Beverly in the windows with some mention of his name'. In 1646 William Dugdale made detailed notes on the heraldic devices depicted.[53]

The surveyor had paced out the grove, and at its largest found it to be 196 by 183 yards. Half of this ground was to be conveyed with the premises of St Bernard's College to Christ Church and ultimately to St John's College, but, as the surveyor remarked in conclusion, it '[stood] commodiously for both the Colleges'. Durham College had three gardens: one to the east of the quadrangle, measuring 43 by 12 yards; one to the north, 11 by 21 yards; and one to the east of the college entrance, 50 feet by 36.[54] For more than a century, the northern garden was enjoyed as the Fellows' Garden of Trinity College, but in 1665 it was to disappear under the first side of the Garden Quadrangle. The garden to the east of the entrance way remained a secluded and sunny enclosure beneath the southern windows of the Chapel until 1737, when it was sacrificed to make way for a wider entrance. The garden to the east of the quadrangle, however, was appropriated to the presidency, and it remains the President's garden today.

## *The Founder's Motivation*

Thomas Pope had an example before him: Audley's foundation of Magdalene College in Cambridge; and the opportunity: vacant and suitable buildings at his disposal in Oxford. He also had the means,

[52] B. H. Streeter, *The Chained Library: A Survey of Four Centuries in the Evolution of the English Library* (London, 1931), 224–5.

[53] Richard Gameson, 'The Medieval Glass', in Richard Gameson and Alan Coates, *The Old Library* (Oxford, 1988), 16–17. Aubrey, *Brief Lives*, 11; Bod. Lib., MS Dugdale 11, f. 148v–149r.

[54] Although it is not mentioned in the survey, there was a fourth garden, today's Fellows' Garden, lying to the west of the entrance, and presumably also accessible via the 'low chamber'.

for he was one of the richest men in the realm. What then of his motivation? On 19 July 1553, Mary Tudor became Queen of England, and on 4 August Pope was sworn in as a member of her Privy Council. The five-and-a-half years of Mary's reign were the climax of Pope's career. He relished the restoration of the Catholic faith to the English Church, and undertook a range of commissions with characteristic devotion and efficiency. On 29 July 1553 he was one of the councillors appointed to arrest Lord Russell and other conspirators in the Duke of Northumberland's failed attempt to secure the throne of England for Mary's Protestant rival, Lady Jane Grey.[55] In February 1554, Pope was one of a number of councillors deputed to remain in London during the Court's absence and take charge of victualling the Tower. On 29 October he was appointed to the commission that examined and assessed the fines of those involved in Northumberland's rebellion.[56] Stowe's account of Mary's reign describes Pope and others standing 'upon the leads' of the White Tower, watching the violent scene below when the rebel Sir Thomas Wyatt was arrested, and remonstrating openly with one of the conspirators as he was brought into custody.[57] Pope put his considerable financial expertise at the service of Queen Mary when, on 15 March 1555, he accepted a commission to examine and balance the accounts of Sir Thomas Gresham, the Antwerp agent through whom Mary raised loans,[58] and he showed his staunch faith when, on 8 February 1557, he was appointed to a commission for the suppression of heresy.[59]

One task which Thomas Pope seems to have found particularly agreeable was the guardianship of the Princess Elizabeth. Elizabeth was the heir presumptive to the throne, a Protestant threat to the Queen, and yet more congenial to Mary's consort, Prince Philip of Spain, than the next in line, Mary Queen of Scots, who was betrothed to the Dauphin of France. As early as 1554 Pope seems to have been in the Princess's company while she was confined under Mary's considerable displeasure at Ashridge. On 8 July 1556 he was chosen to reside with Elizabeth in more gentle custody at Hatfield House in

[55] Samuel Haynes (ed.), *A Collection of State Papers, relating to affairs in the reigns of king Henry VIII, king Edward VI, queen Mary, and queen Elizabeth, from 1542 to 1570, transcr. from authentick memorials left by W. Cecill lord Burghley* (London, 1740), 162.

[56] Haynes (ed.), *A Collection of State Papers* 193.

[57] John Stow, *The Annals of England* (London, 1615), 621.

[58] Thomas Rymer, *Foedera* (London, 1800), xv, 371.

[59] Gilbert Burnet, *The History of the Reformation of the Church of England*, 'A Collection of Records' (London, 1681), ii, pt 2, 311.

Hertfordshire. This is another area, close proximity to royalty, where Thomas Warton found the known facts of Pope's life inadequate, and the *Life of Sir Thomas* contains charming but sadly unsubstantiated descriptions of masques, plays, and courtly entertainment laid on by the kindly gaoler.[60] There is better evidence, however, for Pope's tactful handling of the potentially dangerous proposal of marriage which Elizabeth received from Eric of Sweden in 1558, and he was trusted by the Council to 'open the cause' of the Earl of Devonshire's conspiracy with her in July 1556. One letter to Thomas Slythurst suggests that he took pleasure in discussing events in his newly founded College with his royal charge.[61]

Pope was in genuine sympathy with many of Mary's policies. The Queen took a particular interest in Oxford University, and Crown and gown cooperated willingly during her reign. The state had long presumed on a supply of servants and clerics from the universities, and Mary was now seriously in need of stability in her administration. But the number of graduates had fallen sharply during the reign of Edward VI. The University needed state protection and patronage, in return for which it had already accepted (mostly with reluctance) and subsequently rejected Protestantism. Mary's 1554 gift of six rectories had tripled the University's annual income.[62] Thomas Pope, like Thomas White, founder of St John's College, could hardly have pleased his monarch more than when he established a college that could play a loyal part in her reformed University. The opening chapter of the statutes which Pope gave to Trinity begins with a forthright declaration of the Founder's impeccably loyal motives. Trinity College was established *ad gloriam et honorem eiusdem Altissimi Conditoris* (for the glory and honour of the Most High Creator), to serve the *proventum et publicam patriae meae utilitatem* (success and public benefit of my country), and *orthodoxae fidei religionisque Christianae incrementum* (to build up the orthodox faith and Christian religion). Durham College had been dedicated to the Trinity, the Blessed Virgin Mary, and St Cuthbert, and Thomas Pope chose 'Trinity' to be the name of his new foundation.

The Founder had an educational purpose too. The new college was intended *ad perpetuam pauperum scholarium in Academia degentium*

[60] Warton, *Pope*, 87.

[61] Burnet, *History of the Reformation*, i, 37; TCA Misc. Vol. I, 1/3.

[62] Claire Cross, 'Oxford and the Tudor State from the Accession of Henry VIII to the Death of Mary', *HUO* 3, 140–1.

*sustantionem* (for the perpetual maintenance of poor scholars residing in the University), an objective which brought in a useful return. Pope saw his foundation as a convenient source of literate servants. In December 1557 he wrote to Trinity's first President to request an educated 'poor boy' to be Lady Elizabeth's secretary, and 'a sober fellow' who could serve as a steward. Pope recognized the importance of education for members of his family circle, and urged that Latin and self-discipline be drummed into his young stepson, John Basford.[63]

If Thomas Pope had any personal scruples over having made his fortune from the Dissolution of the Monasteries, these must have been at least in part assuaged by the foundation and endowment of Trinity College. Moreover, he was a rich and self-made man with no living child of his own, and to have his name attached to a permanent institution offered more than mere recognition and prestige. It promised a realistic chance of immortal fame. The College's official title was, and is, 'The College of the Holy and Undivided Trinity in the University of Oxford, of the foundation of Thomas Pope'. Four and a half centuries after his death, members of Trinity remember him in the Founder's prayer, and they sit daily beneath his portrait in the Hall.[64]

[63] TCA Misc Vol. I, 5/13, 7/17, 12/27.
[64] Letters Patent 8 March 1555, TCA Charters A/2.

# 2

# *The College of the Holy and Undivided Trinity*

## *The Foundation of Trinity College*

Trinity College cannot be said to have burst onto the Oxford scene. It was the fourteenth surviving college of the University, and the fourth sixteenth-century foundation. Brasenose dated from 1509, but had a direct link to the thirteenth-century Hall of the same name. Corpus Christi, 1517, had a President, three Professors who lectured to the University, twenty fellows, twenty scholars, and chaplains, clerks, and choristers; it had a clear aim, to strengthen the secular clergy, and a clearly structured modern curriculum. Wolsey's projected Cardinal College, established by Henry VIII as Christ Church in 1546, was grand indeed, with a dean, eight canons, one hundred students (fellows), and eight chaplains. Its magnificent new buildings engulfed Oxford's cathedral. Trinity, however, had no particular distinction. It was to have a President, twelve fellows, eight scholars, and a single, second-hand quadrangle; it was small, poor, and ordinary. The ways in which Trinity was unique, and indeed was a forerunner of some of the most significant characteristics of the Elizabethan colleges in Oxford, were not at once apparent.

The structure and administration of the new College were clearly set out in the thirty-nine chapters of the College Statutes. These were to be strictly observed, 'minding,' said Pope, 'not for any mans pleasure . . . to alter and change any of them', and the President would be bound by solemn oath to uphold and enforce them.[1] Thomas Pope's choice for President fell on Thomas Slythurst BD, fellow of Magdalen College, Oxford, and vicar of Chalfont St Peter, Bucks. According to Thomas Warton, they were old friends.[2] Slythurst had the necessary

[1] Pope to Thomas Slythurst, TCA Misc. Vol. 1, 2/6.
[2] Warton, *Pope*, 246.

experience. He had been a fellow of Magdalen College since 1532 and had held a number of offices there, as dean of arts in 1538, 1539, and 1552, bursar in 1540 and 1541, and dean of divinity in 1543. At the time of his appointment he had been at Chalfont St Peter for ten years, and had recently also acquired the rectory of Chalfont St Giles and a canonry at Windsor. In 1553 he had been disappointed in the election to the presidency of Magdalen.[3]

Thomas Pope had great confidence in his first President. In a Latin address sent to the new college from Tyttenhanger, and dated 1 May 1556, the day that the Statutes came into force, the Founder praised Slythurst fulsomely. He was a man 'so knowledgeable, so equipped by his education, so conspicuous by the excellence of his behaviour, so vigorous in his conduct and practice of affairs and so devoted to virtue and the love of godliness' that he would be well able to steer the infant foundation through its initial difficulties, and indeed be in every way 'the guide in matters spiritual and temporal, and the master of business internal and external' that Pope envisaged as his ideal head of house.[4]

Eleven letters from Pope to Slythurst are preserved in the Trinity College Archive, the majority written in the Founder's own hand. They reveal an effective working relationship. Slythurst made several visits to his patron's home at Tyttenhanger, where the two men worked together on drafting the Statutes. One letter, dated at Clerkenwell on 27 November 1556, shows Pope writing easily on a range of administrative matters relating to college finance, equipment, and personnel. 'I remember you told me at your being with me at Tyttenhanger,' he says, regarding the budgetary deficit. Slythurst, who has informed Pope of an intended benefaction to the library, is told: 'Touching Mr Rawe's books . . . I pray you do therein according as you have written to me.' 'I am content,' continues Pope, that the President should have as many servants as he thinks good, and 'I am likewise pleased' that he should handle decisions regarding the admission of undergraduate battellers. He advises on the best price for stone—'a groat the load, or as cheap as you can'—and on preaching licences for three of the fellows, then lists the various useful items—censers, cruets, altar candlesticks, and other items for the chapel, plus five dozen black chains for the Library and four small

[3] William Dunn Macray, *A Register of the Members of St Mary Magdalen College, Oxford* (London, 1897), ii, 58, 70.

[4] TCA Statutes, Founder's Address, and Chapter 1.

books—which the letter-carrier should also be delivering. A more powerful musical instrument for the Chapel, however, must wait, and meanwhile Slythurst must depend on the generosity of the Founder of St John's College: 'for as much as it is evil carriage of my organs this winter Mr White at my request is content you shall have his little organs till the beginning of Summer when I may convey mine to you without hurting of them.' Pope responds enthusiastically to another request from Slythurst, 'and because ye write you have great need of a standing cup to drink wine in, Mr Southern's money shall be bestowed in two standing cups gilt with covers.'[5]

Thomas Pope's one and only visit to Trinity was on 28 March 1555, the day of his formal conveyance of the premises to the College. The President, however, was not there to meet him. Three days earlier, Slythurst had signed a power of attorney instructing two of the intended fellows, Stephen Markes and Robert Newton, to complete the ceremonial procedure of receiving seisin of the premises in his place.[6] The occasion was witnessed on behalf of the University by John Warner, Vice-Chancellor and Warden of All Souls, Owen Oglethorp, President of Magdalen, and Robert Morwent, President of Corpus. Walter Wright, archdeacon of Oxford, attended, also John Brown, canon of Windsor. The Pope family were there in force: Thomas's brothers-in-law Edward Love and Henry Bryan, his stepsons Ralph Dodmer and John Basford, his nephew by marriage Simon Perrot, and John and Humphry Edmundes from the family of Thomas's father's first wife. A number of local gentlemen had been invited to witness the transaction too: John Bylling, John Heywood, John Myleward, John Lawrence, Bartholome Plott, and Edmund Powell, Esquire. Among the crowd was a young protégé of Queen Mary's called Arthur Yeldard.[7]

Nothing else happened that day. The buildings remained empty.[8] No service was conducted in the Chapel; no meal was served in the

[5] Thomas Rawe was known to Slythurst as a Canon of Windsor; Thomas Southern was the Treasurer of Oxford Cathedral; and Edward Love, gent., was husband to Thomas Pope's sister Alice. TCA Misc. Vol. I, 2/6.

[6] TCA Charters A/3.

[7] Power of Attorney 1555, 27 March, TCA Charters A/3; Foundation Charter ('Deed of Erection') A/4, and endorsement.

[8] According to Anthony Wood the Durham College buildings had been used to house 'scholars of the University upon their own charges, and under the government of Walter Wright.' *Survey of the Antiquities of the City of Oxford composed by Anthony Wood*, ed. Andrew Clark, ii (OHS 1890), 273–4.

Hall. Thomas Pope's plans were still far from finalized and at this date he was actively considering the additional endowment of a school at Hook Norton, Oxfordshire, to be known as 'The Jesus Schoolhouse'.[9] It was almost another year—Lady Day (25 March) 1556—before revenues were handed over to the new foundation, and only then did the first members of Trinity College began to reside.

It had not proved easy to find men to be the fellows. 'It is remarkable,' remarked H. E. D. Blakiston in 1898, 'that not one of the original fellows was qualified under the statutes' (which, of course, were yet to be written).[10] The Statutes stipulated men born in the Founder's own manors, otherwise in counties in which he owned land. There were to be twelve, of whom no more than two should be from any one county, except Oxfordshire, which was allowed five. But the 'Deed of Erection' named only eight men. Stephen Markes was a native of Cornwall, John Barwick and Roger Crispin had been born in Devon, and James Bell in Somerset. Between them they had some limited experience of an Oxford fellowship, Bell at Corpus Christi College for five years, Markes and Crispin at Exeter College for six and seven. Barwick had been a clerk and chaplain at Magdalen. Robert Newton was another West Country man, a fellow on the Devonshire foundation of Exeter College since 1548. The remaining three, John Richardson, Thomas Scott, and George Simpson, were all from Cumberland, and all scholars of The Queen's College.[11]

When the first fellows moved into the College, Robert Newton, one of the two who had formally represented President Slythurst in the ceremony of receiving seisin of the College premises from the Founder, was not one of them; he had instead chosen to remain at Exeter College, where, in October 1557, he was elected Rector. The gaps in the ranks, however, had been filled, and now Arthur Yeldard headed the list. He was from Northumberland, a graduate of Clare Hall, Cambridge, and had briefly held a fellowship at Pembroke Hall, Cambridge. Besides enjoying royal patronage, he had some experience as a private tutor, another factor that had secured Pope's approval. Then there was John Perte, a Warwickshire man, originally

[9] The proposed school at Hook Norton was given royal approval in the Letters Patent of 8 March 1555. There is no corroborating evidence for Warton's assertion of Pope's 'intended foundation' of a school at Deddington: Warton, *Pope*, appendix 16, 331–2.

[10] Blakiston, *Trinity*, 53.

[11] I am grateful to Dr John Maddicott of Exeter College for information on the careers of John Barwick and Robert Newton.

nominated by Pope to a scholarship but now to be a fellow, and three more recruits: George Rudd, born in Westmoreland, another scholar of Queen's; Roger Evans, a Cornishman, fellow at Exeter for three years; and Robert Bellamy, from Yorkshire.

The Founder intended eight scholars on the foundation of Trinity College, but only four had been named in March 1555. There was now a line-up of seven: John Langster (Yorkshire), John Arden (Oxfordshire), Reginald Bray (Bedfordshire), John Comporte (Middlesex), Robert Thraske (Somerset), William Saltmarsh (Yorkshire), and John Harris (Gloucestershire). Langster was 19 years old, Harris 17, the rest 18.[12]

Trinity College was officially opened on 30 May 1556, the Vigil of Trinity Sunday. In his capacity as a public notary, the President of Corpus, Robert Morwent, both conducted the proceedings in the Chapel and recorded them on the opening page of the new College Register, which had been made at the considerable cost of 2*s* 11*d*.[13] Thomas Slythurst took his oath as President, and he was followed in turn by the twelve fellows—Arthur Yeldard went first—and the seven scholars. The President and fellows then proceeded to elect the officers of the College. On the recommendation of Thomas Pope, Stephen Markes was appointed vice-president and Yeldard philosophy lecturer. John Barwick was elected dean, John Richardson and John Perte bursars, and James Bell rhetoric lecturer, and each in turn was sworn in according to the Statutes. Next, Robert Morwent handed over the college seal, which he had received from the Founder, and it was taken immediately to the security of the *gazophylacium*, or treasury. It is a pointed oval measuring 3.5 by 2.5 inches, which depicts a traditional representation of the Trinity—God the Father and Son seated on a throne, with God the Spirit as a dove above them—over Thomas Pope's coat of arms. The day ended in the Chapel as the members of the foundation offered up evening prayers to the most holy Trinity, with singing and music.

The following morning the foundation celebrated Matins and the other canonical hours, followed by Mass, and between the services Slythurst preached to a large congregation which had gathered to wish the new College well. Everyone, including the heads of houses,

[12] The 8th place seems to have remained unfilled, although the early 17th-century 'Kettell's Register' names one 'Starkie' as 'among the first scholars.'

[13] TCA *Computus* 1556, external payments. The following account is based on Morwent's in TCA Register A, 1–4.

was then entertained to 'a splendid and magnificent banquet' largely provided by the Founder's friends and family. The College Register carefully records the names and gifts of these, the very first Trinity College Benefactors. The list is headed by Thomas Southern, Treasurer of Oxford Cathedral, who had already given £20 in gold, and had promised fifty books in his will.[14]

There was quite a feast:

| | |
|---|---|
| Edward Love | 48 rabbits, 3 lambs, 19 capons, 3 suckling pigs, 14 goslings, 62 young pigeons, 2 fallow deer and 1 deer calf |
| Sir George Gyfford, Kt. | 24 rabbits and 12 chickens |
| Master Crocker, gent. | Half an ox and a lamb |
| Master Edmunds, gent. | 1 fallow deer and 1 deer calf |
| Master Anthony Arden, gent. | Half a deer calf, 2 goslings, 1 suckling pig and 1 capon |
| Master Richard Arden, gent. | Bread (worth 6 shillings) |
| Master Platt, gent. | 1 sheep and 2 goslings |
| Master Yates, gent. | 1 sheep |
| Orpwoode of Northleigh | 1 sheep |
| Brian of Cogges | 2 goslings and 2 chickens |
| Master Irish, townsman | 1 gallon of wine |
| Master Furse, townsman | 1 gallon of wine |
| Master Bridgman, townsman | Half a gallon of wine with strawberries.[15] |

When the banquet had finished everyone expressed their profound thanks, and all the guests and strangers departed, praying heartily for the well-being of their hosts. Then there was silence, as befitted the 'future house of study and learning'. The celebrations had been very expensive. Providing for the 'gentlemen's servants', carriage of their various gifts, and the labour and arrangements of the banquet

[14] Southern's will was dated 30 April 1556; he died in 1557. Warton, *Pope*, 324–5 note d.

[15] For details of how these donors were connected to the founder—Platt, for example, 'appears to have married the Founder's uncle's daughter'—see Warton, *Pope*, appendix 13, 325–8. 'Bridgman' may have been Sir Thomas White's brother-in-law.

had cost 18*s* 9*d*. Added to this were costs incurred 'in the feast of Holy Trinity beyond all allocations' amounting to 26*s* 5*d*.[16] By the end of November the fellows were still struggling with the bill, but they received little sympathy from Thomas Pope, who suggested brusquely, 'then the want must be supplied with part of the £12 appointed for reparation of the college and kitchen stuff'.[17]

## *College Finance and Resources*

The first account of Trinity College runs from Lady Day to Michaelmas (25 March to 29 September) 1556. The total income during this period was £184 8*s*, but of this £94 5*s* 8*d* (the statutes said £100) was a one-off 'loan' from the Founder to be used only for the temporary relief of cash-flow problems. The final projected annual income of the College—£226 11*s* 8*d*—was set out clearly in an appendix to the Statute Book.[18] The largest source of revenue was £150 from the rents of the three manors with which Pope endowed the College—Wroxton with Balscote, and Holcombe, both in Oxfordshire, and Great Waltham in Essex. Rents from two parsonages (Bradwell in Oxfordshire and Navestock in Essex) brought in £25, and a portion of the tithes payable from Stoppesley, near Luton in Bedfordshire, was worth £40.

The manor and advowson of Great Waltham had not originally formed part of Pope's endowment. But from the beginning it was all too apparent that the new College was struggling financially. In several important areas—such as building repairs and heating the Hall—the money that had originally been allocated was simply not sufficient. Moreover, Pope had initially neglected to make any financial provision for gaudy days, and for the priests celebrating 'obits'—masses for the souls of the dead—which was a function of the College of particular importance to both Lady Elizabeth and himself. A further cost was the decision taken by Pope to increase the number of scholars to twelve. As a short-term solution, on 10 September 1557 he conveyed his manors of Sewell and Dunthorp in Oxfordshire to Trinity, thereby generating additional income of

16 TCA *Computus* 1556, external payments.
17 TCA Misc. Vol. I f.2/6.
18 'Value of the Lands', TCA Statutes.

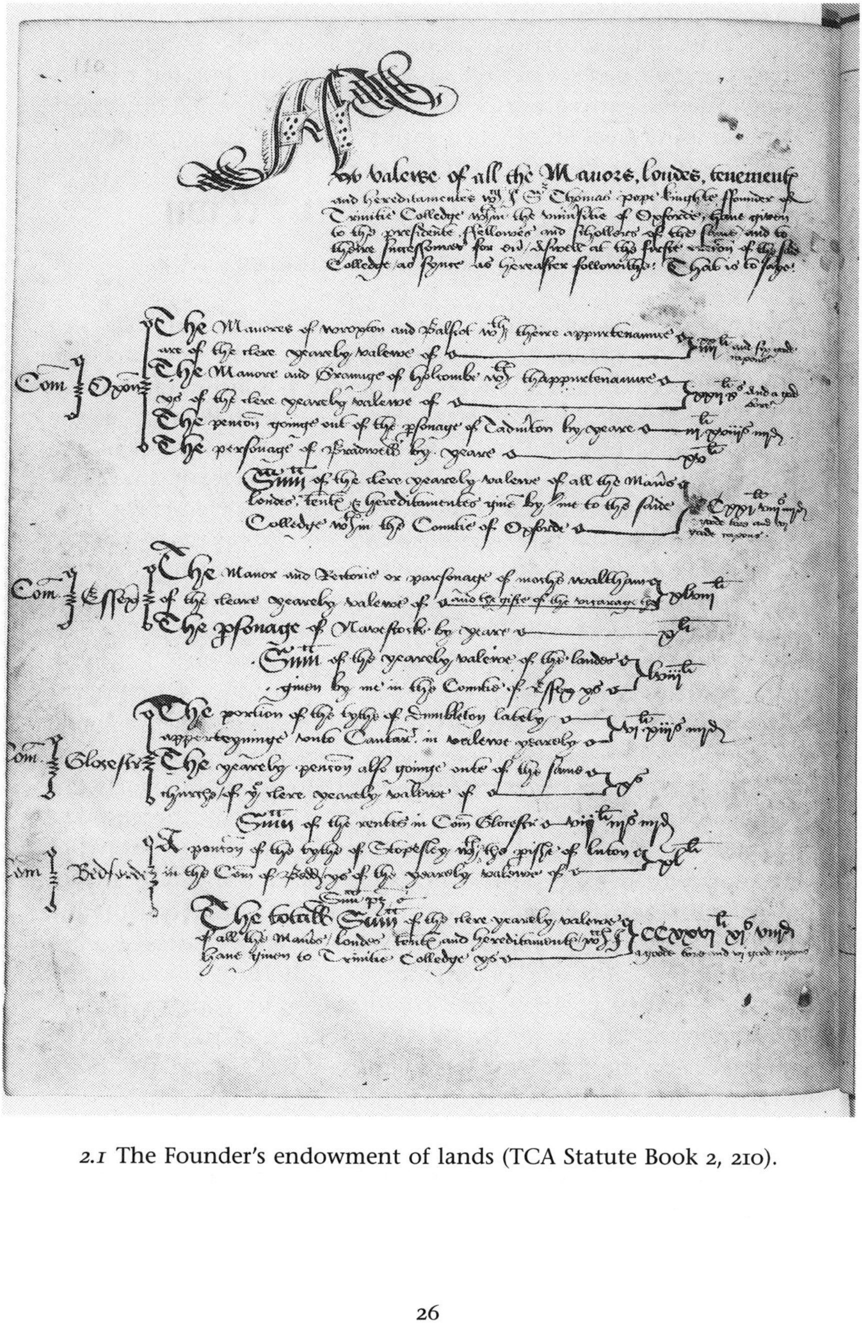

*2.1* The Founder's endowment of lands (TCA Statute Book 2, 210).

£48 8*s*, enough to meet these costs and to finance other such necessities as more candles, increased commons for the President, and payments to one of the fellows to 'play at organs and teach the scholars to sing'. Careful provision was made for the future substitution of other premises of equal or greater value, and on 24 June 1558 Pope paid £900 for the rectory, advowson, and glebe lands of Great Waltham in Essex. Four days later he granted his college the manor and rectory, valued at £48 *per annum*, also tithes and a pension from Dumbleton in Gloucestershire, valued at £6 13*s* 4*d* and 10*s* respectively. Sewell and Dunthorp returned once more to his control.[19]

How the revenue was to be spent was clearly laid down by the Founder, and any surplus (in theory some £17) was to be 'always employed as is declared in the statute'.[20] There was to be an annual audit, held within eight days of the feast of St Andrew (30 November) and a private and secure *gazophylacium*, or treasury, provided for custody of a large strong chest, with three different locks and another lockable cash box within. The keys were held by the dean and the two bursars, and the chest was also to be used for the custody of the statute book, deeds, bonds, and college seal. The room above the Chapel arch was chosen for this purpose; and the chest, with three different locks and another lockable cash box within, still stands today in the secure archive room above the Chapel arch.[21]

Trinity's main overheads—£179—were the stipends and commons of the members of the foundation and household. The stipend was paid quarterly, and the commons comprised a weekly allocation of bread, butter, cheese, and beer. Fellows who held an office received additional payments. The College had six servants on the foundation, headed by the important figure of the manciple or steward, who received a lower rate of commons but the same stipend as that paid to the fellows. Both he and the cook, who was on the same stipend as the scholars, could expect to augment their income by the 'advantages and avails' of their positions.

The Founder's budget made provision for the predictable expenses of the College year. The statutes allowed 20*s* for Chapel expenses—wine, bread, incense, and candles—but this was more than doubled by the addition of £3 from the endowment of Great Waltham and

[19] TCA Statutes; Charters, B/5.2, 6.1.

[20] The Founder signed his assent to the valuation of the college, dated 1 January 1558, in his corrected and witnessed copy of the statutes, TCA Statutes, A/1.

[21] TCA Statutes Chapter 33.

*Table 2.1* Trinity College budget 1558.

| Income | | | | |
|---|---|---|---|---|
| *County* | *Estate* | *Annual Income* | *Additional Payments* | *Total by County* |
| Oxfordshire | Manors of Wroxton and Balscote | £80 | 6 capons | |
| | Manor and Grange of Holcombe | £22 | 1 boar | |
| | Pension from Tadmarton Parsonage | £3 18*s* 4*d* | | |
| | Bradwell Parsonage | £15 | | £121 8*s* 4*d* |
| Essex | Manor and Rectory of Great Waltham | £48 | | |
| | Parsonage of Navestock | £10 | | £58 |
| Gloucestershire | Portion of Dumbleton tithes | £6 13*s* 4*d* | | |
| | Pension from Dumbleton | 10*s* | | £7 3*s* 4*d* |
| Bedfordshire | Portion of Stoppsley, Luton, tithes | £40 | | £40 |
| | | | Total Income | £226 11*s* 8*d* |
| | | | Total Expenditure | £209 11*s* 2*d* |
| | | | Annual Surplus | £17 6*d* |

| Expenditure | | | | | | |
|---|---|---|---|---|---|---|
| Overheads | | | | | | |
| | *Weekly Commons* | *Annual Cost* | *Annual Stipend* | *Annual Cost* | *Total Cost* | |
| *Foundation* | | | | | | |
| President | 2*s* 8*d* | £6 18*s* 8*d* | £10 | £10 | £16 18*s* 8*d* | |
| 12 fellows | 1*s* 8*d* each | £52 | £2 13*s* 4*d* each | £32 | £84 | |
| 12 scholars | 1*s* each | £31 4*s* | £1 13*s* 4*d* each | £20 | £51 4*s* | |
| | | | | | | Total: £152 2*s* 8*d* |
| *Household* | | | | | | |
| Manciple | 1*s* | £2 12*s* | £1 13*s* 4*d* | £1 13*s* 4*d* | £4 5*s* 4*d* | |
| Butler/porter | 1*s* | £2 12*s* | £1 6*s* 8*d* | £1 6*s* 8*d* | £3 18*s* 8*d* | |
| Cook | 1*s* | £2 12*s* | £1 13*s* 4*d* | £1 13*s* 4*d* | £4 5*s* 4*d* | |
| Under cook | 6*d* | £1 6*s* | £1 | £1 | £2 6*s* | |
| Laundress | | | £1 | £1 | £1 | |
| Barber | | | 13*s* 4*d* | 13*s* 4*d* | 13*s* 4*d* | |
| | | | | | | Total: £16 8*s* 8*d* |
| *Officers* | | | | | | |
| Vice-President | | | £1 6*s* 8*d* | £1 6*s* 8*d* | | |
| 2 bursars | | | 13*s* 4*d* | £1 6*s* 8*d* | | |
| Dean | | | 13*s* 4*d* | 13*s* 4*d* | | |
| Organist | | | £1 | £1 | | |
| Logic lecturer | | | £2 | £2 | | |
| Humanities lecturer | | | £1 6*s* 8*d* | £1 6*s* 8*d* | | |
| 4 Priests | | | 10*s* | £2 | | |
| | | | | | | Total: £9 13*s* 4*d* |

*Table 2.1* Continued

| Expenditure | | |
|---|---|---|
| **Household Expenses** | | |
| Kitchen and buttery equipment | £2 | |
| Chapel supplies | £5 | |
| Fuel for Hall and Kitchen | £10 | |
| | | Total: £17 |
| **Feast Days** | | |
| *Obits Date* | *For the Souls of* | *Cost* |
| 25 March (Annunciation) | Founder's parents | 6*s* 8*d* |
| 7 August (Jesus Day) | Sir Thomas Pope | 10*s* |
| 15 August (Assumption) | Queen Mary | 6*s* 8*d* |
| 8 September (Nativity of the Blessed Virgin Mary) | Lady Elizabeth Pope | 6*s* 8*d* |
| 8 December (Conception of the Blessed Virgin Mary) | Margaret Pope | 6*s* 8*d* |
| | | Total: £1 16*s* 8*d* |

Alms

| *Date* | *Given to* | |
|---|---|---|
| 7 August (Jesus Day) | 12 poor men and women | 9*s* 6*d* |
| | Prisoners in Oxford gaol | 1*s* 8*d* |
| | Prisoners in Bocardo gaol | 1*s* |
| Every Friday | 1*s* to prisoners in Oxford gaol | £2 12*s* |
| | | Total: £3 4*s* 2*d* |

College Gaudy Days

| | |
|---|---|
| Trinity Sunday | £1 6*s* 8*d* |
| Christmas Day | 13*s* 4*d* |
| The 4 days after Christmas | £1 6*s* 8*d* |
| New Year's Day | 6*s* 8*d* |
| Twelfth Night | £1 6*s* 8*d* |
| Easter Sunday and 3 days following | £1 6*s* 8*d* |
| Whitsunday and 3 days following | £1 6*s* 8*d* |
| Candlemas (2 February) | 5*s* |
| Midsummer Day (24 June) | 4*s* |
| Michaemas (29 September) | 6*s* 8*d* |
| All Hallows' Day (1 November) | 6*s* 8*d* |
| Ascension Day | 5*s* |
| Corpus Christi Day | 5*s* |
| | Total: £9 5*s* 8*d* |
| | Total Annual Expenditure: £209 11*s* 2*d* |

Dumbleton. The £12 promised for the upkeep of the buildings, however, appeared neither in the statutes nor in the budget, despite the correspondence on the subject between the Founder and the President. Instead the not insignificant sum of £8 *6s 8d* was allocated for the proper celebration of gaudy days: two marks for Trinity Sunday, one for Christmas Day, and half a mark for most of the major feasts of the Christian calendar. The six capons due each year from Wroxton were destined for Christmas dinner, and the well-fattened boar from the estate at Holcombe was scheduled to arrive on the feast of St Andrew (30 November). The resultant roast pork and college brawn were still on the seasonal menu in 1770, when bursar Thomas Warton sent some as a Christmas gift to his friend George Colman.[22]

In Trinity's second year, Pope took steps to increase both the value of the presidency and the resources of the foundation.[23] On 9 July 1557 he acquired by Letters Patent of Philip and Mary the joint ownership of the advowson of Garsington, a parish some four miles south-east of Oxford. The following day the co-owner, Sir Nicholas Hare, quitclaimed his share to Pope, and on 1 December 1557 the advowson was granted ex officio to the President of Trinity. He in turn was bound to provide annually to the College twelve bushels of wheat (the grain used in bread-making), two quarters of malt (used in brewing), and a generous two sacks of coal for each of the twelve days of Christmas.[24]

Where the Founder had not stinted was in provision of ornaments and equipment for the Chapel. 'All the great houses in England must have been full of these spoils of monasteries and churches,' commented Blakiston.[25] In May 1556 the College received 'parcels' of church plate, books, ornaments, and vestments from the Founder, which were followed by two further consignments in January and April 1557. Each delivery was accompanied by a detailed indenture, which served as a check-list. The first is headed by the 'chalice and paten gilt, weighing 20 ounces, three quarters', which have been used in the Chapel throughout Trinity's history. This is Blakiston's description:

[22] *Warton*, ed. Fairer, no. 268, TW to George Colman the elder, 27 Dec 1770.

[23] The convention in the *computus* accounts is to number the years from Michaelmas. The first year ended on 29 September 1556.

[24] TCA Charters B/4.1

[25] Blakiston, *Trinity*, 72.

> it has a nearly hemispherical bowl, a stem ornamented with a plain knop, open tracery between cable work, and an embattlement just above the six-lobed flowing foot, with the crucifix on one face. The paten has a sex-foil depression round an elaborated vernicle, and the liturgical verse "*calicem salutaris accipiam et nomine domine invocabo*" (I will take the cup of salvation and I will call on the name of the Lord), partially repeated on the bowl and foot of the chalice.

It is hallmarked 1527.[26]

At the same time Thomas Pope sent a second chalice and paten, a pipe of silver, an ivory pyx (decorated with silver and gilt and set with counterfeit stones), a copper cross, and censers and two pairs of latten candlesticks for the altar. There was a green-painted desk, a 'wainscot lectern' for the choir, and fourteen books, including illuminated antiphonaries and grails, psalters and choir-books, and two processionals and a gospel book tucked in as a postscript to the indenture. To begin with, the Founder provided ten suits of vestments and six copes, in red, yellow, blue, black, and white, tissue, bodkin, damask, velvet, grosgrain, Bruges satin, and fustian (for Lent). They were embroidered, appliquéd, and woven variously with gold thread, green tissue, scallop shells, birds of gold, and suns, and 'powdered' with crowns and flowers. He also sent altar cloths, a hearse cloth, covers for the sacrament, corporal cases, plain canvas and linen covers for the altars, towels, and cushions and 'a great wainscot coffer to put in all the ornaments aforesaid'.

Everything was carefully checked on arrival, and it was noted that a stole and fannel of black velvet and an alb were missing. These were duly sent on 20 January 1557, along with another cope of red silk, lined with taffeta and embroidered with images of gold; a red velvet vestment with a gold cross in stole-work and embroidered with fleurs de lys, angels, and spread eagles; another of blue silk lined with taffeta and woven with birds and flowers of Cologne; and a black silk cope with gold stripes. For use in the Chapel were two canopies to hang over the sacrament on the altar, three more corporal cases, and two red silk cushions. Pope also dispatched—notwithstanding his earlier protestations about the winter weather—his organs, which, including the carriage from London, cost £10. Then there were pewter utensils for the Chapel: a basin, a staff 'to carry the best cross withal', an incense boat, and cruets. The catalogue continued with another

[26] Ibid., 71–2; TCA Charters C/1.

pyx of ivory, two 'fair bell candlesticks of latten', books, altar and desk cloths, silver-gilt cruets, a water-stoup, sacring bell, pyx (with crucifix and Mary and John), censers, an incense boat, basins, candlesticks, and a cross 'garnished with crystal and stones'.[27]

The third consignment arrived on 12 April. This time ornaments for the Chapel included a banner cloth 'on the one side whereof is painted the Trinity and on the other side our Lady', a wooden crucifix to be placed at the entry to the choir, a wooden image of the Resurrection to be set on the altar at Easter, and a lockable box to keep it in. There were more books, more vestments, and more cloths. Everything in the Chapel was as it should be to meet the Founder's desire that his College should operate 'to the glory and honour of the Most High Creator'.[28]

In setting up the College, the Founder did not neglect the minds and bodies of his members. Alongside the first instalment of chapel plate came books for the library and utensils for the Hall, buttery, and kitchen, listed carefully in a sealed indenture. There were sixty-three books, including all the standard works that would be required reading for a theological degree.[29] Unsurprisingly, Pope had acquired numerous manuscripts from monastic sources, and he also made use of his contacts at Court. The Old Library today has twenty-seven printed books bearing the marks of the royal library at Greenwich, and another fifteen from Hampton Court. Trinity's manuscript books in the Bodleian Library include twenty-six given by Pope. Particularly fine are the works of Isidore, formerly the property of St Mary's, Overey, and a gloss on the Psalms that had come from the library of the Carmelite House in London.[30] A second large consignment of books arrived from Slythurst's friend Thomas Rawe, Canon of Windsor, useful and solid works of theology, and the popular writings of the medieval mystic St Bridget of Sweden.[31]

In the library, the books were chained to shelves above sloping desks to which they would be lifted down to be read. Chains were a costly item, and a memorandum on the back of the indenture of Pope's books records the safe receipt of 'five dozen of chains' as well

[27] TCA Charters C/3.

[28] Ibid. Charters C/4; Statutes Chapter 1.99.

[29] TCA Charters C/2.

[30] For details of all the MSS given by the Founder, see H. O. Coxe, *Catalogus codicum MSS. qui in collegiis aulisque Oxoniensibus hodie adservantur* (Oxford, 1852).

[31] TCA Library Benefactors' Book, Library A/1, no.58. College piety has ensured the survival of all the Founder's books; but of 34 given by Rawe, only 18 remain.

as '2 pot hooks, a fire shovel, a fire fork, a bar of iron to hang the pot therewith, besides three bars of iron [and] 2 dripping pans'. For dining in Hall the Founder provided numerous tablecloths, towels, and napkins, all to be stored in a 'coffer with bars of iron', and pewter salts, plates, dishes, and saucers, while for the kitchen were such basic items as pans, a colander, pestles and mortars of brass and wood, a skimmer and ladle, a 'chopping knife', a frying pan, and '2 trivets of iron one bigger than the other'.[32]

## *Early Difficulties*

Pope and Slythurst had other mundane matters to worry about. They soon learned that the fellows did not like living under the rule of the Statutes. There was an early sign of trouble on 20 August 1556, when George Simpson and George Rudd were caught in breach of Chapter 27, specifically of the stipulation *de muris Collegii non scandendis* (not climbing the college walls). Trinity's gates were locked each evening by the butler (who doubled as porter), at 8 p.m. in winter and at 9 p.m. in summer, and members of College were not allowed to go out at night. The penalty for climbing the walls was perpetual expulsion.

Thomas Pope was horrified and hurt by the two fellows' defiant action, and he had a mind to set a strong example 'in such sort as others might fear to attempt the like'.[33] But at the same time he could hardly afford to lose any of his fellows quite so soon, and he was not by nature a harsh man. A diplomatic solution to the crisis was needed, and, fortuitously, help was on hand in the shape of the Princess Elizabeth, who heard all about Pope's troubles while he watched over her at Hatfield. Pope wrote to Slythurst: 'at the desire or rather the commandment of my lady Elizabeth her grace, and at my wife's request, who hath both sent and written to me very earnestly, and in hope that this will be a warning for them to live in order hereafter, I am content to remit this fault.' There were, of course, conditions. The two men had to 'openly in the hall, before all the fellows and scholars of the College, confess their faults', and in addition they were to pay an appropriate fine. Slythurst was instructed to record in the College Register that the two men were indeed expelled but were then

[32] TCA Charters, C/2.

[33] TCA Misc. Vol. I 1/3.

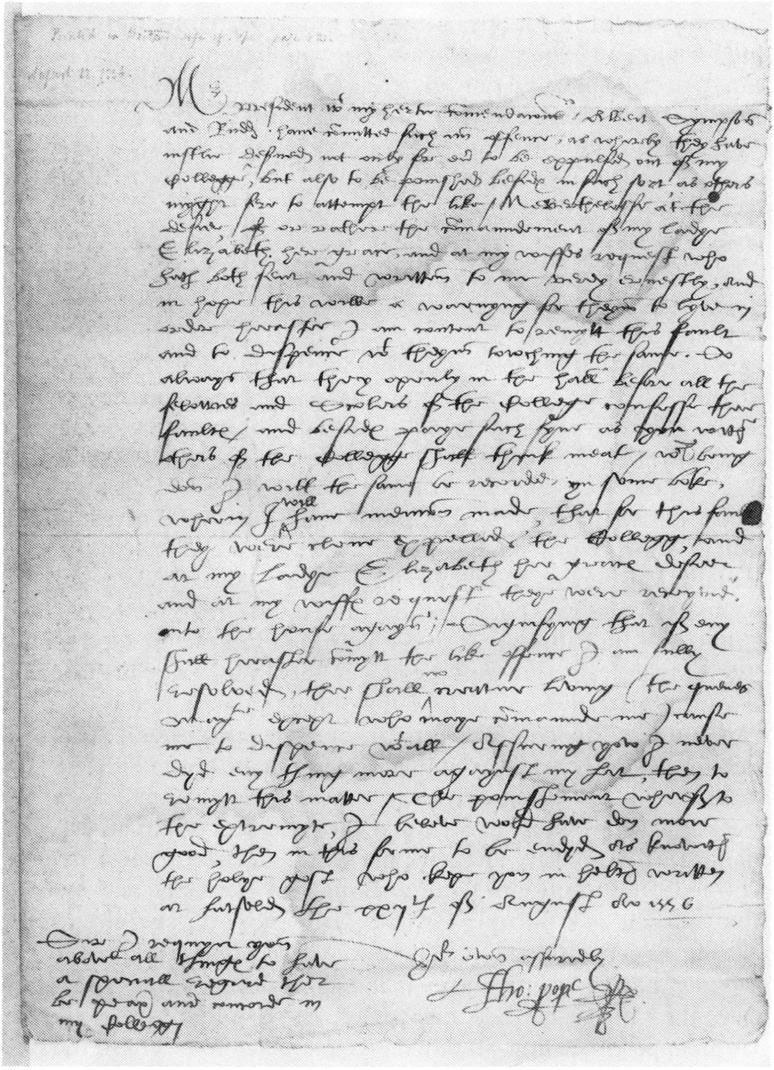

*2.2* Letter of Thomas Pope to Thomas Slythurst, 22 August 1556 (TCA Misc. Vol. I, f. 1/3).

'received into the house again'. And Pope stressed that he would not be so lenient if 'any shall hereafter commit the like offence', for, he said, 'I never did anything more against my heart.' The apologies were duly made, and Simpson and Rudd handed over 7*s* for the purchase of two bombazine curtains for the altar.[34]

The problem which arose in relation to John Perte proved rather more serious and intractable. Originally nominated by Pope to a scholarship, Perte was one of the youngest of the foundation fellows, and served as Junior Bursar for at least the first two years of Trinity's existence.[35] Perte was given the task of writing up a fair copy of the Statutes, for he had a fine and clear hand, although at first his progress was slow. On 24 July 1557 Pope added a postscript to a letter to Slythurst, 'I pray you with my hearty commendations to Mr Perte, desire the same to use speed in my statutes and I will not be forgetful of his pains.'[36]

Pope's confidence in Perte turned out to be misplaced. On 31 March 1558 he wrote again, this time with incredulity. 'You shall receive herein enclosed a letter sent me from Mr Pert such as I thought full little to have received from him, but I think he be not well in his wit. I pray you tell him I have sent you a copy of his letters and willed you to know of him what he means in that he finds fault at my statutes.'[37]

For so it was. The very Statutes in which Pope took such pride and which were 'drawn and collected as well out of the good orders of other colleges as also by the advice and counsel of diverse most sage and wise heads', were not to the liking of Perte nor, Perte had alleged, of others. Stephen Markes was one fellow already known to be unhappy at Trinity. On 15 February 1558 Pope had replied with some astonishment to the insulting news that his vice-president was threatening to resign and go to Hart Hall instead. 'What moves him thereunto I know not, wherefore I would be glad to learn the same . . . praying you in my behalf to say unto him that I trust he will not leave my college except for a further advancement than to go to Hart Hall.'[38] Now the Founder scolded Perte—'I marvel not a little to see him play the wanton'—and blustered—'God will send others in their

[34] TCA Register A f.7 [35] TCA *Computus* 1556, 1556–7.
[36] TCA Misc. Vol. I, 6/15. [37] Ibid., 9/21.
[38] TCA Register A f.16d. In August 1558 Slythurst was recommended by the Queen but was again disappointed in the election to the presidency of Magdalen College, a further advancement with which the Founder would presumably have sympathized; Macray, *Register of Magdalen*, 70, 91.

rooms that will be content.' But more than anything he wanted harmony among the members of his foundation, and faced by the prospect of losing a man whom he had himself chosen for the College, he tried to be reasonable. 'I would,' he concluded, 'he now stayed if it might be at the least for this year, but if he will needs depart, God be with him.' Meanwhile Pope urged Slythurst to ask the fellows 'you shall perceive to mislike the statutes & understand what moves them so to do'.

Perte was summoned to see the Founder in person, and obligingly drew up a list of ten points 'wherewithal he & Marks were offended'. He was blunt in his criticisms of what he saw as oppressive restrictions and unfair requirements made of the fellows. Much time was wasted, he felt, by the stipulation that BAs were expected to attend the rhetoric lectures with the scholars, and he found it 'indecent' that BAs or fellows should have to take their turn at the *narrare*, reciting to the assembled College during dinner. It was also 'unreasonable' that two fellows could not walk in the fields of Oxford without permission, and that the President was able to restrict their use of the Grove. He considered the edict that a man had to take his MA within six months of qualifying for it to be 'very sore', partly for financial reasons, but also because those from far distant counties would not have time to visit their homes. Other perceived injustices included the rules that a junior fellow was allowed to become a priest before his senior, and that a man could be punished if an uncorroborated complaint was made against him. Finally, concluded Perte, it was 'strict' to expect fellows to attend mass at 5 o'clock a.m.

Pope studied these articles of complaint carefully, then sent them to Slythurst for an expert opinion. Between them they denied the validity of some points: 'No such thing in all the Statutes,' Slythurst noted indignantly about the *narrare*. And 'they go not to service till 6 of the clock,' insisted Pope. Other grievances they felt were entirely unreasonable: 'Here he blames all the statutes in Oxford.' After all, as the Founder observed piously, 'fellows and scholars must be in all things commanded by the President.' Nevertheless, Pope conceded that he would 'stay the writing of the stats.' while he considered what moderate adjustments might be made. Central to the difficulty was not the actual requirements made by the statutes so much as their very existence. Many colleges were governed by rules written in the distant past and organized by custom, and to codify life in such detail seemed harsh. Trinity's domestic and religious routines were not untypical of any college, and its educational practices were soon to be emulated elsewhere. Indeed, when Sir William Petre 'refounded' Exeter College in 1566, his new statutes were based in part on those of Trinity.[39]

On 25 April 1558 Pope sent the final version of the Statutes to the College, along with a stern letter of exhortation addressed to all the fellows, which was dutifully copied into the College Register. The statute book is heavily annotated in places. The letter finishes on a characteristically conciliatory note, urging that if any member of the Foundation is still not content, 'I heartily require the same without disturbance to give place unto such others as will obediently live under the same, and when he shall see his time to depart from my said college . . . he shall have my good will & favour.'[40]

No one was less content with life under the Statutes than Thomas Pope's stepson and Elizabeth's only child, John Basford. He was one of a number of young men sent by the Founder to study at Trinity, and he arrived on 13 July 1557 with a letter addressed to his newly appointed tutor, Arthur Yeldard. By 21 December, George Rudd was charged with his education, and was directed 'to read him Erasmus' epistles & Tully's epistles which he shall learn to translate well'. Moreover, Pope insisted to Slythurst, 'command all the fellows and scholars of the college . . . that they speak not one word of English to him'.[41] Pope wrote again with a somewhat softer, more resigned approach: 'you may tell Mr Basford that when you shall advertise me he understands the Latin tongue I will send for him home' and he proffered a large carrot in the promise that he would then advance his career 'further in such place where he shall I doubt not well like his being'.[42] Whit Monday (30 May) 1558, however, found Pope acting as mediator between mother and son. Elizabeth was 'wonderfully offended' at Basford's request to come home and felt that 'her desire to have him [at Trinity] for a while should be sufficient' reason to remain. Thomas suggested indulgently that Basford could take some time out and 'ride to my friends and tenants and make merry there for two or three days'. Slythurst, however, was to use his powers of persuasion and point out that with a year's diligent work Latin 'will

[39] William K. Stride, *Exeter College* (London 1900), 42–3.
[40] TCA Statutes A/1; Register A, 16d.
[41] TCA Misc. Vol. I, f. 7/17.
[42] Ibid., f. 8/19.

be gotten' and that 'what a great offence it is not to obey his mother'.[43] The moral argument had little effect, and by 9 June Elizabeth was 'so much offended' that she refused to read her son's letters, in particular the one explaining why he had refused 'the loan of his horse to his uncle'. Pope felt some presidential assistance might be in order, and beseeched Slythurst 'advise him in what form he shall write'. Meanwhile, he tried a threat of his own, 'tell him from me . . . that having her displeasure he can not have my good will which is I think worth the having.'[44]

Some young men were more grateful for Pope's assistance. A relation of Trinity's first benefactor, Thomas Southern, was promised a place in 1556.[45] Another grateful undergraduate was a 'poor scholar of Bristol' who was admitted in 1558 after a request from 'Mr Dalby . . . the Bishop's chancellor and a man to whom I am beholden', wrote Pope to Slythurst.[46]

The Founder also pulled strings to accommodate two further members of his family as scholars: his nephew Edmund Hutchins, and Lady Elizabeth's younger brother Walter Blount. Hutchins was appointed to a vacant place on 3 October 1556 and Blount on 9 January 1557, an act in clear breach of the statutes, which caused their author some embarrassment: 'When my wife's brother is once placed I will for no mans suit, the Statutes of my College be broken in that point, but that the election shall always be upon Trinity Sunday.'[47] Edmund Hutchins remained quietly in College for two years; the only mark he made was a discreet graffito scratched into an external buttress of what is now the Old Bursary: 'IHS [JESUS] HAVE M[ERCY] O[N] E. HUTCHINS A D 1558'. Walter Blount, however, was less satisfied with the life of an Oxford scholar, and tried hard to leave. There was a family row in December 1557. Pope wrote to Slythurst, 'it is told my wife that her brother hath reported he will no more repair to the college whereat she is not a little offended.' The following May, Pope was outmanoeuvred: 'I pray you give my brother Blount licence to visit his mother who has sent to my wife to obtain him leave. And I trust he will not be long absent.' But in an undated letter of the same year, Pope wrote again, resigned that Slythurst should 'dispense with my wife's brother for his Scholar's Room'. He would, he assured his President, never again override the rules, 'for when I shall go

[43] TCA Misc. Vol. I, f. 12/27. [44] Ibid., f. 13/29. [45] Ibid., f. 2/6.
[46] Ibid., f. 12/26. [47] Ibid., f. 2/6.

about to break my statutes in my own time how may I hope to have them kept after I am gone?'[48]

Pope went sooner than Trinity might have hoped. In the winter of 1558–9 the College was rocked by two deaths. Queen Mary died on 17 November 1558. The accession of Queen Elizabeth, a staunch Protestant, was an immediate threat to the religious observances that were so essential a part of Trinity's purpose and corporate life.

Then, on Sunday 29 January 1559, Thomas Pope died at his Clerkenwell home, seemingly a victim of the epidemic of malarial 'quartan-fever' that, according to Warton, 'seized three parts in four of the people of England; destroying in the general devastation, thirteen bishops, and several other persons, both men and women, of the most eminent rank and quality.' The Founder's interment was everything that Warton could have wished. He was 'magnificently buried' with trappings provided by Henry Machyn, citizen of London and furnisher of funeral accoutrements.[49] In his diary Machyn recorded the ceremonial conveyance of Thomas Pope's remains, 'with a standard and coat, pennon of arms, a target, helmet and sword, and a two dozen of arms'. The corpse was attended by 'two heralds of arms, Master Clarencieux and Master York. Master Clarencieux bore the coat, and Master York bore the helmet and crest.' Thomas Pope had made provision for appropriate distribution of mourning clothes to the poor of the parish: 'forty mantle freeze gowns [given to] twenty men and twenty women; and twenty men bore torches; and the women two and two together, with torches', and for candles, in the shape of 'two great white branches, and four branches tapers of wax garnished with arms, and with four dozen pencils'. An impressive crowd gathered to show their respects: 'Sir Richard Southwell knight, and Sir Thomas Stradling, and diverse other mourners in black, to the number of sixty and more in black, and all the house and the church with black and arms. And after to the place to drink, with spice bread and wine.' The following morning a mass was celebrated, 'with two prick songs, and the third of requiem, with the clerks of London', and then Thomas Pope was buried. 'And that done,' concluded Machyn, 'to the place to dinner, for there was a great dinner, and plenty of all things, and a great dole of money.'[50]

48 Ibid., f. 8/19. 49 Warton, *Pope*, 169–70.

50 *The Diary of Henry Machyn*, ed. John Gough Nichols (Camden Society, first series, 42, 1848), 188.

The loss of the Founder was a heavy blow. The piecemeal nature of his endowment so far left a sense of business unfinished, and his death prevented, in Blakiston's opinion, 'many munificent intentions'.[51] Thomas Pope had taken a closely paternalistic and often rather helpful interest in the minutiae of College affairs. The members of the foundation faced a future of religious and political upheavals, and might have benefited from Pope's experience of living under Protestantism. The new Queen knew about them—two years earlier she had intervened on behalf of two recalcitrant fellows—but they had no idea of what her reign would bring. Trinity College, not yet four years old, was now in a very vulnerable position.

[51] Blakiston, *Trinity*, 74.

# 3

# *Elizabethan Trinity*

## *From Catholic to Protestant*

By his will Thomas Pope left Lady Elizabeth firmly in charge of everything to do with Trinity. He bequeathed to the College £100 to build a wall between it and St John's and 'to enclose the ground belonging to Trinity'. He also bequeathed 500 marks to build a 'lodging at Garsington within the parsonage', which was to be used as a refuge for the College during outbreaks of plague in the city. Elizabeth was to 'undertake the doing thereof' and, should the funds prove insufficient, she was to 'supply the lack herself'. If she wished to remarry, she was first to complete the task of 'furnishing the college with copes, vestments, ornaments, and other church & household stuff', as she had 'faithfully promised' to do. The Founder's will ran to some 5,000 words and included numerous members of his extended family, household, and wide circle of friends, whose 'faithful and unfeigned friendship' he accounted a 'far greater gift than anything' he could bequeath them. There were also many charitable donations to prisoners and the poor 'whereof God knows there are no small number'. Elizabeth was one of the executors and also the residuary legatee. Thomas's trust in her to carry out all his wishes is touching, and, with two pardonable exceptions, was not in the least misplaced. Her promise, he said, 'I do assuredly trust as if I had the City of London bound for doing thereof.' She was his 'most dear and entirely beloved wife' and, he declared, she 'merited a thousand times more than I am able in any way to give her'.[1]

Lady Elizabeth had her first chance to go solo as Foundress within six months, when she had to choose a new President for the College. The 1559 Act of Supremacy declared Queen Elizabeth to be the

[1] Will of Sir Thomas Pope, TNA PROB 11/42b 10 Chaynay. The exceptions were the dispatch of chapel plate and vestments, which arrived in May 1564, more than three years after her remarriage, and the removal of his body from his chosen burial place.

*3.1* Lady Elizabeth Pope, Foundress of Trinity College.

'supreme governor' of the Church of England, and in June her Visitors arrived in Oxford and began the task of imposing the University's second religious U-turn of the decade. The Visitors were not especially severe—Wood considered that their approach was 'mild and gentle, not rigorous'[2]—but nine heads of house were removed from their positions that year, and Thomas Slythurst was one of them. His strong Catholic principles had been one of the reasons why Pope had appointed him. As part of his oath of office, Slythurst had sworn that, in the event of his expulsion, he would utterly re-

[2] Wood, *History*, ii, 140.

nounce all avenues of appeal, and there is no evidence that he resisted the Visitors' decree. Warton and Blakiston followed Wood's assertion that Slythurst died a prisoner in the Tower of London in 1560, but his name does not appear in the Tower's Book of Prisoners, and the exact date of his death and the place of his burial are unknown.[3]

It was Trinity's first election to a vacant presidency, and there was some confusion as to the exact procedure. Following the statutes, the fellows gathered in the Chapel and nominated two of their number, Arthur Yeldard and Stephen Markes, and the vice-president duly sent their names to Lady Elizabeth. But on 22 September, the fellows wrote formally to the Foundress, anxious to explain that they had proceeded to 'a special election' and already selected Yeldard. Lady Elizabeth's reply was dated just one day later, but fortunately she too had 'appointed & chosen Mr Yeldard to be your president, which I trust shall be both for the commodity of the college, and also for all your comfort and quietness'.[4] Yeldard proved to be an excellent choice. His forty-year presidency helped stabilize and unify Trinity in times that were often far from easy. As Thomas Pope had done before him, he neither actively promoted Protestantism nor failed to comply with any reform demanded by the religious and University authorities.

From the beginning there was a rapid turnover in the fellowship. James Bell, the first rhetoric lecturer, had left almost as soon as he had arrived, John Perte in 1558, and Roger Evans the following year. 1560 saw the departures of Stephen Markes, who was both discontented with the Statutes and disappointed in the presidential election, John Richardson, and George Simpson. The scholar Reginald Bray left in 1557, and John Arden and Robert Thraske the following year. Some of the scholars were elected to vacancies in the fellowship, but John Harris stayed in his fellowship for less than a year in 1559, and Comporte, elected as a fellow in 1558, was another who left in 1560. By the tenth anniversary of the foundation only one of the first fellows—Robert Bellamy—and one of the scholars—William Saltmarsh (fellow 1558–67)—were left.

There is no evidence that any of the departing men left for religious reasons, although little is known of their later careers. The Chapel was central to Trinity's corporate life, and in the year following Slythurst's departure, there was little change in the Catholic

[3] Ibid., 142–3; Blakiston, *Trinity*, 76.

[4] TCA Register A f. 24v.

practices that had been stipulated by the Founder. Naturally Sundays and Holy Days were the busiest, with 'first and second vespers, compline and matins, and the other masses and processions' all done according to the ceremonial directions laid out in the Sarum use. The President, with appropriate attendants, celebrated mass on the principal festivals and for the Founder's obit; one of the fellows in priests' orders officiated on lesser feasts and Sundays. The other six days of the week—'working days'—began with one of the priests saying mass before 6 a.m., a service at which all fellows and scholars who were not priests or MAs were expected to be present 'from beginning to end' on pain of losing their commons for the day. The priests and MAs—who were permitted to skip Matins—had the choice of celebrating mass later themselves, or of attending another service later in the day. On Fridays mass was celebrated in honour of Jesus and on Saturdays in honour of the Blessed Virgin Mary, with singing and organ music. Prescribed prayers for Thomas Pope and his family were said daily in the Chapel and both before and after meals. Finally, if the statutes are to be believed, every day ended with the fellows and scholars kneeling by their beds in a spirit of devotion and reverence as they prayed to the Holy Trinity for freedom, salvation, and justification. Personal piety may have been difficult to measure, but public religion was strictly enforced. No one was allowed to talk in Chapel, and irreverent behaviour on the part of fellow or scholar was punished by the loss of commons for up to three days. A fourth offence brought down harsher penalties, culminating in loss of all stipend and commons until the humble miscreant came into line. Undergraduate scholars under the age of 20 could be beaten or flogged by the dean 'if necessary'.[5]

In March 1561 changes were made to the Chapel furnishings, with four yards of 'fetwich cloth', short nails, and long laths, being purchased to make curtains to hang around the altars.[6] The Chapel was a place close to the heart of the Foundress. Within two years of Thomas's death Lady Elizabeth had married again, becoming the second wife of the military commander Sir Hugh Paulet, and on 1 December 1560 the College spent 16*s* on gloves 'given to Dom. Paulet and the lady Foundress'.[7] Sir Hugh was a contemporary of Thomas Pope; they had been knighted by Henry VIII on the same day. Sir

[5] TCA Statutes Chapters 12–13.

[6] TCA *Computus* 1560–1, 20.

[7] Ibid., 19v.

Hugh gave Trinity £20 towards the completion of the College wall in 1566.[8] He was an active Protestant, which may have been an advantage for his actively Catholic wife. The date of his death was probably in December 1572. Twice in her third and final widowhood, Elizabeth was charged with recusancy. In 1578 she was named in a list of papists active in London, accused of having 'Mass commonly in her house', while in 1585 she denied being a recusant but was 'most willing and ready to subscribe £50 for the Queen's service'.[9]

Elizabeth's third marriage in no way lessened her interest in the College. She visited Trinity in June 1565—the College spent 53*s* 4*d* on her Whit Sunday lunch—and again on Trinity Monday 1567.[10] One of her first projects was the construction of the elaborate altar tomb for Sir Thomas, Lady Margaret, and herself, which was built to the left of the altar in the north-east corner of the Chapel. It is curious that the College Register makes no mention of the reburial of the Founder; nor indeed was his removal from St Stephen's ever recorded by that church's wardens, although this silence might be explained by the need to perform Catholic rites in secret.[11] The new tomb may have been contemplated by Elizabeth even at the time of Thomas's death, for although his burial, beside his first wife and child in St Stephen's, Walbrook, was carried out exactly according to the instructions in his will, the date of his death was never added to the inscription there.[12] It is instead recorded (as are the names of both Margaret and Elizabeth) on the new monument in the Trinity Chapel, which is known to have existed by March 1567, when payments are recorded to labourers working in its vicinity, and for lime used 'around the Founder's tomb'. This work seems to have related to the interment of Elizabeth's son John Basford, for the same year's accounts include refreshments for the Foundress's household, when performing his funeral rites.[13] The tomb has two life-sized alabaster effigies, which may have been based on similar figures upon the Founder's tomb in St Stephen's. The figure of Sir Thomas is clad in armour and, like his wife—who, representative as she is of two

[8] The College wrote to thank him on 29 June. TCA Misc. Vol. I f.18/43.

[9] *Calendar of State Papers, Domestic Additions 1566–79* (1871), 551; *Calendar of State Papers, Domestic 1581–90* (1865), 287.

[10] TCA *Computus* 1564–5, 67; 1566–7, 87.

[11] Thomas Milbourn, 'Church of St Stephen Walbrook', *Transactions of the London and Middlesex Archaedogical Society* (1881), v, 327.

[12] John Stow, *Survey of London* (London, 1633), 245.

[13] TCA *Computus* 1567–8, ff. 95–95d.

*3.2* 'Antiquities of Trinity College': the Founder's Chalice and tomb.

women, is more of a 'wifely type' than a portrait—rests its feet on a griffin. The double chains with hanging crosses around the necks of both figures are characteristic of tomb effigies from the reign of Henry VIII, and the shapes of the dagger and gauntlets also suggest an earlier date. The monument was originally painted and gilded.[14] Elizabeth's will referred to Thomas's burial in the College. Elizabeth herself died on 27 October 1593 at Tyttenhanger and, according to her instructions, her body was brought with great ceremony to lie in the vault beside Sir Thomas. Members of the foundation were given new black mourning gowns ('the cloth to be of 13*s* 4*d* the yard' for the President and fellows, 12*s* the yard for the scholars). The scholars were also given 10*s* apiece, and the whole 'household, fellows, scholars, commoners, and whatsoever they be being then resident within the said College' were treated a dinner with 'no want of plenty nor yet superfluity of wine and dainty dishes'. The leftovers were distributed with alms of 20*d* ('up to £5') to the poor at the college gate, while prisoners at the Castle were given alms and 'to every one of them a piece of beef, weighing a stone at the least'.[15]

Trinity has the distinction of being the only Oxbridge college to have a 'Founder's tomb'.[16] Anthony Wood recorded some tantalizing details of what lies beneath when, one evening in June 1691, he met in a tavern:

> Mr Peisley the master-mason of Trinity College, who desired me to come next morning at ten to see the vault of the College chapel opened.
>
> June 16, Tuesday, at ten, I went and the masons opened the door and shovelled the dust off from the steps. I went in with Peisley and 2 candles and found under the north wall a woman's body and on her right hand two men's bodies of 6 feet long, but the coffins rotten with no inscriptions on them. The woman is lady Elizabeth . . . There are also the bones of 2 children.[17]

As the years passed, a spirit of Protestantism stole reluctantly but inevitably over the College. 'Masses' appear in the account of 1556; 'prayers' in the next surviving year, 1560–1. The situation grew more

[14] Lane Poole, 'A Catalogue of Oxford College Portraits', iii (OHS, 1921), 120–1.

[15] TNA PROB 11/83 Dixy.

[16] Maclagan, *Trinity College*, 8.

[17] Wood, *Life*, iii, 364. We may confidently identify the two men as Sir Thomas Pope and John Basford, and perhaps one of the children as the infant Alice. But what of Margaret, and the second child?

serious with the appointment of Robert Horne to the see of Winchester in November 1560. As Bishop of Winchester, he was ex officio the College Visitor, and had the right to make a triennial inspection and the duty to ensure the Statutes were being observed. Horne was, in Warton's words, 'a learned man, but a zealous and active puritan'.[18] In 1561 he 'found Trinity largely hostile to the Elizabethan church'.[19] When the Bishop's Commissary arrived at the College in December 1566, however, all the fellows obediently subscribed to the Thirty-Nine Articles, the essential statement of Protestant orthodoxy, and somewhat surprisingly he found 'no reform' needed.[20] Early in 1570 the three stone altars in the Chapel were demolished. The junior bursar recorded a payment of 4*s* 4*d* to 'stonecutters working in the chapel'. In their place, on 10 February a communion table and bookcases (perhaps to hold copies of the new Prayer Book) for the Chapel were purchased at a further cost of 11*s*.[21]

These changes were not enough. That summer the Queen's commissioners came down heavily on the University, and on 28 June addressed the President, fellows, and scholars of Trinity College in a blunt and threatening letter:

> We will and command you . . . that before the 12th day of July next . . . you cause to be defaced all the church plate and church stuff belonging to your college: in such sort, that it never may be used again . . . And that you so do it, as either one of her Majesty's commissioners may see it; or you the president, by your oath, testify to us . . . Whereof fail you not, as you will answer to the contrary at your peril.[22]

A week after the deadline, the College received a follow-up letter from Bishop Horne, warning them in no uncertain terms that complete conformity was required:

> Whereas I am informed that certain monuments tending to idolatry and popish or devil's service, as crosses, censers, and such like filthy stuff used in the idolatrous temple, more mete for the same than for the house of god, remain in your college as yet un-

[18] Warton, *Pope*, 356, note.
[19] Penry Williams, 'Elizabethan Oxford: State, Church and University', *HUO* 3, 406.
[20] TCA Visitor 1.1/4. [21] TCA *Computus* 1569–70, 124.
[22] TCA Register A, f. 139.

> defaced; I am moved thereby to judge great want of good will in some of you, and no less negligence in other some, as in being so remiss to perform your duties towards god, and obedience unto the prince [Queen Elizabeth]. Wherefore I can do no less, as in respect of my office and care I have of you, but very earnestly forthwith, upon the receipt hereof, will you to deface all manner such trash, as in the church of Christ is so noisome and unseemly; and to concert the matter thereof to the godly use, profit and behoof of your house.

Horne reminded the President and fellows of the 'motion made by the grand commissioners' and, in case they should try quoting their Founder at him, added sternly, 'I have perused the statutes, and do find, that, the same well considered, and the words thereof truly interpreted, you may lawfully without infringing of any part thereof, deface the same abuses.'[23]

It may have been at this time that drastic steps were taken to save some of Trinity's religious adornments. The walls and ceiling of the bursary beneath the Library were painted, the ceiling with a vine-scroll decoration, the walls in 'grey and red bands embellished by a simple floral motif'. The walls were topped by a frieze of acanthus leaves, above which were painted black loops intended to make the whole design resemble tapestry hangings. The style of the painting suggests a date approximately that of Trinity's foundation. It was an effective but low-budget means of decorating the room, and very much in keeping with the values of the young College. In the centre of the southern wall (through which a round-arched door led to the vestry) was painted a large blue and white roundel with 'IHS' in red gothic lettering. This was a common abbreviation of 'Jesus' (being the first three letters of the name in Greek); 'Jesus Day,' as the date of Thomas Pope's obit, had particular significance for the College. The mode of the whole scheme was somewhat old-fashioned, whether consciously or unconsciously; it must have seemed appropriate to a community yearning for the old religion. There is no record of when these decorations were concealed, but three of the walls were whitewashed, using lime, while the south wall and the ceiling were carefully concealed behind a lath and plaster skin. So carefully indeed that they disappeared entirely from the College's

[23] Ibid., f. 138v.

*3.3* 'IHS' roundel on the south wall of the 'Painted Room' beneath the Library.

memory for more than 400 years, and were only rediscovered during building work in 1985.[24]

Most of the Chapel's ornament and equipment had to go. A large quantity of plate was melted down, and in its place came the books beloved of Protestant worship—in the accounts for 1575–6 the bursars recorded the purchase by the dean of six books of Psalms (2*s* each) for the use of the Chapel.[25] Much of the College resigned itself to Protestantism. A significant minority, however, did not. Trinity's first fifteen years saw at least that number of fellows leave the College for the sake of their faith. Many travelled to the English College at Douai, near

[24] Bryan Ward-Perkins, 'Newly Discovered Wall Paintings', *Report* (1985–6), unpaginated; Kathryn Baird, 'Secular Wall Paintings in the Sixteenth and Seventeenth Centuries' (unpublished D.Phil. thesis, University of Oxford, 2002), 313–14.

[25] TCA *Computus* 1575–6, f. 191d.

Rheims, to be received into the Catholic Church, and a number were ordained there or elsewhere on the continent. Nearer to home, Gloucester Hall (now Worcester College) remained a relatively safe haven where Catholicism could be practised privately within the University; outside a college structure, unpalatable oaths and interrogations and the necessity of taking holy orders could be avoided. Thomas Allen left his fellowship after less than a year, and lived the rest of his life at Gloucester Hall, where he was renowned as a mathematician and astrologer. Thomas Warren left Trinity in 1579 (when he would have been required to take holy orders) and spent the next two decades at Gloucester Hall. Both Allen and Warren retained warm feelings for their College; both remembered Trinity in their wills, and both came home to be buried in the College Chapel.

In the two decades following Allen's departure, a number of fellows and scholars are known to have left Trinity because of their Catholic religion. It is impossible to say how many commoners did the same. A large gap was left on the foundation when three of the fellows and one of the scholars left together in 1582. The following summer, the College was rocked by another mass departure, the catalyst for which seems to have been the scandal caused by the appointment of a known Catholic and Balliol College reject, Richard Blount. He had been granted a fellowship at the instigation of his Aunt Elizabeth, using her powers as Foundress to dispense with the Statutes. The news was promulgated with some satisfaction by three members of Balliol, whose letter is preserved among the state papers in the National Archives:

> May it please you to understand that the fifteenth day of this present month of June, there are departed out of our University towards the Seminary of Rheims (as it is credibly reported by their own friends) certain students of Trinity College . . . namely Cecil, Oven . . . and Sir Blount, lately chosen out of our College contrary to the council's letters to be probationer of Trinity College. The man stood for preferment in our house, and for suspicion of his religion was worthily repelled, yet he found such favour with the Lady Paulet that one Trinity Sunday last he was elected as a member of Trinity College. These parties have a long time been noted as enemies to religion, and, Her Majesty's proceedings not withstanding, such has been the witness of that old serpent the Devil the father of lying and the author of all dissimulation, that these could not by just process be convinced for their religion. Yet

*Table 3.1* Fellows and scholars leaving Trinity for their Catholic faith.

| *Date Left* | *Name* | *Scholarship* | *Fellowship* | *Subsequent Career* |
|---|---|---|---|---|
| 1564 | Thomas Allen | 1561 | 1564 or 65 | Gloucester Hall<br>1632 Deathbed conversion to Catholicism |
| 1568 | Edward Hyndmer | 1561 | 1568 or 69 | Retired to live with Catholic patron |
| 1569 | Christopher Wharton | 1559 | 1562 | 1584 Ordained at Rheims<br>1600 Executed at York |
| 1570 | Thomas Forde | 1560 | 1565 | Douai<br>1573 Ordained at Brussels<br>1582 Hanged at Tyburn<br>1886 beatified |
| 1572 | William Sutton | 1561 | 1568 | Jesuit |
| | George Blackwell | 1562 | 1565 | Gloucester Hall<br>1574 Douai<br>1598 appointed 'Archpriest' |
| 1577 | Ralph Swinbourne | 1569 | 1572 | Suspected recusant |
| 1579 | Thomas Warren | 1568 | 1572 | Gloucester Hall |
| 1582 | William Spencer | 1573 | 1579 | Douai |
| | William Wardford | 1576 | 1578 | Douai<br>Jesuit<br>1608 died at Valladolid |
| | Anthony Shurley | 1576 | 1579 | Douai |
| | John Fixer | 1579 | | Douai |
| 1583 | John Cecil | 1573 | 1576 | Douai |
| | John Oven | 1578 | 1582 | Douai |
| | Richard Blount | | 1583 | Douai<br>Ordained at Rome<br>1623 Jesuit Provincial |

*Source*: H. E. D. Blakiston biographical register (TCA Blakiston D/2).

now even according to all expectation their departure has proved that in deed. Which their behaviour whilst they lived amongst us gave us just cause to suspect. Some other there are which (we fear) when like opportunity shall be offered will then manifestly prove unto all that which now they dissemble with many.[26]

[26] TNA SP12/161 no. 13.

Blount had been at Trinity for just three weeks. With John Oven went his brother Walter, who had matriculated as a servitor in December 1581, at the age of 13.

There were many other reasons for leaving, and there was a rapid turnover in the fellowship throughout the century. In the forty-two years 1557–99, 127 men were elected to scholarships of the College, and sixty-nine of these went on to hold fellowships, generally elected well within the seven years for which a scholarship could be held. Another six were elected to the fellowship from outside the College. Nine fellows left within one year of their election. The commonest departure time, in line with the pattern across the University, was the period of six to eight years from election, because this was the time after which a fellow could—or should—be ordained.[27]

## *College Life*

Trinity's BAs were required to take their MA within four and a half years, and MAs to take holy orders within another four years, and their BD within nine. In most colleges, the majority but not all of the fellows were expected to study theology—St John's allowed one quarter to pursue law and one medicine; Magdalen two or three law and the same number medicine—but under the Trinity Statutes it was theology or nothing, an insistence of the Founder's that was to cause problems for the College in later centuries.[28] Ordained priests held many religious and administrative offices throughout the land,[29] but a parochial living was the most common option, and twenty-six of those elected to fellowships at Trinity during the sixteenth century are known to have gone on to hold benefices in the Church of England. Of the foundation fellows, Bell, Simpson, Scott, and Evans all did so. As parish priests they were in a position to marry, they enjoyed a more comfortable standard of living, and they could perhaps aspire to prospects above the headship of a small Oxford college. The very first Trinity men to hold bishoprics were Bernard Adams (scholar 1583, fellow 1588–96) who held the see of Limerick 1604–26,

[27] James McConica, 'Elizabethan Oxford', *HUO* 3, 685.
[28] S. L. Greenslade, 'The Faculty of Theology', *HUO* 3, 295–6.
[29] Ibid., 328.

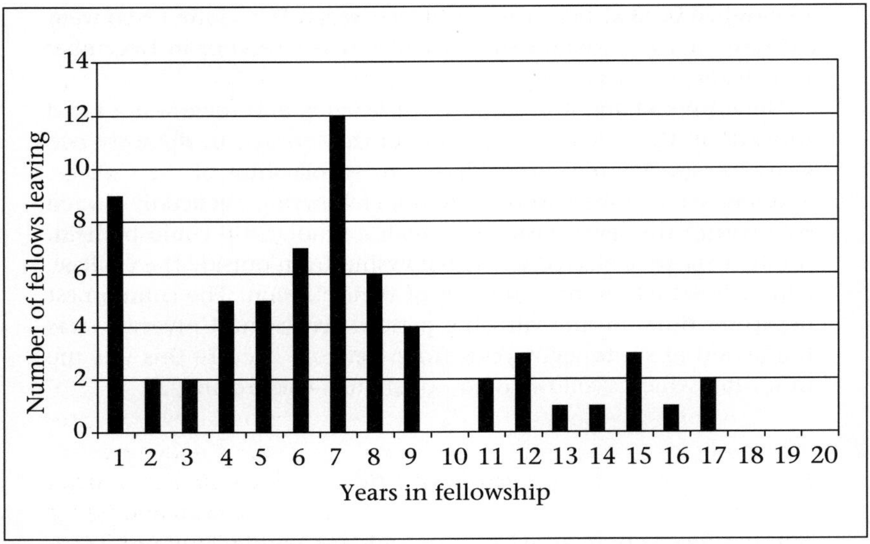


*Fig. 3.1* Tenure of fellowships 1557–1599.

and Robert Wright (scholar 1574, fellow 1581–98) who was appointed Bishop of Bristol in 1623 and of Coventry and Lichfield in 1632.

Those who stayed on at Trinity were required by the Statutes to take higher degrees in the Faculty of Theology: in theory, the Bachelorship of Divinity within nine years of the MA, and the DD, for which a further six were allowed. Once Doctors of Divinity, they were optimistically expected by the statutes 'to preach seven sermons annually in some important church'.[30] Besides Ralph Kettell, who went on to be President, the century's two longest stayers were Robert Avis (scholar 1576), fellow for thirty-seven years (1576–1617), and John Bowman (scholar 1584), fellow for twenty-three years (1587–1610). Both took the BD, neither the DD. They must have been inured to the rigours and dangers of sixteenth-century college life. Oxford was not a healthy place to live, and even in their rural location outside the city walls, the residents of Trinity were vulnerable to disease. The

[30] TCA Statutes Chapter 16.

city was prone to outbreaks of bubonic plague, influenza, 'sweating sickness', malaria, and typhus, pervaded by the foul refuse of the livestock trade, at the mercy of the regular flooding of the river, and surrounded by low-lying meadows which provided an ideal breeding ground for disease-ridden mosquitoes and rats. It is hardly surprising that the mortality rate was high.[31]

When plague struck, Trinity, like other colleges, departed en masse for the relative safety of the country, in Trinity's case the house within the parsonage of Garsington. Four fellows would be chosen to stay behind to mind the College, and the rest, each armed with a stick or other weapons, carried with them such vestments, chapel plate, books, and kitchen equipment as the President and College officers deemed necessary to keep body and soul together.[32] This happened all too frequently. In October 1563 all University lectures and exercises were postponed on account of the plague, and the postponement was twice extended until the autumn of 1564.[33] The Garsington retreat, however, was not yet ready, and on 25 May 1564 the dean and junior bursar rode out to Woodstock to arrange the rental of a house. There were many costs incurred, including the purchase of medicines, a visit from the doctor, and the expenses (*6s 9d*) of a Mr Greenwood who died of the plague.[34] The University decreed another postponement from Trinity Term 1571 until March 1572, and Trinity this time was able to decamp to Garsington, hiring men to convey '*necessaria*' and 'bedding' both there and back again. The senior bursar rode to Abingdon to purchase provisions, while the four fellows left in College had to venture out to Woodstock and Kidlington to buy food and drink. They also invested in an antidote against the plague.[35] The disease raged again in November 1575, and on 3 April 1576 President Yeldard issued formal documentation to Thomas Blocksom, butcher, of Garsington, to facilitate his travel in the College's name as he bought 'for us so many calves . . . as shall serve our necessary use'.[36] Two years later a virulent typhus epidemic spread from the 'black assizes' at Oxford gaol, via the judges and juries to the population at large, and Trinity donated 6*s* to a public collection held to relieve the suffering

[31] James McConica, 'Elizabethan Oxford: The Collegiate Society', *HUO* 3, 648.
[32] TCA Statutes, *ordinatio de Garsington.*
[33] Andrew Clark, *Register of the University of Oxford II 1571–1622*, pt 1 (OHS 1887), 157–61.
[34] TCA *Computus* 1563–4, ff. 58v–59r.
[35] Ibid., 1573–4, f. 131v–133r.
[36] TCA Register A, f. 144, f. 213d.

of the poor.[37] In April 1579 University lectures and exercises were again postponed, and in November 1582 public assemblies were banned, on suspicion of the plague.

Back in College meanwhile, 'consider the plight,' muses James McConica, 'of the undergraduate, rising at 4 in February to attend mass and prayers in an unheated chapel.'[38] The warmest place in Trinity (besides the kitchen) was the Hall. Here there was a fire, here undergraduates were taught, and here the whole College came together to eat. Their diet was 'substantial, limited, monotonous'. Dinner—at midday—consisted of hot meat (usually beef or mutton, or fish during Lent), bread, butter, cheese, and 'small beer'. Supper—5 or 6 p.m.—comprised cold meat (usually beef or mutton), bread, butter, cheese, and pottage (oatmeal steeped in the stock from boiling meat).[39]

As the Hall was central to College life, so dinner was central to the college day. It was invested with formal etiquette, vestiges of which can still be observed four centuries later. The fellows and scholars stood before their places, awaiting the arrival of the President. He sat at the 'first table' and with him the vice-president and two invited Doctors or Bachelors of Divinity (or MAs if need be). The remaining fellows—arranged according to their degrees—sat at a side table, placed at the east (quadrangle) side of the Hall. With them sat the most privileged commoners, sons of noblemen or eldest sons of knights, also those of lower social rank if their parents or friends paid for them to have the same commons as the fellows. Some of the scholars might join the fellows, invited by the vice-president as a reward for good conduct, while the rest sat together at another table. Everyone ate in silence and 'ruminated on spiritual food' which came in the form of a Bible reading brought by one of the scholars or BAs, and explained after dinner by the President or one of the fellows. After the meal the tables were cleared, tablecloths replaced, and basins of water brought out. The prescribed prayers were said by one of the scholars, standing before the President's table, and a loving cup passed round. Then all sat quietly while one of the scholars declaimed 'earnestly, eloquently and briefly' on a theme given by the President or rhetoric lecturer, and the scholars (those who had taken their turn at serving) and

[37] Leslie Clarkson, *Death, Disease and Famine in Pre-Industrial England* (Dublin, 1975), 44; TCA *Computus* 1577–8.

[38] James McConica, 'Elizabethan Oxford', 648.

[39] Ibid., 647.

the servants ate. This was the *narrare*, as stipulated in the Statutes and as objected to by John Perte. Nobody departed before the President; nobody lingered at the table once he had gone.[40]

The Library was a valuable College resource that was reserved for the fellows and graduate scholars, who were each issued with a key. The penalty for leaving the door unlocked was a hefty 6s 8*d* fine, to be spent on new books. The Statutes envisaged more books than the library could hold, and made provision for the surplus to be divided between the fellows in the form of a circulating library. The President and the borrower would each have one half of an indenture recording the titles and dates of receipt, and every year, within a week of Trinity Sunday, the books would be brought together for inspection in the Hall. The Library grew slowly but visibly as the years passed, by means of gifts from fellows, scholars, and commoners. New donations were inscribed with the name and title of the donor, according to a formula laid out in the Statutes. There is no evidence of the circulatory system in use in the early days, but a number of volumes were certainly added to it in 1618 when Edward Hyndmer bequeathed his large library to the College.[41]

The Founder's urgent reminder that members of his College should only speak to John Basford in Latin suggests that the rule to converse only in 'learned languages' was from the beginning a custom more honoured in the breach than the observance.[42] It would be foolish to assume that all the rules set out in the Statutes were in reality enforced. But social distinctions were important in Elizabethan England, and especially so in the University during the chancellorship of Robert Dudley, Earl of Leicester, who sought to enforce the dress code that had evolved in the medieval University.[43] Trinity required all members of the College to appear in ankle-length gowns, their degree marked by the cut of their hood. Doctors of Theology could wear fur on their hoods, and the President alone was allowed tippets (long hanging sleeves) of silk or cloth, or a hood if he chose. No fancy fabrics were worn, nor furs. Weapons could only be carried on a journey, when more practical shorter gowns were also permitted.[44]

Outside the formal requirements of the College routines, there

[40] TCA Statutes Chapter 10.

[41] TCA Statutes Chapter 24; TCA Benefactions B1.3.

[42] TCA Misc. Vol. I, f. 12/27.

[43] Williams, 'Elizabethan Oxford', 423.

[44] TCA Statutes Chapter 17.

were various opportunities to relax. All members were encouraged to go out for walks, although never alone. They were forbidden to spend time around the town or in the suburbs, unless on urgent College or University business, or on their way to give or hear lectures. Undergraduate scholars stayed within the College precinct, unless, with the permission of the dean or logic lecturer, they ventured into the countryside in groups of at least three, for the purpose of 'exercise or mental relaxation'. Certain pastimes were encouraged by the Statutes; surprisingly (for there is no evidence that Trinity ever had a fives court), throwing a hand ball against a wall was expressly 'not forbidden'. But dice, cards, other ball games and anything else that the President, vice-president, or dean chose, were prohibited.[45] There was an obvious practical concern to protect the windows and fabric of the College buildings—every year, the bill for glazing and minor repairs was large—and also a moral one, to protect susceptible young men from the dangers of gambling.

The Christmas Vacation was a particularly special time. Members of the foundation feasted on brawn and capons, luxuriated before an extravagantly large fire—extra coals being sent by the President from Garsington—and, by a noteworthy concession in the Statutes, played cards. Just occasionally, jollifications are mentioned in the *computus* accounts: a 'spectacle' staged for the Trinity feast in 1565, musicians hired at Christmas 1579, and a Christmas play in 1585.[46]

The College grounds were extensive and pleasant, and for obvious reasons were well cared for by the foundation. The grove was reached via a passage through the eastern end of the north range of the Quadrangle. In 1560 a new postern gate was made, and eight keys cut for the President and seven senior fellows, a step worthy of a meeting of the whole fellowship and a decree in the College Register.[47] The following year, a covered walkway was created 'where we planted privet', and in 1580 another decree passed to regulate the care of a new, private garden.[48] There were to be the same eight key-holders, and the fellows agreed to invest in the wages of a skilled gardener, until 'the well-tended garden' could pay for itself, presumably by the internal sale of produce.[49] Further expenditure on plants included

[45] TCA Statutes Chapter 17.

[46] TCA *Computus* 1564–5, f. 66v; 1579–80, f. 232v; 1584–5, f. 276.

[47] TCA Register A f.140.

[48] TCA *Computus* 1561–2, f. 19d.

[49] TCA Register A f. 142.

roses in 1581, plum trees in 1587, and rosemary and paved alleys in 1594.[50]

The accommodation provided by Trinity was basic. Each room was furnished with one or two main beds, depending on space, and, stored beneath, a low, wheeled truckle bed. It was common practice in the University for a fellow to share his chamber with one of the scholars, who performed the duties of a personal servant.[51] Trinity owned some furniture at least: the repair and replacement of beds, cupboards, tables, stools, benches, and shelves is a regular expense in the annual accounts.

## *Undergraduates and Servants*

Between 1550 and 1590 Oxford experienced a sharp rise in the number of admissions of fee-paying undergraduates to the University.[52] An upper limit of twenty commoners was specified in Trinity's Statutes, but this was quickly exceeded. Andrew Clark identified twenty undergraduate commoners in the College in 1565 and twenty-six in 1672; of these nearly half went on to hold scholarships.[53] Commoners were accepted as an ordinary part of the College establishment, living and learning 'alongside the scholars, at table as well as in the classroom'.[54] Undergraduate commoners in Trinity paid between 5*s* and 6*s* 8*d* a year for their accommodation.[55] Food was extra, billed in arrears as termly battels, and so were the fees charged by the fellows who acted as their tutors. In 1555 Trinity was unique in the University in having statutory provision for the education of commoners, since the medieval system of lectures and formal disputations within the various university faculties was no longer providing the modern curriculum needed by England's governing classes.[56] An important innovation made by Pope and Slythurst was to provide for the educational needs of undergraduates in-house, with no recourse to the lectures of the University, although Trinity's

[50] TCA *Computus* 1580–1; 1586–7, f. 294; 1594–5, f. 365.
[51] John Newman, 'The Physical Setting: New Building and Adaptation', *HUO* 3, 628.
[52] Stone, 'Student Body', 16–17.
[53] Clark, *Register of the University 1571–1622*, 24, 42.
[54] James McConica, 'The Rise of the Undergraduate College', *HUO* 3, 44.
[55] TCA Statutes Chapter 10.
[56] J. M. Fletcher, 'The Faculty of Arts', *HUO* 3, 198.

*Table 3.2* The undergraduate timetable as laid out in the Statutes.

| | | | Term | | | |
|---|---|---|---|---|---|---|
| *Time* | *Monday* | *Tuesday* | *Wednesday* | *Thursday* | *Friday* | *Saturday* |
| Before 6 a.m. | Mass | Mass | Mass | Mass | Mass | Mass |
| 6–8 a.m. | Philosophy Lectures *arithmetic, geometry logic, philosophy* | Philosophy Lectures *arithmetic, geometry logic, philosophy* | Philosophy Lectures *arithmetic, geometry logic, philosophy* | Philosophy Lectures *arithmetic, geometry logic, philosophy* | Philosophy Lectures *arithmetic, geometry logic, philosophy* | Philosophy Lectures *arithmetic, geometry logic, philosophy* |
| Before Dinner | 2 hours disputations (working in pairs) | 1 hour disputation (working in pairs) | 2 hours disputations (working in pairs) | 1 hour disputation (working in pairs) | 2 hours disputations (working in pairs) | 1 hour disputation (working in pairs) |
| Dinner | Narrare | Narrare | Narrare | Narrare | Narrare | Narrare |
| 3–5 p.m. | Classical Texts (Humanities Lecturer) *Rhetoric* | Classical Texts (Humanities Lecturer) *Poetry and drama* | Classical Texts (Humanities Lecturer) *Rhetoric* | Classical Texts (Humanities Lecturer) *Poetry and drama* | Classical Texts (Humanities Lecturer) *Rhetoric* | Classical Texts (Humanities Lecturer) *Poetry and drama* |
| | | | Long Vacation | | | |
| Before 6 a.m. | Mass | Mass | Mass | Mass | Mass | Mass |
| Morning | Astronomy Class 1 hour disputation | 1 hour disputation | Astronomy Class 1 hour disputation | 1 hour disputation | Astronomy Class 1 hour disputation | 1 hour disputation |
| Afternoon | *Elegies or verse* | BAs to read something useful | *Elegies or verse* | BAs to read something useful | *Elegies or verse* | BAs to read something useful |

*Source*: TCA Statutes Chapter 15.

scholars were still expected to attend those in logic.[57] Undergraduates were expected to take four years to read for the BA, during which time they attended lectures (giving lectures was a necessary requirement of the MA degree) and performed exercises in the form of disputations, in which the 'opponent' proposed a subject and the 'respondent' answered. When these requirements had been met, the undergraduate would make a formal application to receive his degree. After 1576 he was also required to subscribe formally to the Thirty-Nine Articles.[58]

Trinity offered a comprehensive course of study for undergraduate scholars and commoners alike, working under the daily instruction and supervision of the philosophy ('logic') and humanities ('rhetoric' or 'Latin') lecturers. The Statutes set out in detail a rigorous timetable for term time, and—'lest the scholars should give themselves up to idleness and laziness'—a lighter but still structured programme of work for the Long Vacation, which ran through August and September. This included a thrice-weekly discussion of the globe and the movement of the planets 'or similar'. For the shorter vacations of Christmas, Easter, and Pentecost there were academic exercises to be fitted in around the exhaustive religious activities of the college day, with one of the two lecturers leading a daily declamation practice, the other of reciting verse. An example of each would be performed daily in Hall to the assembled College.[59]

During full term the scholars and commoners spent two hours in Hall each morning at philosophy lectures, and a further two hours each afternoon with the humanities lecturer, who read and 'interpreted' Latin texts from a set list of authors. He had discretionary powers, if he felt his audience would benefit, to turn to more advanced reading material, even Greek (although this eventuality was perhaps so unlikely that no actual Greek author was specified).[60] The following list of books and authors was laid out in the Statutes:

Undergraduate Reading List

Rhetoric

Cicero *de Officiis*
Valerius Maximus

[57] McConica, 'Undergraduate College', 44.
[58] Fletcher, 'The Faculty of Arts', 165, 168–9, 171.
[59] TCA Statutes Chapter 15.
[60] 'The study of Greek was clearly regarded as desirable but improbable.' McConica, 'Undergraduate College', 44.

Suetonius Tranquillus
Florus

Advanced Reading

Pliny *Naturalis Historia*
Livy
Cicero *de Oratore*
Quintilian *Institutio Oratoria*
Quintilian *Declamationes*
Greek authors

Poetry and Drama

Virgil
Horace
Lucan
Juvenal
Terence
Plautus

Arithmetic

Frisius Gemma
Or Tunstall of Durham

Geometry

Euclid (or an easier author)

Logic

Porphyry
Aristotle
Rodolph Agricola
John Caesar

Philosophy

Aristotle
Plato[61]

The income brought into the College by commoners was attractive, but they posed other risks (besides broken windows), in particular that of unpaid bills. With the permission of his family, a young man could depart for another college or institution at any time. Oxford's celebrated tutorial system began with tutors taking financial responsibility for their pupils.[62] At Trinity, Yeldard held a long meeting with all the fellows in his chamber after the 1560 audit and wrote up a de-

[61] TCA Statutes Chapter 15.

[62] McConica, 'Elizabethan Oxford', 493–5.

cree in the College Register, which each of the fellows signed. Each tutor agreed to bind himself in £10 to pay each pupil's debts if they were not settled within thirty days of the end of term.[63]

A decade later the problem of unpaid bills was no better, and Yeldard drew up another decree.[64] A separate account, known as the *Billa Petitionis*, was begun in 1572, and debts were carried over from year to year until they were either settled or written off. Both courses of action required patience. The battels of three undergraduate commoners were noted in the *Billa Petitionis* of 1572 (when the considerable sum of £77 was owing to the College):

| | |
|---|---|
| Bray | *7s 1d* |
| Piggot | *23s 6d* |
| Crispin | £3 *6s* $1^1/_2$ *d.* |

Crispin paid off *7s* the following year, *36s 2d* in 1595, and the remainder the year after. The names of Bray and Piggot, however, were carried forward for almost a century, appearing as late at 1664.[65]

A more effective means of controlling undergraduate finance was caution money, demanded from every member from 1579. Sons of noblemen, knights, and esquires—the 'fellow' or 'gentlemen commoners'—paid a higher rate of 40*s*; those of lower social standing—the battellers—a lower rate of 30*s*. The accumulated cautions provided a useful purse to facilitate the daily cash flow of the College's administration. The different rates charged were a further sign, besides the different tables and values of commons in Hall, of Trinity's recognition of the different social classes within the College. Thomas Pope had foreseen the eventuality of a privileged upper class in his College; indeed, he had allowed members of his own family to be exactly that, and he had paved the way for various exemptions in Chapter 15 of the Statutes, which makes special provision for those excused the standard academic work by 'age, person or circumstance'.[66]

There was an underclass growing too, the servitors, who were exempted from paying caution money and allowed to study in return for a wide range of domestic duties. Their status was less well defined than that of the College servants, who had job descriptions

[63] TCA Register A, f. 140. [64] Ibid., f. 140v.

[65] TCA Accounts III/F/1, *Billa Petitionis*.

[66] McConica, 'Undergraduate College', 44.

and daily commons allocated by the Statutes, and played an important supporting role in the life of the foundation.[67] At the head of the household was the powerful and privileged figure of the manciple, who purchased the food, regulated the dole of commons, planned the President's high-table menus, and liaised with College tenants. Manciples in Oxford often held important positions in the town alongside their College work. The position offered considerable earning potential, not least the profit to be made from battels, the manciple's role equated by Carl Hammer to that of running a college tuck shop.[68] Trinity's first manciple was William Lovercraste, and he doubled as the butler, another position of considerable responsibility. By 1557 Henry Millward had taken over as manciple, and the butler was one James Allwood. There is no evidence whether or not Allwood met the Statutes' criterion of 'a poor scholar eager for an education'. According to the Statutes the butler also acted as porter, keeping the College key, opening the gate each morning, and locking up as dusk fell. He also had a key to the buttery, from which he issued the daily supply of bread and beer, and every evening he would carry all the silver to the President's Lodgings, where it was stored overnight.

The manciple worked closely with the cook, that key worker in any college community. Oxford's college cooks were granted privileged status by the Chancellor's court, and the position offered valuable perquisites. The Trinity Statutes called for an 'honest man, of blameless reputation, hard-working, skilled in his art, and always ready to fulfil his office'. He was assisted by the under-cook, a figure never named in the *computus*, who spent his days fetching wood, lighting fires, drawing water from the well, scouring pots, and turning meat on the spit.[69] Little is known of individual cooks, but Thomas Acton, a Trinity cook who died in 1616, was very comfortably off, owning silver plate valued at £10, including a 'double salt parcel gilt with a cover, a little wine cup gilt, two white little bowls and 9 spoons'.[70]

The final member of the Trinity College household was the laundress. Thomas Pope had been determined that no female servants

[67] TCA Statutes Chapter 11.

[68] Carl I. Hammer, Jr., 'Oxford Town and Oxford University', *HUO* 3, 77.

[69] TCA Statutes Chapter 11.

[70] Helen Clifford, 'Oxford College Cooks 1400–1800', in *Cooks and Other People: Proceedings of the Oxford Symposium on Food and Cookery*, ed. Harlan Walker (Totnes, 1996), 60.

should be attached to his College at all, but had reluctantly made an exception to ensure the supply of clean altar linen and tablecloths. The laundress had to collect and return the washing at the Chapel gate, and she had to be of such an 'age, reputation and condition' that no suspicion could possibly fall on her.[71] In fact, from Trinity's earliest days, many women worked for the College. In 1561 three women worked for three days planting privet in the grove. Women appear regularly and anonymously in the *computus* (although sometimes named as the wives and daughters of male servants), part of the army of casual workers of both sexes who cleaned and carried and performed the countless menial tasks without which the College could not have operated at all.

One independent Oxford tradesman forged a more formal relationship with the College, on account of his loyal service and vital skills. Matthew Udall first worked for the College as a slater, but soon came to be seen as a clerk of works or maintenance manager. In December 1574 a formal resolution was written into the College Register, recognizing his 'slatting, mossing & pargeting for wages by days work' and the way he had repaired 'without wages such small faults and decays of slates in the roof or pargeting in walls, or sealing or paving upon the ground'. He was to be retained on an annual stipend of 13*s* 4*d*, and indeed, in 1583 he was erroneously included by the junior bursar as a member of the official household of servants.[72]

In 1565 the new matriculation statute was adopted by the University, recognizing the presence of more and more commoners in Oxford, and seeking to control them by requiring that all should be presented for matriculation—i.e., that they should swear an oath to observe the university's statutes—within one week of their arrival. A further matriculation statute in 1582 sought to impose religious uniformity, requiring matriculating undergraduates to subscribe to the articles of religion and to royal supremacy. The only penalty that the University could exact on those not complying was to disbar them from taking degrees; it meant, from Trinity's perspective, a further division between classes in the College. Fellow commoners did not need a degree, and often did not bother to matriculate; the servitors do not appear in the College caution book, but they and the scholars seemed almost invariably to matriculate.

[71] TCA Statutes Chapter 11.

[72] TCA *Computus* 1561–2, f. 19d.

Using the University's matriculation register and the College caution account, it is thus possible from 1579 to obtain some limited information about Trinity's undergraduate members.[73] The numbers matriculating and paying caution varied considerably from year to year, as did the number of years for which each individual stayed; but the trend was a steady increase in the College population. At first there was little pressure on the College chambers; as in other colleges, the Reformation had had the effect of reducing numbers in the University, and there was surplus space to be filled.[74] But as the standards of domestic comfort and personal privacy increased in homes across the land, Trinity was under pressure to adapt and expand its accommodation to meet the requirements of its residents. Yeldard embarked on a programme of building cocklofts—attic rooms with dormer windows—into the roofs of the old buildings. Money was often tight, and there were limits to what repairs and improvements could be contrived. In the 1570s such new chambers were built into the north range of the quadrangle. Loggan shows four with windows looking into the quad, and eight, including two in the top floor of the buttery, looking north. The first were completed in 1573, the remainder in 1577, when some £35 had to be borrowed from the 'founder's money' until it could be repaid in the following financial year.[75] Glazing, increasingly a requirement not a luxury, was another continual drain on the College's resources. Many windows were being glazed for the first time, while the glass in chambers, Chapel, and Hall required all too frequent repairs.

To the end of her life, Elizabeth Pope maintained her interest in the College. Two of her later letters are preserved in the Trinity archive. On 5 September 1574 she directed the President and fellows to 'present any such able man as you shall think meet and sufficient into the vicarage of Much Waltham', although, as she made clear, she was passing up her own right to make the appointment 'for this turn & vacation only'.[76] On 12 June 1590 she dictated a long series of instructions about whom the College should elect 'for the supply of your vacant rooms which are and may be at this your Trinity election'. Her advanced age in no way diminished her detailed know-

[73] Transcripts of these sources were made by H. E. D. Blakiston, TCA Blakiston D/1.
[74] Newman, 'The Physical Setting', *HUO* 3, 615.
[75] TCA Accounts, Caution Book I, f. 23d–24.
[76] TCA Register A, f. 23.

ledge of the foundation. First she recommended Francis Field to a probationary fellowship, on account of his seniority. Then, Roger Weston—on account of the 'just causes of his father's great poverty and good desert (as you know) to me and your house, I am contented to show some special favour to his son.' She suggested two further names and then nominated no fewer than seven candidates for scholarships. The Foundress concluded, somewhat peremptorily, with the expectation of a quick and affirmative reply: 'by the next messenger (and this I mean very shortly) [I] shall receive your assurance. And so now troubling you no further, I pray to God for your virtuous and prosperous well doing, and commit you all to the holy and blessed Trinity.' She signed the letter herself, 'your loving friend, Elizabeth Paulet'.[77] Within the week, Field had been duly elected to the only vacant fellowship. Weston had to wait another year.

Lady Elizabeth expected to be obeyed, and indeed, Arthur Yeldard had been at her command for almost his entire adult life. Another of whose loyalty to herself and to the College she could have had no doubt was Ralph Kettell. He was Lady Elizabeth's protégé; he had grown up at King's Langley in Hertfordshire, near Tyttenhanger, and she had sent him to take up a Trinity scholarship in 1579, at the age of 16. By 1598 he was the fourth most senior fellow. Elizabeth Paulet died in November 1593, and in February 1599 Yeldard too passed away. Ralph Kettell was the first of the two nominations sent by the fellows to the Visitor, and he was duly sworn in on 12 February 1599. He was to extend the influence of the Pope family through much of the seventeenth century.

[77] TCA. This letter is pasted into Register A, between ff. 45 and 46.

# 4

# *President Kettell*

## *Ralph Kettell as President*

On 2 May 1642, Ralph Kettell, then aged 79, admitted the 16-year-old son of a Wiltshire squire as a fellow commoner of the College. The youth's name was John Aubrey. Aubrey spent less than four months at Trinity before being summoned home by his father 'for fear' of the Civil War. He pleaded to be allowed to return to Oxford, which he did the following February, only to fall 'sick of the small pox' two months later. When he recovered—'after Trinity week'—he departed for the country once more. Such was the slender acquaintance—barely half a year in total—on which Aubrey based his memoir of Kettell, compiled in the 1680s for the Oxford antiquarian Anthony Wood and published in 1898 by the Oxford historian Andrew Clark. The material in Aubrey's brief life has coloured all subsequent analysis of Kettell's forty-four-year presidency of Trinity.

Aubrey's vivid description of the octogenarian President, as seen through the eyes of a teenager, has undoubtedly brought Ralph Kettell a fame that he might otherwise not have achieved, but at the price of a reputation that he does not, perhaps, entirely deserve.[1] It has, for instance, been accepted unquestioningly that the brain behind Kettell Hall was like a 'Hasty pudding, where there was memory, judgement and fancy, all stirred up together'.[2] In a recent edition of *Brief Lives* he is defined as 'a figure of awe and fun to generations of undergraduates'.[3] Aubrey nostalgically recalled Kettell being baited by the undergraduates, who mimicked his dragging foot—'by which he gave warning (like the rattlesnake) of his coming. Will Egerton . . . would go so like him, that sometimes he would make the whole Chapel rise up imagining he had been entering in'—copied his high-

[1] Aubrey, *Brief Lives* (John Aubrey), 9–17, (Ralph Kettell), 175–83.
[2] Ibid., 177. Aubrey is quoting 'one of the fellows'.
[3] Ibid., 175, the opinion of the editor, John Buchanan-Brown.

*4.1* Ralph Kettell, President 1599–1643, by George Bathurst.

pitched singing voice—'there was one, John Hoskyns, who had a higher, and would play the wag with the Doctor to make him strain his voice up to his'—and ridiculed his Trinity Sunday sermons—'whither a number of the scholars of other houses would come, to laugh at him'.[4] In Aubrey's skilful hands, Kettell's strong personality developed a quality larger than life, and as a result his numerous achievements have all too often been overshadowed by his equally numerous eccentricities. There can be no doubt that Ralph Kettell was one of the great Presidents of Trinity. For more than four decades,

[4] Ibid., 179, 176, 180.

he *was* the College; more than that, he *knew* he was the College. He recorded Trinity's past for the express benefit of its future. He was a vigilant guardian of its members, and steered the foundation through the religious and political minefields of the early seventeenth century. He expanded Trinity's buildings and boosted its finances; and throughout his presidency he fought the College's battles with untiring and dogged determination.

Ralph Kettell is the first Trinity President of whom a portrait exists. His stepson-in-law, George Bathurst, painted his picture from memory in oils, a sad and serious-looking figure, with white moustache, short beard, black cap, and narrow, pleated ruff, and the image was copied, rather flatly, for the Hall. But Aubrey, who had a particular interest in physiognomy, is to be thanked for bringing Kettell more vividly to life with his description of the President's 'fresh ruddy complexion' and imposing stature. 'He was a very tall well grown man. His gown and surplice and hood being on, he had a terrible gigantic aspect, with his sharp grey eyes. The ordinary gown he wore was a russet cloth gown. He was, they say, white very soon; he had a very venerable presence, and was an excellent Governor.'[5]

Indeed he was. One of his first acts was to boost College finances by a *Decretum de Gratiis Collegio Rependendis* (Decree about repaying favours to the College). This was a windfall tax, which all members of the foundation were to be bound by oath to pay, should financial good fortune come their way. On 12 December 1602 the fellows all signed their assent to the measure, which was copied into both the Statute Book and the College Register. They promised to give the College 20 per cent of the annual value of any property they might inherit, and 12.5 per cent of the annual value of any benefice they might accept, and they would bequeath to Trinity 5 per cent of any capital which they might acquire. Kettell led by example and handed over 40*s* from his rectory at Garsington, which was followed immediately by a donation of 20*s* from James Sellar, who was rector of Hickford, Bucks. Four further donations were recorded in the caution book, bringing in another £11 3*s* 4*d* between 1603 and 1617. Three of these related to livings; the fourth was a generous £6 13*s* 4*d* donated by the cousin of an earlier college benefactor, Thomas Warren.[6]

Undergraduate commoners were also expected to make voluntary contributions. There was a university-wide custom that, on going

[5] Aubrey, *Brief Lives* (John Aubrey), 175.

[6] TCA Caution Book I, ff. 9–10.

down, a commoner would present to his college an item of silver plate, its value in accordance with his social rank.[7] At Trinity Kettell soon introduced a Plate Fund, to which a fellow commoner was expected to donate 20*s* at the end of his first year. In 1605–6, £7 14*s* 5*d* was 'received from the President, money collected from convictors coming up, for buying silver plate'.[8] Cash donations continued steadily throughout Kettell's presidency, while the wealthier commoners preferred to give a tankard or a bowl inscribed with their family names and coats of arms. By these means the College store of silver grew rapidly. In December 1626 an inventory was made 'of plate in the butler's keeping'. There were three salts, two of which had been given by Lord Wentworth and Sir John Newdigate, and fourteen 'eared pots', three from the Founder and the remainder presented by undergraduate commoners. The Newdigate Salt, including its engraving, cost £3 12*s*, and was given early in its donor's second year at Trinity.[9] The College had thirty-one bowls donated by members, also two tuns (beer casks), and four tankards, one of them 'double gilt'. Also in the butler's custody were thirty-seven spoons (thirteen 'with knobs' and the rest 'slips'), candlesticks of brass and pewter, salts and basins, tablecloths, napkins, and towels. By 1632 there were thirty-nine bowls and eight tankards, but only thirty-five spoons could be found when the inventory was made.[10]

Other families chose to present plate for the Chapel. Two communion flagons, still in the College, were given by William Pickering (1626) and Richard Bull (1629). Another surviving piece is the exceptionally fine silver-gilt cup and cover, exquisitely engraved with roses, thistles, and acorns, which was given personally to Kettell and subsequently engraved and presented by him to the College. The cup is adorned by a shield pricked with the initials R K. Around the lip is inscribed an elegiac couplet:

*Sit bowrne gratus at hoc Kettell haud dignus honore est,*
*Gratia sit triadi deferor huc igitur*

[Bourne may be grateful, but Kettell is not worthy of this honour.
Let the gratitude be to Trinity; that is why I am brought here]

[7] Stephen Porter, 'University and Society', *HUO* 4, 83.
[8] TCA *Computus* 1605–6, Receipts.
[9] Vivienne Larminie, 'The Undergraduate Account Book of John and Richard Newdigate 1618–1621', *Camden Miscellany XXX* (London: Royal Historical Society, 1990), 198.
[10] TCA Plate 1, ff. 7–8, 20.

*4.2* The Kettell Cup.

and around the cover:

> *Emit Bourne, tenuit Kettell, nunc possidet ista*
> *Sacra domus Triados perpetuo et teneat*
>
> [Bourne bought me, Kettell held me, now the sacred house of Trinity owns me—and may it hold me forever].

The cup is hallmarked 1603 (Plate 4.2).[11]

Under Ketttell's careful stewardship, Trinity's annual income steadily increased during the first decades of the seventeenth

[11] H. C. Moffatt, *Old Oxford Plate* (London, 1906), 156. Kettell was President to three Bournes: Gilbert (scholar 1607) Anthony (1636), and Roger (1638).

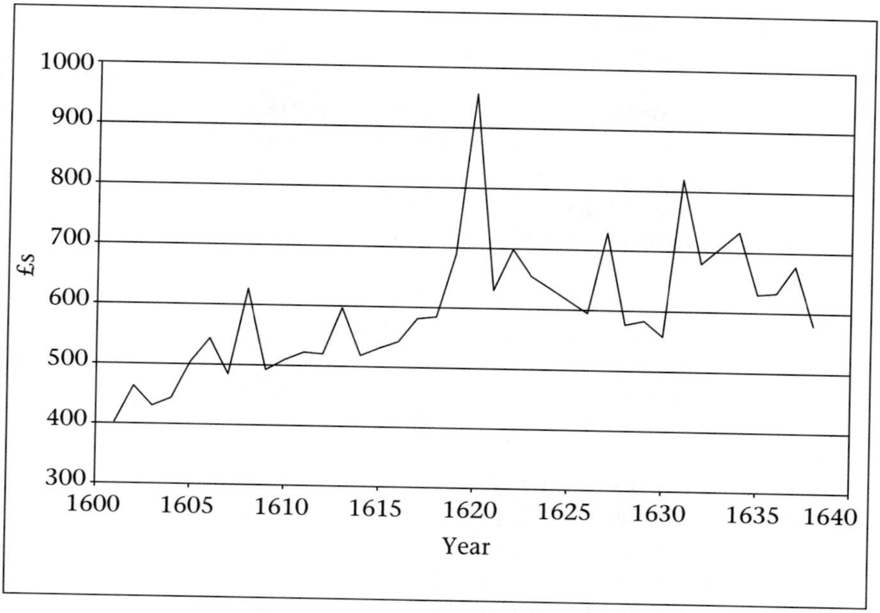


*Fig. 4.1* Trinity College income 1601–1635.

century. Two long leases which had been made at the time of the foundation—of Great Waltham Rectory and the Dumbleton tithes—expired in 1605, and for the first time the College was able to take advantage of the Corn Rent Act of 1571. The Act specified that one third of rent should be 'reserved' and paid in kind at a fixed rate of one quarter of wheat per 6*s* 8*d* of rent owed, and one quarter of barley per 5*s* of rent.[12] This would be translated to the current market price and paid in cash. When harvests were poor the rent would therefore be higher, and the College would be protected against inflated food prices in the market. Since the foundation, the annual rent from Great Waltham had been £48. This now became £32 paid in cash, half at Lady Day (25 March) and half at Michaelmas (29 September). The corn rent was 24 quarters of wheat (worth £8 at the rate of 6*s* 8*d* per quarter) and 32 quarters of barley (worth £8 at 5*s* per quarter). In the year 1605–6, the corn rent brought in £30 8*s* at Lady

[12] A quarter is a unit of volume, equal to 8 bushels (or 190.94 litres).

Day and £32 16*s* at Michaelmas, a dramatic rise in the College revenues. The following year the lease of the Dumbleton tithes was renewed, and again an increase in the real rent was the result. Members of the foundation were given their first pay rise since 1556, in the form of an increase in their weekly allowance for commons. Fifty pounds was set aside for the President, fellows, and scholars, and £4 11*s* for the four members of the household, a very significant addition to the previous annual commons bill of just under £100.[13]

## *The College Buildings*

Ralph Kettell invested every penny that he could in improving the College buildings. The early years of the seventeenth century saw Oxford's colleges, which had undertaken virtually no large-scale building projects since the 1520s, rush to provide more modern and comfortable accommodation. This was an obvious way to attract more and wealthier commoners, whose fees and room rents were increasingly needed to balance the books.[14] At Trinity, where the buildings were nearly two centuries old, this need was particularly pressing, and Kettell embarked on an intensive programme of repair and upgrading that would not be equalled until the second half of the twentieth century. On several occasions the President had to borrow money to complete urgent work. In the year 1602–3 John Sorrell, the College tenant at Great Waltham, loaned £50 to ease a temporary difficulty in completing 'bedrooms above the library against the coming of the honourable Lord Wentworth'. In 1605 the treasury was completely empty, and Sorrell repeated the loan, which was not repaid until 1608, when Kettell himself lent the College £100 for five years.[15] The simplest way to house more undergraduates remained the addition of cocklofts to existing buildings, and these went up in every available roof space, even above the Chapel passage and over the Hall, where there was a 'chamber over high table . . . newly made' and, at the northern end, a 'floor and studies over hall, wholly new'. On the ground floor, Kettell moved the bursary into what had been the vestry in the south-east corner of the quad, and turned the bur-

[13] TCA *Computus* 1605–6, ff. 59v, 71v.
[14] John Newman, 'The Architectural Setting', *HUO* 4, 135.
[15] TCA *Computus* 1602–3, 1605–6, 1607–8, Receipts.

sary into a chamber with a new portal, new study, and new window.[16] Constructing studies within the chambers by means of timber-framed partitions was a straightforward job which could be done in a week. A new study in the 'low corner chamber next the grove' (the north-east corner of the Quadrangle) had a stone window ('Faulkner and boy, 7 days') which was plastered and glazed, and was made of wooden boards ('two men setting up, two-and-a-half days') with wooden shelves and tables. It came in at under 33*s*.[17]

In 1608 Kettell wrote up a detailed record of his first eight years' work. He was satisfied with the condition of the buildings; yet, anxious lest the gamble of such rapid expansion should be misunderstood by future generations, he 'thought it our duty to satisfy our successors and to safeguard our own credits, to report somewhat more particularly what has been done'. His staircase-by-staircase report catalogued new windows, new doors, new staircases, new wainscotting, new plastering, new floors and new studies (Plate 4.3). Trinity now had thirty-four chambers, and a total of sixty-two studies, forty-four of which had been newly built. The four-page description was bound up with the annual *computus* accounts, which year by year reveal the results of his work.[18] Significant revenue was generated by room rents, but even more by the additional payments levied for the use of studies. Between 1600 and 1608, caution payments had doubled, room rents had increased by 120 per cent and payments for the use of studies had shown an almost twelvefold increase. And as the programme of building works continued, so did the rise in Trinity's revenue.

A more ambitious building project by far was the construction of a brand new residential block, which Kettell undertook completely independently of the College, using land leased from Oriel College. Kettell Hall was built on the site of the medieval Perilous Hall and was completed in 1615 (Plate 4.4). It had a door opening directly onto Broad Street, and a private garden with a gate into the College grounds.[19] From the beginning it was used to house members of the College, and made possible the sharp rise in the number of commoners on the College books which is evident from 1617. At the time

16 TCA *Computus* ii, ff. 92v–93.

17 Ibid., 1600–1, f. 7.

18 Ibid., 1608–9, ff. 92–3.

19 In 1898 Blakiston described a 'blocked up doorway at the bottom of the garden'. Blakiston, *Trinity*, 105.

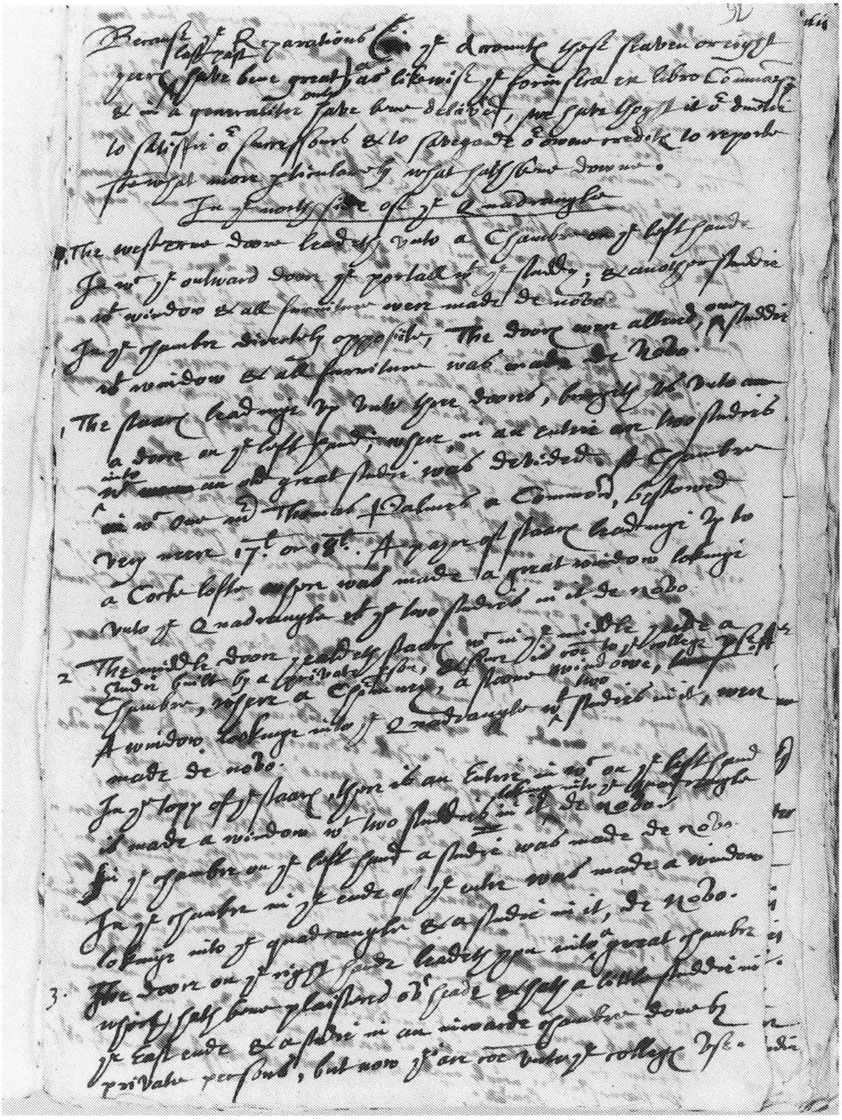

*4.3* President Kettell's College Survey 1608 (TCA *Computus* ii, 92).

*A View of Kettell Hall and Broad Street*

*From a Drawing by Muirhead Bone*

*4.4* Kettell Hall, by Muirhead Bone (Oxford University *Almanack*, 1908).

of Kettell's death, when numbers were very much reduced owing to the Civil War, the Hall was leased to one Anthony Furinfall. Kettell bequeathed the leasehold to his nephew, on the condition that half of the rent was to be paid to his sister Frances during her lifetime.[20]

In 1614 Kettell renovated the President's Lodgings, altering 'inner chambers and exterior buildings' and enlarging and constructing a wall around the garden, the dimensions of which are visible in Loggan's 1675 map of Oxford (Plate 5.2). He did not, however, submit the bill until two years later, when the College finances could stand it.[21] The Lodgings were entered via the central doorway in the eastern side of the Quadrangle (today's Staircase 9). Stairs led to a first-floor landing where two facing doors gave access to the Lodgings and to the Library, and more stairs led up to the cocklofts above.[22] The ancient frame of the presidential front door still remains in its original position, supporting the present door between the Old and Danson libraries. This doorway ceased to be used when President Bathurst created a new entrance to the Lodgings (today's Staircase 10), and for two centuries it was concealed and protected by plaster on the north side and a large book press to the south.[23] An inventory of 'utensils' in the President's custody, taken in December 1634, lists five rooms: the great chamber, the lobby and square room adjoining, the gallery, the chimney chamber, and the lower chamber and study.[24] The great chamber (today's room 10/3) was the President's dining and reception room; in 1634 it was furnished with five tables, six forms, and a wainscot bench. There were four cushions and two pictures of bishops on the walls. Here was kept one useful item of university paperwork: 'the circle for the Proctors', a circular chart by means of which the proctorial cycle could be calculated.[25] Kettell slept directly below in the chimney chamber (today's Bursar's Room, or 10/1). An inventory of his possessions, taken after his death in the summer of 1643, lists various home comforts, including dornock hangings on the walls, a canopy and curtains around the bed, coverlets, a quilt, and two green carpets. Kettell stored a large quantity of linen in his room, ranging from tablecloths and towels of expensive fine diaper and

[20] OUA, Hyp/B/28, ff. 71–4.

[21] TCA *Computus* 1615–16, f. 175.

[22] TCA Plate Book 1 f. ii.

[23] The door was rediscovered in 1888. Streeter, *The Chained Library*, 222.

[24] TCA Plate Book 1, ff. 11–11v.

[25] Falconer Madan, *Oxford Books* (Oxford, 1912), ii, 111. I am grateful to Andrew Hegarty for his elucidation of this obscure item.

damask, to 'eight dozen and one old course napkins' and 'thirty and three pairs of old course sheets and one odd.' He had too a sizeable collection of books (valued at £80).[26]

In 1618 there occurred one of the most renowned events in Trinity's history: the medieval Hall, then approaching its bicentenary, 'collapsed'.[27] The immediate cause of the disaster was the ambitious construction of cellars beneath a building that was already bearing the weight of additional rooms in the roof. However, no fatalities or major calamity were recorded in the annals of the University, suggesting that some partial structural damage may have given sufficient reason to embark upon the building of a more modern replacement. The new Hall took two years to build, and the inconvenience to the College community must have been immense, since during this period the number of admissions remained high. The work cost £700; Exeter College built a new hall at the same time for £1000. Exeter followed the traditional hall design, with a central fire on a brazier, and roof ventilation above.[28] Characteristically, Kettell saw an opportunity to cram additional residents in at minimal expense. Trinity's heating was provided by a hearth and chimney in the west wall of the new Hall, and a full set of cocklofts was built into the roof. There were three new chambers accessible via the stairs opposite the Chapel entrance, and three more by means of stairs running up from the Hall passage.[29] Loggan's 1675 view of Trinity suggests the six chambers were on the west side, overlooking Balliol, each with a fireplace and chimney, and nine smaller rooms, or studies, were on the east, overlooking the Quadrangle. Only £200 was available in the treasury, but £300 was borrowed from the ever-dependable John Sorrell, and Kettell embarked on his, and Trinity's, first venture into active fund-raising, the method 'familiar enough from the Middle Ages to the present day, the dogged soliciting of sums large and small, mostly the latter, from alumni and other well-wishers'.[30] Six donations were received in total. Fourteen pounds came from four old members: one ancient—Edward Cooper (1581); two middle-aged—John Whistler and Thomas Marler (both scholars of 1595); and one just gone down—William Master (1617). A generous £20 was sent by the Bishop of London (a Christ Church graduate), and a remarkable £6 12*s* by an

[26] OUA, Hyp/B/15, ff. 18–19. [27] Kettell, in TCA Caution Book I, f. 46.
[28] Newman, 'The Architectural Setting', 146, 156. [29] TCA Plate Book 1, ff. 1–3v.
[30] TCA Caution Book 1, f. 46; John Newman, 'The Architectural Setting', 137.

Oxford brewer named Wheeler, whose father-in-law, one Alderman Hands, had suggested he make a contribution to the new cellar.[31]

In 1625 Kettell's next large project got under way: it was a 'major refit' of the Library.[32] Not that the Library had been neglected during the earlier renovations; in 1608 the College survey recorded that it had been replastered throughout, and four new desks put in, while in 1613 two new half-desks had been built against the southern wall.[33] The work in 1625 was financed by a notable bequest from one of the College's earliest fellows, Edward Hyndmer, who was a namesake, possibly a kinsman, of the last warden of Durham College.[34] Hyndmer had been elected to a scholarship in 1561 and to a fellowship in 1568. But he was reluctant to take holy orders in the Protestant Church, and resigned his fellowship to live at Ascot, near Wing in Buckinghamshire, under the patronage of the Catholic Sir Robert Dormer and his wife Elizabeth. The largest single bequest in Hyndmer's will—£66 6*s* 8*d*—was to Trinity, 'in which society I was brought up a boy to study', and he also left the College his library, which could be kept or sold to benefit the poor. Hyndmer named the President and fellows of Trinity as his executors, with the desire that 'my body may be buried in the Chapel of Trinity College'. But, the benefactor added humbly, 'If this cannot be by reason of the remoteness of the place,' he was to be buried instead 'in the church or churchyard of wherever God shall appoint my death'.[35]

In the event Hyndmer was buried at Wing on 20 August 1618, and nobody from Trinity was present. William Hollins, the College manciple, set off for Wing on 1 September, and two weeks later Kettell himself rode out to meet with Hyndmer's overseer, in order to sort out probate of the will. He returned with both bursars on 2 October to draw up an inventory of Hyndmer's belongings and take possession of the books. Kettell bought a new sixpenny notebook and carefully recorded the administration of Hyndmer's estate. There were many legacies to pay and many debts to call in, and it soon became

[31] TCA *Computus* ii, f. 205v.

[32] Alan E. Coates, '*Hic loci studiis interdum vacaret*': A History of the Old Library of Durham College and Trinity College, Oxford' (MA thesis, University College London, 1985), 29.

[33] TCA *Computus* ii, f. 92v.; 1612–13, ff. 141v.–142.

[34] Edward Hyndmer, or Henmarshe, was Warden of Durham College *c.*1519–40. See A. B. Emden, *A Biographical Register of the University of Oxford AD 1501–40* (Oxford, 1974), 281.

[35] Will of Edward Hyndmer, TCA Benefactions B 1.1.

clear that no beneficiary could be paid in full. In December 1619 the Hyndmer account was 'viewed' during the main College audit. A 20 per cent 'abatement' was agreed, and the College share reduced to £53. The following year's audit found in fact only £49 8*d* available for the College's use.

Hyndmer's library contained a hundred titles, mainly works of history, theology, and classical authors appropriate to a scholar with humanist interests. Twenty-nine books were in French, twenty-one in Italian, and six in, or partly in, Greek. Only five books were given away: 'Saterthwaite poor-scholar' got two octavo volumes of Cicero and another of the poet Eluridarius, while 'Westlie' had Greek and Latin New Testaments in sixteenmo. Eight works of reference were chained in the Library for common use: a Septuagint Bible, Walsingham's English History, Onuphrius, Genebrand's *Notæ chronicæ*, Copernicus, a French dictionary, Camerarius on ethics and a copy of Linacre's *De emendata structura Latina*. Two of the eight, Walsingham and Camerarius, are still in the Library today. Hyndmer's remaining volumes were distributed among the fellows and scholars, as part of the circulating library.[36]

At least part of the benefaction was devoted to improving the Library facilities. In May and July 1625, £18 was spent on 'six new seats' and £3 16*s* 4*d* on iron bars and locks for chaining and supporting the books and desks. Kettell noted that £27 4*s* 4*d* remained 'to be bestowed on some memorial for the continuance of Master Hyndmer's name'. Beneath the cornices on the ends of the presses facing the central aisle, the inscription *Edvardi Hindmeri donum* (gift of Edward Hyndmer) was painted in gold, at a cost of 11*s*.[37] The inscriptions were subsequently painted over and rediscovered in the late nineteenth century.[38] Just one remains today. In around 1626 a Library Benefactors' Book was procured, and a retrospective record of all donors back to the Founder was written up. The suede-bound volume shows a steady stream of donations to the Library, although the College was also turning to purchase.[39] To supervise the Library, one

36 TCA Benefactions B 1.3, ff. 13v., 21.

37 TCA *Computus* 1625–6, f. 213.

38 B. H. Streeter, *The Chained Library: A Survey of 4 Centuries in the Evolution of the English Library* (London, 1931), 230.

39 TCA Library A1; Coates, 'A History of the Old Library', 27. Sir Thomas Bodley had provided a Benefactors' Register for his library in 1604, and the idea was taken up by many colleges. See Jonathan B. Bengston, 'Benefaction Registers in Oxford Libraries', *Library History*, 16 (Nov. 2000), 143–5.

of the fellows was appointed to the position of librarian; from 1630 the accounts show a quarterly payment of 5*s* for this responsibility, the same sum as was given to the laundress 'above her stipend'.[40]

During Kettell's presidency, the Library was augmented by two major benefactions. In 1640 Richard Rands (scholar 1605, fellow 1610–23) bequeathed to the College land at Hartfield, Sussex, which brought in an annual income of £20, which was dedicated to the use of the Library (and which indeed was the Library's main source of funding for more than three centuries). From Rand's will the College also acquired sixteen books for the Library.[41] The following year, Trinity received a large bequest of books from the estate of Francis Combe, who was the son of the Founder's niece. Combe divided his library and the manor of Abbot's Langley, Essex, between Trinity and Sidney Sussex College, Cambridge, and Trinity marked the gift by making the Library's very first printed bookplate to commemorate his name.[42]

In 1626 Kettell further increased Trinity's comforts by the construction of an elaborate 'privy house' in the grove. It was built in stone (the mason worked for sixty-three days) with a slate roof and wooden fittings. The design may not have been unique, but the pride with which the President described it surely is. The 'doors and partitions serving unto each seat,' he noted in the *computus*, were 'so framed that they may be taken down and removed unto some other new room, when time shall be'. Two or three boards could then be used 'to close up the lower floor; and then the room may serve, during the mean while, to keep coals, wood or any other stuff for public use, until the dung shall be dry and fit to be cleansed'. Human faecal material was an important fertilizer, and Kettell took pains to explain the cunning positioning of a door, which '(immediately under the lower floor and right under the door at which you enter into the house out of the grove) is made six foot deep, whose bottom is nevertheless six foot higher than the bottom of the vault. This door was so placed, that by it the dung might be shovelled out and conveyed with wheel barrows, after it hath some years grown dry, and the use of the room hath been forborne.' To facilitate this removal, the contents of the vault were to be solidified with '126 loads of burrs (as it may be hence collected)'. All this, for just £36 6*s* 4*d*.[43]

[40] TCA Library A/1, no. 129. [41] TCA Charters 10.4.

[42] TCA *Computus* 1629–30, f. 329. The first payment was made for the second term in the year. [43] TCA *Computus* 1625–6, ff. 276, 282.

In January 1631, a second 'house of office' was built, south of the 'ancient' one (presumably that used by the monks of Durham College) which itself stood south of the kitchen.[44] The new building was 19 feet by 12 feet, with 'a sluice on the east side to empty it as need shall urge'. Kettell wrote convincingly of the advantages: 'there is hope that these two houses as they shall be filled *alterius vicibus*, so there will be time and occasion to empty the mould *alternatim* with little labour and no annoyance, that the mould may serve the gardens.'[45]

## *The College Community*

Kettell was a tremendous chronicler of his College. Besides his careful justification of expenditure on the buildings, he also recorded the names and degrees of all members of the foundation in a large and handsomely bound book known to future generations as Kettell's Register. A number was assigned to each new scholar; he himself was number 97. Ninety-two elections were made to scholarships in the years 1600–39, and just under half of those elected went on to hold fellowships. The life of a fellow had become a little more comfortable since the foundation, and quite a lot more remunerative, when the fees of pupils were taken into account. Of twenty-five men elected fellows between 1605 and 1630, only six stayed for less than seven years, and the average tenure was between eleven and twelve. All but four are known to have left in order to take a living.

One member of the foundation involved Trinity in a potentially dangerous scandal. He was the 'controversialist' William Chillingworth (scholar 1618, fellow 1628–32) whose reputation and argumentative qualities naturally caught the attention of John Aubrey. 'My tutor William Browne has told me,' recalled Aubrey, that 'he did walk much in the college grove, and there contemplate, and meet with some cod's head or other, and dispute with him and baffle him . . . He would always be disputing. So would my tutor.' Chillingworth was the godson of William Laud, ex-President of St John's, Bishop of London, and soon to be Archbishop of Canterbury and Chancellor of Oxford. As the story goes, a Trinity old member, Alexander Gill (1612 and 1618, now employed as master at St Paul's School in

[44] It is visible in Loggan's 1675 print of Trinity (front endpaper).
[45] TCA *Computus* 1631–2, f. 4.

London) was in 1628 visiting a friend in the College, one William Pickering. As the two drank together in the buttery, Chillingworth heard Gill toasting Felton, the man who had assassinated James I's favourite, the Duke of Buckingham, and speaking disrespectfully of Charles I. Chillingworth lost no time in informing his godfather, Gill was arrested, Pickering's college rooms were searched, and a number of incriminating letters and poems from Gill were discovered.[46] Chillingworth was an impartial and well-informed thinker, and active in the religious debates of the day. But he was keenly sensitive to the arguments of others, and open-minded to the point of indecision. After lengthy debates with the Jesuit John Fisher, he felt the only course he could take was to become a Jesuit himself. He travelled to Douai in 1630, where he was asked to write up the reasons for his conversion. Unfortunately for the Catholic Church, this led to a reassessment of his recent decision—and in less than a year he was back in Oxford once more. President Kettell was impervious to the arguments of any party, and 'kept himself unconcerned' from religious debate. Aubrey relished his suspicion of Laud, and enjoyed the story of how he once received a gift of venison from the Archbishop:

> the old Doctor with much earnestness refused, and said that he was an old man, and his stomach weak and he had not eaten of such meat in a long time, and by no means would accept of it. But the servant was as much pressing it on him on the other side, and told the President that he durst not carry it back again. Well, seeing there was no avoiding it, the President asked the servant seriously, if the Archbishop of Canterbury intended to put in any scholars or fellows into his college?[47]

The number of commoners increased steadily throughout Kettell's presidency. The annual lists of those for whom caution money was being held give a reasonable idea of how many were in residence, and shows a marked increase in line with an increase in the capacity of the accommodation. The number rises steadily during the decade of renovations, dramatically after Kettell Hall was built, and again, to a lesser degree, once the new Hall was complete. The pattern suggests that the College was generally 'full', and at times may well have been overcrowded.

[46] Gill was tried before the Star Chamber and sentenced to degradation from his degrees, to lose both his ears, and to a £2,000 fine, although this sentence was later commuted. Aubrey, *Brief Lives*, 81.

[47] Aubrey, *Brief Lives* (Ralph Kettell), 176–7.

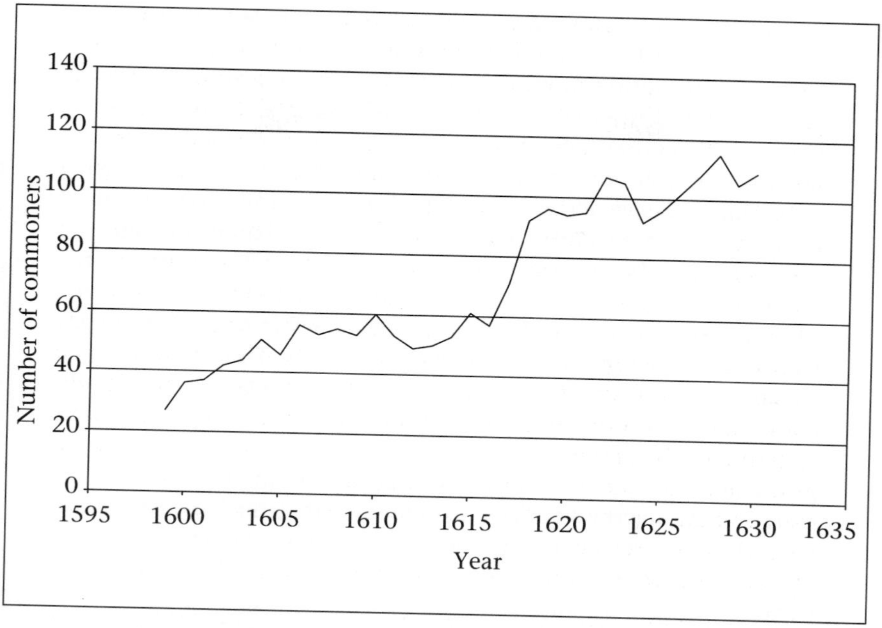


*Fig. 4.2* Commoners in residence (by caution money held) 1600–1630.

Many commoners did not stay to take a degree. Others, such as Francis Potter (1609) stayed for a remarkably long time. He was the son of a former fellow, and the younger brother of a scholar and fellow, Hannibal (scholar 1609, fellow 1613) whose room he shared for some twenty-seven years. His was a simple, scholarly life, exempt from the duties of the fellows and presumably oblivious to the increasingly affluent ways of many of the fellow commoners around him. Aubrey remembered him playing chess with a friend for 'two days together', designing a sundial for the north wall of the Quadrangle, copying the Founder's portrait in oils, and having the idea for his great work (on the Number of the Beast) 'as he was going up stairs into his chamber at Trinity College'.[48]

During Kettell's presidency, the social structure of the undergraduate body seems to have become ever more stratified, ranging from the privileged fellow commoners at the top end of the scale,

[48] Aubrey, *Brief Lives* (Francis Potter), 249–55.

through ordinary commoners, more humble battellers, poor but well enough provided for scholars, and servitors at the bottom of the heap. New rates of caution money were introduced, indicating the significance of the distinct levels of College life. In 1606 Anthony Stocker (son of an esquire), and Robert and Thomas Chetwood (sons of a knight), were the first to pay a new rate of £2 10*s*. The following year, Francis Leigh and Gelley Merrick paid an even higher rate of £3 each, five others paid £2 10*s*, while the original 30*s* and 40*s* rates remained for lesser persons, and an increasing number, mainly plebeians' or paupers' sons, matriculated from Trinity without paying caution money at all. Members of the aristocracy were expected to pay well for the privileges they would receive. In 1609, Thomas Nevill paid £5, and in 1615, £10 was paid for the Blount brothers, Sir Thomas, Bt, and Henry, who were, of course, Founder's kin. In 1614, the brothers Gilbert and Hugh Sheldon paid £8 between them, as did the Newdigate brothers Sir John and Richard. In both cases £5 of this was for the elder son, £3 for the younger. George Calvert (later Lord Baltimore) had achieved some economy when he matriculated in 1594 as the son of a plebeian, although he was to graduate in 1598 as the son of a gentleman.[49] By 1621 he had a knighthood and was a leading minister in the government of James I, and he paid the top rate of £5 for his son Cecil to move in the highest rank of society while at Trinity.

Brothers from more aristocratic families often came up together, and often at a much younger age than did lowlier young men. The Honourable Thomas Wentworth, and his brother Henry (stepsons of the Founder's nephew, William Pope, Earl of Downe) were exceptionally young at 11 and 8. Robert and Thomas Chetwood were 15 and 12, Thomas Pope Blount and his brother Henry were 16 and 13, and the cousins John and Duke Stonehouse came up together aged 15. Lower orders of undergraduate tended to be older. In 1611 William Constable and Edmund Reade matriculated as 'poor scholars', without paying caution. Both were 19. Some youths matriculated as the servants of others: in 1604 £4 was paid jointly for George Horsey and his unnamed servant. The following year 30*s* was paid for both Hector Paulett (son of a marquis and Founder's kin) and for James Biddlecombe, his servant.

Kettell took an active part in the education provided by the

[49] Bromley Smith, 'George Calvert at Oxford', *Maryland Historical Magazine*, XXVI, no. 2 (June 1931), 111.

College. Aubrey remembered him interrupting the lecturer 'one time walking by the table where the logic lecture was read', and another time cracking a joke as the undergraduates worked at their geometry:

> Said he 'I will show you how to inscribe a triangle in a quadrangle. Bring a pig into the Quadrangle, and I will set the college dog at him; and he will seize the pig by the ear and then come I, and take the dog by the tail and the hog by the tail, and so there you have a triangle in a quadrangle.'

According to Aubrey:

> he was constantly at Lectures and Exercises in the Hall, to observe them; and brought along with him his hour glass, and one time being offended at the boys, he threatened them, that if they would not do their exercise better, he would bring an hour glass two hours long.[50]

John Aubrey describes an education that was somewhat haphazard. When he first went up he 'leafed through logic and some ethics' and took time *inter sylvas Academi quaerere verum* (to seek the truth among the groves of Academe).[51] He approved strongly of the Trinity *narrare* as a 'good short speech', and of the logic lectures: 'short and clear, we learned them by heart.'[52] In later life he looked back fondly on the opportunity he had had to read and to indulge his personal interests, observing that 'my fancy lay most to geometry.'[53] He had no plan to take a degree, and, with the confidence typical of a fellow commoner of the time, was secure in the knowledge that a spell at Oxford followed by another at the Inns of Court would meet all his needs as a country gentleman and magistrate.

Other undergraduate members of Trinity, however, while in a similar or better social position, worked rather harder. Sir John and Richard Newdigate came up in 1618; John spent one year at Trinity and Richard two. Their legal guardian, William Whitehall, kept a detailed account of expenditure on their education; this shows regular and considerable expenditure on books, and suggests a serious

[50] Aubrey, *Brief Lives* (Ralph Kettell), 178–80.
[51] Ibid., (John Aubrey), 11. Aubrey is quoting Horace, *Epistles* 2.2.
[52] *Aubrey on Education*, ed. J. H. Stephens (London, 1972), 95, 120.
[53] Aubrey, *Brief Lives* (John Aubrey), 14.

commitment to academic activity.[54] The brothers were aged 18 and 16 when they arrived in College. They had been well prepared by a private tutor and, in Richard's case, by several years at school, to get the most from studying at the University. The fifty titles purchased for them over a two-year period at Oxford reveal a breadth of subjects beyond the grammar, logic, and rhetoric expected at the beginning of the Oxford curriculum. Their reading included 'history, geography, and religious topics, along with plays, polemics, and popular literature attractive to young gentlemen seeking knowledge of the world'.[55] Richard Newdigate stayed on at College for the quarter ending Lady Day 1620, while his brother was 'in the country' and, although only in his second year, took part in University disputations, a significant milestone event which was celebrated by the outlay of 5*s* on 'wine . . . in the Schools'.[56] As a younger son he was expected to prepare himself for a profession, and he opted to stay at College to work through the Long Vacation of 1620, even though, as he regretfully commented in a letter to his brother in London, he found that 'company [was] . . . small and good company exceeding scarce.'[57] The brothers had a fair degree of financial independence, sometimes writing up their own expenses in Whitehall's account book. Also with them in Oxford was their own servant, Peter Oliff.

John and Richard Newdigate's first week at Trinity gives a detailed picture of the experiences of gentlemen commoners settling into the College. The party arrived in Oxford on a Friday—16 October 1618. They had set off from Daventry, travelling via Brackley, where they stopped for beer and cakes, and booked into the Reindeer Inn (in the College's parish of St Mary Magdalen) for one night. There was just time that day to buy 4 shillings worth of lute strings for John and to order their gowns. One-and-a-quarter yards of black cloth, also buckram, ribbon, and silk were required, and the bill, including setting the sleeves and the making up, came to 28*s*. Next day the College

[54] Vivienne Larminie, 'The Undergraduate Account Book of John and Richard Newdigate 1618–1621', *Camden Miscellany XXX* (1990), 149–269. The original document is in the Warwickshire Record Office, CR, 136, B602.

[55] Vivienne Larminie, *Wealth, Kinship and Culture: The Seventeenth-century Newdigates of Arbury and their World* (Woodbridge, 1995), 113.

[56] Larminie, 'Account Book', 205.

[57] Larminie, *Wealth*, 114. The difference between their educational aspirations was even more marked at the Inns of Court. John acquired a superficial introduction to the law as befitted a country gentleman, while Richard studied with the intention of practising law as a profession.

room had to be arranged. Two pence was paid to 'a woman making clean the chambers and stairs', and 4*d* for a pound of candles. Bed staves were procured, and 6*d* spent on 'setting up a bed and cording it'. A jug, nails, a chamber pot, two candlesticks, a standish, and a tinderbox were bought to make the room habitable, and a few less practical items, gloves for Richard, yet more lute strings for John, and four dozen black silk buttons. Payments then had to be made to the College servants. It cost 7*s* 6*d* to enter their names with the manciple, and the same sum was due to both the butler and the cook. The butler's boy required 1*s* 6*d*, the under cook 4*s*, and 'him that divides the commons' 2*s* 6*d*. Finally, 1*s* was paid to the scullery boy (who did the washing up).[58]

Sunday was a quiet day; they acquired nothing but a pound of sugar, an ounce of nutmegs, some ink in a glass, and some paper.[59]

On the Tuesday, numerous items were found wanting: a pewter basin, bellows, fire shovel, a hatchet, and a 'laundress table for clothes'. Fuel for heating was not provided by the College, so two loads of wood had to be cut and carried to the cellar at a cost of £1 6*s*. John and Richard may have brought some books from home. Their first Oxford reading matter was copies apiece of 'Juvenal, Persius and Pliny's *Epistles*', the Articles of Religion (needed to prepare for the matriculation ceremony) and 'a paper book' for each of them. Richard also had Ovid's *Metamorphoses* and a book of epithets, while John chose Horace and a book noted as *A hundred tales*. Both boys had their hair cut. This was the day to meet the College and University authorities: Caution money was handed over to the Bursars, and £1 was paid to 'the schools', perhaps a fee for registration to attend lectures, as they did not matriculate until November. Meanwhile John met up with a lute master, who charged 2*s* and recommended the purchase of yet more lute strings. That day's final requirement was a 'viall stick'.[60]

Their guardian William Whitehall travelled regularly between the family estate at Arbury, in Warwickshire, Daventry, where John and Richard's sisters lodged, London, where John was admitted to the Inner Temple in January 1621, and Oxford. Whitehall returned to Oxford on 1 November 1618, and wrote up the interim expenses incurred by Peter Oliff, who went regularly for wood, candles, paper,

[58] Larminie, 'Account Book', 161–2. [59] Ibid., 162. [60] Ibid.

and food over and beyond what the College kitchen supplied. In the privacy of their chamber they enjoyed apples, liquorice, salad oil, honey, milk, pepper, 'biscuit bread', and cheeses, which came by carrier from home. Soft furnishings from London (delivered by Whitehall's nephew by marriage, Thomas Rode) ensured a standard of comfort far in excess of that enjoyed by the President. There were '24 yards of East India spotted cloth at 20*d* [the yard] for curtains, valance, canopy, carpets and cushions' and thirty-nine ounces of 'fine mocado fringe'. The cushions had to be lined, tufted with mocado, filled with flock, and fastened with six leather buttons. Including the upholsterer's bill, curtain tape and rings, the total cost was £4 2*s* 5*d*. Life was made more comfortable still by the purchase of a close stool with a strong pan.[61]

Robert Skinner, Trinity's vice-president, was the Newdigates' tutor. He was paid £2 4*s* each quarter for 'reading' to them, while the lute master cost 6*s* 8*d*. Rent for their accommodation was paid into the hands of the President: another £1 2*s* quarterly. As their financial guarantor, Skinner witnessed the quarterly payment of their battels to the Bursar. The first term's bill was £9 8*s* 9*d*. The second quarter saw this bill subdivided, however; a debt of £5 17*s* 9*d* had been accrued by John and, as befitted the younger sibling, only £3 15*s* by Richard. No expense was spared when, early in 1619, John fell ill and William Whitehall arrived in Oxford to attend him. Thomas Clayton, the Regius Professor of Medicine, was called in twice for his professional opinion and a range of treatments given, including almond milk, a vomit, plasters of turpentine and olibanum.[62] The overall cost of the brothers' time at Trinity was undoubtedly high, but the social and professional contacts they made were invaluable. One who remained a life-long friend was Gilbert Sheldon (1614), later Archbishop of Canterbury.[63]

A stark contrast can be drawn with the education of Edward Shalcrosse, who was put by his father into the care of Whitehall and the Newdigate brothers in 1619. Ned paid 40*s* caution money, 2*s* 6*d* to the schools, and 11*s* a quarter to his tutor (also Skinner). Shalcrosse's 'chamber and study' cost 3*s* 4*d* a quarter, and he contributed a meagre 13*s* 4*d* to the plate fund. His battels over the year averaged £3 11*s*. The only expenditure he was allowed for personal items was £1

[61] Larminie, 'Account Book', 165–6.
[62] Ibid., 176, 178–9, 184.
[63] Larminie, *Wealth*, 134.

4*s* 10*d* 'for books, a trunk and diverse other things bought by Mr Richard for him' and termly doles of money ranging from 10*s* to £2 4*s*, the latter amount to last him from July until Michaelmas 1619.[64] Such a handsome sum would have seemed a fortune to a servitor. For this lowest class in College, no accounts survive.

Inevitably in a small community, a young man's experiences were largely coloured by his friends and tutor. One who was particularly dissatisfied with Trinity was Thomas Hood, who seems to have been up in the late 1630s, although his name appears neither in the caution account nor in the University's matriculation register. But in 1692 the College wrote to him in the hope of a donation towards the new Chapel, and his reply leaves no doubt that he knew Trinity intimately. Hood's negative comments about the education he received must be tempered by the knowledge that he had just been asked to make a contribution to College funds. Nevertheless, there was much that he needed to get off his chest. He said that he had 'reaped no benefit there. Thither I came illiterate, and so departed. I neither studied or learned anything. My tutor was a good fellow & I was glad of it. He seldom read to me. The best service he ever did me, he rescued me one night from the tyrannical whittlers[65] who always had feuds with me.' By his own account, Hood was the victim of serious bullying while at Trinity:

> Most part of the time I spent in the college was contending & waging war with them, & my other adversaries Mr Gascoigne, Mr Bawdell esq. . . . & Dr Kettell's man . . . Sometimes by the prowess of my fist, my martial feats proved successful in our grove, other times in our quadrangle boldly below the window of our good old limping president who frequently lugged me by the ears; I never pretended to letters, or to the favour of the muses. Blood and war was all my contemplation & practice during my university life among you, and do still carry about me the pitch scalding marks of the frightful whittlers' cruelty.[66]

Kettell was a hands-on President, and 'lugging' Hood by the ears fits in with Aubrey's experience of his disciplinary style. Aubrey recalled with relish the President's feelings about long hair, to which he was 'irreconcilable':

[64] Larminie, 'Account Book', 214–16.

[65] *Oxford English Dictionary*: Whittlers or whiddlers are informers.

[66] Bod. Lib. MS Ballard 49, f. 171. Thomas Hood to Josiah Howe, 15 June 1692.

> When he observed the scholars' hair longer than ordinary (especially if they were scholars of the house) he would bring a pair of scissors in his muff (which he commonly wore) and woe be to them, that sat on the outside of the table. I remember he cut Mr Radford's hair with the knife that chips the bread, on the buttery hatch.

Kettell naturally disapproved of excessive drinking on the part of his undergraduates: 'if any one had committed a fault, he should be sure to hear of it in the chapel before his fellow Collegiates. [He would] have at him that had a white cap on; for he concluded him to have been drunk, and his head to ache.' Aubrey also recalled a public scolding for John Denham during a lecture in the Chapel, this time on account of an unpaid debt. Kettell 'rattled him, and told him, "Thy father (Judge) has hanged many an honester man."'[67]

It is debatable how much truth, and how much myth and college pride, there is in Aubrey's assertion that Kettell 'observed that the houses that had the smallest beer, had the most drunkards: for it forced them to go into the town to comfort their stomachs. Wherefore Dr Kettell always had in his college excellent beer, not better to be had in Oxon; so that we could not go to any other place but for the worse: and we had the fewest drunkards of any House in Oxford.' One of these of course was Gill, and another was Thomas Hood: 'Now and then in the intervals of Mars I used to have a brush with Bacchus either in the cellar or (if I had money) make a brief sally, south of our gate, and took possession of the city cabarets, for which 'twas notoriously known.'[68]

On one occasion, poor Hood threw up in the Chapel after 'an unhappy stroke given . . . by the rough hand of the above mentioned Mr Gascoigne as were near together on our flexible knees'. He 'was in some jeopardy of being expelled the College by zealous Dr Hobbs' had not his 'trusty friend Ettrick' (Anthony Ettrick headed Aubrey's list of friends too) helped him out with some penal Greek verses. But the most commonly employed punishment remained loss of commons. Hood bitterly recalled 'how frequently my name was crossed out of the Buttery Book (particularly for not narraring) until almost starved'.[69]

[67] Aubrey, *Brief Lives*, 176, 178–9.

[68] Ibid., 178; Bod. Lib. MS Ballard 49, f. 172.

[69] Bod. Lib. MS Ballard 49, f. 171; Aubrey, *Brief Lives* (John Aubrey), 15.

Gambling was another problem. Josiah How recounted to Aubrey how Sir John Denham 'was the dreamiest young fellow . . . [who] would game extremely; when he had played away all his money, he would play away his father's wrought rich gold cups.' The Newdigate brothers lost money regularly at cards, but seemingly within an acceptable family budget. Then there were the experiences of Henry Blount, who came to Trinity as Founder's kin, and was a great friend of Francis Potter. Said Aubrey, 'he was pretty wild when young, especially addicted to common wenches . . . I remember . . . he inveighed much against sending youths to the universities, because they learned there to be debauched. Drunkenness he much exclaimed against, but he allowed wenching.'[70]

Ralph Kettell had an active life outside the College. He was a conscientious Rector of Garsington, where he rode to preach every Sunday, Aubrey recalled,

> on his bay gelding, with his boy Ralph before him, with a leg of mutton (commonly) and some college bread. He did not care for the country revels, because they tended to debauchery. Said he at Garsington-Revel, 'Here is hey for Garsington, and hey for Cuddesdon, and hey [for] Hockley. But here's nobody cries hey for God Almighty.'[71]

Kettell was the first President of Trinity to be married, and, again according to Aubrey, 'he had two, if not three, wives, but no child.' No marriage entry was made in the register of Garsington (where the entries only begin in 1602) or in that of the College's parish of St Mary Magdalen, Oxford. But on 25 March 1606, 'Mary, daughter of Mr Dr Rafe Kettle' was baptized at Garsington. Two days later, the baby was buried in the churchyard there. The register also records the burial of 'Mistress Kettle, wife of Mr Doctor Kettle' on 19 April 1623.[72] Aubrey noted that Kettell's second wife was the widow of Edward Villiers, Esq., and the mother of two beautiful daughters. He relished the tale of Kettell as matchmaker:

[70] Aubrey, *Brief Lives* (Sir John Denham), 106, (Sir Henry Blount), 47–8; 'Account Book', passim.

[71] Aubrey, *Brief Lives*, 180. The Boy Ralph is plausibly identifiable as Kettell's step-grandson, Ralph Bathurst (scholar 1837); see Thomas Warton, *Bathurst*, 34.

[72] Oxfordshire County Record Office, Garsington Parish Registers, baptisms 1606, burials 1606, 1623.

> The eldest, whom several of great Estate would gladly have wedded, he would needs dispose of himself, and he thought no body so fit a husband for this angelic creature as one Mr Bathurst, of the college, a second brother, and of about £300 per annum; but an indifferent scholar, red faced, not at all handsome. But the Doctor's fashion was, to go up and down the college, and peep in at the keyholes to see whether the boys did follow their books or no. He seldom found Bathurst minding of his books, but mending of his old doublet, or breeches. He was very thrifty and penurious, and upon this reason he carried away this curious creature.

Elizabeth Villiers was 14 at the time of her marriage to George Bathurst. Aubrey noted that she 'was very happy in her issue; all her children very ingenious, and prosperous in the world, and most of them beautiful'. There were seventeen children born between 1611 and 1628; Trinity's future President, Ralph, was the sixth of thirteen sons.[73]

## *Litigation and Bequests*

Another example of the President's thrifty side is the brown, acidic, and home-made ink with which he invariably wrote. The College archive contains much written in Kettell's crabbed and sloping script, including many replies to, and drafts of, legal documents. He was naturally litigious, and there can be no doubt that he enjoyed going to court. There was indeed a lot at stake in a Chancery suit which Trinity pursued between 1620 and 1622 in order to claim an unlikely benefaction of £500 under the will of John Whetstone, Esq., of Abbotsbury, in Dorset. Whetstone had no link with Trinity. He was 'a mean inconsiderable and vicious person, living altogether on usury and extortion', who one day encountered a formidable and opportunistic local clergyman, the Reverend Ralph Ironside, whose son Gilbert happened to be a fellow of the College. Many years later, Gilbert Ironside, by now Bishop of Bristol, wrote up the story of how the benefaction came about.[74] His father's name had been given, without his permission, to Whetstone as security on a loan by 'one Mr Lawrence Meller'. On learning of the arrangement,

[73] Aubrey, *Brief Lives*, 177–8; Allen Benjamin Bathurst, *History of the Apsley and Bathurst Families* (Cirencester, 1903), 78, and pedigree.

[74] TCA Misc.Vol. I, f. 44/77.

> my father answered that if Whetstone would come to him, he would give the security required, but refused to go to Whetstone as being upon the account of his sordid and scandalous living a disparagement unto him . . . Whetstone coming to my father some hours before Mr Meller, my father among other things talked with him in these words: 'John, you have no child, what will [you] do with all your money?'

Whetstone replied that he was considering a donation of £500 to endow breakfasts for the children of his old school, Winchester College:

> My father told him that was a good deed, and withal acquainted him with a benefactor they had in University College (where my father was sometimes fellow) whose memory was preserved in an anniversary sermon at St Peter's in the East and gaudy in the hall. This pleased the usurer well, who therefore replied, I will give five hundred pounds to the college, where your son is fellow.

Soon after this conversation, Ironside Senior heard that Whetstone was mortally ill, and

> made speed to see his own good motion and the other's promise to be performed, and asking him whether he had put it into his will. He answered no, but that Mr Angel Smith (an old companion of his) had the keeping of his will, & that he had sent Post for him, and doubted not but that he would be suddenly there. My father therefore stays till Angel Smith comes, who looking for the will perceived he had lost it in his journey. For the finding therefore of it, servants are dispatched to look after it, who enquiring of shepherds in the fields at last recover it. The will being brought, my father perused it, and finding it omitted in the will, minded John of his promise to Trinity College and never left till he persuaded him unto it again.

Indeed, Ralph Ironside demanded 'pen ink and paper, which being brought my father wrote the codicil with his own hand, and annexed it to the will'. As Blakiston mildly observed, it was 'not surprising that the codicil, signed "by me, John Whetstone, sick as sick may be, God help me" was disputed by the executors'.[75]

After an order in Chancery, a writ of *executione decreti*, and a petition to the chancellor, the money was at last secured, and in May

[75] Blakiston, *Trinity*, 110.

1622 the College purchased land in Oakley, near Brill.[76] Kettell next turned his attention to an 'annoyance' that had afflicted Trinity since the foundation. The site of Durham College was subject to an annual rent charge of 26*s* 2*d*, payable to the Crown. George Owen and William Martyn, who conveyed the College premises to Thomas Pope in 1555, had covenanted to discharge this rent charge in full.[77] This had never been done, and over the years, Kettell calculated, some £18 had been lost by the College. Like all open and shut legal cases, the difficulty took some time to sort out. In 1623 the Bishops of Canterbury, Lincoln, and Winchester declared that the charge, and £20 compensation to the College, should be paid by one John Walter, who had purchased Owen's other lands. Walter thought otherwise, and so did his widow, the redoubtable Dowager Lady Anne, who resisted until 1632, when she was finally forced to pay £19 12*s* 2*d* via the exchequer.[78]

Meanwhile, there was a second 'annoyance' in the shape of the powerful landowner, Sir George Melsam, and his tenants in Garsington. Melsam had illegally enclosed part of the common land of Garsington, and reduced the value of the rectory by a third, 'from £200 to 200 marks'.[79] Kettell listened to the petitions of his Garsington parishioners, and painstakingly chronicled the local tyrant's 'bloody threats', impounding of sheep and cattle, brutality towards the village poor, and ploughing of common pastureland. He petitioned the Lord Chancellor and the Privy Council, enlisted the support of the Bishop of Oxford, and complained at the Oxfordshire assizes and to the Vice-Chancellor's court. Melsam had been enclosing parts of the common land since 1612, but it was not until 1623, when a Commission of Arbitration was set up, that he finally gave up the fight and sold the manor.[80]

Kettell could be belligerent when the College was under threat, but he was also warm-hearted and kind. Aubrey wrote touchingly of his 'great charity . . . Where he observed diligent boys that he guessed had but a slender exhibition from their friends, he would many times put money in at their windows, that his right hand did not know what his left did.'[81] He made a will in 1636, but the following year

[76] TCA Charters B/9.4–5. [77] Ibid., A/1.
[78] TCA Misc. Vol. I, f. 44/74. [79] Ibid., f. 40/44.
[80] Eve Dawson, *Garsington Before Enclosure* (Garsington, 2001), 28–31.
[81] Aubrey, *Brief Lives* (Ralph Kettell), 180.

crossed out a number of the bequests. As he noted in the margin, the items were 'delivered' already.[82] The main beneficiary was his nephew Fanshawe, and he also remembered his servant Samuel Simson, his clerk, and the poor of Garsington. Besides books, 'such as are already allotted unto the public library of the college', he left nothing to the corporate institution of Trinity College. Instead, he named his step-grandsons, 'the three Bathursts, Master George, Master Edward and Raffe, now abiding in Trinity'. They were to have his silver plate, his books 'to distribute among themselves peaceably and brotherly', and each a pair of gloves and handkerchiefs of the 'second', 'third', and 'fourth sort', a feather bed, two bolsters, a pillow (with pillowcase) and a pair of sheets. George and Edward were to have six handkerchiefs each (they were of course MAs) and Ralph only two, although he was more than compensated by an additional two blankets, a coverlet, and two further pairs of sheets.

Kettell had now entered into his eighth decade. He could look back with some satisfaction on the changes he had wrought in the College, at his new buildings, their sound and commodious chambers, and the healthy influx of increasingly wealthy occupants for them. He had reigned during a time of expansion and prosperity for the University, and Trinity had fared particularly well during his presidency. Did he also foresee some of the troubles that were to come in the final years of his life? In ten years Trinity would be virtually deserted, its members scattered, its treasury empty, its buildings decaying fast. George Bathurst would die as a casualty of the Civil War. The future of the College was with the young man whom Kettell had admitted to the college community, and to whom he intended to hand on some of the basic necessities of College life—Ralph Bathurst.

[82] OUA, Hyp/B/28, ff. 71–4.

# 5

# *Trinity in the Civil Wars and the Commonwealth*

## *The Impact of War*

In September 1645, William Browne (fellow 1642) wrote confidentially from Trinity to his 'most loving pupil', John Aubrey:

> I do seriously advise you to go to Leiden, if you can by any means procure your father's good will. You may live as cheap there as at Oxon, and more safe, and unengaged from . . . a good but declining cause . . . Besides your advancing your abilities in learning you will much better your understanding of the world and state affairs.

Browne had good reason to feel disillusioned with Trinity. For the past two years he had been 'excluded' from his College rooms, and forced to do hard and degrading physical work digging trenches and building defensive earthworks around Oxford. The prosperous college which he had joined a decade earlier was now badly impoverished, even to the point of dissolution, and he and his colleagues were virtually penniless. He may have been guiding Aubrey's studies by post, but there was little academic work being done in Trinity. 'The soldier spoils the scholar for the most part,' Browne wrote frankly to Aubrey.[1]

The city and the University of Oxford were both central to the English Civil Wars. Oxford lay in a front-line position, between the King's support base in the north and the west, and the parliamentary forces raised in London and the south-east. Key battles of the first war (1642–7) were fought in the south Midlands and Oxfordshire, while Oxford, garrisoned for the King between October 1642 and June 1646, was an ideal base for the royalist leaders. The University had a proven record of loyalty to the Crown, and college buildings offered

[1] Bod. Lib. MS Aubrey 12/35.

a plentiful supply of temporary accommodation. Charles himself liked Oxford, and had enjoyed a visit to the University in the summer of 1636, to the general expenses of which Trinity had contributed £12 10s, plus a further 10s 'for the king's trumpeters'.[2] Many members of the court were themselves old members of Oxford.

The masters and bachelors of the University, with few exceptions, sympathized with the royalist cause. After a century of conforming to royal requirements and basking in the favour of four successive monarchs, it would have been remarkable if more than a very small minority had felt otherwise. As the division between King and Parliament had grown, a sense of general uneasiness had crept over Oxford; members of the University were suspected of 'popish subversion' and their hard-won and established privileges seemed to be under threat from Parliament.[3] The fellows of Trinity were staunchly royalist; and the staunchest of them all during the years of war was Josiah How. In May 1637 How had been nominated to a vacant fellowship by the Visitor, and was duly elected, despite Kettell's apparent intention to save money by leaving the place unfilled for a second year.[4] Kettell, How, and several other members of the foundation were regular contributors to the many volumes of laudatory verse which, on every conceivable royal occasion, rolled from the University Press. Ralph Bathurst was a particularly enthusiastic poet in his youth, and penned upbeat Latin verses to celebrate such events as the birth of Princess Anne in 1636 and the arrival of the Queen in Oxford in 1643.[5]

The resident MAs of Trinity who attended the University convocation on 11 July 1642 would have heard a stirring call for a public demonstration of the University's allegiance. It was a letter from King Charles, in York, desperate for money, and offering 8 per cent interest on loans from colleges and individuals. He denied, not entirely convincingly, 'that we intended to make war on our Parliament' and pointed out, not unreasonably, that 'by our perpetual care and

[2] TCA *Computus* 1635–6, f. 51; 1636–7, f. 62.

[3] Ian Roy and Dietrich Reinhart, 'Oxford and the Civil Wars', *HUO* 4, 689–90.

[4] TCA Register A ff. 72d, 75.

[5] Falconer Madan, *Oxford Books, A Bibliography* (Oxford, 1912), ii, nos 840 and 418. Such volumes were 'a feature of Oxford literature 1587–1643 . . . poured forth to welcome or groan over a striking event, whether royal, public, or even private. The official tears . . . which were shed at Oxford must have visibly swollen the Isis'; Madan, 'Introduction', p. x.

protection of such nurseries of learning, we have especial reason to expect [this] particular care of us.' Convocation agreed to the request for financial support, and within a week more than £10,000 was dispatched, raised from University and other sources, so that the name of Oxford University shone at the head of the list of donors to the royal cause.[6] Many colleges sent contributions at once, but Trinity held back until 2 November, when the sizeable sum of £200 was 'lent to his majesty'. An official receipt, signed by the Paymaster General, was carefully placed in the treasury in the Chapel tower, where it has remained, unhonoured, to the present day.[7]

The first soldiers arrived in Oxford on 28 August 1642, when a bedraggled troop of the King's horse, led by Sir John Byron, and charged with protecting the city, rode into town at midnight. Once the initial fear of attack had subsided, they received an enthusiastic welcome from the University population. Preparations for war made a welcome change from academic activity, and commoners and scholars had already devoted much of the long vacation to military exercises and the construction of fortifications. Since the King's 'Proclamation for the suppressing of the present Rebellion' had been read in Oxford Market—two weeks earlier on 13 August—Dr Pincke, the deputy Vice-Chancellor, had been energetically training and drilling 'privileged men,' scholars, and an increasing number of graduates and MAs. Marching through the city streets was most pleasant on a summer's day, and when they were 'hindered by the rain, they marched back again'. Eight days before Byron's arrival, an envious schoolboy—Anthony Wood—spent his Saturday afternoon watching more than 400 volunteers assemble 'with their Arms [in] New Park, where they were instructed in the words of command and their military postures in a very decent manner. So delightful a prospect it was,' gushed Wood (writing some fifty years after the event), 'to behold the forwardness of so many proper young gentlemen, intent, docile and pliable in their business.'[8]

In the actual presence of soldiers, there was a widespread rush to take up arms for real. Despite a clear ban on personal weapons in the Trinity Statutes (except for the purpose of self-defence on journeys and in times of plague), the College had long turned a blind eye

[6] Wood, *History*, ii, pt 1, 438–9. Roy and Reinhart, 'Oxford and the Civil Wars', 694–5.
[7] TCA Caution Book I, ff. 49–49d; TCA Misc. Vol. I, f. 68/110d.
[8] Wood, *History*, ii, pt 1, 442–4.

to their possession. In 1619 John Newdigate had kept a sword and a fowling-piece in College, and made regular purchases of gunpowder, shot, and arrows.[9] During the first eighteen months of the war, the inhabitants of Oxford were required, by means of a series of increasingly urgent proclamations, to hand in small arms and armour which could by used to defend the city. On 24 April 1643, the unlikely figure of Hannibal Potter, Trinity's gentle and tender-conscienced vice-president, arrived at the designated collecting point with a caliver (a shortened musket suitable for cavalry use) and a 'birding piece'.[10] Surely they were not his own!

Meanwhile, on 1 September 1642 a thirty-strong delegacy had been set up to coordinate the university's provision for the troops. Trinity was represented by Nathaniel Simpson, one of the more senior fellows, who had been elected to the foundation as a scholar in 1616. He died in October 1642, and an inventory of his possessions survives in the archives of the Chancellor's Court. Simpson's College room was very comfortably furnished, and he had nice clothes: a surplice, two BD hoods, gowns, cassocks, doublets, hose, and shirts. He owned two pairs of boots, with boot hose, and pairs of buskins and shoes. Simpson's books were valued at over £28 and he rode his own horse (albeit a 'nag with one eye'). Items of a more luxurious and personal nature included an alarm clock, a watch, brass scales and weights, a silver tobacco box, three gold rings, forty-two milled sixpences in an ivory case, and a 'silver case for a beard brush'.[11] The scourge of war had not yet begun to bite.

Oxford had already had its first direct experience of the King's parliamentary enemies. In February 1642, every adult male in England had been required to take the Protestation Oath (although this was designed to uncover closet Catholics rather than royalists). They were required to 'protest to maintain to defend . . . the true Reformed Protestant Religion, expressed in the Doctrine of the Church of England'. Ralph Kettell swore that he would so protest, and all resident members of Trinity did the same: seven fellows, eight scholars, and twenty-eight graduate and undergraduate commoners. Four fellows—Hannibal Potter, Samuel Marsh, Robert Blitheman, and Ralph

[9] Larminie, 'Account Book', 171, 173, 178, 180, 199, 207.

[10] Ian Roy (ed.), *The Royalist Ordnance Papers 1642–1646*, pt 1 (ORS 1963–4), 89.

[11] Anthony Wood, *Athenae Oxonienses*, ed. Philip Bliss (Oxford, 1817), iii, 37. Wood asserts that Simpson died on the day of the battle of Edgehill and was buried in the College Chapel. OUA, Hyp/B/18, ff. 123–4.

Richards—were listed as absent (perhaps deliberately so), as were one scholar and seventeen commoners.[12] But there was no particular cause for suspicion against these men and no recusants were identified in Trinity or elsewhere.

Kettell was certainly no recusant. Aubrey remembered him as a 'right Church of England man; and every Tuesday in term-time, the undergraduates . . . were to come into the Chapel and hear him expound on the thirty-six [*sic*] Articles of the Church of England.'[13] Characteristically, Kettell could not take the Protestation Oath without a small protest of his own, which survives in the form of an indignant handwritten note, attached to the list of Trinity protesters. 'Having been brought up about sixty & three years in this University,' he grumbled, he found the procedure unnecessary, in that it was 'consonant unto the oaths of supremacy & allegiance which I have often taken, [and] that subscription which I have often subscribed & that dutiful prayer which this Parliament time is published for the holy safety of this Church and realm in England.'[14]

On 12 September Oxford was occupied by the parliamentary forces. Sir John Byron and his troop, badly outnumbered by the army being mustered in London, had departed just two days before. The colleges were soon subjected to an unpleasant taste of what they could expect if their side were to lose. Lord Saye and Sele, the Lord Lieutenant of Oxfordshire, came to inspect Trinity, and at once detected a suspicious reek of popery from the two painted altars in the antechapel. Aubrey gleefully recorded the artless (or was it artful?) defence put up by President Kettell: 'My Lord Say saw that this was done of old time and Dr Kettell told his Lordship, "Truly my Lord, we regard them no more than a dirty dish-clout". So they remained untouched.'[15]

The Puritan occupation ended in mid-October, when Lord Saye and Sele was satisfied that Oxford was powerless to assist the King further. But on Saturday 29 October—six days after the indecisive battle of Edgehill—Charles himself rode ceremonially into town and took up residence in the Christ Church Deanery, while his army marched through the city en route to the defence of Abingdon. All the departments of government and offices of the Court were quickly

[12] C. S. A. Dobson (ed.), *Oxford Protestation Returns* (ORS XXXVI, 1955) p. v.

[13] Aubrey, *Brief Lives*, 176.

[14] Dobson, *Protestation Returns*, 117.

[15] Aubrey, *Brief Lives*, 181.

established in temporary locations throughout the city and University, and work began on garrisoning Oxford for real.

Trinity was soon being asked to show its loyalty in ways that were very real indeed. On 19 January 1643, virtually the entire collection of plate was loaded onto a cart and driven away, never to be seen again. It was a great sacrifice of the College's only realizable capital resource. Every crested cup and tankard, every cherished pot and bowl, was melted down and coined into silver pennies with which the army could be paid and the fight continued. The possibility of liquidating some of Oxford's precious assets in this way had already been raised the previous summer by, among others, the Warden of All Souls, Gilbert Sheldon—a Trinity old member with first-hand knowledge of the rich resources that languished in college butteries.[16] During the months of 'phoney war', parliamentarian forces had been vigilantly watching the city, ready to intercept any such transports.[17] Now the mint was set up in the abandoned premises of New Inn Hall, and college plate was easily available. A circular letter was copied out and directed to the 'trusty and well-beloved' of every College, each copy signed personally by Charles himself (Plate 5.1). He was properly grateful—'well satisfied' with their 'readiness and affection' to his service—and in deep trouble, 'as we are ready to sell or engage any of our lands, so we have melted down our plate for the payment of our army, raised . . . for the preservation of our kingdom.' So he had no compunction about demanding that his supporters should do the same: 'lend unto us all such plate of what kind soever which belongs to your college.'[18]

No less than five different lists were drawn up of Trinity's fine collection of plate, recording the donors, the inscriptions, and the weights of each piece. One, very hastily written, noted thirty different inscriptions, beginning with the massive 69$^1/_4$ oz. *poculum parliamentorum donatum Coll. Sancte Trinitatis mense Augusti* 1625 (Parliament cup, given to the College of the Holy Trinity in the month of August 1625).[19] Another enumerated fifty-nine items, down to the pathetic, broken pieces of silver that were still counted among the

[16] Roy and Reinhart, 'Oxford and the Civil Wars', 694. Sheldon does not seem to have presented a piece of plate to Trinity, but he and his brother presumably contributed to the plate fund in 1614. [17] John Twigg, 'College Finances', *HUO* 4, 775.

[18] TCA Misc. Vol. I, f. 68/110; Frederick J. Varley, *The Siege of Oxford* (London, 1932) 37.

[19] In 1625 Parliament was adjourned to Oxford, to escape plague in London. Wood, *History*, ii, pt i, 355.

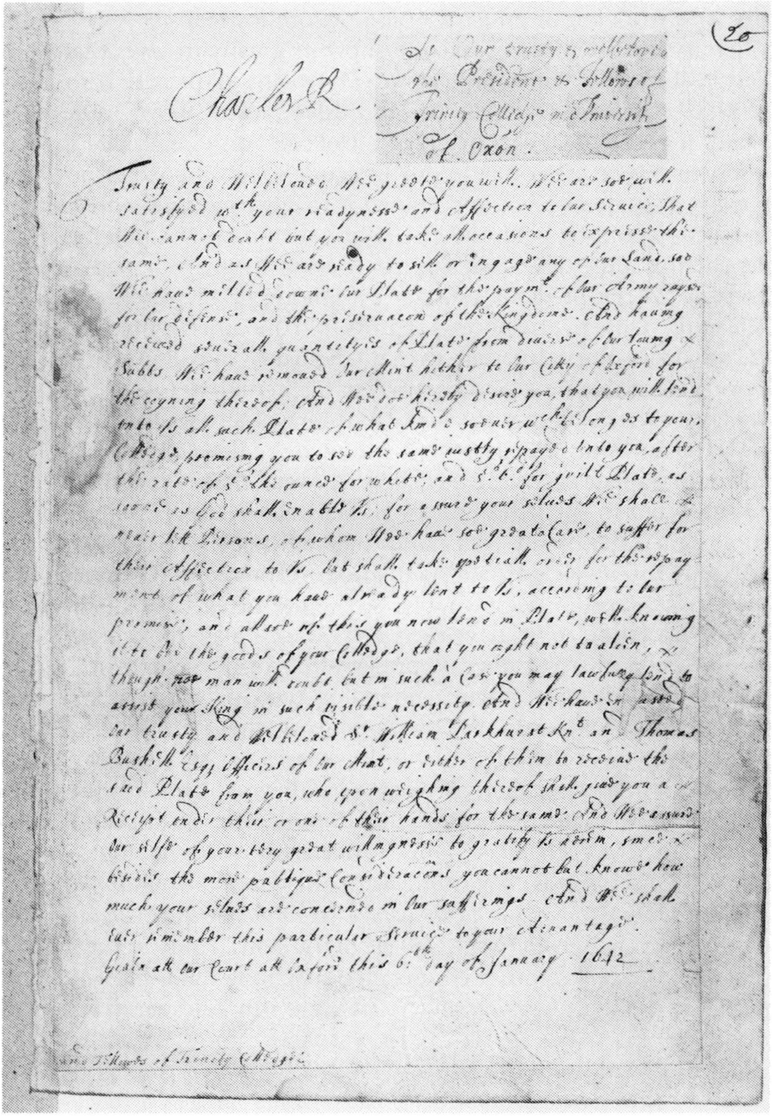

Charles R.

To Our trusty & welbeloved the President & Fellowes of Trinity Colledge in the University of Oxon.

Trusty and Welbeloved Wee greete you well. Wee are soe well satisfyed wth your readynesse and Affection to Our Service, that Wee cannot doubt but you will take all occasions to expresse the same. And as Wee are ready to sell or ingage any of Our Lands, soe Wee have melted downe Our Plate for the paymt of Our Army raysed for Our defence, and the preservacon of the Kingdome. And having receaved severall quantityes of Plate from divers of Our loving Subjects Wee have remooved Our Mint hither to Our City of Oxford for the coyning thereof. And Wee doe hereby desire you, that you will lend unto Us all such Plate of what kinde soever wch belongs to your Colledge, promising you to see the same justly repayed unto you after the rate of 5s the ounce for white, and 5s 6d for guilt Plate, as soone as God shall enable Us. For assure your selves Wee shall never lett Persons, of whom Wee have soe great Care, to suffer for their Affection to Us, but shall take especiall order for the repayment of what you have already lent to Us, according to Our promise; and alsoe of this you now lend in Plate, well knowing it to bee the goods of your Colledge, that you ought not to alien, & though noe man will doubt but in such a Case you may lawfully lend to assist your King in such visible necessity. And Wee have appointed Our trusty and Welbeloved Sr William Parkhurst Knt and Thomas Bushell Esqr Officers of Our Mint, or either of them to receave the said Plate from you, who upon weighing thereof shall give you a Receipt under their or one of their hands for the same. And Wee assure Our selfe of your very great willingnesse to gratify Us herein, since besides the more publique Consideracons you cannot but knowe how much your selves are concerned in Our sufferings. And Wee shall ever remember this particular Service to your Advantage.

Given at Our Court at Oxford this 6th day of January 1642.

[illegible] Fellowes of Trinity Colledge

5.1 Charles I's request to borrow college plate, 6 January 1642 [1643] (TCA Misc. Vol. I, f. 68/110).

College's treasures: 'the relics of Evelin's tankard, $5^1/_2$ oz.', 'two ears of a pot, $3^1/_4$ oz.', and '1 cover of a lost pot, $4^1/_4$ oz.' The King's letter and the lists, together with another official receipt, were put in the treasury. Trinity's 'loan' totalled 130 pounds of 'white' plate and 43 pounds of gilt. At the promised rate of 5*s* the ounce for the former, and 5*s* 6*d* the ounce for the latter, the College could expect future repayment of some £537 from the King.[20] But the final promise in his letter—'assure yourselves we shall never let persons of whom we have so great care, to suffer for their affection to us'—was one that King Charles was never able to keep. And the suffering had only just begun.

It was all very hard for an old man to bear. In Aubrey's opinion, 'Tis probable this venerable Doctor might have lived some years longer and finished his century had not those civil wars come on.' Kettell's authority as head of house, long tested by the insouciant and disrespectful undergraduates, evaporated entirely in the presence of armed troopers. One afternoon, while Aubrey sat listening to the rhetoric lecture in Hall, the two elements of misrule combined with poignant symbolism when a mischievous scholar seized an opportunity to dispense with the unpopular instrument with which the President confined them to lectures. 'A foot soldier came in and broke his hourglass. The Doctor indeed was just stepped out, but Jack Douch pointed at it.'[21] Kettell had admitted Douch to a scholarship in June 1640.

The presence of the royal court brought many shocks for Trinity's octogenarian widower and his celibate colleagues. It was natural that the King's followers should seek accommodation in their old colleges, and natural that, when many commoners had fled, the Colleges should welcome their alumni and indeed anyone else who could help them balance the books. Many members of the court had their wives and families in tow, and Aubrey clearly relished the resulting disruption and spectacle:

> Our grove was the Daphne for the ladies and their gallants to walk in, and many times my Lady Isabella Thynne would make her entry with a theorbo or lute played before her. I have heard her play on it in the Grove myself, which she did rarely.

Even worse:

[20] TCA Misc. Vol. I, ff. 68/110–71/116.

[21] Aubrey, *Brief Lives*, 181. Kettell used to threaten the undergraduates with 'an hour glass two hours long'.

> one time, this lady and fine Mistress Fanshawe (her great and intimate friend, who lay at our college) would have a frolic to make a visit to the President. The old Doctor quickly perceived that they came to abuse him; he addresses his discourse to Mistress Fanshawe, saying, 'Madam, your husband and father I bred up here, and I knew your grandfather, I know you to be a gentlewoman, I will not say you are a whore, but get you gone for a very woman.'

John Fanshawe had come up in 1637 as a fellow commoner, aged 18. He paid £5 caution money, which was returned later the same year. He married Dorothea Kingesmill on 30 March 1639, and four years later he brought her to stay in Trinity.[22] The College authorities were powerless to control the dress and behaviour of such high-spirited young women who had suddenly invaded their cloistered environment. A final insult from Isabella and Dorothea was the way they came 'to our chapel, mornings, half dressed, like angels'.[23]

In his old age Kettell cut an increasingly pathetic figure. Walter Pope remembered him as

> peevish and froward . . . He would stand at the college gate, and observe what persons came to walk in Trinity grove, for that was then the Oxford Hyde Park, the rendezvous of the nobility and gentry. I say, he took notice of all, and usually had a saying to every one of them, which instead of vexing them, made them laugh.

He would then invite yet more ridicule by observing 'to the next of the fellows he chanced to see, "I met some Jack Lords going into my grove, but I think I have nettled them. I gave them such entertainment they little looked for."'[24]

Ralph Kettell died in July 1643, possibly a victim of that summer's 'camp fever', a typhus-like epidemic that led to a sixfold increase in the city's burial rate.[25] He was buried on 5 August, interred in the chancel of Garsington Church, where he had served his parishioners so long and conscientiously.[26]

[22] Lady Isabella was lodging in Balliol. There is no trace, in either the college or the university archives, of John Fanshawe's father—William Fanshawe of Dagenham, Esq.—or of his grandfather; they may however have studied at Trinity, and they may even have been distant kin of Kettell: the name of the nephew who inherited the lease of Kettell Hall was Fanshawe Kettell. See Ann H. Fanshawe, *The Memoirs of Anne, Lady Fanshawe* (London and New York, 1907), 314–15.

[23] Aubrey, *Brief Lives*, 182.

[24] Walter Pope, *The Life of the Right Reverend Father in God Seth Lord Bishop of Salisbury* (London, 1697), 46.

[25] Roy and Reinhart, 'Oxford in the Civil Wars', 710.

[26] ORO Parish Registers, Burials 1643.

## *President Potter and the Siege of Oxford*

Two presidents had governed Trinity for eighty-five years, but the next twenty-one years were to see no fewer than six changes in the headship of the College. Kettell was replaced by Trinity's senior fellow, Hannibal Potter, in an election marred by controversy and ill-feeling. The College Register recorded that William Hawes had not been present to vote, although he had been given written notification of the date and was in Oxford even on the morning of the election day itself. A note in the register accuses him of deliberately absenting himself with the purpose of disrupting proceedings.[27] Walter Pope felt that the position rightly was William Chillingworth's—who 'had the majority of votes but being then at a considerable distance from Oxford, and not able to come suddenly, and take possession, Dr Potter laid hold upon this advantage and was admitted'.[28]

Hannibal Potter had been senior fellow since 1630. He was a man of great piety and very strong principles; and although nervous and timid by nature, he never shrank from doing or saying whatever he felt his Christian duty to be. He had shared a college room with his younger brother Francis for some twenty-seven years, during which he had been quietly tolerant of his sibling's penchant for scientific experiment. Francis 'was always much contemplative,' remembered Aubrey, and 'his genius lay most of all to the mechanics.' In 1637 Francis had succeeded his father in the living of Kilmington, Somerset, where 'his house was as undecked as a monk's cell, yet he had there so many ingenious inventions that it was very delightful.'[29] Hannibal, however, was less than delighted; indeed he deplored any activity that distracted Francis from his duty of caring for his flock. He wrote sternly to Aubrey, asking him not to praise Francis to his face. 'I consider him to be vain, weak, and erroneous in many of his notions (not to say ridiculous) . . . All mathematical inventions are far below the saving of one poor soul.'[30] His language was harsh, but only because he cared so deeply for his brother. Writing again to

[27] TCA Register A, f. 76d.

[28] Pope, *The Life of Seth Lord Bishop of Salisbury*, 47.

[29] Aubrey, *Brief Lives* (Francis Potter), 251–3.

[30] Bod. Lib., MS Aubrey 13/162. The letter is dated 26 May 1653.

Aubrey, he said 'I believe I love him & I seek his welfare more than any man living.'[31]

Hannibal Potter now had the welfare of Trinity as his own charge, and was responsible for its maintenance in almost impossible circumstances. 'From Potter's election till the surrender of Oxford the college has no history,' declared Blakiston dramatically.[32] Indeed, the regular cycles of college days and University terms could hardly be maintained in the face of the disruption caused by war; and it is certainly true that not a single thing was recorded in the College Register between 1647 and 1652.[33] Four fellows and four scholars had been elected in June 1642, three fellows and five scholars in 1643, another fellow and scholar in 1645. The fellowship was younger and less experienced that at any time since the foundation. Indeed, as the wars began, two of the older fellows, Robert Blitheman and Ralph Richards, departed for their country parishes, while George Bathurst volunteered. He was the second of thirteen Bathurst brothers, of whom six were to die in the Civil Wars, George suffering a fatal shot wound to the thigh during the royalist defence of Faringdon in 1644. By 1646 Josiah How (aged 34) was the second senior fellow, and Ralph Bathurst (the fifth brother, now aged 25) the third.[34]

Thomas Warton had no doubt that 'divinity was the profession to which Ralph Bathurst had originally dedicated his life.' As a newly elected fellow, he ignored the war's steady encroachment upon the affairs of the University, and he worked hard at his theological studies, writing up the *Diatribae Theologicae Philosophicae* & *Philologicae* (theological, philosophical and philological debates) that had been held in the Trinity College hall in 1643 and 1644.[35] Warton was impressed by the quality of Bathurst's work, which was 'digested in a masterly manner'. The fullness and exactness of his references, Warton considered, were excellent, showing as they did 'a spirit of theological research, and an extensive knowledge of the writings of the most learned divines'. But as the future of the Church of England began to appear increasingly uncertain, and the demand for

[31] Bod. Lib. MS Aubrey 13/163.1653, 3 August 1653.

[32] Blakiston, *Trinity*, 133.

[33] One reason for this may have been the absence of the register itself, perhaps one of the items taken into safe-keeping by the ejected bursar, Josiah How.

[34] TCA *Computus* 1646–7. How was born 'about 1611' and Bathurst 'about 1620' (*DNB*). It is unclear exactly when the senior fellow William Hobbes (born 1598) vacated his fellowship.

[35] Warton, *Bathurst*, 36–7; TCA OF 2/11.

divines likely only to dwindle, Bathurst felt the need for a more secure career and turned to the study of medicine, although, as he explained many years later to his friend Seth Ward, it was 'only my refuge in bad times, and not my primitive design'.[36]

Trinity's population was diminishing rapidly. Between 1635 and 1640, some sixteen or seventeen commoners had been admitted annually to Trinity, already a sharp decline from an average of twenty-five admissions during the previous fifteen years. But in 1641 and 1642 there were just nine new commoners each year, four in 1643, none in 1644, and just one in 1645. Many undergraduates had been summoned home by their families, and it seemed that nobody was matriculating to take their place.

All able-bodied members of College who were left were required to do their share of war work. A house-to-house count in June 1643 found over 4,000 men between the ages of 16 and 60, of whom some 1,500 were resident in College accommodation, fifty-three of them at Trinity. This workforce was placed in six divisions and each division was set to work one day each week on the city's fortifications. The Trinity contingent was assigned to a division of twelve colleges (768 men in total), and every Monday (subsequently Friday) had 'to be ready at the beat of the drum . . . with their tools, viz, mattocks, shovels, spades, axes, hatchets or bills'. The drumbeat came at 5 a.m., and the working day was from 6 a.m. until 6 p.m., with a two-hour break around noon.[37] Those unable or unwilling to take their turn could opt out, but only on payment of a shilling a day. By means of this forced labour, an extensive series of trenches and earthworks was created in Christ Church meadow, in the New Parks, and around Holywell.

Many of the fifty-three 'Trinity' men thus employed were not undergraduates, scholars, or fellows. The count made no distinction between members and non-matriculated lodgers in the colleges. Across the University, rooms were crammed with a fluctuating population of courtiers and royalist refugees. Oxford was in fact becoming increasingly overcrowded, and in January 1644 the King issued a proclamation that scholars should be sent home from their colleges to make more space for his court.[38] A female resident of Trinity in 1644 was Lady Ann Fanshawe (no relation to President Kettell's

[36] TCA OF2/8. The letter is dated 10 February 1662 (i.e. 1663), but was ascribed by Warton (*Bathurst*, 54–9) to 1663/4.
[37] Bod. Lib. MS Add. D 114, ff. 17, 20, 28, 75.
[38] Roy and Reinhart, 'Oxford in the Civil Wars', 698.

tormentor, Mistress Dorothea). The previous year she had fled from London to Oxford with her sisters and father, John Harrison, and they found lodgings in an unpleasant attic above a baker's shop. The following spring Ann made the acquaintance of Sir Richard Fanshawe, the Prince of Wales's newly appointed Secretary for War, a Cambridge man some fifteen years her senior. The couple were married at Wolvercote Church on 18 May 1644.

Sir Richard may already have been lodging at Trinity; it was where the couple were living the following February when their first child was born. Many years later, Lady Ann recorded the event in her memoirs: 'Harrison Fanshawe was born at Oxford in Trinity College, on Sunday the 23rd day of February, at 9 o'clock at night. He was baptized the next day by Doctor Potter, master of that college . . . He lived for 15 days.'[39]

While their son was dying, Ann and Richard Fanshawe faced the additional grief of separation amid the dangers of war:

> The beginning of March, 1645, [Richard] went to Bristol with his new master. And this was his first journey—I was then lying-in . . . he left me behind him. As it was the first time we had parted a day since we were married, he was extremely afflicted even to tears, though passion was against his nature. But the sense of leaving me with a dying child, which did die two days after in a garrison town, extremely weak and very poor, were such circumstances as he could not bear with, only the argument of necessity.

But Ann Fanshawe was known for her high spirits and resilience. With the help of 'the conversation of many of my relations then in Oxford, and kind visits of very many of the nobility and gentry', she was able to rally her strength. As she recalled, 'It was in May, 1645, the first time I went out of my chamber and to church.' After the service she met Sir William Parkhurst (the officer of the mint) who brought news from Richard, a summons to join him in Bristol, and a very welcome purse of gold sovereigns.

Ann Fanshawe's knowledge of Oxford was limited, and between leaving the city and writing her memoir, she had lived in Madrid, Paris, Hertfordshire, Lisbon, Yorkshire, and Kent. In a separate document she listed her children (six sons and eight daughters christened, six miscarriages) and here she ascribed Harrison's birth to St John's

[39] Fanshawe, *The Memoirs of Lady Fanshawe*, p. xix.

College, and twice noted his burial as 'in the parish church of St John's'. The name of Dr Potter, who baptized the baby, gives credence to her earlier assertion that he was born in Trinity.[40] And given her weakened condition, it seems likely that a subsequent brush with death—on the very day she first ventured outdoors—occurred in the garden of Trinity rather than that of St John's, which would have seemed a long walk from Trinity's main entrance on Broad Street.

> I went immediately to walk, or at least sit in the air, being very weak, in the garden . . . and there with my good father communicated my joy . . . [i.e. the news from Sir Richard]. We—my entire household being present—heard drums beat in the highway under the garden wall. My father asked me if I would go up upon the mount and see the soldiers march . . . I said yes, and went up, leaning my back to a tree that grew on the mount. The commander seeing us there, in compliment gave us a volley of shot, and one of their muskets being loaded shot a brace of bullets not two inches above my head as I leaned to the tree; for which mercy and deliverance I praise God.[41]

Trinity's mount, topped by a mature tree, is clearly visible in Loggan's 1675 view of the College, and would have given a good view of the road. On 15 May Lady Ann left Trinity, and five days later reached her beloved husband in Bristol. One week later, Oxford came under siege for the first time.

Josiah How, meanwhile, had been doing his bit for the war effort. In 1644 he preached a morale-boosting sermon before the King and the court at Christ Church, taking for his text Psalm 4 verse 7, 'Thou hast put gladness in my heart, more than when their corn and wine increased.' The royalist side could be encouraged, he argued, by the fact that 'afflictions which to the wicked are miseries, to God's children appear a kind of severe and not prayed-for blessing, and the rougher sort of love.' In a nutshell, 'The rule that results to us is this: these failings of bounty are blessings, and make no wretched state.' Thirty copies of the sermon were printed, in red letters, apparently by order of the King, but only one is known to have survived the purges of the postwar years.[42]

[40] He was perhaps buried in Merton Chapel (St John the Baptist), which was used by the Court. No registers survive.

[41] Fanshawe, *Memoirs of Lady Fanshawe*, 31–3.

[42] The surviving copy was discovered by Thomas Hearne among the papers of Arthur Charlett (fellow 1679). It is now in the Bodleian.

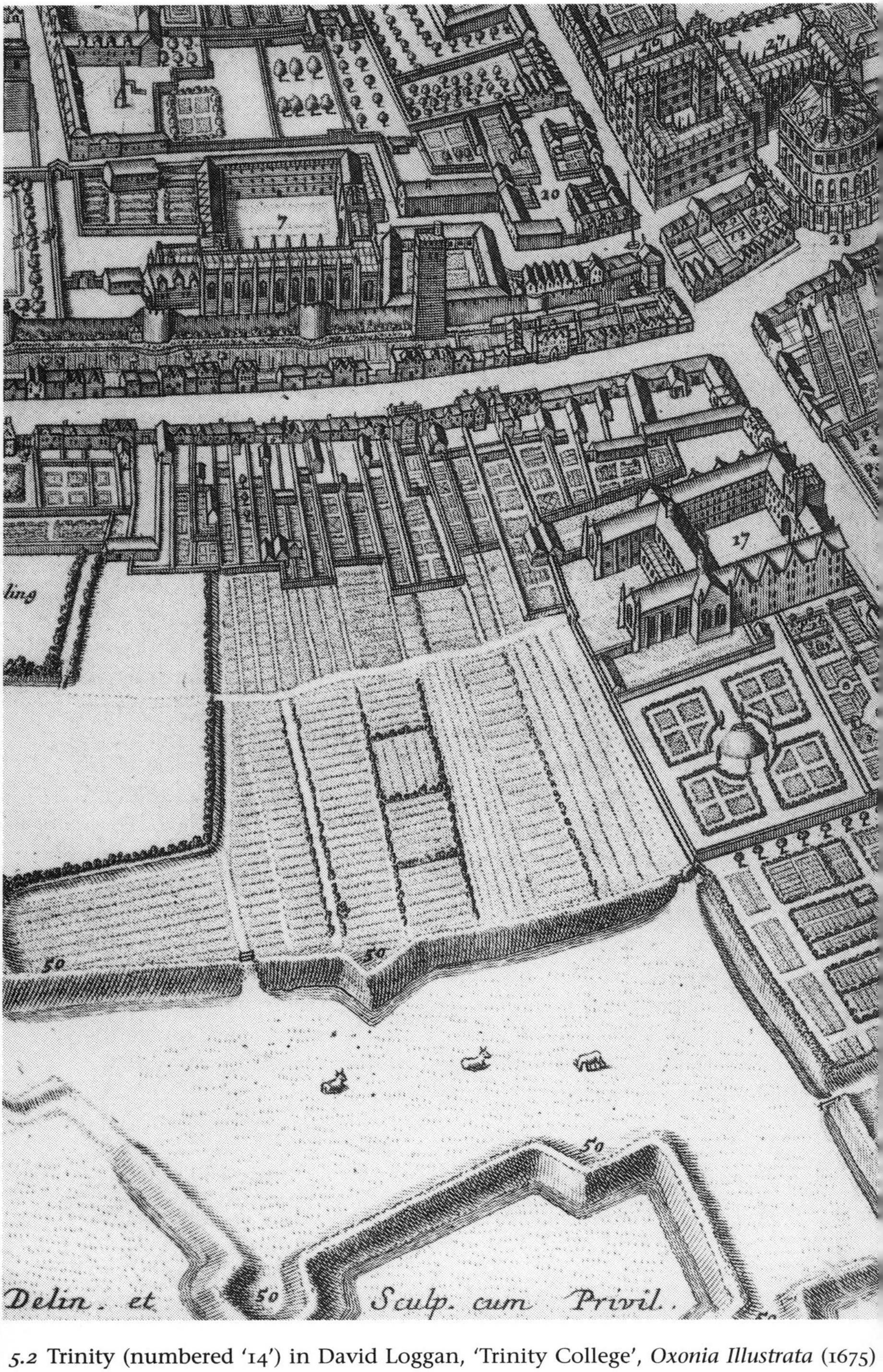


*5.2* Trinity (numbered '14') in David Loggan, 'Trinity College', *Oxonia Illustrata* (1675)

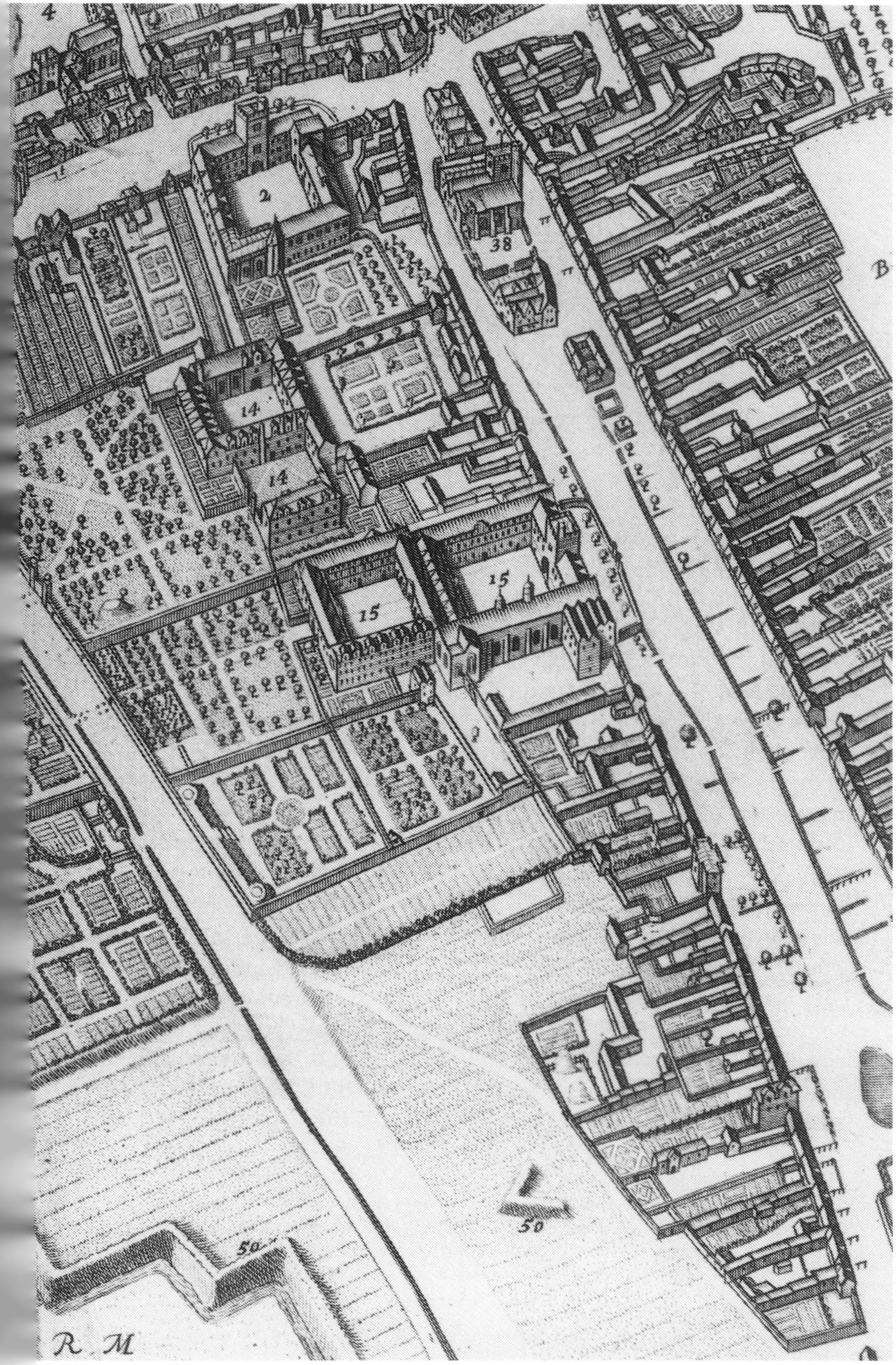
4
2
38
B
14
14
15
15
50
50
R. M.

Life in Oxford became increasingly wretched during 1645 and 1646, and keeping the College solvent became correspondingly difficult. There is a gap in the *computus* account from 1639–40 until 1645–6, but the names of the bursars appear in the record of money placed in or borrowed from the treasury. Surviving accounts of unpaid bills—the *Billa Petitionis*—illustrate the difficulty of collecting money that was owed to the College. In the 1630s the average total owing annually was around £300. In 1647 it was £1,385. Some commoners inevitably left without paying their battels, and debts amounting to £49 had been accrued in this way between 1637 and 1641. But in wartime it was impossible to chase either the absent commoners or the shifting population of lodgers: £106 was owing from 1642, £85 from 1643, and £58 from 1644. One commoner who seems to have been in residence throughout this period was John Coker of Bicester (matriculated 1642). In 1652 he returned to settle four years' worth of accumulated battels, an exceptional act of decency that was emulated by very few others. Moreover, the College's tenants, whose rents supported the foundation, were badly in arrears. Robert Napier, the tenant at Stoppsley, had not paid his £40 annual rent since 1643; nor had anything been recieved from Tadmarton. From Wroxton, £44 was owed for 1646, and not one tenant had paid a penny of his rent in the whole of 1647. The Abbot's Langley rent for 1645 was not received until three years later.[43]

To all intents and purposes, most of Oxford's colleges were now facing the prospect of closure as the conditions of the war made the maintenance of any corporate identity or common purse a virtual impossibility. The terrible truth is that a note in Trinity's *computus* of 1647–8 records payments of arrears of commons and stipends to three fellows 'absent at the time of the dissolution of the college'.[44] There was nothing left to support the foundation, and the fellows and scholars left in residence had no choice but to fend for themselves. They were desperately poor. Samuel Cranford had entered Trinity as a batteller, paying the lowest rate of caution money, in May 1635. He was elected to a scholarship a month later, and to a fellowship in 1640. Cranford died in College in the autumn of 1645, and a pitiful inventory of his belongings was exhibited in the Chancellor's Court

[43] TCA *Billa Petitionis* 1647, 1652; TCA *Computus* 1647–8, f. 105.

[44] Although the meticulous Blakiston seems to have overlooked the ignominious word 'dissolution' in his reading of the *computus*, Trinity should not be ashamed of this fact in its past. It makes the recovery of Trinity's fortunes by the end of the century an even more remarkable achievement. TCA *Computus* 1647–8, f. 104d.

in January 1646. The total value of his possessions was a meagre £6 10*s*. He had two 'desks to lay books out', but 'the rest of his books left unsold' were valued at just £2. The only non-essential items listed—and they were virtually worthless—were '2 maps coloured and framed' and 'one pictured fruit basket'.[45]

During May and June 1646, Oxford was besieged by the parliamentary forces. King Charles had narrowly escaped capture as he crept out of the city, disguised degradingly as a servant in the early hours of 27 April. The city was extremely crowded, food was very short, and the unpaid troops were dangerously mutinous.[46] The surrender came as a great relief to all. The articles of surrender promised that University buildings should 'be preserved from defacing and spoil', but offered no protection to those who had borne arms for the King. At least the colleges could 'enjoy their ancient form of government subordinate to the immediate authority and power of government', and individuals were granted 'convenient time allowed for the removal of themselves and their goods from their lodgings'.[47] One Trinity man on the victorious side was Henry Ireton (1627), famous as one of the regicides who signed the death warrant of Charles I.

The first action of Parliament was to send seven renowned Presbyterian preachers to Oxford, with a brief 'to preach when and where they may think to make most for edification' in the battle for the hearts and minds of the Anglican university.[48] The most senior man in the team was Robert Harris, an old member of Magdalen Hall, an experienced preacher, and the Rector of Hanwell in Oxfordshire. In September 1646, Anthony Wood, who was 'trudging' every day to a 'cockleloft over the common gate' of Trinity, to be coached by his elder brother Edward (scholar 1643), was not impressed by any of the new preachers on offer. They 'made wry mouths, squint eyes, and screwed faces, quite altering them from what God and nature made them' and they had 'antique behaviour, squeaking voices and puling tongues, fit rather for stage players and country beggars to use, than such that were to speak the oracles of God'.[49] Robert Harris's devoted biographer, William Durham, on the other hand, felt that 'his parts were best known in the pulpit; his gifts in prayer were much above

[45] OUA, Hyp/B/11, f. 178. [46] Roy and Reinhart, 'The Civil Wars', 719.
[47] 'Articles of Surrender'. Bod Lib. MS Add D 114, f. 122.
[48] Wood, *History*, ii, pt 1, 490. [49] Wood, *Life*, i, 129, 147.

ordinary; his affections warm and keen, his petitions pithy and sinuous; his language pertinent, unaffected, and without tautologies. Oh how he would buoy up a dull and sinking spirit! How he would warm a cold and frozen heart!'[50]

John Aubrey came racing back to Oxford at the earliest opportunity, arriving on 6 November. His description—'I returned to Trinity College . . . again to my great joy—was much made of by the fellows, had their learned conversation, looked on books—music . . . I enjoyed the greatest felicity of my life'—hardly does justice to the seriousness of the situation around him. Hannibal Potter soon found himself in a very vulnerable position. He was the pro-vice-chancellor, bound to deputize when required for the Vice-Chancellor, the Dean of Christ Church, Samuel Fell. In the spring of 1647, a commission of twenty-four Visitors, including Robert Harris, was appointed, and charged with the 'reformation' of the University. From 1 June they sat at Merton College and commenced the long and often tortuous process of ousting the royalist cause from the University. On 8 October Samuel Fell was summoned to London, where he was imprisoned. But when Fell's keys and books were formally delivered to him, Potter initially refused to accept them. The Proctor—Robert Waring of Christ Church—and Bodley's Librarian—Thomas Barlow of Queen's—had to remind him sternly of his oath before he would agree to act.[51] Barlow enlisted the additional support of Trinity's Gilbert Sheldon, now Warden of All Souls, to help 'fix [Potter] in his determination,' while Richard Baylie, President of St John's, was another who joined in bolstering Potter's wavering resolve.[52]

For details of all these events, we are heavily dependent on monarchist Anthony Wood, who wrote his History of the University after the Restoration. According to Wood, Hannibal Potter, although by nature a timorous and peaceable man and one who hated the limelight, was now ready to shoulder his duty heroically. On 23 October he called a convocation, and having approved a defiant reply to the visitors, 'concluded . . . with a short speech, in which he told the

[50] Durham, *Harris*, 82.

[51] Aubrey, *Brief Lives*, 12; Wood, *History*, ii, pt 2, 528.

[52] Wood, ibid.; Victor D. Sutch, *Gilbert Sheldon, Architect of Anglican Survival 1640–75* (The Hague, 1973), 28.

masters, that seeing the University was then and like to be under a most grievous affliction, that they would as true Christians and adorers of good learning, take all things patiently and behave themselves without tumult and giving offence'.[53] A period of nervous cat-and-mouse resistance ensued. Potter was summoned before the Visitors on 29 October; he wrote back, declining to attend. On 4 November, he and others were summoned again to appear; on 5 November they did so, but gave evasive answers. On 15 November he was called before a parliamentary committee of Lords and Commons in London, and made the same answers again. One by one, the committee found Oxford's leading figures guilty of high contempt and ordered their removal from the University; one by one they ignored the order. 'Not a man stirred from his place,' commented Wood proudly. On 6 January Potter was formally 'removed' from the presidency of Trinity. He stayed in the Lodgings. For three months messengers were sent repeatedly to Oxford and were insulted or ignored. Finally in April, the Chancellor (the Earl of Pembroke) came with soldiers. At Christ Church, Samuel Fell's wife was carried from the deanery still sitting on her chair. At All Souls, Gilbert Sheldon's name was dashed from the buttery book, and he was led away by a troop of musketeers. At Trinity the door of the Lodgings was broken down. But Hannibal Potter was nowhere to be found; he had done the sensible thing, and already fled.[54]

For twelve years, Potter was exiled from Oxford. For a short while he held a curacy at Broomfield, Somerset, but was soon removed from this too, either for using the Anglican liturgy or for 'insufficiency'.[55] In 1653 he wrote to John Aubrey:

> I am (as I have been a long time) in a sad case. My life passes and I can do no good for want of employment. My books, which were my comforters when I could enjoy them, are kept from me for debt and like to be sold for half their worth. I have no accommodation to stir abroad and to seek help. No man will stir for me, and what to do I know not. God help me, and us all in [this] needful time.[56]

[53] Wood, *History*, ii, pt 2, 529.

[54] Ibid., 547, 563, 568–70.

[55] Wood, *History and Antiquities of the Colleges and Halls*, ed. John Gutch (Oxford, 1796), 523 n. 38; Daniel Neal, *The History of the Puritans or Protestant Nonconformists*, 2nd edn. (London, 1754), 315.

[56] Bod. Lib. MS Aubrey 13/162.

## *President Harris*

The next act of the Visitors was an attempt to inspect the accounts and books of all the colleges, while members of the University were called up, college by college, to formally declare their allegiance to the parliamentary government. It was Trinity's turn on 5 May. Three fellows, nine scholars, and twenty-six commoners were summoned; twenty-six in total appeared, and thirteen, including two scholars, submitted. One scholar said he 'never studied state policy and therefore [could] not give any answer to so hard questions'. Another was rebuked for his insolence when 'being asked whether he would submit to the authority of parliament, [he] answered, "yes with all my heart if you'll submit to the king."' Bernard Banger replied that he was 'not satisfied how far' he could submit; which he repeated on 23 May, and on being asked if he would submit to the authority of Dr Harris as President, he replied 'I desire to see the Statutes first.'[57] On 30 June four Trinity names were published in a list of more than sixty men expelled from the University. Two were fellows—Matthew Skinner, son of the exiled Bishop of Oxford, and William Radford; one a scholar, Bernard Banger; and one a commoner, Aubrey's best friend Anthony Ettrick. Two further expulsions followed on 26 October: Josiah How, and William Walker. How and Walker were the bursars, and they had refused to appear before the Visitors at all.[58]

Josiah How is a heroic figure in the archives of Trinity College. James Ingram (President 1824–50) considered him to be the saviour of many of the early financial records of the college, describing in the first caution book how

> the college papers [were] much deranged, and some irrevocably lost during the Rebellion. Many were saved by the care and diligence of Mr Josias How, at that time bursar, who took them into the country with him for a time, instead of leaving them at the mercy of the parliamentary visitors, who had peremptorily demanded them.

How seems also to have taken his keys with him; the day after his expulsion the treasury was broken open by order of the Visitors.[59]

[57] Montgu Burrows, *The Register of the Visitors of the University of Oxford* (Camden Society, 1881), 39, 109.

[58] Blakiston, *Trinity*, 141; Wood, *History*, ii, pt 2, 581.

[59] TCA Caution book I, f. 8d.

As the royalist How was much admired by eighteenth- and nineteenth-century fellows of Trinity, so the parliamentarian Harris was despised. He was assigned the presidency by the Visitors, although in the view of his loyal biographer Durham, he could not be accused of actively usurping the position, as his course had been 'to stand silent, without opening his mouth for any headship at all', until the 'best places' were disposed of without 'any news of any for him'. But 'the smallness of the college, and the situation thereof, did abundantly satisfy him, who never desired anymore than what would keep him from distractions in his studies.'[60] More hostile observers, however, were quick to charge him with pluralism. James Ford (fellow 1806–31) presented his copy of the *Life and Death of Robert Harris* to James Ingram, but not before he had noted in it how Harris had kept the rectory of Hanwell, 'his old love', besides holding Bishopsgate, Hanborough, Buriton, and Petersfield, and receiving payments from his 'Assembly membership' and 'apostleship in Oxford,' giving him a total income of over £1,600.[61]

Harris was also maligned by an unsavoury story promulgated by Anthony Wood after the Restoration:

> a painter at Trinity College, pulling down some boards and shelves, found two bags sealed, and a paper in the mouth of each, which signified that there was £100 in each bag. They were covered with dust about half an inch thick, yet Dr Harris and his wife (solely addicted to money and reformation) presently owned them and said confidently that they were theirs but *oportet mendacem esse memorem* [a liar should have a good memory]. For first he had not been there much above half a year, and the bags were so old and overcovered with dust as if they had lain there 40 years. [Secondly] his wife said at first, they were left there by a friend, who desired her to lay up two bags of £100 a bag, but she refused to take any charge of them, yet he told her he would leave them, and so hid them in that place where the painter found them. [Thirdly] But on better consideration, Dr Harris said that he himself had laid them there, and 'twas money designed for his daughters, and though no man believed, yet this he averred '*verbo sacerdotis*' [on the word of a minister].

Wood supposed that the money had been left by Ralph Kettell, and described how Kettell's heir Fanshawe had come desiring to see

[60] Durham, *Harris*, 40–1.

[61] Bequeathed by Ingram to the Trinity College Library.

the seal and labels on each bag, 'but the old gentleman . . . would neither show bag, or seal, or writing; a manifest argument that they were none of his.'[62] William Durham made no reference to this story in his life of Harris, although, said Wood, it was 'the common discourse of town and country'.[63] Durham did, however, comment on Harris's poor memory for names, and how 'he said "that his memory never failed him", which he presently explained, "because he durst never trust it".'[64]

There is little primary evidence of Harris's decade in office. Durham felt his 'government was such, that it caused a wonder', and 'the foundation . . . honoured him as a father, and he looked upon them, and loved them as children.'[65] Blakiston admitted 'that he seems to have used his almost absolute power in the college with discretion, and to have soon conciliated . . . those members who . . . were allowed to remain without having submitted',[66] and Blair Worden has described Harris's regime as 'more harmonious than puritan'.[67] Information that survives in the archives suggests that with peace in the land and peace in the College, Trinity began to recover its fortunes. The number of admissions picked up at once, although it came nowhere near the pre-war level. Three commoners entered in 1648 and a number of scholars, including three imposed on Trinity from elsewhere. Four commoners entered in 1649, ten in 1650 (including two fellow commoners), four in 1651, eight in 1652. Their experiences were very different from life in pre-war Trinity. Harris 'could not satisfy himself under two sermons weekly,' and the second parliamentary visitation, established in 1653, was particularly focused on the levels of godliness in the colleges.[68]

Surviving *computus* accounts show an increasingly healthy turnover at Trinity. Money became available for much-needed repair work to the neglected College buildings, in particular the Chapel roof.[69] A little could be spared for the garden, where the ambulatory was restored, and shady arbours created in the autumn of 1653.[70]

Ralph Bathurst had submitted to the authority of Parliament, although, by all accounts, he remained at heart a monarchist. He spent

[62] Wood, *History*, ii, pt 2, 624–5. [63] Ibid. [64] Durham, *Harris*, 73, 86.
[65] Ibid., 97. [66] Blakiston, *Trinity*, 138–9.
[67] Worden, 'Cromwellian Oxford', *HUO* 4, 765.
[68] Durham, *Harris*, 42; Worden, 'Cromwellian Oxford', *HUO* 4, 741.
[69] TCA *Computus* 1651, ff. 111–12. [70] Ibid., 1653, f. 120d.

some time away from Oxford, employed as a naval doctor, but by 1654 was back, practising medicine alongside the royalist physician, Thomas Willis.[71] Bathurst was a friend of the leading Oxford figure, John Wilkins, Warden of Wadham, and he regularly met with Wilkins, Seth Ward (fellow of Wadham), and others.[72] Bathurst was active as a covert Anglican, and regularly assisted at illegal ordinations performed by the deprived Bishop of Oxford, Robert Skinner, at his north Oxfordshire rectory. As Warton described it:

> Whenever any candidate solicited to be ordained, he privately applied to Bathurst, who examined him, and appointed a day for meeting him at the Bishop's house. At the time agreed, under pretence of visiting patients, he attended the solemnity at Launton, in which he officiated as archdeacon. This service he executed with the utmost fidelity and punctuality.[73]

When Robert Harris 'began to droop', we are told that Bathurst and Willis attended him faithfully, despite their patient's frequent assertions that they had little hope of dealing with his 'complicated diseases, which were seldom removed; but most of all with old age, a disease which was never cured'. Harris was 80. He was suffering from emphysema, and he endured a long and agonizing final illness. He devoted his last months to 'meditation, prayer, and reading God's book', and when he could no longer sit up and read, and was hardly able to speak, he asked 'his attendants to read scripture to him constantly . . . and while life and language lasted he concluded all prayers with a loud Amen.' His last days were painless, and his passing so peaceful—'his soul, without the lease motion or resistance of body, entered into rest'—that those attending him could not determine the exact time of death, some time in the early hours of Sunday 12 December 1658.[74]

Ralph Bathurst gave an oration at Harris's funeral and composed an epitaph for his grave. He praised the President as 'the keenest judge of character, the gentlest wielder of authority, the most impartial patron of deserving causes', and his college during his presidency for its 'excellent education' and its 'enviable harmony'.[75] And

[71] Warton, *Bathurst*, 39.

[72] Worden, 'Cromwellian Oxford', *HUO* 4, 738–9.

[73] Warton, *Bathurst*, 37. I am grateful to Robert Beddard for confirmation of this activity.

[74] Durham, *Harris*, 50–62.

[75] Warton, *Bathurst*, 125.

then the fellows acted swiftly to avoid any undue visitatorial interference in the choice of a successor. The election was called on Monday 13 December, and the votes were cast three days later. William Hawes, who had caused the disruption at Potter's election fifteen years earlier, was elected unanimously.[76] He did not, however, have long to make his mark on the College. Nine months later, Hawes himself lay dying in the President's Lodgings.

The College Register records only the legal facts of what then happened; indeed, it records them very properly and in great detail. On Monday 12 September, at 5 o'clock, in the presence of a public notary and two of the fellows as witnesses (Ralph Bathurst and John Pettifer), William Hawes resigned. His complicity in the plan to thwart the Visitors yet again can only be assumed. At 8 o'clock, the fellows assembled in the Chapel and heard the vice-president, Thomas Pooler, read out Hawes's resignation and call the election. This time it was held only two days later, at the very moment, according to a marginal note in the register, of Hawes's death. There were two nominations, Ralph Bathurst's close friend Seth Ward, and Bathurst's elder brother Edward, and the fellows had acted alone, as the notary recorded piously, because by order of Parliament, they had no Visitor. Ward was elected unanimously.[77]

It was all done while Bathurst pulled the strings and waited in the wings. The monarchists in Oxford were by now in the ascendancy; Richard Cromwell was the University's new Chancellor, working closely with Wilkins's party; Parliament's rule was almost at an end. Seth Ward was one of the most able men ever to hold the presidency of Trinity, but he held it for less than a year. With the Restoration of the monarchy in 1660 came the restoration of all those who had been removed from their offices, bishoprics, and headships, and from his rural retreat returned the quiet, unassuming Hannibal Potter.

Potter was well suited to the humble and monastic ideals of the founder, but in his lifetime the College had seen a great many changes. The rules for electing presidents had been disregarded, the devout and scholarly routines abandoned. Around Pope's tomb in the Chapel there had been practised a religion that he would have abhorred. Now, the Restoration would bring back many traditions that had been lost by the University, but it would also take Trinity further than ever before from the spirit of Thomas Pope.

[76] TCA Register A, ff. 84–84d. [77] Ibid., ff. 88–90.

# 6

# *President Bathurst*

## *Bathurst Becomes President*

By the time of the Restoration there had developed a strong symbiotic relationship between Trinity College and its alumni, a mutual dependency that was to become central to the College's success and expansion. Old members had the potential to give vital financial assistance to the College, and could exert their influence in the spheres of Church and government. In return, Trinity gratefully accepted the obligation to educate and accommodate their sons.

A good example of the seventeenth-century Trinity man at work was Hannibal Potter's contemporary, Robert Skinner, admitted scholar in 1607 and fellow in 1613. Skinner held his fellowship until he had taken his BD. He left in 1621 for the position of preacher at St Gregory's Church in the City of London, the first in a series of successively more valuable and prestigious ecclesiastical appointments. Skinner succeeded his father as rector of Pitsford, Northamptonshire; served as chaplain to the King; became rector of some four parishes; and, in 1636, was appointed Bishop of Bristol. Five years later he was translated to the see of Oxford. Skinner suffered less hardship during the Civil War than Potter, for although expelled from his bishopric, he was licensed to preach and was allowed to retain his Launton rectory. In 1660 he returned to his see (but not to his palace at Cuddesden, which had been destroyed in the Civil War) and was appointed one of the King's commissioners for the University. So he was well placed to orchestrate the quiet departure of Seth Ward and the re-admission of his old friend to the Trinity presidency. Potter was decreed restored by the Commissioners on 3 August 1660.[1] In 1663 Skinner was appointed Bishop of Worcester, from where he continued to take a keen interest in his old College. His son Matthew,

[1] Wood, *History*, ii, pt 2, 700–1; F. J. Varley (ed), 'The Restoration Visitation of the University of Oxford and its Colleges', *Camden Miscellany* xviii (third series, 79) (1948) 7–8.

*6.1* Ralph Bathurst, President 1664–1704, by Godfrey Kneller (1694).

meanwhile, had been elected to a scholarship in 1640 and a fellowship in 1643.

Potter returned to Trinity in August 1660 and enjoyed the comforts and security of life in his old Lodgings for another four years, seemingly loved and respected by those around him. He died on 1 September 1664 and was buried in the Chapel, the event celebrated by Samuel Dugard (scholar 1662, fellow 1667–72) as a symbol of noble triumph over adversity:

> Pressed with unjuster cares which slashed thy brow
> With cruel wrinkles, clothed thy head with snow
> (whose whiteness puts it on a doubtful score

whether innocence or age may claim the more).
How, sir, how often have you laboured! Thus
You died then to yourself and now to us.[2]

Ralph Bathurst was elected President on 3 September 1664 and assumed his new duties in a seamless transition.[3] He had been senior fellow from 1651 until the restoration of Josiah How in 1660, and had an expert knowledge of the College's finances and administration. No one was better acquainted with the difficulties which Trinity now faced. The 250-year-old Chapel was 'very homely', and calling 'for help to preserve its roof from necessary decay'.[4] Numbers had picked up slowly since the Civil War, but they were far from the boom levels of the 1630s. Bathurst perceived with the utmost clarity that immediate action was required. The Chapel could wait—it waited for another thirty years—until he had raised the profile of the College membership to a sufficient standard to finance the expansion that he dreamed of. What was needed were 'gentlemen of quality' and the way to attract them was to provide more modern and luxurious accommodation.[5]

## *The Buildings*

Bathurst commenced his first building campaign at once, and it was masterly. One of his Oxford friends (another underground Anglican during the Commonwealth period) was an up-and-coming architect by the name of Christopher Wren—a Wadham graduate, a fellow of All Souls who had been Savilian Professor of Astronomy since 1661. Plans were quickly drawn up for a choice of two different new buildings. One was a small square structure with 'Flemish walls' and four sets of rooms on each floor, which was designed to stand in the southern end of the 'garden towards Balliol College', at an estimated cost of £725.[6] The other was considerably larger: a two-storey

[2] Bod. Lib. MS Rawl. poet. 152, f. 40.

[3] TCA Register A, ff. 175–175d.

[4] RB to Henry Whistler, 23 July 1665, TCA Misc. Vol. I, f. 83/127.

[5] 'Gentlemen' or 'persons of quality' was a phrase much used by Bathurst, for example, TCA Misc. Vol. I, 79/124, 85/132, 85/133.

[6] TCA Misc. Vol. 1, 78d./121; Buildings, D.1. Wren's ground-floor plan includes a staircase. The intended site must have been the garden between the Chapel and Broad Street; today's fellows' garden was too small.

two-staircase block with a mansard roof and cocklofts, giving twelve sets of rooms in total, and it was the latter, more ambitious plan that was adopted. The building was designed on classical lines, having a central projection with alcoves, a low triangular pediment, and cruciform windows. It was very French in style, and the height of architectural fashion. The mansard roof—with two slopes on both ends and both sides, the lower slopes at a steeper angle than the upper—had been introduced to England twenty years earlier, but this was the very first example in Oxford.[7]

Such a bold scheme called for powerful patronage, and Bathurst recruited two loyal and willing old members: Robert Skinner, Bishop of Worcester, and Gilbert Sheldon, who in 1663 had been consecrated Archbishop of Canterbury. Such important figures could not be crossed. Bathurst wrote to Skinner at the end of May 1665 to tell him that the new building's foundations were 'about to be laid. We at first intended it in the fellows' garden, but for many reasons have transferred it to the upper part of the grove where it will stand with much more beauty and convenience.' The Bishop disagreed, however, and Bathurst wrote back humbly and hastily on 2 July:

> Having understood your Lordship's dislike of our late purpose to build at the upper end of the grove, we have now in submission to your Lordship's wisdom and advice, transferred it back again to the fellows garden, where we at first intended it, though much against the will of some and the judgment of others, especially Dr Wren who is our chief designer.[8]

Wren's objections were serious and practical ones, but nonetheless the work went on in the Bishop's preferred location. He had not yet given any money to the project.[9] 'We were persuaded from the beginning that we would meet with much false ground thereabouts,' explained Bathurst meekly, 'and accordingly we have found it in three several places, so that we have been forced sometimes to go very deep no less than five yards before we could come to a firm foundation.'[10] In reality, Wren's objections were as much aesthetic as pragmatic. He wanted his building to run north to south, facing down the grove, from where it could be admired at a distance. But he gave

[7] John Newman, 'The Architectural Setting', *HUO* 4, 175.
[8] TCA Misc. Vol. I, 83/128.
[9] Skinner gave £100 in 1666. Benefactors' Book I, 18.
[10] TCA Misc. Vol. I, 83/128.

way with good grace, recognizing the harsh truth that without the support of the College's benefactors there would be no building at all. He wrote to Bathurst:

> My honoured friend, I am convinced with Machiavelli or some such unlucky fellow . . . that the world is governed by words. I perceive the name of a quadrangle will carry it with those you say may possibly be your benefactors, though it be much the worse situation for the chambers, and the beauty of the college, and the beauty of the particular pile of building; and if I had skill in enchantment to represent the pile first in one view then in another, that the difference might be evidently seen, I should certainly make them of my opinion; or else I'll appeal to Monsieur Manzard, or Signor Bernini, both which I shall see at Paris within this fortnight. But, to be sober, if any body, as you say, will pay for a quadrangle, there is no dispute to be made; let them have a quadrangle, though a lame one, somewhat like a three-legged table.[11]

Lesser Trinity bishops also played their part in Bathurst's campaign. Gilbert Ironside, Bishop of Bristol, wrote to request the words of Kettell's Decree *de Gratiis Collegio Rependendis*, 'that by it I may know what obligation there lies upon us by virtue of our oath'. Bathurst seized upon the idea, and large printed copies of the 1602 decree were sent out to former fellows who on the impecunious day of their election had bound themselves to share any future wealth that came their way. Bathurst even sent a copy to Bishop Skinner, 'which the Bishop of Bristol occasioned us to print because himself and some others desired to see it, that they might be reminded of their obligation to the college.'[12] Ironside gave £100, and Seth Ward, now Bishop of Exeter, £50.[13]

Bathurst wrote painstaking letters of appeal to every old member whom he could track down. It was not always easy; that to William Jordan (1631), for instance, was to 'to be left at a silver smith's next door to the Black Swan in Rider's Court near Leicester Fields'. Many drafts of these letters survive in the College archive, and their frequent crossings out and alterations attest to Bathurst's meticulous tactics. The tone was customized to suit the individual recipient, while in some cases a good letter could be copied out and used again and again. Bathurst wielded his epistolatory weaponry to typically good effect in a shrewd letter to Richard Newdigate (1618), now a

[11] Ibid., 82/126. [12] Ibid., 79/123. [13] TCA Benefactors' Book I, 7–8.

justice of the upper bench and MP for Tamworth. The combined elements of flattery—'our poor society which once had the honour of being conscious to have some part of your younger studies'—pathos and nostalgia—'How few and mean our chambers are in comparison of other colleges you may possibly not have forgotten'—exaggeration—'we have of late attempted something which may in courtesy be called a new quadrangle'—name-dropping—'My Lord of Canterbury gave us the first encouragement for it'—College pride—'to give convenient accommodation to gentlemen of quality in any proportion to other houses, most of which have had the good fortune either to be more magnificently endowed or more happily indulged than we'—and even the promise of glorious immortality—'we shall take care to have your Beneficence honourably recorded to posterity'—were a winning formula. The judge replied with £30 in 1670, and with two sons, Richard and John, who came up together in 1688.[14]

Bathurst recorded Trinity's gratitude in a finely bound Benefactors' Book, the *Liber Minervalium*.[15] Its opening page bears his own name and those of the fellows, and the next is given over entirely to Gilbert Sheldon's gift of £100.[16] Bathurst used this volume as a tempting carrot to other would-be contributors, adapting its attractions to suit all pockets and temperaments. In February 1666, he wrote persuasively to Dr Henry Dynham at Bristol 'to let you know that if any friend of yours and ours (especially such as own our college) have a mind to bestow a little of their superfluity upon an honest public work, and to build themselves a lasting monument at a cheap rate, here they may do it.'[17]

Bathurst's draft letters also preserve a few choice phrases that were not in the event ever used. Some were just too ungrateful—'How few [of] our fellows have been benefactors now 110 years (except Mr Rands)'– too arrogant—'my own resolution not to die richer for any church preferment'—or just too downright rude. He clearly thought better of castigating those 'who transfer the wealth of the church to set up lay families which commonly are observed quickly to scatter it by their debauchery'. But generally, the President was not afraid to speak his mind. Sir John Napier (1656), who leased the Stoppsley

[14] TCA Misc. Vol. I, 85/132; Benefactors' Book I, 34; Admission Register A, f. 127r.
[15] *Mineral* = gift in return for instruction.
[16] TCA Benefactors' Book I, i, 1. [17] TCA Misc. Vol. I, 83/127d.

tithes from the College, was an obvious target, and he was taken firmly to task:

> If a tenant, and one who (as we are well assured) has no bad bargain; if the heir of him who often promised, that, whensoever we should attempt a building, he would give us £100; if one that has formerly been a member of our college, and a friend and contemporary to all our present society . . . ; if a rich man, a single man, a son of the church, and a lover of learning, should refuse to encourage such a well meant public work. . . . I cannot suffer myself to doubt but that, when you pay the Lady Day rent, you purpose to accompany it with something that may testify your kindness to us.

Sir John sent £50.[18]

Most of the fellows contributed to the new building. It was a promising investment, which, if it attracted more undergraduates from the higher social classes, would generate a corresponding rise in their income from tuition fees. Bathurst himself gave £100, dedicated to 'putting right deficiencies (*incommodas ordinando*) and repairing the decayed and neglected buildings'. Daniel Danvers and Nicholas Meese each gave £10, Richard Spencer, Thomas Grigg, and Charles Sparkes £5. John Houghton, the cook, gave £10; as a College servant he stood to gain considerably from a more aristocratic clientele.[19] Josiah How, however, may have disagreed with his President's priorities; his gift of £9 was intended for a '*pluteum versatilem* [movable lectern]' for the better reading of scripture in the Chapel.[20]

Past and present members of the foundation were recruited to promote the building campaign by delivering Bathurst's letters in person. At Easter 1665, Henry Kinnemond (scholar 1636–9) called on William Hobbs (fellow 1617–45), Thomas Lambert (1633), and Arthur Charlett (1639) in Wiltshire. Hobbs sent £10, Lambert £20, Charlett £10 and a son, also Arthur, who was elected to a scholarship in 1671.[21] A cheerful letter survives from Nicholas Meese (scholar 1646, fellow 1650) reporting back from a fund-raising trip in the 1665 Christmas vacation. He had first been to importune one Mr Marriott. 'All my poor oratory could prevail for, was an assurance of ten pounds . . . he himself being engaged on building work.' Undeterred, 'I have

[18] TCA Misc. Vol. I, 79/124; TCA Benefactors' Book I, 12.
[19] TCA Benefactors' Book I, 9–10, 15, 19, 22. [20] Ibid., 3.
[21] TCA Misc. Vol. I, 79/124; Benefactors' Book I, 47, 17, 23.

likewise set upon Mr John Trappe, who has promised to present the coll. with a testimony of his gratitude to the value of £5 . . . Mr Bishop I could not meet with, being gone to keep his Christmas abroad.'[22]

Some of the would-be benefactors came up with excellent excuses. Charitable work of their own was a popular one: Walter St John was 'engaged in a pup-like work at this time—the building of a free school and endowing it.' Robert Skinner at first delayed his own gift, 'so soon as I can finish my own undertakings, I shall begin to think of Trinity College. In the meantime, *consilium do* [I give advice].' And besides offering advice, the old members seized the opportunity to ask favours. The Bishop of Bristol had a young protégé on his mind—'I always liked of his father's desire to fix his son in Trinity College.' And William Smith (1645) replied from London on 7 September 1666, the very day that the Great Fire was finally extinguished: 'Although public occasions of this kingdom have drained my purse, the conflagration of this miserable city hurt me more. He who brings this letter is my son . . . I shall be a suitor to you to receive him into your society.'[23]

By July 1665, the trees in the fellows' garden had been felled, and the foundations laid. Bathurst described the position in his letter to Skinner:

> We have now brought it above the ground, and (if the providing of timber do not quite exhaust us) we hope to raise the stonework to the height of the first storey this summer. When that is done, it must stand, as cripples do, to move the compassion of all beholders, till such time as our own diligence & the benevolence of our friends can bring it to perfection.[24]

The building took another three years to complete. In a small ledger—also called the *Liber Minervalium*—the bursars kept careful accounts of the monies flowing through their hands. 'Receipts' include benefactions, payments made by commoners taking degrees, and such extraordinary income as the sale of 'tops of trees'. The 'disbursements' detail payments to workmen; the purchase and transport of timber, stone, and slates; and the cost of writing up the Benefactors' Book. The two builders chiefly employed were Robert

[22] TCA Misc. Vol. I, 79/142.
[23] Ibid., 83/128, 84/130, 80/125, 84/131.
[24] Ibid., f. 79/123.

Minchin and Thomas Strong, who required 'passes in the sickness time' of the plague summer of 1666. During 1665 £535 was laid out, of which £200 had to be borrowed, and in 1668 £12 was paid to 'the widow Minns' as interest (6 per cent) on a loan. The final touches were made in the summer of 1668—Ambrose Hewes was paid 8*s* 8*d* 'for pointing the floor in the N.B. [New Building]'—and it was ready to be occupied. The total cost, approximately £1,500, was double the original estimate.[25] This did not include the expense of panelling the chambers, which was financed by the early occupants, leading to some notable variations in the quality of materials and standards of workmanship. Each resident on the two new staircases [today Staircases 15 and 16] had a private wine cellar large enough to lay down several hundred bottles.

The new building completed, Bathurst pressed on with a wide-ranging programme of College improvements in order to bring facilities and services up to the standard his 'men of quality' would require. In around 1676, a new lavatory or 'bog house' was built in stone and slate.[26] Then, in 1681, the 'old kitchen, and all the buildings about it, being so miserably decayed' were demolished. A strip of land was leased from Balliol College, and a new kitchen built with a yard behind. The new kitchen had rooms above it, reached via a staircase at the west end of the present Hall passage. At the same time, Bathurst 'remodeled the chambers over the hall to a much greater convenience,' doing away with the dormer windows and cocklofts and adding a battlemented front.[27]

The President also had his own family to consider. Three months after his election to the presidency he had married Mary Palmer, widow of the late warden of All Souls. She was related to Anthony Wood, who with his mother, brother, and sister-in-law called at the Lodgings on New Year's Eve 1664 to wish them well. 'They had before sent in sack, claret, cake and sugar to welcome the said married couple. Dr Bathurst was then about 46 years of age, so there was need of a wife,' commented Wood. Warton considered Mary to be 'a woman of admirable accomplishments', but Wood found her 'an enemy to monarchs and bishops . . . a scornful, proud woman'

[25] TCA Accounts III/E/1, 8–16. It is difficult to give a precise figure as some work related to repairs of the existing buildings.

[26] Ibid., f. 45–47d.

[27] R. B. to Bishop of Chester, n.d. [1691], TCA Misc. Vol. I, f. 90/146.

and 'so conceited that she thinks herself fit to govern a college', although it must be noted that Wood's antipathy seems to have related to the frequency, or rather the infrequency, with which he was invited to dine.[28] The President of a now-fashionable college could not be seen to live in cramped and dilapidated surroundings himself, and Bathurst also undertook extensive improvements to the Lodgings, which were conveniently enlarged by the absorption of the large first-floor chamber on the north side of the Durham Quadrangle, which had been traditionally allocated to the senior fellow.[29] Like Kettell before him, Bathurst found himself with two step-daughters requiring husbands. The first wedding ever recorded in the Trinity College Chapel took place on 23 February 1669, when Mary Palmer married Richard Chandler, a gentleman commoner admitted three years before at the age of 17.[30]

In 1682 work began on a second block to accommodate Trinity's fine new members. It was financed by £100 bequeathed by Archbishop Sheldon in 1677, by a small fund-raising campaign, and from the ongoing flow of compulsory donations—the beneficence now routinely expected of new members and of those taking degrees. Between 1682 and 1690, the annual *minervalia* averaged a steady £140. The *computus* of 1681–2 records some £747 received as *minervalia*, of which over £330 was taken from the College treasury and £200 loaned by Bathurst himself.[31] The new block was identical to the Wren building and set at right angles to it, giving the chambers a fine view over the grove. The basic structure of the present garden quadrangle was now in place, although the rooms in the north-east corner, known as the 'back buildings', were reached via the hall passage and the yard. Numbers in residence hardly justified such further expansion, but Bathurst was more concerned with Trinity's image. He explained his motives in a letter to a former fellow, Daniel Whitby. 'Our ambition is not great: all that we aim at is but to be in some measure like our neighbours, and to find rooms for as many as our Hall and our chapel will easily receive, without the help of Kettell Hall and such other too-remote places.'[32] Bathurst no longer required the building which bore his step-grandfather's name. In 1674 Oriel College let Kettell Hall on a forty-year lease to Abraham Finch, cook,

[28] Wood, *Life*, ii, 26, 192, 258, 271, 281.
[29] Aubrey, *Brief Lives* (Francis Potter), 250.
[30] Ibid., 151.
[31] TCA Benefactors' Book 1, 1; *Computus* 1681–2.
[32] TCA Misc Vol. I, 86/135.

*6.2* The Garden Quadrangle, by Dawson Warren, 1801, showing Wren's north range (1665–8), the matching west range (1683–5), and today's Staircase 17 (1728). Note too the sculpted yew hedge.

who paid a rent of 10*s* and two capons.[33] Ironically, however, by 1687 Bathurst was following the example of Kettell and constructing his own eponymous accommodation block, known for 200 years as 'the Bathurst Building' or simply, 'Bathurst.' It had five sets of rooms, and cocklofts. The Bathurst Building stood to the east of the Chapel, approximately on the site of the present Lodgings, and was entered on the north side via the central passageway through the old library side of the quad, and a path across the President's garden (Plate 6.6).

[33] Finch renewed the lease in 1688, and Kettell Hall was leased to his son, William Finch, gent., in 1702. It is not unlikely that some Trinity members continued to live there throughout this period, just as they had when it was leased to Ralph Kettell's nephew, Fanshawe Kettell. In 1716 Oriel leased the Hall to Trinity. Calendar of leases, OCA DELR 7.

## *Admissions*

As Bathurst had hoped, Trinity quickly began to catch the eye of England's wealthier families. Early in his presidency, he began to keep an Admissions Register, recording year by year the names, fathers, places of origin, social rank, and tutors of the undergraduates. The register was compiled retrospectively back to 1648, and then, at some point in 1665, each resident member of the college was summoned to inscribe his own entry. This was the beginning of a Trinity tradition that has continued to the present day. This first registration was done according to social position in the College: one page includes the names of five servitors, whose entry dates range from 1660 to 1665.[34]

Compilation of the register during Bathurst's presidency was somewhat erratic. At times the entries are more or less chronological and include exact dates of admission. Elsewhere they are arranged socially, with commoners of the first order entered first each year, and the servitors and battellers grouped humbly together. Here the admission dates are given by month alone, just by year, or not at all. Bathurst supervised the register carefully, and regularly made corrections or additions to the data included. It was important both for future fund-raising, and also for college discipline and administration. In 1669 Bathurst wrote in the names of that year's tutors, which had in most cases been omitted.[35] President Kettell's register of scholars and fellows, meanwhile, was allowed to lapse.[36] The fee-paying commoners were becoming the dominant force in the College.

From 1664 the annual number of admissions increased, reaching a peak in the first half of the 1670s. There were some boom years, such as 1671, which saw the mass arrival of six young men from County Cork: Laurence Clayton, Vincent Gookin, and George Evans, who entered as fellow commoners, William Romayne and Thomas Farren, commoners, and Zachary Braylay, servitor. During Bathurst's presidency there was a measurable rise in social status, evident in the number and proportion of young men entering as commoners 'of the first order' and as fellow or gentleman commoners ('the second

[34] TCA Register A, f. 28. [35] Ibid., ff. 41–3.

[36] TCA Kettell's Register. The final entry was of William Radford (scholar 1640).

*Table 6.1* Trinity College admissions 1661–1700.

| *Year* | *Total admissions* | *Noblemen commoners* | *Fellow commoners* | *Percentage above commoner* | *Commoners* | *Battellers* | *Servitors* | *Percentage below commoner* | *Other/ don't know* |
|---|---|---|---|---|---|---|---|---|---|
| 1656–60 | 61 | 2 | 13 | 24.6 | 31 | 0 | 9 | 14.8 | 6 |
| 1661–5 | 90 | 8 | 16 | 26.6 | 48 | 3 | 4 | 7.7 | 11 |
| 1666–70 | 116 | 12 | 24 | 31.0 | 75 | 2 | 7 | 7.8 | 1 |
| 1671–5 | 139 | 6 | 25 | 22.3 | 83 | 0 | 25 | 18.0 | 0 |
| 1676–80 | 135 | 16 | 22 | 28.1 | 70 | 1 | 26 | 20.0 | 0 |
| 1681–5 | 119 | 25 | 4 | 24.4 | 62 | 3 | 20 | 19.3 | 5 |
| 1686–90 | 126 | 33 | 3 | 28.5 | 66 | 0 | 22 | 17.5 | 2 |
| 1691–5 | 99 | 19 | 0 | 19.2 | 59 | 4 | 16 | 20.2 | 0 |
| 1696–1700 | 93 | 18 | 0 | 19.4 | 54 | 4 | 17 | 22.3 | 0 |
| 1661–1700 | 917 | 137 | 94 | 25.2 | 517 | 17 | 137 | 16.7 | 19 |

*Source*: TCA Admissions Register A.

order'). In 1666 a staggering 40.6 per cent of new undergraduates entered at a rank above that of commoner.[37]

According to the College Statutes, the first order was restricted to the sons of 'noblemen' (dukes, marquesses, earls, viscounts, and barons) or the eldest sons of knights, who were all entitled to dine at the President's table. At this highest level of society, Trinity's new and fashionable image made relatively little impact. In the years 1650–89, Trinity was indeed one of the colleges where the social elite were concentrated. Behind Christ Church (which educated almost 30 per cent of Oxford's noble undergraduates), Trinity ranked with Queen's and Magdalen, these three colleges between them admitting another 27 per cent. These proportions, however, were little changed from the situation in the first half of the century.[38] It is in the next level down the social scale that a real difference can be observed. Bathurst's new building was attractive to the ambitious squires and landowners of England, and to the nouveaux riches who were struggling to move upwards in society, much indeed as the founder had done a century before. These were the families who were especially eager to enter their sons at Trinity, and who could afford the additional expenses of the fellow commoner, and increasingly of the first order. During Bathurst's presidency, more and more young men entered as commoners of the first order, willingly paying the extra caution money and expenses concomitant with the 'noble' lifestyle in College.

An undergraduate's matriculation status had serious financial implications, and families had to weigh up the likely expenses against the level of dignity gained in the College. Samuel Barker was the son of an esquire. He entered as a fellow commoner in March 1675 and paid £8 caution money. He then paid another £2 'to make his caution ten pounds', thereby raising his status to a level that technically he did not merit.[39] In 1679 John Sayer, the eldest son of John Sayer, esquire and citizen of London, similarly upgraded his rank in the admissions register from the second to the first order.[40] In 1690 John Moore entered as a commoner but quickly went up two levels, presumably having found his original rank uncomfortably low for the son of a knight.[41]

[37] 32 admissions, 7 noblemen, 6 gentlemen commoners.
[38] Porter, 'University and Society', *HUO* 4, 62–3.
[39] TCA Admissions Register A, 69; Caution Book 2, f. 12v.
[40] Ibid., 91. [41] Ibid., 134.

After 1680, however, there was a dramatic reduction in the number of undergraduates entering in the second order as gentleman commoners—just three admitted in the last two decades of Bathurst's presidency—while the number in the first order increased. It is surely no coincidence that during the 1690s, Trinity had the reputation of being the most expensive college in the University, attractive for those who wished to flaunt their wealth at the very highest level, but not necessarily a good choice for gentlemen of more limited means.[42]

Trinity was by now financially dependent on the sons of wealthy families, and was willing to excuse any intellectual deficiencies that they might have. A remarkable ignorance of Latin grammar and spelling is evident in the admission entry of Richard Shuttleworth (1688). Shuttleworth described his place of birth as '*Durham in comitatu Bishoprich*'—patiently corrected by Bathurst to '*Episcopatu Dunelmensi* [in the bishopric of Durham]'—his age as '*annorum cersitur 16*'—corrected to '*circiter* [aged about 16]'—and his rank in College as '*prime ordinis*'—corrected to '*primi* [of the first order]'.[43]

At the lower end of the social scale, there was a corresponding rise in the number of servitors, who traditionally paid no caution money and worked their way through College. Some took the role of personal servant to a fellow or nobleman commoner. William Capel (1696) seems to have been attached to Bathurst himself, and to have enjoyed a close relationship with the President.[44] In exceptional cases, entrance as a servitor could be the route to a highly successful career. Thomas Sykes entered Trinity as a servitor in 1660. Two years later he was elected to a scholarship; in 1667 he became a fellow and tutor (one of his pupils was the lowbrow Richard Shuttleworth); in 1691 he was appointed Lady Margaret Professor of Divinity; and on the death of Bathurst in 1704, he was elected to the presidency of the College. Between 1670 and 1690, Trinity admitted four or five servitors each year. The position was a vital means of access to the University for the sons of poor men, and Trinity, with its large number of privileged undergraduates, was able to provide many such places. The rank of batteller, however—a commoner who paid the lowest rate of caution money and who shared some of the servitors' menial duties—was soon to disappear almost entirely. Between 1670 and 1690, only four battellers were admitted to Trinity, and two of these,

[42] Porter, 'University and Society', 63.
[43] TCA Admissions Register A, 104.
[44] Warton, *Bathurst*, pp. xvi, 183.

Edmund Lovell in 1690 and Thomas Prowse in 1683, had entered first as servitors. Lovell was the son of a gentleman, Prowse of a plebeian father. From 1679 the servitors appear in the caution account, charged a bottom rate of £2 10*s* and listed by their surnames alone. Rules drawn up for the servitors illustrate their status as the College underclass. They were expected to run errands for the commoners and fellow commoners, during meals and at other times; they were forbidden to 'battel above 40*s*'; and they ate in the buttery, after Hall had been served.[45]

The fellows were growing increasingly concerned by inappropriate and lax behaviour in the Hall, and they sometimes struggled to control the College's undergraduate population. On 9 April 1673, Anthony Wood observed an unruly scene when Trinity provided the customary refreshments following the admission of Abraham Campion (fellow 1665) as Senior Proctor. 'Proctors took their places,' noted Wood. 'Great rudeness. At Trinity College the undergraduates and freshmen came up into the hall; scrambled for biscuits; took away bottles, glasses, etc.'[46] In 1683 it was decided that the dean should keep a record of decisions made by the President and fellows at the 'yearly scrutiny or at other times'. The range of activities and practices forbidden by these College orders—'no bachelor scholars to wear hats in college . . . No clans or common meetings to be kept in any chamber after nine at night'—gives a good indication of what the junior members were doing at the time. During the 1680s and 1690s a number of College orders were agreed, with the purpose of tightening the standard of behaviour, and improving the efficiency of Trinity's domestic administration. No one was to leave the Hall and then eat in the buttery or kitchen; everyone must 'put on' at once for what they ate or drank in Hall, staying in their place until the butler and manciple had 'passed by'; the bursar was to inspect a man's room before returning his caution money; no one was to leave dinner or supper early without leave from the senior person there; no ordinary commoner was to 'sit, walk or make any stay in the kitchen, buttery or cellar'; on 'Fridays and other fasting suppers' the grace was still to be said properly; no guests were to be brought in without permission; and commoners were to be 'crossed off' if they had not paid their battels within six weeks of the end of term.[47]

[45] TCA *Liber Decani* I, ff. 7, 8d, 10, 10d, 13.

[46] Wood, *Life*, ii, 261–2.

[47] TCA *Liber Decani*, ff. 6–15.

Despite these efforts to maintain discipline, the college was drifting insidiously away from the spirit of the Founder's Statutes. In the sixteenth century, those who missed prayers went hungry. In 1688, no undergraduate was allowed to miss more than twice a week, or pay a 2*d* fine for each offence. 'According to the late Visitor's instructions,' recorded the dean, 'all be reckoned *tardy* that come in after the end of the first psalm; twice tardy is equivalent to once absent.' There was a similar relaxation in gate hours. The College gates were to be shut 'after Christ Church great bell has done tolling' [9 p.m.] but members could be admitted for another 'half an hour after in winter, and an hour in summer'.[48]

## *Undergraduate Life*

The President enjoyed the society of his undergraduates. In 1761 Thomas Warton published *The Life and Literary Remains of Ralph Bathurst*, using as a source the recollections of Bathurst's nephew. 'Lord Bathurst has been pleased to inform me,' wrote Warton,

> that he was entered in Trinity College at fifteen years of age, when Dr Bathurst, his uncle, was upwards of eighty; and he remembers to have been often charmed by his conversation . . . No man ever possessed a greater share of cheerful, engaging, unaffected wit, that although he maintained the most exact discipline in his college, his method of correction chiefly consisted in turning the faults of the delinquent scholars into ridicule, in which expedient he always effectually succeeded; and that all the young students admired and loved him. The cast of his conversation was rather satirical, but mixed with mirth and pleasantry. He was remarkably fond of young company.[49]

John Harris was elected to a scholarship in 1683, and a surviving fragment of his autobiography attests to this view of Bathurst, and indeed to the popularity and growing reputation of Trinity College.[50]

[48] Ibid., f. 11d.

[49] Allen, Lord Bathurst (1700), was the eldest son of Ralph's youngest brother, Sir Benjamin Bathurst.

[50] Extracts of Harris's autobiography were made for Thomas Warton and preserved among his papers. Blakiston made extracts from the extracts (TCA Blakiston C/4; quoted in Blakiston, *Trinity College*, 170–6) and these are the only copies which survive.

*Table 6.2* Timetable circa 1685.

| *Time* | *Exercise* | *Participants* | *Location* |
|---|---|---|---|
| 7 a.m. | Logic and Physics lectures | All students 'in distinct classes' | Hall |
| Mid-morning | Lecture from tutor | All undergraduates | Various |
| 10 a.m. | Disputations in Logic and Physics | | Hall |
| | Latin Declamations | | Hall |
| Noon Dinner | Narrare | | Hall |
| 2 p.m. | Exposition | | Hall |
| Mid-afternoon | Lecture from tutor | Undergraduate scholars, many other undergraduates | Various |
| 5 p.m. | Disputations | Bachelors to dispute undergraduates to listen | Hall |

*Source*: Autobiography of John Harris (1683).

Blakiston considered that Harris was 'evidently priggish'.[51] He was certainly very proud to be a Trinity man:

> Trinity College was at this time . . . very famous and full of students; gentlemen being very fond of placing their sons under so excellent a governor . . . For certainly no college ever had more exercise done in it, nor better performed . . . The education and manner of life in this college was manly and gentle and free from abundance of the pedantry and impertinence in other houses.

Harris strongly approved the rigorous instruction offered by Trinity, and from his account it is possible to construct the daily timetable.

The exposition each afternoon was 'on the best Greek and Latin authors, where the young scholars were made to construe and to give the sense in a manly way; [and] the lecturer explained the text grammatically and historically.' Bathurst himself attended most of these exercises 'if he were well and in town'. In addition 'many tutors' required their pupils to be present at afternoon lectures as well, and 'to make a theme or Latin verses every week; which the undergraduate scholars did also, and their exercises were produced in the hall at the fellows' table every Saturday at noon.' During the Long Vacation, this programme of studies continued three days a week. The

[51] Blakiston, *Trinity College*, 172.

College order book shows regular attempts made by the fellows to enforce academic work. For example, in 1688 it was agreed that 'they all be constant at disputations, whether it be their turn to dispute or not.' The dean, or moderator, would call on 'at least four of 'em . . . in what order he pleases, without any regard to seniority; and that more especially he call forth that as be most negligent'. Two years later, it was agreed to impose swingeing fines of up to 10*s* on those who failed to take their turn in divinity disputations.[52]

Bathurst maximized the potential of his available tutorial staff to provide a wide-ranging and modern curriculum. Harris heard lectures on 'experimental philosophy and chemistry' and took 'a very tolerable course of mathematics'. From 1688 the scholars had the option of taking additional classes in Hebrew from the Jewish scholar Isaac Abendana.[53] After Harris had taken his BA, he himself was invited by the President to teach mathematics 'to such as were inclined to learn, which he did, and showed them the practical and useful part, and how to apply it to business and the advantages of life'.

One very important aid to education was the lower library, which was established on Bathurst's initiative in 1683.[54] Trinity was the first college in Oxford to attempt to provide books for the undergraduates, and a room beneath the fellows' library was set aside for the purpose. Harris approved again. It was 'a very good collection of philosophy and mathematical books of all kinds as also of the classics placed in a room . . . where every undergraduate had the liberty to go and study as long as he pleased, which was a mighty advantage to the house, and ought to be imitated by other colleges.' In 1688 the fellows agreed that all undergraduate 'sconces'—the twopences for missing prayers, and sixpences for being caught red-handed in the buttery or cellar—be used at the end of each year for the purchase of some 'useful book or books' for 'the Juniors' Library'.[55]

One undergraduate who took a minimal interest in his studies was Edmund Verney, who entered Trinity as a commoner of the first order in January 1685. His letters home give a detailed account of his life

[52] TCA *Liber Decani* I, ff. 11d, 15–15d.

[53] From 1687 to 1695 Abendana was paid quarterly at the rate of 10*s* per pupil. The largest number of pupils seems to have been 3, in the third quarter of 1687–8; TCA *Computus*, 330.

[54] Bathurst gave £20 to '*bibliethecae in usum juniorum primitus instruendae*' ('firstly to set up a library for the use of the young men'), TCA *Liber Minervalium* II, f. 1.

[55] TCA *Liber Decani* I, f. 11d.

in Trinity, and illustrate the vital importance of social proprieties and appearances to a young gentleman at University.[56] Indeed, his father, Edmund, the heir of Sir Ralph Verney of Claydon, was hardly any less preoccupied with clothes than was he was. The new undergraduate, known to his family as 'Mun', was very proud of his 'new silver hilted sword, his new striped morning gown', and his 'six new laced bands whereof one is point de Loraine'. He arrived in Trinity on 23 January 1685, paying £10 caution money, £1 10*s* for utensils, £15 'for the new building', £2 for the common room, and £1 8*s* to the college servants. The previous day his anxious and indulgent parent had handed to the carrier a carefully packed trunk and a box, and had written the first in a long series of parental letters: 'your old hat I did not send neither, for it was so bad I was ashamed of it.' But he had tucked into a pair of old breeches 'five laced bands . . . and a new pair of laced cuffs. And your two guineas in your fob, and a new knife and fork in your great pocket'. Edmund senior had also dispatched a large box of tuck: oranges and lemons, brown and white sugar, brown and white sugar candy, raisins ('good for a cough') and nutmegs. And then he had settled down to wait for a reply. He waited for nearly a fortnight.[57]

Mun's first letter home begins, 'My honoured father, I want a hat, and a pair of fringed gloves very much, and I desire you to send me them if you possibly can before Sunday next, for as I come from church, everybody gazes at me and asks who I am.' The hat was dispatched, but Mun wrote again two weeks later:

> I find you could not buy me any fringed gloves, until you knew what was generally worn in the university by reason of the death of our most excellent King Charles the Second . . . There are two or three commoners in our house . . . that have bought their black clothes, and plain muslin bands, and cloth shoes and are now in very strict mourning.

Fortunately he was saved from any social solecism when Edmund senior consulted with the Provost of Oriel, and discovered that 'here and there some particular person might go into mourning, and

[56] Frances Parthenope Verney and Margaret M. Verney, *Memoirs of the Verney Family during the Seventeenth Century* (London, 1907), ii, chapter 55.

[57] Ibid., 414–16.

that would be all.' He sent instead a new silver seal tied in a handkerchief.[58]

At this date it was still customary, even for the wealthier undergraduates, to share a chamber. Mun lived with his kinsman Denton Nicholas, and in June wrote to suggest some domestic improvements. Edmund was annoyed:

> you say he has bespoke a new table and cane chairs, which will amount to £3 apiece between you. But I do not understand why you should be at that unnecessary charge, as long as you have that which will serve your turn, neither do I like the vanity. You do not tell me whether you are matriculated yet or no.[59]

In February 1686, Edmund's elder brother Ralph died, aged 20. Their father was distraught, and movingly described how 'my heart is so incurably pierced with grief for the loss of my dear child that I can no more be comforted than Rachel was.' He was a devoted father, and felt justified in his constant worry over his own health and that of his children. But by 15 February he had rallied somewhat. 'I have drawn a fresh bill here,' he wrote, 'to buy you a black cloth suit. And I have a new black beaver hat for you, which I will send you next Thursday in a little deal box, with a black crepe hatband, black mourning gloves, and stockings and shoe buckles, and three pairs of black buttons for wrist and neck. And I have also sent you a new French caudebeck hat to save your beaver. The box is to keep your beaver in; nobody uses hatcases now.' Mun was similarly anxious to do and say the right thing. He wrote home on 23 February,

> Now seeing it has pleased Almighty God to make me acquainted with the sorrows and afflictions of this world, by taking from me my only brother, I hope it will be a means to make me fear God, and honour you and my mother, and by doing I hope I shall render both you and myself happy. I have made myself a new black cloth suit, and a new black morning gown, which with new muslin bands and cloth shoes will stand me in very near ten pounds.[60]

Edmund senior was also corresponding with Mun's tutor, Thomas Sykes, and taking a close interest in his son's academic activities. In the summer of 1686 he learned both that Mun was to recite in the University theatre and also that Trinity was in the grip of a serious

[58] Ibid., 416–17. [59] Ibid., 418. [60] Ibid., 421–2.

outbreak of illness. On 21 June he informed his son that he had heard from Nicholas's mother that 'the small pox was very rife in Oxford, and particularly in your college, of which I wonder that you take no notice. If this be so I would have you leave . . . I would have you prefer your welfare and health before the honour of speaking in the theatre.' Writing again three days later, however, he advised, 'I pray that when you speak in the theatre do not speak like a mouse in a cheese.'[61]

Thomas Hearne considered Sykes 'a great tutor'.[62] He was more conscientious than his pupil may have wished. Mun was taken to task in September when his tutor—'unto whom you are very much obliged. Take my word for it'—complained to his father that he was skipping afternoon lectures. The tone and content of this correspondence reveal Sykes's awareness of just how heavily the tutor–pupil relationship was weighted in favour of a rich young pupil, whose attendance was ever voluntary. Edmund wrote to his son, 'if all others should forbear coming to them as you do, the lectures must fall, which are a support to the college, and so by degrees Arts and Sciences, and learned societies must dwindle away and dissolve to nothing.' But, at the same time, 'Pray let me know by the next post those particular reasons [for not attending], and if I like them, I will do what I can with civility to get you excused.'[63]

A month later Mun was in much more serious trouble, and on the point of expulsion. Sykes reported that 'Mr Verney' had stayed out overnight

> with another or two of the college, and that with some other provocation has occasioned Mr vice-president to cross his name with the others. I suppose he will give you some account of where he was, he is unwilling to do it here, and that makes the business so much the worse. I suppose he will scarce ask for his name again, and I presume the vice-president will not give it him of his own accord, and so what will be the issue of it I know not. He speaks of removing himself to some other college.

Sykes was in an unenviable position:

[61] *Memoirs of the Verney Family*, 425–6. Oxford experienced regular outbreaks of smallpox throughout this period (Porter, 'University and Society', 46). At Trinity, Henry Oborne (1687) and Samuel D'Assigny (1691) both contracted the disease in the summer of 1691 (Thomas Sykes to RB, TCA Misc. Vol. I, 89/142–3).

[62] *Hearne* I, 128.

[63] *Memoirs of the Verney Family*, 428–9.

> I hope he will not deny but that I have behaved myself to him in all things as a tutor ought to do, and been civil to him as far as I could, but as to this business I can only be sorry for this, but cannot remedy it. It is against both the discipline of our college and the university in general to lie out at nights.

Sykes had pleaded in vain with the vice-president; he had also failed to persuade Mun to apologize. And if his pupil left, he would suffer a significant drop in income. In the event, the disciplinary stalemate was conveniently resolved by the ongoing smallpox epidemic. There were 'sixteen or seventeen' cases in Trinity and the majority of commoners fled to their homes. By December Mun's 'fault' had been forgotten, and Sykes could write to Edmund, 'the sooner your son returns to me the more welcome he will be.'[64]

Then, as now, it was the extracurricular activities that made undergraduate life truly memorable. John Harris justified his best 'whim, or flip'—although it all went dangerously wrong—with the observation that Bathurst 'loved dearly to see the young gentlemen of his college discover something of fire and spirit in their diversions, and would pass by any little excursions provided they were not vicious nor injurious'. Freschville Croom (1685), owner of the £50 Cremona violin that was inadvertently destroyed in the course of the 'bright moonshine night' in question, doubtless saw things differently:

> Two young gentlemen . . . were dressed up like Roman statues, and by means of a ladder placed in the two niches of the new quadrangle, which were left vacant for the statues of some eminent benefactors. As soon as these had their cue, Harris got into the fellows' room, and with a great deal of counterfeited surprise and horror tells them that he feared the college was haunted; for that there were human figures standing in the niches of the new buildings. Two of the fellows went out with him: saw them standing there to their very great surprise; but they had not courage enough to venture to go near them without more company. But while they were gone to fetch this out of their common room, a young fellow-commoner happened to go through the court with a violin in his hand, on which he had been playing in the grove; he had been that evening drinking in company, and had got himself pot valiant. As he passed by, one of the statues hemmed to him, and by that means discovered himself to the gentleman, who, after having

[64] Ibid., 429–31.

> stared at him some time, flies to a heap of rubbish that lay hard by, and snatching up some pieces of bricks, soon pelted one of the statues down, and broke the window adjacent to that niche. The statue had no remedy but to leap down upon him, which it did, breaking his fiddle and demolishing him very much and withal bestowing many kicks and cuffs upon him, and then together with the other statue got away to his chamber. By this time the then dean and some more of the fellows had mustered up courage enough to make a visit in consort to these statues, but when they came into that quadrangle, they found the niches empty and no statues there. The rest ridiculed the dean, who said he had actually seen the figures himself; and in the truth of that he was supported by Harris, who affirmed that he saw them also, as did the other fellow the dean's first companion. While the dispute held, the groans of Croom affected them, for that was the name of the hero that had stoned the statue till he had fetched him down upon his head. They approached him, took him up, and examined him nicely. But he finding the violin broke fell into such a passion that they could get nothing out of him but curses against the devil, who he said, had leaped upon his head, beat him and broke his violin.

There was of course an inquest in the morning. Croom could remember nothing besides getting drunk, falling over, and breaking his precious violin. The dean and his companion maintained their story, and Harris confirmed it,

> but did it in such a manner that the President saw into the whole affair, and telling the dean and fellows that they were either drunk or mad, invited Harris to dine with him, and made him tell the whole contrivance; and he expressed himself to be as sorry as the contrivers were that Croom's drunken valour had disappointed them of the pleasure of frightening the fellows (if they should have ventured to exorcise the statues) by dreadful voices and speeches which were ready prepared for that purpose.[65]

## *The Fellowship*

Such irresponsible complicity cannot have endeared Bathurst to his fellows. Following the example of Merton in 1661, the low chamber to the south of the Hall (today's 'Old Bursary'), was converted 'to the

[65] Blakiston, *Trinity College*, 174–6.

*6.3* The Common Room (Old Bursary) fireplace, 1664 (*Country Life*, 1930).

end that the fellows might meet together in the evenings after refection, partly about business but mostly for society's sake, which before was at each chamber by turns'.[66] The common room was open

[66] By 1680 there were at least 9 senior common rooms in Oxford; Newman, 'The Architectural Setting', *HUO* 4, 172; Anthony Wood, *The History and Antiquities of the Colleges and Halls in the University of Oxford*, ed. John Gutch (Oxford 1786), 528.

to the fellows, MAs, and fellow commoners, each paying a £1 admission fee. On 2 March 1681, an agreement was drawn up and signed by the twelve fellows, twelve fellow commoners, and five scholars, that future payments would be diverted from the 'annual expenses' and set aside 'for wainscoting'.[67] On 30 April 1681 articles of agreement were drawn up with the Oxford carpenter Arthur Frogley to panel the room in Flanders oak, at the rate of 7*s* 'per square yard plain wainscot' and £6 for the 'chimney piece with carving and ornaments' (Plate 6.3). The Benefactors' Book records their donations totalling £54 towards this project.[68]

The fellowship had become more stable than at any time in the College's history, but the longer tenure came at the price of a hitherto unknown degree of disaffection. Scholars often had an anxious wait for fellowships to become vacant, while the fellows waited with equal impatience for livings. The increased competition for places inevitably caused rivalry and jealousy. Eighty-five scholars were elected between 1600 and 1704. Those who did not wish for a college career often departed after four or five years, with their Bachelor's degree, or after six or seven, with their Master's. But twenty-three stayed on past the seven years allotted in the Statutes. In the 1660s fourteen new fellows were elected. But in the 1670s there were only five, two of whom had waited nine years, and one who had waited eight. In the 1680s there were six new fellows, of whom two were of nine years' standing, and another two of eight.[69] Of fourteen who held their scholarships for nine years, only six were elected to fellowships. It is hardly surprising that there were regular disputes.

In 1688 Richard Lidgould (scholar 1679) made a desperate appeal to the Visitor, Peter Mews, Bishop of Winchester, against the election to a fellowship of Walter Fifield (scholar 1681). The Statutes demanded that priority should be given to candidates in order of seniority, and Lidgould also complained that the wealth of Fifield's family should render him ineligible. The Statutes were not to be broken lightly, and the College sought legal advice from Thomas Bouchier, the Regius Professor of Civil Law.[70] Lidgould's appeal was

[67] The term 'fellow commoner' was used in the College to refer to all above the rank of 'commoner'. [68] TCA Misc. Vol. I, 100/176; Benefactors' Book 2, 8.

[69] The Statutes were circumvented by giving a year of grace after the upper age of 24, and 'assuming' a scholar was elected at the age of 16. Bathurst's nephew, Villiers Bathurst (scholar 1671), held his scholarship for an exceptional 11 years, whilst in the employ of Charles II. [70] TCA Visitor I, 12/24.

rejected, but the Visitor was not always so compliant to the wishes of the President and fellows. The following year Mews wrote to the College on 22 May to demand the election of John Brideoake (scholar 1682) to a vacant fellowship; and he wrote again on 30 May to demand why his instruction had been ignored.[71]

It was only natural that the fellows were thinking carefully about whom they wished to add to their number. Forty fellows were elected between 1660 and 1704, and they stayed for an average of fifteen years. Nine remained for over twenty-five. The average tenure would have been higher were it not for three fellows expelled during or at the end of their probationary year. One of these was John Shirley (fellow 1673). Bathurst penned a memorandum that he and the seven senior fellows found Shirley 'wholly unsuitable (*minime idoneum*)', while Anthony Wood noted that he was 'turned out for having a wench in his chamber, drinking'. Shirley had certainly behaved abominably towards Wood at the University Act. This was the annual celebratory event, precursor of today's Encaenia, which the Sheldonian Theatre had been built to accommodate in 1664–9.[72] Traditional eremonies included a procession of professors and University officers, services, sermons, formal disputations and recitations, the awarding of degrees, and a satirical speech by an appointed *Terrae Filius* (son of the earth). It was in this role that Shirley 'spoke a speech full of obscenity and profaneness', libelling Wood and his newly published history of the University, which, he said, was based on 'shitten papers' and 'was best fit to return there again'.[73]

Another fellow of whom the College wished to be rid was Stephen Hunt (scholar 1672, fellow 1681). Hunt was to some extent a victim of the religious unrest which had again swept the country between the accession of the Catholic James II in 1685 and the arrival of the solidly Protestant William and Mary in the 'Glorious Revolution' of 1688. Monmouth's rebellion had caused considerable excitement within the University, and at Trinity Philip Bertie (1683) had 'trained a foot-company of scholars in the grove' ready to defend their monarch.[74] Oxford's, and Trinity's, leading figures, however, were as determinedly Anglican as loyalist, and, at some point, Hunt had converted to Catholicism. To the Visitor, Bathurst accused Hunt of being 'a

[71] Ibid., 14/32–40. [72] Newman, 'The Architectural Setting', *HUO* 4, 172.
[73] TCA Visitor I, 6/14; Wood, *Life*, ii, 266–7. [74] Wood, *Life*, ii, 149–50.

recusant . . . and most notoriously obnoxious'. On 21 December 1688, he was summoned to a meeting of the President and senior fellows and 'with the unanimous consent of the seniority' informed that his fellowship was 'void', on the grounds that he had not taken his BD.[75]

Bathurst's presidency was dogged by a number of direct challenges to his own authority. He was indeed vulnerable on two counts, both clear breaches of the Statutes: first, that he had not taken his DD; and second that, after his appointment as Dean of Bath and Wells, in June 1670, he spent too much time away from Oxford. His position was weakened in 1684, when the Visitor, Bishop George Morley, instructed the College to appoint Robert Michell (scholar 1675) in place of Stephen Fry (fellow 1677–84), who, although a Doctor of Medicine, had not taken holy orders within the prescribed seven years. Everyone in Trinity wanted Fry, and two years earlier Morley had permitted him to stay on temporarily for 'the college's convenience, in having a physician among you', there being 'no want of priests'. But Robert Michell petitioned the Visitor in person, and convinced him that without the fellowship to which he was legally entitled, he would be 'utterly undone'. Feelings ran high on both sides. Morley refused to receive a petition in person from Fry, and Bathurst vented his anger in a cross letter 'not sent': 'I might farther add that Mr Mitchell came first into the foundation by a trick, under a pretence of an intended benefaction . . . which was never made good to the value of one penny.'[76] With episcopal support, Michell was victorious over Bathurst, and held his fellowship until 1720; with presidential support, Fry remained in his Trinity rooms until 1707.

There was more trouble the very next year, when John Willis, a fellow of fifteen years' standing, accused Bathurst variously of excessive absence, holding the too valuable deanery, and of financial corruption. Bathurst had a strong defence against the charge of absenteeism, for a precedent had been set when Bishop Morley himself granted permission to attend to the deanery in 1672.[77] Against the other accusations, Bathurst defended himself robustly, and countercharged Willis with jealousy and lust, partly caused by 'that unlucky window of yours that looks towards the Turle'.[78] Willis was expelled in June 1685.

[75] TCA Visitor I, f. 14.
[76] Ibid., 9/17; 11/20–23b.
[77] TCA Visitor I, 4/10–11.
[78] Ibid., 4/17, 24/54–7.

## *The Chapel*

Bathurst's last and greatest work was the Trinity College Chapel. He had dreamed about it for three decades, and it was to be the most magnificent place of worship in Oxford. For the sake of completing it—'with a resolution equally noble and disinterested', said Warton—he turned down the offer of a bishopric—'a much more honourable and eminent station', said Sykes.[79] There was no doubt that the work was long overdue and the southern walls of the old Chapel and treasury had become positively dangerous. Indeed, as Bathurst wrote to a potential benefactor, the fellows had to 'venture [their] lives every day' in the face of a possible collapse.[80] Bathurst set out his hopes in a long letter to Nicholas Stratford (fellow 1663–71), now Bishop of Chester. 'I doubt not but your Lord may already have heard of our last summer's attempt for rebuilding the south side of our college . . . ,' he began, 'always homely and mean enough, but of late grown very infirm and ruinous, especially in the roof of the chapel and walls of the treasury and gate house.' Bathurst described the plans, and the advice given by 'the worthy dean of Christ Church and other able judges in architecture', to have a larger chapel, built on entirely new foundations, and better aligned with the corners of the existing quadrangle. He himself was going to be the most generous benefactor. 'The shell, or outward bulk of all (as the walls, roof, pinnacle, windows etc) I hope, by God's blessing, to be able to finish at my own charge; but for the inward furniture and ornamental parts (as wainscot, seats, screen, altar piece, marble fretwork and the like) we must make bold to solicit the charity of such good friends as are willing to contribute to so pious a work.'[81]

The Durham College Chapel was demolished in the summer of 1691. Bathurst left Thomas Sykes and Roger Almont in charge, while he spent some time in his Wells deanery. Sykes wrote to him on 10 August: 'All the old building is in a manner down and the new advanced farther than you can easily imagine.' The surveyor, Mr Phips, was in charge of paying the workmen, but the two fellows had to do a deal with a suitable stonemason. 'The day after you parted hence,' Sykes

[79] Warton, *Bathurst*, 63; Thomas Sykes, *A Sermon Preached at the Consecration of the Trinity College Chapel*, Epistle Dedicatory, unpaginated.

[80] TCA Misc. Vol. I, 94d/164. [81] Ibid., 90/146.

informed Bathurst anxiously, 'Mr Almont and I was with one Kemster, to whom we showed the model of our chapel, and took what advice he could give us concerning it. But upon further discourse . . . he demanded near as much more as Peisley had offered you to do it for before you left us.' Worse, the two men found they could 'not get rid of him without a gratuity for his journey hither. All that we could do therefore was to clap up a bargain with Peisley as soon as we could, and upon the best terms we could get, lest after he had conferred with Kemster, as he did the next day, he should rise his price upon us.'[82]

Peisley had worked for Bathurst before.[83] He now contracted to construct the Chapel stonework at *9s 6d* the perch or pole, 'to be measured in such a manner as is not usual, and as we believe will be to your advantage,' reported Sykes on 3 September. The new building was well under way when last-minute changes were made to the plans. The Chapel's main architect may have been Henry Aldrich, the dean of Christ Church, and designer of All Saints' Church (now the Lincoln College library) at the southern end of Turl Street. But the only evidence for his involvement is the Chapel's similarity to All Saints' and Bathurst's reference to Aldrich's advice on the building's location. In the winter of 1691–2, Bathurst sent Phips to Sir Christopher Wren with a printed copy of the design, and brought back a verbal report on the unsuitability of the proposed pinnacles. Bathurst wrote to Wren on 25 February 1692, to ask 'for your thoughts concerning our design, and particularly of the pinnacles, which as they were superadded to our first draught, so, I must confess, I would be well content to have omitted with your approbation.'[84] Wren replied just a week later. He had studied the design, 'which in the main is very well, and I believe your work is too far advance to admit of any advice'. He ventured on a number of suggestions, however, of which one was of serious structural importance: 'two sorts of cornice, [the mason] may use either'; 'a change of the stairs, to leave the wall next the porch of sufficient scantling to bear that part which rises above the roofs adjoining'; and 'another way to the rail and baluster, which will admit of a vase that will stand properly upon the pilaster'. And he dispatched 'a little deal box, with a drawing in it' by the Oxford carrier.[85]

Research undertaken at the time of the Chapel's tercentenary sug-

[82] TCA Misc. Vol. I, 89/142.

[83] TCA Accounts III/E/1, ff. 46d, 47d, where his name occurs in relation to the 'bog house'.

[84] TCA Misc. Vol. I, 92d/153.

[85] Warton, *Bathurst*, 69–70.

gests that a sketch of the Trinity Chapel now in the possession of All Souls College is the very same drawing that was sent in the little deal box. It follows the engraving, but incorporates most of the changes which Wren suggested in his letter. Bathurst had another engraving made, which used almost all of Wren's suggestions for the ornamentation of the building (Plate 6.4). It omitted an ornate second doorway in the area of the Founder's tomb, presumably because, as Wren had supposed, the work was already too far advanced.[86]

Bathurst commenced a new round of fund-raising, sending out the 'scarce yet finished delineation of our whole design' together with further reminders of the decree *de Gratiis Collegii Rependendis* (decree about repaying favours to the College). The Trinity bishops were importuned, and replied with donations of varying generosity. The fellows travelled the land with letters addressed to likely old members. The bursar, Arthur Charlett, wrote to report on his mixed progress in London in December 1691. Some recipients he found 'more easy at the second visit than at the first'. Anthony Etterick (1640) had been of real assistance, and he hoped 'to find the good effects of his solicitations with our friends in the House of Commons'. But another old member had 'pressed me very much to declare what others gave. I thought it best to avoid an answer.'[87] Josiah How had a particularly negative response from one of his earliest pupils, Thomas Hood, who demanded to know 'how can I be so unkind to the precious memory of your founder . . . as to contribute the least spill of money to the prostrating and demolishing any part of his benefaction which will be forgot as soon as the new chapel is hallowed.' Despite his antipathy to the project, however, Hood still sent his 'humble service to your president and the rest of your venerable and reverent society', and asked them all to 'take care to advance my ingenious godson Vincent Philips'.[88]

Having demolished the treasury, Trinity found itself suddenly in need of a bank. Large sums of money were passing through the College, and in 1691 the decision was made to deposit £100 with the Oxford goldsmith, Daniel Porter.[89] Another important way of financing the ongoing work was to take out loans. In 1693 Trinity borrowed £200 for a year from Corpus Christi College, and in 1694 £200 from

[86] Matthew Steggle, 'New Light on Wren and Trinity Chapel', *Report (1995)*, 40–3.

[87] TCA Misc. Vol. I, f. 99d/150.

[88] Bod. Lib. MS Ballard 49, f. 172–3.

[89] TCA *Computus* 1691, f. 366.

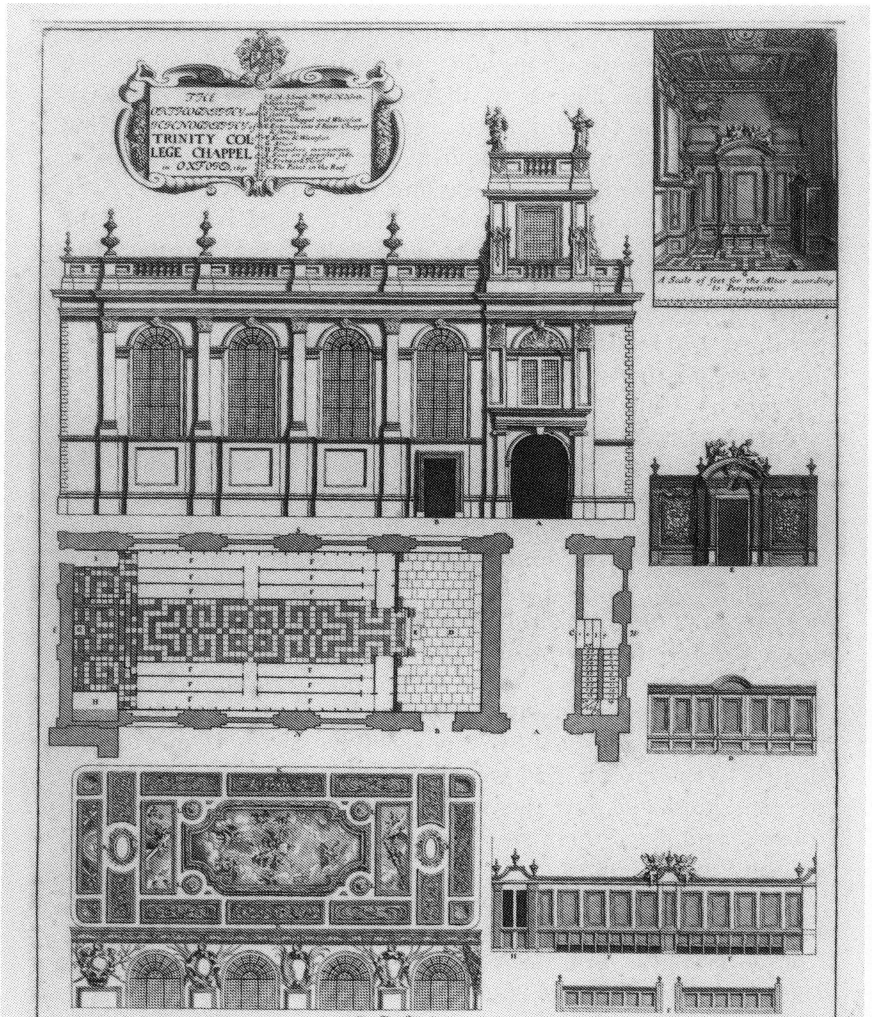


*6.4* 'The Orthography and Iconography' of the Trinity College Chapel, 1694.

Thomas Rowney, £100 each from William Taylor and Joseph Penn, and Charles Cole, and a further £200 from the University.[90]

The carpenter responsible for much of the building work was Arthur Frogley, the quality of whose work was already evident in the beautifully panelled common room. The accounts of 1691 record payments totalling £230 to Frogley. On 9 November 1693, Bartholomew Peisley signed articles of agreement relating to 'Paving with marble the Inner Chapel' with 'the best black and white Italian marble' in blocks one foot square and one inch thick, to be laid according to the printed design. He was paid at the rate of *2s 9d* per square foot, and received five guineas on completion, while the 'extraordinary over-work in the steps' was to be agreed separately. He also bound himself in £20 to a ten-year maintenance contract.[91] The Chapel ceiling was decorated with the finest plaster work, and in the centre, a painting of the Ascension executed by the Huguenot refugee, Pierre Berchet.

It is much to the regret of College historians that no bills were kept recording details of the Chapel's exquisite wood-carving. Five different woods were used. The stalls and panelling are of oak; the carving on the reredos is in lime and pear; the veneered panel above the altar walnut; and the veneering of the reredos, the alcoves, the altar rail, and the screen are of Bermudan cedar or juniper. Blakiston had no doubt that 'the beautiful lime and cedar carving' was by Grinling Gibbons. Arthur Oswald, writing in *Country Life*, felt 'no one, on seeing the extraordinary virtuosity of the work, could possibly suspect any other authorship.'[92] Michael Maclagan thought more cautiously that 'the pear and limewood, above the altar, is stylistically at least as good as anything Grinling Gibbons wrought elsewhere.'[93] Besides the sheer perfection of the craftsmanship, and some characteristic Gibbons motifs, the best evidence to ascribe Trinity's altarpiece to Gibbons is the travel journal of a 1695 visitor to Oxford. Celia Fiennes enthused over the 'beautiful magnificent structure' and the 'very fine carving of thin white wood just like that at Windsor, it being the same hand'. She could literally breathe in the beauty of the place: 'The whole chapel is wainscoted with walnut tree and the fine sweet wood the same that the Lord Oxford brought over when High

[90] TCA *Computus* 1691, f. 375, 383d.
[91] TCA Charters F/1/1; TCA Misc. Vol. I, f. 99/175.
[92] *Country Life* (8 March 1930), 358.
[93] Blakiston, *Trinity*, 165; Maclagan, *Trinity College*, 7.

*6.5* The Chapel interior (J. R. H. Weaver, 1938).

Admiral of England . . . It is sweet like cedar and of a reddish colour, but the grain much finer and well-veined.'[94] The Chapel, when new, was pervaded by the perfume of these scented woods. *Halat opus, Lebanique refert fragrantis odorem* (the work smells sweet, and carries the aroma of fragrant Lebanon), wrote Warton in 1748.[95]

Further doubt arises as to the identity of the sculptor responsible for the four figures on the Chapel tower—'conjectured to be the work of Caius Cibber', ventured Maclagan. The identities of the figures themselves are better recorded, and three still bear traces of their distinguishing features. Theology (south-west corner) holds a Bible, Astronomy (north-west) an orb, and Medicine (north-east) a snake entwining a stick. The fourth statue—Geometry—has lost all the mathematical instruments which appeared in early prints.

The new Chapel was consecrated on 12 April 1694, in a ceremony performed on behalf of the Visitor by John Hough, Bishop of Oxford. The inaugural preacher was Thomas Sykes, whose eloquent sermon was published with a warm 'epistle dedicatory' to Ralph Bathurst, praising him variously for his good government of the College, his encouragement of piety and learning, his bounty in giving so generously, and his kindness 'to this college in general, and in particular to myself'. Sykes took for his text the apt words of King Solomon in 1 Kings 8:18, 'And the Lord said unto David my father, whereas it was in thy heart to build an House unto my name; thou didst well that it was in thy heart.'[96] The Bathurst coat of arms was carved on the north side of the tower, the College arms on the south.

Visitors to Oxford were enthusiastic. Celia Fiennes mentioned it in her opening sentence: 'There are several good colleges; I saw most of them. Wadham Hall is but little; in Trinity College is a fine neat Chapel, new made, finely painted.'[97] When, in 1698, the landlord of Golden Cross Inn was required to take an incognito tourist—actually Tsar Peter the Great of Russia—on a hurried tour of the city, Trinity's Chapel was the only collegiate building of any kind included in the

[94] Celia Fiennes, *Through England on a Side Saddle* (London, 1888), 27–8. 1790s undergraduates had no doubt that the carving was by Gibbons. John Skinner described the Chapel 'bedecked with ornaments by Gibbons / In rich festoons of flowers and ribbons'; Bod. Lib. MS Top e.41, f. 261.

[95] Warton, *Bathurst*, p. xxiii. 'It needs a keen nose to detect it now,' commented Arthur Oswald in 1930, *Country Life* (8 March 1930), 358.

[96] On his retirement in 1980, Michael Maclagan (fellow 1939) presented a copy of Sykes's sermon to the College Library.

[97] Fiennes, *Through England*, 25.

imperial itinerary. The visit was described by William Williams, underkeeper of the Ashmolean Museum, who found the Tsar

> a very uncouth fellow, wearing a long black wig and a rather fine kaftan with gold buttons. He stoops heavily; his hands were dirty and scratched, as if he had a rash. He was not properly shaven, although I could not see his whole face adequately, because his hideous wig was enormous, and he himself did his best to hide his face . . . The Tsar arrived at ten o'clock on Friday evening; they say he had drunk two bottles of vodka. Very early in the morning, he visited the bookshop, the town-hall and the theatre, and from the Museum, where he had spent little more than a quarter of an hour, he departed to the chapel of Trinity, but it seems he was recognized and his entourage grew against his wish, and the students and citizens ran to see him, so he turned back and immediately left the city.[98]

Bathurst had many reasons to feel proud of Trinity, and well satisfied with the results of his devoted and sacrificial headship. 'Were it not for the love I bear to that worthy society . . . ,' he had written to the Visitor in 1689, 'and if I did not hope to be still more useful to the college than it can be to me, I would not care to stay there a week longer.'[99] A story of his 'zeal for his college' towards the end of his life was current in the eighteenth century. In sentiment, if not in detail, it has the ring of truth. 'Balliol College had suffered so much in the outrages of the grand rebellion,' related Warton,

> that it remained almost in a state of desolation for some years after the restoration: a circumstance not to be suspected from its flourishing condition ever since. Dr Bathurst was perhaps secretly pleased to see a neighbouring and once a rival society, reduced to this condition, while his own flourished beyond all others. Accordingly, one afternoon he was found in his garden, which then ran almost contiguous to the east side of Balliol College, throwing stones at the windows with much satisfaction, as if happy to complete his share in completing the appearance of its ruin.[100]

Tragically, in the last years of his life, Bathurst was neither able to see his College, nor even to remember what he had done for it.

[98] Arthur MacGregor, 'The Day the Tsar Came', *Ashmolean* (Spring 2003), 9. William Williams's account is translated from Casper Meyer, *Storicheskii vestnik 100* (1905).

[99] TCA Register B, f. 16.

[100] Warton, *Life and Literary Remains*, 203. Today's Fellows' Garden may have been given up to Bathurst's private use when the Bathurst Building was put up.

Evelyn described Bathurst as 'stark blind, deaf, and memory lost' in June 1704.[101] Lord Bathurst told Thomas Warton that his uncle had been blind 'for some time' before his death, while William Capel, Bathurst's servitor, wrote movingly of the President's senility:

> How often for an hour together in the evening, have I heard him tell of things done within the compass of his own knowledge, with such particular and enlivening expressions, that methought I heard, and saw them all! How often have I heard him repeat the stories of ancient times so punctually, as though he had been an interested actor in them! And yet, now not one glimpse of many of those does he retain, not one circumstance can he remember![102]

Documents in the College archive, however, testify to Bathurst's involvement in the minutiae of college administration as late as 1703, when the *Liber Devillantium* (Book of Absences) includes shakily written notes of room allocations promised to fellow commoners.[103] His will, dictated—'my bad eyes not permitting me to write it myself'—on 29 August 1698, is long and lucid, and was amended by a number of codicils, the latest dated 25 August 1703.[104]

Ralph Bathurst died on 14 June 1704. According to Warton, he fell and broke his thigh

> while he was walking in the garden, which, on the failure of his eyes, became his favourite and only amusement. Under this malady, he languished for several days. It is said . . . that at first, and for some time, he refused to submit to the operations of the surgeon, declaring, in his tortures, that there was no marrow in the bones of an old man.[105]

Bathurst had originally asked to be buried in the chancel at Garsington, but in the event he was interred in the College antechapel, beneath a marble lozenge inscribed with a brief Latin epitaph of his own composition. His funeral was simple, done according to his wishes for burial 'with the utmost privacy and frugality, without speech or sermon'.

Ralph Bathurst's will included many characteristically generous

[101] *The Diary of John Evelyn*, ed. E. S. de Beer (London, 1959), 1108.

[102] Warton, *Bathurst*, 183. Warton is quoting a letter dated 24 December 1703, 'communicated' to him by Mr Payne, prebendary of Wells Cathedral, grandson of Bathurst's nephew by marriage and beneficiary, Richard Healy (Warton, *Bathurst*, pp. vii–viii).

[103] TCA Coll. Govt. IV/9.

[104] TCA Benefactions, B/3.1.

[105] Warton, *Bathurst*, 182.

*6.6* The Chapel and Bathurst Building from the south, *c.*1860.

bequests. He remembered the poor in the parish of his birth, as well as in Garsington, Wells, and in every parish in the city of Oxford. He bequeathed £150 to Trinity, and £20 worth of books to be selected by two of the fellows for 'the two libraries'. 'Small books' were to be distributed to undergraduate members of the College judged 'to be like to make the best use of them'. The 'statutable servants' were to have a guinea each, and the 'common servants' 50*s* between them. Each servitor was to receive 10*s*, and Bathurst's own servitor £10. His private servants were each remembered in the will.[106] Bathurst's most significant and most enduring legacy to Trinity was the College's new buildings. What he did not leave, however, was an obvious successor. Now he was dead, and who was there to continue the great President's work?

[106] TCA Benefactions B/3.1

# 7

# *Trinity in the Eighteenth Century*

## *The Presidents*

Trinity College elected four Presidents in the eighteenth century, of whom, sniffed Blakiston, 'no worse need be said than that they are too insignificant to figure in the *Dictionary of National Biography*.'[1] The first was Thomas Sykes, in his early sixties and in poor health. The second name sent to the Visitor had been that of the senior fellow Roger Almont (fellow 1666), who had, according to the antiquarian Thomas Hearne (a resident of Edmund Hall), 'lived so obscure a life in the college . . . 'tis hard to know his character'.[2] Sykes enjoyed eighteen months in the headship, during which time he renovated the Lodgings.[3] Then he died of 'gout in the stomach' on 14 December 1705, and was buried in the Chapel. 'An honest man,' concluded Hearne, 'and a learned divine.'

On Sykes's death, there was still no obvious successor to Bathurst. The eight senior fellows were Roger Almont, Henry Barker (fellow 1684), Robert Michell (1684), Iön Beachamp (1685), John Barber (1689), Thomas Hasker (1698), Henry Hale (1699), and Edward Cranke (1700). Almont was nominated once more, but the majority of votes went to a second representative of an earlier generation: William Dobson (fellow 1676) who since 1679 had been rector of Cliddesdon with Farley in Hampshire. Dobson was an 'honest man and a good scholar, who by his prudence,' remarked Hearne acidly, ''tis hoped will raise the drooping credit of the society, which formerly had men of note in it, but now has not one.'[4]

Thirty years as a parish priest were poor preparation for the challenges of college government. In the early years of his presidency, Dobson's authority was severely tested by an unpleasant row that

[1] Blakiston, *Trinity*, 185. [2] *Hearne* I, 128, 153.

[3] Sykes spent over £200 of his own money on the Lodgings, and bequeathed to Trinity a further £300 (TCA Benefactors' Book III, f. xv). [4] *Hearne* I, 153.

began with the expulsion of a gentleman commoner, Henry Knollys (1704), and escalated into the public exposure of serious divisions within the fellowship. Dobson's own account of what happened is somewhat unedifying:

> When the Dean put the usual sconce for missing prayers upon [Knollys's] name, he struck it off in defiance, which you know is flying in the face of the government of the college; and these things we passed by in hopes he would in time be prevailed upon to behave himself like a gentleman . . . but he went on and grew still more insulting. At length to crown the rest, he made a public disturbance in the chapel, while divinity disputations were performed, and with some others setting up a loud laugh (an unheard of insolence) to affront the vice-president in the execution of his office; And to show what we were to expect for the future, he owned . . . that he came there with premeditated designs to affront the vice-president, and that he would affront him whenever he met him.

With the support of the vice-president, John Barber, and the senior bursar, Thomas Hasker, Dobson formally expelled Knollys on 27 October 1707. He wrote sternly to the young man's cousin that to have him back would 'be the most effectual way to sink the college. For I can't think any gentlemen will venture their sons here, when we have made ourselves unable to govern them.'[5]

Knollys's tutor, John Gwinnet, and the two lecturers, Henry Overton and Francis Finch, resented Dobson's high-handed approach. They penned a glowing testimonial for their ex-pupil, who had 'acquitted himself with reputation by constantly attending the Greek lecture for one whole year, although that is an exercise which has not in our remembrance been performed by or ever . . . required of fellow-commoners'. A second document, signed by four fellows, certified to his good character 'not being known or in the least suspected to be guilty of cursing, swearing, lying, or any other profane discourse, immoderate drinking, whoring or any other vice or immorality whatsoever'. His only offence, indeed, was to have 'laughed in the chapel . . . at the time of divinity disputations,' and to have 'kicked at the cat of Thomas Hasker clerk and Bursar of the college, which cat (as it was said) ran afterwards into the chapel'. Although he had 'behaved with incivility towards some of the

[5] Dobson to John Foyle, 10 November 1707, *Hearne* II, 82–3.

society' he had not been given the opportunity to explain or apologize.[6]

There were further repercussions. Dobson wrote darkly of Knollys's bad influence, which had begun to 'infect others with prejudices against the college'. Gossip was rife in the University. Hearne believed that two fellow commoners departed the College in sympathy, and Gwinnet was 'put out of commons' for supporting them. One observer, John Pointer, recorded Knollys's expulsion as one of the main events of the Oxford year but thought he 'was afterwards restored'. On the other hand, on 1 December, Stephen Fry (fellow 1677–84) and John Budgen (scholar 1694–1701) 'were likewise expelled upon the same account espousing Mr Knollys's cause'.[7] Fry and Budgen both lived in college rooms, and their departure was perhaps the most serious outcome of the whole affair. Fry was 'very rich and . . . [had] lived all his time at the college' and Budgen might have been 'a good benefactor if they had dealt prudently'. Dobson's defiant attitude—'it may be better for us to lose £500, than have the company of one so prejudiced and soured against us'—may have cost Trinity double that amount. At his death in 1710 Stephen Fry left £1,000 to Stone's almshouses in Oxford.[8]

In 1713 Dobson was viciously satirized in a speech intended to be spoken by the *Terrae Filius*. It was suppressed by the Vice-Chancellor but subsequently published and read widely:

> *Receipt for a Head of House of the Dobson Type:*
> Recipe an old heavy country parson, extract all remains of common sense, and common honesty; and then put in gravity, formality, hypocrisy, and pretended conscience, of each a large quantity.

[6] Ibid., 84–5. The list of 10 signatories is headed by Drs Fry and Budgen; the fellows were Gwinnet, Overton, Finch, and Cranke, who collected Knollys's caution money for him on 29 July 1708 (TCA Caution Book B, f. 83d.). Cats are of course a traditional means of vermin control. John Skinner suggested a large eighteenth-century feline population when he wrote of an undergraduate going 'to shoot another cat / in famed Bog Alley' in 1793, referring to the passage to the privy house behind the hall (Skinner, 'Letters', f. 145). As recently as 1962 Terry Bird (1960) made use of a 'master cat' to catch mice on Staircase 12 (*Report* (2001), 81–2).

[7] John Pointer, 'Chronology of Oxford University', Bod. MSS Rawl Q. f. 5, f. 21.

[8] *Hearne* II, 77. Hearne asserts that Fry 'burned his will in Mr Nourse's chamber in Kettell Hall'; ibid., 78. Francis Nourse (1693), a lawyer, seems to have been another Trinity graduate settled comfortably in college accommodation. He was a signatory to the testimonial supporting Knollys; he took back his caution money in March 1708 (TCA Caution Book B, f. 81d).

Add of stupidity, *q. suff.* [a sufficient quantity].
*Fiat compositio simplex* [let the mixture be simple]: give him the degree of Doctor in Divinity and then . . . *Caput Mortuum* [a worthless residue].
NB The use of this sort is to vote and act as the others bid them.[9]

Dobson's political views may have contributed to his unpopularity in a university that was, for the most part, staunchly Tory. In 1721 he orchestrated the election to the fellowship of a junior scholar, Charles Bayley, over the heads of no less than four senior candidates. Hearne wrote disapprovingly of the President's political machinations, noting that the four overlooked scholars were 'Tories, whereas this Bayley is a great Whig. The head, Dr Dobson, was for this Bayley, which gained him the ill will of many.' News of the 'nice and unexpected majority' was promulgated gleefully in London by the *Whitehall Evening Post* as a harbinger of 'a different state of affairs in the college, to the great joy of his majesty's well-wishers in the university'. Hearne was sure the Visitor would overrule the 'unstatutable election', but Bayley remained securely in his fellowship for the next four years. Dobson seems to have got away with such a clear breach of College custom during an interregnum in the diocese of Winchester. [10]

William Dobson died in 1731, and this time the College elected a much younger man, George Huddesford, who was a fellow of just nine years' standing. Huddesford's presidency lasted for forty-four years and 292 days, a college record that seems unlikely ever to be broken.[11] His years of office were pleasantly lacking in dramatic events, notable mainly for the development of antiquarian interest in the College's past. When Huddesford died in 1776, there was some expectation that the headship would go to Thomas Warton (fellow 1751), then at the height of his powers, active and respected in the academic and literary worlds. Warton's loyalty to Trinity and experience of college administration could not be questioned, and his life of the Founder, published in 1772, had been a labour of love that was universally well received. 'No person but myself would have under-

[9] *The speech that was intended to have been spoken by the* Terrae-Filius (1713); *Hearne* IV, 243.

[10] *Hearne* VII, 250; *Whitehall Evening Post* (June 8–10, 1721). Bayley left in 1725 to take the College living of Navestock. The Visitor, Bishop Jonathan Trelawney, died on 19 July 1721; his successor, Charles Trimnell, was consecrated on 19 August.

[11] 5 July 1731–21 April 1776 (a leap year). Ralph Kettell comes a close second, with 44 years and some five months; the exact date of his death is unknown.

taken it,' he wrote simply to a friend.[12] Warton himself had assumed the position was his; but on 14 May 1776 he wrote with sad resignation to tell his sister Jane that 'by an unforeseen cabal formed in the society, I am not the President'.[13] Richard Hele (fellow 1767–86) gave more details to a friend: 'I was much deceived in my account to you about the future President. Mr Chapman is nominated by the Visitor, and in order to exclude Mr Warton, Mr Jesse was returned with him.' Joseph Chapman had been a fellow for less than six years, and Charles Jesse for less than three.

> Three of the senior fellows, Drs Peisley, Parker and Wilmot, turned the election against Mr Warton. By what motive they were actuated, I know not, but in my opinion the college is essentially injured by their choice. Exclusive of his literary character, I think Mr Warton was by nature formed for this appointment. . . . It is needless to inform you that he is one of the best-natured men that ever lived. To this amiable quality is added a sincere regard for the college, which, I am fully persuaded, would have improved and flourished under his guidance.[14]

It was not to be. Chapman was duly appointed, and he occupied the Lodgings for the next thirty-two years. 'A tall, dignified, well-wigged Head of a House,' remembered George Valentine Cox. 'Like his successors at Trinity he seems to have preferred a quiet easy life.'[15]

## *The College Garden and Buildings*

Life in eighteenth-century Trinity was certainly quieter and easier than it had ever been before. The most remarkable achievement was the creation of a new college garden. Following the fashions in Oxford and England, the fellows devoted a considerable amount of energy and money to the transformation of their informally wooded grove into one of the most exquisite and ornamental gardens in the city. It was, in the opinion of Howard Colvin, 'the most ambitious

[12] *Warton*, ed. Fairer, letter 290, TW to Richard Hurd, 19 January 1772.

[13] Ibid., letter 325, TW to Jane Warton, 14 May 1776.

[14] Andrew Dalzel, *History of the University of Edinburgh from its Foundation, with a memoir of the author* [by Cosmo Innes] (Edinburgh, 1862), i, 15–16.

[15] G. V. Cox, *Recollections of Oxford* (London, 1868), 158.

of all'.[16] A contemporary guide, Thomas Salmon, described Trinity's Garden Quadrangle as 'one of the beauties of Oxford, not only on account of its buildings, but its situation, opening into one of the finest and most spacious gardens in town'.[17] Work began in 1706.[18] Almost at once the significance of the changes was marked by the adoption of a new name: in 1709 the £200 legacy of William Bourchier (1675) was used in part 'to embellish the public garden (lately the grove) and lay it out in a new design'.[19]

Trinity's four acres of grove were divided into three parts, the largest being the expanse of geometric grass plots and pathways that Salmon so admired. Following the coronation of William of Orange in 1689, England and Oxford had been caught up in a craze for the 'Dutch style' of horticulture, with dwarf trees, topiary pyramids and pilasters, and intricately cut evergreen hedges dividing the ground into regular compartments.[20] At Trinity, yews were planted along the St John's College wall, around the northern and eastern sides of the President's garden, and in a long hedge extending westwards down to the College's eastern boundary. Williams's print of 1733 (Plate 7.1) shows these hedges trained and cut to resemble panels, the width of each section calculated to correspond with the wide gravel paths.[21] This feature was maintained with meticulous care for more than a hundred years. In 1794 the eminent landscape gardener Humphrey Repton visited Trinity, and spoke warmly of the way 'the ancient style of gardening [was] very properly preserved' there: 'I should doubt the taste or any improver who could despise the congruity, the utility, the order, and the symmetry' of the 'hedges and straight walks'.[22] The yew hedge was 'so perfect in its kind,' wrote Robert Southey in 1807. 'You would hardly conceive that a vegetable wall could be so close and impervious, still less, that anything so unnatural could be so beautiful as this really is.'[23] A number of the original yew trees, now

[16] Howard Colvin, 'Architecture', *HUO* 5, 852.

[17] Mr Salmon, *The Foreigner's Companion through the Universities of Cambridge and Oxford* (London, 1748), 62.

[18] John Pointer, 'Chronology of Oxford University', ff. 5, 18.

[19] *'In horto publico (nuper arbusto) ornando et in novam formam disponendo.'* TCA Benefactors' Book III, 20).

[20] Mavis Batey, *The Historic Gardens of Oxford and Cambridge* (London, 1989), 96–7.

[21] William Williams *Oxonia Depicta* (Oxford, 1733), plate XLV.

[22] J. C. Loudon (ed.), *The Landscape Gardening and Landscape Architecture of the late Humphrey Repton* (London, 1840), 112.

[23] Robert Southey, *Letters from England: by Don Manuel Espriella* (London, 1807), ii, 68–9.

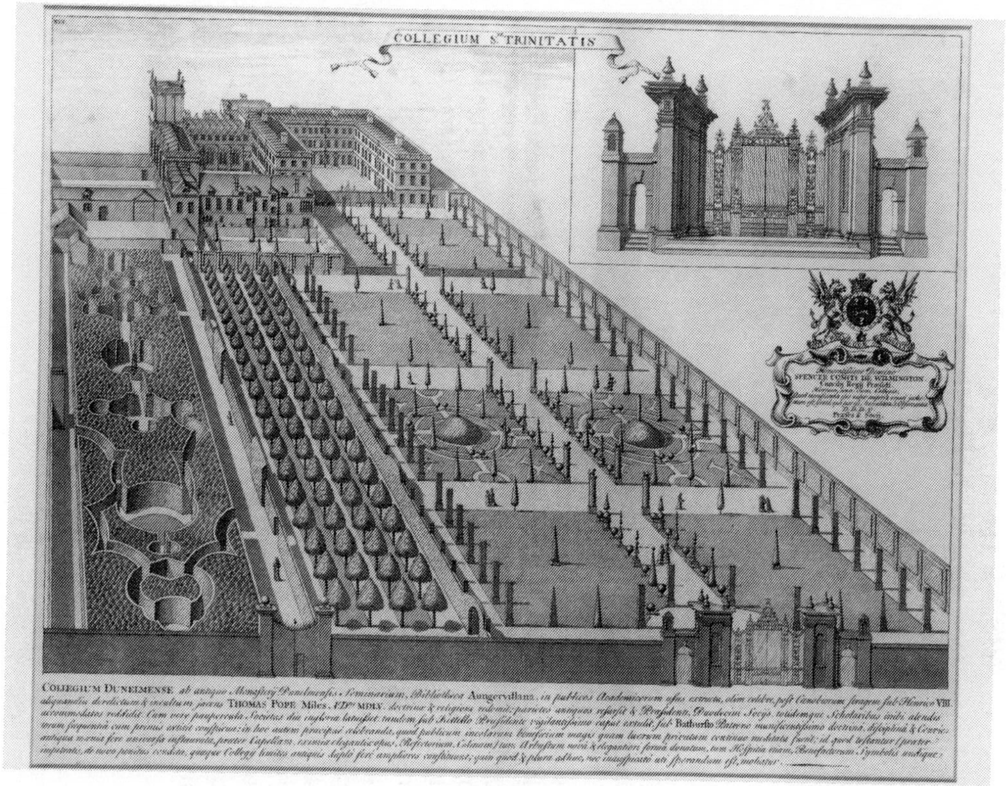


*7.1* The eighteenth-century garden, in William Williams, *Oxonia Depicta* (1733), plate 45.

*7.2* The initial of 'Richard Piers' (Benefactors' Book III, f. 28).

growing naturally, are still to be found in the garden at the beginning of the twenty-first century.

A wide path led down the garden from the 'inner quadrangle'—'separated by a beautiful iron gate and palisade, adorned with magnificent stone pillars'[24]—to a new wrought-iron grille, or gate, through the bars of which passers-by on the road were offered 'an agreeable prospect' of Wren's quadrangle.[25] To pay for the gate, sixty-five individuals subscribed a total of £224 12*s* 6*d* in 1713; and at the same time an almost identical sum was laid out on the trees, hedge plants, ornaments, and other garden expenses. The gate was erected in the spring of 1713, set between imposing baroque piers that were the work of Bathurst's master mason Bartholomew Peisley. The piers cost £52, and another £40 was expended on six vases to top the piers, and on stone steps leading up to the gate from the garden.[26] In 1718 the unknown illustrator of the Benefactors' Book sketched the gate as a pun on the name of Richard Piers (scholar 1702) (Plate 7.2).[27] Over the years

[24] Salmon, *Foreigner's Companion*, 62.

[25] *A Pocket Companion for Oxford* (London, 1759), 70. This guidebook contains an early version of an unlikely tradition associated with the gate: 'When the workmen were sawing the stones in order to build the piers, in the heart of a large block was found a toad alive, which had undoubtedly been there a considerable time.'

[26] TCA Misc. Vol. I, f. 104v/178. No *computus* accounts are extant for the years 1696–1718. Peisley's son, Barnard, was a scholar of Trinity 1709–15, and fellow 1715–28.

[27] TCA Benefactors' Book III, f. xxviii. Similarly the 1717 entry for William Chambers depicts the garden quad, and some of the garden's topiary ornaments in the foreground (ibid., f. xxvii.)

two traditions have attached themselves to this gate. The first, which may have begun as a jibe aimed at the Whiggish president of a Tory college, is that it would only be opened when 'the true king came into his own' (i.e. a 'Jacobite' descendant of the exiled Catholic James II), the second that the gate is in fact purely ornamental and incapable of being opened at all.[28] Either side of the central path ran a line of intricate topiary pillars, and the grass plots were ornamented with symmetrical mounds, heraldic designs, evergreen obelisks, tall slender pyramids, and closely trimmed spheres. The pillars at the corners of the intersecting paths were topped with beasts. All these details may be observed in Williams's print (Plate 7.1).

The second part of the garden lay to the south of the open paths, grass, and topiary. In January and February 1713, forty-eight lime and forty-eight Dutch elm trees had been bought and planted at a total cost of £18 19*s* 5*d*. The limes were set in a double avenue, running parallel to and reached via entrances at either end of the long yew hedge. This was the beginning of Trinity's celebrated 'Lime Walk', which endured in various incarnations until the last decade of the twentieth century.[29] The branches were pleached into an overarching canopy, and one of the earliest surviving photographs of Trinity, taken circa 1860, shows members walking in the shade of a high and vaulted roof (Plate 7.3).

In the third part of the garden, to the south of the lime walk, the elms were planted in a geometric arrangement of trees, known as the labyrinth, or wilderness. Pointer found it 'extremely delightful with a variety of mazes, in which 'tis easy for a man to lose himself. Here and there in this labyrinth are placed benches, inviting students to sit down and study. In the middle of all is a neat fountain with artificial flowers on the surface of the water.' Salmon wrote of the 'wilderness, adorned with fountains, close arbours, round stone tables, and other embellishments'.[30] This part of the garden was modified as the century progressed. The 1750 *Pocket Companion for Oxford*

[28] Maclagan, *Trinity College*, 14. The regular opening of the gate for functions in the garden nicely scotches both traditions at once, although the difference in level between street and garden has always rendered the entrance somewhat impractical.

[29] The first of the original lime trees 'went' in 1902; the last was felled in 1963. Although replacement trees were planted in the avenue at various dates, in 1990 the decision was made to incorporate the remaining lime trees into a 'woodland area.' *Report* (1963), 9; (1989–90), 3.

[30] *Pointer's Oxford Guide* (1749), 88; Salmon, *The Foreigner's Companion*, 62.

*7.3* The Lime Walk, *c.*1860 (Album of Henry E. Hulton (1858), TCA OM 8).

approved of the way that 'the lesser division to the south has been lately laid open to the rest, planted with flowering shrubs and the whole much improved.' The 1788 edition recommended to visitors its 'pleasing solitude, consisting of shady walks, with a wilderness of flowering shrubs, and disposed into serpentine paths'.[31]

Once the garden was established, the fellows turned their attention to the buildings. In 1728 the medieval north range of the Durham Quad was demolished, and replaced by a stylish three-storey construction more in keeping with the College's fashionable appearance (today's Staircase 17). President Dobson headed the catalogue of benefactors, with gifts totalling £160. An old member, Samuel Trotman, and a former fellow, Richard Hale, each donated £100, and the fellows and scholars between them contributed some £130.[32] A whole page of the Benefactors' Book was used to commemorate the Earl of Guildford's 1737 gift of a 'wrought iron gate of exceptional workmanship' which suitably beautified and modernized the College's Broad Street entrance, and at the same time solved the problem of the impractically narrow medieval gateway.[33] Gentlemen's carriages could now be driven up to the inner gate under the Chapel tower, around an elegant oval lawn in front of the Chapel, which some years later was made wider, and more elegant, by the westwards relocation of the stable-yard wall.

Meanwhile, in 1732, the *Oxford University Almanack* had published a remarkable view of the Trinity buildings from the garden, showing a grandiose extension to the Garden Quadrangle in the form of colonnaded wings projecting from the north and south ranges (Plate 7.4). A very similar view appeared as the *Almanack* of 1756. There is no evidence to suggest that such a scheme was ever costed, nor of any obvious need for so much additional accommodation, but in 1760 the undergraduates were discussing the idea avidly. Brownlow North (1760) wrote to tell his father:

> there is now some talk of pulling down our President's Lodgings, & building up that side of the Quadrangle in a handsome manner, if all the members of the college will contribute. Mr Wise has made a very handsome offer, which is, that if the fellows will contribute their share, he will double their sum total, & give as much as all of them together. The President is the only objection, who does

[31] *Pocket Companion for Oxford* (1750), 70; *Pocket Companion for Oxford* (1788), 53.
[32] TCA Benefactors' Book III, 45, 47–8. [33] Ibid., 61.

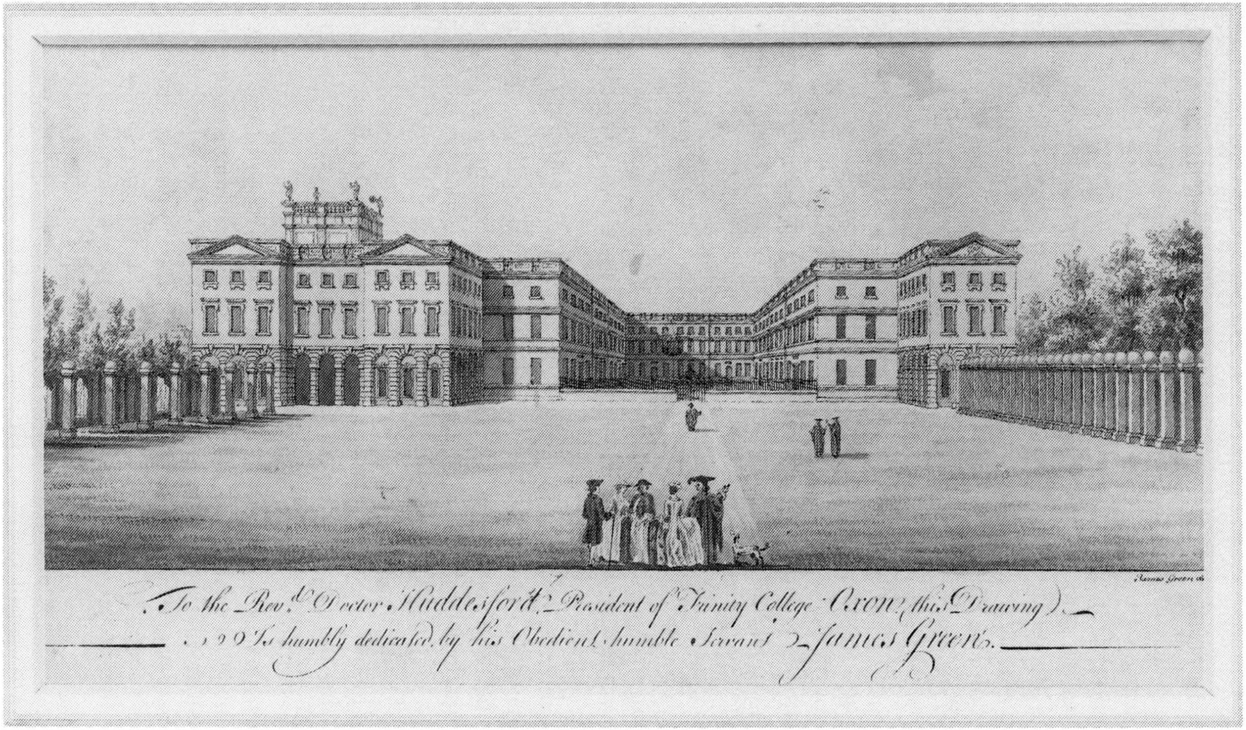
To the Revd. Doctor Huddesford, President of Trinity College Oxon, this Drawing
Is humbly dedicated by his Obedient humble Servant James Green.

*7.4* Projected extension to the Garden Quadrangle by James Green, *c*.1750.

not choose to be turned out of his Lodgings; I dine with him today.[34]

## *College Administration*

In 200 years, Trinity had come a long way from the plain accommodation and monastic routines set out in the Founder's Statutes, but legally they were still very much in force. The eighteenth century was punctuated by painful disputes and regular stand-offs as members of the foundation attempted to bend the rules further and further away from their original severity. Ways were found to re-interpret some of the more inconvenient stipulations, while others were simply ignored as successive Visitors took an increasingly pragmatic line on enforcement. Jonathan Trelawney (Bishop of Winchester 1707–21) tended towards a progressive view, and in 1711 he tentatively supported Richard Piers's appeal to be allowed to hold his scholarship for longer than nine years.[35] In 1713 he delivered an authoritative opinion on the question of seniority, in effect giving carte blanche for the statute on taking higher degrees to be dispensed with. Those prevented by 'reasonable impediments' from taking the expensive doctorate in divinity, he considered, should not lose their seniority when it came to the question of electing officers. 'I cannot but think,' he reasoned, 'considering the tenor of your statutes, that poverty or the meanness of a man's circumstances should be a good reason for his not proceeding to that chargeable degree.' The only distinction that should be given to doctors was 'an honorary precedence in the hall and chapel and all public processions'.[36]

Seniority was an issue of particular importance because it affected a fellow's income. In the sixteenth century his stipend and commons had provided an acceptable standard of living; now the majority of his income came from other, often less transparent, sources within the College. A single volume of the *computus* account had once recorded everything about the College's financial year; now it had evolved into a formal record of the 'old rents' and a fossilized account of selected outgoings. Trinity's annual housekeeping surplus,

[34] Bod. Lib. MS North D23 f. 116. Brownlow North to the Earl of Guildford, 27 May 1760.

[35] TCA Visitor I 18/46.

[36] TCA Register B f. 61.

the 'increments', was divided between the President and actual fellows (those who had completed their probationary year), the President receiving a double share. But other monies were the preserve of the President and six seniors only. In 1717 the Dean listed these 'profits' as *musea* (study rents), 'decrements' (a termly charge levied against damages), *caena* ('dinner') and heriots (a manorial death duty, traditionally the 'best beast' of a deceased tenant).[37]

An even more important source of revenue, which appears nowhere in the *computus*, were the lump sums, or 'fines', payable by tenants when leases were renewed. Although leases were made for twenty-one-year terms, it was the custom across the University to renew them after seven. The fine would be calculated as a multiple of the land's 'clear value', in the knowledge that the College tenants (who bequeathed their leases and sublet the land as de facto owners) made far more from it than the 'reserved rent' that they paid to the College landlord. In 1755 Trinity's fines were set at one and a quarter times the annual rent; in 1777 they were raised—broadly in line with other colleges—to one and a half times the clear value.[38] Sizeable sums were generated in this way. Generally, 20 per cent went to 'domus' (the College), and the rest was divided between the President and fellows. In 1784 and again in 1791 the tenant at Holcombe paid a fine of £360. In 1801 the estate at Filkins was let to a new tenant, who paid the College £2,800, of which, exceptionally, £2,350 was allocated to the College 'for the discharge of the college debts'.[39] The prudent Blakiston considered the system to be 'a great obstacle to economy and regularity of expenditure',[40] and to allow a lease to 'run out' meant, in the short term, a sizeable loss. In July 1772 the fellows resolved not to renew the Bradwell lease, but cushioned their own incomes by agreeing to borrow the fine from the College treasury, to be repaid 'when the estate there shall fall in'.[41]

To make the system of fines work to the College's advantage, it was necessary to build up sufficient knowledge of the estates in order that their true worth could be calculated, and the tenants persuaded to pay realistic fines. In 1772 bursar Warton addressed the Earl of Guildford, old member (nobleman commoner 1721), benefactor, and

[37] TCA *Liber Decani* I, f. 19.

[38] J. P. D. Dunbadin, 'College Estates and Wealth 1660–1815', *HUO* 5, 270–7. The tenant of Trinity's largest estate, the Earl of Guildford at Wroxton, was renewing his leases every four years; TCA Leases, Wroxton.

[39] TCA Fine Book B, unpaginated.

[40] Blakiston, *Trinity*, 203.

[41] TCA Order Book B, f. 55.

Wroxton tenant, with cautious obsequiousness when he wrote to warn him of a raised fine:

> We hope your Lordship will not think our demand [£190] unreasonable. We are well assured that the lease will bear this advance, and we have raised our fines on many other estates in the same proportion. In the meantime we take the liberty to observe that no account is ever made to our college for the timber growing on your lordship's pleasure grounds, and belonging to us by lease. I mention the circumstance in further justification of our proposal.[42]

The earl paid up, but baulked at another 'considerable advance' four years later, and Warton had to arrange a new survey and valuation in some haste. The following year a lengthy dispute began, over Trinity's right to mark and fell trees on the estate, and the earl's son, prime minister Lord North (nobleman commoner 1749), broke off from the affairs of state to rail against his own Alma Mater:

> It appears to me of the first importance to your lordship, & your family, to get rid of the tyranny of Trinity College which is really become insupportable. Your Lordship cannot doubt of my readiness to contribute to so desirable a deliverance by every means in my power. As to the . . . gentlemen I do not wish to resent their unhandsome and ungrateful conduct to your lordship, but I do most cordially wish to be fairly quit of them.[43]

A College meeting was convened in February 1778 to discuss the expediency of cutting that timber 'as shall appear to be of full grown and least conducive to the ornament of the premises'; and in May it was suggested to the earl that a payment in lieu of timber might be added to the rent when the lease was next renewed. Legal opinion was sought, and the case, favourable to the College, sent to the earl in June 1780. It was now the College's turn to threaten. Early in December a gracious 'benefaction' of £100 arrived from Wroxton, with the news that the terms of the lease could be changed.[44]

A bursar's inattention to detail or ignorance could be costly. In 1776 Trinity was allocated, under the 1775 Filkins Inclosure Act, 460 acres

[42] *Warton*, ed. Fairer, letter 298, TW to the First Earl of Guildford, 19 July 1772.

[43] Ibid., letter 331, TW to Earl of Guildford, 14 October 1776; letter 333, same to same, 3 November 1776; letter 341, same to same, 5 December 1776. Bod. Lib. MS North adds. C.4 ff. 179–82, Lord North to Earl of Guildford 16 August 1777.

[44] TCA Order Book B, ff. 131, 135, 157, 165.

in the parish of Filkins, in lieu of rectory tithes. But this rated amongst 'the poorest farmland in the parish', and was not improved by inadequate hedging of the new fields by the College.[45] Late eighteenth-century bursars began to produce copious notes in numerous notebooks, listing sub-tenants, the sizes and locations of their holdings, and the condition of their cottages. The management of the estates became ever more organized as the century progressed.

While the senior bursar dealt with the cottages and the estates, the junior kept the accounts and managed the domestic side of College life. The various concomitant perks—such as 'poundage' (a proportion of bills paid)—which the office generated were well earned.[46] There were many time-consuming responsibilities, and these came to a head in the weeks before the December audit. In 1765 Thomas Warton wrote to a friend, the philologist and philosopher James Harris, 'it is out of my power to be of the Christmas party at Salisbury this year; for I am engaged in the unclassical office of Bursar.' He was similarly unable to visit his niece Charlotte in the Easter Vacation of 1787, being 'obliged to go on a progress,' or triennial tour of the College estates.[47] The bursars were often responsible for sizeable sums, for example the £1,000 borrowed at 4 per cent to purchase the great tithes of the college living of Hill Farrance in 1776. They were also personally liable for the money they handled, and they found it necessary to keep their own private cash books. In 1779 Thomas Warton had an account with Child's Bank, on Trinity's behalf, but in his own name. The balance on 14 December stood at £1,620.[48] The following December it was decided that 'Mr Child of Temple Bar London [should] be the college banker, and all tenants and others be directed by the bursars to pay all sums due to the college at his shop.'[49] At times there was sufficient surplus money available to dabble in investments. At the close of the 1771 audit it was agreed to purchase, through Child's Bank, £100 of East India Bonds,

[45] *Victoria County History for Oxfordshire*, vol. xvi forthcoming, 'Filkins: Manors and Estates: Economic History' (unpublished draft by V. R. Bainbridge).

[46] As the century progressed, many of these perks were replaced by regular payments, e.g., in 1784 poundage from bedmakers and barbers was exchanged for £5 p.a. (TCA Order Book B, f. 189).

[47] *Warton*, ed. Fairer, letter 157, TW to James Harris, 3 December 1765; letter 529, TW to Charlotte Warton, 27 March 1787.

[48] Cash Book of Thomas Warton: TCA Accounts I/C/1, unpaginated. A letter and statement from John Keysall of Child's Bank, 14 December 1779, is pasted into the book.

[49] TCA Order Book B, f. 169.

in addition to the £400 which the College already held, and a further £100 was invested the following year.[50] After the 1792 audit it was agreed to invest, through the bank, £300 in 3 per cent consolidated annuities; but by 1795 'it having been found impossible for the bursar to comply with the order . . . owing to the necessary and unexpected expenses of the college' the plan was abandoned.[51]

Housekeeping finances were controlled by means of the annual Broad Book, which was used to record the elements of the five separate payments—battels, servants' wages, College and University charges, tuition, and accommodation—which appeared on each member's quarterly bill.[52] Every quarter a double leaf of the Broad Book was used to record the complexities of domestic outgoings and to calculate what remained as 'increments'. An annual charge of 10*s* 6*d* appeared against the names of the non-resident MAs 'for the single article of writing their names . . . on the books'.[53] Every effort was made to encourage prompt payment by members of College. In 1769 it was decided that a servant's battels should be added to his master's. In 1771 it was agreed that no member could take a degree until all his arrears were paid. By 1778, however, unpaid bills were mounting. Two fellows, Mr Jesse and Mr Davie, were appointed 'to assist the bursars in recovering debts', and any member who did not pay his battels within eight weeks was to have his name 'crossed off the books' by the butler and manciple. Five years later the period of grace was reduced to one month.[54]

Warton once described himself as 'almost constantly involved in the rotation of college offices, some of which are very troublesome'. In the decade 1770–80 he held an office every year: 1770 Dean, 1771 Junior Bursar, 1772 Senior Bursar, 1773 Vice-President, 1774 Dean, 1775 Junior Bursar, 1776 Senior Bursar, 1777 Vice-President, 1778 Junior Bursar, 1779 Senior Bursar, 1780 Vice-President.[55] Such a rigid pattern rendered it inevitable that the junior fellows had to wait their turn before they could expect to hold any office at all. In December 1717 ten fellows and five scholars signed an agreement that the 'profits'

[50] Ibid., ff. 49, 59. The bonds were 'drawn out' of the bank in October 1776; ibid., f. 107. [51] TCA Order Book B, ff. 261, 273.

[52] Joseph Davie, 'Explanation of the bursar's broad book' 1779, TCA Accounts II/C/1.

[53] TCA Order Book B, f. 7.

[54] TCA *Liber Decani* I, f. 29; Order Book B, ff. 27, 127, 183.

[55] *Warton*, ed. Fairer, letter 290, TW to Richard Hurd, 17 January 1772.

*Table 7.1* Elements of a termly battels bill 1779.

| | *Article* | *Details* | *Commoner* | *Gentleman commoner* |
|---|---|---|---|---|
| Battels | Drawer | For sweeping the Hall | 3*d* | 3*d* |
| | Battels | Weekly totals from kitchen and buttery books | variable | variable |
| | Salads | Weekly totals from manciple's salad book | variable | variable |
| | Decrements | Against damages | 2*s* 6*d* | 5*s* |
| | Coal | | 1*s* 3*d* | 1*s* 3*d* |
| Servants wages | Barber | | variable | variable |
| | Bedmaker | | 10*s* | 10*s* |
| | Cook | | 3*s* | 4*s* |
| | Undercook | | 2*s* | 3*s* |
| | Under butler | Paid once in the year | 5*s* | 5*s* |
| | Knives | | 3*s* | 4*s* |
| College and University charges | Garden | | 2*s* 6*d* | 2*s* 6*d* |
| | Common Room | | variable | variable |
| | Lamp | | 1*s* | 1*s* |

| | | | | |
|---|---|---|---|---|
| | Library | Graduates/Undergraduates | 1*s* or 6*d* | 1*s* or 6*d* |
| | Reparations | Buildings maintenance | 4*s* | 6*s* |
| | Lectures | Paid by all under 7 years' standing | 2*s* 6*d* | 2*s* 6*d* |
| | Linen | | | 2*s* 6*d* |
| | Bodleian Library | Graduates only | 1*s* | 1*s* |
| | University Lectures | All under degree of MA or BCL | 6*d* | 6*d* |
| | Arts Culets | All arts students under MA | 2*d* | 2*d* |
| | Law Culets | all 'who have put on a civilian's gown' | 2*d* | 2*d* |
| | Bachelors' gallery | All BAs and BCLs | 6*d* | 6*d* |
| | Clerk of St Mary's | | 1*d* | 1*d* |
| | Prayer Book | one charged to each fresher | | |
| Tuition | Tuition | Payable for 16 terms | 2 gns. | 3 gns. |
| Accommodation | Rooms | Fixed charge, payable to college by all under seven years' standing | 1*s* 8*d* | 1*s* 8*d* |
| | Studies | Remainder of 'room rent' payable to President and senior fellows | variable | variable |
| | Window tax | For every room inhabited | 9*d* | 9*d* |

*Source*: 'Explanation of the bursar's broad book', TCA Accounts II/C/1.

which had 'customarily' been enjoyed by the President and six senior fellows should 'always remain entire to them', and that the junior fellows would revoke all claims to the offices of vice-president, dean, or bursar (although they were still 'deemed capable of being chosen, whenever the electors shall think fit').[56] The junior fellows and scholars who promised to 'use all lawful endeavors to oblige' their successors to commit to this, presumably agreed in anticipation of their future promotion to the exalted senior ranks.

In the same way, the tradition that elected the senior scholars to the fellowship endured almost to the end of the eighteenth century. It was not until seventy years after Charles Bayley had been elected so outrageously out of turn that a new scholar, David Allen, wrote home excitedly to his father, 'the whole college is nearly petrified with astonishment, Mr President and fellows having contrary to all precedent . . . rejected the two senior scholars and elected the third: it makes a wonderful change in our constitution.'[57]

## *College Life*

This was the conservative background against which changes in the Statutes had to be made. In 1734 Benjamin Hoadly (Bishop of Winchester 1734–61) struggled to reconcile common sense with the Visitor's traditional responsibilities. In his heart he supported Thomas Hughes (fellow 1734) who wished to take a degree in medicine rather than study for his BD. 'It might have been for the benefit of the college (if the founder had permitted it),' he mused, 'to have had one or two of the fellows bred up to the study and practice of physic.' But at the same time, the intentions of the founder were very clear, and at first the bishop suggested an uneasy compromise. He would not 'turn him out of his fellowship for not going into orders,' but Hughes must 'be obliged to study so much divinity, as may enable him with credit to perform all the statutable exercises of the college.' But by 1751 Hoadly had further analysed the motives of the Founder, and his views had hardened. 'Now, as every founder is quite a voluntary and arbitrary agent in his own free design,' he declared firmly,

56 TCA *Liber Decani* I, f. 19.

57 Blakiston, *Trinity*, 191. The fellow in question was James Alexander (scholar 1786) who in 1790 pipped both John Robinson (scholar 1784) and Jeremiah Scholefield (scholar 1785, fellow 1794).

> and may found a college for what purposes, and for what professions alone, he pleases . . . and as the founder of Trinity College has sufficiently declared his intention to be to provide for none but artists, priests, and divines . . . This I apprehend to be exactly of the same effect, as if he had said in words, 'They shall all be priests', although there be not college livings enough to provide for them all, and although the number of priests in the world be already more than sufficient: or they shall lose the right of my college.

Hoadley's detailed arguments ran to 'twenty-eight folio pages of paper'—'I am sensible I have been very tedious,' he acknowledged in his accompanying letter. But although he knew his views would be unpopular, his episcopal conscience could not allow him to rule otherwise.

> If I, as visitor, now knowing this . . . should grant a dispensation to anyone who has devoted himself to another profession; I should not but esteem myself . . . a wilful discourager of the observance of the statutes; and guilty of encouraging and authorising the persons thus dispensed with, to eat the bread appointed by the founder for others. This would be, in me, a great iniquity.[58]

The Statute's demands regarding divinity were being observed in a more and more perfunctory manner as the eighteenth century progressed. The Chapel was not the centre of College life that it once had been. In 1758 President Huddesford and the resident fellows lightened their burden of religious duty by drawing up a rota whereby all fellows 'in orders, resident or not, shall take care of the chapel each a week in his turn, by himself or proxy'. In 1770 it was decided that the porter should be paid 5*s* a year 'for taking care of the altar'.[59] Ten years later he was given 'sole care of the chapel and bell'. His daily duties included 'giving notice to the reader . . . a quarter of an hour before the hour of early morning prayers', ringing the bell for late prayers (7.45 a.m.) and evening prayers (5 p.m.) and 'at all times [attending] the chapel during services'. By 1790 the fellows found it necessary to keep a formal record of who was reading the services in Chapel, and the payments they received.[60]

Greater rigour was expected of the undergraduates. The year 1786

58 TCA Register B, ff. 67–8; Visitor I f. 26/71–2.
59 TCA *Liber Decani* I, ff. 24, 29.
60 *Liber Capellanorum A*, TCA College Government VI.3.

saw the institution of 'the imposition of some literary exercise' on all who missed prayers more than twice in a week, although two years later this was relaxed to allow four absences.[61] Some of course were more devout in their religions observations than others. William Legge (Lord Lewisham; second earl of Dartmouth) and Frederick North (Lord North) (noblemen commoners 1748 and 1749) were reputed to have been 'as regular as Great Tom. . . . they never missed early prayers in their college chapel *one* morning, nor any evening when not actually out of Oxford.'[62] Several old members made generous gifts to the Chapel which they had loved as undergraduates: 1770 saw the presentation of fine silk altar hangings and service books—valued variously at £105 and £125—by John Folliott (commoner 1751) and of two very large silver candlesticks—£94—by Thomas Whitby (fellow commoner 1763).[63] But many others shared the fellows' lack of enthusiasm. John Skinner's juvenile verses paint a convincing picture of the agony of wintertime chapel attendance in 1792:

> Now shuffling to the chapel door
> Behind two sloven students more
>   I follow up the aisle.
> Displeased, good natured Chapman stares
> For nearly half done are the prayers,
>   And lessons read meanwhile.
>
> With chattering teeth and noses blue
> We creep together to our pew
>   Responses quavering out;
> So cold is our devotion then
> That by my faith the best of men
>   Scarce know what they're about.
>
> At length the benediction said
> The President he takes the lead
>   And fellows follow fast;
> Scholars and commoners behind
> Precedence, form, nor order mind,
>   The devil catch the last.'[64]

When it came to the Library, the Statutes were patently insufficient.

[61] TCA *Liber Decani* I. ff. 41–2, 45.

[62] *Gentleman's Magazine,* lxviii (1798), 282–3.

[63] TCA *Liber Decani* I f. 28; the Benefactors' Book illustrates the gifts, 96.

[64] Skinner, 'Letters', f. 53.

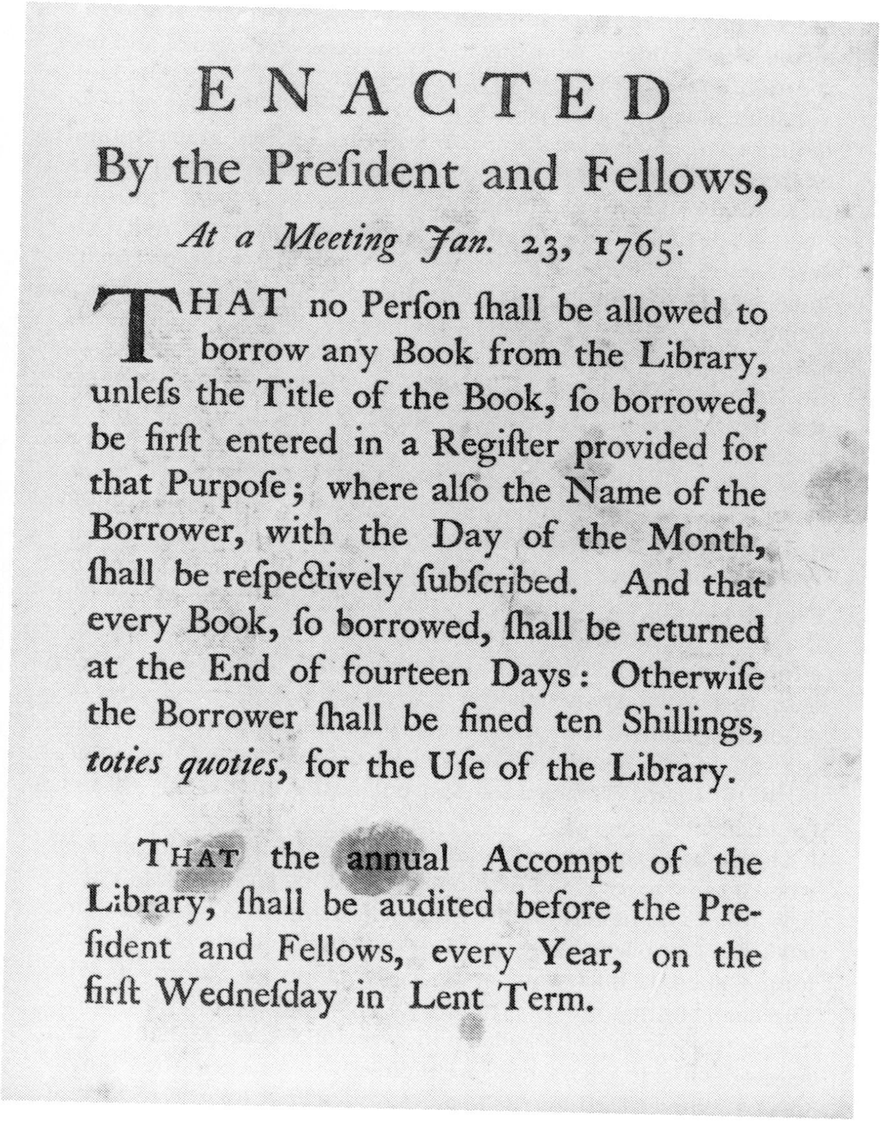

ENACTED

By the Preſident and Fellows,

*At a Meeting Jan.* 23, 1765.

THAT no Perſon ſhall be allowed to borrow any Book from the Library, unleſs the Title of the Book, ſo borrowed, be firſt entered in a Regiſter provided for that Purpoſe; where alſo the Name of the Borrower, with the Day of the Month, ſhall be reſpectively ſubſcribed. And that every Book, ſo borrowed, ſhall be returned at the End of fourteen Days: Otherwiſe the Borrower ſhall be fined ten Shillings, *toties quoties*, for the Uſe of the Library.

THAT the annual Accompt of the Library, ſhall be audited before the Preſident and Fellows, every Year, on the firſt Wedneſday in Lent Term.

*7.5* Library Rules 1765.

In 1763 the Library's care and management were formally given over to the vice-president, who was to see to 'necessary repairs' and use the money received as fines on the purchase of books 'which he himself shall judge most proper'. For these responsibilities he received money charged *pro bibliotheca*, 1*s* from every resident graduate, and 6*d* from every undergraduate member of the College. The Library's main source of income remained the income from Rand's 1640 bequest. Some dozen or so volumes were purchased each year, and there was regular expenditure on routine cleaning and upkeep. Library Rules were drawn up in 1765, and printed copies distributed (Plate 7.5). In 1771 and 1783 shelf lists of the Library were compiled, and in 1783 a borrowing register was put in place.[65] The most famous user was, of course, Samuel Johnson, who stayed in Kettell Hall and found the Library so conducive to work, he declared, 'If I come to live at Oxford, I shall take up my abode at Trinity.'[66] As a token of his thanks, he presented a fine edition of Virgil set in Baskerville type. The Library was now one of the last surviving links with Trinity's earliest history, and it had a strong antiquarian appeal. In 1767 William Huddesford (fellow 1757) wrote a detailed description of the painted glass in the windows.[67] A reasonable innovation in 1788 was the use of the Library permitted to 'scholars of two years' standing,' although, as a pencil note in the Junior Bursar's Order Book makes clear, this was 'in gross violation of the statute'. Two years later, a decision was made that undergraduate commoners of two years' standing should also be admitted to the Library 'on paying one guinea to the librarian'. This was crossed out firmly in ink, but without comment.[68]

The Statutes governing the scholars were particularly impractical when it came to residence requirements. Having taken their MA, they had little to do besides waiting for a fellowship to fall vacant. Some left Trinity for places at other colleges where the elections were open: John Gilbert (scholar 1713) was elected fellow of Merton in 1716; Thomas Huntingford (1769) fellow of New College in 1773; Francis Meade (1778) fellow of Magdalen in 1784; and George Richards (1785) fellow of Oriel in 1790. Others went directly to careers in the Church. In 1701 Samuel Farthing (scholar 1696) departed for the rectory of Crowcombe, Somerset, and Cornelius Belgrave (1697) left to become

[65] TCA *Liber Decani* I, f. 25–25d. TCA Library: Rules: E/1; Shelf lists B/3–5; Borrowing register C/1.

[66] Quoted by Thomas Warton, *Boswell's Life of Johnson* (Globe ed., London, 1893), 90.

[67] TCA OF 6/1.

[68] TCA Order Book B, ff. 215, 231.

rector of North Kilworth in Leicestershire. Henry Dodwell (1760) resigned in 1766, and spent the next fifty years as rector of Harlaxton and Colsterworth in Leicestershire. More commonly, graduate scholars augmented their stipends by taking jobs as curates while they waited anxiously for a fellowship at Trinity. Even interpreting the Statutes' limit on absences (no more than twenty days each year) as a requirement to return to the College every twenty days to renew one's leave, this was still a costly, time-consuming, and, in winter, uncomfortable burden. As Thomas Warton put it, 'a scholarship but half maintains / and college rules are heavy chains.'[69]

The crux of the problem was the Statutes' unrealistic demands, and in 1768 five scholars, all MAs, petitioned the Visitor, John Thomas, for relief. Their complaint was bitter:

> it seems evident the Founder did not in the least foresee the present slowness of succession in his college, nor the . . . inconveniences and hardships, because the most particular directions which are laid down in the statutes for the succession of scholars to fellowships relate to, and suppose the succession of bachelors to the said fellowships; the succession of scholars of the degree of master of arts being mentioned there as a casual and unlikely case.

Nor had Thomas Pope planned for 'not only the *slow* but the *uncertain* succession to fellowships' which made it all the more imperative that they should 'have every opportunity given them of forming such connections as shall seem most likely to conduce to their future advantage in case they should be disappointed in their views at college'. President Huddesford lent his support with a declaration that he and the fellows were 'thoroughly convinced of the reasonableness of this petition'. The Bishop's reply was 'in the affirmative'. He was inclined to allow absences of up to forty days for the scholars, and a corresponding extension from forty days to six months for the fellows.[70]

In 1791 President Chapman (who twenty-three years before had been the senior petitioning scholar) seized an opportunity to make the case for even more protracted absences: up to a year for fellows; up to three fellows (with 'especial' permission) allowed 'to leave the kingdom'. The Visitor, Brownlow North, acquiesced meekly; he was himself in Rome when the petition eventually reached him, and

[69] Thomas Warton, 'The Progress of Discontent', in *Poetical Works of the Late Thomas Warton*, ed. Richard Mant (Oxford, 1802), ii, 193.

[70] TCA Register C, ff. 78–80.

about to depart on a trip to Naples 'to which place you will direct, if further occasion require'.[71]

Junior fellows who stayed in residence were often forced to endure a state of considerable under-employment in the College, with neither an office to perform nor pupils to teach. The majority of new undergraduates were allocated to their tutor by the President; to be a tutor became de facto another college office. In 1720 nine of fifteen undergraduates admitted were taught by George Shepheard; in 1740 thirteen pupils were divided between four fellows; by 1760 there were just two tutors, Thomas Warton and Harry Parker. There were three in 1780, but John Filkes taught five out of eight men admitted. Fellows who were in holy orders regularly found second jobs as clergymen. In return for the parish income they undertook some parochial work and employed a curate to perform the rest. Warton was delighted to be offered the rectory of Kiddington in 1771, and was the enthusiastic author of *Specimen of a Parochial History of Oxfordshire: Kiddington* (1781).[72] But he never had any intention of actually serving the parish himself. In 1788 he wrote bluntly to his curate, W. F. Mavor, 'I presume you have no objection to the old terms of half a guinea per Sunday. In case of a burial on weekdays (a very rare case) you will please to charge me a crown each time. Fees for a marriage, etc, are to be your own. You will please to begin on next Sunday.'[73]

Another option was a life largely of idleness. The Scottish professor, Andrew Dalzel, accompanied an aristocratic young pupil, Lord Maitland, to Trinity in the summer of 1775. Although he appreciated the open friendship and convivial welcome of the common room, he was shocked how 'very little study goes on at Oxford except among a few book-worms that shut themselves up, and do not associate with others.' His only first-hand experience of 'the English Universities' was his few months at Trinity, and he was later to condemn the way that 'dissipation, idleness, drinking, and gambling are also to be learned there. [They] are huge masses of magnificence and form, but ill calculated to promote the cause of science or of liberal inquiry.'[74] The generally hard-working Thomas Warton certainly en-

[71] Ibid., f. 82.

[72] 'You will be surprised to see my account of so small a village take up three large quarto paper books' Warton wrote to John Price on 13 October 1781; *Warton*, ed. Fairer, no. 398.

[73] Ibid., no. 544, TW to W. F. Mavor 28 January 1788.

[74] Dalzel, *History of the University of Edinburgh*, i, 14.

joyed regular lapses: in 1773 he admitted cheerfully to his friend, Bodley's Librarian John Price, 'What with turtle-eating, claret-drinking, etc etc, I was so dissipated and hurried when I left Oxford that I had not time to call upon you, nor to do many things which I ought to have attended to.'[75] Warton's biographer, Richard Mant (scholar 1795), considered that although Warton's 'panegyric on Oxford Ale' was 'a burlesque', nevertheless his 'fondness for ale and tobacco, the subjects of his muse, was by no means feigned'. Warton spent many an evening in 'pot-house snug', and liked of a morning 'to repair / to friendly buttery; there on smoking crust / and foaming ale to banquet unrestrained / material breakfast!' Indeed, as he also observed, 'Nor less by day delightful is thy draught / All-powerful ale! whose sorrow-soothing sweets / oft I repeat in vacant afternoons.'[76]

More than half of Trinity's eighteenth-century fellows ended their lives as parochial clergy. Warton was rather the exception in having no wish to remove himself from Trinity in this way. But he well understood the frustrations endured by many of his colleagues:

> These fellowships are pretty things,
> We live indeed like petty kings:
> But who can bear to waste his whole age
> Amid the dullness of a college,
> Debarred the common joys of life,
> And that prime bliss—a loving wife!
> O! What's a table richly spread,
> Without a woman at its head!
> Would some snug benefice but fall,
> Ye feasts, ye dinners, farewell all!
> To offices I'd beg adieu,
> Of dean, vice-pres.—of bursar too;
> Come joys, that rural quiet yields,
> Come, tythes, and house, and fruitful fields![77]

The eighteenth century saw a significant shift in the expectations of Trinity's fellows, who now felt that the College had a responsibility to provide them with livings. At the time of the foundation Trinity had owned three advowsons: Garsington in Oxfordshire, and Navestock and Great Waltham, both in Essex. Garsington was the preserve of the President, who might appoint one of the fellows or

[75] *Warton*, ed. Fairer, letter 301, TW to John Price, 16 August 1773.

[76] Thomas Warton, 'A Penegyric on Oxford Ale', *Poetical Works*, ii, 181n., 185–6.

[77] Thomas Warton, 'The Progress of Discontent', *Poetical Works*, ii, 194.

*Table 7.2* Eighteenth-century livings.

| *Benefice* | *Population and value*[1] | *When and how acquired* | *Incumbents (date elected to fellowship)* | *Date of incumbency* |
|---|---|---|---|---|
| Vicarage of Navestock, Essex | 623 | Foundation endowment | Samuel Lord (1702) | 1703–1724 |
| | | | Charles Bayley (1721) | 1725–1734/5 |
| | £13 3*s* 9*d* | | Thomas Bell (1708) | 1735–1763 |
| | | | Thomas Chapman (1742) | 1763–1788 |
| | | | Joseph Davie (1774) | 1788–1792 |
| | | | John Filkes (1776) | 1792–1830 |
| Vicarage of Great Waltham, Essex | 1475 | Foundation endowment | Henry Oborne (scholar 1689) | 1703–1721 |
| | | | Edward Cranke (1700) | 1721 |
| | £18 13*s* 4*d* | | Nicholas Tindal (Exeter College 1707) | 1721–1740 |
| | | | Francis Seely (1729) | 1740–1755 |
| | | | William Burrough (1741) | 1755–1797 |
| | | | George Somers Clarke (1781) | 1797–1837 |
| Rectory of Rotherfield Greys, Oxon. | 677 | 1687 gift of Thomas Rowney (former steward of the college manors) | Henry Barker (1684) | 1720–1740 |
| | | | Thomas Wilkes (1702) | 1740–1745 |
| | £10 12*s* $8^1/_2$ *d* | | Francis Wise (1718) | 1745–1767 |
| | | | Harry Parker (1741) | 1767–1782 |
| | | | William Townsend (1762) | 1782–1785 |
| | | | Richard Hele (1767) | 1785–1802 |
| | | | John Bankes Moulding (1781) | 1802–1814 |

| | | | | |
|---|---|---|---|---|
| Rectory of Oddington-on-Otmoor, Oxon. | 158 | 1700 Gift of Ralph Bathurst | John Bruere (1732) | 1746–1777 |
| | | | Gilbert Parker (1747) | 1777–1795 |
| | £12 16*s* $^{1}/_{2}$ *d* | | William Flamank (1777) | 1795–1817 |
| Rectory of Barton-on-the-Heath, Warwicks. | 137 | 1704 Purchased | John Rodd (1731) | 1743–1782 |
| | | | James Wilmot (1752) | 1782–1807 |
| | £12 17*s* 11*d* | | Jeremiah Scholefield (1794) | 1808–1846 |
| Rectory of Farnham, Essex | 330 | 1728 Bequest of Richard Hale (1689) | Barnard Peisley (1715)[2] | 1727–1738 |
| | | | James Read (1715) | 1738–1745 |
| | £23 8*s* 9*d* | | Henry Yardley (1731) | 1745–1756 |
| | | | Nathaniel Geering (1733) | 1756–1785 |
| | | | Charles Jesse (1773) | 1785–1793 |
| | | | Thomas Wisdom (1776) | 1794–1825 |
| | | | William Greenhill (1798) | 1825–1849 |
| Perpetual curacy of Hill Farrance | 438 | 1732 Bequest of John Geale (scholar 1702) | Harry Parker (1741) | 1743–1782 |
| | | | Thomas Warton (1752) | 1782–1790 |
| | *n/a* | | John Bankes Moulding (1781) | 1790–1793 |
| | | | Charles Jesse (1773) | 1793–1820 |

*Notes*: 1 As published in the 1810 University Calendar; 2 Peisley was presented to the living by Richard Hale.

*Source*: TCA College Registers.

scholars to a curacy (Bathurst appointed Roger Almont);[78] the other two when they fell vacant were offered in turn to the twelve fellows, according to their seniority. By 1732 the number of livings available to Trinity fellows had risen to seven, and of seventy-six eighteenth-century fellows, twenty-eight resigned their fellowships to take one. Eleven fellows left for non-Trinity parishes.

The new livings came to Trinity by a variety of means, largely in response to the evident need. In the decades following the Restoration, the religious conflict between the government and the University's Anglican leaders had led to a sharp decline in the number of livings becoming available to Oxford clerics, and thus a considerable rise in the average tenure of Oxford fellowships.[79] With his characteristically practical approach, in 1700 Ralph Bathurst purchased the advowson of Oddington to help meet this deficiency; and four years later, the College itself invested £360 in the living of Barton-on-the-Heath.[80] The rectories of Rotherfield Greys and Farnham, and the perpetual curacy of Hill Farrance, all came to Trinity by the goodwill of men with first-hand knowledge of college life. Hill Farrance did not at first provide more than a small second income, and was held pluralistically by Harry Parker, Thomas Warton, and John Moulding. In 1793, the stipend was augmented by £105 per annum, taken from the increase in the great tithes from Navestock. Great Waltham became a better prospect in 1740, after Francis Seely spent £120 of his own money and £80 of the College's on renovating the house.[81]

It was impossible to predict when each living would fall vacant; most commonly this occurred when an incumbent died. Oddington and Barton were both in the College's gift for forty years before the first presentations could be made. Many Trinity rectors and vicars were long-lived: John Rodd held Barton for thirty-nine years, John Filkes held Navestock for thirty-eight, and Nathaniel Geering Farnham for twenty-nine. Twenty-year incumbencies were common. But a few fellows waited for a remarkably short time before receiving a living: Samuel Lord was presented to Navestock after a single year in his fellowship, and Charles Bayley succeeded to the same living after just four years in his (Thomas Wilkes having turned it

[78] *Hearne* I, 153. With characteristic spite, Hearne interpreted this as Bathurst's solution to the problem of Almont's 'notoriously' poor tutorial skills.

[79] G. V. Bennett 'Against the Tide: Oxford under William III', *HUO* 5, 31, 34–5. The economic depression exacerbated this shortage by rendering some livings uneconomic.

[80] TCA Benefactors' Book III, 11; Title Deeds Barton on the Heath, 3–6.

[81] TCA Register B, f. 83.

down). The average wait, however, was nineteen years, and the uncertain succession was a constant source of tension. In 1778 the fellows agreed that having accepted a living, a man could resign it for another that became vacant within the year. He would have the same period of grace to return to his fellowship, but only if he undertook to 'give up all right and claim to any college living' in the future. In 1785 Charles Jesse was given unique dispensation to accept Farnham for one month 'with an intention of ascertaining the value thereof' and without losing the right to take another. In the event he held Farnham until 1793, when he resigned it to take the newly augmented Hill Farrance.[82]

Fellows whose influential friends and families could present them to livings outside the College list were fortunate, especially if they were eager to marry. The tale of William Benwell (scholar 1784) is especially poignant. While still a scholar (in December 1788) Benwell became engaged to Penelope, the daughter of his friend and patron, John Loveday of Caversham. Learning that his love for Pen was reciprocated was to William 'the dearest discovery in the world', but, as the impoverished curate of Sonning in Berkshire, he could see no immediate prospect of marriage. In 1790 he was elected fellow of Trinity, and the following year appointed the College's lecturer in Greek. William devoted himself to his Trinity pupils—characterized by John Skinner as 'meek Benwell . . . with manners mild / and heart as pure as nursing child'[83]—and waited patiently for a suitable parish or other employment. In August 1793 he stood for the under-mastership of Winchester College, but lost out to an old boy of the school. Four months later his hopes were raised by the offer of a university living, that of Hale Magna in Lincolnshire, only to be cruelly dashed when he realized that the parish income would never support a wife and family. William Benwell accepted Hale, but continued to teach at Trinity, while another eighteen months went by.

At last, in June 1795, he received from a family friend the offer of the rectory of Chilton in Suffolk, and the news that he would be able to take possession the following March. On 20 June 1796, Pen wrote in her diary, 'I was married to my dearly loved Mr Benwell, after a great many years of uninterrupted and strong attachment. We could neither of us scarcely persuade ourselves that it was really at length to be.' In his diary William wrote a prayer: 'May God in his infinite mercy bless our union and grant us very long the sustaining comfort

[82] TCA Order Book B, ff. 147–9, 195.

[83] Skinner, 'Letters', ff. 265, 267.

of each other's society and affection.' The loving couple spent two weeks on honeymoon, then they travelled to the Loveday family, resident at Milton, Oxfordshire, and found the parish in the grip of a typhus epidemic. The ever conscientious William 'rightly felt it was incumbent on him to visit the sick'. He succumbed to the fever on 28 August, and on 6 September he died. William Benwell's final words were a request that his friend John Hind should be given the 'splendid edition of Addison's works which had been given to him by Trinity College'.[84]

The atmosphere in the Trinity common room was not always harmonious. Some disputes between the fellows went on for years, and an uncongenial member, once elected, could be difficult to remove. Richard Hedges (fellow 1720), for example, was in dispute with his colleagues for more than five years. Accusations made against Hedges included financial misconduct and neglect of the divinity disputations, besides 'calumny, drunkenness and profaneness'. Hedges considered that he had been unfairly deprived of holding the office of bursar; Huddesford, on the other hand, declared him to be 'by no means an unexceptionable candidate . . . he having by his intemperance and idleness incurred so many debts that his fellowship was then under a sequestration for the satisfaction of his creditors.' Hedges accused the President of forcing him to sign a false confession, and of depriving him of his commons excessively. Huddesford insisted that Hedges had been 'treated with candour and tenderness'. The situation was further complicated by the tragic scandal of 1728, when a Trinity graduate, Robert Jennens (first order, 1722) had committed suicide, his mind seemingly disturbed by the deistic views of his college friend Nicholas Stevens (probationary fellow 1728), whose letters, critical of orthodox Christianity, were found in Jennens's desk. Stevens resigned and went abroad, taking with him another member of the College.[85] Now, claimed Hedges hysterically, the President was also charging him with 'favouring the heretical opinions of Mr Stevens'. Hedges first appealed to the Visitor, Richard Willis, in March 1727; in August 1732 the Bishop sent a final declaration of his

[84] Sarah Markham, *A Testimony of her Times* (Salisbury, 1990), 8–22. Addison's works, also Bacon's, were presented to Benwell in 1787, in recognition of his winning two university prizes (TCA Order Book B, f. 211). In 1808 John Hind became Pen's second husband, when, after 24 years as a fellow, he finally succeeded to a Magdalen College living (Markham, *Testimony*, 82).

[85] V. H. H. Green, 'Religion in the Colleges 1715–1800', *HUO* 5, 435–6.

expulsion, backdated to February. When it was all over, numerous documents were transcribed carefully into the College Register, while one of Hedges's friends wrote to congratulate him on his 'deliverance from a nest of villains'.[86]

The most disruptive malcontent of the eighteenth century was the obsessive and depressive George Somers Clarke (scholar 1774, fellow 1781). By the time of his first appearance in the extant records, Clarke must already have been deeply unpopular among his colleagues. In May 1784 he dispatched a long and detailed complaint to the Visitor, appealing generally against 'partiality' in the college administration and a 'spirit of repression' in the College, and at the same time bringing a direct challenge to the legality of Joseph Davie's fellowship.[87] On 29 September 1784, the dean noted that Clarke had been deprived of his commons for refusing to appear before the President 'on statutable business', but that on 27 October he had humbly 'made a submission' and been restored. Four years later, Clarke appealed against Davie again, also against Warton, on the grounds that they had not taken their BD. When, in 1792, Clarke was himself dean, he took the opportunity of 'tearing out two leaves pertaining to him' from the book. The crime was discovered a year later, and Clarke was 'censured . . . & declared an improper person to be entrusted hereafter with any college office'. A further humiliation was the knowledge that the missing pages were rewritten by his old enemy Joseph Davie.[88] When in 1797 President Chapman presented Clarke to the college living of Great Waltham, did he feel any compunction on behalf of the parishioners?[89]

## *Undergraduate Life*

What, meanwhile, of the undergraduates? Across the University, the eighteenth century saw a steady decline in the admissions of all classes of commoners. There were many reasons for this. It was

[86] TCA Register C, ff. 1–7; Visitor I, f. 25/69, G. Williams to RH.

[87] TCA Visitor I f. 95/147. [88] TCA *Liber Decani* I, ff. 50d–52.

[89] Clarke was vicar of Great Waltham until his death in 1837, although from 1824 he resided in Chelmsford Gaol for contempt of the consistory court. The story of his tragic disintegration from conscientious parish priest to deranged parish liability is told in Michael Beale 'George Somers Clarke—a Perverse Spirit', *Essex Journal*, 30 (1995), 20–4, 56–61.

harder for young men of lower social backgrounds to win scholarships and fellowships, because places on college foundations were now becoming an attractive option for those higher up the social scale. Similarly poorer graduates, who had no influential friends, were struggling to find worthwhile career opportunities in the Church. The increasing affluence and inherent expense of College life was another deterrent to poorer families, who saw little prospect of financial return from investing in their sons' education.[90] This rise in the social status of Trinity's fellows and clergymen can be seen in the career of Harry Parker (grandson of a baronet) who entered as a commoner in 1731 and was elected to a scholarship two years later and a fellowship in 1741. He held both the college living of Rotherfield Greys (from 1667), also the nearby living of Glympton (from 1676), until his death in 1782, not finding it necessary to resign from either when he succeeded to the baronetcy.

At the aristocratic end of the social scale, university education was also less attractive than it had been in former centuries. The traditional emphasis on the importance of intellectual polish conferred by knowledge of classical literature was declining in relation to the perceived need for social skills and elegant accomplishments. Moreover, it was increasingly feared that undergraduates risked being not only debauched by lax discipline and riotous living, but also corrupted by the subversive political ideas of their tutors. [91] Trinity was known for its 'extreme Toryism',[92] which inevitably carried a dangerous taint of Jacobitism. William Pitt (1727) studied at Trinity for little more than a year. In 1754 he condemned Oxford passionately in the House of Commons, describing how he had seen 'what would have been high treason anywhere else. He saw and heard, but this last summer, several persons of rank and standing in the University walk publicly along the streets singing God bless Great J our King.' Pitt claimed to have seen pictures of the Pretender in shop windows, and 'the very streets,' he said, 'were paved with Jacobitism.'[93] Whether this was true or not was hardly material. William Pitt seemed to believe it, and he sent his son to Cambridge.

By the last decade of the century, the revolution in France was bringing different anxieties to bear. One Trinity commoner, sympa-

[90] Stone, 'Oxford Student Body', 40. [91] Ibid., 49–50, 55.
[92] G. V. Bennett, 'University, Society and Church 1688–1714', *HUO* 5, 381.
[93] Oxford, Exeter College, Bray MSS, R Blacow–T Bray, 3 December 1754.

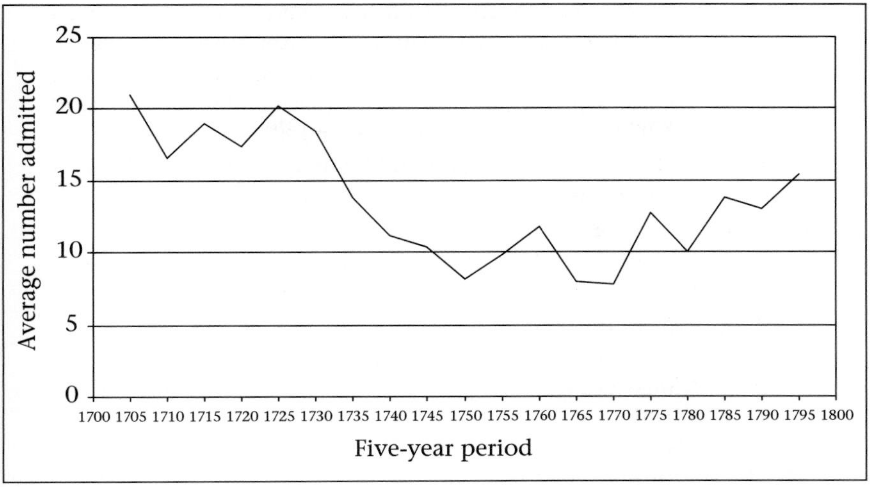


*Fig. 7.1* Eighteenth-century admissions.

*Source*: TCA Admissions Registers.

thetic to the extreme politics abroad, was Walter Savage Landor (1793) 'notorious as a mad Jacobin'. Landor was a brilliant scholar, but outspoken and rebellious. As a freshman he had refused to conform with the custom of wearing powdered wigs to dinner. '"Take care", said my tutor, "they will stone you for a republican." The Whigs (not the wigs) were then unpopular; but I stuck to my plain hair and queue tied with black ribbon.' [94]

Between 1741 and 1770 Trinity admitted an average of just nine undergraduates a year, and numbers in residence remained low throughout the century. From 1754 a Room Register was kept, which tells of empty rooms throughout the College. Many gentlemen commoners took second rooms for their servants, which was of course another expense.[95] The political danger of Oxford may have been exaggerated in the minds of anxious parents, but they had no shortage of evidence for the high cost of university life. William Pitt wrote home in April 1727 to explain his 'wild and boundless' battels bill, which he attributed not 'to my extravagance, but to the custom of

[94] Robert Southey to Humphry Davy, John Forster, *The Life and Works of Walter Savage Landor* (London, 1976), i, 29.

[95] TCA Room Register A.

this place; where we pay for most things at a too high rate.' His case was made plausible by the letters sent by his tutor, Joseph Stockwell, hinting that 'several young gentlemen of Mr Pitt's gown have besides made the college a present of a piece of plate of £10 or £12,' and advising that it was 'customary and creditable to a gentleman of family to be attended by a footman.'[96] Pitt's account for the first Quarter of 1727 was as follows:

| | £ | s | d |
|---|---|---|---|
| Battels | 15 | 0 | 0 |
| Lambert his wages | 4 | 4 | 0 |
| Three months learning French and Entrance | 2 | 2 | 0 |
| For a Course of Experimental philosophy | 2 | 2 | 0 |
| For coat & breeches & making | 5 | 18 | 0 |
| Booksellers bill | 5 | 0 | 0 |
| Cambrick for ruffles | 1 | 4 | 0 |
| Shoes, stockings | 1 | 19 | 0 |
| Candles, coal, faggots | 3 | 10 | 0 |
| Pocket money, gloves, powder, tea etc. | 4 | 4 | 0 |
| For washing | 2 | 2 | 0[97] |

In 1760 Brownlow North made earnest efforts to disguise his overspending, when he wrote to his father:

> I have received both your letters about coming to town; But I find I have misunderstood you about the Quarter Day. I imagined those twenty guineas were to last me till Lady Day, & then that we were to begin our regular quarters, & accordingly calculated them to to last til Tuesday next. I have therefore but a few shillings remaining. But if you remember, you gave me five guineas to set me up in some necessaries. There is almost a guinea & half remaining of that, which if you will give me leave to borrow of you, & pay me at the quarter day, I can come up.[98]

Trinity made regular attempts to restrain the behaviour of the junior members. In 1788 the dean noted a new schedule of penalties to be imposed 'upon any undergraduate he shall find intoxicated':

| | |
|---|---|
| The first offence— | Translation [into Latin] of 'a paper in the *Spectator*.' |

[96] Stanley Ayling, *The Elder Pitt, Earl of Chatham* (London, 1973), 30–2.
[97] Lord Roseberry, *Chatham, His Early Life and Connections* (London, 1922), 544–5.
[98] Bod. Lib. MS North, d. 23, f. 111.

| | |
|---|---|
| Second offence— | Translation of a sermon |
| Third offence— | Two sermons |
| fourth offence— | Confinement to college for a week, strict attendance in hall and chapel, two sermons to be translated, 200 'lines to be repeated'. |
| Fifth offence— | Father or friend to be informed. |
| Sixth offence— | Rustication for four terms [i.e. one year].[99] |

A year later, undergraduates were forbidden to 'give dinner or supper' without their tutor's written permission.[100] Wine drinking was by now a well-established habit in the College. In 1752 the system of licensing retailers was abolished, and Oxford had a thriving direct trade, dominated by the wholesale vaults around Carfax, inns, and coffee-houses.[101] Trinity was also laying down its own wine, which was being drunk in hall dinner, in the common room, and in members' rooms. There were large cellars beneath the new kitchen, and small, lockable, private vaults in the cellars beneath the Garden Quadrangle. Warton identified the management of the wine cellar as one of the pleasures of an Oxford fellowship:

When calm around the common room
I puff'd my daily pipe's perfume!
Rode for a stomach, and inspected,
At annual bottlings, corks selected.[102]

In 1792 later the dean came down heavily on Alexander Colstone (1789) and Stawell Chudleigh (1791) who 'having intoxicated themselves' went on to destroy 'a silver tankard and a silver pepper-box'. Not only were they required to replace the broken items, they were gated for two weeks, during which time they had to be constant in Hall and Chapel and deliver a 'daily exercise' to the reader of prayers, and they were also to lose (i.e. delay taking their degree for) one term.[103]

The most humiliating punishment in the College's armoury was to enforce a public apology in Hall. In March 1779 William Matthews (1775) stood up and said:

[99] TCA *Liber Decani* I, f. 46. [100] Ibid., f. 49.

[101] Fay Banks, *Wine Drinking in Oxford 1640–1850*, BAR British Series 257 (1997), 1.

[102] Warton, 'The Progress of Discontent', *Poetical Works*, ii, 197.

[103] TCA *Liber Decani* I, f. 50.

> the displeasure of my superiors has been justly provoked by my reciting in this place a ludicrous declamation, containing a passage so palpably obscene as not even to shun detection under the disguise of ingenuity. It has been judged impossible for anyone to be so ignorant as to recite this passage without comprehending the drift and purport of it. Now I cannot but be conscious that [this] is a crime to which no punishment is adequate.

Then it was the turn of Henry Boulter (1777), who began:

> In no circumstances does obscenity admit of any defence, but to design or even hazard the publication of it before our superiors is an aggravation of a crime enormous in its own nature. Impressed with a due sense of this reflection & conscious of having unguardedly violated the laws of decency by inserting a ridiculous & obscene sentence in a late declamation, I am obliged in this public manner to express my regret for such an impudent proceeding . . . I have nothing left but to submit myself to their clemency.

The sentence on both miscreants was 'loss' of one term, plus confinement to College, constant attendance in Hall and Chapel, and delivery of a weekly exercise to the dean, which was to continue until Trinity Monday, some three months away.[104]

The earliest picture of the Hall interior is a sketch by the watercolourist J. H. Pyne, who accompanied Skinner's friend, Dawson Warren, to Trinity in 1801. The panelling and plaster ceiling date from 1774, as does the painting of the arms of Queen Mary and Philip of Spain over the fireplace. In a prominent position stands the 'griffin lectern', which was presented by Richard Beckford, the college butler, in 1723, as a focus for the daily *narrare* recitation (Plate 7.6). The lectern cost a remarkable £66 (of which Beckford contributed £50), an indication of the status of the senior college servants.[105] When performed well, the *narrare* received 'just applause'; at other times the nervous or diffident 'gownsman' would resort to reading from a text concealed in his cap. Skinner relates an amusing breakdown in

[104] TCA *Liber Decani* I, ff. 34d–36. 'Loss of a term' meant in effect a delay of a term before taking the BA.

[105] Clare Hopkins 'The Beckford Lectern', *Report* (1998), 57–60. Traditionally known as the 'griffin' (as in Thomas Pope's and Trinity's coat of arms), the lectern is in fact a double-headed dragon (Thomas Pope's and Trinity's crest). There is nowhere to rest a book, because the *narrare* was a recitation, not a reading exercise.

*7.6* The Hall interior and Beckford lectern, by Dawson Warren, 1801.

junior–senior relations when a novice's inept performance incurred the displeasure of the corpulent vice-president John Moulding.

And here en passant, I will state
A dialogue we heard of late
Betwixt Vice-Pres and chap,
Who, not a friend to spouting, stood
At Griffin's head in surly mood,
The verses in his cap.

But not being able to see well
To read them there, much less to spell,
He silent kept his place.
Silent meanwhile were gownsmen all,
At least five minutes in the Hall,
Full staring in his face.

He, blessed with impudence enough
Now smiled, now looked grim and gruff,
At verses now would peep;
Now with cap tassel he would play,
Now turn his body quite away
From where the fellows keep.

Moulding, vice-pres, with visage round
As is a cheese of twenty pound
Or moon in harvest week,
Than those not boasting more pretence
To features emanating sense,
At length began to squeak:

Why, why, you stupid fellow, why
Are you thus silent, and not try
Your tongue for to unloose?
Better behaviour, Sir, I beg,
You stand as foolish on one leg,
As any silly goose.

This sharp reproof when Freshman heard
A moment at fat Moulding stared
Not knowing what to do.
But slow returning to his seat
He spluttered out in rage and heat,
I ain't more goose than you.[106]

The harshest punishment that could be inflicted was expulsion. One of Trinity's most famous alumni to be sent down was Walter Savage Landor, whose tutor, William Benwell, allegedly 'shed tears when his favourite pupil was obliged to quit the college'.[107] The obligation to quit was self-imposed, and brought about by an act of drunken aristocratic hauter: he incurred the penalty not for shooting at another undergraduate across the Garden Quadrangle, but for not owning up like a gentleman.

> In the morning I had been a-shooting; in the evening I invited a party to wine. In the room opposite there lived a man universally laughed at and despised . . . and it unfortunately happened that he had a party on the same day, consisting of servitors and other raffs of every description. The weather was warm, and the windows were open. The consequence was that those who were in my room began

[106] Skinner, 'Letters', ff. 69, 71.

[107] Forster, *Walter Savage Landor*, 26.

> rowing those in his, who very soon retorted. All the time I was only a spectator . . . but my gun was lying on another table in the room. I had in my back closet some little shot, and I proposed, as they had closed the casements, and the shutters were on the outside to fire a volley. It was thought a good trick; and according I went into my bedroom and fired. Soon the president sent a servant to inform me that Mr Leeds had complained of a gun being fired from the room in which I entertained my company, but he could not tell by whom. So that he insisted on knowing from me, and making me liable to the punishment.[108]

Gun ownership was tolerated throughout the century. Dogs, equally necessary to the sporting activities of young gentlemen, were considered a nuisance, however, and the College tried hard to ban them, or at least, to restrict their ownership to only the wealthiest members. In 1778 the fellows agreed that the porter could 'sconce every gentleman one shilling for his own use whose dog shall be seen in the college, and this as often as their dogs appear within the iron gates'.[109] Only in December 1800 were undergraduates banned from keeping firearms or gunpowder in their rooms, and 'every person detected in so doing, or bringing any in' was to be fined 5*s* and 'severely imposed by the Dean'.[110]

## *College Servants*

From 1776 the gentlemen commoners had their own common room, on the ground floor of Staircase 5 (today's surgery).[111] The following year it was found necessary to raise their caution money (set at £21 in 1770) to £30, and expressly to forbid individuals from hosting dinners or 'entertainments' in the Hall or common room 'on any occasion or pretence whatever'. Those of three years' standing could remove to the fellows' common room; BAs meanwhile gained their own common room above the buttery.[112] The new common room had its own servant, as did the majority of its individual members.

[108] Ibid., 32–3. Forster's opinion is that Landor would have returned, but for financial difficulties.

[109] TCA *Liber Decani*, f. 32.

[110] To 'be imposed' was to be set written work. Ibid., f. 62. A later interlineation hints at a defence attempted by some undergraduate lawyer: 'or carrying any out'.

[111] TCA Order Book B, f. 93.

[112] Ibid., ff. 29, 113, 115, 121.

Their scouts, or bedmakers, although employed directly by the young men whom they served, were now coming under college control. From 1777 a 'master' was required to exhibit in the bursary a 'written character from [his servant's] last place'. In 1784 it was agreed to fix their wages at 12*s* per quarter; four years later it was ordered that 'no females be employed as bedmakers, or servants, in the college; and that all servants depart the college before ten at night'.[113]

Other college staff were being brought similarly under the College's direction. In 1775 the Junior Bursar noted that 'in lieu of perquisites' the two cooks were to receive annual salaries of £80 and £50, and the 'kitchen man' £2 above his present wages. Within four years, however, this decision was revised to restore an element of incentive, with salaries set at £50 and £40, and a 'gratuity' of up to £10, payable quarterly at the rate of 'fifty shillings then allowed or disallowed as their conduct shall have merited'. In 1781 the manciple was allotted an annual stipend of £50.[114] Rarely do we know the names of the college servants at this date. One exception was the butler, Richard Beckford, and another was Richard Bradley, 'for fifty years servant of Trinity College', whose portrait was engraved by Albert Hoffay in 1826.

John Skinner's verses reveal just how heavily dependent on servants even the ordinary commoners now were. On a winter morning, Skinner is roused simultaneously by the College bell and by his scout who brings a light and puts out his breeches and great coat. By the time he returns from prayers there is a fire blazing in his rooms and water boiling in a kettle. He washes and shaves, and at half-past eight sits down with a friend to a leisurely private breakfast of hot rolls, brown bread and butter, tea with sugar and cream, all delivered from the buttery. After a morning spent reading, walking, and skating, they hurry back to college to have their hair dressed and powdered by the college's high-speed 'highland barber, far-famed Duff'. After dinner, Skinner takes his turn to host dessert for a dozen or so friends from both inside and outside the College. He provides the port, but each guest has his own account with 'a wily fruiterer called Baloon'. Ignoring the bell for evening chapel, 'time quickly passes, mirth and song do not the heavy hours prolong,' and the young men drink and doze around the fire until nine. Then the scout reappears, bearing supper trays of 'boiled fowl, salt herrings, sausages / cold beef,

[113] TCA Order Book B, ff. 111, 189, 221.

[114] Ibid., ff. 91, 151, 175.

and brawn, and bread and cheese / with tankards full of ale'. The uneaten remains are his perquisite,

> although in some respects he earns
> The solace of these good returns
> For putting them to bed.
> As many a curse, and many a kick
> And many a pinch, and many a lick
> They give while being led.[115]

Walter Savage Landor may have sneered at the 'servitors and other raffs' in Richard Leeds's rooms, but in fact, no servitor had been admitted to Trinity since William, the son of Lewis Williams of Dollgellau, Merionethshire, entered on 20 May 1763. In February 1792 the College heard that the Reverend John Bowles (servitor 1734) had bequeathed to Trinity £2,700 in 3 per cent consolidated annuities, to be used to provide 'exhibitions' for six servitors. President Chapman and six fellows met and agreed that Chapman should 'apply to one of the Trustees for the same'. Their discussions went so far as to set the caution money for the new servitors at £8. But on 20 June the full fellowship met 'at an especial meeting' to 'determine on the question "whether the re-establishment of the order of servitors, which had been long discontinued, was or was not beneficial to the college".' It was not, they decided—presumably because no servitor would be able to provide the level of service now expected—and the legacy was therefore 'relinquished'.[116]

The lack of detail of academic work in this chapter largely reflects the lack of interest shown in it by the majority of Oxford's eighteenth-century members. Few undergraduates were taking degrees and few fellows were taking higher degrees. The final decades of the century, however, saw an increasing number of educational reforms, and these were to come to fruition in the early years of the next century. The days of the port-quaffing gentleman commoner and the time-serving fellow were almost over.

[115] Skinner, 'Letters', f. 79.

[116] In fact, Bowles's bequest was still received in 1807 and was used to replace the Hall roof. TCA Order Book B, ff. 249, 253, 305.

# 8

# *Tommy Short's Trinity*

## *Undergraduate Education*

The first recorded case of 'exam nerves' in Trinity College occurred in May 1818, the victim the 17-year-old John Henry Newman (1816). 'I am sure I felt the tortures of suspense so much,' he wrote later to his mother,

> that I wished and wished I had never attempted it. The idea of '*turpis repulsa* [shameful rejection]' haunted me. I was not very well. My head ached constantly . . . I constantly reverted to it in my thoughts, in spite of my endeavours to the contrary. Very few men thought I should get it, and my reason thought the same. Even he with whom I am most intimate [John Bowden] thought my case desperate and betted against me.[1]

Newman was one of the eleven candidates competing for a Trinity scholarship; he was one of the first generation of undergraduates for whom examinations were becoming significant personal milestones and all too regular ordeals.[2]

The Oxford University Examination Statute, passed in 1800, was but the harbinger of a future in which daily life would be structured around exams and shaped by results. An Oxford BA could no longer be attained merely by fulfilling residence requirements and making set responses in a formulaic examination. Now, candidates were expected to reach a minimum standard in grammar, rhetoric, logic, moral philosophy, the 'elements of maths and physics', and the 'elements of religion', about which they would be questioned publicly by three out of a board of six appointed examiners. Candidates who aimed at an 'honours' degree would be examined by all six.

[1] *Newman Letters & Diaries*, 53.

[2] In 1816 Trinity had offered its first 'open' scholarship; i.e. candidates were no longer required to be undergraduate members of the College. See *Newman Letters & Diaries*, 47–8.

*8.1* Tommy Short, fellow 1816–79, circa 1860 (Album of Henry E. Hulton (1858), TCA OM 8).

From 1807 honours were awarded separately in classics and in mathematics. In the early days the examinations were oral, and conducted at the rate of six candidates a day.[3] Such reforms had an inevitable impact both on the methods of college teaching and on the attitudes of those being taught.

Trinity, like most other colleges, had already been responding to the evident need for some regularization of teaching standards.[4] As early as 1789, all undergraduates had been subject to oral

[3] V. H. H. Green, 'Reformers and Reform in the University', *HUO* 5, 626.
[4] M. G. Brock, 'The Oxford of Peel and Gladstone 1800–1833', *HUO* 6, 7.

examinations in the College Hall, which were held twice yearly in the 'Lent' and 'Act' (i.e., Hilary and Trinity) Terms in the presence of the President and fellows. They were then 'distributed into classes according to the proficiency which the tutors shall judge them to have made' and handed a list of books to read for the next term.[5] The fellows were also offering incentives to encourage greater academic effort. In 1788 two annual cash prizes of five guineas each had been instituted, for which all undergraduates were 'required' to submit a 'Latin declamation or English essay or both'.[6] In 1809 these internal examinations were refined, with a decision that they should be 'conducted upon the plan of the responsions in the schools'.[7] No more than six individuals were to be examined at the same time, and they were to be examined 'in one science at least in addition to divinity and two classical authors to be chosen by [the student] himself, notice given to dean or tutor on previous Saturday'. The name used for today's internal examinations—'collections'—is derived from the way candidates would collect together their own choice of books. Meanwhile it was also decided to use the 'literary prize fund' of 1788 to buy book prizes for 'those who distinguish themselves' in these exams.[8]

The first Trinity man to achieve university honours was Henry Dryden (1805); the first to achieve a first class was John Wilson (1806).[9] Dryden succeeded to a baronetcy in 1818, and from 1824 until his death in 1837 was perpetual curate of Leek Wooton, Somerset. Wilson went on to a fellowship and the presidency of Trinity, 1850–66. The career of neither was dependent on his exam success; and yet, Wilson's six immediate successors all had first-class degrees.[10]

In 1800 Trinity's tutors were Henry Kett (fellow 1784) and Jeremiah Scholefield (fellow 1794). Kett took on his first two pupils in March 1785; between 1799 and 1808 he was one of the two main tutors in College. Kindly and able, Kett was popular with his pupils and, unlike many of his contemporaries, took a personal interest in their lives; at

[5] TCA *Liber Decani* I, f. 48.

[6] Ibid., f. 44. The President subscribed 2 guineas annually, six fellows 1 guinea each, four fellows half a guinea.

[7] 'Responsions' was introduced in 1808 as a preliminary examination in Greek, Latin, and either logic or Euclid; it was taken after one year, or during the second year in residence. M. C. Curthoys, 'The Examination System', *HUO* 6, 352.

[8] TCA Order Book B, f. 311. The Prize fund was restored to its original purpose in 1822.

[9] Results are taken from *University Calendar*, published annually.

[10] The 7th, Arthur Norrington (ironically for the deviser of his eponymous table), had a second.

*8.2* 'A View from Trinity College', Henry Kett by Dighton (1807).

his death it was justifiably said that he had 'united the character of friend with that of tutor'.[11] 'My learned tutor—whom all we / think wondrous wise at Trinity,' wrote John Skinner in the winter of 1792, when he and his friend Dawson Warren would devote a morning—three and a half hours' work—to reading Virgil and Demosthenes in preparation for one of their two weekly classes with Kett.[12] His quaint and endearing mannerisms first earned him the sobriquet 'Father Kett', while his long face and straight, bony nose led to incessant teasing and the crude nickname 'Horse'. 'His figure's

[11] *Gentleman's Magazine* (August 1825), 184.

[12] Skinner, 'Letters', f. 57.

awkward, gaunt, and thin, / His face an ell from front to chin,' rhymed Skinner. 'Our Kett's not a poet? / Why how can you say so? / For if he's no Ovid, / I'm sure he's a Naso,' cracked the poet laureate, Thomas Warton.[13] Kett was famously caricatured in Dighton's 'A View from Trinity College' (Plate 8.2).

Although he participated in the University's examination reforms—he was one of the classical examiners in 1803–4—Kett had a vision of university that provided a modern, multi-disciplined, but essentially liberal education. He used 'a course of lectures, which [he] occasionally read to his pupils' as the basis for a manual of education, *The Elements of General Knowledge* (1802). By 1815 there had been eight editions, each conscientiously updated to include all the latest reference works. In the sixth edition (1806) Kett acknowledged additional information 'obtained from the *Encyclopaedia Britannica, Imison's Elements of the Arts, Robertson's History of America* and *Tytler's Elements of General His*tory'. Kett's *Elements* was 'designed chiefly for the junior students in the universities, and the higher classes in schools'. 'I have considered young men,' he explained in his introductory chapter, 'with a view to their most important relations in life, as Christians, as students, and as members of the British Empire, the welfare and prosperity of which depends upon the usefulness of their attainments, and the respectability of their conduct.' Kett arranged his material in six 'classes': the Christian Religion, Language, History, Philosophy, Polite Literature and the Fine Arts, and the Sources of National Prosperity. 'History' included chapters on the Jews, the Greeks, the Romans, modern Europe, and England; 'Philosophy' covered logic, mathematics, and 'the works of nature', with three chapters on the animal kingdom, botany, and mineralogy and chemistry. 'National Prosperity' was divided into agriculture, commerce, foreign travel, and the professions ('I the barrister, II the physician, III the clergyman'). Finally, an appendix supplied 'Lists of the most approved authors, including the best editions of the classics'.[14] Less successfully, Kett published *Logic Made Easy* (1809) and attempted a female counterpart of *The Elements*, using the romantic

[13] Skinner, 'Letters', f. 5. The full name of the poet Ovid was Publius Ovidius Naso. For Warton's verse see *The Annual Biography and Obituary* (London, 1826), 13–25. Kett deflected ridicule by making jokes against himself. 'An oat!' he exclaimed, when a note came through his door, and 'I'm off for a trot down the High Street.'

[14] Henry Kett, *Elements of General Knowledge*, 6th edn. (London, 1806), pp. title-page, vi, xi–xxiii, 6.

story line and epistolatory structure of *Emily, a Moral Tale* (1809) to discourse on moral issues, general knowledge, and natural history. In 1808 Kett gave up his college tutorship, seemingly frustrated by the essentially conservative nature of the new system.[15]

Trinity's most famous nineteenth-century fellow and tutor was Tommy Short (commoner 1807, scholar 1808, fellow 1816–79). He himself had achieved an honours degree (equivalent to a third class) in 1811, and had five years' experience as an under-master at Rugby School, where he was renowned as a gifted teacher.[16] He was a college tutor for forty years, during which time he came to be revered by his pupils—and their sons—for his no-nonsense approach and unrivalled knowledge of the undergraduate psyche. Roundell Palmer (scholar 1830) remembered Short as 'a naturally clever man, of shrewd masculine sense, and a caustic ready wit, of great generosity also, and kindness of heart'. Palmer's other tutor, Isaac Williams, might have been 'remarkable' for his 'genius . . . acquirements . . . moral qualities . . . modesty and humility', but it was Short who had 'the gifts necessary for understanding and managing the young men'. As Palmer recalled admiringly, 'he had been idle when young, fishing when he ought to have been reading,' and was 'rather too unclerical a clergyman; his life was blameless, but his speech was not always decorous. But we liked him, and thought much of his criticism, his praise, or blame, and he never lost our respect.'[17] Isaac Williams rather disapproved of his colleague's style, particularly the way 'he seemed almost incapable of looking on college matters in a moral or religious light.'[18] When William G. Cole (scholar 1854, fellow 1859–70) breakfasted with Short on the morning of taking his MA, Short required him to read the Thirty-Nine Articles aloud, while 'he moved about all the time' talking to his scout, Mrs Tanner, and disappearing frequently into his study. But when Cole got to the 'passage about obedience to "the commandments which are called moral",' Short 'interrupted . . . to enquire which were the immoral commandments'.[19] Such irreverent humour had obvious undergraduate appeal, and Short was physically attractive too: although he 'lacked height,

[15] Green, 'Reformers and Reform', *HUO* 5, 626.

[16] Edwards, *Oxford Tutor*, 29–34.

[17] Roundell Palmer, *Memorials, Part I, Family and Personal* (London, 1896), i, 116–17.

[18] *The Autobiography of Isaac Williams*, ed. Sir George Prevost (1892), 80.

[19] *Breviarum*, 21–2. Towards the end of Short's life, his younger colleagues kept a notebook where they recorded verbatim his oft-told anecdotes and other amusing stories about him. They called it the '*Breviarum* or Short-notes'.

his clean cut features—the nose being rather of the Wellington type—well-opened blue eyes, black wavy hair, firm mouth and chin, made him, even in old age, a handsome man.' Or so he seemed to his devoted biographer, C. E. H. Edwards.[20]

John Henry Newman was one of Tommy Short's very first pupils. His letters and diaries provide fascinating insights into the educational progress of a Trinity undergraduate of his day, albeit a particularly highly strung and assiduous scholar. Newman came into residence in June 1817—in order to 'keep' the term towards his BA—but did not begin regular academic work until October, when he was both pleased to discover that his tutor had a reputation for strictness, and disappointed not to start work at once. On 28 October Short directed Newman to lectures, 'Tacitus, every morning but Thursday; one in Cicero on Wednesday, Mathematics three times a week. This is little enough, but of course they begin with little, to see what I can do.' Newman was soon gratified to find himself advanced rapidly up the maths class, and praised for his Latin declamation: 'I was stopped by the fellow [Kinsey] who looks over the declamations and to whom we recite them, and told by him that mine did me much credit.' Newman saw his first college collections as an opportunity to show off:

> I believe I have made something like a dash and therefore I am a little anxious lest I should not fulfil my engagement. Every one must take up some Greek, Latin, Mathematics, and Divinity. I have taken the whole of Xenophon's *Anabasis* (*Retreat of 10,000*) (*one* book would have done and I chose all *seven*) two tracts of Tacitus, the 5$^{th}$ book of Euclid (the hardest . . .) and the gospels of Luke and John. This is rather fagging for a month or six weeks.

Meanwhile Newman was delighted with the maths class, where all but he and his best friend Bowden had abandoned Euclid for logic:

> We shall finish Euclid's Elements this term, and go to Trigonometry or something of the same kind next. If any one wishes to study much, I believe there can be no College that will encourage him more than Trinity. It wishes to rise in the University and is rising fast . . . In discipline it has become the strictest of Colleges. There are lamentations in every corner of the increasing rigour; it is laughable, but it is delightful, to hear the groans of the oppressed.[21]

Short was proud of Newman, if at times exhausted by him. In later

[20] Edwards, *Oxford Tutor*, 11.

[21] *Newman Letters & Diaries*, 35, 43–5, 47–8.

life he would recall nostalgically 'his bringing the Book of Psalms to Collections, and when we asked him to name the prophetical Psalms, he started with the second and went through them all. Oh dear! He ran you down with his answers.'[22]

For his second term's collections, in February 1818, Newman prepared 'five books of Herodotus, Virgil's *Aeneid*, Mechanics, and the Pentateuch, Joshua, Judges and Ruth. Both the tutors seemed very glad to see me and shook hands with me.' They also presented him with a book prize, Port's *Lexicon Iconium*. The two tutors had found the man to whom they wished to award their open scholarship. 'On Wednesday April 29 about breakfast time Mr Wilson and Mr Short called for me . . . they wished me to stand this year, because they would wish to see me on the foundation.' There were five examiners: the President, who had two votes, and the four college officers. Newman stood against four other 'in-college men, and six out-college, viz one from Exeter, one from Merton, two from Worcester—one from Rugby and one not of the University'. The examination took four days:

> They first made us do some verses—then some Latin translation—then a Latin theme—then a chorus of Euripides—then an English theme—then some Plato, then some Lucretius, then some Xenophon, then some Livy. Most of the Latin and Greek we had to construe off to them. What is more distressing than suspense? At last I was called to the place where they had been voting: the vice-Chancellor [President Lee] said some Latin over me; then made me a speech. The Electors then shook hands with me, and I immediately assumed the Scholar's gown.

Newman described his feelings to his mother: 'when I heard the voice of the Dean summoning me before the Electors, [I] seemed to myself to feel no surprise. I am told I turned pale.' Throughout the years of his scholarship, Newman was under additional pressure to prove Trinity right to have chosen him.[23]

As an undergraduate, Newman followed the widespread practice of employing a private tutor, in his case a senior scholar of the College.

[22] *Breviarum*, 44–5.

[23] *Newman Letters & Diaries*, 51–3. The meritocracy of the elections was not always transparent. Joseph Smith once told James Pycroft that a candidate 'would have been elected scholar of Trinity . . . but we perceived he was too near-sighted for the duty of marking the names in chapel.' Pycroft, *Memories*, i, 82.

From Michaelmas Term 1818, James Adey Ogle (scholar 1812) coached Newman and Bowden in mathematics for two hours a day, for which they paid him £50. When in February 1819 Ogle was appointed as the College logic and mathematics tutor (he was allowed to use a non-resident fellow's 'sitting room . . . as a lecture room'), they continued to see him privately for an hour a day (£30).[24] Newman and his family considered Ogle's 'terms very high', compared to college tuition at three guineas a term, but he quickly became one of Newman's closest friends. The weekend before Newman 'left Oxford for good' in February 1846, he 'called on Dr Ogle, one of my very oldest friends, for he was my private Tutor, when I was an undergraduate. In him I took leave of my first College, Trinity, which was so dear to me.'[25]

While the College tutor had to consider the needs of a class, even a hall full of pupils, a private 'coach' could meet the precise requirements of an individual, and such intensive tuition was increasingly regarded as essential for all serious honours candidates. The pupils' fees provided a good second income for many junior fellows and recent graduates.[26] During the term of Newman's university finals, however, John Wilson saw him privately for 'always two, sometimes five hours every day', and 'would not hear of a remuneration'.[27] The College's reputation was now at stake. 'I am in no common situation,' wrote Newman in September 1820:

> The very few honours that have ever been taken by men of our College, the utter absence of first classes for the last ten years, the repeated failures which have occurred, and the late spirit of reading which has shown itself among us, render those who attempt this autumn objects of wonder, curiosity, speculation, and anxiety. 'Unless,' I am told, 'success at length attends on Trinity this examination, we have determined it is useless to read.'[28]

Tutors and pupils alike were inexperienced in preparing for finals. Newman aspired to a double first, and during the 1820 Long Vaca-

[24] Ogle's room: TCA Room Register B, unpaginated, 1825. As private tutor: *Newman Letters & Diaries*, 57, 61.

[25] Ibid., 49. Newman, *Apologia pro Vita Sua* (Oxford, 1967), 213.

[26] A. J. Engel, *From Clergyman to Don* (Oxford, 1983), 4.

[27] *Newman Letters & Diaries*, 92.

[28] Ibid., 87. In fact Trinity had had a number of Firsts in the previous decade: and 1820's relative lack of success had no impact on subsequent entrants. However, compared to today's figure (20–25% Firsts) in Newman's day a First was a comparatively more difficult achievement.

tion he stayed up at Trinity in a fever of swotting, 'reading' for twelve hours a day and six days a week. He was given special permission to study in the College Library. 'The goal seems now to be so full in my sight, that I do not feel the want of friends,' he informed his father. But, as he also admitted, 'he had Trinity College, its garden and library, all to himself; and in his solitude, as pleasant as he found it, he became graver and graver.'[29] In September he was able to write home optimistically:

> By the end of the week I shall have finished, thoroughly, I hope, Aeschylus, Newton, and half of my Livy. I am now reading at the rate (I whisper a great secret) of from 13 to 14 hours a day. I make hay while the sun shines. When term commences, I shall not be able to read so much; besides, if I can, I wish to have little or nothing to do the week before my examination.

On 8 November he confessed that 'the rhetoric of Aristotle I fear I have determined to throw aside, and with it my hopes of a first class in Classics. I really think my success is very, very precarious.' Four days later however his spirits had rallied, 'I will not deny that I have moments of terror, but, except those moments, I am cool and in spirits. . . . I think I may attain a first class in mathematics and a second in classics.'[30]

In the event, Newman managed neither. The examinations began a day earlier than he had expected and were a disaster. With hindsight he realized that 'he had over-read himself . . . lost his head, utterly broke down, and after vain attempts for several days had to retire.' On 1 December 1820 he wrote, 'when I got into the schools, I was so nervous, I could not answer half a dozen questions. The nervousness, I may add the illness, continued whenever I approached the schools, and, after a week's procrastinated efforts, I have this morning retired from the contest.' Newman failed completely in maths, and in classics his name appeared 'in the lower division of the second class of honours, which at that time went by the contemptuous title of "under-the-line", there being as yet no third or fourth classes.'[31]

Newman was quick to acknowledge that in the light of his failure, Trinity was not unkind. 'The authorities of the college instantly

[29] *John Henry Newman: Autobiographical Writings*, ed. Henry Tristram (London, 1956), 45–6.

[30] Ibid., 47; *Newman Letters & Diaries*, 80, 88, 92–3.

[31] Ibid., 94.

assured me I had done all I could,' he wrote to his mother. But he felt the bitter disappointment of his tutors, that after 'formidable out-college opponents had been put aside' for him in the scholarship exam, there should have been such 'an untoward incident in the first start of a great reform'. His tutors were not experienced in preparing candidates for examinations, and the pressure they put on Newman was considerable. Short encouraged his pupil to attempt the English Essay Prize,

> that you may distinguish yourself in the Rostrum, and prove to the world, what is already well known to ourselves, that the purity of our Elections is un-sullied. For should your old competitor of Worcester obtain high honour in the Schools, sneerers will not be wanting to amuse themselves at our expense.[32]

Newman did not compete for the essay prize, but remained in college to consider his future. In the summer of 1821 Short fixed him up with an income of £100 from 'a man of our college for a private pupil. I am to begin with him after the long vacation'. The following January he acquired a second pupil through the agency of William Kinsey (fellow 1815–44).[33] So when, in April 1822, he decided to try for an open fellowship at Oriel College, his 'Trinity friends' were startled, and 'pained also, for they were sure it would end in a second miscarriage. They had not the shadow of a hope of his succeeding.' The examination lasted for five days, during which:

> we had to do a Latin Essay, a translation of some Spectator, answers to twelve Mathematical and Philosophical, and to ten logical questions; besides construing passages in nine Greek and Latin authors before the Electors. . . . The examination throughout was most kind and considerate, and we were supplied with sandwiches, fruit, cake, jellies, and wine—a blazing fire, and plenty of time.[34]

Even so, Newman's anxieties returned. When, on the second day, Short invited him to lunch, it was for him the final throw of the dice. Short told the story for the rest of his life:

> Newman . . . came to me after the first paper, which was an essay, and said: 'I have made a complete mess of it and broken down entirely.' I happened to meet Tyler, one of the [Oriel] Fellows; he said

[32] *Newman Letters & Diaries*, 95, 102.
[33] Ibid., 110, 120.
[34] Ibid., 130–1.

> to me 'Tell me something of your man Newman, for he has written by far the best essay.' Of course I did not tell Newman what I had heard, but I said: 'You go on with the examination as though you had no chance, and were only an unconcerned spectator.'[35]

It was good advice. On Friday, 12 April, Newman was told of his success, and the whole college was jubilant. 'The news spread to Trinity with great rapidity,' he recorded:

> I had hardly been in Kinsey's room a minute, when in rushed Ogle like one mad. I then proceeded to the President's, and in rushed Ogle again. I find that Tomlinson rushed to Echalaz's room, and nearly kicked down the door to communicate the news. Echalaz in turn ran down stairs. Tompson heard a noise and my name mentioned, and rushed out also, and in the room opposite found Echalaz Ward and Ogle leaping up and down, backwards and forwards. Men rushed in all directions to Trinity to men they knew, to congratulate them on the success of their college.[36]

## *The Boat Club*

College pride was growing very strong in the early nineteenth century. It was manifested in academic honours and in sporting glories. So now let us take a moment to welcome those readers who have looked up 'Boat Club' in the index. Rowing and sailing on the Isis had been growing in popularity for some decades, as alternatives to the traditional recreations of walking or hunting. Rowing, offering as it did not only an opportunity for exercise, but also the close comradeship of training and the thrill of competition, was soon to leave rival sports far in its wake. The first eight-oar races between Oxford colleges took place in 1815.[37] By the 1830s, competitive rowing was an important, although as yet quite informal, feature of Trinity life. James Pycroft (1831) recalled how 'a college boat sometimes was

[35] Short believed too that he had helped Newman's chances by telling the Provost of Oriel something of Newman's family circumstances; *Breviarum*, 45–7. Newman also always remembered this day. Visiting his old tutor in 1878 after 32 years away from Oxford, he was able to thank him again for the lunch of lamb cutlets and fried parsley; Edwards, *Oxford Tutor*, 42–3.

[36] *Newman: Autobiographical Writings*, 62–3.

[37] Christopher Dodd, *The Oxford and Cambridge Boat Race* (London, 1983), 33.

purchased by a private subscription amongst the crew who proposed it, but generally there was a voluntary rate levied on all the men, it being considered that the boat and its anticipated victories were for the honour of the college generally.'[38] The official Eights' Charts were kept from 1837, when no Trinity boat competed. But the very next year the Trinity crew went up three places—from eighth to fifth—gaining two 'by Worcester and Christ Church taking off' and on the last night bringing 'great credit to the college by the very great pluck displayed in the race to bump BNC'.[39]

Trinity's first rowing Blues were John Cox (1839) and Edward Breedon (1838), who in 1842 rowed in the sixth Boat Race, Oxford's first victory on the Westminster to Putney course. Already, rowing was no casual pursuit. John Cox rowed in five college Eights, competed twice at the Henley Regatta, once in the Boat Race, and once 'against the Leander at the Thames Regatta'.[40] Both Cox and Breedon are represented in the earliest known depiction of a Trinity crew, dating from 1842; this print, published as a generic representation of University rowing, has been coloured by hand to show Trinity at the Head of the River (Plate 8.3). In 1842 Trinity bumped University to go head on the first day of Eights. Four days later they were bumped by Oriel to finish, as they had started, in second place. It was a memorable race, and one that achieved immortal status through the pen of Thomas Hughes, author of *Tom Brown's Schooldays*, whose brother George happened to be the Oriel stroke. In the breathless passage in *Tom Brown at Oxford*, quoted below, the fictitious 'St Ambrose' has been changed back to Oriel, and Hughes's 'Oriel' to Trinity:

> The boat's length lessens to forty feet, thirty feet; and surely and steadily lessens. But the race is not lost yet; thirty feet is a short space enough to look at on the water, but a good bit to pick up foot by foot in the last two or three hundred yards of a desperate struggle. They are over, under the Berkshire side now, and there stands up the winning post, close ahead, all but won. The distance lessens, and lessens still, but the Trinity crew stick steadily and gallantly to their work, and will fight every inch of the distance to the last. The Trinity men on the bank, who are rushing along some-

[38] Pycroft, *Memories*, i, 49.

[39] TCA JCR B/BC/vii/1, *Ye Chronicles of Ye Trinity Boat Club 1837–1862*, unpaginated.

[40] E. Morgan, *University Oars* (London, 1873), 176. This book is based on a survey of Blues, undertaken to refute the commonly held belief that rowing was dangerously unhealthy.

*8.3* 1842 racing boat, showing Trinity as Head of the River.

> times in the water, sometimes out, hoarse, furious, madly alternating between hope and despair, have no reason to be ashamed of a man in the crew. Off the mouth of the Cherwell there is still twenty feet between them. Another minute and it will all be over one way or another. . . . The Oriel stroke is glorious . . . Tom had an atom of go still left in the very back of his head, and at this moment he heard Drysdale's view holloa above all the din; it seemed to give him a lift, and other men besides in the boat, for in another six strokes the gap is lessened and Oriel has crept up ten feet, and now to five from the stern of Trinity . . . Another fifty yards and Trinity is safe, but the look on the Captain's face is so ominous that their coxswain glances over his shoulder. The bow of Oriel is within two feet of their rudder. It is a moment for desperate expedients. He pulls his left tiller rope suddenly, thereby carrying the stern of his own boat out of the line of the Oriel, and calls on his crew once more; they respond gallantly yet, but the rudder is against them for a moment, and the boat drags. Oriel overlaps. 'A bump, a bump' scream the Oriel men on shore. 'Row on, row on,' screams Miller. He has not yet felt the electric shock, and knows he will miss his bump if the young ones slacken for a moment. . . . A bump now and no mistake; the bow on the Oriel boat jams the oar of the Trinity stroke, and the two boats pass the winning-post with the way that was on them when the bump was made. So near a shave was it. Who can describe the scene on the bank?[41]

Trinity had to wait another nineteen years before going Head of the River. On the first night of the 1861 Eights, they bumped University College 'within a few hundred yards' of the start. On the second, they bumped BNC 'without much effort'. On the third, they bumped Exeter 'after a hard struggle', and on the fourth, they bumped Balliol to go Head, where they remained on the fifth and sixth nights. 'The rowing of the Trinity men has been the theme of general admiration,' enthused *Bell's Life*, 'such a college crew not having been seen on the Isis for some time.'[42] Trinity remained invincible until 1865, a glorious period of dominance, which has been matched only once in the ensuing 140 years.[43] The crews were

[41] Dodd, *Boat Race*, 30; T. Hughes, *Tom Brown at Oxford* (London, 1903), 140–1.

[42] *Bell's Life in London* (19 May 1861).

[43] Their decline between 1865 and 1868, however, was all too swift: 1865 from Head to 3rd—'disastrous'; 1866 3rd to 9th—'college star evidently on the wane'; 1867, 9th–11th—'again an unfortunate year'; 1868, 11th–16th—'Trinity which was the Head of the River

Eight, 1861.
Bow C. A. Garnett ---- 10.7.
2. C. Wyatt-Smith ---- 11.1
3. H. E. Hulton ---- 10.10
4. A. O. Hardy ---- 10.0
5. A. R. Poole ---- 12.2
6. H. B. Rhodes ---- 11.6
7. J. A. Thompson ---- 11.7
Str. H. Couchman ---- 12.0
Cox. H. W. Wilkie ---- 7.9


*8.4* Trinity College Head of the River Eight, 1861.

photographed (Plate 8.4), an album was purchased, and a clerk from Lincoln's Inn, one Gerald Surman, was employed to write up the annals of the Boat Club in two volumes entitled *Ye Chronicles of Ye Trinity Boat Club*.

Trinity's first rowing double Blue was Arthur Poole (1859), in 1861 and 1862. The second was Meredith Brown (1863). Already an experienced oarsman when he came up from Radley School, Brown went on to become the only Trinity oarsman to row three times in the Boat Race. Brown himself summed up his achievements modestly:

having gone down night after night ever since, being now only one place from bottom'. (*Ye Chronicles of Ye Trinity Boat Club*).

> In 1863 I went to Oxford, where I rowed in the University Eight in 1864, 1865 and 1866, besides rowing in College Eights, and University Fours and Pairs for four years. I rowed at Henley three years, besides Paris, Kingston, Walton. I calculate I was in training for rowing more than four months in each of the eight years 1858–1866.

Unsurprisingly, he did not take a degree. Henry Schnieder (1862) described the typical training regime of his day:

> Rise early, take a walk for about half an hour, during the course of which spurt once or twice at full speed for a distance of about 200 yards to improve the wind, a cold bath, breakfast consisting of beefsteaks and mutton chops (not necessarily underdone), bread or toast, butter, and tea . . . No further exercise is then required till after lunch . . . Lunch consists of bread, butter, and lettuce or watercress, and half a pint of ale. Then comes the rowing for the day. Dinner at six; a joint of beef or mutton, potatoes, cabbage, bread, lettuce or watercress, and a pint of ale. After dinner a few plain biscuits and two glasses of port wine each. Sometimes a cup of tea is allowed about eight o'clock; once or twice also during the training fowls are allowed for dinner, and sometimes eggs for breakfast . . . Pastry in any shape, and cheese, are never allowed, and the men are on their honour not to smoke. The hour for bed, is (if I recollect right) ten o clock. On Sundays the crew take a walk of eight or ten miles, instead of the rowing.[44]

'I believe that rowing and training, and all the rest of it, did me not only no harm but a vast deal of good,' wrote John Cox cheerfully in 1873.[45]

The senior members did not at first see rowing and training, and particularly 'all the rest of it', in quite such a positive light. Tommy Short called the boating men 'hydro-maniacs,' and would write to the fathers of his pupils, advising they be forbidden to join the college crew. The scholars he could persuade more directly. According to the memoirs of James Pycroft, Thomas Lewin (scholar 1825) 'being famed for athletics, had thoughts of joining the boat, but soon received a hint that it would not do'. Indeed, 'the rowing or the uproarious set, who behaved like big schoolboys' had the reputation for 'extravagance and midnight uproar', and their bump suppers, held in celebration of every successful race, were 'unusually uproarious with speeches, hurraying, and songs various'. A large part of Pycroft's

[44] Morgan, *University Oars*, 333–4.

[45] Ibid., 176–7.

*Oxford Memories* is given over to such riotous representatives of 'the fast set'. 'These were the men who made night hideous with drunken and noisy wine parties—men who knocked in late and bribed the porter not to put down their names.'[46]

## *College Life and Discipline*

As a freshman, John Henry Newman was intimidated by the seemingly hardened drinkers around him. His first invitation 'to take a glass of wine' left him bemoaning how:

> they drank and drank all the time I was there . . . They drank while I was there very much, and I believe intended to drink again. They sat down with the avowed intention of each making himself drunk. I really think, if any one should ask me what qualifications were necessary for Trinity College, I should say there was only one,—Drink, drink, drink.[47]

Newman may have been unduly sensitive to the high spirits of his contemporaries, but he was not alone in identifying a problem of excessive alcohol consumption. Pycroft described how:

> a man who was almost mad when excited with wine, in a room unfortunately nearest the President's study, once stood on a table and, enacting a shuffle and cut among the glasses and dessert dishes, made a speech and then sang a song with a chorus of men as excited and loud as himself.[48]

Trinity could be an anarchic and unruly place. The number of undergraduates in residence almost doubled in the early years of the nineteenth century, and, within the precincts of the College, the proportion of junior to senior members was higher than it had ever been.[49] By the 1820s the average annual number of admissions exceeded twenty, only slightly beneath the boom years of 1615–35, when the full twelve fellows had generally been in residence. There are many possible causes for this rapid expansion, not least the rise in

46 Pycroft, *Memories*, i, 18, 47.

47 *Newman Letters & Diaries*, 36.

48 Pycroft, *Memories*, i, 35.

49 This was the pattern across the University. M. C. Curthoys, 'The Unreformed Colleges', *HUO* 6, 146–7.

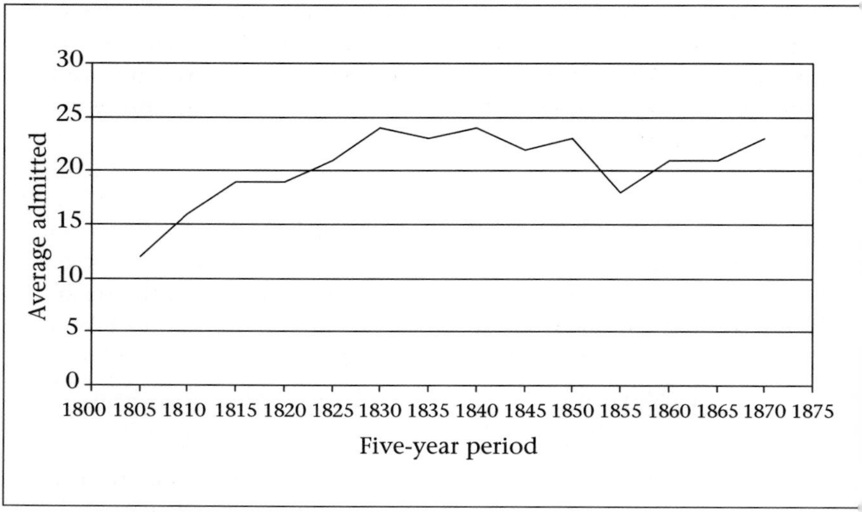


*Fig. 8.1* Average admissions 1801–1870.

the population as a whole. The Industrial Revolution created both a larger middle class and more career opportunities for graduates, in Church and business; and degrees, proof of both industry and ability, were becoming an attractive and valuable qualification.[50]

There was a long struggle to get the increased undergraduate population under control, and decanal records show strenuous and repeated attempts to enforce discipline. In 1803 it was agreed that any BA 'seen lounging about the college in his hat (either in the Quadrangles or garden) be regularly sconced half a crown—and that every undergraduate so offending, be punished by an imposition [a written exercise]'. Impositions could also be incurred by undergraduates for failing to take their turn at the *narrare*, and from 1806, for missing or 'loitering about' during the University sermon, being absent from the declamations, or coming in more than fifteen minutes late for dinner. When, in May 1805, Henry Wyniatt (1801) refused to do an imposition, he was forced to sign a humiliating apology in the dean's book.[51]

[50] Lawrence Stone, 'Oxford Student Body', 59.
[51] TCA *Liber Decani* I, ff. 63, 65d–6, 68–9.

One month later the fellows took measures to cope with a new 'practice of throwing stones, & breaking windows [which] has prevailed of late to the great Disgrace of the College'. Any such offence was now punishable by rustication, and the following year the same sanction was to be applied to 'any bachelor or undergraduate, who shall disturb the college by noise, riot, or intoxication'.[52] In the case of Pycroft's table-dancer, neither he, nor the party's host was sent down; rather the owner of the rooms, who had 'lent [them] to a friend—the practice sometimes of men who, near the end of their residence, were indifferent to the wear and tear of the furniture to be passed on to their successor'.[53]

The fellows were particularly keen to tighten up on all aspects of Chapel attendance. In May 1819, Thomas Wyatt had his BA deferred for two terms, which was the length of time he had 'absented himself from the chapel upon excuses, discovered to be groundless & frivolous'.[54] Despite his irreverent attitude, by 1821 Wyatt was in holy orders and installed in the living of Wroxton cum Balscote, which he held until his death in 1853. The fellows were provoked into drawing up a new decree, dated December 1820, which was communicated by the Dean to the undergraduate members of the College as a standing order:

> The President & Fellows have observed with deep regret, that notwithstanding their frequent injunctions, *proper attention is not paid at divine service in the chapel* & that with very few exceptions, *the habit of not making the responses seems to be general* among the undergraduate members of the College. To put an immediate stop to this system, & to ensure decorous behaviour from every individual during his attendance upon the sacred offices of religion, the President, in unison with his society, has directed the Dean to report to him the names of those gentlemen who thus continue inattentive to their religious duties, *in not regularly joining in the responses*, having determined to suspend the degree, & to refuse letters testimonial for Holy Orders to all those gentlemen, who may in future be observed habitually offending in this important particular.[55]

One group who did not long withstand the increasing rigour of work and severity of punishments were the gentlemen commoners,

[52] This rule had been attempted before in relation to the custom of giving 'gracious wine' to guests at graduation, but it was now to be 'strictly enforced'. Ibid. ff. 67, 69.

[53] Pycroft, *Memories*, i, 35.

[54] TCA *Liber Decani* I, f. 72.

[55] Ibid., f. 73.

whose rapidly diminishing portfolio of privileges hardly made their increased expenses worthwhile. The new rules hit them hard. From 1797 gentlemen commoners had been 'expected to attend prayers and to do all other exercises [though they were excused the *narrare*] with the same regularity as commoners'.[56] In 1809 they were denied the right to dine at High Table, but confined to their own table in Hall.[57] In 1822 there was an attempt to restrict their extravagant menus to a mere 2*s* 3*d* for dinner. At the same time they paid double the caution money of ordinary commoners (£60 as opposed to £30; or even £80, if they were natives of Ireland or 'any other distant province').[58] A small—and presumably lonely—rump persisted, their aristocratic sensibilities assuaged by the act of signing in as commoners *superioris ordinis* (of the higher order) rather than as mere *inferiores*. Twenty-six gentlemen commoners were admitted between 1821 and 1835—and then there were none; with the solitary exception of the Honourable William Ward, Baron Ward of Birmingham, eldest son of the Honourable William Humble Ward of Birmingham, deceased, who on 13 March 1840 entered as a migrant from Christ Church, bearing the long disused title of nobleman commoner and a testimonial of his good behaviour from the Dean.[59] Ward's career at Christ Church had been somewhat chequered, for he was rusticated for Hilary and Trinity terms 1837, and was out of residence for much of 1838. During this period his private tutor was Thomas Legh Claughton of Trinity (fellow 1832–42), who remained touchingly convinced of his pupil's good intentions, and whose diary tells a story of vigilant devotion. 'My heart is heavy tonight,' he confided on 9 February 1838, 'on my pupil's account. He appears to be forming habits of idleness—and to be commencing what he may think a life of indifference. I have done all in my power to guide him gently in the right way.' It was a relief when he breakfasted with his pupil ten days later, and they had 'a long and serious conversation about his future plans. He intends to read for honours, even if it is Easter 1839 before he goes up.'[60] Ward's name remained on the books at Trinity for two terms, but he was not given a room, and he never did take his degree.

[56] TCA *Liber Decani* I, f. 55.
[57] TCA Order Book B, f. 309.
[58] TCA Order Book C, ff. 9, 15.
[59] TCA Admisison Register C, f. 5.
[60] LPL MS 1835, ff. 12d, 14. I am grateful to Judith Curthoys for information about Ward at Christ Church.

In the ongoing disciplinary battle, Trinity's most serious punishments were handed down by a 'Common Room', to which a miscreant would be summoned to face the combined wrath of the gathered President and fellows. This may have been 'a ceremony to make a young man quake,' but generally, the majority of commoners showed little respect for their elders. Frederick Meyrick (scholar 1843, fellow 1847–60) remembered Joseph Smith (fellow 1824–52)[61]—'his essential quality was pompousness'—as 'a constant joy to the undergraduates; some story about "the Bursar" was always afloat.' Smith was redoubtable when Meyrick and the other scholars warned him of a plot to throw 'an explosive ball into [his] study, where he generally sat after tea. "Is it gunpowder?"' he asked mildly. 'Then I sit here tonight.'[62]

'You only heard of the President when a common room was called' in Pycroft's day,[63] and the head of house seems to have been similarly distant to Newman. Thomas Lee returned from the College living of Barton to take up the presidency in 1808. He had held a fellowship between 1784 and 1807, but had been out of residence since 1790. When as a freshman Newman called on President Lee, he was told that 'he left all such questions, as Mr Newman asked, to be answered by the tutors.'[64] Lee was Vice-Chancellor at the time, and the University Bedel, George Cox, remembered how he 'went through his quadrennium of office (from 1814 to 1818) . . . in calm, easy-going days, and in an amiable, unobtrusive manner . . . In his private and college life he was highly esteemed; he also played a steady second violin part in a quartet.'[65] The Lees regularly entertained college guests to dinner in the Lodgings; in March 1822, Newman took his violin along to a 'Music party at the President's . . . we played chiefly Haydn's symphonies.'[66]

Thomas Lee was succeeded by James Ingram (fellow 1803–17) in

[61] Smith was senior bursar 1827/8–28/9, 1834/5–38/9, and 1842/3–51/2, and junior bursar 1833–4.

[62] Frederick Meyrick, *Memories of Life at Oxford and Elsewhere* (London, 1905), 11–12.

[63] Pycroft, *Memories*, i, 52

[64] *Newman Letters & Diaries*, 39.

[65] G. V. Cox, *Recollections of Oxford* (London, 1868), 192–3.

[66] *Newman Letters & Diaries*, 126. Newman preserved an invitation from Mrs Lee to dine during his finals. Dinner was at 4.30. She graciously gave him permission to decline: 'altho she will be sorry not to see Mr Newman as several of his friends dine at the Lodgings and that she likewise thinks an hour or two in a pleasant party would do him good, yet if he wishes not to accept any invitation until his arduous task is over, she and the President will be fully aware of his motive.' Ibid., 93 n. 2.

1824. Ingram frequently struggled to maintain his presidential poise as he combined his own serious academic research and writing with the governance of an undergraduate college. 'Any noise in quad was at any time liable to draw old Ingram from his lair,' mused Pycroft, with the consideration born of *A Retrospect after Fifty Years*. 'No doubt for a busy and studious man, and devoted antiquary, a lot of thoughtless, noisy youths must have been very irritating.' Ingram left much of the administrative minutiae to Short and the college officers, and if he did have to deal first-hand with undergraduates he could exhibit a marked lack of self-control. When Charles Graham (1831) 'one evening, just under the President's desk in chapel, sank on his side and fell asleep', the President 'began pounding the side of Graham's head with open palm. Graham sprang up in a maze, and before he knew where he was, he felt a tremendous thrust in his back that sent him staggering out of the chapel.'[67] When annoyed by late-night revelries, Ingram burst in on a wine party and threatened to beat a drunken undergraduate about the head with 'a heavy and sharp-edged French horn'. When he discovered a ban on expensive breakfast parties being flouted, he hurled a basket of 'kidneys, cutlets and broiled chickens' to the ground in Broad Street. And 'once a noisy party in the quad near his door, and not far from his study window, were cracking a tandem whip. Out rushed Ingram, snatched the whip from one man's hand, and flipped and flanked about right and left most vigorously while the men ran screeching with laughter away.' The undergraduates were quite sure that Ingram 'had attained some celebrity as a Cornish wrestler' in his youth.[68]

Tommy Short was regarded as the real fount of college authority, and his success lay in his confidence in dealing with the young men around him. He was 'one of the best of tutors to keep the men in order,' considered Pycroft. 'At lecture he showed a degree of grammatical accuracy and a certainty in his familiar negative, "you're wrong" not common with other tutors.' He was equally outspoken and direct with parents. When James Pycroft's father sought advice on his son's likely expenses, Short told him to '"not calculate on less than £200 a year". He afterwards in conversation remarked, "I prefer to be explicit; but I do meet with some great fools."'[69] It was

[67] Pycroft, *Memories*, i, 53. Pycroft never forgot the grief of the undergraduate body when Graham was drowned in a sailing accident on the Isis, a tragedy which led to the introduction of the first water safety measures; ibid., ii, 74–5.

[68] Ibid., i, 53–4, 57–8.

[69] Ibid., i, 58–9, 121.

a great advantage to Short that the undergraduates believed so implicitly in his ability to detect lies, and were willing to submit to his rulings.

Others of the fellows were not so successful. In 1831 Trinity was rocked by an unprecedented attempt by the undergraduate body to unite in a fight against what they believed to be unfair treatment by the dean. The trouble began with 'a system of outrages against the property of individuals & the college'—smashing windows—and culminated in the following demand, which was personally addressed to President Ingram:

> At a meeting of the undergraduates of Trinity College held on Monday the 31st day of October the following Petition was unanimously agreed upon:
>
> That in the opinion of this meeting a Petition should be presented to the President praying for a redress of grievances, stating that the meeting had been called not to set the college authority at defiance but humbly to suggest that the impositions set by the present dean for minor offences are of the most unprecedented length & are found to interfere extremely with college study, & that his excessive severity is prejudicial to college discipline. That this meeting looks with the most unqualified disapprobation at the breaking of the Dean's windows & disclaims all knowledge of the offender. That this meeting trust the Revd the President will not lightly treat this our unanimous petition as we consider it the only respectful manner in which we can make known our reasonable grounds of complaint.

This eloquent document was signed by no less than fifty-three undergraduates, nine of them scholars. The dean, Henry Michell, had held his fellowship for only fifteen months; clearly neither he nor Ingram knew what to do next. There was an emergency meeting of President and college officers in the Lodgings on 5 November. Michell 'laid before the meeting an account of the impositions set by him. It was agreed that the impositions were not of great length nor was there any foundation for the imputation of severity.' The scholars were called in, and 'reprimanded', but no action was taken against the commoners for another two weeks. On 19 November, the 'senior undergraduate members' were summoned before the College audit, and—in the notable absence of the President—were scolded by Tommy Short (acting as vice-president) who forced them to admit 'the impropriety of the proceeding'. The petitioners thus divided, the protest fizzled out. Those who 'made the same acknowledgement' were let off 'the imposition determined on for the offence'; but from those who did not, it was 'strictly exacted'. One week later, four undergraduates were permitted to leave for other colleges; then, after 'further outrage', presumably in the form of broken glass, it was firmly agreed 'no more *liceats* should be granted'. Michell wrote up the proceedings in his decanal book as a victory for 'college regulations', but he had resigned from his fellowship by the end of the year.[70]

A more successful dean, in 1840–1, was Arthur Kensington. He recorded no incidents in the dean's book, but 'left to posterity, twelve rules' for the practical assistance of his successors.

1. Be sure to have postponable lectures on Thursdays between 9 & 11.
2. Do not forget to give out Chapel Lists on Saturday evening, and to have subjects for exercises etc. put up before Hall lecture on Monday.
3. Look well after the marking scholars [who kept a register of chapel attendance] who will plague you exceedingly, if you do not, by their carelessness.
4. Never miss Surplice Prayers—cast your eye over the men yourself. This will save you an immensity of trouble, as you will see at a glance if it is right, whilst you are on the spot.
5. Be sure to tell every Freshmen Chapel & Exercise regulations. Explain about the Fine, & tell them what purpose is applied, & put up no notices in Hall.
6. In summer terms have the garden gate locked at 10.30 and not 10, & just walk through the garden before you go to Church.
7. · · · Tell every man who comes to you about his degree 5 things twice over:

   To go to the President for Declamation
   To attend chapel with it on degree morning
   To put down name at Vice-Chancellor's
   To breakfast with dean etc. . . .

[70] The Buttery Book for the week beginning 28 October 1831 shows fifty-four undergraduates in residence, and five fellows. Ingram was away. TCA Buttery Book 1831 Sept.–1832 March; TCA *Liber Decani* I, ff. 76–8. Michell seems to have felt no lasting ill will, for, having changed his name to Luttman-Johnson, he sent two sons to Trinity in 1858 and 1868.

And tell them before they go to the schools to pay college fees to you, & state the amount viz MA £6 1s, BA £3 16s.

8. Never omit sending for men if they have done anything wrong.
9. Do not be ακριβοdικαιος [a stickler for the rules] on account of small faults if not very frequent, and never refuse anything that is asked you in a straightforward way, unless you have some particular reason, & abstain from asking questions if you mean to grant it.
10. If you suspect anything going on wrong without being able to fix on individuals speak about it at your large lectures.
11. Appeal to good feelings etc if rules are violated, if the offender has any; if not be down on him sharp.
12. Avoid bringing reprobates before the college as much as possible, except where the offence is pretty manifest & the punishment therefore certain.[71]

This shrewd policy may have served Kensington well during the Oxford career of one of Trinity's most notorious undergraduates, Richard Burton. The main source of his notoriety is in fact his own highly coloured account, which has been taken on trust by generations of biographers. Burton came to Trinity from Italy. He was a talented linguist, he was sexually experienced, he was accustomed to a considerable degree of personal freedom, and he was arrogant. Not surprisingly, he took an instant dislike to the restrictive rules of college life, the uninspiring and pedagogic teaching methods, the callow society of most of his contemporaries—'I felt as if I had fallen among *épiciers*' (grocers)—and the British climate. Nor did he enjoy the food:

> It consisted of hunches of meat, cooked after Homeric or Central African fashion. and very filling at the price. The vegetables . . . were plain boiled, without the slightest aid to digestion . . . This cannibal meal was succeeded by stodgy pudding, and concluded with some form of cheese, Cheshire or double Gloucester, which painfully reminded one of bees'-wax, and this was called dinner.

As Burton told the story, he arrived full of good intentions to work for a first and win a college fellowship, but very soon abandoned all hope of an academic future—'the fellows of Trinity were nice, gentlemanly men, but I by no means wished to become one of the

[71] *Liber Decani*, ff. 80–1.

number'—and spent his time fencing, rowing, and playing practical jokes. After two terms and a long vacation in Germany, he resolved to get himself rusticated, which—so he claimed—he did by ostentatiously going to a forbidden steeplechase, and by impugning the honour of the fellows by the insulting suggestion that they might not return his caution money. Burton gave a fine description of his defiant departure from Oxford in a tandem:

> driven boldly up to the college doors. My bag and baggage were stowed away in it, and with a cantering leader and a high-trotting shaft-horse, which unfortunately went over the beds of the best flowers, we started from the High Street by the Queen's Highway to London, I artistically performing upon a yard of tin trumpet, waving adieu to my friends, and kissing my hand to pretty shop girls.[72]

The eloquent silence of the college records, however, suggests a less exciting year in college, and the buttery book tells a mundane and rather more credible story. Burton went down, with his fellow undergraduates, on the last day of Hilary Term 1841.

James Pycroft divided his contemporaries into a number of distinct sets. Besides the boating men, he admired 'the Scholars' set [which] was as it should be, sober, intellectual, and in every sense improving,' while he himself aspired to be 'intimate with reading men'. He recognized too

> a more rational class. Such were the late Sir Crawley Boevey, Hunt, Pulteney, and others, whose fathers could afford to let them keep horses and hunt—men who did not pretend to be studious or hard-reading men; but who went quietly through the academical course and had little difficulty with their degrees.

Tommy Short was of course able to differentiate appropriately between the different sets in College, taking 'the rougher class of men' himself, and handing the amiable Pycroft over to 'Poor Williams! Among the wilder set of Trinity he was as much out of his element as a high Church missionary among the wild tribes of Timbuktu.' Short was 'very keen and sharp', enthused Pycroft,

> idle excuses went for nothing with him; the reading men met much encouragement, and the hunting and sporting men were rarely refused leave of absence from lecture. I think he had a secret

[72] Isabel Burton, *The Life of Captain Sir Richard F. Burton* (London 1893), i, 69–78, 82, 88–90.

satisfaction in the remark, then often heard, that Trinity turned out more red coats than most of the colleges twice its size.[73]

A final type of undergraduate identifiable in 1830s Trinity was the 'religious set . . . We called them the saints, they were all very low church.' In Pycroft's eyes, they 'consisted of two or three who held together and were chiefly distinguished by their absurdly preaching to every one else'.[74] By the beginning of the nineteenth century, religion in college had sunk to a very low ebb. Stories abounded of biblical ignorance uncovered in examinations. Newman, strongly evangelical in his younger days, was regularly shocked by the irreverence—to him, the apostasy—of his contemporaries. 'O how the Angels must lament,' he sighed, as he contemplated the 1819 Gaudy, 'If there be one time of the year in which the glory of our college is humbled, and all appearance of goodness fades away, it is on Trinity Monday.'[75] Nothing was more important to him than his Christian faith: 'It is my daily and (I hope) heartfelt prayer, that I may not get any honours here, if they are to be the least cause of sin to me,' he wrote shortly before his finals.[76]

Newman never discussed, or expected to discuss, religion with his tutor. Tommy Short's biographer, C. E. H. Edwards, knew him as 'a high and dry Tory Churchman, who could see nothing specially incongruous in a Bishop discussing the breed of sheep during the pauses of a Confirmation service caused by a broken window being mended. He kept up the old custom of bowing ceremoniously in hall and chapel' but disapproved of anything ostentatious, like fasting, which 'always called forth some witty and caustic remark'. Only once did Short betray the existence of a spiritual side to his life, to his former pupil and colleague, Thomas Claughton, who had recently been raised to a bishopric:

> I dined with him one evening at the President's . . . We strolled into the garden after dinner, and suddenly dear old Short (we were quite alone) stopped, and he knelt on the grass and said; 'Claughton, give me your blessing.' I was much moved by it, as you can imagine.[77]

[73] Pycroft, *Memories*, i, 14, 104, 155, 186.

[74] Ibid., i, 147, 150.

[75] *Newman Letters and Diaries*, 66. [76] Ibid., 48.

[77] Edwards, *Oxford Tutor*, 44, 49, 54. Claughton was consecrated Bishop of Rochester in 1867, when Short was 78.

Isaac Williams deplored the low level of religious activity—'very dead'—when he took up his Trinity fellowship in 1831. He made it his duty not to miss the University Sermons, but found them 'a great trial of patience, and on Saints' days I was often nearly the only one in church listening to the usual hack preacher, who was reading some old sermon . . . earning his five guineas in a manner unedifying and unprofitable to all but himself.' A quondam Trinity scholar, John William Hughes (scholar 1813), complained to Tommy Short about his 'only solitary silent witness': '"I wonder what Williams admires so much in me; he is the only person in the university who comes to my sermons on Saints' days. It is very complimentary of him, but it puts me to a little trouble . . .".'[78] Williams himself was extremely active on the religious front. His dealings with his close friends, James Froude, John Keble, and Newman, were largely centred on Oriel College, but, as Williams recalled it, the Oxford Movement—Anglicanism's affirmation of its links to the early Church, and its restoration of the High-Church ideals of the seventeenth century—actually started within the very precinct of Trinity College:

> the circumstance which I most remember about that time was a conversation with Froude which was the first commencement of the 'Tracts for the Times.' He returned full of energy [Froude had been travelling abroad with Newman] and of a prospect of doing something for the Church, and we walked in the Trinity College Gardens and discussed the subject. He said in his manner, 'Isaac, we must make a row in the world. Why should we not?'[79]

By 1840 there was a strong culture of Anglo-Catholicism in the College. James Laird Patterson (1840) and Edward Augustus Freeman (scholar 1841) were two of the four founder members of the inter-collegiate 'Mason's Brotherhood of St Mary'. The brotherhood was 'founded for the study of ecclesiastical art upon true and catholic principles' at the end of 1844 and was to consist of up to ten resident members, one to be chosen master and another appointed amanuensis. They agreed to hold 'an annual commemoration on ye feast of ye purification of S: Mary' and to preserve 'rules and all other documents in manuscript only'. At their first meeting, held in Freeman's rooms on 2 February 1845, the four 'brothers' enjoyed a discussion

[78] *Autobiography of Williams*, ed. Prevost, 52.
[79] Ibid., 62–3.

on 'the superiority of high-pitched or low-pitched roofs'. New members accepted their invitations to join, rituals for 'chapters' were devised, and additional rules were adopted, many in the form of non-binding 'suggestions' left to the individual's discretion, as the brothers aspired to 'rise early', to 'be moderate in food', to 'devote some time' to serious study each day, to 'receive the Holy Communion, if possible, every week', and to 'try in all ways to bring others to the love of God'.[80]

A devout Trinity diarist of this period was Wharton Booth Marriott (scholar 1843), whose daily routine centred on his various affiliations with like-minded members of his own and other colleges. Their numbers in Trinity were sufficient for them to be a significant force in college life, daring even to discuss 'the propriety of a Petition from undergraduates to the Head in favour of decreased expenses and stricter discipline'. In March 1846, Marriott also became:

> a member of the Decade [an influential university essay-reading society], and of the Hermes,[81] a kind of anti-Decade, whose first meeting, a very successful one, was held in Coleridge's rooms, last Monday. I am to open the next debate . . . on the motion that circumstances were more favourable to the development of the Fine Art in ancient than in modern times.[82]

Marriott developed a particularly close friendship with his contemporary Frederick Meyrick (scholar 1843). 'I never yet met with the man before whom I could pour out my *whole* self, or rather my *two* selves,' Marriott confided to his diary, 'but my *better* self seems to yearn for such a friend as Frederick—and he seems not disinclined to meet me half way.' Meyrick in turn admired Marriott's 'great strength of character. He was strong in body, strong in mind' and took 'a leading position among us . . . His healthy muscularity and genial wit and humour were very useful to repress any morbid tendencies towards asceticism.'[83] The scholars of 1840–3 were an exceptionally close brotherhood. Meyrick wrote of their 'Trinity ethos':

[80] At some point the Brotherhood changed its allegiance to the Holy Trinity. A minute book and various papers relating to the Brotherhood were given to Trinity by a son of Frederick Meyrick (scholar 1843, fellow 1847–60) in 1941, and subsequently preserved by President Weaver. TCA DD28.

[81] M. C. Curthoys and C. J. Day, 'The Oxford of Mr Verdant Green', *HUO* 6, 285.

[82] Diary of W. B. Marriott, TCA REF, 12 and 26 March 1846.

[83] Frederick Meyrick, *Memories*, 22.

> Chiefly it resulted from our loyally accepting and realising the true idea of college life. We loved to regard each other, Fellows and Scholars, as members of one family, our Founder's . . . We were a family of brothers, emulating not envying one another, gladly learning from each other, without jealousy one of another, and possessing for a time a common family character.[84]

They were as oblivious to the College boat as its crew were ignorant of their high ideals. But Tommy Short knew, and disapproved, of both. 'I remember . . . when there were some eighteen undergraduates of the Tractarian School in this College, who tried to set up what they called a Trinity ethos!' he would boast. '*I* threw not only *cold* water, but *dirty* water, upon their ascetic practices.'[85]

## *University Reform*

Short was unable, however, to stem the tide of change. For the first half of the nineteenth century, the fellows of Trinity still lived under the restrictions—and the freedoms—of the Founder's Statutes. The pressure for places was reduced by the greater range of career options open to the scholars: Henry Davison (scholar 1824) became Chief Justice of Madras; Herman Merivale (scholar 1825) served as Under-Secretary of State for the Colonies, and for India; Edward Twisleton (scholar 1826) was Commissioner for Poor Law, for Public Schools, and for the Civil Service; Roundell Palmer (scholar 1830) entered politics, and became, ultimately, Lord Chancellor; George Bowen (scholar 1840) was variously Governor of Queensland, New Zealand, Victoria (Canada), Mauritius, and Hong Kong; Erasmus Brodie (scholar 1850) became a schools inspector; and Charles Alderson (scholar 1851) Chief Charity Commissioner.[86] An increasing number also held fellowships at other colleges. Twisleton was a fellow of Balliol from 1830–8. Palmer was elected fellow of Magdalen in 1834, Nutcombe Oxenham (scholar 1829) fellow of Exeter in 1832, and George Kettilby Rickards (scholar 1829) fellow of Queen's in 1836. Wharton Booth Marriott left Trinity for a fellowship at Exeter

[84] Frederick Meyrick, 'Narration of Three Years of Undergraduate Life', in *Memorials of W. B. Marriott*, ed. Fenton J. A. Hort (London, 1873), 57–8.

[85] *Breviarum*, 48.

[86] The careers of 19th-century Trinity alumni may be studied in M. H. Green, *Admissions in the Nineteenth Century* (1901).

College in 1846. An 'open' fellowship could be subject to a highly competitive examination, such as that taken by Newman at Oriel in 1822. Trinity's fellowships remained closed until 1843, when George Ormsby, exhibitioner of Lincoln College, was elected. The second non-Trinity scholar elected to a fellowship was William Stubbs (1848), who had been an exhibitioner at Christ Church.[87]

Those scholars who took the time-honoured course of a fellowship at Trinity were still very much 'migrants' for whom the position was but a stepping-stone in a traditional clerical career.[88] They too found more openings in the Church at home and abroad. Of the thirty fellows elected between 1800 and 1850, twenty went on to hold benefices, but only six of these were Trinity livings. In 1825 the fellows took the decision to establish an 'Advowson Fund' with the express purpose of purchasing livings 'in order to accelerate the succession of the Members of the Foundation'. Some £465, raised by voluntary contributions (diverted from the fellows' share of the college increments), was invested in 3 per cent stocks, and several large bequests were made in favour of the fund. Henry Kett bequeathed £500 in 1825, and Anne, the widow of President Lee, £300 in 1843.[89] But they were responding to the needs of a past generation. Only one living was ever purchased, that of Newbold Verdun in Leicestershire, which cost £3,750 in 1843.[90] In 1850 Trinity received by the bequest of James Ford (fellow 1806–31 and vicar of Navestock) £4,000, intended to be invested for the purchase of advowsons. Royal Licence was obtained in 1860, but no advowsons were ever bought.[91] It was already clear that the demand for parochial preferment was not what it had once been, and by the 1880s the fund had become rather an embarrassment.[92]

Many fellows took advantage of the rules that allowed them to live, and work, away from college. In 1824 it became necessary to draw up a rota by which 'the non resident fellows whose attendance may be required for the transaction of business in college [could] be

[87] See Green, *Admissions*.

[88] M. G. Brock, 'The Oxford of Peel and Gladstone', *HUO* 6, 22.

[89] The first decision was taken in March 1823, TCA Order Book C, f. 25.

[90] TCA Title Deeds, Newbold Verdun 11.

[91] Ford left to Trinity another £4,000 to endow exhibitions from the Grammar Schools of Canterbury, Ipswich, and Brentwood (TCA Trusts 8).

[92] TCA Trusts 7. In 1885 the trustees agreed to widen the purpose of the fund in order to use it for improvements in college livings.

summoned up,' and not until the audit of 1833 was no summons necessary.[93] Between 1824 and 1857 the senior fellow was one George Griffinhoofe (fellow 1797); but from 1805 he was absent as the vicar of Catterington in Hampshire. Griffinhoofe was sincerely troubled by the thought of occupying a fellowship that might benefit another man, and he regularly intended to resign. But to give up a position that was legally his, and which paid a stipend for no work at all (he was regularly excused the annual Trinity Monday visit on medical grounds) was to his family, proof of insanity; Griffinhoofe's brother Thomas (commoner 1798) wrote regularly to the President on the subject over the course of thirty years.[94]

As Oxford's student body increased in size, the inadequacies of the collegiate structure became apparent, and the problems and possibilities of reform were debated widely. The fellows of Trinity recognized that the College's role, essentially, was as an educational establishment, as opposed to the religious institution it had been once. Tutors were central to this work, and yet—*pace* Thomas Short—to be a tutor was a temporary job, mainly attractive to young and single men, and one that offered no professional career structure, no prospects of promotion or incentives to undertake research. The official means of teaching—lectures—was obsolete. 'No reading man in any time thought there was much use in the college lectures,' complained Pycroft. 'The worst part of it was that the lectures broke in on all that time, from ten o'clock till one, which is most valuable for private study.'[95]

Numerous proposals for change were argued over publicly. James Ingram went anonymously into print to defend the autonomy of the colleges against those reformers who would see all teaching given over to a hierarchy of properly qualified professors.[96] Trinity made various efforts to reduce costs, a perennial area of popular criticism. In April 1850 a Parliamentary Commission was appointed, with a brief to inquire into the statutes and practices of Oxford and Cambridge Universities and colleges. The fellows of many colleges,

[93] The requirement was clarified in December 1825: orders were to be agreed by the President and seven actual fellows, and signed by the President and four actual fellows. TCA Order Book C, ff. 39, 53.

[94] TCA, Old Bursary Drawer 9, correspondence 1825–55.

[95] Pycroft, *Memories*, i, 76.

[96] *Apologia Academica or Remarks on a Recent Article in the Edinburgh Review* (London, 1831).

including Trinity, were reluctant to recognize its authority, or to make any return beyond a polite acknowledgement. Even George Griffinhoofe was recruited to add his voice to their expressions of disquiet: in June 1852 Thomas Griffinhoofe sent in 'the enclosed memorial, with the addition of my brother's signature, which he inserted with evident approval'.[97]

But when the Commission's Report—the 'Blue Book'—was published, in May 1852, it could not be ignored so easily. Its recommendations concerning the colleges themselves were wide-ranging: costs should be reduced, fellowships should be subject to open competition, and stipulations about taking holy orders should be abolished. Its recommendations concerning university examinations—four separate honours schools, in theology, moral philosophy and philology, jurisprudence and history, and mathematical and physical science—portended serious difficulties for the existing teaching arrangements in the colleges.[98]

In 1850 James Ingram was succeeded by John Wilson. The new President was a loyal and serious college man, experienced in the offices of tutor and bursar, and by no means blind to the inadequacies of the present college administration. Wilson at once began an urgent correspondence with the Visitor, Charles Sumner, without whose approval no reform of Trinity was possible. In 1853 Sumner came on an official visitation to Trinity and was presented with a detailed and comprehensive 'summary paper', of 'changes which appear to us to be necessary either in themselves or under the altered circumstances of the time in order to the better fulfilment of the duties of our foundation'. There was, as yet, no way of getting away from the Founder, and the document continued with 'questions upon the construction of our statutes' arranged under eight separate headings.

Thomas Pope would surely have approved the way that 'chapel services' were addressed first, taking precedence over both 'education' and 'expenses'. Wilson wrote eloquently of the need for 'instruction or guidance such as would be supplied by *sermons*' and for more regular celebration of Holy Communion. The fellows had considered a way to address the need for more specialized teaching, and the training of the junior fellows. By increasing the lecturers' stipends, it was felt, they could be required to give daily tutorials, and would gain 'at

[97] TCA Statutes B/1 Visitation Commission volume.
[98] W. R. Ward, 'From the Tractarians to the Executive Commission', *HUO* 6, 317–22.

least two hours . . . useful employment'. Other suggestions included the establishment of exhibitions as a means of keeping promising undergraduates who had failed to win scholarships; a library for the use of junior members; and some thorough reform of college finance. But, as Wilson admitted glumly, most of these proposed reforms 'were not in accordance with the spirit of our statutes', and he feared that 'even legislation could not annul the moral force of the college oath.'[99]

In 1857 a body of 'ordinances' was put in place by the Commission, addressing, in a limited way, some of the problems of the old Statutes. Five of the fellowships were now open to laymen, and one could be held by a professor. The Governing Body was empowered to ignore the Statutes that were being ignored already—regarding religious practice, educational methods, and domestic arrangements—and to bring in their own regulations in their place. But these had the feel of temporary measures; the next presidential election, for example, had double the formalities, as both the Founder's Statute and the new Ordinance were read aloud.[100]

The college buildings and facilities were in some ways easier to modernize. Early in the century, an extensive programme of repair and improvement began, with the purpose of expanding the College's capacity. The 'low chamber' to the south of the hall was converted into a 'new bursary' (today's 'old bursary'), while the former bursary beneath the Library (now a bursary again) was annexed to the Lodgings for the use of the President's servants. In 1810 the 'uninhabited garrets, or lumber rooms' above the kitchen were 'converted into two good attics'. The following year new rooms were built over the common room and bursary, using the £500 legacy received from the college lodger, Warton's friend and Bodleys' librarian, John Price.[101] A new room 'formerly [a] laundry' was created in the Bathurst Building, where the existing four rooms were 'repaired, improved' and in one case, 'papered'. Both the Bachelors' Common Room and the Gentlemen Commoners' Common Room were restored to their original purposes. In 1822 the books and bookcases of Bathurst's juniors' library were carted off to the tower in order that it could be converted into two sets of usable rooms. The 'back build-

[99] TCA Visitation Commission; Ward, 'Tractarians', 22.
[100] TCA Register D, 243–5.
[101] TCA Benefactors' Book III. John Price had been living in Trinity since 1789.

ings' in the 'pump court' were recognized as 'less eligible' than others. Internal reorganization in 1826–7 found space for 'five additional members' but at the cost of some 'having bedrooms only'. These rooms tended to be occupied for only a short time until they could be 'exchanged for better, as vacancies occur'. In 1826 the study of a ground-floor set [on today's Staircase 13] was converted to a bedroom in order that two brothers might share. A survey at about the same date found sixty sets of rooms 'not including Common rooms and offices'. Trinity was, for the most part, full. Room Lists of 1847 and 1849 even name members 'sleeping in the library'.[102]

The public parts of the College were similarly refurbished. In the summer of 1821 the skirting boards of the staircases were painted, and the 'garden privies' painted and repaired. Since 1795 a second 'lavatory block' had also been available in the Dolphin Yard, a useful addition to the College site in the 1780s.[103] In 1822 the statues on the Chapel tower were taken down and replaced 'with new ones of Bath Stone at £30 each', while it was agreed that 'the tower be rebuilt as far down as the first moulding, if necessary.' 'Medicine', which seems to have been in the best condition, was placed in the President's garden, where it remained until the tower was next repaired, in the 1960s. In 1823 the Chapel was given an inner door covered with crimson baize; three years later it was 'thoroughly cleaned and washed' and 'the broken parts of the ornamental work' repaired. At the same it was agreed that the hall ceiling should 'undergo a thorough repair', while the panelling should be painted 'a stone colour' and the walls 'distempered' in a lighter shade of the same.[104]

These changes were mainly cosmetic. Without a new programme of building works, and without a new set of Statutes, there was little more that could be done. The Library underwent a major refurbishment in 1850, when the bequest of James Ingram's library doubled Trinity's holding of books. The bookcases were raised to ceiling height, but nothing was done to meet the reading needs of the undergraduate body. On 21 September 1866, President Wilson wrote to inform the fellows that he intended to resign at the end of the Michaelmas Term, a decision, he said that did 'not arise from any

[102] TCA Room Register C; Order Book C, f. 3.

[103] TCA Order Book C, f. 11. At the same time outer doors were fixed to several staircases and to the privy. 'Such alterations as can best be contrived' were mooted for the servants' privy, but, sadly, 'none' were made.

[104] TCA Order Book C, ff. 15–16, 21, 29, 59.

sudden or hasty resolution but [was] the result of much consideration'.[105] He retired to spend the last seven years of his life in rural seclusion at Woodperry House, not far from Oxford.[106] Some felt that he was 'worried into resignation by Mr Wayte [his successor] and the junior fellows', a theory which Wayte firmly denied.[107]

Tommy Short, with characteristic candour, used to say, 'College rooms are pleasant places to live in; they are not pleasant places to die in.'[108] Charles S. de L. Lacy (1866) remembered evening encounters with Short—an 'old gentleman of the old school'—with fondness:

> The dear old man was not very often in residence, he had long since ceased taking any lecture, and was only up for a few weeks during the term. We often used to wonder how much port old Tommy drank during his life, I daresay for many years a bottle a night. In his old age no doubt a couple of glasses was all he took, but they were sufficient to get into his head just for a short time, and he used to come out of the Common room and shuffle through the Pig and Whistle [passage] . . . —and look doubtfully at his staircase, which was diagonally across the Inner Quad. Any of us standing about used to give him an arm; I have often done so. 'Thank ye, my boy, thank ye. I'll do the same for you another time' he would say.[109]

In 1876 Short retired from the College and returned to the Warwickshire village of his birth. He saw no reason, however, to resign his fellowship, and before his death on 31 May 1879 he returned to Trinity at least once, when he participated in an event which he barely understood, but which was to shape the future of the College in ways which he would have deplored.

105 TCA Register D, 205.

106 Only one of Wilson's fourteen predecessors (Hawes) resigned; four of his five immediate successors did so (the fifth, Pelham, died in office). Presidents elected since the 1926 Statutes have been obliged to retire at 70.

107 TCA OF 12, no. 4, 3; no. 5, 16. The undergraduates joked that Wayte had forced Wilson, who had only one arm, into resignation, by insisting on the addition of a minute hand to the clock on the chapel tower. 'He used to go into the quadrangle,' asserted Edmund Bagshawe (who came up in 1874, eight years after Wilson's departure) 'and, waving his arm, cry to the clock—"they can give you a new hand but I can't get one."' (OF 12, no. 5, 15–16.)

108 *Breviarium*, 55–6. Different advice was given to John Pervical, when Benjamin Jowett was urging him to seek headship of a college: 'These headships of colleges, although not very distinguished positions, are good places in which to grow old.' Jowett to Percival, 15 March 1874, in Temple, *Percival*, 50.

109 TCA OM 14 Lacy, 'Oxford', 3.

# 9

# *President Perceval*

## *Trinity in the 1860s*

Students of mid-nineteenth-century Trinity life are greatly indebted to the inventors of the camera. Photographs were being taken in Oxford as early as 1842—one of the first to experiment with the new process was a scholar of Trinity, William Basil Jones (1840)[1]—and by 1861 there were ten professional photographers in the city.[2] Many undergraduates were collecting photographic prints in albums, and it had become customary to exchange studio portraits with one's friends. Sanford G. T. Scobell (1857) preserved a set of twenty Oxford scenes, nine of them of Trinity, and thirty-four undergraduate portraits, many accompanied by the autographs of his contemporaries. Several of the same faces appear in the album of Charles R. Bradburne (1857). Henry E. Hulton (1858) preserved the earliest dated College group, taken in 1861: eighteen young men informally arranged around a sapling to the east of the President's garden. One of the first group photographs taken in the Garden Quad is preserved in the album of John L. G. Hadow (1864): the man looking through the window appears to be Tommy Short (Plate 9.1).[3]

One 1867 freshman, Randall Thomas Davidson, stands out from the other undergraduates of his day. He was recovering from a serious injury received fourteen months before (a friend had accidentally shot him in the lower back as they returned from shooting rabbits), and it was his destiny to be Archbishop of Canterbury.[4] Davidson, the

[1] I am grateful to Giles Hudson of the Museum of the History of Science for this information.

[2] *The Oxford Directory* (1861), 85.

[3] TCA DD 258 Scobell; OM 7 Bradburne; OM 8 Hulton; OM 11 Hadow.

[4] Davidson saw the accident as a turning-point in his life; at the very least it brought him to Trinity when he had expected to win a scholarship to Corpus. At first partially paralysed, he eventually recovered his mobility except for a slight limp. At Trinity he suffered from headaches and memory loss, missed two of his first three terms, and

*9.1* College group, *c.*1865. Staircase 7 (now 14) is the traditional place to take such pictures. (Album of John L. G. Hadow (1864), TCA OM 11).

eldest son of an Edinburgh merchant, was admitted to Trinity on 12 October 1867, and, despite his health problems, was given rooms on the top floor of the Garden Quadrangle. 'They are very good for a freshman,' he informed his parents, and 'my sitting room has a lovely look out upon the coalhouse tiles. My bedroom has a wee window into the quad.'[5] Heating was provided by the traditional coal fire, but the rooms were lit by gas lamps, which had been installed in the 'quadrangles, staircases, buttery, kitchen & privies in the backyard' by decision of the President and fellows in 1857.[6]

Davidson's first friend at Trinity was Thomas G. S. Mahon. 'I don't know what Mahon or I should do without one another,' he told his mother. 'The other freshmen who are up are none of them . . . nice men at all, and it is rather a bore being alone at table with them.' The nice thing about Mahon was the fact that Davidson had known him at Harrow School. 'The old Harrow men here are very kind,' Davidson noted on his third day in college; and doubtless the Wykehamists and the Rugbeians had similar experiences. By 23 October, Davidson was able to tell his father of 'a very nice Rugby man in the next rooms to mine—called Lucy. He and I are great friends.'[7] The twenty-one men admitted in 1867 had come from fourteen different establishments, but of these only two were not public schools. One hopes that John Merryweather (Lincoln Grammar School) and Richard Ward (Edgbaston) had something in common besides their socially inferior education.[8]

Davidson and Mahon were 'together in everything in the work line'. In his first term, Davidson had eleven lectures a week (including one on Saturday morning) on Thucydides, Virgil's *Eclogues*, mathematics, and the Gospel of Luke. 'Hurrah!' he wrote on 6 December, the day of his 'smalls' exam: 'I shall never have to open a Euclid

'collapsed' on the second day of his finals. He always recalled his Oxford years as 'a time of disappointment'. G. K. A. Bell, *Randall Davidson* (London, 1935), i, 18–21.

[5] Now Staircase 14, room 12.

[6] TCA Order Book D, 105. Trinity's first ever gas bill was for £11 12*s* for 46,400 cubic feet of gas consumed in the six months ending in March 1858, TCA Accounts I/F/6.4; The Act for Gas Lighting in Oxford was given royal assent in May 1818, but the concept had not met with the immediate approval of the fellows; TCA OB Drawer 24.

[7] LPL Davidson II, ff. 1–3. This was William Charles Lucy, as opposed to another of Davidson's friends, Charles Sethward de Lacy Lacy (1866).

[8] TCA Admissions Register C, 67–9. Eleven of the public-school boys came from 'Clarendon' Schools: Charterhouse, Harrow (4), Rugby (3), and Winchester (3). The others were from Blackheath, Bradfield, Cheltenham, King's College London, Leamington, Marlborough, Rossall, and Tonbridge.

again.' His daily timetable was much the same as John Skinner's had been, sixty years before:

| | |
|---|---|
| 8 a.m. | Chapel, which must be attended 4 times a week. |
| 8.30–10 a.m. | Breakfast. In your own rooms. At what hour you please. |
| 10–1 p.m. | Lectures. One hour each . . . |
| 1 p.m. | Luncheon (if you take it). Some do. Some don't. |
| 1–5 p.m. | Miscellaneous Impulses. No one *works* between 1.30 and 5. |
| 5 p.m. | Chapel—for those who don't go in the morning. |
| 5.30 p.m. | Dinner in Hall. |

Then I generally go out for about an hour after hall, and then settle to work for the evening. Supper, if you desire it, at 9 p.m.[9]

Davidson took his Sundays seriously. 'I am much disappointed with the *chapel* here,' he wrote to his mother on his first Monday in Trinity. 'There are only *two* sermons in the term! and *no organ*!!! Of course one goes on Sunday to *Church* where there is a sermon, but you must also attend service *twice* in chapel on Sundays . . . No one seems to know whether it is sandalwood or not. It does not smell.'[10]

In his first term, Davidson joined the Union Club and the Harrow Club, and throughout his years at Oxford he took a keen interest in politics as a member of the Canning Club. His health precluded rowing, but he enjoyed paddling a canoe, 'something I do now and then in the way of amusement', and played fives—'rather too expensive—1*s* 6*d* each per hour! besides balls'—and racquets, for which he even won a cup. One early highlight was a 'very jolly' day out at his old school, made possible by the advent of rail travel to Oxford: 'I was asked on Friday night to fill a vacant place in a drag which was to take a football eleven from Paddington down to Harrow.'[11]

One of Davidson's contemporaries was the Etonian Charles Lacy (1866), who wrote his memoirs many years later, while under the strong and heady influence of nostalgia. He remembered Davidson as 'a great friend of us all, especially of the Harrow men', and was

[9] TCA Admissions Register C, 1–2. Since 1850 'Smalls' was the part one examination (Moderations), as opposed to finals or 'Greats'. Of the 21 undergraduates admitted in 1867, 17 took honours degrees. There were four firsts, nine seconds, and four thirds (including Davidson).

[10] LPL Davidson II, f. 1.

[11] Ibid., ff. 2, 5, 7; Bell, *Davidson*, 19. The Great Western Railway had arrived in Oxford in 1844.

particularly proud that they had played in a scratch billiards competition together. The rose-tinted Trinity of Lacy's memories housed 'such a band of brothers' that they were the envy of all other colleges. He and his '*fidus* Achates' (best friend) Cecil Clay were never punished by the college authorities—'by persistent wrong-doing we established ourselves, as it were. . . . I suppose they liked us.' He took his degree (a pass) with virtually no work— 'How we managed it I do not know . . . I don't think I ever read at night for any exam.' In his fourth year he and three friends took rooms in a former hotel, the Shakespeare, where they 'kept open house and had a glorious time'. And when it snowed, the snow was 'quite a foot' deep. That was in Hilary Term 1867, the occasion of the first of many outrageous pranks, when:

> we thought it necessary to block up the passage between the two quads called the 'Pig and Whistle'. Taking the precaution of putting a pebble in the lock of the garden gate . . . we had unlimited snow for our purpose. It was a fine moonlight night, and it was a weird sight seeing the whole college working, very silently, filling in this passage. By three o' clock that morning we had it all filled up solid.[12]

One afternoon during his final term at Trinity, Lacy met the Dean as he walked up from the river, and nonchalantly admitted his part in 'a disgraceful scene' which had occurred three nights before on Staircase 7 (now 14):

> the only staircase in college which had straight, wide, shallow, flights of stairs, and [where] we began Pandemonium, tobogganing down the flights of stairs on tea-trays, or trying to, and bringing down all the contents of the landings, tea-kettles, baths, brooms and everything into the Quad. Here we got worse, and began throwing the things about, and bowling the tea-kettles through the ground floor windows; and a copper tea-kettle does make a splosh going through a window. We went on at this rate

[12] TCA OM 14 Lacy, 'Oxford', 7. Davidson explained the name 'Pig and Whistle' to his father as 'a low public-house kind of place where everyone turns in.' (LPL Davidson, II, f. 2.). One occupant, F. J. Stewart (1936) was informed by President Blakiston, 'Ah yes. . . . We always put the Lorettovians in the Pig and Whistle. They seem to make congenial hosts,' *Report* (1998) 65. Such a resort, conveniently near to the hall, seems to have evolved spontaneously and existed by force of necessity in the years between the closure of the Gentlemen Commoners' Common Room opposite and the opening of the Beer Cellar below.

> for about half an hour, and then Cecil and I went out of college, stating to the Porter the time-honoured fiction that we had been having tea with the Dean. The next morning there was a melancholy row of battered kettles, and broken brooms, and hardly a whole pane of glass.

On hearing of Lacy's involvement, the Dean said, ' "I was afraid of it, I was afraid of it, but did not like to ask. How can I keep the junior men in order if you senior men set such an example?" And he burst into tears.'[13]

Randall Davidson sent his parents vivid descriptions of the main players on the college stage. The tearful Dean was Alfred Plummer (fellow 1865–75), whom he found 'a pleasant, jovial, round faced, dark individual with bushy whiskers and considerable ideas of his own dignity. I don't think much of his bible lectures.' Davidson liked William G. Cole (fellow 1859–70). He was 'the bursar, and man to whom one applies for leave for anything', who, despite his 'discontented look', had 'almost . . . [a] kindly smile'. Then there was Henry G. Woods (fellow 1865–79, 1883–7), who taught composition. Davidson found him 'a young fellow . . . with an unhappy look. He is a great scholar and (as is generally believed) an atheist. That accounts for his unhappy look. I don't much like him.' Robert W. Raper (scholar 1861–5, tutor 1869–82, fellow 1871–1915), lectured to Davidson on Virgil and Thucydides. He was 'a young and very nice man—only just taken his fellowship and quite an undergraduate in spirit still. He is not yet in orders, which all the others are. Indeed I don't know if he is going into the Church. He is very handsome. I like him very much indeed.'[14] Davidson was wrong on one point: Raper was the atheist, Woods a devout Christian.

## *President Wayte*

Finally, there was:

> our noble president, 'Sammy Wayte.' He is fat, short, sulky, ugly, and stutters. At least he says peh peh peh for some considerable period before he says anything. Without exception he is the most silent man I know. I went with the other freshmen to breakfast with him and every one of us tried in turn to draw him out. It was

[13] TCA OM 14, 'Oxford', 15. [14] LPL Davidson II, f. 12.

9.2 Samuel Wayte, President 1866–78.

> no good at all. He would not say more than peh peh peh, yes, or, rarely, peh peh peh, indeed? He has a way of saying two or three words very slow and then two or three very fast.

Davidson found the President's preaching in chapel 'really painful and almost inaudible. He walks sideways—has a head in about the same proportion to his body as a tadpole's, but withal is a kind hearted old fellow with a great deal of sharpness in his own way.'[15]

Samuel William Wayte was in his mid-forties when Davidson was an undergraduate at Trinity. 'It is difficult to imagine that, when I came to Oxford [in 1868], Mr Wayte was only as old as I am now,'

[15] Ibid.

wrote Martin H. Green (fellow 1872–1927), when he heard of Wayte's final illness in 1898. 'I have always heard that he never seemed young at any age.'[16] Wayte was a very able tutor—in which capacity he had served the College throughout the twenty-four years of his fellowship—and an extremely competent administrator. He was junior bursar from 1854 to 1858, senior bursar until 1866, and continued to manage the College estates as President. Blakiston considered him a financial 'genius'.[17] Wayte's presidency saw many useful reforms eased quietly and painlessly into place. In 1867, the charge made on battels for 'charities' was discontinued. The following year, the ancient office of manciple was abolished, as it no longer gave 'satisfaction to the college'. Instead, an 'additional cook' was appointed, to 'market and be responsible for the management of the kitchen, and prepare the kitchen accounts for the Butler'. Meanwhile, the time-honoured custom of allowing the undergraduates' 'dinner remains' to the servants was replaced by a cash 'commutation', and the left-overs 'returned to the kitchen for subsequent use'. Such changes were invariably made for the sake of efficiency and cost-cutting. In December 1867 the dinner hour was altered to 6 o'clock, but on the considerate understanding 'that during the boat-races in summer term it should be at 5.30'. Meanwhile it was agreed that the college accounts should be printed, but that the word 'private', in the title was 'not to be understood in any way as debarring the President or any of the fellows from communicating the accounts to any of their friends who may be interested in University matters'.[18] In 1871 Wayte gave up the rectorship of Garsington—held by every President since the foundation—and saw it become a regular college living.[19] He had no scruples about diverting money from the advowson fund to practical use in improving college livings for both incumbents and parishioners. He also gave long and faithful service to the University, as Secretary to the University Commission 1854–8, an 'influential though silent member' of the University Council, a curator of the University Chest, and a Guardian of the Poor.

There was at times something ludicrous about President Wayte. Arthur Bernard (1871) once stayed in the Lodgings, and related how 'the President conducted him to bed each night, and was led to acknowledge that he always looked under his bed before getting into

[16] TCA Wayte no. 10. [17] Blakiston, *Trinity*, 235.
[18] TCA Order Book D, 206, 208–9, 212. [19] Ibid., 218–19, 235.

it.' Another guest, E. A. Freeman (scholar 1841, fellow 1845–7), once 'came down to breakfast very fierce because the button at the back of his shirt-collar had come off . . . the President retired and soon returned with a "housewife" [a sewing box] of such vast dimensions that he was greeted with a shout of laughter.' When, at an excruciating presidential party, Archibald Robertson (scholar 1872, fellow 1876–86) fell asleep 'so soundly that even the departure of all the other guests failed to rouse him', Wayte went to embarrassingly elaborate lengths to wake him, knocking a heavy book to the floor while standing 'in such a position that his guest on waking should not have to meet his eye'. While travelling on the continent—which he would do 'with company of a tedious and expensive kind' in the shape of 'some undergraduate whom he thought industrious and knew to be poor'—Wayte persisted in wearing a ridiculously inappropriate top hat, 'raising the raillery of Mr Wayte, of Eton [a cousin] . . . whom he chanced to meet in Normandy'. Indeed, his attachment to his 'topper' was so strong that when his hat-box was temporarily misplaced on a German train, he refused to leave Heidelberg railway station without it.[20]

Members of the College may have laughed at Wayte's foibles but they universally admired his motives. On one occasion he spoke 'with pleasure' to James F. Cornish (1870), of how, as bursar, he had 'made it possible for men of modest means to come to Trinity—for before that time it had been in great measure the resort of horsy, hunting men with heaps of money.' If there was an elite, it was presumably to be found in the Claret Club, but those at the earliest recorded dinner—held on 24 April 1870—would scarcely have passed muster among the cream of British society. The President was the Sydney-born Etonian Edward Fanning (1866), who by 1900 was 'in business' in Australia. The Secretary, Rugby-educated Herbert Kemball Cook (1867), was the son of an 'esquire', as were four of the seven other members and honorary members. Thomas Legh Claughton (1866) was the son of a Trinity clergyman, later a bishop; John Hammond Morgan (1866) the son of a medical doctor.[21]

Wayte was deeply sympathetic to the problems of the 'scouts and their widows and their children. He found his gown useful for concealing soup or wine, that he would carry to some sick connection.'

[20] TCA Wayte no. 4, 1; no. 5, 9; 'Samuel William Wayte', *Temple Bar* (December 1898), 586, 588–9.

[21] TCA JCR: C/CLA/v/1, unpaginated.

In 1870 the bursar was authorized to 'provide an entertainment for the college servants' during the Long Vacation. In 1875 the College agreed to pay half the pension contribution—a 'deferred annuity of £30 commencing at age 60'—of 'any college servant', and half the premium to insure a servant's life for £100 while he was in the College's employment.[22]

The President's life in College was centred on the undergraduates, 'not limited to those who were likely to get Firsts, but extended to all of less scholarly promise'.[23] He offered to coach Edmund Bagshawe (1874) in his 'Rudiments', for he 'could not bear anybody to fail . . . and used to instruct the men who were going in'.[24] When the President discovered that James Cornish was 'very ignorant of mathematics' he invited him to join 'a band of duffers to whom he gave instruction for several hours a week'. Sir John Bridge was another who remembered Wayte with gratitude for the 'careful and constant tuition, unasked and unpaid he had given him in mathematics all his time'.[25] The President's pastoral concern for the junior members even induced him to support the college boat, especially when it was doing badly: 'Though he had never rowed, and was not built for running, he would appear upon the tow-path when the eights were "on", and getting a good start, would amble along a little way, making encouraging remarks while breath sufficed.' When Trinity had been bumped on the first two nights of racing, 'the President appeared at the starting point, with the inevitable umbrella, and began to run with the boat.'[26] He was also a keen student of college history. 'Not long before his death,' recalled H. E. D. Blakiston, 'knowing I was studying the history of the college, Wayte sent me a large box of prints, well framed & furbished up.'[27] Such thoughtfulness was typical. Invariably modest, but never one to hinder progress, he was the first President of Trinity to be photographed (Plate 9.2); and the last not to have his portrait painted.[28]

When Wayte resigned his office, on 12 September 1878, there was widespread astonishment. He retired to Clifton, where he lived until his death on 7 September 1898. Everyone who knew Wayte

[22] 'Samuel William Wayte', 587, 589; Order Book D, 265.
[23] TCA Wayte, no. 6, 23. Memoir of Howard G. Daniell-Bainbridge (1875).
[24] TCA Wayte, no. 6, 23. Memoir of Howard G. Daniell-Bainbridge (1875), no. 5, 11.
[25] 'Samuel William Wayte,' 584–5; TCA Wayte, no. 3.
[26] 'Samuel William Wayte', 587; TCA Wayte, no. 5, 10.
[27] TCA Wayte, no. 13.
[28] He was asked in 1879, but declined. TCA Order Book D, 298.

*9.3* 'Prize Birds': the new President Percival crows over his defeated rival, Henry George Woods (Shrimpton 1878).

remembered him as 'more than popular' (James Cornish); 'dear old Sammy' (Edmund Bagshawe); 'a voiceless cause of harmony and good feeling' (*The Times*); a man of 'real benevolence' (the *Guardian*); 'Kindness was his great characteristic', (H. G. Daniell-Bainbridge); he was 'a pleasure to work with' (Henry G. Woods). Their praise was sincere, and amply justified by the evidence. 'Few people have shown more clearly how much can be effected by the silent influence of a thoroughly good life,' said 'a friend', quoted by Blakiston.[29] But there was another reason why Samuel Wayte was so highly esteemed by members of the College. They were comparing his quiet and self-effacing style with the autocratic and high-profile headship of his successor John Percival, surely the least popular appointment since the Puritan Robert Harris had been imposed on the College at the end of the Civil War.

## *The Presidential Election of 1878*

Coincidentally, Percival came to Trinity from Wayte's new home of Clifton, where he was the highly successful first headmaster of Bristol's new public school. He had just two years' experience of an Oxford fellowship (at Queen's) and no previous connection with Trinity. The only thing he had in common with his predecessor was a double first, in 1858, and that would have been a triple had not ill-health forced him to abandon his history finals after a brilliant start in the first two papers.[30] In September 1862 Percival had been a surprise appointment at Clifton, at the remarkably young age of 27. Tall and handsome, with a dominating physical presence and an awesome speaking manner, he was supremely self-confident, ambitious, and energetic. Percival was an active liberal and a keen supporter of Gladstone. His life was driven by strong Christian principles, rigid self-discipline, a tireless work ethic, and a personal agenda for comprehensive social reform. In the sixteen years of his headship, Clifton had grown from nothing to over 600 pupils. Percival had implemented an extensive building programme: classrooms, laboratories, lecture rooms, a sanatorium, sports facilities, a swimming bath (one of the earliest in the county), a chapel, and a library (which he paid

[29] 'Samuel William Wayte', 589; TCA Wayte, no. 5, 4; *The Times* (13 September 1898); the *Guardian* (14 September 1898); TCA Wayte, no. 6, 23); Blakiston, 235; TCA OF 17/4.2, H. G. Woods, 'College Loyalty, a Sermon', 2.

[30] Temple, *Percival*, 6–7.

for himself) 'had risen from the ground as by an enchanter's wand'.[31] Meanwhile, he had modernized the traditional curriculum, made science and a modern language compulsory, and actively recruited the very best masters he could get. Percival believed in social inclusivity. He promoted the integration of day boys, and established the first Jewish house at any public school in England. He always led by personal example: he was the most munificent benefactor; the most devout and diligent Christian; the pre-eminent all-rounder. Nor were his activities limited to his actual sphere of employment; he exerted his influence and his fund-raising skills towards a first-grade school for the population of Bristol, and on behalf of the city's fledgling University College. Another innovation was Clifton's school 'mission' by means of which he aspired to awaken the social consciences of his pupils and help 'the spiritually, materially, and educationally deprived' of a poor district of Bristol. Further afield, his magisterial gaze reached even as far as the unmarried mothers of his home county of Westmorland and in neighbouring Cumberland.[32]

John Percival was nowhere in the frame in August 1878 when Samuel Wayte, with typically selfless naïvety, announced his intention to resign. His principal reason seems to have been a desire to be near his elderly father, and a conviction that it would be wrong to be anything less than a full-time head of house. The fellows urged him to reconsider, and suggested he should apply to the Visitor (who alone had the power to overrule the Statutes) for leave of absence. But, as Wayte wrote nobly to his vice-president, 'the great advantages which I have myself received from my membership of the College seem to me to lay me under an obligation to refrain from doing that which might turn out to be a great injury to it.'[33]

College gossip, however, quickly promulgated a second reason for Wayte's departure: that he had intended the presidency for Henry Woods. Wayte never spoke on the matter explicitly, but nor, in later life, would he deny that this had been his expectation. When Edmund Bagshawe, 'greatly daring', made a tactful enquiry, Wayte just looked at him 'but without any sternness, and said nothing'.

[31] O. F. Christie, *Clifton School Days* (London, 1930), 24.

[32] Potter, *Headmaster*, 33–5, 39, 44–8, 58, 84–8, 98–100.

[33] 'Samuel William Wayte', 585; TCA Register D, 240. Wayte's letter is dated 12 September 1878, and concludes with a characteristically generous offer to restore some of the Old Library glass. After the 1878 election, Henry Woods officially reiterated the 'delicate scruples' over 'domestic reasons' that made Wayte 'temporarily unable to reside in Oxford' and prompted his resignation (Woods, 'College Loyalty', 3–4).

Woods was engaged to be married to Margaret (Daisy) Bradley, daughter of the Dean of Westminster. While Trinity's Statutes, partially reformed following the Oxford Act of 1854, now allowed eight of the twelve fellows not to be in holy orders, celibacy was still required of them all.[34] The President, on the other hand, had always been allowed to marry, although he was still required to be a priest. Wayte, it was supposed, believed that Woods was a man 'far more necessary to the college than himself'.[35]

Just beyond the College wall, there was another Oxford head with his own plans for the Trinity presidency. Benjamin Jowett, most prominent and outspoken of university reformers, and Master of Balliol since 1870, wanted a place in the University for a friend. He and Percival had been correspondents as early as 1869, when Jowett had lent enthusiastic support to the plans for University College, Bristol.[36] Jowett looked forward to enjoying Percival's galvanizing presence in Oxford, but he also desired the appointment for Percival's own sake. The headmaster was known to be suffering from mental and physical exhaustion at Clifton, and running a small college would be comparatively undemanding. Jowett's first hope had been to get his friend in at his old college, Queen's. But on 4 October he wrote to Percival's wife Louisa:

> From what I can learn I imagine that the Election at Queen's is a foregone conclusion . . . meanwhile there is another Headship vacant in Oxford—Trinity—and a rumour has reached me that there may be a chance of Dr Percival being elected. I have written to those of the Fellows whom I know, to urge them that they could not do a better thing for the College, and for the University. Do not be sanguine, but there is a chance.[37]

There were several Trinity fellows whom Jowett knew very well. The 'most popular and influential' was Robert Raper, who, as a layman, was not eligible to stand for the presidency himself.[38] Raper had spent one term at Balliol in 1861, before being elected scholar of Trinity. He admired Jowett greatly, and Jowett reciprocated his feelings. In the Long Vacation of 1868, Raper joined Jowett at a reading party at Pitlochry, 'a charming fellow,' wrote Jowett to his friend Florence

[34] The new Statute was sanctioned by the Visitor in January 1870, TCA Order Book D, 225. For a discussion of why Oxford colleges clung to the celibacy rule, see Engel, *Clergyman to Don*, 54–6. [35] TCA Wayte, no. 5, 6.
[36] Temple, *Percival*, 34, 262–3. [37] Ibid., 64–5. [38] TCA Wayte, no. 13.

*9.4* Robert W. Raper, fellow 1861–1915, by Brian Hatton (1914).

Nightingale, 'who comes here of his own accord to help me in Plato: and he is a real help for he is an excellent scholar & has very good taste.'[39]

A second fellow over whom Jowett held sway was Robinson Ellis (scholar of Balliol 1852, fellow of Trinity 1858–93). Jowett had supported Ellis steadfastly as he recovered from a suicide attempt made on 16 January 1869. 'A dreadful thing has happened here which grieves me,' wrote Jowett to Nightingale:

> Poor Ellis of Trinity . . . a very faithful friend and pupil of mine . . . has been for the last seven years really insane being as I think

[39] BCO Jowett, III, N/208. Published in E. V. Quinn and J. M. Prest, *Dear Miss Nightingale: A Selection of Benjamin Jowett's Letters 1860–1893* (1987), as no. 170.

> I told you in a state of divided consciousness & in the most awful suffering. During the last year he appeared better because he never spoke of his misery. But on Friday night he could endure no longer & shot himself in the forehead with a revolver: Alas Alas he is not killed & may possibly recover with the loss of one of his eyes—his mind never.

Jowett had been pulling strings to help Ellis's career: 'I had just made an arrangement for him to have a large class in Latin Philology. It is just possible that this which he had greatly desired may have increased the trouble of his mind.'[40]

As Ellis recuperated, Jowett visited him loyally and sent regular bulletins to Florence Nightingale. It soon became apparent that Ellis's injury was not as bad as at first feared. 'He has partially lost the sight of his right eye but this appears to be all. He told me that he did it under the impression which he has had for years that some one was going to put him to a horrible & cruel death. When he found out he had not succeeded he ran out to the surgeon at 5 o clock in the morning. He is wonderfully good & patient & perfectly rational.'[41] On 19 February Jowett wrote to Nightingale again. 'Thank you very much for your suggestion about Mr Ellis. He shall not go back to his rooms. The surgeon who attends him says that he expresses regret that he did not succeed. The ball has been at last extracted & the eye sees nearly as well as ever.' Jowett kindly invited Ellis up to Pitlochry for the Long Vacation. They were together at St Andrews on 1 October. 'Since what he calls "his accident",' reported Jowett solicitously, 'his mind appears decidedly better. He has translated nearly all of Catullus into corresponding English metres very ingeniously.'[42]

A third fellow of Trinity with strong Balliol connections was Arthur Lionel Smith (exhibitioner of Balliol 1868, fellow of Trinity 1874–9, fellow of Balliol 1882, Master 1916–24). And a fourth was Charles Gore (Scholar of Balliol 1870, fellow of Trinity 1875–98) who, as Vice-Principal of Cuddesdon College (1880–4), kept a picture of Benjamin Jowett on his study wall.[43] Archibald Robertson (scholar 1872, fellow 1876–86) was close to Gore, and joined a small group who met weekly in his rooms to study the Greek New Testament. Gore, however, was far from close to the strongly agnostic Raper, who was 'excited both

[40] BCO Jowett, III, N/229, published in Quinn and Prest, *Dear Miss Nightingale*, no. 184.

[41] Undated, Quinn and Prest, *Dear Miss Nightingale*, no. 185.

[42] BCO Jowett, III, N/234, 256, 261.

[43] G. L. Prestige, *The Life of Charles Gore: A Great Englishman* (London, 1935) 38.

by the positive and uncompromising nature of Gore's convictions, and by his habit of walking about the garden with his arm enfolding an undergraduate's neck, in what was later called "the Cuddesdon cuddle".'[44]

The election was scheduled to take place on 28 September, but one week before, the University Commissioners granted a postponement to 22 October. It was the last election to be conducted along the lines laid out by Thomas Pope, and ten fellows took part. The most senior was the vice-president, Thomas Short, now aged 89, who managed two shaky signatures in the College Register. John Gent (scholar 1863, fellow 1869–86) declaimed on Short's behalf the required chapter of the foundation Statutes, and the other necessary parts of the formalities. Then each fellow in turn wrote two names on a paper laid on the altar, and the names of the two receiving most votes—John Percival and Henry George Woods—were taken by deputation to the Visitor, Edward Browne, at Winchester.[45]

It is remarkable that the College Register contains no record at all of the Visitor's reply, although the formal Latin address to every elected candidate, Harris excepted, had been so preserved in every election since the foundation. Bishop Browne could, in theory, select either man, but tradition demanded the choice of whoever had received the majority of votes, in this case Percival. The archival silence speaks eloquently of the unhappiness of a divided fellowship. As the years passed, various stories about the election began to circulate, and Robert Raper was popularly blamed for the outcome. Edmund Bagshawe declared himself 'not surprised' that Samuel Wayte 'never mentioned' Raper's name at all.[46] It would have been characteristic of Raper to relish such a reputation. He enjoyed having others in his power, and had 'a penchant for intrigue'. One contemporary remembered him as 'a very potent personal force. He acted through and upon others.'[47]

Many years later Archibald Robertson wrote an account of what happened, prefaced by such pious sentiments as befitted his subsequent career as a bishop. 'There was a total absence of rivalry,

[44] Ibid., 22–3. [45] TCA Register D, 243–5.

[46] TCA Wayte, no. 4, 16.

[47] Laurie Magnus, *Herbert Warren of Magdalen* (London, 1932), 165. A later story, promulgated by Tommy Higham, told of him tricking two suffragettes into believing that Balliol was Trinity. See Dennis Burden 'A College Story Partly Authenticated', *Report* (1990–1), 68–71.

self-seeking or bitterness in the election, before it or after it,' he claimed. 'We were all of us desirous to do simply what was best for the College.' Robertson felt that Woods was a 'likely candidate' but that 'there was a feeling, shared by many of the fellows, that the College wanted new blood, and that Woods's time had not quite come. As Raper constantly reminded us, we had "the whole clerical world" to choose from.' Raper, although he first suggested Percival, 'seemed disinclined to act upon it and was regarded as a supporter of Woods'. John Gent 'would have supported Raper' but came down in favour of Woods. The others in the Woods camp were Martin Green and Tommy Short, the latter 'hardly realising that there was another serious candidate'. Robinson Ellis and Charles Gore wanted Percival, and Robertson and the other junior fellow, Henry Whitehead, 'hardened in favour' of him too.[48]

In the days before the election, Henry Woods was quite in the dark. 'I know no more now about the intentions of the Fellows than I did,' he confided in a letter to Daisy on 14 October, 'but Ellis told me that Mr Percival had been down on Saturday to see the house, & after inspection said that if he was offered the place, he would take it.'[49] Former fellows were anxious for news. Indeed, precedent suggested that the new President might be chosen from their ranks. Archibald Robertson would have liked to vote for North Pinder (scholar 1847, fellow 1851), who held the college living of Rotherfield Greys, while William Cole, now rector of Newbold Verdun, had been the second nomination for the presidency in 1866.[50] On 16 October Cole wrote to Albert Watson of Brasenose to ask directly, 'who is likely to be elected at Trinity next Thursday? Your letter shall be committed to the flames as soon as read. If you do not like to venture what you yourself expect let me know the general feeling.'[51]

Finally, 'the eve of the election came,' recalled Robertson, and 'we had a prolonged discussion in Raper's rooms . . . Next morning . . . before the time for chapel had come, Raper announced himself a convert to the side of Percival. This decided the election.'[52] That evening both Woods—'very vexed'—and Raper both wrote to Cole, who was

[48] Temple, *Percival*, 66–7. [49] TCA OF 17/5.1.

[50] Temple, *Percival*, 66; TCA Register D 207–9.

[51] TCA Newbold Verdun Letter Book, 83–4.

[52] Temple, *Percival*, 67, TCA Register D, 243–5. Robertson's memoir is wrong on one important point. He lists Franklin Richards as a Woods supporter, but Richards was not at this time a fellow.

utterly dismayed by the result. Partly he blamed Wayte, whom he felt had 'acted very strangely', and he was also 'surprised by Ellis'. Cole doubted whether Ellis knew Percival at all.[53] To Woods he said, 'I heartily wish they had elected P at Queen's. Why didn't they?' The victor was, he conceded, 'of course a first rate man' and he advised Woods to think very carefully before resigning. 'If you were to leave Oxford hastily for work which you like less well you would always regret it afterwards. I think you will find P a pleasant man to work with.' To Raper, however, he wrote, 'I am afraid after this life will be less comfortable in college.'[54]

It fell to Archibald Robertson's 'painful lot' to explain to Tommy Short that a complete stranger was to be the new President. And the unworldly Robinson Ellis had the task of taking the good news to Clifton. Ellis's conversation with Percival was to become famous in the annals of anecdotes. This is the Herbert Warren version: 'The flattered Headmaster expressed surprise. "I don't wonder you're surprised," said Ellis, "but, you see, our choice is so limited." The Headmaster then offered him tea, saying, "My wife is waiting for us in the drawing-room." "Oh, but Percival" exclaimed the fellows' envoy, "one of the recommendations was that you were not married." '[55] An alternative story runs thus: Percival—'I am married, but Mrs Percival is upstairs to-day as she is not well.' Ellis—'Ah . . . (hopefully) . . . then she *is* in poor health.'[56] Percival was not only married, he arrived in Oxford with a household of six children and numerous servants, and two rooms above the Library had to be annexed to the Lodgings to accommodate them all.[57]

Louisa Percival had a character as strong as her husband's, but her manners were softer, and she had the crucial ability to render his lofty ideals intelligible to others. Percival's biographer, William Temple, described her 'marvellous gift of sympathy and her infectious vitality [which] endeared her to all who met her'. Without his wife's warm and supportive presence, Percival's achievements would have undoubtedly been fewer. He also loved Louisa deeply. When she

53 Cole later amended this opinion.

54 TCA, Newbold Verdun, 84–5, Cole to Raper 23 and 24 Oct. 1878, to Woods 24 Oct. 1878. Cole was in an awkward position as an undergraduate friend of Percival's, and a regular visitor when Percival was a Master at Rugby. He concluded his letter to Woods with the vindictive hope that 'he will come down on Ellis & get something useful out of him.'

55 Magnus, *Herbert Warren*, 111.

56 Temple, *Percival*, 66.

57 TCA Order Book D, 295. The College agreed to defray the expense up to £260.

died, not long after his election to the see of Hereford in 1895, his grief was 'almost overwhelming'. Although he maintained his unemotional public face, 'late in the evening he often went to the terrace walk beside the river—a very secluded place—and there sobbed alone until he could bear to go to bed.'[58]

Opposition to Percival's election was orchestrated by a number of the former fellows, who were the very first generation of Trinity men to make the painful discovery that their love for the College gave them no power to direct, only great potential to be hurt by, the actions of their successors. Alfred Plummer, now Master of University College, Durham, was particularly angry, and was instrumental in the drafting and circulation of a strongly worded 'memorial' which was 'based on the following considerations':

That, contrary to a wisely cherished tradition, never violated before, a gentleman wholly unconnected with the college has been made its President.

1) That thereby the continuity of the college has been broken, and the President, instead of being a link between past and present, resident and non-resident members, is an obstacle, however involuntary, to cordial relations between them.
2) That such an election implies that no person fit to hold the office of President could be found among the Members of the college, and involves a very unmerited slight to the present and former Fellows and Tutors.
3) That the bestowal of such an honour on one who has done nothing for the College is singularly unfair to those who have devoted the best years of their lives to it.
4) That this grave responsibility has been incurred by a mere majority of the electors, whereas absolute unanimity could scarcely have justified it.
5) That thereby widespread dissatisfaction has been caused, and discord has been introduced into a Society hitherto singularly united.

'We observe, with surprise,' the document concluded, 'that this momentous step has been taken at a time when a large proportion of the electors are very junior members of the university, and when

[58] Temple, *Percival*, 104, 139, 142.

consideration for the late President might have been expected to withhold them from an act which could not fail to be deeply distasteful to him.'[59]

Randall Davidson, recently appointed a chaplain to the Archbishop of Canterbury, swiftly dissociated himself from the protest. 'I am so sorry you can't sign the paper,' wrote Robinson Duckworth (fellow 1860–76) to him on 7 November:

> It is being sent out by Pinder, Plummer, & myself to all the MAs & BAs of Trinity, & will be signed by an overwhelming majority of them, I expect, & sent in at the Audit in December next. I shall be satisfied if we do something to check the speed of this priggish 'ασ–τογγια [heartlessness] on which young Oxford prides itself. Of personal disappointment I do not feel the faintest shade. But I am ashamed of my college & have seriously contemplated (like others) removing my name from the books.

Furthermore, Duckworth claimed, the Visitor made 'no secret of the reluctance with which he has had to sanction this offensive proceeding'.[60]

The memorial was fairly soon 'withdrawn'. Cole admitted that he found the election 'monstrous' and 'shameful' but also felt that he 'could not possibly have signed', and he repeatedly urged his friend Plummer to accept the election with good grace. The two men expended much effort in analysing the voting, and Cole was forced to conclude that 'all the electors had little confidence in Woods.' He was particularly disturbed by the suggestion of Jowett's interference, and even went so far as to draft a letter to the Master of Balliol. Cole managed to convince himself at least that 'under these circumstances what is needed is a hard-working man universally recognised as first rate . . . Such a man we have in P.' Moreover, he added reasonably, 'Something too is due to P himself . . . Are we to act so unhandsomely to him as to tell him the College has since changed its mind? Surely in acting so the college would stultify itself in the eyes of the world.'[61]

Various details were reported in the newspapers. On 14 November, John Henry Newman wrote from the Birmingham Oratory to R. W. Church, the Dean of St Paul's: 'I am flabbergasted . . . by the retirement and succession of Trinity Heads. What does it all mean?' And

[59] Bod. Lib. G. A. Oxon C287 no. 158.

[60] LPA Davidson, vol. 523, ff. 3–4.

[61] TCA Newbold Verdun Letter Book, 86–7, 89, 91, Cole to Plummer 26 and 30 Oct. and 1 Nov. 1878, to Duckworth 6 Nov. 1878.

the Dean replied, 'There is a kind of buzz, like a disturbed beehive, among the old Trinity men about the election. Many of them . . . are very wrath with the indignity to the College, as if it could not produce a fit head. I believe it is a bit of youthful *protervitas* [impudence].'[62]

## *President Percival*

John Percival was accustomed to facing opposition, and had never yet allowed it to stand in his way. A number of caricatures were published on the theme of his election to Trinity. In one Wayte was depicted as an undertaker, with the Chapel as his hearse; In another Percival became a 'Prize Bird' wearing a rosette and crowing over Woods from the top of the College gate (Plate 9.3). Louisa Percival was amused by the latter, and purchased a copy in Shrimpton's shop on Broad Street.[63]

The man with the most reason to feel let down, Henry Woods, behaved with exemplary dignity. On 10 November he preached in the Chapel on the subject of 'College Loyalty'. His sermon began with a paean of praise for Samuel Wayte, whose motives, he said, had been 'so strangely and falsely misinterpreted'. Woods urged his listeners to be sensitive to bad publicity for the College, and to feel 'an increased sense of corporate union', as when a bereavement draws 'more closely together the other members of the family'. Although there were some who believed that 'college feeling stands in the way of university reform'; he, however, saw it as 'the source and spirit of much that is good in the life which we live here'. In lofty tones he warned his listeners against 'a misapplication of College Loyalty'. To 'protest, when protest can do no possible good,' he declared, was 'a very spurious form' of the emotion. Finally, the preacher turned his thoughts to the new President—who, not being a member of the College family, presumably did not share the 'sacramental bond' he was talking about—'I am sure that we shall all welcome him heartily and loyally.' Such laudable sentiments did no harm to the cause of a would-be President waiting in the wings. The undergraduates clubbed together to buy him and Daisy a 'handsome' wedding present,[64] and the couple were duly married and set up home on

[62] *Newman Letters & Diaries*, xxviii, 421.
[63] Temple, *Percival*, 76.
[64] TCA OF 17 4/1.

Holywell. In the event, Woods did not have to leave Trinity after all. Percival petitioned the University Commissioners for him to be elected under a clause of the new Statutes then being drafted, and the commissioners in return suggested a 'course best calculated to attain the object of the college'. The fellowship made vacant by Woods's marriage was suspended, and, under section 36 of the Ordinance of the 1872 Commission, Woods was retained as bursar and tutor, his stipend increased by an 'amount equivalent to the value of his fellowship'.[65] When the new Statutes came into force in 1881, he was quietly restored to his fellowship once again.

Percival could not leave Clifton until Easter 1879, but throughout the winter he travelled up to Oxford for the College meetings, which, by all accounts, could be difficult. When H. E. D. Blakiston came to research the history of the 1878 election, he felt that Percival had been shown 'less than fair play'.[66] The problem was that the new President did not understand the rules. He betrayed a tendency to treat the fellows as subservient schoolmasters, and had no experience of being *primus inter pares* in the governing body of a college. Christie felt it was Percival's 'masterfulness which hindered him from being the ideal ruler of a college . . . He could not brook opposition; he could scarcely acquit the opposer of disloyalty.'[67] Blakiston had no doubt that Percival 'made great mistakes through want of tact'.[68] Charles Gore was a fellow throughout the Percival presidency, and developed a 'deep admiration for [his] character and influence'. On a personal level, however, he recalled how 'we felt that a strong righteous will was expressing itself among us with profound astonishment at our being content to be such fools as we were.'[69] When Percival left Trinity, Robinson Ellis felt it incumbent on himself to communicate his regret for the way the fellows had on occasion behaved. 'Some scenes at College meetings have left a painful impression on my memory,' he acknowledged, 'and I have from time to time tried to express to Mrs Percival my sympathy.'[70]

Within a year of the election, a draft statute was being circulated, which vested all authority in the College meeting: 'The President shall in the performance of his duties be subject to the direction of

[65] University Commissioners to Percival, 19 March 1878, TCA Register D, 251.
[66] TCA Wayte, no. 13. [67] Christie, *School Days*, 27.
[68] TCA Wayte, no. 13. [69] Prestige, *Gore*, 23.
[70] Letter dated 18 November 1886, Temple, *Percival*, 91.

the College; and anything done by him may . . . be modified, countermanded, or reversed by the College.' Percival voiced his opposition in a forthright memorandum: 'If the President . . . is to be subject to the constant interference and direction of a college meeting as to the mode in which he sets about and performs his recognised duties . . . the clause must in practice be proved to be either inoperative or intolerable.' The document resonated with the key words and phrases of his headship: 'real vigour and efficiency in administration'; 'judging [individuals] by the results of their work'; and the 'vigour and enthusiasm of officers'.[71]

Percival's tried and tested technique for getting his own way was simply not to 'accept or admit defeat'. He would submit his proposals repeatedly, 'with a combination of unruffled patience and unswerving persistence which was peculiarly irritating to those who thought that a proposal was killed by defeat on a division'.[72] The fellows of Oriel College were subjected to considerable pressure to sell the freehold of Kettell Hall, without which the President's grandest plans for college expansion were not viable. In February 1880 Percival and Woods were authorized to 'enter into negotiations' with Oriel, and an offer was made in May. The Provost and fellows of Oriel declined to sell, primarily because Kettell Hall was the oldest property the College owned in Oxford. In October, the resident fellows of Trinity were appointed 'a committee to carry on negotiations' and 'such plans as may be necessary for the conduct of the negotiations' commissioned, which were shown to the fellows of Oriel the following February. Meanwhile, Percival had written personally to Vice-Provost D. B. Monro in January, to urge him not to thwart 'one of the most beautiful & effective things in Oxford'. He wrote again in April to hasten Oriel's decision, with the hope that the Oriel Governing Body might 'delegate the negotiations to a committee, so that they need not have to drag on & wait for some further college meeting . . . it would be a convenience to us . . . to be able to settle the matter by Trinity Monday.' Oriel obliged on 22 April, voting 6:5 in favour of the sale, but stipulating that it should not be completed until the plans were finalized. In June, Trinity's fund-raising circular was drafted, stating that 'Oriel College

[71] Temple, *Percival*, 72–3. [72] Ibid., 75.

has declared its willingness to sell to us the freehold of Kettell Hall with its garden' and accompanied by a printed elevation of a grand new accommodation block. Finally, on Lady Day 1883, the purchase was sealed.[73]

Despite their formal nature, minutes of College meetings—the Order Books—hint of division and resistance. When, in March 1879, Percival wished to have a copy of the Founder's Chalice made for the cathedral at St Alban's, it was agreed 'under proper safeguards, if after due enquiry made, the resident fellows consent'. At the meeting which authorized Percival and Woods to begin negotiations for the purchase of Kettell Hall as a prelude to a new Front Quadrangle, 'the residents [were] empowered to proceed, if they think fit, with the erection of a building for rooms in the Dolphin Yard.'[74] Such a suggestion was an empty gesture, and Percival surely knew it. A remarkable number of committees was established during his presidency, and only rarely was he trusted to act alone (Table 9.1). His determination was difficult to check, particularly as he was in most cases quite prepared to meet the cost of getting his own way. The committee on college servants, for example, recommended that two new gardeners would be employed, Percival having offered to pay 10*s* a week towards their wages. The location of the President's new stable did provide the fellows with a small opportunity to thwart him. Although it was originally hoped that both a new workshop and a new stable could be built in the Dolphin Yard, and agreed that, if this was not feasible, the stable should be given priority, an unminuted meeting in August—when Percival was away—decided that 'the workshop only should be erected.' Percival was to endure greater inconveniences during the building and laying out of the Front Quadrangle, but with his mind fixed on higher things, he made the sacrifice with characteristic stoicism. One important innovation of these years was the creation of the office of Domestic Bursar, 'Mr Woods desiring to delegate the duties of that office' in December 1886.[75]

[73] TCA Order Book D f. 309, 312–13, 315, 319, 322; New Buildings B.1 'Proposed New Buildings' circular, undated; OCA GOV 4 B1/2/2, 13 Oct. 1880, 22 April 1881; OCA DL 1.6, Percival to Monro 4 Jan. and 20 April 1881.

[74] TCA Order Book D, 297.

[75] Ibid., 329–30; Order Book E, 5–6, 22, 27.

*Table 9.1* Committees formed during Percival's presidency.

| *Purpose* | *Members* | *Date* |
|---|---|---|
| Provision for servants' retirement | Resident fellows | 1880 May |
| To communicate with architect for new building | President, Woods, Raper | 1880 October |
| To draft fund-raising circular | President, Woods, Raper | 1881 October |
| The Millard Lectureship | President, Woods, Senior Tutor | 1882 March |
| Stipend of Estates Bursar | President, Gent, Raper | 1882 June |
| Tutorial Finance | President, Ellis, Woods, Whitehead | 1882 June |
| New Statutes | President and Bursars | 1882 June |
| To investigate work and payment of college servants | President, 2 Bursars | 1882 June |
| Creation of office of Domestic Bursar | Percival, Raper, Cannan | 1883 February |
| Fitting up of undergraduate library | Ellis, Raper, Green, Cannan | 1885 March |
| Stipend of Millard Lecturer | Percival, Woods, Raper | 1885 April |
| Location of President's stable | Percival, Woods, Raper | 1885 August |
| Statute on appointment of supernumerary fellows | Percival, Woods, Raper, Gent | 1886 May |
| Tutorial arrangements | Percival, Woods, Raper, Cannan | 1886 July |

*Source*: TCA Order Books D and E.

## *The Jackson Building*

Some of the ideas which Percival presented to the fellows were breathtaking in their ambition. College expansion was central to his whole reform strategy, and he wanted not merely a new building, but an imposing new quadrangle. Trinity's outward appearance was to be transformed, just as it had been by Bathurst's Chapel two centuries earlier. At Clifton, Percival had sought out the best schoolmasters; now he employed the best architect he could get—'the maker of modern Oxford' and fellow of Wadham, Thomas Graham Jackson.[76] Robert Raper was later to complain that 'Jackson's buildings are irregular, and I think him a bad architect. I still wish we had employed the man I originally suggested as both builder and architect, one Collins, who restored Tewkesbury Abbey and Winchester Cathedral, having started life as a stone mason—with a trowel in his hand.'[77] There is no evidence that Trinity even considered Raper's idea as a serious alternative. Easily the most popular architect in Oxford, Jackson had no truck with the Gothic Revival of the early Victorian period, and had introduced a modern, eclectic style of building—John Betjeman dubbed it Anglo-Jackson—to the University. His new Examination Schools were the embodiment of the university reform which Percival so desired.

In December 1880 Jackson drew up an elevation for a proposed new quadrangle that would stretch from the east window of Balliol's new chapel (1857) to the west side of Kettell Hall, and more than double Trinity's Broad Street frontage. Gone were the cottages, and in their place an ornate and eye-catching gateway. Gone too was the Bathurst Building, replaced by undergraduate (and presidential) accommodation provided in six staircases, which would fill the space between the east end of the Chapel and the garden lying west of Kettell Hall. The whole quadrangle would be clearly visible to public scrutiny through the railings on Broad Street, and it would stand both as a potent symbol of the reform Percival hoped for within, and also as a means to its achievement. To accommodate more of the undergraduates within the College precincts would bring them under the

[76] *Oxford Journal*, 13 October 1900, 5.

[77] Raper to Woods, 10 Sept. 1884, TCA 'New Buildings' box E/1.3.

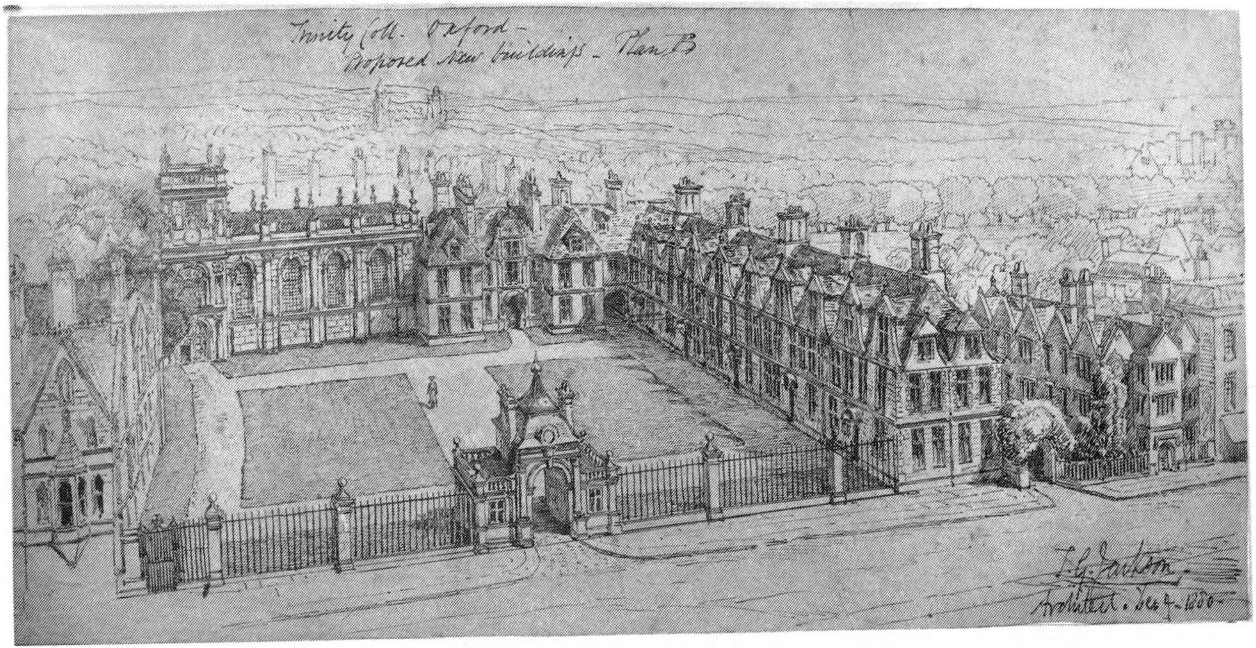


*9.5* Jackson's design for the Front Quadrangle, 1880.

disciplinarian eye of the President, and make them subject to his educational ideas.[78]

The following June, Percival drafted a detailed proposal 'for the use of the fellows'. He estimated the cost:

| | |
|---|---|
| Block from Kettell Hall to the Grove . . . 25 to 30 sets of rooms | 10,000 |
| Rebuilding or enlargement of Bathurst | 6,000? |
| Laying out New Quadrangle, New Porters' Lodge, Iron Railings etc. | 2,000 |
| Price of Kettell Hall including transfer | 3,300 |
| Equivalent for loss of rent for our cottages & Kettell Hall stable | 113.10*s* p.a. |

He budgeted to meet this cost as follows:

| | |
|---|---|
| From President and Fellows | 3,300 |
| from other subscribers[79] | 6,000 |
| advowson Fund | 2,000 |
| Suspended fellowship | 1,000 |
| Borrowed money | 9,000 |

Regarding the size of the loan, he estimated that, given the increase in rents which the new building would accrue, the final burden on college finance would be £150 a year for thirty years. 'Should the scheme be thought impractical or imprudent,' however, he suggested a startlingly bold scheme, which 'would not only enable us to carry out our present purpose, but would also effect a permanent saving which for myself I should be glad to see extended throughout the university.' He then proposed that the presidential stipend should be cut to £400 or £500 per annum, but held in tandem with a professorship, 'the duties of the office and the work which a head of house can do for his college or the university have under various influences become so restricted that the office might in all cases be held in conjunction with a professorship, and would under such an arrangement be adequately remunerated.' Percival had no doubt that this could be done 'in almost every college in Oxford without appreciable loss,

[78] TCA 'New Buildings' B/2; William Whyte, 'Oxford Jackson: Architecture, Education, Status and Style 1835–1924' (unpublished D. Phil. thesis, Oxford University, 2002), 103.

[79] 'I hope (though I know too little of our constituency to speak with confidence),' he conceded honestly.

if only,' he added modestly, 'due care were taken that Headships should be filled by men of some rank.' Perhaps this was impossible at the present time, but 'if it can be made statutable,' he urged, 'I shall be quite ready in view of the general advantage, to guarantee that, so far as I am concerned, it shall come into operation within 5 years.' The saving in stipend, some £600 per year, would not merely fund any 'good building scheme' the fellows wanted, but would be able to 'double the number of its scholars and thus very considerably to improve its position in the university and enlarge its sphere of influence.'[80]

No wonder Gore found Percival 'very bracing'.[81] Faced with such a prospect, the resident fellows hastened to agree on a fund-raising circular, which was sent out with copies of Jackson's design (Plate 9.5) and a statement of the President's aspirations. The new buildings 'would comprise a block containing 25 to 30 sets of rooms, a new Lecture Room, Undergraduates' Library and Magazine Room, such as the best Colleges have already added to their buildings.' By opening out the existing kitchen garden, stable yard, and 'green in front of the chapel', there could be added 'to the college a feature of great beauty, as the quadrangle so formed would be one of the finest in Oxford'. The circular reassured old members that there was 'no intention' of adding to the number of undergraduates, but, deploring the existing situation whereby 'more than one-half of the whole body are obliged to live scattered about in lodgings', he mooted the possibility—a veiled threat to old members with sons—that without a new building it might be necessary to 'reduce the number of undergraduates to a point at which it would become difficult . . . for the College to maintain its position with other leading Colleges'. The circular concluded with a reminder that 'the existing chapel was built by subscriptions in former times', and, following the example of Bathurst, Percival advertised his own promised benefaction of £1,000 or a year's stipend. Eight thousand pounds was the sum indirectly suggested for old members to provide.[82]

Ironically, the fellows baulked at just one thing, their 'sentiment' preventing the demolition of the Bathurst Building 'for some years'. To Jackson it was 'a rather uninteresting building containing some not very convenient chambers', and in January 1883 he reported with-

[80] TCA 'New Buildings', A/1.
[81] Prestige, *Gore*, 23.
[82] TCA 'New Buildings' B/1.

eringly on what might be done 'to make it worthy of its place' in the new quadrangle. Jackson felt the College would need to 'reface it and to raise the walls and roof so as to get a good 2nd floor. It would also be desirable to build a new staircase.' The total cost, 'if as I expect the front wall and end walls proved too weak to bear refacing' would 'approach £2,000', while the 'sole advantage . . . in point of accommodation would be the improvement of the two attics.'[83]

Percival was equally annoyed when he saw the final plans. 'The departure from the general character & effect of your original elevation was a surprise, and I may say a disappointment,' he wrote to Jackson on 14 March, 'as that was circulated among subscribers, & the new one seems inferior.'[84] But they pressed on. By January 1884 the foundations for a three-staircase three-storey block were virtually complete.[85] As the building grew, various amendments were made to the design, generally with the intent of rendering it 'even more idiosyncratic and showy'.[86] In May 1884 it was agreed to spend a further £208 10s on 'additional ornamentation' of the two southern gables, which were the part most visible from Broad Street. In January 1885 another 'extra' was 'red lead putty instead of ordinary putty to glazing in all casements'.[87]

Henry Woods took a large share of the responsibility for seeing the work through, and showed a bursarial interest in the practical minutiae of the design. His initial questions for Jackson covered six sides of paper: 'Dry gravel for filling in. Does this keep out damp?'; 'How is the mortar made?'; 'Mouldings of woodwork. Are there any parts where these might be dispensed with and plain substituted?'; 'Water. What provision in case of fire?'; and '? Slow combustion grates. Place to put kettle on.'[88] Woods wrote to Percival on 19 December 1884, to report on the pantries, ventilation, and the 'roof of W.C. I rather think it may be worth while to have the boarding & felt under the slates, because the extra warmth gained would probably make all the difference in frosty weather.'[89] Four new lavatories were situated at the northern end of the building, a welcome alternative to the distant facilities of the Dolphin Yard.[90] Provision in case of fire was becoming a serious consideration in the modern city. Trinity had

[83] Thomas Graham Jackson, *Recollections: The Life and Travels of a Victorian Architect*, ed. Nicholas Jackson (London, 2003), 153.
[84] TCA 'New Buildings' E/2.2.
[85] Ibid., E/2.7.
[86] Whyte, 'Oxford Jackson', 103.
[87] TCA 'New Buildings', C/2.
[88] Ibid., C/6.
[89] Ibid., E/1.4.
[90] TCA Building Plans, C/3.1.

subscribed to the Oxford Volunteer Fire Brigade since 1873 (when they paid a guinea for the year),[91] but the College was now reluctant to go to any additional expense for the sake of protecting the new building. Against the advice of the 'Water Co's engineer' to lay a 3-inch main 'as far as the hydrant', in November 1883 it was decided to retain the existing 2-inch pipes. In May 1885 Jackson wrote pointedly to Woods, 'the time has now come to connect our water supply with the main and the Engineer again repeats his opinion that the 2 inch main will not have force of water enough to throw as high as the new building.' Moreover, the 2-inch hydrant would be 'useless as it would not fit the apparatus of the fire engines in use at Oxford.' The cost of converting the pipes was £13.[92]

In Michaelmas Term 1885 the first undergraduates took up residence in the New Building, as it was still being called in the mid-1960s.[93] There were thirteen sets of rooms on the central staircase, and eleven plus a fellow's set on the southern one. Each undergraduate had an inner lobby, a sitting-room, a bedroom, and, in most cases, a pantry. The first fellow to live there was Charles Cannan (fellow 1884–98). Cannan, a brilliant Cliftonian who had won a scholarship to Corpus in 1877, had been recruited by Percival to boost Trinity's teaching. He was to be renowned as a tutor as much for his hearty sporting enthusiasms as for his 'intellectual force', and from his arrival he devoted himself to the creation of Percival's new quadrangle. Arthur Quiller-Couch (scholar 1881) wrote appreciatively of his tutor's contribution: 'no one who has not been a party in such an experiment ['to build its new and gracious quad and double its numbers'] can realize how ticklish a business it is and how laborious for somebody. That somebody, of course, was Cannan . . . [who] more than anyone carried the business through.'[94] Cannan enjoyed two sitting-rooms and two bedrooms on the first floor; by the 1920s this set, with its commanding view of the college gate and of the south-

[91] TCA Order Book D, 256.

[92] TCA 'New Buildings' E/2.28. Students of fire safety will be interested to learn that Trinity's first ever fire drill was held on Thursday 17 Nov. 1887 at 2.30 p.m (TCA Memo Book I, 17).

[93] President Norrington wrote somewhat confusingly of both 'our present New Buildings' and 'the 19th Century New Buildings', in his account of 'The College Buildings', *Report* (1964), 14.

[94] Temple, *Percival*, 76 (quoting Herbert Warren); Q writing in the *Oxford Magazine* 23 January 1920, published in *Some Recollections of Charles Cannan 1858–1919* (Oxford 1920) 17.

*9.6* The New Building in 1886: photograph sent to subscribers.

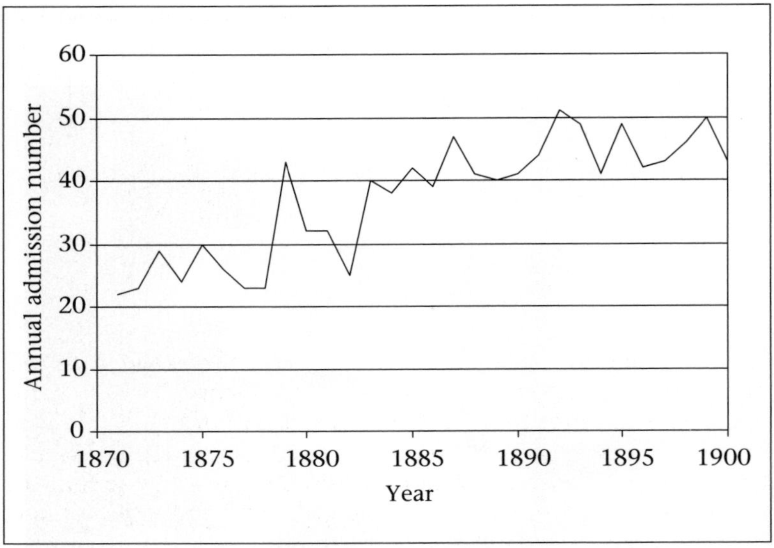


*Fig. 9.1* Admissions 1871–1900.

*Source*: TCA Admissions Register C.

east frontier of Balliol College, was to become the perquisite of the dean. Three undergraduates were accommodated above the lecture room and reading room at the northern end of the building.[95]

In January 1887 Percival sent out his official thanks to all subscribers. The 'Benefactors' were listed in detail, and each was sent a photograph of what had been achieved (Plate 9.6). Besides Percival's £1,000, nine fellows had contributed £1,650, and sixteen former fellows £1,111. Twenty-seven ex-scholars had given £722, which included £100 each from Lord Lingen (scholar 1837), now an honorary fellow, and a loyal old Cliftonian, Edwin Bean (1869). Finally, twenty old members had sent donations, which totalled just £657 10*s*, but included the first of many considerable benefactions Trinity was to receive over the ensuing decades from William Hunt (1861), who sent £300, and Harold C. Moffatt (1878), who gave £100. The total of all subscriptions was £5,140 15*s*; the total expenditure (including entrance gates, laying out the quadrangle, and 'conversion of the cot-

[95] TCA Building Plans, C/3.10. For the Dean's rooms: Higham, *Dr Blakiston*, 19 and n. 1.

tages into rooms') £14,789 15*s* 8*d*. Trinity therefore was 'burdened with a debt of about £8,000, and in a time of falling rents and general depression'. It was a not inconsiderable burden. At the adjourned 1884 college audit, it was agreed to 'take steps for applying so much of the Advowson Fund as may be available' towards paying some of the bills. Percival invited old members once again to lend their 'support and assistance'.[96]

## *The Undergraduates*

Despite Percival's denials, the size of the College had increased markedly from the very beginning of his presidency. This was partly in line with the growth of the University as a whole, as it welcomed a large influx of middle-class students from Britain's burgeoning public schools and reformed itself both educationally and administratively to meet their various requirements.[97] But it also owed much to the new President. Trinity's reputation had formerly been modest but was now rising fast. Herbert Warren credited Percival with a rapid transformation of the College: 'Always distinguished, it had rather gone to sleep and fallen behind. He certainly raised and roused it.' Warren noted too how 'the barometric curve of its honours list began to mount'.[98]

Some undergraduates, it hardly needs saying, found Percival's rule 'irksome'.[99] He had the habit of treating them as if they were at school. Arthur Galpin (scholar 1879) remembered:

> during my first term finding one day on my table a printed paper signed by the President and containing a string of questions rather after this style: 'Are you reading for an Honour School or for a Pass Degree?' 'How many lectures do you attend a week?' 'How many hours do you give to private study during the week?' and so forth. I thought it a little inquisitorial, but, not being versed in the methods pursued by Heads of Houses in general, I felt no particular vexation. Far otherwise was it with the second and third year men. The place was soon buzzing with a strange blend of ridicule and indignation. Other colleges were highly amused. The caricaturist of the day at once had Percival up in

96 TCA Building Plans, B/3.4. The published account is out by 5*s*. Order Book D, 357.
97 Stone, 'Oxford Student Body', 65–9.
98 Temple, *Percival*, 76.  99 Ibid., 74.

> Shrimpton's window as a sandwich man, displaying on his board the derided questions and wearing the plaintive look of one who has missed fire.[100]

The increasingly post-public-school ethos of the University was reflected in the progressively more hearty and wholesome activities of the undergraduate body. Sports teams began to proliferate, and rhetorical skills were honed in debates. Trinity's Debating Society was founded in March 1873, meeting in members' rooms and chewing over such classic themes as 'Any reform in the House of Lords would prove detrimental to the interests of the country', 'That the agitation for the so-called rights of women is mistaken in principle and ought to be strenuously discouraged', and 'That the abolition of capital punishment is undesirable'. Attendance averaged under twenty before Percival's arrival. By 1882 it was not uncommon for more than forty to attend, and on 25 October 1885, no less than fifty-two turned out for the first debate to be held in the new Junior Library, when A. E. W. Mason moved 'That the Conservative Party is a thing of the past', a motion of which Percival would surely have approved.[101] Trinity's sports teams were run on ever more responsible and business-like lines with the inauguration of the Consolidated Athletic Fund (also known as the Amalgamated Clubs) in 1883, with its own bank account and Charles Cannan as treasurer.[102]

Percival longed to control the moral lives of the undergraduates as he had those of his Clifton schoolboys. When, in 1909, he was invited back to Oxford to preach a Sunday evening sermon at St Mary's, he voiced his heartfelt horror of the mentality that he had fought, largely in vain, to reform. To appreciate the full effect, the following passage should be intoned menacingly in a broad Westmorland accent:[103]

> Those of you who have come . . . from one or other of the best of our public schools, accustomed there to the moral responsibilities of the prefect's acknowledged and accepted position, and having been very jealous of the purity and honour of your corporate life

[100] Temple, *Percival*, 74.

[101] TCA Debating Society Minute Book 1873–95, JCR A/3/1.1.

[102] TCA JCR, A4 1/2, 2/1.

[103] Or as Henry Newbolt put it in *The Twymans* (Edinburgh, 1911), in 'the lingering North-country accent that gave so curious a distinction to his voice, and the unconsciously melancholy cadence that softened its strenuousness with a grave beauty of resignation' (quoted in Temple, *Percival*, 21).

and of every individual's contribution to it, knowing as you do what a purifying, strengthening, and uplifting influence that system of sixth-form responsibility and authority had had upon the common life of your house or school—such members . . . must have felt when they first found themselves in the extremely individualistic society of their college, no man seeming to recognise any responsibility for the character, conduct or tone of his neighbour, as if they had suddenly dropped into some lower stream of social intercourse.[104]

In Trinity Chapel the undergraduates were subjected to regular exhortations. 'I shall never forget those evenings,' wrote Galpin:

The Chapel lighted up in its primitive way by rows of candles fixed on to the pews—the splendid carvings of Grinling Gibbons just catching the gleam here and there—and Percival standing in the President's stall at the west end, his head slightly on one side, his fine, clean-cut features showing up against the candle-light with a strange chiaroscuro effect, his voice retaining still the accent of his northern home as he upheld the sanctities of life and poured vials of scorn on all that was "low and degraded."[105]

Percival's expectations regarding the behaviour of junior members were quite unrealistic. 'I have heard him, in the chapel of Trinity,' recalled Octavius Christie (1886),

impliedly divide his undergraduate congregation into two classes: (1) the Whites, hard-reading scholars, steady, conscientious men (preferably teetotallers and non-smokers) destined to be clergymen, schoolmasters, writers on Social Reform, philanthropic manufactures of great municipal activity, or Radical Members of Parliament; (2) the Blacks, hunting men, betting men, frequenters of billiard-rooms, taverns and houses of ill-fame—the sporting, the low-toned, the lewd, the cynical. As a matter of fact, more than ninety per cent of us at Trinity were neither Black nor White, but of various hues of Grey. In after-life some of us Greys have doubtless degenerated into darker shades, and some few may even have clarified ourselves into Whites. Our moral complexion was not finally determined at Clifton, nor at Oxford.[106]

[104] Temple, *Percival*, 70. Percival had himself inaugurated the Sunday evening preaching services, writing to the vicar of St Mary's in April 1880 of his anxiety 'to do some little work for the undergraduates, and having long felt that Sunday evenings afford an opportunity which might perhaps be turned to good account'; ibid., 87.
[105] Temple, *Percival*, 21. [106] Christie, *School Days*, 23–4.

Arthur Quiller-Couch has been identified as a distinguished Trinity 'grey'. A brilliant scholar and a dutiful undergraduate librarian, he was also a member of the Claret Club, and began his celebrated career as a novelist in order to pay off his undergraduate debts.[107] Percival once reprimanded him with 'What! Another new pair of trousers. . . .!'[108] Quiller-Couch was one of a rapidly growing band of Cliftonians at Trinity. In 1878 Percival had expressed his desire 'to do something towards making a centre for Old Cliftonians at Oxford', and parents who had so admired his methods were only too happy for their sons to continue in his care. Despite Percival's impossible ideals, it would have been surprising if the undergraduates were not influenced by their President. They were not long out of school; and they knew he had the power to send them down. Raper claimed that he had 'been compelled to apologise to the college wine merchant' for the significant drop in consumption, although he told this story against both Percival and Gore.[109]

## *Science Teaching*

Percival was strongly committed to the teaching of science. In 1873 Trinity had been taken somewhat by surprise by a bequest of £8,000 from one Thomas Millard, Esq., a man with no known connection to the College, who stipulated that his benefaction should be used for the advancement of mathematics and science. Conscientiously, the fellows sought to employ the money in an appropriate way, and agreed to offer a £200 lectureship to 'the candidate elected for physics at Merton fellowship in October' on condition that Trinity undergraduates should be admitted to 'the scheme of combined lectures' shared by Merton and Magdalen Colleges. A. S. L. Macdonald was succeeded by Lazarus Fletcher of Balliol in 1876, and by Alexander MacDonnell in 1878. In June 1878 Wayte took expert advice before purchasing 'books likely to be useful' to students reading for Natural Science schools.[110] Two of the first acts of Percival's presidency were the appointment of a new Millard Lecturer, the 'outstanding

[107] Potter, *Headmaster*, 160; Quiller-Couch and A. E. W. Mason were appointed undergraduate librarians for 1885–6, at a joint stipend of £15; TCA Order Book E, 8.

[108] Potter, *Headmaster*, 27.

[109] Ibid., 160. Prestige, *Gore*, 23.

[110] TCA Order Book D, ff. 252, 277; Keith J. Laidler, 'Chemical Kinetics and the Oxford College Laboratories', *Archive for History of Exact Sciences*, 38 no. 3 (1988), 229–30.

researcher' and 'inspiring teacher' Harold Dixon (Millard Lecturer 1879–85), and a convenient arrangement to share teaching with Balliol, who provided an underground laboratory beneath the north-east corner of the Balliol Hall.[111] In 1885 Percival urged the construction of a 'mechanical workshop' (agreed on condition it was 'not in the college garden'). The Millard Laboratory was opened the following year in the south-west corner of the Dolphin Yard, and advertised to 'men who are going to be engineers or architects', 'men . . . who wish to use close and accurate observation of natural phenomena as a mental cultivator', 'medical students, who are required to pass a preliminary examination in mathematics and physics', and 'law students, who wish to acquire a knowledge of technical terms and scientific principles'.[112] Dixon's initial offer to admit women was declined by both Percival and Jowett, who were under pressure from the women's colleges not to allow it. The year 1885–6 saw the first female attendance at any Trinity College lectures: Florence Rich of Somerville, and Dixon's wife who acted as her chaperone.[113]

The Millard Laboratory contained six rooms packed with modern scientific equipment:

a) A Lecture-Room furnished with apparatus for illustrating the principles of Mechanics and Hydrostatics, and provided with a supply of electricity from both dynamos and accumulators, and an electric projection lantern.

b) An Experimental Room, in which experiments involving the use of complicated apparatus can be done. This room contains a standard Clock with electrical attachments, a chronograph, testing machines, and various forms of measuring instruments. Instruments for determining the velocity of flow of liquids.

c) An Engine Room, which contains a steam engine and boiler, gas engine, three dynamos, transmission and turbine dynamometers . . .

d) A Machine Room, containing two Whitworth lathes, one lathe with micrometer dividing head by Cook & Sons, York, and three light lathes, together with drilling, planing, and milling machines, and a full supply of engineers' hand tools.

111 Laidler, 'Chemical Kinetics', 329; TCA Order Book D, ff. 300, 304.

112 TCA 'The Millard Laboratory, Oxford', undated prospectus.

113 Chaperones were considered necessary for solitary females at lectures until the First World War. Pauline Adams, *Somerville for Women* (Oxford, 1996), 33, 40.

e) An Instrument Room, devoted to electrical testing, and containing galvanometers, electrometers, and other electric measuring instruments, and various forms of incandescent and arc lamps, and photometric apparatus.

f) A Book Room, containing books of reference, apparatus used for drawing and machine construction, planimeters and integrating instruments.[114]

## Percival's Frustration at Trinity

Despite his apparent success, many people sensed that Percival was not happy at Trinity. How could he be, when he had:

> a dream of undergraduate life so ordered that every young student during his earliest residence . . . should be first of all instructed by some gifted and inspiring teacher in what we might call the ideal history and ideal purpose of his college and the university around it, and made familiar with its great names and its inspiring examples, and thus stirred to feel at the outset the greater possibilities of his own manhood and what should be his preparation for it.

So he preached in 1909:

> We may dream also of an undergraduate college life more self-governed than hitherto, in which, through the influence of the most thoughtful, the most instructed, the most high-minded among you, there shall be no tolerance for the man of bad language, or low tone, or wasteful extravagance, or sensual vice, or any form of bad example or influence, bringing discredit on the society and moral risk to those who enter it.[115]

As early as the winter of 1881–2 Benjamin Jowett was expressing his concern over Percival's frustration at Trinity, which was exacerbated by his grief following the death of his youngest son, Freddie, in a riding accident on Port Meadow in June 1881. 'I sometimes fear you are disappointed with Oxford,' wrote Jowett. 'No wonder that the sky should seem dark and heavy to you after the calamity . . . If you are depressed it makes you less fit for work in College, and in the Uni-

[114] 'The Millard Laboratory'.
[115] Temple, *Percival*, 71. This sermon was preached on 21 Feb. 1909.

versity. And you are no longer able to take that hopeful view of things which is the soul of success.'[116]

Characteristically, the President sought to occupy himself with good works. In October 1882 he renewed his links with Bristol and accepted a canonry at Bristol Cathedral—'an opportunity for Christian work in Bristol that I should . . . do wrong to decline'—and instituted Sunday evening sermons there, for the preaching of which he donated a pulpit.[117] He threw himself into a project to start evening schools in Bristol, whither he would travel as required. One of the committee described his intimidating presence 'awful as an Alpine peak', as he sat 'listening with grave patience to our fumbling reports, beaming encouragement on hopeful suggestions . . . chilling us to the marrow when it came to inviting explanations as to why the bright ideas of the previous meetings had got no further.'[118]

One cause in Oxford to benefit from Percival's immediate support was that of female education. On 7 February 1879, he attended a meeting for subscribers to a Hall for women undergraduates; three weeks later he seconded the proposal that it should be called Somerville Hall, and accepted the position of chairman. When the committee met on 5 March, he agreed to chair two sub-committees, charged with the appointment of a lady principal, and with acquiring premises for the new Hall. All this was before he moved to Oxford. Subsequent meetings he hosted in the Lodgings at Trinity, where, during the mid-1880s, he and Louisa were 'at home' to any Somerville undergraduate who wished to take tea with them on Tuesday afternoons.[119]

Equally close to Percival's heart were the educational needs of the poor. Those who could not afford college charges had, since 1868, been allowed to matriculate as Unattached Students, and permitted to reside in lodgings licensed by a delegacy set up for the purpose.[120] Two Censors (one after the passing of the new University Statute of 1882) supervised their activities. When in 1882 Benjamin Jowett became Vice-Chancellor, he at once began a series of improvements of the facilities and tuition provided for the Unattached Students, and

[116] *The Times* (27 June 1881), 9; Temple, *Percival*, 78.

[117] Temple, *Percival*, 78–80.

[118] Memoir by Vaughan Nash, quoted in Temple, *Percival*, 80–1.

[119] Adams, *Somerville*, 14, 114.

[120] Alan Bullock, 'A Scotch University added to Oxford? The Non-Collegiate Students', *HUO* 7, 194.

when, in December 1882, Percival heard the censorship was vacant, he seriously considered taking it on.

He suggested the idea to Jowett:

> Supposing you to be at a loss for a suitable man, should you think it a mad thing for me to offer to undertake it, resigning Trinity for the purpose . . . I don't suppose I shall ever be able to do much good for Trinity; and if I were to go they might probably elect Raper, who would make a very suitable head in many ways. As Censor of the Unattached, I suppose I should be pretty free to work out a good system, and the work would interest me more than anything else in Oxford.

Jowett was horrified. 'I would strongly advise you not to hint to anyone an intention or desire to give up the presidentship,' he replied. 'It would be a great error.' The Master tried to encourage his friend:

> I think you are also mistaken about your success at Trinity. You have surely got on very well. Does not the college increase in numbers? You have helped female education; you have gathered a pleasant society about you and your hospitality is greatly valued. No one who has a great deal of energy will long be popular in Oxford . . . If you leave Trinity at all you should either go to a Bishopric or to the Deanery of Bristol.

Percival slept on this for a week and then wrote again:

> What set me thinking of the unattached Censorship was my long-cherished belief that the system might develop into something really creditable to the University, and of service to the country. It is not that I feel uneasy where I am. The college is in a much better condition in various ways than when I came; but I expect it would go on well in its quiet little way under any fairly good head; and if there is an opportunity of doing a really good piece of work, life is short and it might be worth while to try it.

He did, however, acknowledge 'the force' of Jowett's argument, and suggested as a compromise the statement that 'the President of Trinity has agreed to perform the Censor's duties without salary till June 1884, if required.'[121]

[121] Percival to Jowett 29 Dec. 1882, Jowett to Percival 31 Dec. 1882, Percival to Jowett 8 Jan. 1883; Temple, *Percival*, 83–5.

Even before the New Building was complete, the College had turned its attention to the new President's Lodgings. Thomas Jackson was asked to produce new plans, which he felt could be achieved at 'a moderate cost', and he suggested that up to eleven sets of rooms could be created out of the old Lodgings. He had re-inspected the Bathurst Building, and found 'the structure is even weaker than I had supposed.' On 15 March 1885 Robinson Ellis wrote to Thomas Jackson, 'I have never been more pleased than with the result of our college meeting today. We determined by a large majority to pull down 'Bathurst' and erect a President's house on the spot, still retaining the time-honoured name.' Tenders were sought, and a quotation from Parnell & Son to do the work for £5,928 was accepted.[122] It was a struggle to keep costs down, and in March 1886 Jackson wrote optimistically to Percival that if they were to 'lump together' the alterations to the old Lodgings, 'and if possible save a few hundred out of that to go to the other part of the work . . . I believe we shall pull through for the money—but only just.'[123]

Ellis called the prospect of the new Lodgings a 'delightful issue'. Jackson claimed to 'like this quadrangle as well as anything I have done at Oxford'. In May 1886 the *Oxford Magazine* welcomed it as 'a real picture, and the College is to be thanked for adding a new and original effect to those which the Quads of Oxford already possess. One critic was quoted as describing it as 'beautiful: it beats Botticelli.'[124] Only the man expected to take up residence was unmoved. In 1884 Percival's name had been discussed as a possible candidate for the headmastership of Eton; shortly afterwards he was asked, though declined, to stand for Harrow. In November 1886 he was offered the headmastership of Rugby, and accepted with alacrity.

Robinson Ellis received 'the unpalatable news' in a note from Louisa Percival at 5 p.m. on 17 November. The next day Percival wrote himself, offering to resign at any date 'most convenient and most advantageous to the college'. 'I should not fancy that any of the fellows would be anxious to hasten it,' replied Ellis. Percival's

[122] TCA 'New Building', C/3.5; Jackson, *Recollections*, 154. The fellows determined on the name 'Bathurst Lodgings' (TCA Order Book E, 1), but, as was to happen with 'the Cumberbatch Building South' in the 1960s, and 'Ogston House' in the 1980s, it failed to catch on.

[123] TCA 'New Building', E/2.36. The final cost was £6,769 19*s* 10*d*, including £200 for the 'conversion of old house into rooms', 'New Building', B/4.

[124] Jackson, *Recollections*, 175; *Oxford Magazine* IV (1886), 162.

*9.7* The Woods family in front of the Lodgings, photographed for the University *Almanack*. The figure to the left is Charles Cannan (fellow 1884–96).

presidency, he declared, 'must for ever be remembered as epoch-making'. Neither the new buildings, nor the enhanced reputation of the college, would have been possible without Percival as the college's 'Pope'.[125] But Trinity had not loved John Percival as Clifton had done, and neither at Rugby nor in his subsequent appointment as Bishop of Hereford was he to achieve the greatness of his first headmastership. His Oxford years were marred by continual conflict, much of it caused by his aura of priggish superiority. He lacked the personal skills and gift of friendship which were the basis of Jowett's success and enduring reputation as Balliol's greatest Master. Percival was very quickly forgotten. His name has never been associated with the buildings he inspired in the way that Bathurst's has with the Chapel and Garden Quadrangle. Indeed, his greatest achievement at Trinity is known today as 'the Jackson Building'. Percival's large and imposing portrait (paid for with a £100 gift of Henry Woods in 1897) was rescued from the disused coal cellar of the Lodgings in 1993, only to be consigned to the relative loneliness of the SCR back stairs.[126] The sad truth was he was heartily glad to leave Trinity, and Trinity was equally relieved to see him go.

The presidential election of 1887 was the first conducted according to the new Statutes, which had come into force in 1881 (they are dealt with in the next chapter). The fellows met in the Common Room on 16 March, and voted unanimously for Woods.[127] Thomas Jackson wrote to offer his congratulations, and to address some of the finer points about his new home. Henry and Daisy had the pleasure of choosing the range for the kitchen, the 'dinner lift' to the dining-room, and the brass 'furniture' of the bell pulls. In August, Jackson finalized the design for the 'chimney piece frieze' in the drawing-room and suggested 'among conventional rosettes' the initials JP and HGW.[128] The Woods family—Henry, Daisy, and two of their sons—posed with Charles Cannan in front of their fine new home for the *Oxford Almanack* of 1888 (Plate 9.7).[129] It must have seemed like a just reward after nine patient years of waiting. It is ironic then, that Daisy Woods, like the man who had kept her out, was to find life in the Lodgings very frustrating indeed.

125 Temple, *Percival*, 92.
126 TCA Benefactors' Book IV, f. 31.
127 TCA Register D 262.
128 TCA 'New Buildings', E/2.43, 45, 49.
129 Preserved among 'Papers, Documents etc. relating to Trinity College Oxford, 1878', TCA College Government, V/9.

# 10

## *Late Victorian and Edwardian Trinity*

In the final week of his final term at Trinity, Hugh Legge (1889) took his leave of President Woods. 'I went round to see the Cocker,' he wrote in his diary. 'The old gentleman was very pleased at my getting through schools'—Legge had stayed up for an extra term and, against all expectations, scraped a pass—and they 'had a long talk about the College'. During the closing years of the nineteenth century and the early years of the twentieth, Oxford colleges enjoyed very close relations between senior and junior members. Woods was widely respected as President of Trinity, and Legge was one of the most influential undergraduates of his generation. By 1900 he was ordained, and working at the College Mission in the East End of London, with which Woods was actively involved. The relationship, however, had not always been so cordial.

In May 1891, for instance, Legge and his friend Park Goff (1888) had been summoned by Woods to explain their conduct on the night of the Pembroke College Bump Supper. 'I was in a state of complete prostration,' recorded Legge. 'Park Goff was pretty well done too.' They had returned to Trinity:

> at about 10.30. As I got out of the cab I came a howler on my face & so did Goff . . . It seems the Dean [David Nagel] was at the Lodge & was an interested spectator of my being carried in. He then got Park carried to his digs by Smith the porter & some other chaps while he (the Dean) kept the lodge which was very funny.

The next day, the two undergraduates were interviewed by Nagel, Legge sporting 'two great gashes, one on the top of my nose & the other on my upper lip'. 'Park had an elaborate story about being sober until he fell down & then being knocked silly,' Legge wrote in his diary. 'I told the Dean candidly that I was blind. He said, "You are a ruffian". I laughed & he laughed too & said "There is an air of comicality about it too". He then told us we should hear of it again.'

The following day they were interviewed by the President,

who 'seemed ill at ease', and the day after, a Saturday, they were 'hauled before the College at about 9.30 . . . It was in Common Room. Mullins fetched me. I marched up & found all the Dons seated in conclave . . . It was short & to the point. The Cocker asked me if I was "intoxicated". I said I'd already told him I got drunk.' At 10.15 Legge and Goff went to Woods's study to hear the College's verdict:

> He informed us that they felt bound to accept Park's version & only hoped for his sake it was true, & that I was to go down when I'd kept my two terms . . . & was to be gated at 7 till then. I . . . couldn't help feeling a little annoyed. The Dons have as usual behaved like fools . . . Trinity is pitied in general for having to put up with them & their school discipline.[1]

This sorry episode is typical, both of undergraduate behaviour at this date and of the fellows' inability to deal effectively with it. Committed though they were to scholarship, higher education, and multifarious good works, the individual members of the Trinity Governing Body, like those of every other college in Oxford, spent a large proportion of their time struggling to cope with the jolly japes of their pupils. John Percival's new buildings stood firm, but his efforts to reform the ethos of Trinity life had left no visible mark. The majority of Trinity's members were drawn from a small sector of English society, and the College community was both conservative and complacent. In three and a half years, Hugh Legge developed a love for Trinity that was to prove deep, sacrificial, and enduring. It was rooted in a confident acceptance of his natural right to be there. Going down after his finals, he observed patronizingly:

> I honestly believe that they'll have no peace till they get a good firm dean. We had glorious rows but never a scrap of bad feeling. Now they have wretched rags—& endless bad feeling. I'm very angry with old Chadder who is wildly sick with the Cocker because the Cocker is not a gentleman which he cannot help. Chadder ought to be above such silliness. The Cocker's a ripping old chap if you take him right & allow for his oddities.[2]

## *Trinity College under the New Statutes*

'The Cocker' would doubtless have been flattered and amused by such praise. When not engaged on disciplinary matters he had many

[1] Bod. Lib. Legge e. 2855, 145–8, e. 2896, 94. [2] Ibid., e. 2896, 94.

other presidential duties to perform. These were clearly defined by Trinity's new body of Statutes, which had been sealed by the University Commissioners on 16 June 1881 and given royal approval on 3 May 1882. The College's officially stated purpose was unchanged, at least as far as Thomas Pope's sixteenth-century objectives were concerned. The glorification of God, benefit of the public good, strengthening of the orthodox faith, and provision of a perpetual place of study for poor scholars all remained, albeit in a Latin quotation in the preamble. Otherwise, the new Statutes were in English, arranged in fifteen chapters, each divided into numbered paragraphs. The new rules were clear and succinct. Trinity's primary function as a place of education was stated in chapter VIII paragraphs 8 and 10: the College would give 'courses of instruction' for members *in statu pupillari* for a minimum of twenty-four weeks in the academic year, and also provide 'religious instruction' which was to be given by a fellow, office-holder, or the President.[3]

The President was now elected by a simple majority of the fellows (in case of a tie the vote of the junior fellow being withdrawn). His oath was a single-sentence 'declaration' in English, and he was required to reside in Oxford for seven months of the year, including six weeks in each of the three university terms. His stipend was set at £1,200, and should he hold another office, his total income could not exceed £1,600. If the President was incapacitated in any way, either he or the fellows could petition the Visitor for his retirement on a pension of up to £500 (half of which was to be taken from the 'emoluments' [profits] of his successor). The President could be deprived of office for gross misconduct or bankruptcy. His responsibilities were as follows:

a) custody of the college muniments and upkeep of the register and admissions books.
b) superintendence of the college property.
c) enforcement of the Statutes and regulations, and general superintendence of education, discipline and administration.
d) the option of teaching or holding a college office.[4]

Government of the College was highly centralized, and the role of

[3] TCA Statutes E/3.

[4] TCA 1882 Statutes, Chapter I. The first three presidents elected under these statutes, Woods, Pelham, and Blakiston, took (a) very seriously, each writing the official record of his election himself (TCA Register D, 262, 268, 273).

the President was pivotal. Henry George Woods, the first President elected under the new Statutes, was a gifted administrator with an intimate understanding of the College's ways, and the wheels of college life turned smoothly under his headship. In 1896 Woods was succeeded by Henry Francis Pelham, himself no stranger to Trinity, and another with considerable experience of Oxford administration. Pelham had held a scholarship at Trinity for four years (1865–9) and a fellowship and tutorship at Exeter College for twenty.[5] Since 1889 he had been Camden Professor of Ancient History and a fellow of Brasenose. The stronger and fully internal candidate Robert Raper, by all accounts, declined to stand.

As Woods had once supported Wayte and Percival, so he now relied on his bursars, in particular Robert Raper. H. E. D. Blakiston (fellow 1887) was a loyal lieutenant as junior bursar during the presidency of Pelham. Unlike Percival, both Woods and Pelham were content to be *primus inter pares*, and the College was run harmoniously through the weekly meetings of the President and fellows. Important decisions were taken at the termly 'stated' meetings and officially recorded in the Order Book. Ongoing business was conducted more informally at weekly meetings held in the Common Room every Wednesday during the term. Three times a term, outside tutors were invited to 'lecturers' breakfasts' where the academic and disciplinary troubles of the undergraduates were discussed. Woods kept his own memoranda of all these meetings in a small lockable notebook. Pelham—as with almost everything else—did the same.[6]

The closing decades of the nineteenth century saw a series of small but expedient improvements to the College buildings and facilities. In June 1887 the room adjoining the fellows' library, formerly part of the Lodgings, was 'fitted up' as a more comfortable reading room (it had a fireplace).[7] In 1892 a suggestion by H. E. D. Blakiston to allow 'certain undergraduates' to use the fellows' library without supervision was rejected as 'undesirable', but seven years later the fellows

[5] Like Woods at Trinity, Pelham had vacated his Exeter fellowship on his marriage, but continued as a tutor until re-elected under new statutes.

[6] President's Memoranda of College Meetings, TCA Memo Book 1. In March 1893 it was agreed to hold lecturers' breakfasts twice-termly, on the 2nd and 6th Wednesday (191). The Governing Body still meets weekly on Wednesdays during term; three meetings are 'stated', where formal decisions are ratified.

[7] The reading room and Library were to be given a communicating door, if possible; there was no memory of the existing and original presidential front door, walled up in Bathurst's time (TCA Memo Book 1, 8)

agreed that it should be opened for some four hours a day, under the care of a library clerk.[8] Electric lighting was first discussed in February 1890, and was gradually installed throughout the College, beginning with the cottages in November 1893, the 'old buildings' in July, and the 'new buildings' the following May. In June 1901 it was decided to electrify the Hall, and finally, in November, to try 'temporary . . . specimen' electric lights in the Chapel.[9] Another popular Victorian innovation was the bicycle. In November 1896 Woods first noted talk of a 'bicycle stable', and in March 1898 the fellows agreed to proceed with the creation of such a storage facility in the basement of Kettell Hall, at a cost not exceeding £35. Users were charged a termly rent of 7*s*, and an 'assistant' was employed to undertake necessary bicycle maintenance, chargeable on battels at 1*s* per repair.[10]

Kettell Hall returned to the College fold in October 1898, when the tenant, the ancient historian John Henry Mee, moved out. In 1893 Mee had been granted a five-year extension to his lease in lieu of the considerable sum of £2,000, which he had spent on improvements during his tenancy. These included a new kitchen, a music room, panelling, and drainage.[11] In May 1898 Raper took charge of drawing up a scheme to convert the building into undergraduate rooms, while the music room, in the garden to the west of the Hall, became a lecture room.[12] The cottages had been accommodating undergraduates since 1885, and a full renumbering of all staircases in October 1899 marked this final integration of the last part of the Front Quadrangle. The cottages became Staircases 1–3, Kettell Hall 4, and the Garden Quadrangle 12 to 17. One early occupant of the cottages was Hugh Legge, who wrote cheerfully of his first day at Trinity, 'The porter directed me to my rooms, just over the Lodge and very jolly . . . This is a very old building & I have to bend double going up stairs

[8] TCA Memo Book 1, 147; Memo Book 2, 184. The Library was to be open at the following times: 9–10, 12–1.15, 6–7, 8–9. The Librarian's name and pay are not known, but in October 1901 he asked for a rise, and received a £3 bonus at the end of the year. (TCA Memo Book 3, 19, 21).

[9] TCA Memo Book 1, 79, 225; TCA Order Book E, 96, 103, 176, 179; TCA Memo Book 2, 250; TCA Memo Book 3, 23. The Chapel lights were made permanent in March 1902, (Memo Book 3, 39). In the Long Vacation of 1893 Blakiston recorded how 'the smaller rooms & bedrooms were supplied with one light each, the larger rooms with one pendant lamp and one reading lamp with wall plug' (Records of Trinity College Oxford 1887–, 69).

[10] TCA Memo Book 2, 78, 186, 196.

[11] Ibid., 183, 187.

[12] Ibid., 150, 152.

& can touch the roof of my bedroom with my head. Sitting room also very low.'[13]

The Kettell Hall lecture room (Lecture Room C) was the third in college, the others being on the ground floor of Staircase 5 (A) and above the buttery (B). Facilities for science tuition were augmented, at Nagel's suggestion, by the building of a teaching laboratory adjacent to the facility provided by Balliol, and linked to it by means of a door through the boundary wall. Work on the new laboratory began at Easter 1896, and was completed in the Long Vacation, at a cost of some £450.[14]

One change of great magnitude was mooted in the closing years of the century: the possibility of enlarging the Hall, which was now too small to accommodate the entire college comfortably.[15] Balliol's new hall, more than twice the size of its medieval predecessor, had been a daily reminder of what might be done since it rose above the Trinity skyline in 1877. In October 1889 the fellows discussed a number of radical alternatives: 'plans by Mockford' for a northward extension of the Hall into the buttery; 'mov[ing] forward the Bursary and Common Room'; or constructing 'a gallery for tables'. The subject was allowed to lie for some years, but in January 1897 a committee reported its majority view that a new hall in the Dolphin Yard would be 'impossible'. Blakiston then proposed the southward extension of the existing Hall, and, at a special Sunday meeting, it was agreed to employ Thomas Jackson to draw up plans for an enlarged Hall and a new Common Room, the latter to be situated in the fellows' garden. Jackson's designs were duly received and placed in the Library for consultation, and there the matter rested.[16] Such a great project required a visionary leader in the Percival mould, and Pelham, like Woods before him, was focused on the daily minutiae of college administration.

The largest undertaking of this period was the provision of first-rate and permanent sporting facilities for the undergraduates. For some years Trinity had been renting a barge where crews could change into their rowing attire; but it was 'old, inconvenient, [and] too small for the increased numbers of the College'. For cricket and

[13] Bod. Lib. Legge, e. 2606, 208–9.

[14] TCA Trinity College Records 1887–, 113.

[15] In June 1898, for example, the bursar was given authority to 'arrange overflow dinner in Lecture Room B', TCA Memo Book 2, 158.

[16] TCA Memo Book 1, 69; Memo Book 2, 88, 108.

football a field was rented at Cowley, but the pitch used for football was prone to flooding, and the whole area was under threat from housing development. In 1887 Woods launched an appeal for £700 for a new barge, giving the first £100 himself. By February 1888 (estimated cost now £850), 165 members had pledged some £535, in sums ranging from the pounds and guineas of recent graduates to the £20 of Charles Cannan, £25 of triple-Blue Meredith Brown, and £100 of the loyal H. C. Moffatt (1878). The new barge (final cost £928 6*s* 10*d*) was ready in time for the 1889 Torpids.[17] Its ornate superstructure stood well amongst the college barges that lined the river, and its brightly painted dragon figurehead was a distinctive Trinity touch (Plate 10.1).[18] The barge came into its own each year in Eights Week, when it would be crowded with Trinity men and their families.

A new sports ground was a more difficult and expensive project, and the search for a suitable site took almost a decade. In May 1890 abortive negotiations were opened to purchase a field from Merton—'as Balliol & New have done', noted Woods. Three years later the fellows were discussing the possibility of leasing a cricket ground from Brasenose.[19] Finally, in 1898, it was agreed to buy a ten and a half acre site from Magdalen College, 'part of a large field, lying to the left of the path leading from Mesopotamia to the Marston Road'. In July an appeal was sent out to old members in the names of Pelham, Raper, Cannan, and the captains of the Boat Club and of the College cricket, rugby, and association football teams. The fellows had subscribed the £500 purchase price, but £1,200 was required to prepare the ground and erect a pavilion.[20] The final account totalled some £3,260, and the published list of subscribers was prefaced by a friendly letter from Raper, dated in January 1902. He had undertaken a large part of the fund-raising work himself:

> You may be interested to hear all that there is to tell about the New Games Ground towards which you so kindly subscribed a year or two ago. The land has been purchased, levelled, and fenced; the Pavilion built, neighbouring houses planted out, a bridge over the

[17] TCA Benefactions C/1; JCR B/BC//iii/2.3.

[18] The barge ended its life as a tea-room near Shillingford Bridge. The only surviving part is the figurehead which was purchased from the owner of the tea-room by David Woodrow (1938) and bequeathed by him to Trinity in 1999.

[19] TCA Memo Book 1, 83; Memo Book 2, 64,

[20] 'Printed Matter issued by Trinity College during one Academical Year, 1898–9' TCA Coll. Govt. V/10, 70.

*10.1* The College Barge in *c.*1901. The figurehead is a dragon, the carved figure on the balustrade is a gryphon (TCA DD 3, Geoffrey Christie-Miller).

> Cherwell made; and the ground has now for some time been in full working order giving satisfaction to Cricketers and Lawn Tennis players in summer, to Rugby and association players and Hockey players in winter: and even if the light-hearted amusements now popular in this island are destined to disappear before the steadier tramp of troops in training, there will still be room and to spare for drills, parades, manoeuvres, and inspections.[21]

The South African War was uppermost in everyone's thoughts. In 1899 a significant proportion of the undergraduate body were in the Officer Training Corps, and there was a daily conflict between drill and chapel, where compulsory attendance was a battle being lost by the college authorities. In May 1889 the fellows agreed to a shortened service three days a week—'one lesson, one psalm, one canticle'. Two years later there was no improvement in attendance, and in April 1891 Woods withdrew an 'offer to make himself responsible for the rule about chapel' and noted instead that 'the question of roll-call' would be considered for the coming Michaelmas Term. By March 1893 the number of men opting for the roll call, which was held in Hall, had reached thirty. Pelham took an equally realistic—or defeatist—attitude. In April 1899 he conceded that 'Early Parade' counted 'as Chapel or roll call', and, in March 1906, he agreed that choir practice would also be acceptable.[22] Both Woods and Pelham were troubled by well-meaning outside enquiries into the provision made for college servants (who worked seven days a week) to attend chapel. In February 1892 Woods felt obliged to interview the 'senior bedmaker' on the subject, but 'deferred' a suggestion by Gore to consider a 'special service' for the servants. In June 1900 the President received another circular enquiry on the same subject. 'College does not see its way to alter present regulations,' Pelham noted firmly.[23]

Living in the Lodgings, the President was somewhat aloof from the College. 'The Cocker (and his brilliant little wife) we were all fond of but saw them all too seldom, recalled Cyril Alington (scholar 1891) of Henry and Daisy Woods.[24] The couple built a house at Boar's Hill, where Daisy retreated whenever she could. She did not appreciate being known simply as the President's wife, and she found Trinity's restrictive routines frustrating and the hearty uniformity of the

[21] Scrapbook of E. B. W. Nicholson, Bod. Lib. G.A. Oxon C. 287, f. 109.
[22] TCA Memo Book 1, 57, 115, 243; Memo Book 2, 186; Memo Book 3, 12.
[23] Ibid., 1, 147; 2, 226.
[24] TCA OF 24/2, Alington to President Norrington.

majority of undergraduates highly uncongenial. A decade after leaving Trinity, she wrote bitterly of a visit to Oxford, 'O how pleasant to have escaped from the circle of purgatory where the Angel with the scourge continually drives on the herd of hurrying souls.'[25] Daisy Woods aspired to the literary world. Her first published poem appeared two years after her marriage, in *The Garland of Rachel by Divers Kindly Hands* (1881), which was edited and printed by Henry's friend, the Provost of Worcester and publisher Henry Daniel. Daisy's first novel, *A Village Tragedy*, came out in 1887. Only a very few members of the College interested her, but to these she was extremely kind. The undergraduate poet Laurence Binyon (scholar 1888) was invited regularly to Boar's Hill to meet writers and poets of her acquaintance.[26]

In the Easter Vacation of 1897, Woods confided in his vice-president, Raper, the news that he intended in the summer to resign the headship on account of 'the injurious effect of residence at Oxford' on his wife's health. The surprising announcement was made in *The Times* on 10 June.[27] Woods took a parish living, first at Ffestiniog in North Wales, and then at Little Gaddesden in Hertfordshire in 1899. This life was no more interesting to Daisy but at least it allowed for long spells of continental travel. Between 1904 and his death in 1915, Woods served as Master of the Temple in London. Here he became well known as a preacher, while Daisy was able to move freely in London's literary society. Henry Woods was unfailingly supportive of his wife's writing career. Her obituary in *The Times* paid tribute to his 'constant appreciation and encouragement', and how he was 'in the days before typewriters . . . her unwearied amanuensis'.[28] Although by the time of her death, in 1945, Margaret Woods's work was largely forgotten, she has been subsequently described as 'one of the most distinguished women writers of her day'.[29]

Henry Pelham (he had no nickname) and his wife Laura made less

[25] Harvard, Houghton Library, Margaret L. Woods to William Rothenstein, 20 Nov. [1898], bMS Eng 1148 (1641, item 13).

[26] Binyon's poem 'The Garden of Criticism' was published in the *Oxford Magazine* during his first term, and his first book, *Primavera*, was published by Blackwell in 1890: John Hatcher, *Laurence Binyon Poet, Scholar of East and West* (Oxford, 1995) 18, 20–2.

[27] TCA Memo Book 2, 103; *The Times* (10 June 1897).

[28] *The Times* (4 December 1945).

[29] Martha S. Vogeler, 'Margaret L. Woods', *Late Nineteenth and Early Twentieth Century British Women Poets*, ed. William B. Thesing, vol. 240 of *The Dictionary of Literary Biography* (2001), 355, 360.

*10.2* The hall of the President's Lodgings, 1897 (TCA Gabriel Woods).

of an impression on the undergraduates than their predecessors. Pelham was the Camden Professor of Ancient History. He had an international reputation as an ancient historian, and was widely respected for his writings on Rome, although, partly on account of trouble with his eyes, he never did produce the definitive history of the Roman Principate that his friends hoped to see. Whenever he could, Pelham tended to delegate the problems of Trinity's junior members to the Dean. Alan Lascelles (1905) paid an evening call at the Lodgings when he came up for the scholarship examination in December 1904. 'He is a quaint old fossil, visibly nervous and still more visibly bored,' the aspiring candidate wrote in his diary. 'As we departed, after a rather chilly visit, he wished us Good Morning (it was pitch dark) politely and firmly.'[30] Another undergraduate diarist,

[30] *End of An Era*, 13.

the Australian James Walker (Rhodes Scholar 1904) wrote of a 'rather wearisome evening' dining with three others in the Lodgings. Once a term he would pay his respects to Mrs Pelham, a 'ceremony... viewed rather in the light of an official duty than a pleasure because the hostess is such an appallingly bad conversationalist'.[31] Given the number of undergraduates in College, it is difficult to imagine that Laura Pelham saw the ceremony any differently.

On the morning of 11 February 1907, the College heard that the President, who had been unwell since Boxing Day, was dangerously ill, and by the evening, that his life was despaired of. Next day Walker took an early train to London—to watch the state opening of Parliament—and on his return was informed of Pelham's death. In his diary he recorded with interest the events that followed. The 'senior undergraduate', Robert MacSwinney, chaired an after-dinner meeting in Hall, and 'a record attendance' agreed on a wreath and a letter of condolence to Mrs Pelham. The next day a 'record gathering' attended a 'very impressive' memorial service in the Chapel. The funeral took place on the afternoon of 14 February. Walker joined the other undergraduate commoners in the Garden Quad (scholars and BAs assembled in the Chapel Quad, and fellows, MAs, and doctors in the Hall) and walked behind the Vice-Chancellor and University officers in a procession—another 'record'—to the University Church. Pelham was buried in the Walton Street cemetery, where the undergraduates lined the path from the gate to the grave.[32]

## *The Fellows*

Under the new Statutes, the number of fellows was set at 'not less than ten nor greater than twelve', although, under certain conditions, it could be reduced as low as nine. The foundation invariably tended to the lowest figure possible, for the revenue from any vacant fellowships could be usefully employed elsewhere. Up to seven fellows (elected with or without examination) were deemed 'official', their holders residing (at least at first) in College and performing the offices of tutor, lecturer, or bursar. The remainder, up to a limit of eight, were 'non-official', elected after examinations that were so

[31] TCA Walker, 237, 240. [32] Ibid., 353, 356–8.

structured as to make places 'accessible from time to time to excellence . . . in every branch of knowledge recognised in the Schools of the University'. The non-official fellows could be required to teach during the first two years of their appointment only. Each fellowship was tenable for seven years, but a fellow could be re-elected any number of times, on condition that he was 'engaged in some work of learning, science or research', and he could continue indefinitely without re-election if he held a College office. A fellowship could also be extended for five years, if the fellow was elected to a University post. Only single men were eligible for election, but once elected, non-official fellows could marry as they chose. Official fellows were required to vacate their fellowships on marriage, but could then be re-elected to the vacancy, provided that at least three unmarried official fellows were in residence.[33]

Charles Cannan (fellow 1884–98) was the first official fellow elected under the new Statutes (Woods's re-election excepted), and the brilliant scholar and linguist Charles Norton Edgcumbe Eliot (fellow 1884–95) was the first non-official one. Eliot held a tutorship between 1885 and 1886, and was then given College approval to devote himself to the study of Turkish and Arabic. In 1888 he was appointed Third Secretary at the British Embassy in St Petersburg; and the College meeting obligingly recorded its approval of the substitution of Finnish for Turkish in March 1890. Eliot continued both his linguistic studies and his diplomatic career as chargé d'affaires at Tangiers between 1892 and 1895, but eventually resigned from Trinity while serving as the Second Secretary at Constantinople.[34]

The President and fellows were serious about introducing specialists to their number in order to strengthen the teaching in College. In December 1894 Woods consulted Sir William Anson, the Warden of All Souls and Trinity's law lecturer, as to the 'conditions necessary' for a law tutor. Trinity's first fellow in law was Sydney Cornwallis Peel who, after lengthy discussions, was allowed a year's leave of absence in order that he might reside in chambers and 'fit himself' to take 'final honours work'. Peel undertook to return in October 1896, but he wrote in May informing the College that he now intended to resign and pursue a career at the bar. He enclosed a cheque for £101, his stipend for six months, but Pelham returned it with thanks. The view of the fellows was that he was fully entitled to emoluments

[33] TCA 1882 Statutes, Chapter 2.

[34] TCA Order Book E, 20, 60.

until the point he announced his intention not to return.[35] Other appointments were more fruitful. In June 1896 the fellows were debating the 'recognition' of English Literature. The first Trinity undergraduate desirous of taking the new school was John Miller Hamilton (1894). An outside tutor, Ernest de Selincourt of University College, was found, and Hamilton took a second in 1898.[36] Reginald Tiddy, fellow of University College, was appointed Trinity's classics lecturer in June 1903. In December 1905 Pelham wrote to offer him a Trinity fellowship, and a tutorship jointly in Classics and English Literature.[37]

The range of conditions attached to the new fellowships could cause some confusion. Paragraph 13 of chapter 2 of the Statutes allowed the election of a man in holy orders (or intending to take them within one year), with the specific task of providing 'religious instruction'. H. E. D. Blakiston (scholar 1881) was appointed under this clause in June 1887. Twelve days later, at an adjournment of the same College meeting, he was also appointed classical lecturer, and the duty of chaplain was divided between him and the Revd W. H. Price (at £10 a term). Having completed his probationary year, Blakiston found it necessary to seek clarification as to the exact nature of his fellowship, and his 'office' was defined as 'a lectureship for the purpose of religious instruction'.[38] When, in 1895, Blakiston was appointed an official tutor, the fellows again looked no further than the ranks of college graduates for a chaplain, and the choice fell this time on Michael Furse (1889), who had had considerable experience of working with the College authorities as the senior commoner of his year.[39]

Another internal appointment was that of David Nagel (Millard Scholar 1882–6), who from 1888 held a lectureship, and from 1890 an official fellowship as science lecturer and demonstrator under the Millard lecturer, Balliol's Sir John Conroy. Nagel succeeded Conroy as head of the laboratory in 1901, receiving a stipend of £325 and £170 for laboratory expenses. Nagel was a gifted and painstaking teacher,

[35] TCA Memo Book 2, 14, 30, 32, 80.

[36] Ibid., 68, 72.

[37] The time of his election was 'arranged' with Univ. TCA Memo Book 3, 90, 149.

[38] TCA Order Book E, 35–6, 39, 49.

[39] Furse took responsibility, for example, for smoking concerts in March and November 1890, and in November 1891, and on one occasion took personal responsibility for any 'disorderliness'. Memo Book I, ff. 80, 95, 135.

much loved by his pupils, although, as we have seen, rather less successful as Dean.[40] Maurice Davidson looked back fondly on his days in the Balliol–Trinity laboratory:

> The atmosphere here was one of the greatest friendliness. The place was in fact rather like a very select social club in which all the members knew each other, and over the activities of which Nagel seemed to preside in an informal way, almost like an old secretary whom everyone knew and loved, and to whom everyone went for advice and help . . . From four o'clock onwards tea and cake were available.[41]

A fellow's stipend was £200 'clear of Income Tax', and an additional £100 was payable to tutors or lecturers, besides the fees they received via the tuition fund. One of the most significant innovations in the new Statutes was the establishment of a pension fund. The College contributed up to £250 yearly from corporate revenue, and the tutors up to 10 per cent of the tuition fund. Pensions were payable in cases of ill-health, or on retirement after twenty-five years of teaching, which was the maximum period for which a tutorship could be held. With no celibacy rule and a retirement pension, an Oxford fellowship was no longer a step in a clerical career; it had at last become a recognized profession in its own right.[42] Even within a small college such as Trinity, a measure of promotion was possible. In 1892 it was agreed to increase Cannan's stipend as tutor from £250 to £310, with further £10 increments yearly until 1896. Blakiston, newly appointed as tutor, was to receive the basic £250.[43] On his marriage in 1891 Cannan set up home in a house on St Giles'. Many dons resided in North Oxford with their families. Even the bachelor Martin Green decided to move out of College from Michaelmas 1898. He was then 48.

This period saw the ending of clerical Oxford and of college livings as an integral part of the establishment. The Advowson Fund, established when the majority of fellows were waiting to take up parochial church work, was now obsolete. The new Statutes allowed it to be used for the enlargement and improvement of the College

[40] Edmund J. Bowen, 'The Balliol–Trinity Laboratories, Oxford, 1853–1940', *Notes and Records of the Royal Society of London*, 25 no. 2 (December 1970), 229.

[41] Maurice Davidson, *Memoirs of a Golden Age* (Oxford, 1958), 21–2.

[42] TCA 1882 Statutes, Chapter 6; *Clergyman to Don*, 158–67. A fellow's pension was not to exceed £250; this compared with up to £400 at richer colleges (163).

[43] TCA Order Book E, 79–80.

buildings, and for the purchase of land for building purposes. Advowsons could be sold and the money arising used in the same way.[44] In 1887 the sale of Oddington was negotiated, and the £1,600 raised was used to pay part of the debt on the new building, although the transaction was complicated by the agreement to pay interest to the purchaser until the living became vacant.[45] A considerable amount of presidential time was now taken up by the problem of finding suitable incumbents for parishes. In 1887 no Trinity man, fellow or graduate, could be found to take the living of Hill Farrance, and it was finally presented to a member of Hertford College. When it became vacant again in 1900, Pelham was reduced to writing to the bishop for suggestions.[46] In 1891 Ford End was presented to a recent Trinity graduate, Alan Armitage (1879), and three years later it was offered to an even younger member of the College, Arthur Shearly Cripps (1887). When, six years later, Cripps departed for the African mission field, the living was refused by two Trinity men.[47] Meanwhile the churches, rectories, vicarages, and parishes for which the College was responsible were a constant financial drain. President Woods went personally to inspect the structural defects of Ford End church and vicarage in November 1891. He reported that the £150 outlay on the vicarage had been met by H. E. Hulton (1858), rector of the College living of Great Waltham, and a regular, generous benefactor. But the 'serious cracks' in the church remained. After one winter in Ford End, Harold Grindley (1885) sought help with the 'dilapidations' and was told firmly that the College could 'not find more than £50'. When Great Waltham became vacant in 1906, the fellows felt obliged to augment the living by £50 per annum from College revenue before they even began the search for an incumbent.[48]

## The Undergraduates

The new Statutes did, in theory, open Trinity to a wider social mix. The University's new Statutes had removed the necessity of religious tests for matriculation, and Trinity was now open to men of all

[44] TCA 1882 Statutes, Chapter 9.
[45] TCA Order Book E, 31–2.
[46] TCA Memo Book 2, 228.
[47] TCA Memo Book 2, 226, 238.
[48] TCA Memo Book 1, 139; Book 2, 226, 228, 236, 242, 258; Book 3, 131, 155, 193.

*Table 10.1* Percentage of admissions from public schools, sampled decennially 1870–1910.

| *Year* | *Number admitted* | *Clarendon schools*[1] | *Main public schools* | *Fringe public schools* | *All public schools*[2] | *Non-public schools* |
|---|---|---|---|---|---|---|
| 1870 | 19 | 47.4 | 26.3 | 15.8 | 89.5 | 10.5 |
| 1880 | 32 | 50 | 40.6 | 6.3 | 96.9 | 3.1 |
| 1890 | 40 | 22.5 | 57.5 | 12.5 | 92.5 | 7.5 |
| 1900 | 42 | 45.2 | 45.2 | 0 | 90.4 | 9.6 |
| 1910 | 44[3] | 43.2 | 31.8 | 11.3 | 86.3 | 13.6 |

*Notes:*

1 That is, Charterhouse, Eton, Harrow, Merchant Taylors, Rugby, St Paul's, Shrewsbury, Westminster, Winchester.

2 This classification of schools is based on the lists given in Tables 23.A1 in *HUO* 7, 565–6.

3 Excluding 4 Rhodes Scholars.

faiths.[49] Nonconformists were no longer required to compromise their beliefs, but were allowed to attend daily roll-call instead of chapel services.[50] Nor were there geographical restrictions to scholarships. In October 1892 it was even decided to hold a scholarship exam 'at two centres in Australia' during the following year.[51] In reality the Statutes made little difference to Trinity's social composition. The College population stabilized at an intake of between forty and fifty, almost all from the same small number of public schools. Non-public schoolboys were as likely to be from other British universities as from grammar or other schools. Joshua Holden (Millard Scholar 1890), who came up from Wyggeston School, Leicester, and took a first in Natural Science, was very much an exception. By 1900 he was teaching at a non-public school in West Yorkshire.[52] Holden's scholarship would have sufficed to finance his studies, but not the social activities that were part of most undergraduates' lives. Most of the scholars came from public schools too. Only occasionally did the College authorities made a small gesture towards their less affluent members. In May

[49] One scholar of 1882—Simeon Moses—was a Jew. I am grateful to his descendant John A. S. Abecasis-Phillips for information about him. TCA Register D, 257.

[50] 'Decanalia' of Archibald Robertson, TCA Dean B/1. Participation in chapel services was encouraged, however, by the timing of roll-call ten minutes earlier.

[51] TCA Order Book E, 84. President Woods's memoranda reveal a great deal of effort put into this scheme, but no Australian scholar was in the event elected.

[52] M. H. Green, *Admissions in the Nineteenth Century* (Oxford, 1901), 80.

1897 it was agreed 'to give some help to [the] senior scholars of this year (few and poor) in entertaining at the scholars' wine' on Trinity Monday, and in May 1906 the Boat Club was given permission to raise a fund to take the Eight to Henley, on the understanding that they were 'not to dun poor men for subscriptions'.[53]

Trinity had long had a small overseas contingent: sons of planters from the Caribbean and of expatriate administrators from the Indian subcontinent, and, later, representatives of Australia's emerging professional class. The College's first Australians, the Tasmanian-born Reibey brothers Thomas and James, were grandsons of a celebrated female convict, Mary Haydock, transported (aged 13) in 1794 for horse stealing, and of Thomas Reibey, first mate on the whaler *Britannia*; their father, also Thomas Reibey, was a wealthy and respected landowner and businessman.[54] Trinity's first American was William Murison (1869). The Silesian Baron von Zedlitz (scholar 1889) came up from Wellington College and signed the Admissions Book with the familiar first names of George, William, Ernest, and Edward. He was not the only 'foreigner' to have been previously Anglicized in some public school.

One important group of overseas members were the Rhodes Scholars. They came from the USA, the British colonies, and Germany, their studies financed by the munificent endowment of Cecil Rhodes. Trinity first received a questionnaire from the trustees of Rhodes's will in October 1902, and the fellows convened a special College meeting to draft their answers, which were carefully considered and amended before being returned. The College's response was positive: up to three Rhodes scholars would be welcome to apply each year; they would be given rooms and expected to read for honours.[55] Trinity's very first Rhodes Scholar was a South African, Charles James Gardner, from St Andrew's College, Grahamstown, admitted in 1903. The following year came two Americans, William Crittenden of California and David Porter from Maine. In the first ten years of the Rhodes Trust, Trinity admitted thirty-one Rhodes Scholars. Twelve were from South Africa, eight from the United States, four from Canada, three from Germany, two from Australia, and one each

[53] TCA Memo Book 1, 106; 3, 201.

[54] *Dear Cousin, The Reibey Letters*, ed. Nance Irvine (1995 edn.) 3, 14, 19, 110. Thomas Reibey went on to be Premier of Tasmania. I am indebted to James's great-great grandson, Barton R. William-Powlett (1958), for introducing me to this fascinating family.

[55] TCA Order Book D, 187–8; TCA Memo Book 3, 61, 63.

*Table 10.2* Overseas admissions in the nineteenth century.

| *Year* | *Name* | *Country of Origin* |
|---|---|---|
| 1806 | Kellerman, Thomas Penny | Jamaica |
| 1806 | Wylly, Thomas Brown | Bahamas |
| 1806 | Lancaster, Thomas Farrer | Jamaica |
| 1814 | Conn, Robert | Curaçao |
| 1814 | Bathurst, Charles | India |
| 1815 | Sulivan, Robert | India |
| 1816 | Wilson, Philp | Tobago |
| 1817 | Blake, Martin | Antigua |
| 1817 | Partridge, Robert Wynyard | India |
| 1817 | Clement, Richard | Barbados |
| 1823 | Holder, Caddell | Barbados |
| 1829 | Harris, Charles | India |
| 1831 | Holder, Coulthurst | Barbados |
| 1835 | Payne, David Richards | Jamaica |
| 1835 | Thomas, George John | India |
| 1837 | Singer, George | Jamaica |
| 1840 | Reibey, Thomas | Australia |
| 1840 | Reibey, James Haydock | Australia |
| 1842 | Crewe, Henry | India |
| 1854 | Cox, James Dalrymple | Australia |
| 1860 | Robertson, Robert Henry | Jamaica |
| 1862 | Robertson, George Pringle | Australia |
| 1869 | Murison, William Alexander | USA |
| 1870 | Bayley, Henry | India |
| 1873 | Kennedy, Edmund Charles | Guernsey |
| 1881 | Wilson, Walter Frederick | Australia |
| 1883 | Broomfield, Reginald Cobden | Australia |
| 1884 | Young, George James | Australia |
| 1889 | Von Zedlitz, Baron George William Ernest Edward | Silesia |
| 1889 | Mant, Reginald Arthur ICS | Australia |
| 1890 | Bonnin, Alfred | Australia |
| 1890 | Semsey de Semse, László | Hungary |
| 1891 | Hinshelwood, Alfred Ernest | Australia |
| 1891 | Gomes, Augusto José | Hong Kong |
| 1891 | Wright, Charles Henry Conrad | USA |
| 1892 | Martius, Alexander Carl Eduard Wilhelm | Germany |
| 1893 | Mirza, Wasif Ali | India |
| | Mirza, Naseer Ali | India |
| 1894 | Johnston, Harold Featherston | New Zealand |
| 1898 | De Liedekerke, Comte Charles Honoré Elie Marie Joseph | Belgium |
| 1898 | Huidekoper, Reginald Shippen | USA |

*Source*: TCA Admissions Registers B and C.

from New Zealand and Jamaica. Richard Cadman (scout 1901–68) regarded the new arrivals with some trepidation. Sixty years later he recalled, 'we thought, "Oh this is going to be awful." But they're all right, you know, they broaden the mind of the ordinary undergraduate.'[56] When James Walker (Western Australia) first arrived in College, another Australian (William Sandover, born in Fremantle but admitted from Clifton College in 1902) was hurriedly produced to talk to him. During his first term, Walker attended an 'At Home' hosted by F. J. Wylie, the Rhodes Agent, who advised the assembled Scholars not to 'express opinions about Oxford . . . we were not qualified to do so. . . . He felt sure we would find the life quite different.'[57]

The purpose for which Cecil Rhodes established his scholarships was simple, and it was one which the fellows of Trinity could only applaud. He intended that selected young men, particularly from the British colonies and the United States (a former colony whose loss he deplored) should experience the best of English civilization and culture, and return home equipped to extend the influence of the British Empire.[58] Foreigners who came on their own terms were regarded with more suspicion. Two 'Mohammadan Princes', Wasif Ali Mirza and his brother Naseer, sons of the Nawab of Moorshedabad, were given a very chilly welcome in 1893, when the fellows agreed to admit them only under pressure from John Percival, their headmaster at Rugby. Woods wrote reluctantly to Percival in October 1892, conceding that the brothers would be admitted to Trinity on condition that they lived in a separate house 'under the charge of a responsible tutor or guardian. The College . . . wishes its responsibility to be considered as little more than minimal.'[59]

Discrimination on the grounds of race and religion was almost universal in Oxford at this date.[60] Men from overseas were few and far between, and mere possession of a foreign name was sufficient qualification to be considered exotic. It is now time to introduce readers to Arthur Mario Agricola Collier Galetti-di-Cadilhac (scholar 1894). Some of you will know him already, as Gordouli. Galetti-di-Cadilhac was born in Essex, and attended Cheltenham College. But his Italian

[56] Richard Cadman speaking to Susan Cooper, *Sunday Times* (9 April 1961).
[57] TCA Walker, 18–19, 26.
[58] George R. Parkin, *The Rhodes Scholarships* (London, 1913), chapters 2 and 3.
[59] TCA Memo Book 2, 164–5.
[60] For example, to find 'Indians, etc' in Foster's *Alumni Oxonienses* it is necessary to turn to the very end, where they are arranged chronologically.

forebears made a nickname inevitable, and he came to be called Gordouli, after a popular brand of Egyptian cigarette.[61] When Alan Lascelles came up in 1905, a tradition concerning him was being handed down to new members of the college:

> Gordouli was a Trinity man . . . whose room looked out on Balliol quad, which made him liable to Saturday night serenading, and possibly getting bowls thrown through his windows. His real name was not Gordouli, but he was a foreigner and Gordouli (a well-known cigarette-maker in those days) was the nearest the Balliol men could get to it.[62]

For it was during Galetti-di-Cadilhac's three years at Oxford that the now traditional rivalry between Trinity and Balliol Colleges was first manifested, and, quite unwittingly, he became the focus of Balliol undergraduates who would gather late at night and chant the following lines over the dividing wall:

> Gordouli
> Face like a ham.
> Bobby Johnson says so
> And he ought to know.

Robert Johnson was a scholar of New College (1893). By 1898 the chant had become a song, which later acquired a refrain—Bloody Trinity!—and a response—Bloody Balliol! And so began a tradition of feuding strong enough to be transmitted to every succeeding generation of undergraduates for more than a century.[63] The long frontier was a recent, and perhaps provoking, innovation: Trinity's front quadrangle (1886) was overlooked by Balliol's Brackenbury Building (1869); behind Trinity's Garden Quadrangle the peace of the Master's garden had been exchanged for the bustle of the Balliol Hall (1877). Various factors contributed to the continuation of the feud. Sporting rivalry fanned the flames in the early years of the twentieth century, when the Trinity and Balliol First Eights jostled for position in the top division. Now Trinity would sing:

> Balliol, Balliol,
> They can't r-o-w

[61] G. Norman Knight, 'The Quest for Gordouli', *Balliol College Record* (1969), 35–46.

[62] *End of an Era*, 46 n.1.

[63] Knight, 'Gordouli'. Knight speculates on the facial features of Bobby Johnson, which may have led to these lines being sung.

Joe Legge says so
And he ought to know.

Joe, alias Hugh, Legge (1889)—was the Trinity rowing coach.

Undergraduates on both sides were jealous of their own college's reputation. Balliol had prospered under Jowett's long mastership (1870–93) and was renowned for its progressive ethos and intellectual brilliance. Trinity was heartier and reactionary. Balliol had the highest proportion of 'black' undergraduates (by which adjective all non-whites were described) in the University; they were not encouraged to apply to Trinity. The majority of Balliol's overseas students were in fact from India, sponsored by the Indian Civil Service. They were always a very small group, but their existence was a popular subject for humour, and one about which many white Balliol students were sensitive. Strong racist overtones soon attached themselves to the chanting over the College wall. Before the First World War, Trinity men were singing: 'Balliol, Balliol, Bring out your black men,' and in 1919 Thomas H. Cathrall (1914) was punished by the Dean for changing a news-vendor's poster 'Negro Riots in Cardiff' to read 'Negro Riots in Balliol' and pasting it up on the cabman's shelter in the centre of Broad Street.[64]

Another very important reason for the enduring popularity of the feud must not be forgotten. The protagonists on both sides (who after all had a great deal in common) found it all great fun. Alan Lascelles was one of a close group of Trinity–Balliol friends, for whom 'ragging' was an important part of daily life. After Lascelles's twenty-first birthday party—'It was very successful, and Trinity was very suitably roused after dinner'—Charles Lister (Balliol 1906), was sent down, having got extremely drunk on Pol Roger and 'used words far from secular to the Rev. the Dean'. Lister was given a tremendous ceremonial send-off by more than a hundred undergraduates. His Trinity friends paraded 'in black overcoats and craped opera-hats . . . with large arum lilies in our hands and a wreath of copper-beach leaves' to Balliol, where Patrick Shaw Stewart (Balliol 1907) made a speech in which he 'touched lightly on the feud between Trinity and Balliol, with a passing reference to Gordouli of pious memory'. Three years later, Lascelles mingled with the London crowds on the night of George V's coronation, and his natural response to the charged

[64] The verse concluded 'Jack Johnson says so / And he ought to know.' Jack Johnson was a Black American boxing champion between 1909 and 1915.

atmosphere of the occasion was to sing 'Gordouli all down the Strand'.[65] Even as an undergraduate, he clearly recognized that the ungentlemanly behaviour the feud required was a healthy mental release in the repressive society of Edwardian England. 'Where else, save in the garden quad, will one find delirium in making hunting-noises at the moon?' he confided in his diary. 'Where else can we escape the pall of conventionality, the clog of responsibility, so utterly that we can say with perfect sincerity, "Nothing matters"?' And where else could young men of his class hurl drunken obscenities and stones over a wall?[66]

The admissions process was now highly organized. By the closing years of the nineteenth century, printed literature was sent to explain the procedure to all applicants for places as commoners. Application forms were available from the President, who required 'some recommendation' and 'formal testimonials'. An Entrance Examination was held in the Easter Vacation for admission the following October, which was recommended as 'the best time to commence residence'.[67] The College expected new undergraduates to have passed Responsions before coming up, and the examination could be taken at four times in the year: early December, March, mid-June, and late September. In March 1899, Geoffrey Christie-Miller's father was eager for him to attempt Responsions as early as possible. 'Perhaps the sooner the better,' agreed Raper. 'It gives another chance in case of failure.' Raper's pessimism was justified. Christie-Miller received the news from Senior Tutor Blakiston, on a postcard addressed to the Grand Hotel des Palmes, in Palermo: 'You were ploughed in Euclid . . . NS [*non satis*, i.e.,'not enough'], & Latin Prose. You passed in grammar & arithmetic. Your books were not read. You have evidently a good deal to make up. Meanwhile I hope you will have a pleasant holiday in Sicily.'[68]

Christie-Miller was successful in the Entrance Examination in May 1900. Latin prose, translation 'of easy unprepared passages from Latin and Greek authors', and an English essay were all compulsory, while optional papers included 'Additional Classics', mathematics, 'some part of Chemistry or Physics', and 'A period of modern history to be studied on books approved by the President'.[69] Scholarship examinations were even more highly organized. In March 1887 negotiations

65 *End of an Era*, 45–7, 102–3. 66 Ibid., 44.
67 'Regulations for Undergraduates', TCA Christie-Miller, 1/2.
68 Ibid., 8/1–2. 69 Ibid., 1/1.

were opened with Wadham to examine jointly, and soon Trinity was combining with a number of other colleges. In the year 1899–1900, three scholarship examinations were held, with printed advertisements, application forms, timetables, and lists of candidates. Trinity joined with Balliol and Christ Church in a Natural Science scholarship examination, which began on 21 November 1899; with Wadham for an open scholarship (i.e. Classics) on 30 November, and with Merton and Brasenose for a Modern History Exhibition on 24 January 1900. Each examination lasted five days. Compared to many colleges, Trinity's number of scholars was low, and the introduction of an Exhibition Fund under the new Statutes was an attempt to address the deficiency. Chapter 3 paragraph 9 of the Statutes provided for up to £250 from corporate revenues, in addition to certain money from trusts, to be used in 'giving assistance' to needy and deserving members of the College, for the purpose of 'promoting study and improvement' among the undergraduates. By means of the shared examinations it was also possible to interview a wider field of candidates who might otherwise not have considered Trinity at all. There were thirteen candidates for the 1899 Natural Science scholarships, and one place at Trinity, chemistry preferred. Only one man put Trinity as his first choice, and only two placed it second (as opposed to ten who preferred Balliol). The entrance regulations also made some attempt to attract the more able students: those who showed 'sufficient merit' in the scholarship exam were offered the possibility of 'precedence over all other commoners'.[70]

## *College Life and Discipline*

Hugh 'Joe' Legge came up in October 1889, a 'red-haired bruiser' who held the public school heavyweight boxing title.[71] He was immediately at home in the College environment, which in many ways was not much different from his public school, Haileybury. Despite a confident attitude—'I got things a bit ship-shape & then asked the porter where the rear [lavatory] was (it is always requisite to know this)'—he was nonetheless very anxious to learn the unwritten rules of his new life. On his first evening the freshmen dined alone in Hall ('sole

[70] The balance between Trinity and Wadham was more even. Of 67 men, 11 were applying only to Trinity and 4 only to Wadham. 'Printed Matter', TCA Coll. Govt., V/10, 2–20; TCA Christie-Miller, 1/1.

[71] *The Times* (18 October 1944).

. . . liver & bacon, mutton, beer, apple & blackberry tart'), but the next day they were joined by the rest of the college. 'After Hall it is etiquette for each table to go en masse when it has finished,' he noted in his diary. 'Individuals don't go out alone.' After dinner Legge went to the Playhouse with two school friends at other colleges, and here he discovered another inadvertent solecism. 'It is etiquette to go to the theatre without cap & gown as the proggins [proctors] do not book you it not being etiquette to do so. We three went in caps of course not knowing, as did several other Freshers.'[72]

Another witness to the strong behavioural codes of this period is Thomas Stone (1895). In 1901 Stone was invited to address an audience of schoolboys on the subject of 'Oxford and its life', and he drew heavily on his own experiences. A fresher, he explained,

> soon meets others, very often at coffee, a very usual way of becoming acquainted with men of your college, both Seniors & Freshers. You will get an ordinary visiting card in hall, handed by scout: 'Coffee. 7.45'. You send an answer back, on your own, or back of the other, & will probably meet half a dozen freshers & some seniors in the man's rooms, & you sit & smoke & talk. Other seniors will send or leave cards in your rooms, & then you go & return the call or leave your card. Then you meet other men at football, or boating, or lectures & so on. There is a certain amount of etiquette.[73]

Legge received regular invitations to breakfast from the senior undergraduates. 'Breakfast here consists of much the same things always,' he commented. 'Fish 1$^{st}$ course, Meat 2$^{nd}$ course, or eggs etc, omelette 3$^{rd}$ course, bread & marmalade or jam etc at end & smoke after.' Printed order forms were provided for the convenience of the kitchen and the scouts who delivered both breakfast and lunch to members' rooms. The breakfast menu included, 'fowls, chops, steaks, mutton & veal cutlets, sausages, kidneys, bacon, porridge, eggs & bacon, buttered eggs, omelettes, eggs, ham & eggs', while, in season, the poultry and game section of the lunchtime choice was roast fowl, duck, pheasant, partridge, wild duck, and blackcock. Legge was highly amused when some second-year hosts, 'Elger and Goff in 6.B.', entertained a second-year man by mistake, having written 'Hitchings' not 'Hichens' on his invitation, but he was very embarrassed when he himself was in error. 'I made a gruesome mistake

[72] Bod. Lib. Legge, d. 2606, 208–9, 212. [73] TCA DD 72 Stone.

this morning', he wrote on 31 January 1890, when another undergraduate

> asked me to brekker on Saturday. Being in an upside down state of mind I went this morning. Of course he was there alone & rather surprised to see me. I felt awfully awkward & insisted on going but he meanwhile yelled to his scout out of the window & ordered me 2 mutton chops. I was very sorry & very angry with myself as I'm afraid [he] hasn't much money, but I can make it up to him later on.[74]

Christopher and Noel Chavasse, the twin sons of the Bishop of Liverpool, came up in October 1904, and found their days 'very full up with invitations. It is rather hard work to fit in time for work.' They had strong characters, and, like their parents, were committed to the Temperance Movement. Noel was quick to praise one of his new friends, John P. Argenti (1904): 'although he is awfully rich and his father sends him musty bottles of choice wine, he is not in the least fast and hardly ever touches wine or smokes.' Under the pressure of their peers, however, their teetotal stance quickly softened. 'Last Sunday we had rather a scare,' wrote Noel to his mother on 24 October 1904, 'we thought there was to be a smoking concert, freshmen specially invited and a great many Freshers got very nervous. About four came to consult us . . . We decided to strike and not go, but to our relief we found that it was only a College Meeting about a concert.' By the Freshers' Drunk of 1905, however, they were more ready to conform:

> It was quite a mild affair, only one fresher drunk, and he is going to get ragged by some of the second-year men because it is bad form for a Fresher to get drunk. One awful man named Gurney did not come to the Drunk, and five of us went to look him up about 12 p.m., it so happened that all the other freshers did the same, and there was an awful squash on the stairs up to his room and an awful row too. He was not in his room so his furniture was spread about a bit, nothing broken, and his coal spilt about. Then we went up to his bedroom, and found him, where do you think? Under the bed in a mortal funk, a few boots were cast at him and then everyone went out, they were too disgusted with him to touch him.[75]

[74] Bod. Lib. Legge, d. 2606, 221, 225, 332–3; d. 2607, 56–7; TCA Coll. Govt., V/10, 44–5.

[75] Ann Clayton, *Chavasse Double VC* (London, 1992), 24–5. Although we might expect grammar-school outsiders to be the victims of bullying, Gurney was in fact an Etonian.

In the close-knit community of the College it was difficult not to take an interest in sport, and undergraduates were subjected to considerable pressure to participate. Members of the Boat Club were hard to resist, although Legge could hardly have been a more enthusiastic victim. On Tuesday 14 October he recorded cheerfully in his diary: 'After lunch was tubbed [coached on-shore] by Tuckett & Lowry [Boat Club secretary] & am very sore, my clothes sticking to me whenever I sit.' One year later the roles were reversed. 12 October 1890:

> After hall, after coffeeing in Theo's rooms Lowry & I went round the freshers' rooms to get men to row as is customary. One man in digs in the Broad said he was paralysed down one side when we asked him & we felt very awkward, but it couldn't be helped. Another (in my old rooms) was a tall fattish youth & he said "I don't think I'll row. I came up *to play golf.*" I nearly burst with laughing however we persuaded him to try rowing.

The next day, Legge took out

> a Hungarian fresher who came down under charge of F W Hall [scholar 1886]. He does not know a word of English & weighs 14 stone 7 lbs being somewhat fat & suggestive of German beer. The process of coaching him was odd. F W Hall had to go in the boat & translate into German what the coach said to this chap. The effect was ludicrous.[76]

James Walker did not record the names of the 'two men [who] came around to enlist recruits for rowing' but he was soon 'persuaded to take up this sport'. He preferred the more individual pastime of boxing, however, and here his obvious talent promised greater glory for Trinity. With some satisfaction, Walker recorded his first Oxford boxing lesson on 27 January 1905: 'The instructor found that I was an extremely promising pupil . . . As a matter of fact, Dad taught me everything years ago . . . From what I saw of his other pupils I think Western Australia could shake them up a bit.' Walker's training programme involved work in the gym and long early-morning walks, often in multiple layers of clothing as he struggled to keep his weight

[76] Bod. Lib. Legge, d. 2606, ff. 215–16; d. 2608, 103, 105. The word 'fresher' is a classic usage of the 'Oxford–er' (e.g. breakfast—brekker, rugby football—rugger, association football—soccer, cup final—cuppers) which emerged at Harrow *c.*1870 and became endemic in public schools, Oxford, and the upper middle classes between *c.*1870 and 1940. See J. R. de S. Honey and M. C. Curthoys, 'Oxford and Schooling', *HUO* 7, 549.

down, but often also in the congenial company of sympathetic friends. Walker in his turn spent many an afternoon cheering on one College team or another. Even on the day that he won his boxing Half Blue, he interrupted his preparations to watch Trinity beat Oriel at hockey. The Varsity Boxing and Fencing match took place on Friday 9 March 1906 at the Town Hall. Walker won by a knock-out, 'I caught him full on the jaw with my right and he went down like a log.'[77]

Members of Trinity still hunted, but the concomitant expense made it more and more a minority activity. Alan Lascelles was obsessive about hunting, although he found it a struggle to keep up with the higher echelons of undergraduate society. His Trinity friends included John Gore (1903), the Hon. Guy Charteris (1905), and Oliver N. 'Chubby' Chadwyck-Healey (1905), a group whose wealth, status, and academic brilliance bought them an easy aloofness from the majority of their peers, but, not unnaturally, incurred some resentment. They spent a great deal of time in Balliol College. Lascelles dined regularly as a guest of Balliol's exclusive Annandale Club, and in the Long Vacations of 1907 and 1908 he joined two Balliol reading parties in the Alpine chalet of the Balliol don 'Sligger' Urquhart.[78] He cared nothing for the debts that he ran up, nor for the disapproval of some Trinity contemporaries. 'I think they hate us,' he confided in his diary on 5 March 1908:

> They believe we're 'fast'; we go out hunting, and we only dine in hall six times a term. We know men in other colleges, and we don't seriously support our own in athletic departments. These really are very valid indictments from a very large section of the Oxford world. The college feeling is pushed to the most absurd limits, and the ideas about games are v. little better than those of a public school. Heaven knows, no one is fonder of Trinity than I am, but I do fail to see that because any particular dull individual happens to have been allotted rooms there for the same period as I have, I should therefore prefer his society to that of a less dull individual in another college.[79]

[77] TCA Walker, 239–42. On at least one occasion, Walker suffered serious concussion after boxing. In October 1906, he consulted an 'eye specialist' about his 'wracking headaches', and was prescribed reading glasses (206, 314–15).

[78] *End of an Era*, 24, 31–2, 40, 44, 48.

[79] *End of an Era*, 43–4. Reflecting on his schooldays at Marlborough, in 1920 Lascelles admitted of his contemporaries that he 'despised them all secretly, because their forebears had been county-cricketers, and mine masters of the Branham Moor' (315).

One occasion when the hunting men rode to win College glory was the annual Grind, or point-to-point steeplechase. The earliest reference to such an event is a note of a sweepstake draw preserved in the album of Sanford G. T. Scobell (1857).[80] James H. Orr (1898) had in his album a photograph of the impressive 'Trinity coach at the Varsity Grind' (Plate 10.3). Geoffrey Christie-Miller preserved race cards from 1901, when he rode 'G J Edward's Swannell' round a course at Garsington, and 1902, when the event was held at Northmoor, and he rode his own brown gelding Up-to-Date, in his own colours of white with dark blue sash and cap. Christie-Miller and Up-to-Date won the Cup and purse of £8 in 1903, when the Trinity Grind was held jointly with Magdalen's, and was followed by a dinner at the Randolph Hotel.[81] Alan Lascelles was bitterly disappointed when he failed to win the College Grind of 1909. 'It was a great blow, as I'd schemed to win it for the last twelve months,' he lamented. 'I wonder how many people would believe that I minded the fiasco of that race about forty times more than I minded missing my shadowy chance of a First?'[82]

The senior students were strong role models, although not in the way that President Percival used to hope. As a freshman, Hugh Legge paid particular attention to what was expected in the way of riotous behaviour. Sunday 27 October:

> This morning at about 3 I was woken up by a frightful row in Braybrooke's rooms just opposite mine (his sitting room). It must have been a lot of drunk chaps I think. They came upstairs & kicked up a shindy outside my bedder & I prepared for a row but they didn't come in.

The night of 5 November, with its long-standing tradition of Town and Gown hostilities, was a natural opportunity to experiment in this direction. With a number of friends, he 'paraded the streets looking out for a row but beyond being hooted & yelled at a good bit in the Corn: the town didn't notice us much'. Returning to College, they gathered in the rooms of Evelyn Waddington (1889), where they found:

> Turner, Lyon, Ryves, Boas . . . We got jovialler & ended by a rag. I smashed the tongs & then we tried breaking other things like

[80] TCA DD 267 Scobell.
[81] TCA Christie-Miller papers, 6/1–3.
[82] *End of an Era*, 52.

*10.3* The Trinity coach at the Varsity Grind, 1900 (TCA DD 296, G. W. M. Orr).

> Samson.[83] I managed to draw up one leg of the tongs into 2 bits & wine glasses & bottles etc were smashed all over the shop. Meade danced a step dance which was rather effective. After that the out-college men went & we ragged about again. Darbishire (who climbed over) then hailed us through the window, so after much exertion I tore down the iron framework outside to prevent one getting out & he jumped in. We then ragged about the Quad & were joined by O'Neill, Harrison, Thursfield & Wellby, whom we went to see. Everybody else seemed to be in bed. We went & saw Slocock at one time. He was very fit. At about 1.30 I got to bed.[84]

Legge was extremely proud of this episode. Next morning after Chapel he learned that:

> last night as I was rambling about with Meade & [Waddington] I went up to a good many people & told them that if I hit them in the eye they'd remember me. It so chanced that I met our missionary at Stratford (there is a college mission there) & said this to him. Today he told someone that he had met 3 young fellows who were a disgrace to their college. Rather funny!

Better still, it had come to the ears of the bursar. Two days later, Legge went for a tutorial after evening Chapel:

> Raper in great form & asked me if I took much interest in Samson. I said yes. He then chatted a bit about him & suddenly said, "I don't think he should be emulated in private life." I, seeing he referred to Waddinton's window . . . smiled & said I thought on the contrary, that the development of physique ought to be encouraged. Raper grinned & said there were limits. I grunted & went.[85]

The fellows were remarkably tolerant of destructive behaviour within the College community, although, short of sending down the majority of their junior members, there was often little that they could do. The rule against bonfires in the quadrangles was breached so frequently that President Woods was moved to remark on the absence of one on the night of 5 November 1889. The 'feeling of the Common Room [was] against doing anything' when the Vice-Chancellor invited representatives to a meeting about bonfires and fireworks 'after College races' in February 1891. Indeed, when the

[83] The Old Testament judge, famous for his violent outbursts and physical strength.
[84] Bod. Lib. Legge, d. 2606, 233–4. [85] Ibid., 234, 237.

undergraduates requested 'leave' to celebrate five bumps in Torpids with a bonfire and fireworks, permission was formally granted by the College. Whether it was legal or not, when they were confronted by several dozen inebriated young men hurling broken furniture into the flames, the Dean and the few fellows in residence could only observe from the sidelines. On the morning of 6 November 1892, Nagel, Raper, and Blakiston brought the names of twenty participants to President Woods to be reprimanded and fined. Financial penalties were in reality a means of licensing a range of undesirable, but everyday, activities. At a Stated Meeting in December 1889, Woods noted that 'The Bursar will be supported in putting [a] fine of £1 on playing football in the quadrangles.'[86] The bursar was Raper, and he had an equally forbearing attitude to unruly behaviour at dinner. 'Gentlemen coming from homes where bread-throwing is habitual,' reads his exquisitely ironic notice of about 1900, 'and finding a difficulty in conforming suddenly to the unfamiliar ways of a higher civilization, will be permitted to continue their domestic pastime, on a payment of 5/- [5s] a throw, during their first year. After that the charge will be doubled' (Plate 10.4).[87]

An undergraduate's coming of age was frequently the occasion for a lavish private dinner, and such occasions often culminated in a bonfire in the Garden Quad. Following a riotous bonfire and considerable damage (a bath thrown through a window) on the night of 22 October 1892, Woods put up a stern notice threatening the imposition of fines. Nine days later Bonfire Night was celebrated with a torch-lit procession and two bonfires. Legge and Noble, two fourth-years who had fed the fire, were gated (confined to their lodgings after 10 p.m. for the following term) and fined £5; eighteen others were fined £1. Woods made a note: 'in seeing these gentlemen said fine would be reduced in the case of anyone who said that he had not put anything on the fire, but no one took advantage of this.' Legge and Noble were subsequently let off the gating when they assured the President that the bonfire had been 'unpremeditated', and when he reflected that the 'sentence [was] disproportionately heavy'.[88]

[86] TCA Memo Book 1, 69, 73, 109, 170, 223.

[87] Two copies of this notice survive in the College archive, one preserved by Clara Coxon, the daughter of M. W. Patterson (TCA DD 30), the other in the collection of Geoffrey Christie-Miller (TCA Christie-Miller, 1/8).

[88] TCA Memo Book 1, 167, 169, 171.

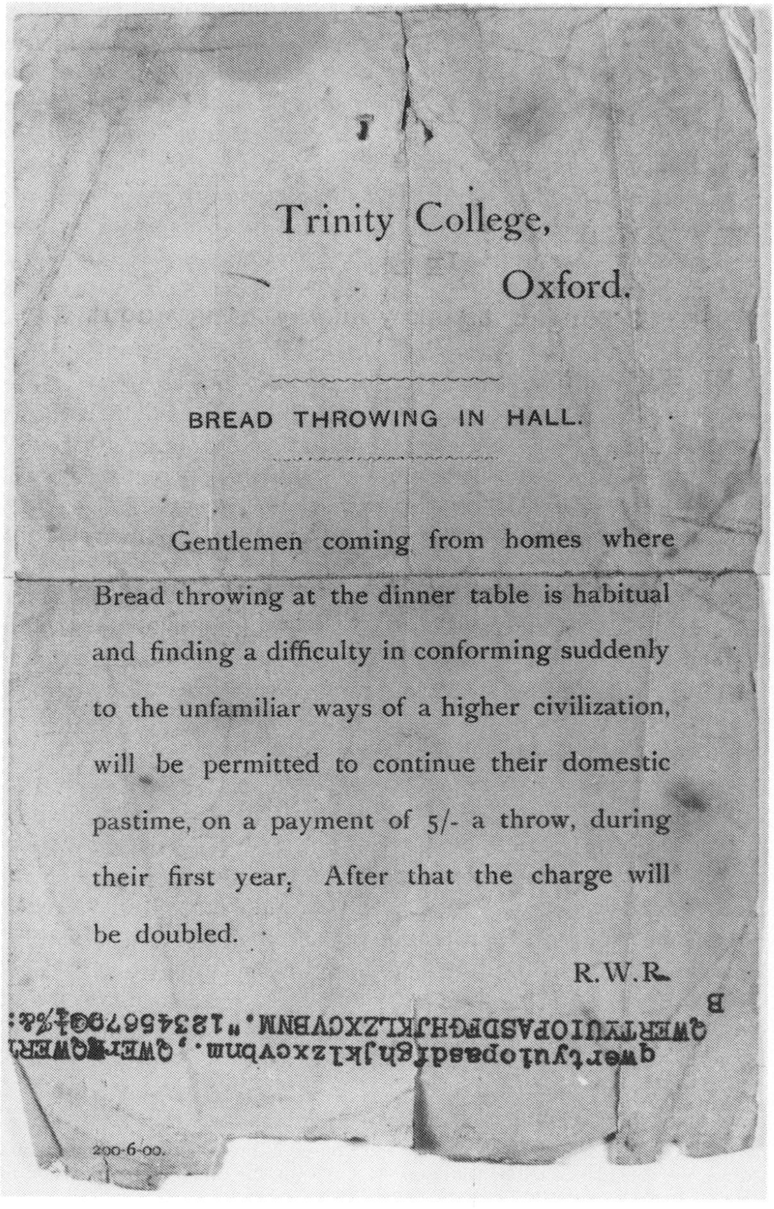

Trinity College,

Oxford.

BREAD THROWING IN HALL.

Gentlemen coming from homes where Bread throwing at the dinner table is habitual and finding a difficulty in conforming suddenly to the unfamiliar ways of a higher civilization, will be permitted to continue their domestic pastime, on a payment of 5/- a throw, during their first year, After that the charge will be doubled.

R.W.R.

200-6-00.

*10.4* R. W. Raper's bread-throwing notice (TCA DD 30, Mrs Clara Coxon).

Perhaps aware that too-heavy penalties might only exacerbate trouble, the fellows agreed the following November that those 'present only' at a bonfire should pay just 5*s*, while men 'seen to take an active part' would be subject to 'a heavier fine'. In the event, two men were fined £2 (Henry Foster (1892) also paying double the cost of a door which he had put on the fire), eight were fined £1, and forty-three 5*s*.[89] H. A. Prichard (fellow 1898) once sent a friendly caution to Geoffrey Christie-Miller: 'Should you be likely to want illumination in the Quad tonight—you ought to think to apply to have some faggots out—before it is too late to arrange for it—in order to avoid the possibility of damage.'[90] Geoffrey Christie-Miller ( who celebrated his coming of age with a dinner on 15 March 1902) kept the menus of numerous such occasions, including that of his friend Horace E. W. Young (1900) whose birthday dinner on 6 December 1901 was followed by a musical party in his room and a large conflagration in the quad, with bagpipes, and a photographer on hand to record the scene.[91]

Bonfire Night 1895 was the occasion of a serious fire, which gutted the rooms of a freshman, James Hugh Thomas, on the ground floor of Staircase 14. Thought to have been started by 'the incautious throwing of a squib', the blaze was noticed at 11.30 p.m. by Charles Fox Burney, the Hebrew lecturer of St John's. According to one press report:

> he gave an alarm, and a number of St John's men promptly deserted their own bonfire and scaled the wall, and joined the Trinity undergraduates in vigorously exerting themselves to keep the flames under by means of cans, baths, and jugs of water. The Volunteer Fire Brigade were summoned by telephone, and 22 members under the command of Second-Officer F. Symonds, with hose-cart, escape, and appliances, were quickly on the spot.

The entire contents of Thomas's rooms were destroyed, also the 'ceiling of the sitting room, doors and windows', and further damage was done by the 'hasty removal' of the contents of the rooms adjacent and above. Blakiston estimated the total repair bill at £200. 'A good supply of water was obtained from a hydrant in the quadrangle,' the

89 TCA Memo Book 1, 189, 223.
90 TCA Christie-Miller 8/28 undated.
91 TCA Christie-Miller 5/3; TCA OM 29 Young.

*10.5* Bonfire at the coming of age of Horace E. W. Young (1900), 6 December 1901 (TCA OM 29).

press report approved, 'and enabled the Brigade to effectively cope with the flames'.[92]

The incident resulted in a further rule 'absolutely forbidding the introduction of fireworks into the college' and the servants were required to report infringements. But bonfires continued to be lit. Alan Lascelles remembered two in Trinity Term 1907:

> After schools were over, there was a good deal of indiscriminate revelry. On the night they finished we all dined at No 20 Holywell—about fifteen of us. Adjourned to college 9.40 and donned pink cardboard masks with elegant black moustaches. Having padlocked and in other ways obstructed the three gates into the garden, we climbed in through the window on No 5 with a detachable bar, and lit a bonfire in the middle of the path, following it up with a picturesque pyrotechnic display. Another bonfire had been lit in the garden quad, with the idea of drawing the Dean; but he, unfortunately, was at a Masonic dinner, and didn't appear till late. When he *did* come, he was quite sulky. In a hurried flight back through the window I tore my trousers from the knee to the ankle and left the greater part of my shin on the window ledge.

And, after a 'succulent dinner' at the Gridiron:

> In college more serious-minded men had been at work for some two hours on the bars of No 14 cellar [where combustible material was stored] with a steel-saw; these were by way of giving way any moment, so a preliminary bonfire was started with three chairs and a tin of methylated. But the supplies were long in coming, and only strenuous efforts kept the Dean from extinguishing it entirely. When they did come, there was a v. cheery warmth. It was a very wild night, and a very fitting finale.[93]

There were three things that the President and fellows were unwilling to tolerate: damage outside the precincts of the College, 'drunkenness', and personal disrespect. Strong intervention became necessary when a number of glass windows in Balliol rooms overlooking the front quad were smashed, and the sub-dean Michael Furse sent a warning letter to all undergraduates urging those responsible to 'give in their names . . . at the office'.[94] The additional

[92] Blakiston recorded the incident and preserved an anonymous press cutting in 'Records of Trinity College 1887', 94–5. The telephone had been installed in the Lodge in June 1894 (TCA Memo Book 1, 253).

[93] *End of an Era*, 29–30.

[94] TCA Christie-Miller, 1/5.

office of sub-dean had been found necessary, for obvious reasons, and Michael Furse's 'muscularity' was a useful asset in the post.[95] The College authorities came down very strongly on the rugby team in March 1892, when a complaint was made against them by the London and Great Northern Railway Company. One man was accused of indecent exposure, and others of damage to the First Class compartments. When the President asked for 'names', Stokoe and Noble admitted the second charge, and President Woods gave them four days to raise £85 from the team 'mainly to save legal proceedings on the part of the company, & as a preliminary step'. Two members of the team were sent down until October, four more (including John Percival's son Lancelot) until the end of term. Six players, however, 'cleared themselves' by a simple denial that they had committed any offence or been 'disorderly or drunk'.[96]

It was the ungentlemanly 'disorderliness' of 'drunkenness' that the fellows particularly disliked. Underpinning their generally lenient attitude to heavy alcohol consumption was a simple belief that gentlemen neither got drunk nor told lies, and all Trinity men were presumed to be gentlemen, at least until proven otherwise. This explains, for example, how the Claret Club was able to retain its 'privileges' after the most outrageous excesses, none of which, in the official record, are associated with drunkenness at all. Not that regular efforts were not made to curb the club's activities. When in December 1889 the club applied for permission to dine in a 'separate room', the 'unanimous feeling' was against it. The bursar was instructed instead to suggest 'fewer guests and smaller numbers' invited to join. The 'unusual conduct' of two Brasenose guests at the club dinner in March 1893 led to a 'Special Meeting' of the fellows, and the suspension of the club. One BNC member 'broke whole windows (with woodwork) in Mr Comyn's room, he being in bed at the time', while the other 'cut in a disfiguring manner the hair of Mr Vlasto'. A grovelling letter of apology led to a one-year reprieve in October 1893, but it lasted only until the following January. This time individual members were made to sign 'a pledge that they will not in future as individuals on club nights or non club nights encourage or take part in disturbances or damages'; moreover, they were to understand that this promise was to apply to every man elected to the club in future.[97]

[95] M. C. Curthoys, 'The Colleges in the New Era', *HUO* 7, 141.
[96] TCA Memo Book 1, 149, 151.
[97] Ibid., 197, 219, 231.

The consequences of being found guilty of drunkenness were serious. Francis Muglington (1890) 'used obscene language to the scholars' while under the influence of alcohol on Trinity Monday 1892, and he was sent out of College and confined to his lodgings after 10 p.m. for the whole of the next term. The scholar Baron von Zedlitz was sent down for drunkenness after the 1893 Bump Supper, while John Hawkins (1892) was sent down after being 'drunk and disorderly again' in May 1894.[98] On the other hand, the College was ready to believe any explanation for apparent inebriation or promise of reform. George Meade (1889) almost forestalled a complaint from his outside tutor by convincing President Woods that he 'had become a teetotaller' in June 1891. Hugh Legge escaped rustication for his disgraceful behaviour after the Pembroke Bump Supper in May of the same year, because he had recently suffered from concussion. Three weeks before he had experienced an urge to 'try and put a gown round the statue of Sir Thomas Pope our founder' over the door to the Hall passage. He fell and 'was knocked silly,' he wrote next day in his diary. 'They thought I was killed at first: I made such funny gurgles in my throat & they chucked water on me & gave me brandy.' And another to escape rustication for drunkenness was Albert Charles (scholar 1893), who successfully pleaded the 'effect of liquor due to bilious attack' in February 1894.[99]

Trinity regarded as 'a very serious matter' the offence known as 'direct insubordination'.[100]Alan Lascelles went too far on 5 March 1908:

> Rather a memorable night. Things were stagnant, so Denis Anson and I devised a scheme by which a line of ornaments [i.e. chamber pots] might be hung from one side of the quad to the other, not merely from window to window, but from chimney-pot to chimney-pot, aloft and inaccessible. A feature of the idea was that the Dean should unconsciously supply one of the ornaments, which I purloined during Hall. It worked beautifully, and the college awoke next morning, to find the horizon obscured by three homely vessels, looking like new planets . . . The scouts unfortunately got them down quite early, but the diaconal machinery had been set in motion, and perhaps accelerated by the discomforts of the night.

[98] Ibid. 1, 125–7, 129, 163, 217, 239; Memo Book 2, 29.
[99] TCA Memo Book 1, 121, 125, 239. [100] TCA Decanal, B.1.

> Eventually Guy [Charteris] and I were interviewed singly. The Dean's point was that (a) a fellow of the college had been insulted; (b) the perpetrators must have got on the roof. We took up an attitude of reluctant participation and hinted at vast numbers of fellow conspirators. (b) of course we could at once dismiss . . . the whole thing being done by an ingenious system of throwing a lacrosse ball with a light string attached from one quad to another and then making a running noose around the chimney. (a) was more serious, and to admit that I had taken his Basil-pot [a reference to Keats's poem *Isabella*: 'For cruel, 'tis, said she, to steal my basil-pot away from me'] would have involved being sent down. So I had to invent a wild Irish friend, a soldier, who had been in college that night, and being ignorant of all Varsity tradition had violated the Dean's honour.

Despite his jaunty attitude—'Idiotic no doubt, all of it; but there's a marvellous lot of enjoyment in these nocturnal adventures, and it's damned good practice lying one's way out of them next morning'—Lascelles was sufficiently worried to send a telegram to a friend at Aldershot, in case a letter of apology should be required.[101] To blame an outsider was in itself a high-risk strategy, threatening as it did bad publicity for the College. When in 1892 a 'stranger' introduced by Park Goff (1888) was under suspicion of damaging a window frame, Goff was threatened with immediate rustication. But when Goff gave a solemn denial to Woods that he had brought in any guest, and when Raper 'stated unofficially' that he had overheard a member of the College say he had seen Goff throw the bath through the window himself, the matter at once became less serious.[102]

The law student and future judge of the Australian Supreme Court, James Walker, was shocked by the lying and cheating that he saw in Trinity. On 12 October 1906, he sat an examination for the Commoners' Prize Exhibition, 'a money prize given on the result of College exams to test how much reading has been done during the Vac. . . . It was rather disquieting to see various men secretly using books to answer the questions.'[103] Conversely, Walker's contemporaries would doubtless have been dismayed by his reaction when he was summoned to the dean at the end of Hilary Term 1905, after 'a crowd' had invaded his room, and 'by throwing coal out of my windows, had broken a lamp'. 'I had no trouble whatever in clearing

[101] *End of an Era*, 42–3.
[102] TCA Memo Book 1, 167, 169.
[103] TCA Walker, 309.

myself,' he wrote vindictively, 'and there is a nice row waiting for the evil doers on their return to College next term.'[104]

Disciplinary matters notwithstanding, the fellows and undergraduates enjoyed generally close relationships. All members of the College could expect regular invitations to breakfast and dine with the fellows. College societies enjoyed regular patronage from senior members. The longest-lasting of these was the debating and paper-reading Gryphon Club, founded in November 1881, and, after several revivals, still in existence at the end of the twentieth century. Between 1883 and 1911, no less than sixteen fellows (not to mention President Pelham) appear in the Gryphon's annual photographs.[105] M. W. Patterson (fellow 1997) was there in 1900 and 1904, and he also lent his support to the Shakespeare-reading Gargoyle Club, which was founded in 1900. As an honorary member, Patterson attended two meetings in June 1901, reading Rowley in *The School for Scandal* and Banquo in *Macbeth*, and accompanying the club to its annual dinner in March 1902. In June 1904 he took his future wife, Clara Burdett, to the Trinity Ball, and to another 'impromptu dance' in the College Hall.[106] 'He was extremely popular,' recalled Clara in later life, 'and rather alarmed me when we were engaged by saying he would like to build a house in Trinity so that it could always be filled with undergraduates.' In the early years of their marriage Clara 'knew, and constantly saw, many undergraduates'. She continued to befriend her husband's pupils, and was regularly accompanied by them to summer reading parties on the Isle of Wight. [107]

Neither Woods nor Pelham taught during their presidencies, but they kept careful records of the undergraduates' academic progress as reported at the lecturers' breakfasts, and in the brief, termly collections. At the end of Michaelmas term 1889, Hugh Legge wrote in his diary, 'The Dean gave me back my logic papers with S = [satisfactory double minus] on them. The Pre said I should do better & shook hands & I went.'[108] Every generation of undergraduates experiences the tension between academic work and leisure. In January 1890 Hugh Legge was both working for law prelims and training for Torpids. 'Oh these loathsome, beastly books,' he wrote on 22 January. 'The older I grow the more I hate the sight of 'em & yet I

[104] Ibid., 66–7. [105] TCA JCR C/GRY/iv/1. [106] TCA Christie-Miller.
[107] TCA JCR C/GAR/ii/1; TCA Christie-Miller 3/5; DD 32 Coxon.
[108] Bod. Lib. Legge, d. 2606, 23.

have to begin to work hard now & get through these exams. It is really difficult working here.' As a prospective member of the Torpid crew, the main changes in his regime were the regular hours set aside for sleep, and the concomitant reduction in alcohol consumption. He rose at 7.15—'cold bath'—retired at 10.30—'Be in bed'—and conscientiously observed dietary restrictions. One evening Harold Dowdell (Millard Scholar 1887) made a mechanical dog which Legge had bought

> steeplechase down the table. It was awfully funny & we shrieked. Raper saw it & sconced Dowdall which was very funny. (Raper told Furse later on that he didn't know whether to take it to the High Table & play with it or to sconce Dowdall at first.) We aren't supposed to drink sconces at the Togger table but we finished this one & had less beer afterwards ourselves.[109]

The reduced drinking made little difference to his work, and Legge was one of five undergraduates summoned to the lecturers' breakfast of 30 April 1890, and 'admonished' by Woods in the presence of the law lecturer, Sir William Anson.[110] By the beginning of his second year, however, the reluctant student was more in control of his academic work. 'I am going to map out my day roughly like this,' he wrote on 13 October 1890: '8 am chapel & breakfast, 9–1 read, 6–7 read, pm 9–11 read or 8–10 sometimes perhaps. That gives 7 hours a day & ought to do.'[111]

Legge enjoyed the lectures of Charles Cannan for their entertainment value. 'His lectures are amusing because we always argue with him,' he noted in his first term. 'Cannan appears to have had a logic lecture which I missed, not realising it,' he confessed a few days later. 'I am sorry, they are so funny.' Martin Green's classes were less useful—'I ought to have gone to a lecture in A on unseen with Green but cut it as I thought it more important to do bookwork'—and he regularly missed the law lectures of J. B. Moyle at New College—

[109] Bod. Lib. Legge, d. 2607 ff. 42, 46, 62–3. The traditional rules for sconcing in Hall were not codified until *c.*1970. This instance presumably qualified under 1) (b) 'other unseemly behaviour' (DD 100 Burden 8/1).

[110] TCA Memo Book 1, 82. Woods regularly reprimanded men for their lack of work, for example, Bertram Gibson (1887), 'ploughed in Law Prelim., the result of idleness merely', and Edward Packard (1887), whose refusal to enter his name for Law Prelims was deemed to equate to a plough (39, 42).

[111] Bod. Lib. Legge, d. 2608, 105. It did for a pass degree in December 1892 and he got his Blue in 1893.

'awful drivel & I always slide off into a daydream.' 'Cheeky little chap!' wrote Legge, when Moyle informed him it was time to take his law prelims.[112]

Some of the teaching in Trinity was uninspiring for both sides. On Tuesday 29 October 1889 Legge wrote in his diary, 'I had to go to Raper about an essay on Maine. He said mine was the best he'd had which pleased me as I wrote it slick off in ¾ hour without making a rough copy.'[113] When Christopher Chavasse failed his history Schools in 1907, his twin was quick to blame the tutor. 'I feel dreadfully cut up about Chris,' he wrote to their mother. 'I think it is most awfully hard lines and that Patterson is nothing else than a lazy fool. I have always disliked him. Now I hate and despise him from the bottom of my heart.'[114] Cyril Lace (1922) enjoyed Patterson's reading parties in the 1920s, but recalled a remark of W. D. Gibbon (1899) that 'he guessed Patters was using the same notes as he had at the beginning of the century.'[115] Indeed, a popular impression of his approach to teaching—'Patters Patters, nothing matters'—was immortalized some years later by Sir Cyril Hinshelwood.[116] In Patterson's defence, however, it should be noted that Christopher Chavasse's other achievements had included an athletics Blue, and when, without changing his tutor, he retook his finals in 1908, he got a very satisfactory second.

Although the general rule was that an honours degree in a single school should be taken in three years, but a joint degree was allowed four, the tutors had discretionary power to grant a fourth year to any deserving candidate. In December 1907 Alan Lascelles and Guy Charteris applied for a fourth year for reasons that were almost entirely social. Lascelles recorded in his diary:

> I convinced Prichard that I was too young to take Greats next year, and Prichard convinced the college, and I convinced father of the conviction of the college, so all is well. Guy, by a similar process, has obtained a fourth year for his Law, and we are going into digs in Michael Street. Perhaps the best term of all, this last.[117]

Most of the undergraduates at Trinity received exactly the education that they required, and left Oxford suitably equipped to play

112 Ibid., d. 2606, 219, 225, 229–30, d. 2607, 56.
113 Ibid., d. 2606, 226.
114 Ann Clayton, *Chavasse*, 23, 33.
115 Gibbon, as headmaster of Campbell College, gave Lace his first job. C. B. Lace to Bryan Ward-Perkins, 27 April 1986 (TCA DD 32 Coxon).
116 TCA Higham 3/1.
117 *End of an Era*, 38.

their part in the government of Britain and its Empire as administrators, lawyers, teachers, and clergymen. Of the forty men admitted in 1889, thirteen went on to take holy orders. When Martin Green published *Admissions during the Nineteenth Century* (1901), he found that in 1900, ten of those forty were employed in various capacities by the Church of England, six in imperial government, and another six teaching at home and abroad. Five were practising law, two were in academic life, and one each practising medicine, farming, and in the army. Michael Furse was a fellow of Trinity. It is impossible to say how many had been helped in their career by Robert Raper, who was renowned across Oxford for his ability to place graduates in suitable positions by means of his extensive network of friends. Indeed, he claimed to have in his gift more places for public and grammar schoolmasters than he had pupils to fill them. In December 1892 Raper chaired the first meeting of the Provisional Committee of the Oxford Appointments Committee, precursor of today's Careers Service. The committee charged a fee to graduates who were recommended to vacant posts notified by schools and government agencies, a process that in its early days was very dependent on Raper's patronage and encouragement. When he stood down from the chairmanship in 1899, it was very fitting that Raper should suggest his own successor, secure a useful appointment for a friend, and at the same time ensure his own continued influence. Who else but Trinity's chaplain, Michael Furse?[118]

## *The College Mission*

One of the class of '89 to enter the Church was Hugh Legge. In 1900 he was working as a 'permanent resident' at the College Mission in the East End of London. The year before he had published a twenty-page history of the first eleven years of the Mission's existence, a remarkable record of Victorian altruism, heartily approved and generously supported by numerous Trinity men, John Percival not the least. The Trinity College Mission was opened on 13 January 1888 in a church on Tenby Road, Stratford, 'the slum in which the mission is situated'. Credit for the establishment of the Mission was attrib-

[118] Timothy Weston, *From Appointments to Careers: A History of the Oxford University Careers Service 1892–1992* (Oxford, 1994), 23, 26–31.

uted to Thomas Legh Claughton (1826), since 1877 Bishop of St Albans, while the first missioner was Charles Baumgarten (1887), who established 'a parochial organisation in the district, which was carved out of St John's parish, and got together a congregation out of the neighbourhood'.[119] Baumgarten worked hard on the creation of links with the Great Eastern Railway Company, parties of whose employees were brought to the College for annual summer outings. Fifty-one railwaymen came on the first outing, on 23 May 1888, which was commemorated by an illuminated scroll.[120] Typically, the College's guests would be given tours of Oxford by undergraduates, 'who are often thus led to see the sights of Oxford for the first time. What the G.E.R. men learn about Oxford it is impossible to say.' The railwaymen would be treated to 'a big luncheon in the Hall', with 'speeches by the President, etc.', and this was followed by 'river excursions, cricket matches to see, and plenty of occupation for all'. Then they would be given supper 'in different men's rooms . . . followed by singing and smoking until it is time to go'. Those running the Mission had no doubt of the success these outings had in 'breaking down class prejudice, one of the chief aims of a University settlement. The men from Stratford never have another such day in their lives.' From 1892 a return visit was held, 'the *Social Dinner*' in the newly built mission hall. In 1899 ninety-five sat down to 'dinner, speeches and songs', of whom twenty-eight were Trinity undergraduates and old members.[121]

In September 1891, Baumgarten left for a post in South Africa, his health 'ruined' by the hardness of the work. Before his departure he had the satisfaction of seeing 'the Great Hall, two club rooms, and accommodation for one resident' opened, at a cost of over £2,000, all raised by Trinity members. Two years later, a 'Mission House' was complete, accommodating three 'residents', and providing a billiard room, 'reading, games, and committee rooms', and a 'club kitchen'. There was also a boys' club—of two rooms, one large, one small—behind the church, and the further outlay had exceeded £2,500. College pride was, as usual, at stake. 'Few other missions could boast of such buildings,' said Legge, 'and in all the sixty clubs of the Oxford House federation . . . not one can boast of finer premises.' In 1896 the

119 Trinity would have been unusual not to have a mission. There can have been few streets in the East End of London not allocated to one institution or another. *The Trinity College Mission 1888–1899*, 5, 9.

120 TCA Coll. Govt., V/9.

121 *Mission 1888–1899*, 9–11.

Mission launched its 'Ladies' Settlement' an occasion patronized by HRH the Duchess of Albany, in whose honour 'Tenby Road decorated itself . . . The windows looking towards the street were hung with old shirts and pairs of trousers, for all the world like the tattered standards . . . that adorn the aisles of our cathedrals.'[122]

The centrepiece of the Mission, so far as Trinity men were concerned, was opened in 1898: a rented semi-detached house at 60 Romford Road, home to a fluctuating population of old members who gave their free time to support the social work of the Mission. Hugh Legge saw his role as 'combining the functions of a priest with those of a genteel mendicant, a recruiting sergeant, and a keeper of a common lodging house (for Trinity men)'. There was a 'Common Room . . . decorated in blue and white', while the house was 'adorned with Trinity photographs, oars, and other trophies'. Here Trinity men could stay overnight for free, for several days at 3*s* 6*d* a night, or permanently 'for about 30*s* a week (beer included)'. Homely touches included a gong 'rigged up' from a tin bath and a broken poker, and 'tied up with a Trinity ribbon (this reminds us of a "Dilke" in the Garden Quad)'.[123] One early resident was Hugh Blakiston (scholar 1891) who acted as bursar, and combined his day job at *The Times* with the captaincy of 'a flourishing company of the Church Lads' Brigade' for 'the less rough boys'—and a paper-reading 'newspaper club' for their fathers. Presidents Woods and Pelham both ventured to address the club, the former on 'Don Quixote', the latter on 'the German Emperor'.[124]

By 1899 the Mission had a staff of three: the missioner, the Revd H. Mosley ('not a Trinity man, but . . . learning how to be one'), his assistant, Harry de V. Watson (Trinity 1891), and the 'parish nurse'. The missioners took care of the 'religious work', while Legge and the laymen concentrated on the social side. Club members subscribed 1½*d* a week, and enjoyed billiards, 'other games in plenty', a 'nigger troupe', 'entertainments of sundry kinds', 'biscuits and ginger pop for refreshments', football, cricket, and rowing on the River

122 *Mission 1888–1899*, 10–12.

123 Ibid., 14–16. James Walker recorded the celebration of a 'Dilke' when the Trinity Torpid bumped Merton 26 February 1906: 'This consists of gathering in the Quad in a compact mass, beating baths with pokers or fire brushes, and yelling and cheering at the top of their voices . . . It is an institution of very many years standing and was originally established to annoy Wadham when they were head of the river.' If true, this would date the first 'Dilke' to 1850. (TCA Walker, 237).

124 *Mission 1888–1899*, 16–17.

Lea—'which reminds Oxford men of the Cam', joked Legge. The children (and adults) were divided into 'two very distinct classes', those from 'respectable homes' who owned 'Sunday clothes', and those from 'more or less disreputable homes', who did not. There were two sets of Sunday school classes, two Bands of Hope, and, for the superior class only, a Children's Guild (raising funds for missions to Africa).[125]

All of this was supported, and largely funded by, the undergraduates and old members of Trinity. Balliol's Charles Lister went as a volunteer worker in the summer of 1908, and, as befitted a man sent down for abusing the Trinity dean, poked gentle fun at its homely but worthy atmosphere. 'There is a programme of the day neatly framed in every room', he wrote to a friend:

| | |
|---|---|
| Breakfast | 8 a.m. |
| Matins | 8.30 a.m. |
| Prayers | 9 a.m. |
| Luncheon | 1 p.m. |
| Evensong | 6.30 p.m. |

I like the meals and hours of orison sandwiched together. One might spend the whole day between the Lord's table and one's host's ditto.[126]

## *Old Members*

The old member had been a valuable, but distant, member of the Trinity community since the seventeenth century. Now he was becoming more valuable and less distant. E. W. B. Nicholson (1867) was, from 1882, Bodley's Librarian in Oxford. For many years he collected the communications that he received from his old college, and various other items of Trinity interest which came his way. Pasted into a scrapbook, they fall roughly into two groups: invitations to send money and invitations to social events. The financial requests were regular, and no longer confined to the exceptionally large building project. Besides the New Building of 1882, Nicholson received a begging letter from the solicitor of Sir George Cox Bt (scholar 1845), and

[125] Ibid., 13; Mission Annual Report 1898–9.

[126] *Charles Lister: Letters and Recollections*, ed. Lord Ribblesdale (London, 1917), 31.

appeals for subscriptions to such objects as Henry Woods's wedding present (1879), the Raper portrait fund (1909), a silver altar-cross for the Chapel 'which we feel has long been a want', the new barge, and the new cricket and football ground.[127]

One important innovation in the lives of old members was an annual dinner, held for many years at a London venue. The first was held in 1884, and its success led to a repeat venture 'on a larger scale' on Trinity Monday (1 June) at the Café Royal on Regent Street. These dinners were open to 'past and present members' and organized by the diners themselves. In 1885 Nicholson received a simple invitation from J. H. Morgan (1866); the following year the invitation was more lavishly printed, and the date had been changed to 'the first day of the University Match . . . in accordance with a very generally expressed desire'. There was a set menu—8*s* 6*d* for those who paid early, 'excluding wine'. By 1889 there was an organizing committee of eleven, and in 1894 it was agreed that the dinner should be brought to Oxford.[128] The Gaudy remained a dinner for past and present members of the foundation (fellows and scholars), but in 1900 there began a new tradition, a 'second gaudy' for former commoners. That year they began 'with 1850' and invited all who had subscribed to the cricket ground, whether or not they were 'on the books'.[129] In 1899 Trinity sent out its first published *Report* to all members on the College books, summarizing the main events (offices, appointments, publications, deaths, and benefactions) of the year.

The 1899–1900 *Report* noted 'between thirty and forty' Trinity members on active service in South Africa; that of 1901–2 listed four undergraduates who had volunteered.[130] Trinity deaths in the South African War numbered four: George Tomkins Norman Barton (1895), Edward Erskine Wilmot-Chetwode (1897), Claude Seaton Du Buisson (1894), and Daniel Legge (1895). All ranks of the College joined in erecting a suitable monument to them, in the shape of a memorial window above the scholars' table in Hall, and a second gaudy was held in Commemoration week, to which were invited all members 'who had been engaged in the recent war'.[131]

[127] Nicholson scrapbook, 51, 93–4, 98, 100, 106.

[128] Ibid., 113–14.

[129] To be 'on the books' required the payment of annual dues for all BAs and non-graduates. TCA Memo Book 2, 219.

[130] *Report* (1899–1900), 3; (1901–2), 4.

[131] Ibid. (1902–3), 5. Unfortunately 'not many . . . were able to accept', and some who did were 'detained . . . in connexion with the King's Birthday Review'.

Dining in Hall (and dessert in the Common Room) was given additional interest by a rapid influx of portraits. Between 1889 and 1899 Henry Hulton donated pictures of four illustrious alumni—Lord Selbourne (Roundell Palmer, scholar 1830), Professor E. A. Freeman (scholar 1941), the Bishop of St Alban's (Thomas Legh Claughton, 1826, scholar 1828, fellow 1832–42), and the Bishop of Oxford (William Stubbs, fellow 1848)—while his gift of £500 was spent on portraits of Henry Woods and James Bryce (scholar 1857). In June 1897, Woods was put in the embarrassing position of returning a cheque for £100 to George G. Ramsay (scholar 1857, Professor of Humanity at Glasgow University since 1863) when he discovered the Professor intended it for a portrait of himself.[132] Portraits of Albert Venn Dicey (1830) and Isaac Williams went up in 1901 and 1902. In 1904 old members subscribed towards a suitably imposing image of Randall Davidson by Hugh Rivière, the largest picture in College, which was exhibited in the Royal Academy before being placed in Hall. Subscribers could have their own print at home, for half a guinea. Meanwhile, many of Trinity's early pictures were loaned to the Oxford Historical Portrait Exhibitions of 1904 and 1905.[133]

Trinity was rightly proud of its past, and of the distinguished names on the books. The College looked with satisfaction on the steady progress of graduates moving into influential and worthwhile positions at home and abroad. There was pleasure to be had in the promise of sporting successes: in 1906 an anonymous donor gave 'a silver centre-piece', being a four-foot-high replica of the gryphon lectern, which was 'to be inscribed with the names of those who obtain certain successes on the river'.[134] Confidence was in the air. None of them knew what was to happen in 1914.

[132] TCA Memo Book II, 116.
[133] *Report* (1899–1900), 3; (1900–1), 3; (1901–2), 4.
[134] Ibid. (1905–6), 7.

# II

# *President Blakiston*

## *Blakiston Becomes President*

Herbert Edward Douglas Blakiston was not Trinity's first choice for President in 1907. On 19 February, he himself wrote 'by the wish of *all the Fellows* . . . [and] by our *unanimous vote*' to offer the headship to Robert Raper. The election would be 'warmly approved by all generations of the college', he insisted. 'We know that no one has the interests of the college more sincerely at heart, and we rely greatly on your sagacity and influence.' The fellows had discussed Raper's frailty—he had been 'always delicate', and was now six weeks short of his sixty-fifth birthday—and they were ready 'to support [him] loyally, and do everything in [their] power to make the office as easy as possible'. 'For myself,' Blakiston added, 'I urge you more even more strongly than I did before; if you will discuss any point of detail with me, I should hope to prove this change to be for your own good, as well as for that of the college.'[1]

Raper's answer was hardly unexpected. 'I am deeply sensible of the great honour done me & of the gracious terms in which the proposal was made,' he replied, and

> if I had only my own pleasure & convenience to consider I would unhesitatingly comply with the wishes of the Fellows; but I have to take into account the permanent wishes of the college & I am convinced that these would be better promoted by the election of a younger, more efficient, and more presidential Head.[2]

So the chance came to Blakiston. It was mooted quite casually in a note from Melville Patterson: 'If Raper refuses, why not you? I hope

[1] Blakiston preserved a draft of this letter, TCA Blakiston F/7. For Raper's health, see Laurie Magnus, *Herbert Warren of Magdalen* (London, 1932), 165.

[2] This letter was dated by Raper, 1 March 1907, but corrected by Blakiston to 28 Feb. Blakiston had asked Raper 'not to decide off hand', and Raper had 'taken time to think the matter over'. TCA Blakiston F/9.

*11.1* H. E. D. Blakiston on a walking tour in the Lake District, 1891. Left to right: F. W. Hall (scholar 1886); Laurence Binyon (scholar 1888); Blakiston; Frank D. Mackinnon (exhibitioner 1889); J. Hugh Thursfield (exhibitioner 1888); Henry P. Plumptre (1889).

so.'[3] Blakiston was elected on Sunday 17 March 1907.[4] Ten years earlier (when Woods's resignation left an unexpected vacancy) he had dreamed of the possibility, and confided in the chemistry lecturer, Sir John Conroy, that he believed 'the Presidentship is the proper and only object of one's career at the College.'[5] He was twenty years younger than Raper, and there was no doubt of his efficiency. He had experience of multiple college offices: chaplain, tutor, senior tutor,

[3] Patterson made this suggestion on the day that Blakiston wrote to Raper, ibid., F/8.
[4] TCA Register D, 273. [5] BCO Conroy Papers 1 B 20.

and domestic bursar, and was known to be 'a man of much acumen and of business like habits'.[6] But was he more presidential? His later reputation certainly suggests not. 'It would be a great mistake to write of Dr Blakiston mainly as a figure of fun,' begins Tommy Higham's *Dr Blakiston Recalled*, a brief biographical memoir which then proceeds to dwell largely on 'the circumstances of his home life', his 'niggardly habits', his 'ridiculous' snobbishness, his 'undistinguished appearance', his 'physical disadvantages', his 'unsociable ways', and his 'obsession with finance'. Blakiston was extremely short-sighted, and his nickname, 'Blinks', dated from his schooldays at Tonbridge.[7]

One person, at least, was apparently dismayed by Blakiston's election (or, at least, came to deplore it in after years): Joanna Cannan, the youngest of Charles Cannan's three daughters. Theodore Fletcher, the central character of her 1931 novel *High Table*, is a thinly disguised and rather cruelly caricatured Blakiston. He is 'clumsy, paralysingly self-conscious, a coward', 'one so ill-equipped for ordinary life [that he] inevitably falls back on books', and one who shrinks 'from life, love, action, emotion and risk behind the defensive medieval fortifications of an Oxford college'.[8] Fletcher is presented as *tertius gaudens* in the election to the mastership of 'St Mary's College'. The candidates kept out are Dr Quears—'a small man with pink cheeks, neat snow-white hair and beard, blue eyes, a girlish mouth . . . clever and disagreeable . . . with a passion for power', who is clearly Robert Raper—and Professor Haughton, less easily identifiable but conceivably drawn as the antithesis of Charles Cannan himself. Haughton is known for his 'roars of laughter and dirty jokes'; at the Oxford University Press, Cannan's menacing silences earned him the nickname of 'the alligator'.[9] The Cannan family held Trinity in deep affection, and Joanna's sister May treasured Arthur Quiller-Couch's description of her father as 'little less than the College's second founder'.[10] To women who perhaps dreamed of their father as President, the shy bachelor Blakiston must have seemed a poor alternative. He was to reside in the Lodgings for thirty-one years.

[6] *The Times* (10 October 1917). [7] Higham, *Dr Blakiston*, 1–7, 27.

[8] Anthony Quinton, Introduction to Joanna Cannan, *High Table* (Oxford, 1987) pp. vii–viii. I am grateful to Martin Maws, the OUP Archivist, for his insights into the career of Charles Cannan. [9] Cannan, *High Table*, 89.

[10] Obituary of Charles Cannan in the *Oxford Magazine* (23 January 1920), published in *Some Recollections of Charles Cannan 1858–1919* (Oxford 1920), 17, and quoted by May Cannan in *Grey Ghosts and Voices* (Kineton, 1976), 1.

*11.2* Blakiston on his election to the presidency in 1907.

Between 1881, when he was elected scholar, and 1938, when he retired from the presidency, he spent just one year away from Trinity, teaching sixth-form classics at Clifton. Blakiston's character was shaped by the traditions, fortunes, and expectations of the institution to which he devoted his life, while the reputation of Trinity in the twenty-first century still bears distinct traces of his influence.

Trinity College was the great love of Blakiston's life. To write its history was the fulfilment of a cherished ambition. His *Trinity College* was published in 1898, and was a work of considerable scholarship and lucidity. 'I wish I could make a second edition, with more space and longer quotations,' he wrote to Michael Maclagan (fellow

1939) in 1940; but the bankruptcy of the publishers prevented it. Blakiston was particularly proud of the painstaking research that went into his Trinity writings, although careful not to boast. 'My summary in Foster's Oxford Men is all right,' he informed Maclagan, and that in the *Victoria County History* 'I hope . . . [is] adequate.'[11] In 1888 he was appointed the 'college recorder', an office which was created for him personally, and which provided a vehicle for projects such as the updating of Bathurst's series of Benefactors' Books, which had been abandoned in 1838. Now he commenced a new folio volume, bound in red leather and fastened with brass clasps, and backdated the entries to include several major gifts received in 1867. Like Kettell before him, Blakiston was inspired to keep biographical records and to chronicle the College's achievements for posterity. He began to write up each term's 'Records' in a fine, suede-bound volume, a practice that in 1898 evolved into the annual publication of the *College Report*.

Blakiston's research was meticulous, both into the archives of the College and into the lives of its distinguished alumni. He created a comprehensive register of members of the foundation (he himself was number 801) and a meticulous directory of commoners admitted in the years before the first Admissions Register begins.[12] Every chapter of Blakiston's *Trinity College* contains a roll call of the great and the good on the foundation and the 'commoners' tables'. Writing on the nineteenth century, he paid tribute to the 'many . . . who are qualifying for the honour' of bringing posthumous glory to the College by appearing in the *Dictionary of National Biography*.[13] He was jealous of Trinity's secrets, however, and in 1924 provoked the equally scrupulous Charles Mallet to express his frustration publicly. 'I could wish that Dr Blakiston had permitted me to use the college documents,' he lamented in the footnotes of *The History of the University of Oxford*.[14]

As the father of his college, Blakiston showed equal devotion. He developed a life-long habit of collecting news of Trinity's members, punctiliously clipping reports of their marriages, careers, and deaths from *The Times* each morning, and welcoming them (not always

[11] TCA Maclagan, Blakiston to Michael Maclagan, 6 and 29 April 1940.

[12] TCA Blakiston D/1–3.

[13] Blakiston, *Trinity*, 187, 227.

[14] Charles Edward Mallet, *A History of the University of Oxford* (London, 1924), ii, 160, n. 2.

successfully) when they came back to visit the College. Higham praised Blakiston's 'kindness, especially towards the young', and Weaver his 'simple, even child-like, kindness'. He took a particular interest in the children of his contemporaries.[15] One favourite was Bevil, the eldest child and only son of Arthur Quiller-Couch (Q). When, in the summer of 1909, Bevil failed the entrance examination 'in everything except algebra and Latin grammar', the President wrote encouragingly to his father:

> Of course we ought to drop him: but in consideration for you, & I must say owing to a favourable impression of the boy himself, Nagel & I cannot bring ourselves to do it. So he must have a shot in September . . . I hope very much things will come all right & that he will do well when he gets here.[16]

Bevil came up in January 1910, but was sadly unappreciative of the President's intended kindness. 'Blakiston has played the complete fool over my rooms,' he grumbled to his father. The rooms were 'alright but a good ten minutes walk from College up in Wellington Square . . . his reason being that they are kept by one Ray a daughter of an old scout of yours which has precious little to do with me.'[17]

Blakiston's indulgent and avuncular approach was tested severely on the last night of Mods in March 1911, when

> there was repeated unpleasantness to the Dean. A bonfire was lit . . . in the front quad, explosions thrown several times, a gate chained up—some hooliganism by individuals but no general disorder. Next morning the big door & other places were found to be inscribed "Dean Black spectre" . . . & on the grass "Bloody Dean" in white paint.

The Black Spectre and Bloody Dean in question was the Revd R. H. Lloyd, also chaplain of the College. 'Your boy was seen to light the fire,' Blakiston informed Q, 'but denied bombs . . . It transpired however that his boots—of all in college—were spotted with white paint. He then said to Lloyd he had been present but got sprinkled with the paint.' Only when Blakiston asked him to produce 'compurgators' ready to swear *'that they saw him not do it'*, did Bevil admit his

[15] Higham, *Dr Blakiston*, 2; J. R. H. Weaver, 'Memorials: Herbert Edward Douglas Blakiston DD', *Oxford*, 8 (1943), 38.

[16] Arthur Quiller-Couch papers, TCA DD 36, Correspondence, H. E. D. Blakiston (10 July 1909).

[17] Bevil Quiller-Couch papers, TCA DD 36 add, 3.1 A/9 (18 January 1910).

involvement. 'I think it is rather a turning point,' the President wrote optimistically to Q. 'I must say he was quite decent with me; he lied freely to Lloyd, & my subsequent viva caused him some confusion, but I think his decision to spare his friends was honest, & having owned up he took the consequences properly.' Indeed, 'I do not think you need be much distressed . . . about the lying to Lloyd.' (Q was less certain about Bevil's untruthfulness, however, preferring to call it 'equivocation'.)

Both Blakiston and Q were inclined to blame the dean. He was 'a kindly fellow', but Q did not consider him 'particularly strong or tactful in his handling of youth', and Blakiston would not 'say anything about [him], except that he is more suited to the work which he is taking up in October', Lloyd having declared his intention to exchange the civilized life of Oxford for more congenial existence on the foreign mission field. Blakiston was also so determined to blame the incident on Bevil's old school friend, Henry Graham (1909), who had 'persistently tried to use our leniency towards [Bevil] as a means of whittling away his own punishment', that Q felt he had to remonstrate. Bevil had given him a frank account, he wrote firmly. He had admitted to 'Dean Black Spectre', but another man, not Graham, was responsible for the painting on the grass. Graham was 'a good fellow if trusted: but . . . by nature apt to turn sullen if wrongly suspected'. Blakiston used his presidential prerogative to limit Bevil's punishment to going down early, and being gated in his lodgings the next term, but his conscience was not quite clear: 'I am afraid the unofficial fellows will blame me for not sending him down,' he admitted.[18]

Blakiston's paternalistic attitude to the junior members was underpinned by a realistic acceptance of what the College was required to provide. As he once remarked in a sermon:

> Some of you come here to study for service in Church or State, some to advance the frontiers of knowledge; some to form useful connections; and some to sow your wild oats in a place where the harvest will prove less expensive than in London, or Paris, or Rome.[19]

[18] Arthur Quiller-Couch papers, Correspondence, H. E. D. Blakiston (18 and 20 March 191), 1; TCA Blakiston 'Correspondence Chest', Quiller-Couch to H. E. D. Blakiston (19 March and 29 April 1911).

[19] Higham claimed to have been present at this sermon, but quoted the phrasing as remembered by Professor Ewert: Higham, *Dr Blakiston*, 28.

Undergraduate behaviour was particularly wild in the years before the First World War, and the authority of the dean was correspondingly weak. Lloyd was succeeded by Reginald Coupland, official fellow and lecturer in ancient history since 1908. The departing dean briefed his successor on likely miscreants, and Coupland kept detailed records of his own wearisome dealings with them. Frank Chadwick (1910) for example, had a bad reputation already: 'R.H.L. reports . . . : "With Luttman-Johnson in hurling things from M.W.P.'s room November 1911. With Pemberton & Luttman-Johnson in bonfire after midnight in Feb 1912. Goes to bed very late."' In November 1912, Chadwick was sent down until the end of Hilary Term 1913, guilty of 'forcibly obstructing [Coupland's] passage from Garden to Chapel Quad'. The JCR protested, boycotting Hall dinner on 5 November, holding daily meetings and presenting a petition to the fellows, and Chadwick's father came in person to appeal 'for leniency without protesting the justice of the sentence'. Blakiston and Coupland bowed to the pressure and Chadwick was permitted to return at the beginning of Hilary Term.[20]

The College was now turning a blind eye to all drunks but the legless, and to all but the most dangerous and provocative bonfires. On the night that the Torpid came out of training in February 1914, Coupland noted that the senior commoner of 1913, Roger Cranage, was 'offensively drunk. Shouting & cursing (Balls, God Damn, etc) & violently resisting efforts of friend to get him to bed. Much of this outside my windows . . . Warned that "dead drunkenness" meant sending-down.' In June 1914 John Purvis (1912) was 'detected by Kilbey [the porter] & President v. drunk. Crouching on grass & fell over on his back. . . . Assisted by K to his rooms. Unsteady on his legs, but not "leggers".' Coupland interviewed Purvis the next morning, and 'warned that he was *nearly* "leggers" & that would probably have meant sending-down'. The previous term Purvis and John Macbeth (1911) had been hauled before the dean when they were caught 'in the putting of faggots, taken from the boot-hole, on a bonfire, lighted by the Back of College after 1.30 a.m. Fined 10*s*. Asserted that he had never heard of the distinction made between a bonner in Garden Quad & a bonner by Balliol.' Coupland was still prepared to believe that gentlemen tell the truth.[21]

[20] TCA Decanal D/3. 33. Chadwick showed his gratitude by a large legacy, which Trinity received in 1938. [21] Ibid., 36, 150.

Almost without exception, Trinity's undergraduates were the middle-class sons of country landowners and the urban professional classes. The President controlled the admissions process, and Blakiston resisted applications from those he considered unsuitable, in particular from 'black men', as all non-whites were designated. He was far from alone in this, but he was to become notorious. In the years before the First World War, the India Office was actively promoting the admission of Indian students to Oxford, and Blakiston was doggedly refusing to comply. In 1910 he took refuge in a statement that although unable 'to reserve vacancies for Indian students', Trinity would 'consider suitable candidates' if they applied. When Indian students did so, he had no difficulty in keeping them out. In January 1911 Blakiston wrote to Syed Ozari, an Indian student resident in Oxford, that 'testimonials from persons not known to me would be no use', and to A. B. Agaskar, a graduate of the University of Bombay, that his application was 'too late'. In February he replied to the headmaster of the Leys School, Cambridge, that his Indian pupil, P. T. Rajan, would do better elsewhere, as his application was too late to secure rooms. 'I should add that we have not had an Indian at this college for nearly twenty years, and are not anxious to encourage Indian students to come to Oxford.' In May, Daya Shankar, another unattached student in Oxford, asked for advice as to 'the possible way of my being successful' and Blakiston replied, 'I cannot give you any hope of being accepted as a candidate at this college next year, any more than this year.'[22]

In 1917 Blakiston, as Vice-Chancellor, came under pressure from the Secretary for Indian Students at the India Office. 'Indian educated opinion [was] naturally perplexed' by the published information that only two colleges, Trinity and Magdalen, refused to admit Indians, seemingly on the grounds of 'race only'.[23] Finally, in October 1920, Udharam Maniram Mirchandani, the son of a revenue officer from Hyderabad, and a former pupil of Sind College, Karachi, was admitted to read for entrance to the Indian Civil Service. The dean, Tommy Higham, felt no surprise or disapproval that Mirchandani was discriminated against while up at Trinity. 'Usually we refused Indians, on the ground that they would lose us our South African connection; and [one South African] showed by his demeanour when Mirchandani became a fellow undergraduate of Trinity that this ex-

[22] TCA Blakiston, Correspondence, 'India Office', uncatalogued. [23] Ibid.

cuse was far from idle.' Higham 'liked' Mirchandani, however, and 'respected his feelings'. So he persuaded the undergraduates 'for a time' to substitute 'bring out your white man' for the more usual anti-Balliol song.[24]

Higham succeeded Coupland as dean in 1914. R. H. Lloyd's replacement as chaplain, meanwhile, had been recruited by none other than Robert Raper, who must have relished the arrival of a brilliant young Balliol scholar with a tendency to 'Roman fever'. This was Ronald Knox (fellow 1910). He described his election in *A Spiritual Aeneid*:

> Just before I went in for Greats, I received through my brother (who had been at Trinity) a suggestion which was to determine my outward circumstances for many years. Partly through him, and partly through my Eton friends, I already enjoyed the friendship of that venerable figure in Trinity common-room, Mr R W Raper. Mr Lloyd, then chaplain of the college, was to leave in two years' time; and a fellowship then vacant was naturally ear-marked for a future chaplain. The suggestion that I should allow myself to be proposed took me completely by surprise.

Knox was welcomed graciously by the Trinity Common Room—'whatever misgivings they may have had about my ecclesiastical future, my colleagues made room for me without any hint of suspicion or disapproval'—and, after an initial period of loneliness, by the freshmen of 1911:

> they found me already ordained and in full work, and treated me as an institution of the place; and when I began to be at home on Wednesday evenings with coffee and port and barrow-loads of bananas, even official restraints slipped away, and I felt an undergraduate once more.

He was 23.[25]

The cassock-wearing, Latin office-reading young cleric was well aware that his 'views did not quite "go down"'. Nevertheless, he 'had no difficulty in making friends', describing:

[24] T. F. Higham, 'The Balliol–Trinity Frontier' (1932), TCA Decanal C/1.3. The name of the South African undergraduate has been removed, because his dates do not correspond with those of Mirchandani, and Higham was clearly mistaken in his identity.

[25] R. A. Knox, *A Spiritual Aeneid* (London, 1918), 84–5, 89. Knox's brother was Wilfred (scholar 1905) who used his research notes on 'a series of controlled experiments in the college gardens, whether tortoises really preferred yellow flowers' as 'the basis of an essay on the inductive method'. Penelope Fitzgerald, *The Knox Brothers* (London, 2002), 63.

> Dinners in the Old Bursary, where the staid portraits of Trinity men long dead seemed to look down scandalized on the frivolity of a later generation . . .—dining and bathing in the Long Bridges backwater, convoyed in a flotilla of punts, long Wednesday evenings when the interval ailments of motor-bicycles were discussed exhaustively among heaps of banana-skins.[26]

Ronald Knox paid particular tribute to the 'sparkling gift for friendship' of Reginald Tiddy, Trinity's English tutor, who divided his time between Trinity and his cottage in the Cotswolds village of Ascott-under-Wychwood, where he showed a keen interest in local dialects and traditions, and was a passionate morris dancer. In Oxford he was the 'moving spirit' of the University branch of the English Folk Dance Society, and a close friend of its leading light, Cecil Sharp. Tiddy's main focus of academic research, the Mummers' Play, dovetailed nicely with his enthusiasm for rural life and customs. The Trinity College garden was the venue of one of the earliest displays of morris dancing before the 'raised eyebrows' of a university audience. Tiddy danced on a public stage in February 1913, when the Society appeared in the OUDS production of Dekker's *Shoemakers' Holiday*. 'Surely never in real life and never before on the stage were there such glorified Morris dancers,' enthused the *Oxford Journal*:

> Their long golden boots were a joy in themselves; their harmoniously shaded ribbons streaming everywhere as they danced, their black hats with black and white brims, their little bells and everything about them was of the finest, and the way those Morris dancers leapt into the air and played leap-frog, some of them of sober years and solid proportions, was wonderful to see.[27]

Perhaps the most evocative of all the images of the golden years in Trinity before the First World War are to be found in the elegant photograph album of David Ritchie (1911). Ritchie appears in immaculate cricket whites in the team pictures of Trinity Oxford vs Trinity Cambridge, of the Trinity Triflers vs the University Authentics, and of the 'Tics' vs Magdalen. In perfect evening dress, he stands among the survivors of the Magdalen and New College balls. And, as a member of the privileged Trinity elite, he poses in the fellows' garden in the exquisite attire of the Claret Club for a photograph

[26] Knox, *Spiritual Aeneid*, 105–6.

[27] [David Pye], 'R. J. E. Tiddy—A Memoir', in R. J. E. Tiddy, *The Mummers' Play* (Oxford, 1923), 14–18; *Oxford Journal* (5 February 1913).

taken to mark the dinner of 17 June 1914 (Plate 11.3). None of the nine undergraduates present that day would ever attend another Claret Club dinner and, by 1918, four of them would be dead.[28]

## The First World War

On 4 August 1914 Great Britain declared war on Germany, and members of Trinity rushed to enlist. Blakiston saw the outbreak of war as 'the greatest crisis in [the College's] history since the siege of Oxford in the Civil War'. One hundred and fifty undergraduates had been in residence in Trinity Term 1914, but just fifty came up in October, and only thirty of those remained by the end of term. During Hilary and Trinity Terms 1915 the undergraduate body numbered twenty-five young men who were 'ineligible for service, as aliens, as medical students, or for special reasons'.[29] The group photograph taken in the summer of 1917 shows a mere fourteen junior members of the College. One was a Belgian refugee and eight were Rhodes Scholars, six of them American. On 2 April 1917 the United States entered the war, and its Rhodes Scholars hurried home to enlist. Wyatt Rushton (Alabama, 1916), was the very first Rhodes Scholar from his state, and on the threshold of a promising career in journalism. Initially rejected for military service on account of his poor eyesight, he made his own way to Paris, where he joined the American Red Cross and later US military intelligence. Rushton was one of four Trinity Rhodes Scholars to die in the war, tragically succumbing to illness on board ship returning home in February 1919.[30] In Trinity Term 1918 Blakiston was photographed with just six undergraduates, and listed another three as absent. Many College servants joined up too. In December 1914 it was agreed to pay a weekly allowance of 7*s* to the wife of Cadman, scout since 1901, and a year later, of 3s *6d* to the wife of the porter Kilbey.[31]

Early in 1915 the fellows began to depart. In January James Brierly (fellow in law 1913) and Thomas Higham (fellow in ancient history 1914) were granted leave of absence to take commissions in the 7th Wiltshire Regiment and the 9th Oxford and Bucks Light Infantry

[28] TCA, OM 33, Ritchie. This album was purchased for Trinity by the assistance of Andrew Rudebeck (1963). [29] *Report* (1913–14), 1; (1914–15), 1–3.
[30] TCA DD 288. [31] TCA Order Book E, 299, 310.

*11.3* The Claret Club 1914 (Album of David M. Ritchie (1911) TCA OM 33).

respectively.[32] 'Both my Trinity colleagues, Higham and Brierly, are gazetted, poor dears,' wrote Tiddy to a friend. He himself had been rejected repeatedly for service overseas. He was 34, asthmatic, and 'so short-sighted as to be almost helpless without his glasses'; but he wanted to play his part. 'It seems to me that officers will stand a very poor chance of surviving this war, but I cannot really see how I can keep out of it, having had quite a fair amount of happy life, when these poor kids are being shot like this,' he wrote in September 1914. Finally, in February 1915 he secured a commission in the 4th Oxford and Bucks Light Infantry, and in May 1916 he departed for France.[33] In March 1915 Ronald Knox offered his services to Shrewsbury School 'in place of a master absent on account of the war'. He was glad of a respite from religious duty while he struggled to resolve his difficulties in the Anglican Church. Next, in April, Harold Prichard (fellow 1898) took up a post in the War Office and J. R. H. Weaver (fellow in modern history 1913) began work in the War Trade Department. Two of the fellows who were above conscription age also did their bit. In 1917 Henry Stuart-Jones was required to 'interrupt his revision of Liddell and Scott [the Greek lexicon] for important work in the War Office Intelligence Department', and in October 1918 Melville Patterson took up 'educational war work in France'.[34]

When a fellowship became vacant, it was suspended under special Emergency Statutes. Seven such statutes were passed between March 1915 and October 1916, giving the fellows dispensation from residence requirements, extending terms of scholarships and lifting age limits so that their holders might return after war service, and removing the restrictions on certain funds so that revenue could be diverted to general college purposes.[35] Three fellowships became vacant during the war. On 15 July 1915 Robert Raper passed away. His loss was 'a shock even to those who were aware of the state of his health', and it left 'a gap in the College . . . which will be keenly felt', wrote Blakiston in the *Report*. On 22 September 1917 Ronald Knox resigned, on the eve of his reception into the Roman Catholic Church. And, on the night of 10 August 1916, the short-sighted and golden-booted morris dancer Reginald Tiddy, who had joined up in the hope of

[32] TCA Order Book E, 300.

[33] Tiddy, *Mummers' Play*, 22, 27, 46.

[34] *Report* (1913–14), 1; (1914–15), 1–3; (1917–18), 1; TCA Order Book E, 300–2, 304. Knox, *Spiritual Aeneid*, 186–7.

[35] Order Book E, 302, 306–7, 309–10, 316.

saving a younger man's life, was killed by a shell falling in the trenches near Laventie.[36]

The Common Room was becoming an increasingly lonely place. Blakiston missed Raper for reasons both personal and practical, and he planned an apt memorial—'a sort of heraldic biography'—to the man who had to all intents and purposes held the gift of the presidency for so long. In 1921 Raper's coat of arms was placed, with an inscription, in the centre of the window to the left of the fireplace in Hall, surrounded by the arms of the six Presidents he had known. Raper was also commemorated by the gift of his portrait in pastel by the artist Brian Hatton (1905), who had fallen in action at Katia in April 1916.[37] Blakiston took on the estates bursarship (an office he found so congenial that he kept it until his retirement in 1938), and depended more and more on the support of David Nagel, who had succeeded him as both senior tutor and domestic bursar in 1907. Nagel was also providing such science tuition as was required by Trinity and Balliol, doing 'much of the Chemistry teaching in the University', and serving additionally on the Government Science Teaching Committee.[38] Both men were exhausted by their administrative burdens. Secretarial and office assistance was provided by Charles Honey, bursary clerk from 1894 until his death in 1948.

In 1917 Blakiston shouldered the additional and considerable duties of the vice-chancellorship. 'During the war had to deal with the finance and special conditions of an almost empty university for 4 terms,' he recorded in 'Memoranda' of his life which he sent to *The Times* in anticipation of his obituary. Blakiston's bent was for the 'careful economy' that the situation demanded, and he was proud of his achievements in reorganizing the University's finance boards and instituting a Reserve Fund.[39] He also rose to the occasion when statesmanlike ceremonial was required. At a luncheon in Magdalen College, for example, he proposed the toast to a 'delegation of distinguished Italian professors', 'speaking throughout in Italian', and the next day accompanied the party to lunch with the Duke of

[36] *Report* (1914–15), 4; Order Book E, 324.

[37] HEDB to P. W. Sergeant, TCA War Memorial Library, Returned Letters, uncatalogued; *Report* (1918–19), 4–5; (1920–1), 6. The Presidents were: Wilson, Wayte, Percival, Woods, Pelham, Blakiston.

[38] Blakiston to Lord Curzon, Oct. 1917, TCA, Blakiston, Correspondence Chest, 1917.

[39] 'Memoranda' of his life sent by Blakiston to F. S. A. Lowndes (1887) at *The Times*, *c.*1930, TCA, Blakiston papers, G/2. The memoranda were returned by Charles W. Brodribb (1897, also on *The Times*) to President Weaver in 1942.

Marlborough at Blenheim.[40] At the other end of the social scale, Blakiston recognized his duty to undertake very different visits in relation to the war. 'Would you like to go and see sometime the widowed mother of one of our kids who has been killed—the third son to perish in the War?' asked Tiddy in a letter from the front in July 1916. 'Her name is Mrs Randall, 17 Abbey Place, St Ebbes.'[41]

The strains of the vice-chancellorship had a marked effect on Blakiston's health. He told Higham that he had 'nearly died under chloroform' in August 1918, and recorded in his 'Memoranda' that he was 'seriously ill but managed to keep going' in 1919 and 1920.[42] In September 1920 he wrote frankly to an old member in Australia, 'The Vice-Chancellorship for 3 years on top of all the College work . . . has taken a great deal out of me . . . I have decided that a fourth year is out of the question. Everybody wants everything done at once.'[43]

Throughout his career Blakiston's contribution to the University was impressive, or as J. R. H. Weaver put it in an obituary, 'peculiar and valuable'. His knowledge of Oxford's 'history, ceremonial, and official routine' was second to none. But he was at heart 'essentially a "College" man. The well-being of Trinity, its members and material possessions, the maintenance of its tradition, and the preservation of College "independence" generally, were the absorbing interests of his long official career,' considered Weaver. Blakiston played an active part in University politics. His 'opposition, as it usually was', was directed mainly towards anything that might threaten his beloved College: to government grants to the University, to the admission of women, to the creation of the New Bodleian Library.[44]

During the First World War, Trinity's financial problems mirrored those of the University. For the year 1914 the College's expenditure had exceeded its income, which was reduced by half in the years

40 *The Times* (21 May 1918). Blakiston had visited Italy on three occasions, 'a few days' in March 1888, and during the Easter vacations of 1900 and 1902, TCA Blakiston papers, B/3.

41 Tiddy, *Mummers Play*, 51.

42 TCA Blakiston, G/2; Higham, *Dr Blakiston*, 18. (Higham tempered this information with his view that Blakiston, 'when out of sorts, was more miserably absorbed in his own sensations than most people'.)

43 TCA War Memorial Library, Blakiston to R. E. Thwaites, letters returned to sender, uncatalogued.

44 Weaver, 'Blakiston', *Oxford*, 37.

1915–17. Tuition fees, which had totalled £3,533 in 1913, were only £579 10s in 1915; admission fees dropped from £265 in 1913 to a low of £20 in 1918, and receipts from room rents fell from their pre-war level of £1,617 to just £174 in 1916. Blakiston economized where he could, beginning with a cut of his own pay from £1200 to £800 for the years 1915 to 1917, and £1100 in 1918. On Raper's death, Nagel agreed to be vice-president on a salary reduced by £50 a year. 'It would be of great assistance,' Blakiston suggested to the old members in October 1915, 'if a good many of those qualified could proceed to the M.A. next year; others might help by replacing their names on the books.'[45]

As early as October 1915 the President was turning his thoughts as to the best way to commemorate the Trinity men who died in the war. 'It will probably be possible to find a conspicuous place for a brass or a slab of marble, with an appropriate frame or supporters, to contain the full Roll of Honour,' he suggested in the *Report*.[46] By the summer of 1917 he was considering a memorial volume of photographs and tributes, and he wrote to the bereaved families to request contributions. His letters were a genuine expression of his own deep sorrow at the College's loss, and, as replies show, they brought much comfort to the bereaved families.[47] The first Trinity casualty came during mobilization: the accidental death of Edward Cohan (1907) on 5 August 1914. The first Trinity man killed in action was James Gilkison (1903), who fell at Le Cateau on 26 August. Before the year's end seven more Trinity men had been killed, including the brothers Villiers Downes (1909), who died on 18 October of wounds received at St Omer, and Archer Downes (1911), who died on 20 November of wounds received at Bailleul, and Trinity's Olympic athlete and record-breaking hurdler, G. R. L.'Twiggy' Anderson (1908), who fell at Hooge on 9 November.

In Trinity, Blakiston and Nagel were struggling to preserve what they could of normal college life. In January 1915 fifty rooms were allocated to OTC officers attending month-long courses of instruction provided by the War Office. 'This has been most useful in providing employment for those of the servants who have not been able to join the army,' reported the President. It also provided a vital boost to

[45] *Report* (1914–15), 3.

[46] *Trinity College, Abstracts of Receipts and Payments* for the years ending 1913–20; *Report* (1914–15), 7.

[47] TCA Blakiston, D/7.

college revenues. Military usage brought another benefit, which was to be enjoyed by subsequent generations of undergraduates. This was the conversion of the Millard Laboratory into a bathhouse 'with furnace, boiler and a row of full-length baths' for the use of the officers.[48] This facility was a great improvement on the pre-war arrangements described by Higham:

> The only baths provided for undergraduates . . . were foot-baths, commonly called by a name which I represent in the anagram RUZBEEFREMS. There was one of these to each room—a saucer of fairly solid metal about 3 ft. in diameter and eight inches deep. Outside it was painted brown and inside white. It had a turn-over rim drawn to a point in one place to form a spout; and with it went a large zinc can and an earthenware vessel of the same capacity, called a 'browner'. If hot water was required the full can would be set close to the room's coal fire in winter-time, or in summer upon the gas-ring on the stairway. The browner served for carrying off waste—a labour performed, like the filling and carrying of the can, by the scout and his 'boy' on the stair.[49]

The bathhouse still left something to be desired by the standards of most middle- and upper-class homes. Aidan Crawley (1926) found the baths a 'spartan touch . . . two quads and several stone passages away' from his rooms in the New Buildings. 'When the snow was on the ground one was apt to wash only when mud from the football field had made it essential.'[50]

By March 1916 Trinity had been formally organized to accommodate its military residents. Companies of over 100 cadets were 'billeted in the New Buildings and the Cottages, with reading and recreation rooms in Kettell Hall; and the Hall [was] given up to them as a canteen, while a High Table and an Undergraduates' Table . . . found accommodation in the Old Bursary.' In imitation of Oxford college life, the officers were allowed to use the College tennis-courts and the barge—'their boats have done well in competition with those of other companies'—and posed for group photographs with the

[48] There is no corroborative evidence for the story that, at the end of the war, the War Office presented Blakiston with a bill for this improvement, to which he replied with a demand that they either remove the baths or pay the cost of their removal, and pay additionally 'for the depreciation of the building'. According to Higham, Blakiston told the story 'with many a private and public chortle' at acquiring the bathhouse for nothing. *Dr Blakiston*, 26.

[49] Ibid., 25–6.

[50] Aidan Crawley, *Leap Before you Look* (London, 1988), 60.

President in the Garden Quadrangle. The sports ground, however, was 'devoted to hay and sheep for the relief of the dwindling resources of the Consolidated Clubs Fund'.[51]

The Rhodes Scholar Robert Coffin (Maine, 1916) spent one year in Trinity, which he described as the 'finest' of his 'whole life', and in August 1917 he wrote to Blakiston from an officer training camp in Maine:

> I shall return to Trinity no matter how long the interim before peace comes. The instant war is over and I can disengage myself from the army, I shall hurry straight to Oxford & to my work again . . . We had a very fine trip across and we got a submarine off Northern Ireland.

It was the most cheerful letter preserved by Blakiston from the melancholy contents of his postbag that month. He also kept the memorial card sent by the parents of David J. Davies (1915) who fell 'while in command of a "Tank" on July 31 1917, the day before his 20th birthday', and the circular letter of 20 August by which the Bishop of Liverpool and Mrs Chavasse expressed their feelings at the loss of their son Noel (1904), a captain in the Royal Army Medical Corps: 'He used to tell his friends that he was not really brave, but that the thought of the men of his Battalion, whom he knew and loved, lying out in the open bleeding to death, was more than he could stand.' Noel won the VC at Guillemont in August 1916, and a Bar to the VC at Wieltje, 31 July–1 August 1917. The citation reads:

> For conspicuous bravery and devotion to duty when in action.
>
> Though severely wounded early in the action whilst carrying a wounded soldier to the dressing station, Captain Chavasse refused to leave his post, and for two days not only continued to perform his duties, but in addition went out repeatedly under heavy fire to search for and attend to the wounded who were lying out.
>
> During these searches, although practically without food during this period, worn with fatigue and faint with his wound, he assisted to carry in a number of badly wounded men, over heavy and difficult ground.
>
> By his extraordinary energy and inspiring example he was instrumental in rescuing many wounded who would have otherwise undoubtedly succumbed under the bad weather conditions.

[51] *Report* (1914–15), 1; (1915–16), 1; (1917–18), 1.

This devoted and gallant officer subsequently died of his wounds.

The Bishop also sent a personal letter and a notice about his youngest son Aidan, who was 'missing'. Another man 'missing', since 3 May, was William Gale (1913), whose father wrote of his desperate hope that he might still be alive: 'when last seen he was unwounded & ahead of his men, & their theory is that he was probably taken prisoner.' Percival Wace (1902) had been missing since the Battle of the Somme. His mother wrote to the President on 26 August, "I am not going to give up hope of seeing my boy back before the end of the War, but as the W.O have now concluded that he was killed . . . you had better perhaps alter the record on your college roll.'[52]

One particularly poignant letter in Blakiston's correspondence from August 1917 was scrawled in pencil by J. Gilbert Laithwaite (1912). He was 'in trenches, & have been since June—it is not so entirely unpleasant as one had expected except for the mud: we are also rather lucky in our district—on a ridge with a wide view into the German country—rather like a smaller Birdlip.' Among the 'Oxford people' he had met was

> a Trinity fresher of 1914 . . . Monckton, who never came up . . . Somebody met Thomson not long ago, & said he was very cheery, & had a good job—Transport Officer . . . Perhaps you have heard about Latter? He resigned his Staff captaincy to come out here to his old Battalion as a full lieutenant, & is now up somewhere near Nieuport, I believe. Brunner was in the Mesines show . . . Bown is in hospital at Harrogate—he expects to come out here again very soon. We seem to have been losing very heavily lately—Peel [Geoffrey Peel (scholar 1913), killed in action 18 July 1917], Raper, especially . . . I am running Signals & Intelligence for my battalion & so get many curious souvenirs in the way of Boche papers . . . All this district must have been a terrible shambles in April & May: we are in the old German lines, & one cannot dig a foot down without turning up bodies—our own as well as theirs, while in the open, where German guns still have observation, people are still lying after four months. Everything is of course battered to pieces, though it is not as bad as the Somme country.[53]

52 TCA Blakiston, Correspondence Chest, '1917' drawer, uncatalogued.
53 Ibid.

## The War Memorial Library

Five Trinity men had fallen in the Battle of the Somme, thirteen in the Gallipoli campaign. The University Roll of Service, published in 1920, included the names of some 820 Trinity men who had served in the War. One hundred and fifty-three were dead.[54] The oldest of these was Blakiston's exact contemporary William Bolitho (1881), Lieutenant-Colonel of the Royal 1st Devon Yeomanry, while the youngest was Gordon Murray, accepted for admission in 1917. Peace, when it came, did not bring an immediate cessation of the death toll. Among the last names to be posted on a list in the chapel was that of Bevil Quiller-Couch, who fell victim to the influenza pandemic while serving with the army of occupation in Germany on 6 February 1919.

Trinity held no celebrations to mark the end of the war: there was no college community to hold them. Only eleven undergraduates were in residence on 11 November 1918, but sixty-four by the end of Hilary Term 1919, and 106 in Trinity Term. Peace brought with it a new range of difficulties, not least the sudden shortage of rooms. During 1919 and 1920 the undergraduate body was the largest it had ever been, with 165 men in residence in Michaelmas Term 1920. The pressure for space led to some rooms in the Garden Quadrangle being 'made to suffice for pairs of brothers or friends' for the first time. Tuition was suddenly required for large numbers of students, and temporary substitutes had to be hastily arranged for the fellows still on war service. Trinity's law tutor, James Brierly, remained in Constantinople (Istanbul) until the autumn of 1919, but his former pupil, the Rhodes Scholar Laurence Crosby (Maine, 1913), stepped in 'with great success' in Trinity Term. There was a backlog of increasingly urgent repairs to the buildings both in the College and on the estates. Blakiston calculated a loss of some £24,000 during the war. 'Supplies of fuel and other necessaries' were limited, and all meals had to be taken in Hall.[55]

The administrative work was harder than ever, and David Nagel's health broke down under the strain. On 27 September 1920 he died

[54] E. S. Craig and W. M. Gibson, 'Trinity College', *Oxford University Roll of Service* (Oxford, 1920), 395–428. Trinity lost some 18.5% of those who served, compared to the University's average of about 20%. See J. M. Winter 'Oxford and the First World War', *HUO* 8, 19, although Table 1.1 (p. 20) gives an erroneous figure of 10.54% for Trinity's losses.

[55] *Report* (1918–19), 1

of sclerosis, 'brought on by prolonged over work,' said the President. Nagel was 58. In the *Report*, Blakiston praised Nagel's 'devoted, and indeed excessive, service' to the University, 'in connection with all the delegacies, courses and examinations in Natural Science, including the new Committees for Forestry and Rural Economy'. To J. C. Hutson (1904) he wrote, 'for myself I feel that after 38 years friendship & 33 years co-operation, I can hardly go on without him.' Nagel had not missed one term of residence since Michaelmas 1882; Blakiston had missed only three.[56]

On Trinity Sunday (15 June) 1919, a memorial service was held in the Chapel. Blakiston read out the Roll of Honour, arranged in order of seniority, and gave 'a special address'.[57] Although not known for his stirring preaching—quite the opposite in fact—Blakiston's love of the Chapel and of the Anglican liturgy could make him an inspiring speaker there. 'The quiet beauty of his voice and the perfect inflexion of his sentences as he celebrated the Holy Communion in the College chapel' remained 'a living memory' for Kenneth Kirk (fellow and chaplain 1922–33).[58] In July 1919 Blakiston convened a meeting of 'non-resident members representing different generations' to discuss what form a permanent memorial to the dead should take. It was agreed unanimously that although only the Chapel 'seemed appropriate for the erection of a mere monument', no 'decorative object could be placed [there] without endangering the harmonious effect of the original design'. (They rejected the President's sketch, which still survives on the back of an envelope, of 'a sort of monument against the South wall' of the antechapel.) The committee decided therefore that a 'simple list of names' should be placed in the antechapel, and an appeal should be made for 'a really large sum' to be used for 'something certain to be permanently beneficial to Undergraduate Members of the College'. A new JCR was discussed, also a cloister in the fellows' garden. J. Hugh Thursfield (exhibitioner 1888) favoured the foundation of a fellowship, while J. H. Fowler (scholar 1880) suggested a statue in the garden, perhaps of Pitt, and L. S. R. Byrne (1882) wrote from Eton, 'I want before I die to see two minor improvements in the Garden Quad, turf and a balustrade.' The President, however, suggested a library.[59]

[56] *Report* (1919–20), 2; Blakiston To J. C.Hutson (17 October 1920), TCA War Memorial Library, returned letters, uncatalgued. [57] *Report* (1919–20), 8.

[58] Kenneth Kirk, 'Memorial of H. E. D. Blakiston', *Oxford* (1943), 40.

[59] *Report* (1918–19), 8; TCA Benefactions C/3, War Memorial Library, Appeal Circular.

To build a new library had always been Blakiston's ambition.[60] He could picture it already: 'a long and lofty room, 35 to 40 feet broad by 80 to 90 feet long, with bays of high bookcases and galleries over them on one side and tables between low floor-cases on the other side next to a row of large windows. There would probably be a half-basement for storerooms, heating furnace, etc.' He had also chosen the site, 'an area of about 110 feet by 100 feet . . . east of the New Buildings and extending from the College garden on the north to the houses and shops, nos 48 to 53 Broad Street, on the south'.[61] The 1880 Ordnance Survey map shows a complexity of plots and buildings in this area, which Trinity had been buying up piecemeal since the completion of the Jackson Building. In 1890 the College acquired the land behind 51 Broad Street and in 1893 the site of Bliss Court (48 and 49 Broad Street). B. H. Blackwell's occupied the shops at 50 and 51, and the White Horse was number 52. The missing piece needed for the Library was the back of no. 53 (today called Marriott House), and this was finally secured during 1920.[62]

In March 1920 Blakiston began sending out appeal literature, each circular accompanied by the printed Roll of Honour, and a personal letter from a member of the committee, in most cases himself. A bundle of envelopes, returned to the College with 'addressee unknown', reveals the immensity of the task, and the writer's tremendous dedication to both the recipients and the object of his letters. His appeal was often understated—'I think you will be interested in the enclosed papers'—but he invariably filled both sides of the paper with friendly gossip about the College and its members. 'I have not seen your name lately as the biographer of disreputable empresses,' he began to P. W. Sergeant (scholar 1889). And to F. J. Skinner (1857), 'there are not many of your year surviving, but I see the senior Scholar Lord Bryce not infrequently, & 2 others Marshall & Ramsay sometimes. The Roll of Honour enclosed includes two sons of contemporaries of yours.' By his own calculation, Blakiston had written 1,200 of the 1,300 appeal letters sent out by the beginning of 1921. By September 1921 'well over £15,000' had been pledged, of which over £13,000 was already received and invested in National War Bonds.[63]

The project took eight years to complete, from the sending of the

[60] TCA Maclagan, Blakiston to Maclagan (29 April 1940).

[61] TCA War Memorial Library, Appeal Circular.

[62] J. F. Wright, 'College Expansion Eastwards, 1880–1965', *Report* (2000), 61, 63, 65.

[63] *Report* (1919–20), 7; TCA Blakiston, G/2; *Report* (1920–1), 5.

first appeal. By 1923 the fund was large enough to assure the 'eventual success of the scheme', and by 1924 the plans were 'completed after constant consultation' between Blakiston, Weaver, members of the committee, and the architect. This was Joseph Osborne-Smith, but the design, as everybody knew, was Blakiston's, and he wrote obsessively to Osborne-Smith about the finer points of the work. In one letter (four sides of foolscap, typed) dated 24 June 1924, he listed no less than eleven major concerns: the windows at the north end ('it will be better if you make them the same height from the ground as the west windows'); the water supply ('I should like to have some kind of tank . . . [leading] to a blind-well in the garden'); the design of the 'the Librarian's room' ('the rest of the space can be made into a store room'); the heating ('the Library . . . will hardly be warm enough with only the five radiators under the windows'); the proposed window at the north end ('we do not want any window at all' and 'the design . . . is unnecessarily ornate'); the proposed door ('too short and too broad'); the outer doorway ('still unsatisfactory'); the panels between the windows and the pediment ('too deep'); the balustrade ('we think . . . there should be urns . . . There are very good ones on the Sheldonian'); the staircases to the galleries ('we can leave it to a future generation'); and, finally, the 'very difficult question' of the columns. 'If single pilasters with Ionic capitals are necessary,' mused Blakiston, 'then they may as well be fluted,' and he sent 'a paper giving the actual measurements of a bay of All Saints' Church . . . It is curious that my original plan with four bays of 15 feet turns out to be exactly the same as All Saints.'[64]

At last in February 1925, the work began. The builders chosen were Parnell & Sons, who had built both the Jackson Building and the Lodgings. The ground was cleared, the basement excavated, and the foundations laid on a 'most satisfactory' bed of gravel. The work proceeded slowly, largely because of the 'great difficulty in securing an adequate and regular supply of the Clipsham stone', large blocks of which were needed for the columns.[65] Meanwhile, Blakiston's greatest concern of all was for the symbolic trophy over the entrance (which was taken down to make way for the Cumberbatch Building in 1964–6). In October 1924 he had confided in H. C. Moffatt that he doubted Osborne-Smith's 'ability to design good and suitable orna-

[64] Blakiston to J. Osborne-Smith (24 June 1924), TCA War Memorial Library, 'trophy', uncatalogued. [65] *Report* (1924–5), 5; (1926–7), 5.

*11.4* Entrance to the War Memorial Library, 1928 (*The Times*).

ment. He really ought to get the assistance of someone who is more of a sculptor.' In July 1925 he wrote to the architect, 'your design is much more suitable than the previous one, but we fear it is still too crowded and in certain details rather stiff: e.g. the flag-poles are too heavy, the flags too flat, the two daggers and pistols awkward, and the centre too crowded . . . Mr Weaver would like to see one more attempt.' Weaver travelled regularly to Osborne-Smith's London office. The London firm of Farmer and Brindley were eventually commissioned to carve the trophy, and by February 1926 they too were receiving challenging correspondence. 'Great care must be taken to get the St. Andrew's cross correct in its lines,' insisted Blakiston. 'The Saltire crosses are counter-charged heraldically.' And regarding the 'upper trophy', 'Can you send me a fresh drawing (perhaps based on Torregiane's wreath) . . . ?' (Plate 11.4 shows the final appearance of the trophy.)[66]

The Library roof went on in the winter of 1927–8, and the interior was fitted up in the spring. The six long elm tables were the personal gift of H. C. Moffatt, designed by himself and made in his own workshops from trees felled on his estate at Hamptworth. Each had six places, 'separately lighted by night' (Plate 11.5). In the Easter Vacation of 1928, some 10,000 volumes were placed on the shelves, the contents of the first-floor library in the Jackson Building, and 'large sections of modern and useful books' from the fellows' library.[67] With characteristic efficiency and economy, Blakiston wrote to Weaver on the subject. There were valuable books, he pointed out, such as a first edition of 'Doughty's Arabia Deserta . . . It might be sold; at any rate it ought not to be left in open shelves. . . . It is no use wasting books which have a fancy value.' On the other hand, there were 'many volumes of absolute rubbish, e.g. works of unimportant Trinity men, presented by them, which Green [Librarian 1871–1921] had not the courage to throw away; and worthless books sent by conceited Americans.' In Blakiston's view, there were other books brought over from the old library which were 'of no use to the ordinary reader . . . The removal of them would set free many feet of valuable space.'[68]

But Weaver, as Librarian, had firm ideas of how the Library should be run. He wanted 'a clean chronological divide' between the old and

[66] TCA War Memorial Library, 'trophy', letters of 20 Oct. 1924, 17 July 1925, 3 Feb. 1926.

[67] TCA Library, F/8, War Memorial (New Library) Fund, Report to Subscribers (30 September 1928).

[68] TCA Library, F/3.

11.5 Interior of the War Memorial Library, 1928 (*The Times*).

new libraries, and he fixed the date at 1800. More recent books were on open shelves and card-catalogued, and he suggested an ambitious extension of opening times to seven and a half hours a day. The Library was open from 10 a.m. to 1.15 p.m., from 5 p.m. to 7.30 p.m., and from 8.15 p.m. to 10 p.m. Books could be borrowed between 12.15 and 1.15 p.m., and from 5.45 to 7.30 p.m.[69] The clerk was F. W. Dubber. In 1930 Weaver estimated library expenditure at £330 for books and binding, and £170 for administration. To support this level of expenditure Richard Rands's 1640 benefaction and the residue of the war memorial fund were considered ample.[70]

Even before the first stone was laid, gifts of books had been pouring in for the new library. Sir George Whitehead donated £500 War Loan Stock to be used for the purchase of English books in memory of his elder son James, as well as sixty-one volumes of the Transactions of the Camden Society and the Royal Historical Society from his father's library. David Nagel bequeathed the choice of his books, of which 295 volumes 'including some long sets of scientific periodicals' were selected. The executors of William Sanday (1866), who had held both the Ireland chair of Exegesis of Holy Scripture and the Lady Margaret chair of Divinity, gave 172 volumes—'mostly important works on theology'—from his personal library. The mother of Henry J. G. Moseley (scholar 1906, killed in action at Gallipoli, 10 August 1915) presented twenty-one 'finely bound volumes . . . being the Eton prizes of her son'. Some gifts were perhaps more useful than others. In 1922 Miss G. E. Troutbeck gave a 'handsomely bound copy of the Bible, given to her uncle, Canon R. Duckworth, by two members of the royal family', while from the grandson of Walter Savage Landor came a bust of Trinity's notorious alumnus, 'modelled at Rome in 1839 by John Gibson for Joseph Ablett'. In 1923 Blakiston announced in the *Report* that a share of the income from the Lingen Fund (established by Lady Lingen in memory of her husband, Lord Lingen (1837)) was to be devoted to the purchase of classical books, and suggested that 'similar funds for special departments of study would be more and more necessary in the future. (If given as memorials such volumes can be distinguished by a special book-plate).'[71]

Blakiston celebrated the year 1927–8 as an '*annus mirabilis* for large benefactions to the college', and by 'the college', he meant not so

[69] TCA Library, F/8.

[70] Ibid., F.6. Library funds were also augmented by decanal fines.

[71] *Report* (1919–20), 8; (1920–1), 5–6; (1921–2), 7; (1922–3), 6–7.

much the President and fellows as the undergraduate body. On the death of the former librarian Martin Green, his sister Jane gave £1,000 which was invested for the future endowment of the Library. Sir Mackenzie Dalzell Chalmers (1865), civil servant, county court judge, and permanent under-secretary at the Home Office, died on 27 December 1927, leaving Trinity as his residuary legatee. Some £40,000 came to the College (worth £1,900 p.a.). It was free of any trust, and at that time was the largest addition to the College's endowment since the foundation. Following Chalmers's own suggestion, the bequest was used in part to establish a Law Library 'for the use of the Law tutor and his pupils' in a room conveniently opposite Landon's set on Staircase 16.[72]

The parents of Trinity's war dead were drawn to create memorials within an institution where the young men grew not old, as they who were left grew old.[73] Sir George Whitehead, Bt, (1880) was twice bereaved. His elder son and heir, James Hugh Edendale ('Jim') Whitehead (1909), died of illness contracted on active service on 13 March 1919. His younger son, George William Edendale Whitehead (accepted for admission in 1914), was killed in action at Lauwe, near Courtrai, on 17 October 1918. In 1924 Sir George and Lady Whitehead conceived a plan by which they could enrich the lives of young Trinity men in the way they had once hoped to support their sons. For an experimental period of five years, they funded a 'travelling studentship' worth £300, to enable a man intending 'to adopt a business career' to 'have four or five months of instructive travel between leaving Trinity and settling down to work in one of our Cities'. The recipient would visit some of Britain's colonies, and also 'perhaps one or two Foreign Countries [which] should help to correct any tendency to insular pride and aloofness. Such a trip should make a man . . . "think Imperially".' Sir George further suggested that each holder of the bursary should produce a written report for the College Library, and he hoped very much to make their acquaintance himself. The first award was made in 1925, to Charles R. Prichard (1921), who visited Canada and the United States, and the second in 1926 to

[72] The Chalmers Law Library was moved to the basement of Staircase 14 in 1961–2, and is now integrated into the main library.

[73] From Laurence Binyon's poem 'For the Fallen'. Binyon does not appear in the Trinity Roll of Service although he spent the summers of 1915–17 as a volunteer medical orderly in France; John Hatcher, *Laurence Binyon Poet, Scholar of East and West* (Oxford, 1995), 198–210.

Arthur T. Maxwell (1923) who travelled through Kenya, Southern Rhodesia, and South Africa.[74]

In November 1927 Sir George settled £6,000 in securities to endow the James and George Whitehead Travelling Studentship in perpetuity. It remains today Trinity's most valuable student award. Until his death in 1931, Sir George would invite the recipient to talk about his travels over dinner, an occasion that could be fraught with anxiety. Adam D. Marris (1925) had to be hounded by his tutor for even an 'interim report' on his months in Canada: 'Marris was asked to supply evidence that he had spent two months profitably in the Dominions. This is the evidence,' wrote Philip Landon witheringly, and the report was returned by Sir George with a letter criticizing both its presentation and statistics. Lady Whitehead wrote to enquire about the typing of the reports. 'More rubbish for the Library,' noted Blakiston glumly.[75]

The War Memorial Library was finally opened on Saturday 10 November 1928. A service in the Chapel and the subsequent ceremony were attended by the families of many of Trinity's fallen members, but not by the architect, Osborne-Smith, who had died in January 1928. After an address by Michael Furse (1889), now Bishop of St Alban's, Blakiston read the Roll of Honour, and the congregation walked from the Chapel to the Library. The Bishop declared the building open and dedicated the memorial panel, which listed the names of the dead between a Latin inscription and a quotation from a funeral oration by Pericles, 'by giving their lives they gained the renown that grows not old.'[76]

Blakiston had of course designed the panel himself. He was rightly proud of the new Library, but his obsessive interest in it, and his snobbishness, became increasingly exasperating to the younger fellows. The President's attitude to the Library was immortalized in Hinshelwood's nursery-rhyme parody entitled 'This is the box that Blinks built'. The last verse runs:

> These are works of learning all forlorn
> That are not sufficiently nobly born
> To live with the work
> of Sir Bernard Burke

[74] TCA Trusts 15, A/1 (schedule), B/1925/1–2, 1926. [75] Ibid., A/1, B/1925/1, 1928/1–2.

[76] *The Times* (12 November 1928); *Report* (1927–8), 6. The quotation is taken from Thucydides, book 2, chapter 43.

That sits on the shelf
Designed by Himself
That stands in the Box that Blinks built.

According to Higham, Blakiston become 'engrossed for long periods' in *Burke's Peerage, Baronetage and Knightage*.[77] He prefaced the autobiographical memoir which he sent to *The Times* with details of his descent from Sir Matthew Blakiston, Bt, Lord Mayor of London in 1760. One anecdote about him relates an undergraduate breakfast guest observing 'what a wonderful collection of miniatures!' To which his host replied, 'They're not a collection. They're my ancestors.'[78] When Michael Maclagan was elected to the fellowship in 1939, he sent the President a pedigree showing how their two families were related. Blakiston was delighted: 'I am struck by the unevenness of the generations,' he wrote. 'I seem to be your mother's mother's sixth cousin.'[79]

## *Trinity in the 1920s and 1930s*

The Trinity Common Room had a very different profile in the years after the war. Seven new fellows were elected between 1920 and 1929:

Philip A. Landon, law fellow 1920–1952
Edward G. T. Liddell, physiology fellow 1921–1940
Cyril N. Hinshelwood, chemistry fellow 1921–1937
Kenneth Kirk, fellow and chaplain 1922–1933
Henry Price, philosophy fellow 1924–1935
Robert Hall, economics fellow 1927–47
Ronald Syme, ancient history fellow 1929–49

Tommy Higham saw a clear division between the President, the three older fellows (Patterson, Weaver, and himself), and the seven younger members of the Governing Body, and he gained a great deal of secret enjoyment from a satirical portrayal of his younger colleagues as a subversive band of rebels whom he dubbed 'the fellaheen'. After Blakiston's retirement, Higham wrote up an untitled history of the 'fellaheen'. It begins:

[77] TCA Higham, 3/1. [78] Higham, *Dr Blakiston*, 5.
[79] TCA Maclagan (29 April 1940).

> Long ago, when the darkness was very dark, before that gentle luminary The Little Man [President Weaver] had ascended with his starry consort [his wife Stella] to the throne of Bogo [Blakiston] in the Triune Kingdom [Trinity] it so happened that the monstrous virgin Primeval Might was overpowered by an ugly but clever Devil, whose name, being translated, is Insubordination.

Seven 'pups, but almost human' are born, 'creatures later to be known as the "Fellaheen"', and 'in course of time, Bogo, bachelor king of the neighbouring country, adopted the ungainly bastards one by one, giving them some control, as instructors, over a troglodyte population only less human than themselves [the undergraduates]'.[80]

As Blakiston was the official historian of the College, so Higham was the unofficial historian of the Blakiston years, and his records give a fascinating insight into Blakiston's characteristics and foibles in later life. In the latter years of his presidency Blakiston came to be seen as increasingly eccentric and difficult. The small size of the SCR community, and the considerable amount of time that the fellows were expected to spend together, caused inevitable tensions. Many comic verses (mostly by Hinshelwood), cartoons (mostly by Higham), and jokes at the President's expense circulated behind his back. Breakfast and dinner in College were the norm even for those fellows with wives and kitchens of their own in Oxford. Higham found Blakiston's company almost intolerable at breakfast, at least if his illustrated verse ('Chuffle, chuffle, Chup, Chup, Chup, Bogo is gobbling his grapefruit up') is anything to go by.[81]

Equally infuriating was Blakiston's driving. He was the first Trinity President to own, and drive, a motor-car. Charles Honey's daughter Joan remembered its arrival in the 'house (formerly a stable) next to our house in Parks Road. He used to invite . . . visitors for "drives". It was one of my childhood delights to observe him starting off. The car, containing himself and his alarmed guest, would leap about four feet into the air and come down with a bump.'[82] Higham was one of the fellows who were invited in turn to take their place in the passenger seat. Another Trinity nursery rhyme copied into Higham's book runs:

80 TCA Higham, 3/3.

81 Ibid., 3/4. The cartoon was drawn on a card, and addressed to Ronald Syme.

82 Memoir by Joan Honey, TCA DD 289 Honey.

Drive seven-horse
To Banbury Cross
To see my Lord North is incurring no loss;
With a hoot every minute
And a cat-fish-skin cap,
And the Chaplain to read me an obsolete map.

Higham's footnote to this rhyme is worth reproducing in its entirety:

> HEDB was owner-driver of a Seven-horse-power Austin car. Owing to his defective sight, he drove nervously, with constant use of the horn, and he preferred to have one of the Fellows at his side. Dr Kirk as chaplain often took this post . . . When the North family relinquished their tenancy [of Wroxton Abbey], it was thought by some of the fellows that the terms on which they were allowed to discharge their final obligations as tenants were over-lenient.
>
> HEDB purchased a cat fish skin cap when on a visit with F. W. Hall (President of St John's) to the Scandinavian countries. He wore this while motoring in this country. His stock of early Ordnance Survey maps was seldom if ever renewed.[83]

Blakiston's tight grip on College finance was more than just an irritating eccentricity; it was a policy that affected the wider college community. Blakiston also had a reputation for meanness. Although powerless to prevent a College decision to put Edward Liddell in charge of a Baths Committee in 1929, he was known to begrudge the expense of a more convenient fellows' lavatory:

Hey Liddell Liddell
Made a place for a piddle
At the foot of the Common Room stairs.
The fellaheen laughed to see such sport—
When the bill is on Duggie, who cares?

The sobriquet Duggie derived from the well-known bookmaker Douglas Stewart's advertisement, 'Duggie always pays.'[84]

Another nursery rhyme addressed the question of Blakiston's misogyny:

Blakiston, Blakiston where have you been?
Oh I've been up to London to preach to the Queen . . .

[83] TCA Higham, 3/3. [84] Ibid.; TCA Order Book E, 411.

Blakiston, Blakiston, did you say the right thing?
Oh I said, Ma'am you're civil, but, please, where's the king?

The fellows had heard rather too much of Blakiston's success in talking to Queen Mary when he was invited to preach before the royal family at Sandringham in the early 1930s. The Windsor Castle Librarian, remembered how he had kept her 'spellbound by his knowledge of bric-a-brac'.[85] According to Higham, Blakiston 'loved to relate with schoolboyish glee' how as Vice-Chancellor he had revenged himself on Oxford's women students, whose demands for full membership of the University were finally granted, against his wishes, in 1920. Blakiston suggested the name of *Societas Mulierum Oxonii Privatim Studentium* for their 'Society of Home Students'. 'This looked innocent enough,' sniggered Higham, 'but, as he well knew . . . it would most often appear in the abbreviated form "Soc. Mul. Ox. Priv. Stud." suggesting a stud-farm of obstinate bovine creatures.'[86]

Other dominant characteristics of Blakiston's personality were his conservatism and his racism, and these, more than anything else, were to attach themselves to the reputation of the entire College. He was intractably opposed to the new Statutes written for all the colleges after the Asquith Commission of 1919–22. Trinity's were drafted in 1924, and the following year Blakiston wrote in the *Report*, 'Many of the changes . . . are naturally bureaucratic in character, and will greatly increase the burden of accounts, statistics, and reports.'[87] Smaller changes met with equal disapproval. He was adamant in his refusal to consider an application from a girls' friendly society to use the College tennis courts in 1923, and rejected out of hand a suggestion from the undergraduates to introduce a new system of paying for teas at the cricket ground in 1925.[88]

With the exception of Mirchandani, no Indian student was admitted to Trinity during Blakiston's presidency, nor for more than a decade after his retirement, and the College's reputation for racism grew. The Chinese writer and artist Chiang Yee strolled down Broad Street in November 1940. 'I went to have a look at the beautiful lawn of Trinity College with its many well-shaped trees,' he wrote. 'I remembered having heard that Trinity is now the only college which does not admit Orientals. My flat face could not be disguised, so I

[85] Higham, *Dr Blakiston*, 6–7, TCA Higham, 3.1.
[86] Higham, *Dr Blakiston.*, 21–2. [87] *Report* (1925–6), 1.
[88] TCA JCR A4/6.36,45.

passed on without entering to avoid misunderstandings.'[89] When T. R. Anantharaman (Rhodes Scholar 1951) determined to apply to Trinity, the Warden of Rhodes House was 'somewhat perplexed' by his choice, and 'spent a sleepless night or two figuring out the diplomatic and other implications of [his] possible rejection'.[90] One story current in the 1930s, and promulgated by Richard Hillary (1937) in his best-selling *The Last Enemy*, related how the white Armenian Noel Agazarian was rejected by Blakiston on the grounds that 'when the last coloured gentleman had been at Trinity, it had really proved most unfortunate.'[91]

'We were a small college of less than two hundred, but a successful one,' said Hillary. Certainly Trinity's fellowship was very distinguished academically. Tommy Higham, although belonging to a generation which published very little, was a distinguished classicist who held the post of Public Orator for nineteen years, and was renowned for his elegant Latin speeches at Encaenia and other occasions. He expected the highest standards from his pupils, and invited them to transcribe their best pieces of work into his treasured *Liber Aureus*. Edward Liddell's research in the physiology department was centred on the study of reflex action and the nervous system, an area in which he led the field. In College he was an able, though a formidable teacher. Of Hishelwood, Harold Hartley wrote:

> As a college tutor, [he] was unsurpassed. All his pupils became his friends . . . Both in tutorials and in lectures the clarity and vision with which he could present a subject appealed both to the clever and to the dull. He was an ideal supervisor of research. By his daily presence in the laboratory and his close attention to any detail of their research his students were imbued with his own critical attitude towards techniques, evaluation of results, and style of presentation.

Cyril Hinshelwood's graduate pupils in the Trinity laboratory assisted in the experiments that went into his first book, the ground-breaking *Kinetics of Chemical Change in Gaseous Systems* (1926).[92] Their work-

[89] Chiang Yee, *The Silent Traveller in Oxford*, 4th edn. (London, 1948), 17.

[90] T. R. Anantharaman, 'Three Years at Trinity', *Report* (1988–9), unpaginated.

[91] Hillary, *Last Enemy*, 12–13. The same story is told in Maurice Bowra, *Memories* (London, 1966), 337.

[92] This album of Greek and Latin prose and verse was passed by Higham to James Holladay, and given by him to the Trinity Archive, TCA DD 50; 'Sir Cyril Hinshelwood', *DMB*.

*11.6* Lavatory block (1795) converted to Laboratory (1920).

place between 1920 and 1929 was the old 1795 lavatory block, now converted into a research laboratory (Plate 11.6). After 1929 Hinshelwood moved to the old Millard Laboratory, now reconverted to its original use after a decade as the College bathhouse (Appendix I). Both Liddell and Hinshelwood were elected to the Royal Society, and went on to hold Oxford professorships: Hinshelwood was appointed Dr Lee's Professor of Chemistry in 1937, Liddell to the Waynflete chair of Physiology in 1940. Equally eminent in their work were Ronald Syme, knighted (1959), and appointed Camden Professor of Ancient History in 1949, and Robert Hall, created Lord Roberthall (1969).

Such distinguished tutors notwithstanding, if the Norrington Table had been invented then, Trinity would have languished near the bottom.[93] In writing of the College, Richard Hillary was using very

[93] Brian Harrison, 'College Life, 1918–39', *HUO* 8, 105.

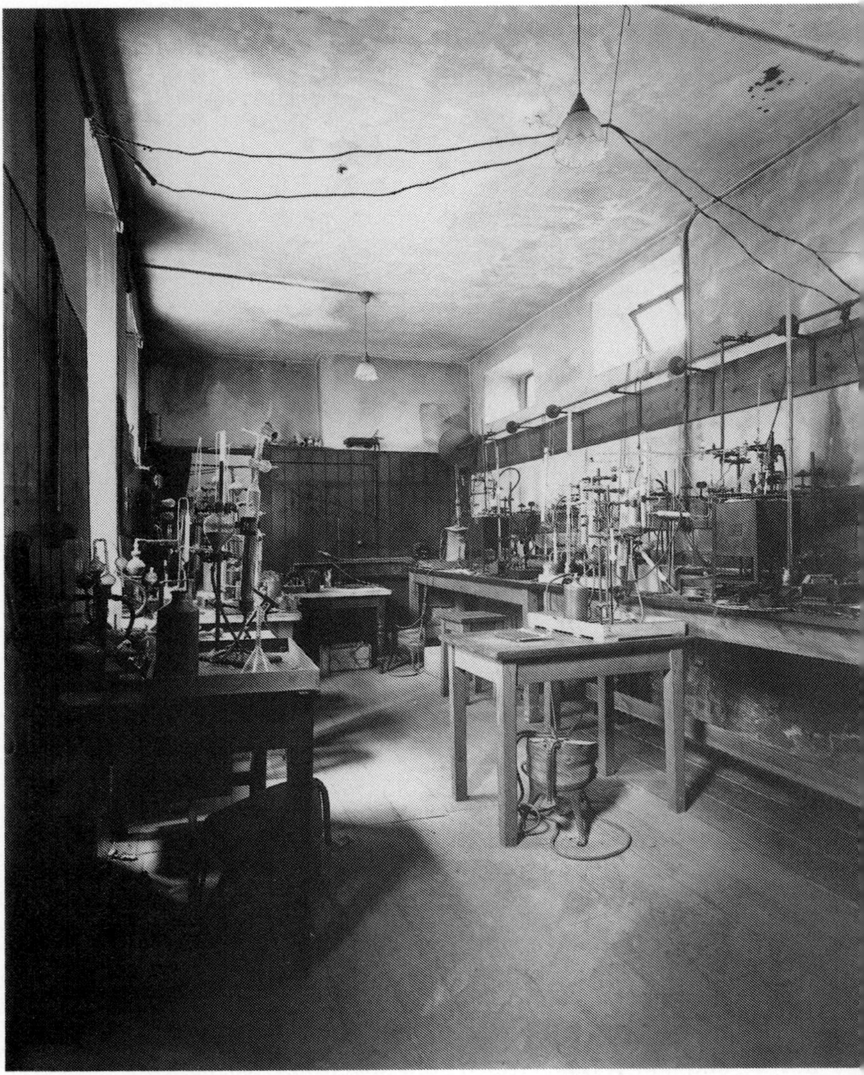

*11.7* Laboratory interior, 1921–9.

different criteria to define 'success'. 'We had the president of the Rugby Club, the secretary of the Boat Club, numerous golf, hockey, and running blues and the best cricketer in the University,' he claimed. Trinity was a hearty place, and proud of it. 'The sentiment of the college was undoubtedly governed by the more athletic undergraduates,' explained Hillary:

> Apart from the scholars, we had come up from the so-called better public schools . . . and while not the richest representatives of the University, we were most of us comfortably enough off. Trinity was, in fact, a typical incubator of the English ruling class before the war.[94]

Aidan Crawley won 'minor glory' at Harrow, when he won the 'top History Scholarship' to Trinity in 1926. But when he arrived, he found that the work 'was not exacting. It was necessary to read a few special books but the rest was familiar ground. I set about enjoying myself.'[95] Terence Rattigan (1930) allegedly 'said he was not going to make the mistake of working. He was determined to be a writer and did not want to be "marked out for life by getting a degree".'[96] Proof of sporting prowess opened as many doors as did academic honours. As Hillary put it, 'I went up for my first term, determined, without over-exertion, to row myself into the Government of the Sudan, that country of blacks ruled by Blues, in which my father had spent so many years.'[97] Blues on the books were just as useful to the College as were Firsts. The University's own handbook made the point that to be Head of the River was 'a kind of symbol or index of the general prestige of the college'.[98]

Trinity's standing as one of Oxford's leading sporting academies gave it a distinct identity and ensured a regular supply of applicants. Success in this area was owing, to a very great extent, to Philip Landon, law fellow and, for thirty years, 'the very model of domestic bursars'.[99] Landon's particular loves were rowing, rugger, and Etonians. This was encapsulated in a Landon clerihew attributed to Hugh Trevor-Roper and Gilbert Ryle:

[94] Hillary, *Last Enemy*, 10. [95] Crawley, *Leap Before you Look*, 57, 60.

[96] Michael Darlow and Gilliam Hodson, *Terence Rattigan, The Man and his Work* (London, 1979), 46.

[97] Hillary, *Last Enemy*, 11. [98] *Oxford University Handbook* (1932), 119.

[99] Austin Farrer, obituary of Philip Landon in the *Oxford Magazine*, quoted in *Report* (1961), 4.

*11.8* Philip Landon, fellow 1920–56, in his rooms on Staircase 16.

At Vincent's dining with abandon
Blues surround me, Philip Landon.
With this grace, my food I sweeten:
Eat, and if you can, be Eton.[100]

Landon held court in his rooms almost nightly, and entertained invited undergraduates to conversation, music, and beer. Austin Farrer wrote of the 'force of that kindness which had delighted and encouraged generation after generation of undergraduates'.[101] Crawley

[100] TCA Higham, 3/5. Michael Maclagan once asked Trevor-Roper if the attribution was correct, and 'was not contradicted'. Vincents Club, founded in 1863, is notable for the number of Blues among its members. [101] Farrer, obituary of Landon.

*11.9* Trinity VIII Head of the River, 1938.

remembered that 'anyone could go and have a drink in his rooms'; in fact, not all were invited; Landon had little to do with Trinity's scholars, and a particular dislike, for example, of the activities of the Trinity Players.[102] The experience of the classical scholar Michael Longson was that 'unless you were a blue or something like that, you did better to keep away.'[103] Landon's photograph albums are an impressive record of Trinity teams (in addition to the annual Vincent's picture), and the pages chronicle the College's steady climb, throughout the 1920s and 1930s, to the very top flight of University sport. In 1938 Trinity went Head of the River for the first time since 1864, and

[102] Crawley, *Leap Before you Look*, 65; R. M. Collins (1947), talking to Clare Hopkins (12 September 1991).
[103] Michael Longson, *A Classical Youth* (London, 1985), 86.

*11.10* Trinity Athletics Team Cuppers winners, 1938.

maintained the position for a record six years (there were no races during the Second World War) until 1949. In 1937 Trinity provided five members of the Oxford XV that played Cambridge at Twickenham. In 1938 Trinity had five athletics Blues, and won cuppers in athletics, golf, and rugby. J. D. Eggar, one of two cricket blues that year, made the top score for Oxford against the Australians. In 1939 the College had Blues in association football, golf, hockey, rowing, rugby, shooting, and skiing, and University representatives in lacrosse and water-polo. Trinty's top all-rounder during this period was Michael Walford (1934), who was a triple Blue (in cricket, hockey, and rugby) for three consecutive seasons, 1936–8[104] (Plates 11.9–11).

Landon was active in ensuring that suitable applicants came Trinity's way. He was on the Governing Bodies of four public schools: Kelly College (of which he was an old boy); King's College,

[104] R. A. Powell and F. M. M. Forster, 'Far Beyond the River', *Report* (1990–1), 50–3.

11.11 Trinity Rugby XV Cuppers winners, 1938.

Canterbury; Malvern; and St Edward's, Oxford. Sporting talent was a definite asset for candidates hoping to read law. The Etonian Alan Tyser has put on record the remarkable chain of events that led to his admission in January 1939. He was a close friend of Derek Graham (1936), one of the victorious 1938 Trinity VIII. The crew had lost its number 5, Henry Melvin Young (1934), who had gone down that summer. 'By an accident of life,' said Alan Tyser modestly, 'I filled the bill.' He had been 'always going to read the law', and he was an experienced Eton rower. Landon invited Tyser to sit the Trinity entrance examination at the end of Michaelmas Term, 1938:

> It was so important that I was successful that I was given the college entrance paper the night before to make absolutely certain that I did a bit of research. Which I did . . . [I] had dinner in college with a whole lot of friends and then I sat this examination in

what is now the Senior Common Room and happily it all turned out well.

Four months after Tyser's admission, Trinity retained the Headship of the River.[105]

Tommy Higham, like Landon, enjoyed the company of his pupils. Michael Longson knew he was 'always welcome at Tommy's house in Northmoor Road'.[106] Aidan Crawley valued the way that at Trinity 'younger dons called me by my Christian name and expected me to do the same to them.'[107] The fellows and undergraduates shared various social activities. James Lambert (scholar 1930, fellow 1938) remembered junior and senior trips to the pictures—'films were much better in those days and we often went off to a cinema after dinner.'[108]

It was a pleasant and comfortable life. 'We took the advantages of privilege very much for granted,' admitted Michael Longson. Crawley had 'a large sitting room and two bedrooms' in the New Buildings. The scout Walter Lynes looked after him and two others. 'One could always have lunch in one's room with two or three guests and could also have dinner there if one ordered it a day in advance. Male friends could sleep in the spare room at any time. Lynes looked after us all.'[109]

The last decade of Blakiston's presidency saw considerable work on the College buildings. In 1929 a second bathhouse was constructed in the Dolphin Yard, and the first reconverted to its original use as a laboratory, where Cyril Hinshelwood and E. J. Bowen conducted their research. In 1930 £600 was allocated for improvements to the College kitchen. The Chapel was extensively restored between 1932 and 1934, after the discovery of a serious infestation of death-watch beetle in the roof: 'the mischief must have been going on for at least a century,' thought Blakiston. The beams were replaced by steel girders, and the wood which could not be replaced was treated with 'the strongest insecticides known'. The parapet and balustrade were refaced with new stone, and a damp course put in above the cornice. The total expense came to more than £4,500. In 1936 the cottages were found to be 'suffering from dry-rot, death-watch beetle and in

105 Alan Tyser (1939), talking to Clare Hopkins (24 January 2004).

106 Longson, *Classical Youth*, 95.

107 Crawley, *Leap Before you Look*, 59.

108 James Lambert, notes on Trinity fellows in the 1930s, TCA Higham, 3/3.

109 Longson, *Classical Youth*, 90; Crawley, *Leap Before you Look*, 59.

many places from inferior masonry', and they too were restored, with 'new and uniform rough-cast' facing.[110]

Tommy Higham was Dean between 1919 and 1931, and he did his bit to modernize the behaviour of the undergraduates. He faced a number of difficulties, not least that the College was full of ex-service men, some of whom had held high positions in the army, and not unnaturally resented petty college regulations. They were also sentimental about Oxford's traditions, resisting 'any movement to efface the Oxford they might have known five years before'. Higham himself looked back to:

> pre-war days when . . . it was not unusual to wreck the rears and pile the rear-seats [lavatory seats], together with furniture from rooms, in generous profusion upon a bonfire; and to light a bonfire first in one quad and then another, to keep the Dean running. I was determined that tradition should be broken in this respect at least, and dealt with wanton breakage and unauthorised bonfires severely.[111]

In another respect Higham was a great deal more lenient. Where the feud against Balliol was concerned he was not only tolerant of a certain amount of damage, he seems positively to have relished the sentiment behind it. Indeed, when he relinquished the deanship in 1932, he wrote a thirty-page essay entitled 'The Balliol–Trinity Frontier . . . A Study in Social History'. In the early 1920s, he recorded, 'the "vendettula" . . . was taken over by the rowing men, to whom it had always in the main belonged, and [became], on both sides of the wall a rallying point in college life.' His Balliol counterparts agreed. When Balliol had hurled over the wall a trench-mortar that had been presented to the College by the War Office, the Junior Dean of Balliol had tempered his apology with the satisfaction that it 'was the first thing that had really united the college since the war.' One fairly typical frontier incident occurred on the last night of Hilary Term 1931, when falling masonry had left a 'large hole' in the wall of the fellows' garden. 'Some noise attracted me to the place, close on midnight, but no one was visible', wrote Higham:

> I asked the Night Porter to ring up Balliol, and then join me in the Bursary garden, where I lay in wait . . . It was rather cold, but the cat and mouse game was amusing. I waited till a head emerged,

110 TCA Order Book E, 418; *Report* (1931–2), 5; (1932–3), 5; (1936–7), 7.

111 T. F. Higham, 'The Balliol–Trinity Frontier', TCA Decanal, C1.3, 9–10, 13.

> and then identified Bury, a Wykehamist of Alpine tendencies.... [Next] a party of four came tumbling through in a great hurry. Curtis was the first. I was afraid he might shout the others back when he saw me; but they were out almost too soon—Chadwyck-Healey, Russell, and R. A. Lyle, headfirst in a jumble of falling stones, with the Junior Dean of Balliol in full cry behind them . . . They paid £1 apiece cheerfully enough, remarking that a hole into Balliol could really not be resisted.[112]

Another fascinating historical vignette is Higham's collection of papers relating to the General Strike. On 3 May 1926 the Vice-Chancellor issued a proclamation requesting 'all citizens to enrol themselves as volunteers for the maintenance of essential services', and urging undergraduates to register for voluntary work away from Oxford. In Trinity, Blakiston pinned up a notice announcing that he would 'give leave to go home, at once or at any time' for the purpose. On 10 May the Vice-Chancellor issued a further announcement that examinations were postponed. The first two Trinity strike-breakers departed on 4 May, and by the time the strike was called off on 12 May, 153 had left Oxford, and 160 were employed in some capacity or another. 'Of the remaining 15,' noted Higham, 'eight were prevented from service by ill-health or special circumstances'; three were 'aliens'; only four 'had scruples'. Volunteering offered a pleasant vacation from the undergraduates' usual activities, and a chance to experience work of a type usually denied to men of their class. The registration form allowed for three choices of 'Work Volunteered for'. William Olivier (1923) listed: '1. Driving own car or any other—own 3 seater car; 2. Look after livestock. 3. Work on Railway', and under 'Qualifications and Remarks', he put 'Healthy—Educated Eton'. Many of the undergraduates had quite a good time. John Shearer (1925) wrote to Higham on 10 May, having departed in a party to Hull:

> We had quite a comfortable journey, but found on arrival . . . five hundred Cambridge men had already arrived and supplied all the dock labour required. After several hours we were fed, on bread and 'bully' beef, by the crew of a cruiser, and then came an offer of jobs on the tram. Cole, Lloyd, and I expect to start on that to-morrow morning, and are now housed in quite a good hotel . . . by becoming a car conductor I shall at last realise one of my earliest ambitions!

[112] T. F. Higham, 'The Baillol–Trinity Frontier', TCA Decanal, C1.3, 28–9.

George Addleshaw (1925) found no work at all at first, but then 'went to the Tramways Office at Westminster. They wanted Oxford men, and at once gave me the job of conducting from Shepherd's Bush to Uxbridge.' Iver Krabbé (1925), meanwhile, enjoyed a stint as 'a special constable and also in addition a lorry driver'. Blakiston was reminded of the war except, as he remarked in the 1925–6 *Report*, 'There were no casualties.'[113]

Herbert Blakiston was the last Trinity President with the right not to retire. But at the end of Trinity Term 1938, he startled his colleagues by the announcement that he would be resigning on 1 September. He was acting, as he had done throughout his adult life, for the sake of the College, leaving while 'his health and powers were unimpared' and hoping that he could be useful in retirement as an adviser. He moved to a large house not far from Oxford on Boar's Hill. The move was a great personal sacrifice. As he told Higham, it felt 'like committing suicide'.[114]

Like Presidents Wayte and Woods before him, Blakiston was glad to assume the role of elder statesman, although when it began to seem that a second war was inevitable, he rather regretted that he had not stayed on at Trinity to face it. 'I should have been better off [regarding travel] & perhaps useful in College!' he wrote gloomily to Weaver. He kept himself busy working on his College lists, corresponded with the older of the old members, and when occasion offered, wrote to his successor with pertinent, and probably unwelcome, advice. In May 1940, for example, he suggested 'utilizing the large pile of *good paper* which had accumulated in the tower . . . If I was still in authority, I should very soon now, when paper-pulp is even scarcer, have 9/10$^{th}$ of the account books etc sorted out and disposed of.'[115]

But he was not in authority, and he also wrote to Trinity's new President about his death. 'I am leaving the College a substantial sum . . . intended to preserve my memory usefully . . . I should hope that my legacy will be large enough to give me a place in the annual commemoration of benefactors.' (It did.) He asked further that, whether he was buried or cremated, his funeral service—'not merely a memorial service'—should be in the Chapel. (It was.)

[113] TCA Higham, 5, *Report* (1925–6), 3.

[114] TCA Order Book D, 475–6; Higham's obituary of Blakiston in *The Times* (30 July 1942).

[115] TCA Blakiston, F/14, 31 May 1940.

Furthermore, if cremated, could his ashes be interred in the antechapel, 'privately & without any further ceremony?' (They were.) He hoped too for a memorial in the Chapel that he had loved and served with such devotion, 'preferably in the form of a marble lozenge in the floor of the antechapel, where there is a vacant space next to Bathurst'. (Members of College and visitors can pay their respects there today.)[116]

Blakiston's final request was characteristically practical. 'Will you put this where it will be found if we should both be bombed at the same time?' he asked.[117] Oxford was not bombed, and neither was Boar's Hill. But on Tuesday 28 July 1942, while walking in Boar's Hill in the direction of Oxford, Blakiston stepped suddenly in front of a motor car being driven by a solicitor from Abingdon. He was fatally injured and died the next day.[118] 'How much Trinity owes to him in things intangible is difficult to express,' wrote Higham in the *Oxford Magazine*.[119]

[116] TCA Blakiston, F/14, 26 June 1939.
[117] Ibid., 17.
[118] Inquest report in the *Oxford Mail* (6 August 1942).
[119] 'The Rev H. E. D. Blakiston', *Oxford Magazine* (5 November 1942).

# 12

# *President Norrington*

## *The Second World War and President Weaver*

John Reginald Homer Weaver, commonly known as Reggie, was Trinity's President during the Second World War. He was the senior fellow at the time of his election, for Patterson, fifteen years his senior, had retired with Blakiston in 1938. The new President paid tribute to Patterson's 'courtesy, geniality, and habitual kindness', and many would have said the same about Weaver himself. 'He was totally unbusinesslike, but marvellously hospitable,' remembered James Lambert. 'We all rallied round and kept the College going.'[1] Weaver was a quiet and unassuming figure, who exuded an air of 'indefinable distinction' and a 'sense of noble leisure'.[2] His twin passions were architectural photography and roses. He spent several vacations travelling in Spain, and a large and fine collection of his photographs of Romanesque buildings was deposited after his death in the Victoria and Albert Museum. In Trinity Weaver created a rose garden between the War Memorial Library and the Jackson Building, where on at least one occasion he was mistaken for the College gardener.[3] Stories abound of the President's gentle unworldliness. David Mitchell (1945) climbed into College 'early one summer morning' and met Weaver in the rose garden, 'examining the blooms he so cherished . . . "You're up betimes Mitchell,"' murmured Weaver vaguely.[4] It was generally felt that to all intents and purposes Trinity was governed by Philip Landon.

The President's easygoing attitude to College administration was well suited to the war years, when Oxford's institutions had to adapt

[1] For dates and subjects of fellows, please refer to Appendix III. *Report* (1937–8), 2; James Lambert, reminiscences on presidential elections, TCA DD 20 add 2.

[2] Austin Farrer, 'J. R. H. Weaver', *Oxford Magazine* (1965).

[3] For Weaver's photographs of the garden see TCA Photographs 17. The photograph of the Chapel interior (Plate 6.5) is by Weaver.

[4] David Mitchell 'The Melvin Young Bursary' (8 July 1989), TCA DD71 Mitchell.

rapidly to greatly changed conditions. At first, the war's impact on College life seemed small, for Trinity remained full of undergraduates, their days busy with tutorials, meetings, and regular bursts of physical activity. In December 1939, for example, Weaver was able to report that the College rooms were 'filled to the utmost', and a year later, that Trinity still 'maintained its own XV' in rugby football. By the end of 1944 Trinity was the fourth largest college in the University, and had more of its own members in residence than any other college except New College.[5]

In September 1939 conscription was introduced for young men of 20. The University responded by offering war degrees, the qualification for which was a certificate, awarded after a shortened course of study with termly examinations, and a period of military service. In December 1941 the conscription age was lowered to 19, and the following year it was reduced still further to 18. Now matriculation was also offered to cadets enrolling on six-month courses at the University. In 1944–5, sixteen 'regular freshmen' were admitted to Trinity, and eighty-six service cadets. By the end of June 1946, 318 cadets had matriculated at Trinity.[6] One such young man was Denis Eve, who came up as an RAF probationer in October 1942. The admissions system was wholly centralized, and the entrance examination was a sheet of thirty questions to be answered at home and posted to 'The Director of Studies, RAF cadets, Wadham College'. The paper covered mathematics ('Can you solve quadratic equations?'); physics ('Do you know anything about astronomy?'); electronics ('Can you mend (a) a cycle lamb (b) a wireless set?'); history and philosophy ('Would you prefer to study the rudiments of Moral Theory or the History of Political Theory from 1760?'). The final question was 'would you have gone to a University if there had been no War?' Eve was notified of his assignment to Trinity by a printed letter from the Air Ministry.[7]

Another to matriculate as an RAF cadet was Stephen Cooper (1943). Like countless undergraduates before and since, he found the ceremony 'the greatest farce yet'. He had to wear his new uniform ('I will have to spend my time sewing lots of buttons on') under his new gown ('15*s* 5*d*. No coupons. It is a stupid little thing but we have to wear them in lectures'). 'Won't we look sweet,' Cooper wrote to his parents. 'Nigel [his friend Nigel Poston, naval cadet] of course will

[5] *Report* (1938–9), 1; (1939–40), 8; (1942–4), 1.
[6] Ibid. (1944–6), 3–4. [7] TCA Eve.

wear bell bottoms & a gown!' Stephen Cooper wrote out his weekly timetable for his parents:

> All Sunday is free.
> Monday & Friday, 9.10–5.30 is RAF work.
> Tuesday, three one-hour lectures between 10 and 1, and between 5 & 7 I see my tutor.
> Wednesday, Physics practical between 10 & 1, and 2.15 & 4.15.
> Thursday, 3 lectures in the morning, & I see my tutor between 6 & 7.
> Saturday, 3 lectures between 10 & 1.[8]

The traditional beginnings and ends of term had by now been suspended for most undergraduates. As early as April 1940, the members of the JCR were discussing the implications of a 'proposed long vac. term', and fifteen 'signed their intention of coming up' if it counted towards their degree.[9] In December 1943, Stephen Cooper had just twelve days of 'leave at Christmas from December 17 a.m. to December 28 p.m.'

Trinity had to adapt quickly to accommodate the academic requirements of its wartime members, a process complicated by the disappearance of many tutors. In September 1939 Robert Hall departed for an assistant secretaryship in the Ministry of Supply, while Ronald Syme took a post in the Ministry of Information. Hall spent much of the war travelling between Whitehall and Washington, while Syme, after stints in Belgrade and Ankara, did his bit for 'Anglo-Turkish interests' as a temporary Professor of Ancient History and Classical Literature at the University of Istanbul. Early in 1940, Tommy Higham put his knowledge of Greek at the service of the Foreign Office. His Latin also stood him in good stead when, in April 1941, he was given 'special leave' to go with Weaver (who was representing the Vice-Chancellor) and Professor Entwistle of Exeter College on a twelve-day visit to Lisbon, where the party conferred an honorary degree upon Dr Salazar, the Portuguese 'Prime Minister'.[10]

Next to leave Trinity was Anthony Peck, who spent much of the war as a staff officer in the Middle East.[11] The College's history and

[8] TCA Cooper, letters home 10 Oct. and 16 Nov. 1943. Most clothing was rationed, only available with clothing coupons. [9] JCR Minutes, TCA JCR B 3/1, 165.

[10] The background to this visit would merit more research: it was presumably part of a British strategy to keep Portugal neutral.

[11] *Report* (1939–40), 1–2; (1940–1), 1–2; (1941–2), 2.

chemistry tutors departed during 1941, Bruce Wernham to the RAF, Michael Maclagan to the War Office, and James Lambert to the Royal Engineers and the Far East. Lambert served as a chemical warfare officer under General Slim, and later as a scientific adviser to Lord Mountbatten. Tom Sewell (1946) got to know him in the Burmese jungle where

> James had a wonderfully laid back approach to the war, and accepted his extraordinary uprooting with philosophy and a dry wit which brought the air of a Senior Common Room to our mess in a bamboo *basha*. 'Not pheasant again!' he remarked, when the tinned bully beef came round for the umpteenth time.[12]

Trinity's Senior Common Room was now seriously depleted, and College offices changed hands again and again. The estates bursarship, finally yielded by Blakiston to Robert Hall in 1938, passed to Landon (who was absent owing to pneumonia for much of Trinity Term 1940), while the senior tutorship went from Higham to Wernham to the President. Ronald Syme relinquished the position of Dean to Lambert, who was succeeded in turn by Peck, Maclagan, Professor Ewert, and Austin Farrer. Farrer disliked the role, particularly the requirement to sleep in College, but shouldered the responsibility with characteristic aplomb. A sign on his door read:

> The Junior Dean
> May best be seen
> From 10 a.m. to 10.15.[13]

Ewert also assumed the new and vital role of Trinity's 'chief ARP [Air Raid Precautions] officer'. The College was grateful for the assistance of two former fellows who still retained their rooms in Trinity, Edward Liddell (attached in 1940 to Magdalen as Waynflete Professor of Physiology) and Cyril Hinshelwood (now Dr Lee's Professor and a member of Exeter College). Liddell supervised the growing number of medical students, while Hinshelwood resumed the chemistry tuition from his former pupil Lambert. The Trinity teaching laboratory entered into honourable retirement in 1941, when the new Physical Chemistry Laboratory was opened on the edge of the University Parks.[14]

[12] Tom Sewell, 'James Lambert in Burma', *Report* (2002), 64.

[13] Philip Curtis, *A Hawk among Sparrows: A Biography of Austin Farrer* (London, 1985), 118–19.

[14] *Report* (1940–1), 2; (1941–2), 2.

Another development, unthinkable in peacetime, was the accommodation of second-year Balliol undergraduates in the Jackson Building, while Balliol was given up to the Political Intelligence Department of the Foreign Office, and, from 1943, to the entertainment of visiting allied troops.[15] Roy Jenkins (Balliol 1938) was grateful for this 'great and indeed surprising generosity', as he lived 'first on the ground floor at the back looking across to the Library, and then, during a summer term of perfect weather and the fall of France, on the first floor at the front with a fine comparative view' of the two college chapels.[16] The war saw something akin to a truce on the Trinity–Balliol frontier, although in January 1940, the JCR President Peter Marrian (1936) spoke disparagingly of 'evacuees, who found themselves unable to accept the hospitality offered them by the College', and, two years later, Balliol men were accused of using 'obscene language' in the JCR Suggestions Book. There was a brief renewal of hostilities in June 1942, when the JCR President Nigel Anderson (1938) 'advised that there should be no more raiding of our so-called neighbours as the two Deans had been having words'. Honour was satisfied when 'the President answered in the affirmative to the question, "is the pouring of verbal excretement over the wall still allowed?"'[17]

Oxford's undergraduates, like the population at large, had to grow accustomed to a more austere way of life. On his arrival, John Harper-Nelson's scout, North, showed him the one scuttle of coal that was his daily allowance.[18] Denis Eve was sent an amended copy of the college 'Regulations', with the '6 glass-cloths and 6 dusters' each reduced to two, and the '3 table-cloths' crossed out altogether.[19] The obscure requirement of 'Toilet covers', however, remained on the list of what to bring up: '[they] seem to be what Auntie Walsh said they were, but I *don't* want them,' wrote Stephen Cooper to his parents.[20] While the Battle of Britain was being fought in the skies above south-east England, the JCR was much exercised over the Bursar's refusal to give individuals 'their own ration of tea' on the grounds that the College was 'a catering establishment'. At a meeting on 13 October

15 Addison, 'Second World War', 170, 178; John Jones, *Balliol College A History*, 2nd edn. (1997), 280.

16 Roy Jenkins, 'Chancellor's Address [on opening Staircase 18]', *Report* (1991–2), 5.

17 JCR Minutes, TCA JCR 3/1.2, 159, 197, 213.

18 John Harper-Nelson, *Oxford at War* (Northbridge, W. Australia, 1996), 6.

19 TCA Eve.

20 TCA Cooper, SDC to his parents, 10 October 1943.

1940, members discussed the introduction of gummed labels to save envelopes, and the question of when the JCR fire would be lit.[21]

Conditions at Trinity were generally acknowledged to be exceptionally good. Roy Jenkins was impressed by the arrangements that he found in place. Balliol had 'already gone in for gas fires and for all meals, save only tea, to be served in hall'. Trinity, however:

> considerably improved on all that . . . In place of all meals in Hall there were hot luncheons in the winter and lobster luncheons in the summer which were borne by the same old scouts, and could be eaten with guests in one's rooms . . . For long afterwards, whenever anyone asked whether Oxford in the first year of the war had not been a sad decline from the splendours of peacetime, I said that, on the contrary, it had put my standard of living up by about a half.[22]

Everyone agreed that Trinity owed its fine cuisine to Philip Landon's 'touch of magic'.[23] As James Lambert recalled:

> Landon took over the gardens on the College estates at Wroxton, which grew vegetables, and persuaded the wealthy father of two undergraduates with an estate in Scotland to send him two whole deer a week during term, so Trinity was fed like nowhere else in Oxford.[24]

To facilitate the bursar's catering operations, the Governing Body agreed in October 1942 to defray the 'running expenses (registration, insurance, garage & petrol) of the Bursar's motor car' until further notice.[25] Landon also registered the President and fellows as the owners of fifty hens, which lived on the College sports field under the care of the groundsman Hodgkins and his son. Ducks were introduced to the President's garden, to the annoyance of Sproule Bolton (1940) and Philip Zimmerman (1939), who in October 1941 suggested that the birds 'should be muzzled at all times and especially in the early morning'.[26] Many undergraduates believed that Landon owed

[21] JCR Minutes, 3/1.2, 171, 173.

[22] Roy Jenkins, *A Life at the Centre* (London, 1991), 35.

[23] *Report* (1952–6), 3.

[24] James Lambert, 'Philip Landon', TCA 20 add 2.

[25] TCA Order Book E, 500.

[26] To which 'the President replied that impersonal remarks when at tea with the President might work wonders,' JCR Minutes, A3/1, 189. There is no known link between these birds and the ducks which have come, on and off, to breed and nest in the College garden since the late 1980s.

his domestic bursarial genius entirely to his dealings on the black market, but there were no complaints from members of 'the best fed college in Oxford'. For his first day's breakfast, Stephen Cooper enjoyed 'sausage, scrambled egg & fried potatoes' and for lunch, 'soup, cheese, salad & butter' and wrote to his parents 'we can buy some cold meat, such as spam or pressed beef to go with it.'[27] The Sunday evening JCR meeting, where grievances about food were traditionally aired, now witnessed such unusual scenes as that of 8 March 1942, when the food committee reported that 'the standards of meals in hall had been well maintained . . . thanks to the untiring energy & resourcefulness of Eyles [the chef] & further that the one request for hot sausages had been granted.' On 29 November 1942 it was 'unanimously agreed . . . that a message of commendation' be sent to Eyles.[28]

Three hundred years earlier, members of colleges had joined with the residents of Oxford in building defences to protect the city in the civil war. Now they were united again, against the very real threat of air raids. Regular drills were held, and non-attendance was a serious disciplinary offence. Trinity was divided into three 'divisions' to cover the three main quadrangles. As a resident of Staircase 11, John Harper-Nelson was in the Second Division:

> responsible for the protection of the Chapel, Chapel quad, Staircase 10, the Tower, kitchens, bathrooms and lavatories. The undergraduates were placed into four squads, armed respectively with hoses, stirrup pumps, ladders, and shovels. Each division was divided into sections consisting of one or two men from each squad so that, in theory, there would be hose-men, stirrup pump men, chaps with ladders and chaps with shovels to dig us out if all else failed.[29] Those of us detailed for duty had to be in college from 6 p.m. onwards and, if there was an air raid alert, to remain up and fully dressed until the All Clear. On the alert, two members of the section were to go up onto the top of the chapel tower.

Where, needless to say:

[27] TCA Cooper, SDC to his parents, 6 October 1942.

[28] JCR Minutes, 3/1.2, 199, 211, 219. The reputation of William Eyles has been besmirched by the publication of an uncomplimentary sonnet by Cyril Hinshelwood (known for his 'queasy stomach') which concludes with the lines: 'Yet still I think, and this thought courage gives / Fate harms him not who eats of Eyles and lives'; *Report* (1967), 7.

[29] The shovels, in fact, were for throwing incendiary bombs down from roof-tops, before covering them with sand.

> the temptation to make the clock strike thirteen at midnight proved too much for some, but the most confusion could be caused in the early morning when a long night's watch could be enlivened by adding a couple of chimes to four or five o'clock and watching the panicked rush for baths and breakfast.[30]

The fear of bombs was very real. From the Chapel tower watchers could see a 'wavering glow that lit the horizon' as fires raged night after night in London and Birmingham. Across the University, static water tanks were built to provide sources of water for fire-fighting. Trinity had three, in the Garden Quadrangle, the rose garden, and 'close to the south wall' of the main garden, the latter intended for the protection of the New Bodleian. The pool in the rose garden, a rare survivor until 1964, became a much-loved feature of the College in the postwar years (Plate 12.1). Another precaution was the removal and storage of most of the carving in the Chapel and antechapel. Arrangements were made for undergraduates to take shelter if necessary in the basement of the New Bodleian (which they were to reach via Broad Street). Trinity's own cellars were approved as shelters, but considered by the College to be 'inconvenient', a statement that can only have added to the general suspicion of Philip Landon's activities.[31]

One casualty of the London blitz was the College Mission. During the winter of 1940–1, the missioner, E. H. Knell, wrote of how 'night after night, to the accompaniment of gun-fire and exploding bombs, we serve tea and sandwiches to the people who crowd into the shelters built on our premises, and each succeeding morning reveals the extend of the damage done to the district.' On the night of 19 April 1941, the Mission church received a direct hit by a thousand-pound bomb, 'entirely demolishing it and damaging the Club buildings beyond repair'. In the *College Report* Weaver reported the sad news that the Mission was to be closed at the end of August 1941, 'for the duration of the war. Besides the destruction of the Church, the evacuation of at least half the population of the district and the impracticality of social work during the "black-out" period contributed to the decision.'[32]

[30] Harper-Nelson, *Oxford at War*, 29–30.

[31] *Report* (1940–1), 9; TCA Dean C/3; Harper-Nelson, *Oxford at War*, 31.

[32] *Trinity College Oxford Mission Report*, 1941–7; *Report* (1940–1), 4. The Mission never reopened, but Trinity continued its involvement in the East End of London through medical missions to hop-pickers during the 1950s and 1960s. Subsequent social outreach by Trinity undergraduates has included camps for Borstal boys, and voluntary work in Oxford schools.

*12.1* Sir Arthur Norrington and James Lambert walk by the pool in the Rose Garden, 1964.

Back in College the authorities were concerned to maintain what they could of Trinity's cherished traditions. In October 1942 Weaver circulated an urgent appeal—'on the grounds of preserving and handing on a good College tradition'—that Sunday chapel 'which has always been regarded as a corporate obligation on all resident members of the College' should be better supported.[33] In the JCR, the undergraduates had a rather different Oxford tradition on their minds. No one had any experience of a Commem Ball, but 'Mr Marten said that before the war the College used to hold a very good dance'. Even as the meeting recognized that 'under war-time conditions, the expense was too great', members were nominated to form a Dance Committee. The JCR minutes of this period are a poignant

[33] Dennis Eve preserved Weaver's circular carefully, also his own drawing of a Stuka bomber dropping its load on the Chapel.

mixture of responsibility—worrying about the blackout, and responding to 'a request from the Bursar for voluntary work on the lawns and grounds'—and frivolity. Undergraduates frequently discussed the possibility of subscribing to the *Sporting Life*, as well as 'the merits, demerits & desirability' of extending the hours for women visitors and whether 'double summer time should allow the fair sex to remain in College twice as late'.[34] They were not unaware that, for some of them, this was their last year of life. By the end of the war, nine members of 1939 would be dead, thirteen of 1940, sixteen of 1941, five of 1942, and three of 1943.

And so the years of war passed. Trinity's death toll was very great indeed. The Roll of Honour placed in the chapel listed 133 names, beginning with Brigadier Frank Hole Witts (1906), killed commanding the 8th Infantry Brigade, and ending with the 18-year-old Norman Dawe (1945), killed while serving as a Royal Artillery cadet, and Sergeant Air-Gunner Gordon Dean, of the Common Room staff. One name not on the list was that of Count Albrecht Bernstorff (Rhodes Scholar, Germany, 1909) who was executed for his part in the plot against Hitler. Nationally, losses in the Second World War were about half that of the First, but the proportion for Oxford University was considerably higher, and at Trinity it was over four-fifths of the number who fell in 1914–18. One reason for this was the high number of undergraduates joining the University Air Squadron, and thence the RAF, where casualty rates were appallingly high throughout the war. Over a third of Trinity's war dead were in the RAF, and flying seemed to have a particular appeal for many sportsmen: 'In a fighter plane, I believe,' said Richard Hillary, 'we have found a way to return to war as it ought to be, war which is individual combat between two people, in which one either kills or is killed.'[35] Six members of the 1938 VIII were killed on active service; four of those six, including Hillary, were in the RAF. One of the two survivors, Frank Waldron (who was seriously wounded serving with the Scots Guards), had been prevented from joining by air-sickness.[36]

At the end of the war Weaver looked forward with relief to the 'transition to approximately normal conditions', and was pleased

[34] JCR Minutes, A3/1, 201, 203, 207, 245.

[35] Paul Addison, 'Oxford and the Second World War', *HUO* 8, 180–1; Pat Utechin, *Sons of this Place: Commemoration of the War Dead in Oxford's Colleges and Institutions* (Oxford, 1998), 6; Hillary, *Last Enemy*, 16.

[36] The Marquis of Aberdeen, 'Captain F. A. L. Waldron', *Scots Guards Magazine* (1989).

that, as far as College sport was concerned, it seemed to be business as usual. 'Games and Athletics have been resumed in full measure,' he reported, 'and with a zest reflected in the unprecedented attendances of spectators at the Boat Race, at Lords, and at Twickenham.' In 1946 Trinity 'stroked by R.Wakeford, VC' retained the Headship of the River, and won cuppers in seven-a-side rugby, swimming, water-polo, and the Relay Races. In the first two years of postwar competition, the College had no less than twenty-four University representatives: at rugby football, cricket, association football, hockey, lawn tennis, squash, swimming, and Eton fives.[37] The demobbed Stephen Cooper returned to Trinity in October 1947, and was inspired to take up rowing the following February. He wrote in his diary: 'The great thrill of the term was the Torpid races. I think it was with them that I found my soul. I realised that once again I was an undergraduate. Trinity did very well and I decided that I would get myself into a Torpid next October.'[38]

The 1947 Bump Supper epitomized both the general sense of joy that things were back to normal, and the fact that nothing could ever be quite the same again. Michael de Lisle (Rhodes Scholar 1946), had arrived in Trinity after two years as a prisoner of war in Italy. He enjoyed the euphoria of 'true Epicurean happiness' and revelled in 'the deep shade under the limes and all the colours of grass and flowers' in the College garden. For him the bump supper was 'a great meal in hall', although 'rationing allowed no extras beyond a fish course.' The highlight of the evening celebration was when:

> an Exeter man from across the Broad (disguised in a Trinity blazer) came in to announce that fifty of their men were fighting inside Balliol with their backs to the wall. This was the signal for a general exodus, though most people dashed to don old clothes before the start of the real fun of the evening.[39]

One month earlier, on 19 April 1947, a service of Commemoration had been held in the Chapel, and another Roll of Honour placed in the War Memorial Library and antechapel, designed to match the board of the 1914–18 war. The Greek lines were chosen from a funeral oration of the orator Hyperides: 'never have men fought for a nobler

[37] *Report* (1944–6), 1, 18–19.

[38] TCA Cooper, Diary (1948, February 'memoranda').

[39] Michael de Lisle, *Over the Hills and Far Away* (Cape Town, 1999), 166–7.

*Table 12.1* Endowments of scholarships and undergraduate prizes 1938–1947.

| *Date* | *Donor* | *Value* | *Object* |
|---|---|---|---|
| 1938 | Frank Chadwick (1910) bequest | £23,000 | Open scholarship in modern languages; second scholarship in modern subjects |
| 1940 | William Dalrymple Fanshawe (scholar 1876) | £500 | Assistance of members reading for holy orders |
| 1940 | Walter Haskett-Smith (scholar 1878) | | Fund to give assistance to undergraduates |
| 1942 | John Evan Williams (1881) | £3,000 | Leaving exhibition from Marlborough School with preference to Trinity |
| 1943 | Colonel Geoffrey Christie-Miller (1900) in memory of Stephen Christie-Miller (1938) | £6,000 | Bursaries with preference to sons of Trinity men, otherwise unable to afford a university education |
| 1943 | Miss Alberta Wake Gearing in memory of her godson, Henry Melvin Young (1934) | £2,500 | Exhibition, with preference to ex-RAF men or sons of RAF men killed in the war |
| 1944 | Executors of H. E. D. Blakiston | £6,000 | One or more entrance or postgraduate scholarships or exhibitions. |
| 1945 | Basil Cozens-Hardy (1903) in memory of Graham S. Cozens-Hardy (1941) | £100 | Annual commoners' prize for jurisprudence |
| 1946 | Alan Francis Titley (1919) | £2,000 | Scholarship or Exhibition in Natural Science |

*Source*: *Report*; TCA Benefactors' Book IV.

cause or against a stronger enemy or with so few on their side.'[40] A committee of fellows and old members met to plan an appropriate memorial, and their decision chimed with the general feeling of facing up to a changed world. The 'visible part' of the memorial was to be a new gateway between the garden and the Garden Quadrangle. This was erected in September 1949, bearing a bronze plaque and an inscription devised by Tommy Higham: *Suos Domus Luget Laudet* (The College mourns and praises its own). But the main objective was to raise a fund 'to assist relatives of Trinity men (though not excluding others) to enter the College or to continue in residence, where need arises'. The period 1938–48 saw a remarkable number of scholarships and prizes endowed, all with the intention of preserving something of Trinity's pre-war spirit. Colonel Geoffrey Christie-Miller (1900) whose fourth son, Stephen, was killed at El Alamein, wanted preference 'to be given to the sons of former members of Trinity, and special regard paid to character and personality as judged by interview and record'. Holders of the Henry Melvin Young exhibition, named after a hero both of the Trinity Boat Club and of the 1943 Dam Busters raid, were intended to be 'former members of the Royal Air Force, or . . . the sons of those who have served and lost their lives in that service'. These exhibitions would help 'Commoners of the best type to come to the College' wrote Weaver in the *College Report*. Another benefactor was John Evan Williams, who both bequeathed money to the College and endowed a leaving exhibition from Marlborough. Weaver wrote somberly:

> Benefactions such as this, which help link the college to a great school, are of special value, and never more so than at the present time, when Colleges have to be taking thought for the maintenance of their numbers and their traditions in the difficult years which lie ahead.[41]

Weaver had no need to worry about falling numbers; but he was very right to fear the end of College traditions. Ironically, the stipulations of many of these named exhibitions were to be among the first casualties. State funding of higher education was soon to render such awards largely redundant.

[40] TCA Benefactions C/4. The lines are taken from *Eptaphios*, chapter 19; the translation is by Tommy Higham.

[41] *Report* (1941–2), 8; (1942–4), 16–17; (1944–6), 15.

## College Expansion under President Norrington

The most noticeable changes in the two decades following the Second World War were the increased size of the college and its increased financial dependence on the State. From these two closely linked factors, almost every significant development of the second half of the twentieth century has followed. Some external financial support had been available to individual students since 1902, in the form of grants from local education authorities, but this had been an insignificant drop in Trinity's coffers. In the immediate postwar years, however, the majority of Trinity undergraduates—and thus the College—were receiving funding from government sources.[42]

Numbers were up for the very obvious reason that servicemen were returning to finish their degrees: in 1946 and 1947, 90 per cent of places were reserved for them. This was an option even for those who had taken a war degree already; moreover, the government had in 1943 promised full grants to all whose higher education had been interrupted or deferred because of military service.[43] Now government spending policies continued to boost higher education. The 1944 Education Act, which extended compulsory education to the age of 16, sharply increased the potential number of applicants; and the University Grants Committee funded both additional teaching posts and improvements to accommodation, without which colleges would have found it harder to increase their numbers. Michaelmas Term 1948 saw a record number of 289 junior members at Trinity. The College was not used to having to turn candidates away. 'Owing to state aid, the pressure of numbers on the University continues to be severe,' wrote Weaver in 1949. And yet, the increased number of undergraduates was undeniably useful: 'as their swollen numbers decline, the Colleges . . . will have to face increasing financial stringency.' Whereas before the war, internal revenue (fees, charges, and trust funds) had been about equal to external ones (estates and investments), by 1950 internal revenue totalled £26,500 and external £17,000.[44] The decision was made 'to stabilize the number at

[42] Daniel I. Greenstein, 'The Junior Members, 1900–1990, a profile', H.O 8, 46, 49; J. P. D. Dunbadin, 'Finance since 1914', ibid., 672.

[43] Addison, 'Second World War', 186–7.

[44] 'Trinity College', *Abstracts of the Accounts of the Colleges* (Oxford, 1935).

*12.2* Trinity College group, 1950. President Weaver is twelfth from the left in the front row. To his left are Austin Farrer, Michael Maclagan, Tommy Higham, and James Lambert. To Weaver's right are the President of the JCR, Philip Landon, and Patrick Nowell-Smith.

approximately 200' by 1953, when the ex-service boom would have ended. Weaver calculated this as a 17 per cent increase on the pre-war figure, and 37 per cent higher than in 1914.[45]

More difficult decisions were required during the presidency of Weaver's successor, Arthur Lionel Pugh Norrington (commonly known as Tommy). 'We all knew Weaver was due to retire in 1952,' recalled James Lambert, 'and had two definite Trinity candidates in mind.' It fell to Lambert, as Vice-President, to make the necessary enquiries. The first, Robert Hall, said 'he really didn't want to leave his present job so early,' but Arthur Norrington offered to 'come in two years. So we simply chose Norrington, and prolonged Weaver with the Visitor's permission.' There was no job description, and certainly no advertising.[46]

Norrington was an extra-professorial fellow of the College—as Secretary to the Delegates of the Oxford University Press—and he was also a Trinity old member. He had matriculated in 1919, so had first-hand experience of life in an over-crowded college. As President he was energetic, compassionate, and visionary. In the fifteen years of his presidency, Trinity was to undergo a radical transformation. Initially, Norrington was reluctant to expand the College any further. The number of 200 allowed every member to live in College for two years, 'to the great benefit of the undergraduates, as we believe', he wrote in 1956. Trinity was now the third smallest college in the University, above only Hertford and Corpus, but its size could not be pegged for long. In an article on 'Numbers in Residence' in the *College Report* for 1952–6, Norrington predicted a coming 'emergency'—the postwar baby boom, which was likely to bring a 40 per cent increase in applicants around 1964–6. Trinity planned to respond to the 'bulge' by increasing the intake by 10 to 15 per cent, reaching a new total of 230 during 1963–6.[47] But then, with the sudden ending of national service in 1958, the College was faced by an unexpected and early 'crush', when the school-leavers of 1956 and 1957 competed for places with those of 1958 and 1959. It was agreed to meet this crisis by increasing admissions from October 1957, and limiting undergraduates to just 'four or five terms living in college'.[48]

[45] *Report* (1947–8), 4; (1947–9), 1, 4–5.

[46] The nickname Didymus (Doubting Thomas) derived from his arrival at Winchester College, when he questioned many school customs. See the obituary by Michael Maclagan, *Report* (1982–4), unpaginated; T. C. A. Lambert, reminiscences on presidential elections.

[47] *Report* (1952–6), 7–8.

[48] Ibid., (1956–8), 3–4.

## *The Quatercentenary*

The possibility of new accommodation was mooted as early as 1956, but first there was the pressing problem of the existing College buildings, most of which were in serious need of renovation.[49] During 1954, some £8,000 was spent on urgent repairs to the Jackson Building, the Hall, and the President's Lodgings. In February 1955 the bursar, Patrick Nowell-Smith, estimated that another £80,000 would be needed to complete a twenty-year programme of work, which would include restoration of the stonework of the Chapel and Garden Quadrangle. Here the soft Headington freestone used in the seventeenth and eighteenth centuries had suffered particularly badly from air pollution, reacting with sulphur dioxide to form a vulnerable and flaking skin of calcium sulphate. The problem was by no means unique; the characteristic appearance of much of Oxford at this date was of black and blistering antiquity. Much of Trinity's disfigurement was hidden beneath the creepers that covered the Garden Quad, the south face of the Chapel, and the north side of the Durham Quad, although the creepers too were suspected of causing damage.[50]

The financial implications of such widespread decay were serious. The college was already running an annual deficit of some £3,000, which was due largely to the sharply rising cost of running the College. Charges to undergraduates were being increased steadily—Robin Fletcher hoped to raise a 'small surplus' in 1955[51]—but there was no likelihood of funding the necessary work out of ordinary revenue. Trinity made another loss on its domestic operations in 1960, when it was agreed to increase charges by £5 a term, and begin accepting conferences the following year. It was 'a ticklish business', admitted Nowell-Smith to the bursar of Queen's, writing on the instruction of the Governing Body to discuss the possibility that the Estates Bursars' Committee might petition the government to support colleges' buildings as it did their undergraduates.[52] In 1954 Trinity agreed to set up a Building Fund, to appeal for financial help from old members, and to assign several recent benefactions to this urgent need. A

[49] Ibid., 8.
[50] 'Oxford Historic Buildings Appeal' circular (TCA Maclagan, 'Trinity College' album).
[51] Report on 'College Accounts 1954', TCA Bursarial Minutes 1948–55.
[52] Ibid., 21 August 1952.

particularly valuable bequest—his entire estate, including copyrights—had been received in 1948 from the novelist and playwright A. E. W. Mason (1884). Besides regular royalties, Trinity could negotiate large payments for the sale of film rights. In 1952, for example, a five-year extension of rights on *The Four Feathers* was sold for £1,500, and on *The Drum* for £750.[53] A particularly welcome addition was the large and unexpected bequest of Hugh C. Cumberbatch (1904), nephew of another major Trinity benefactor, H. C. Moffatt (1878). Cumberbatch left almost his entire estate to Trinity, including his uncle's extensive collection of English silver and furniture. Death duties were particularly heavy (just £65,000 of an estate valued at over £300,000 came to the College), but the bequest was nonetheless a timely and useful one. The furniture (subject to double death duties if sold) was distributed through the College rooms.

The year 1955 was the quatercentenary of Trinity's foundation. As Norrington admitted, it was 'an occasion for which no recorded precedents afforded any guidance', but the celebrations, orchestrated by Trinity's domestic bursar, Robin Fletcher, and his St John's counterpart (St John's being just six months younger) were universally acclaimed as a triumph. On Monday 20 June, a joint ball was held, on a scale never before attempted. There were three dance floors, 1,250 dancers, and a bridge over the wall between the two college gardens, and it was 'a beautiful night, leading into a cloudless dawn'. On 27 June (Trinity Saturday), Trinity held a commemoration service at the Cathedral, with an address by Kenneth Warner, Bishop of Edinburgh (Trinity 1909), and the *Te Deum* sung to a setting by Basil Harwood (1877). In the afternoon Trinity and St John's shared a joint garden party—'a family affair, with no outside guests'—and in the evening a joint concert of chamber music in St John's, followed by a cold supper and fireworks in the Trinity garden. 'A most friendly message of congratulations' was received from the Master and fellows of Balliol College, and a telegram from the Vice-Chancellor of Durham University, 'mindful of our ancient connection'.[54] Trinity and St John's were fêted in the local and national press. There were lengthy articles in *Country Life*, *The Times*, the *Manchester Guardian*, and the *Observer*, while the *Illustrated London News* commissioned and published a series of drawings of college life by Bryan de Grineau. Michael

[53] *Report* (1952–6), 8; TCA Accounts, Bursarial Committee Minutes 1948–55.

[54] 'The Quatercentenary', *Report* (1952–6), 23–5.

Maclagan produced a 'delightfully written and informative' College history, and was invited to give a talk on BBC Radio Midland.[55] Another notable event of the year was the erection of a new effigy of the Founder in the niche above the entrance to Hall.

The Quatercentenary Appeal was launched in November 1955, with a target of £100,000. By July 1956 gifts and promises of £42,000 had been received, and by the end of December 1957 over 900 individuals had subscribed. The College was now in regular, formal contact with its alumni, not merely by means of the *Report*, but also through the agency of the newly established Trinity Society. The Society was formed by, and for, the College's old members, and owed much to the energy of its first chairman, Sir Cecil Kisch (1903). The first meeting was held at the United University Club on 2 July 1954, and its first Oxford weekend was attended by some eighty Trinity men in October 1956. Besides maintaining contact between College friends—an early project was a comprehensive address book—the Society's second objective was to support and enhance the life of the College. Gifts of the Society in the early years included a set of three engraved glass goblets, by Laurence Whistler, which were placed in a cabinet in the Senior Common Room.[56]

Despite the generosity of Trinity's members, the greater part of the cost of restoring the buildings was eventually met by the University of Oxford's Historic Buildings Fund Appeal, which was launched in May 1957 and in fifteen months had reached its target of £1.75 million. A supplementary appeal for £500,000, launched in 1963, met its target within a year. Trinity was one of twelve colleges assisted by this fund to transform their dark and crumbling piles into the smooth pale edifices, with their clear lines and sharp corners, which seem so characteristic of Oxford today.

The work began in September 1957, on the north side of the Durham Quad. Working on a 'big climbing-frame of scaffolding' masons removed the top six inches of stone, and set in its place new blocks of Bath stone. They proceeded to the north side of the Garden Quad (the front of Staircases 15 and 16), which was completed in the spring of 1959, and then to the south (Front Quad) side of the Chapel. This was a project which brought the College 'near to

[55] *Country Life* (23 June 1955); *The Times* (24 June 1955); *Manchester Guardian* (25 June 1955); *Illustrated London News* (25 June 1955), 1143–6; *Radio Times* (17 June 1955).
[56] *Report* (1952–6), 22–3.

*12.3* Staircase 16 during refacing work, August 1958.

disaster' during the Easter Vacation of 1959. In order to remove the stained glass windows, internal scaffolding was erected in the Chapel, and 'inflammable soft-board' put down to protect the top of the panelling. But, as Norrington explained in the *College Report*:

> It was laid in contact with the metal reflectors of two assemblies of concealed lighting . . . It was not long before the trap was sprung. Soon after dark somebody—presumably a party of visitors—turned on the lights for long enough to set the soft-board smouldering, turned them out again, and left in innocent ignorance of what they had set in train. At about 6.30 the soft-board burst into flames.

The fire brigade were quickly called, and the fire was extinguished. But then

> a Fire Officer came back, about 10.30 p.m., to see if all was well, [and] he turned on the lights again . . . This period of illumination was long enough to cause the next length of soft board to start smouldering, and some time before midnight flames broke out

> again. It was the vacation, and there would normally have been 'no one about in the quad', but fortunately Mrs Norrington was giving a dance for her younger daughter's 21st birthday . . . An amateur fire-fighting squad from the Lodgings was at work in a few seconds . . . But it was a narrow escape, and some of us got no sleep that night.[57]

The main surfaces of the Chapel were refaced in Bath stone, with Portland at ground level, and Clipsham for the window sills and the capitals of the pilasters. Next up was the Tower, where, although 'the four ladies [had] suffered greatly from exposure', the decision was made not to attempt the replacement of the statues, mainly owing to 'the practical difficulty of providing substitutes' and the realization that they 'might not please'.[58] 1961 saw work completed on the west side of the kitchen—'necessary . . . but only visible from Balliol'—and a beginning made on the north side of the Chapel, which was finished the following summer. In 1963 it was the turn of the west side of the Garden Quadrangle (the front of Staircases 12 and 13), and in 1964 of the Old Library side of the Durham Quad ('washing [and] some minor patching and renewals'), the piers to the gates on Parks Road ('perished beyond repair'), and Kettell Hall. The very last buildings to be done were the south side of the Garden Quadrangle, the east face of the Hall, and the south face of the Common Room. By the end of 1967 the tremendous work of restoration was declared complete. The final cost had been over £200,000, of which three quarters had come from the Oxford Historic Buildings Fund.[59]

A considerable amount of other work had been going on at the same time. In 1948, 'a notable, and noticeable, addition to the College buildings' was the gatehouse built between the Dolphin Yard and St Giles. This building was designed as a flat for a married fellow, and until 1965 was the home of the chaplain, Austin Farrer, who worked 'in a room at the top of the house, to which he gave the Aristophanic title of Phrontisterion (thinking shop)'.[60] In 1954 the capacity of the War Memorial Library was increased by a third by the

[57] *Report* (1959), 12–13.

[58] Ibid. (1960), 13–14. The opportunity was taken to put back the original statue of medicine, which had been placed in the President's garden when new statues were made in 1822.

[59] *Report* (1961), 13; (1962), 13; (1963), 18–19; (1964), 12; (1965), 11; (1966), 13–14; (1967), 15. In fact, a certain amount of work remained, including the St John's side of the garden quad (finished in 1979) and the east wall of the Chapel (postponed indefinitely in 1979).

[60] Curtis, *Hawk Among Sparrows*, 125.

construction of a gallery along the eastern side. At the same time, the 'damp and unhealthy' Common Room Stores was redesigned with improved access and 'up-to-date equipment', while the 'old JCR' above the buttery was 'enlarged, redecorated, and provided with a bar'.[61] The 'mean and unsanitary' porter's cottage in the Dolphin Yard was demolished and replaced by garages for fellows' cars, and a two-storey flat above. The first occupant was Alexander Mulligan, Norrington's butler and SCR steward.

In the Long Vacation of 1959 the College was confronted by 'an unexpected emergency' when the Hall ceiling was found to be in a highly dangerous condition, likely to collapse at any time. 'The Incorporated Association of Preparatory Schools was about to hold its annual and time-honoured conference here, and it was decided to take a chance on the ceiling staying up a few days longer,' wrote Norrington nonchalantly in the *College Report*. Then, in September, the eighteenth-century plaster was pulled down. The new ceiling, put up in the Long Vacation of 1960, was an 'exact replica' of the original—thereby qualifying for a grant from the Oxford Historic Buildings Fund—but with 'modification of the plaster' intended to absorb and deaden sound. The walls and ceiling were decorated in a bold and modern paint scheme, primarily yellow and grey, with touches of red in the ceiling. The finishing touch was 'modern "chandelier" lighting', in the guise of white plastic pendant shades (Plate 12.4). The finished effect 'surpassed our expectations', said Norrington and all agreed it had been done just in time. For on 4 November 1960, Trinity was honoured with a visit by the Queen and Prince Philip, who came to Oxford to lay the foundation stone of St Catherine's College and to lunch with the Vice-Chancellor (Norrington) in his college. The royal standard was flown from the Chapel tower, Her Majesty took sherry in the Lodgings, and 'connexions and friends of the College, with their families, thronged the lawn in the front quadrangle.' The lunch that followed in Hall has achieved semi-mythical status for the number of things that went splendidly awry. Prince Philip, on hearing an explanation of the celebrated 'Trinity Salad' (a Robert Raper creation, 'inspired by a passage in the 11th book of Homer's *Iliad*'), replied, 'That's all right, I have been brought up to eat *whatever* is put in front of me.' During the meal the Lord Lieutenant fainted, and, on being given the news by the Regius Professor of

[61] *Report* (1947–8), 15; (1952–6), 37; Bursarial Committee Minutes, 21 March 1955.

12.4 Hall lunch, cafeteria style.

Medicine, his wife fainted too. Next on the floor was the most senior of the College scouts, Richard Cadman (then three months short of his eighty-seventh birthday), who had tripped on a trailing gown.

Finally, the catalogue of mishaps culminated in a near-disaster for the Chancellor, who was resuming his seat after proposing the Loyal Toast. The scene was described by Robin Fletcher:

> The chair, behind which the vigilant Mr Mulligan (a scout) had been stationed for its withdrawal and propulsion, refused to move forward into place. It had become entangled in the Cancellarial gown and Mr Macmillan, Prime Minister at the time, sat down on thin air and almost to the ground before the situation could be retrieved. He is said to have uttered no complaint but simply to have enquired, 'Is the Press present?' to which luckily the answer was 'no'.

Most of these details came out a long time later. But no absence of journalists would have prevented the furore had an eighteenth-century plaster ceiling come down on the heads of the Queen, the Prime Minister, and the assembled 'Heads of Houses, Professors, and other prominent people in the University, and City, all the Fellows and Emeritus Fellows of the College, and twenty undergraduates, chosen by lot by the JCR'. The Queen had coffee afterwards with undergraduates selected to represent the colleges and achievements of the University. 'We've had a wonderful lunch,' she remarked to David Evers, the JCR Secretary, 'bodies all over the place.'[62]

## *New Buildings*

Another area of College found to be in dangerously poor shape was the Broad Street cottages. The 1937 'rough cast facing' was now 'shabby and unsightly'; the 'seventeenth-century masonry beneath was in . . . a parlous state'; and the rooms, Norrington felt, 'ranked very low as "comfort stations" in the technical sense'.[63] In a compromise between an efficient new building and a restoration of an important part of Broad Street's architectural legacy, the front façade

[62] *Report* (1960), 1–2. I am indebted to Hugo Brunner (1954) for his ongoing researches into this event. See his article 'The Queen and the Duke of Edinburgh at Trinity', *Report* (1998), 43–4.

[63] *Report* (1965), 12. The cottages, of course, were particularly lacking as 'comfort stations' in the modern sense too.

*12.5* The Cottages during restoration work in June 1968.

of the cottages was carefully rebuilt and refaced in stucco, behind which a new porter's lodge and undergraduate rooms were erected 'within the existing roof-line'. The architects were Pinckheard & Partners, and the builders Kingerlee Ltd. In 1972 the project won a Civic Trust award.[64]

The restoration was an expensive undertaking, costing around £70,000, with no real enlargement of the College achieved. In 1969 a new fund-raising appeal was launched, partly to pay for the work on the cottages, partly to endow further tutorial fellowships, and partly to finance out-of-college accommodation. The request was curiously understated: 'We meant to launch an Appeal more than two years ago,' said Norrington's circular letter, 'but the financial climate was discouraging. It is not encouraging now, but time presses.' This time the target set was £200,000. Old members stumped up loyally, and in three years just short of three quarters of this sum had been raised.

There were few projects of the Norrington years that were to prove unsuccessful, but one was the widespread replacement of coal fires by electric heaters. The President's hope that 'any loss of antique cosiness will be made up for, or at least condoned, by the saving in labour and convenience, and perhaps by an increase in actual warmth' was sadly wrong on the latter count. In the exceptionally cold winter of 1962–3, Terry Bird (1960) lived on the ground floor of Staircase 12, where his electric fire generated just enough heat to cast a red glow on the floor. He witnessed:

> on too many occasions for any doubt, an astonishing sight. The mice came out and lay in straight lines along the red reflection from the two-bar electric fire as it struck the floor. This struck me as an amazing natural phenomenon, part of the privilege of being at Oxford. If Virgil had seen this, perhaps he would have described it in the Georgics.

In 'the pre-Christmas cold spell' of 1976, domestic bursar Richard Popplewell discovered by experiment that 'in one room . . . both bars of the fire (5p per hour) served only to raise the ambient temperature from 6 to 9° C.' His proposal to install gas fires instead was adopted *nem. con.*[65]

[64] *Report* (1968), 16–17; TCA Accounts, BF 17/2.

[65] Terry Bid, 'Mice Again', *Report* (2001), 81; TCA BF 3/10 'Magistratos', 'Heating of college rooms—proposal to install gas fires', 2 May 1977.

A heavy load fell on the members of the Bursarial Committee during Norrington's presidency. The committee consisted of the President, both bursars—Nowell-Smith was replaced by John F. Wright in 1955—and various members of the Governing Body. Besides the ongoing building programme within College, the College estates demanded their attention. One particular problem was Wroxton Abbey, the Jacobean house built by Thomas Pope's nephew, which had for centuries been the centrepiece of Trinity's most valuable estate. But the historical connection with the North family (indirectly descended from the Founder) had been broken when the eleventh Lord North had died in 1932, at the age of 96. The contents of the house had been sold at auction (Trinity purchasing the fine contemporary portrait of Thomas Pope, which now hangs in the Lodgings), but the College had experienced considerable difficulty in finding a new tenant or purchaser. The house had finally been let to one Lady Pearson, who by 1959 had eight years to run on her lease. She ran a restaurant, and opened the house to the public. In July 1960, at the age of 80, Lady Pearson gave an interview to the *Oxford Times*: 'We never thought of "showing" at first, but keeping up a large Jacobean house is difficult.'[66] The Abbey's roof alone needed £25,000 to repair it, and a report by the College surveyor gave the forty-bedroomed property a 'minimal' value, with the possibility of raising £4,000 to £8,000—and the probability of engendering considerable 'odium'—if it was sold 'for demolition'.[67]

Rather tentatively, the College put Wroxton Abbey on the market in the spring of 1963, with an advertisement in *The Times* welcoming private offers in advance of a public auction. And, not for the first or the last time, a Trinity man came forward to help: Loyd Haberly (Rhodes Scholar 1921), now Dean of Arts of Farleigh Dickinson University, New Jersey. The house was sold to Farleigh Dickinson for £30,000 and, after extensive refurbishment, began a new existence as an 'overseas campus' for graduate students 'in History or Literature', with a new name, Wroxton College, and Haberly as the first Principal.[68] At the other end of the housing spectrum, Trinity's cottages were becoming another financial liability. Trinity owned some sixty cottages in Wroxton and Balscote. They were stone-built with

[66] *Oxford Times* (29 July 1960).

[67] 'Wroxton Abbey', Bursarial Committee Minutes, Jan. 1959; 'Wroxton Abbey', *Report* (1963), 8–9. [68] TCA Accounts, BF 8/2 'Wroxton College'.

thatched roofs, and the College surveyor considered that their 'uniform and unspoilt appearance' made Wroxton 'one of the prettiest villages in North Oxfordshire'. They were also in poor repair, and had inadequate water supplies and drainage. Most were occupied by workers from the aluminium factory and the ironstone company, who paid an average rent of 4*s* a week, while the estimated cost of new thatching alone was £700. The College agent recommended they should be sold, wherever possible, to the tenants, who could undertake their own modernization. In 1954 seven cottages were disposed of, raising £2,000, and it was agreed the College might have to accept £100 or less for others.

The College meanwhile was investing heavily in the College farms, by building barns and workers' cottages, concreting yards, and improving water supplies.[69] An increasingly important source of income from Wroxton was from opencast ironstone mining (the first agreement had been signed during the First World War), although this involved the College in unpleasant controversy in 1958, when John Wright was forced to defend Trinity's policies in the letters page of the *Oxford Magazine*. The bursar was proud of the College's commitment to the local community and environment, and he wrote of 'miles of hedges and thousands of trees planted' while he claimed the fertility of the land was often improved.[70] By this date the estates were playing a more minor part in Trinity's finances, since an increasing amount of the College's endowment was now invested in securities and equities.

The main preoccupation of the Bursarial Committee, and perhaps the greatest of all the achievements of the Norrington years, was the erection of a new building, and the total redesign of the entire south-east area of the College site. This included the ramshackle premises of 53 Broad Street, renamed Marriott House in honour of Charles B. Marriott (1886) who had bequeathed his residuary estate to the College in 1946. By 1960 several possibilities were being discussed, and serious consideration was given to two alternative schemes that would provide a minimum of twenty-five sets, two or three fellows' rooms, and a new lecture room. One was a large U-shaped building on the site of the cottages, which would project northwards into the

[69] Report 'College Estates—Capital Improvements', 1952, Bursarial Committee Minutes 1948–55.

[70] TCA Accounts BF 7/7; *Oxford Magazine* (23 Oct., 13 Nov., 20 Nov. 1958).

front quadrangle; the other was a taller block situated at the south end of the rose garden.[71]

Then, in February 1961, Robin Fletcher suggested that the College consider the possibility of building at the north end of the rose garden, with a projection northwards into the garden from the Library. Fletcher and Norrington were eager to use the modern ideas of 'a young man on his mettle', and opened negotiations with the Surrey-based architects, Robert Maguire and Keith Murray. The first plans for the new building were produced in January 1963. They included a 'revamp' of the Library façade, the demolition of Blakiston's ornate entrance, a four-storey block with semi-basement fellows' rooms and a ground-floor lecture room, a 'swimming pool' in the rose garden, and more undergraduate sets linking Kettell Hall and the Blackwell's building. The response from the fellows was favourable in principle, but concern was raised at the estimated cost of £156,000. The swimming pool was costed at £4,500: Fletcher envisaged 'something small and refreshing for the hottest months. It is intended for the use of Fellows and undergraduates, should probably be about 5′ deep and needs to have water running through it.'[72]

It was agreed in March 1963 that such a luxurious feature could be dispensed with. Fletcher insisted that the College was 'not concerned to be uneconomically parsimonious', but still the cost could hardly be justified.[73] It was time to begin negotiations with another well-placed Trinity man, this time Julian Blackwell (1950). Blackwell's bookshop had been using the Library basement for storage since it was opened in 1928, and the company needed to expand its premises further. It was agreed that Trinity should build an extensive basement beneath the Library quadrangle, which would be leased to Blackwell's on a twenty-one-year lease at a rent based on 9 per cent of the capital outlay (estimated at £60,000).[74] 'The whole plan was worked up with the interests of both parties in mind,' said Robin Fletcher in the *Oxford Magazine*, and the arrangement was indeed to prove profitable for all concerned.[75] The work was scheduled to start in the summer of 1964, and was completed in time for the residents to move

[71] TCA Accounts BF 4/3, 'Architect's Partnership'.
[72] Ibid., BF4/4, Fletcher to Maguire, 21 Nov. 1962, Estimated Costs 4 Dec. 1962.
[73] Ibid., 29 March 1963.
[74] Ibid., JFW to Ministry of Agriculture, 26 May 1964.
[75] R. A. Fletcher, 'The Cumberbatch Quadrangle at Trinity College', *Oxford Magazine*, (Trinity Term 1966).

*12.6* Architect's model of the New Buildings, 1964.

in (lacking only curtains and desks) at the start of Michaelmas Term 1965.

On Trinity Monday, 6 June 1966, the new buildings were opened by Tony Crosland, former fellow in economics, now Secretary of State for Education and Science. Crosland declared himself 'delighted that the new development had not cost a penny of public money. "There is no quicker way to my heart",' he told the *Oxford Times*.[76] The two blocks of accommodation were named the Cumberbatch Building North (Staircase 4) and the Cumberbatch Building South (Staircase 3), in honour of the benefactor who had helped finance their

[76] *Oxford Times* (10 June 1966).

construction. Following the speeches, refreshments were served in the new lecture room, which had been named the Danson Room, after another major College benefactor, Colonel John R. Danson (1910). The College was now larger by thirty sets of rooms (including six in Marriott House), and four additional rooms for fellows. The design of the new building was a delicate combination of modern and traditional concepts. The building materials were the very latest, with concrete blocks and ribbed rubber flooring, but residents still had separate bedrooms and sitting rooms. Staircase 3 had six 'duplex' rooms, which were half-way to bedsits, with steep steps up to a sleeping platform above the door. One short-lived feature of the new development was a small fountain between Kettell Hall and the Blackwell's Building. As the 1976 *College Report* explained:

> Recent members who recall with affection the simple pleasure of testing the efficiency of their favourite brand of soap powder by sprinkling it into the fountain . . . will no doubt be sad to learn that the Bursar has given up the struggle and had it planted with bulbs.[77]

The College was extremely proud of what had been done. Fletcher praised the architects fulsomely: 'the texture of their buildings, blue engineering brick to first floor level, shuttered concrete and panels of 8 inch square concrete blocks above, with teak windows and slated roofs, blends well with the stone of the neighbouring buildings.'[78] But the greatest publicity was given to the official opening, on 16 June, of the 'superb grotto' that was the new Blackwell's basement, now to be called the Norrington Room. The room contained 160,000 books on two and a half miles of shelves, and was to feature in the *Guinness Book of Records* as 'the largest underground bookseller's space in the world'.[79]

## *Expansion of the Fellowship*

The new fellows' accommodation was badly needed, for the fellowship had been growing in line with the increase in junior members.

[77] *Report* (1976), 22. [78] Fletcher, 'Cumberbatch Quadrangle'.
[79] e.g. *The Guinness Book of Records*, 17th edn., ed. Norris and Ross McWhirter (London, 1972), 146.

A significant event in the University's development was the 1949 decision by the University Grants Committee (UGC) to recognize the dual status of College tutors who were also University lecturers, by contributing to their salaries from the Common University Fund (CUF), thereby making it possible for colleges to finance additional posts.[80] In 1949 Trinity's Governing Body had comprised the President, eleven fellows, and three professorial fellows. Several new faces were familiar ones: Anthony Crosland (scholar 1937) replaced Robert Hall in 1947; James Holladay (scholar 1939) succeeded Ronald Syme in 1949; and Robin Fletcher (1946) already University lecturer in modern Greek, was elected in December 1950, to assume the role of domestic bursar in 1951. Additional fellows were elected to meet the College's expanding teaching requirements. In 1952 Trinity elected its first fellow in modern languages, Frank Barnett, who was chosen from 'an exceptionally large field', to meet 'an urgent need'.[81] A second modern linguist, Cyril Jones, was appointed fellow in Spanish in 1963, as part of an arrangement to share the teaching of 'minority subjects' with St John's and Worcester College. Two years later, English had its own Trinity tutor again (the first since Reginald Tiddy) in the shape of a fourteenth tutorial fellow, Dennis Burden. New professorial appointments included the first occupant of the chair of the history of art, Edgar Wind, in 1955, and David Lack, Director of the Edward Grey Institute of Field Ornithology, in 1963.

The most rapid growth in the University as a whole was in the area of science. In 1964 Peter Fisher was appointed as Trinity's first fellow in physics, and Irving Wood took up a research fellowship, his work based at the National Institute for Research in Nuclear Science at Chilton. In the last year of Norrington's presidency, 1969, the College appointed its first fellow in politics and sociology, Roderick Martin. There were now twenty-four members of the Governing Body: the President, eighteen tutorial fellows, and five professorial ones. In 1970 two additional new members became fellows by special election: Alistair Crombie, University lecturer in the history of science, and Peter Hazzledine, University lecturer in metallurgy. To accommodate their growing number, in 1965 the SCR took over the

[80] 'Finance since 1914', *HUO* 8, 652–3.

[81] *Report* (1950–2), 2.

'tower rooms' above the chapel arch, which were renamed the Landon Room.

## *The Middle Common Room*

The days of a recent graduate proceeding directly to a College fellowship had passed, but those intermediate stages of academic promotion that are today taken for granted were only just developing in the 1960s. Trinity advertised its first two Junior Research Fellowships in 1967. Three years earlier the College had recognized the needs of postgraduates within the community of junior members by the appointment of Cyril Jones as its first Tutor for Graduates. In 1964, Trinity had twenty-nine postgraduate students, twelve reading for the D.Phil., six for the Diploma in Education, five for the B.Phil., three for the B.Litt., two on the 'Overseas Service Course', and one reading for the Certificate in Statistics. Less than half of them were Trinity graduates; several were married. The Middle Common Room came into being on 11 November 1964, when its founding members 'dined as a corporate body in the Gallery of Hall', and on 12 May 1965 an inaugural committee meeting was held in the Tower rooms. The MCR's first president was Christopher Brearley (1961), its secretary Michael Jones (1960), and its committee comprised Alexander Mackinnon (1955), Christopher Jackson (1963), and David Hamer (1964). Priorities at their first meeting centred on their college rights: they wanted representation on the Furniture Committee for the new building, and on the Library Committee. In their second meeting, on 8 June, the committee concentrated on amenities: 'an actual MCR room', with 'coffee making machinery'. For the first year they budgeted on a turnover of £150 (£1 per member per term). By October Trinity's graduates had acquired a room on Staircase 11 (they moved to Kettell Hall in 1973), and the 'drinks cupboard was now open'; indeed, the pleasures and problems of trusting members to pay for their drinks have been a perennial theme of MCR history. On hearing that Cyril Jones was to become Senior Tutor, the MCR resolved to 'exert diplomatic pressure' to demand the appointment of their own choice of Tutor for Graduates, Dennis Burden.[82]

[82] TCA MCR 1, 2, 5.

## Student Identity

Such an act of self-determination would have been unthinkable to pre-war 'commoners' of the College. It must be time to start using the word 'student'. Norrington accepted the designation with some reluctance, first using it in the *College Report* of 1958 as 'a convenient American term' to describe junior members, both undergraduates and graduates.[83] The traditional 'undergraduate' was accustomed not to question disciplinary rules (however much he might seek to flout them) or the decisions of the Governing Body, and he owed his strongest loyalty to his College. But this model did not work so well for the young men of the 1950s. The two decades following the Second World War saw a growing resistance to the traditional College rules. They were still enforced, but with dwindling conviction. The gate hours were particularly inappropriate for battle-hardened army officers, or those who had been held (unsuccessfully in the case of Michael de Lisle, for he had twice escaped) as prisoners of war. The wave of high spirits that accompanied the postwar generation to Oxford turned most of the restrictions into a game. De Lisle's most famous exploit was to climb into Balliol College via an open window on Broad Street, only to find himself trespassing in the bedroom of the Master and his wife.[84] For Stephen Cooper, the complicated route by which he (and three female friends) climbed into College on the last night of Eights 1949 was a highlight of his Oxford life:

> I changed out of my D.J. & went into the Broad. Proctors very busy & not much excitement. At midnight I met three nurses from the Wingfield whom I knew slightly & we all climbed into Trinity by way of St John's. When we got to the Bursary we ran into one of the dons and decided to evacuate. I got scratched going through the Pres. Garden. We nearly ran into some more Dons in the garden. Great fun & it was something I had wanted to do for a long time.[85]

Ten years later the College rules were still there to be broken, and the repercussions could still be grave. Ian Flintoff (1957) successfully

[83] *Report* (1958), 5 [84] De Lisle, *Over the Hills*, 168.
[85] TCA Cooper, Diary (25 May 1949).

ignored a gating by crawling on his hands and knees beneath the split door of the Lodge, but in Trinity Term 1959 he was very famously sent down (while playing Hamlet) for having a woman staying in his rooms. 'It was a very serious breach of the college regulations,' Norrington allegedly said to *The Times*. According to the *Daily Mail*, Flintoff said 'I don't bear any ill will for either the President or the Dean . . . The thing that annoys me is the regulations as they stand.'[86]

It takes a 'student' to criticize his Alma Mater in the national press. Students identify with a national, even an international community of those that study; they are approximately equal in dress and wealth; they know their rights, and they question the rules that govern them.[87] In theory the 1962 introduction of maintenance grants and the payment of fees by local education authorities rendered all students financially equal; in practice it meant that the poor were not as poor as they once might have been. In theory it also meant that students would be admitted from a wider range of social backgrounds; in practice Trinity remained for many years a bastion of the independent schools. In 1951 Trinity's Senior Tutor, Tommy Higham, began keeping individual files to control the growing quantities of paperwork that admissions now required. The College was in a group of colleges for a shared admissions process, but this did not interfere with the President and tutors' control of the selection procedure, and it seemed only natural to Higham to favour candidates on the traditional grounds of class and family. One individual's file from 1953 contains a note from Philip Landon, 'The boy referred to is the heir to [a] baronetcy. He sounds attractive,' while another includes a pedigree drawn up by Michael Maclagan to show the candidate's descent from an Irish earl. Higham corresponded with one of his own former pupils about their shared desire to have a third generation of the family at Trinity.[88]

In 1960 Michael Maclagan, who had succeeded Higham as Senior Tutor two years earlier, wrote to the *Guardian* to deny an explicit slur in the previous day's leader column. 'Selection is made by the whole body of teaching fellows,' he insisted, 'and it is their policy to admit the best candidates from as wide an entry as possible.'[89] The

[86] Ian Flintoff, 'Memories of Cadman', *Report* (2003), 83; *The Times* (12 June 1959); *Daily Mail* (12 June 1959). A 'gating' was confinement to the College premises in the evening.

[87] See Keith Thomas, 'College Life', *HUO* 8, 204–5.

[88] TCA Admissions.

[89] *Guardian* (11 May 1960).

published statistics suggested otherwise. In April 1961, the *Oxford Magazine*, followed by various local and national papers, identified Trinity as the College with the highest proportion—80.6 per cent—of admissions from independent schools. Second highest was Christ Church, with 70 per cent. Further statistics proved that those colleges 'at the top of the list socially . . . [were] academically near the bottom of the list with under 50% of Firsts and Seconds'. 'More good boys apply to us from Independent Schools,' argued Maclagan. He also wrote to the *Daily Telegraph*: 'The college tries to give the sons of old members a decent run for their money. But they are not preferred to better candidates who have no connection with the college.'[90]

The belief that Trinity favoured public-school candidates and members of particular families was one that affected the College for many years, even after it was no longer the case. The same was true of Trinity's reputation for racism. The Indian Rhodes Scholar T. R. Anantharaman (1951) detected a link:

> It became obvious to me within a few days of my entering the portals of Trinity in October 1951 . . . that my admission was not all that welcome to many at the College, particularly the large group of Etonians there. Some of the grammar school boys assured me that I had nothing to worry about, since they also felt equally unwelcome, the public school boys looking down on them also!

Anantharaman 'rather enjoyed . . . [his] special status and importance as the first "black man" in Trinity' and he had no difficulty in making friends. In some ways a turning-point for both him and the College was one particularly unpleasant incident in 1953, when he persuaded an African friend ('a paramount chief from the Gold Coast') to join him for dinner in Hall:

> The moment my friend and I reached my usual table in the bottom right hand corner of the Hall that night I could sense some tension all around and overheard some whispers and murmurs amidst rather unpleasant stares at the two 'black men' from many a pair of white eyes! When the Grace was finished, all the English students marched off suddenly from our table with obvious signs of indignation and disgust on their faces. My guest and I went through the meal in silence at the table which was by now all our own.

[90] *Oxford Magazine* (27 April 1961); *Daily Telegraph* (28 April 1961).

*12.7* David Raven surveys the daffodils in the JCR, 1963.

Later, Anantharaman learned that the 'dissidents' had gone to the JCR and written in the Suggestions Book 'words to the following effect: "why on earth was a bloody nigger admitted into our hall tonight?"' Many in Trinity were shocked into active sympathy with the victim, and Anantharaman was 'goaded' into joining 'programmes planned to promote racial unity'.[91]

It was during Anantharman's three years at Trinity (in Eights Week 1952) that eight undergraduates (and one of their sisters) put on black make-up and grass skirts and paddled past 'the immemorial mangrove trees of the Cherwell' in a 'Balliol War Canoe'.[92] Balliol responded overnight, and the following morning a battered old taxi, covered in such inscriptions as 'Keep out—Men? at work—Trinity

[91] T. R. Anantharaman, 'Three Years at Trinity', *Report* (1988–9), unpaginated.
[92] TCA DD 122.

*12.8* Students in the Beer Cellar, 1980.

Passion Waggon', was found outside the Trinity Lodge. In some ways the 1950s and 1960s were the golden age of Trinity–Balliol rivalry. Frontier incidents reached a breathtaking level of inspiration and finesse, while also, it must be admitted, causing a considerable level of damage. The traditional feud was now in the public domain. When, on 6 March 1961, a party of Trinity students hired a large public-address system and broadcast a muezzin call from the 'minaret' of the Balliol Chapel, the escapade was reported widely in the press. Indeed, the Oxford correspondent of *The Times* had been invited to watch from the windows of the Tower rooms, where the tape recorder was situated.[93] When, in the summer of 1963, Balliol students turfed the floor of the JCR and planted daffodils in it, the dean, David Raven, posed for a photograph for the *Oxford Mail* (Plate 12.7). Such

[93] Memoir of Christopher Williams (1957), *Report* (1990–1), 46–7.

behaviour seemed perfectly natural to Norrington, who reported the feat in the *College Report*, along with the observation that 'the protracted celebrations by Balliol of its 700$^{th}$ anniversary took place . . . and were unfortunately attended by very bad weather.'[94]

One sine qua non of corporate student life is of course the bar. Trinity's Beer Cellar was opened in the summer of 1967, with a new staircase down from the Pig and Whistle passage, and a newly tiled floor. The JCR were quick to add a dart board and a juke box. 1979 was an important year in the Beer Cellar's history, when the opening hours were extended to '10.30 p.m. five nights a week', and profits from the 'various machines' were used to provide half-price beer on 'jazz, rock and folk-music evenings'. The following year saw the installation of 'Space Invaders', perhaps the most famous animated computer game of all time, and one which brought 'new-found' wealth to the JCR committee, who financed a 'Greek night . . . supported by ouzo, retsina and other Greek delicacies'.[95] One even more vital element of the modern JCR was present too: women.

[94] 'Various News', *Report* (1963), 9.
[95] 'The Junior Members', *Report* (1979), 19; (1980), 17.

# 13

# *Modern Trinity*

## *President Ogston*

Norrington's successor was a Balliol man. Alexander George Ogston (known as Sandy) was the first Trinity President since Percival to have had no formal connection to the College. According to James Lambert, his name came up during a round-table discussion—'Charles Phillips strongly recommended Sandy Ogston, ex chemist and physiology fellow of Balliol, now a professor in Canberra. A lot of us knew him, because he dated from the old joint Balliol–Trinity Laboratory days.'[1] In his first 'President's Letter' Ogston did not hesitate to admit that his 'acquaintance with the College [was] patchy' and that he proposed to 'do' nothing 'with' the College during his presidency.[2] What he did do, in fact, was facilitate the modernization of many of Trinity's customs, and foster the burgeoning independence of the students.

Sandy Ogston was not one to persist with outmoded social customs. Indeed, his 'liberalism in some matters . . . sometimes came as a surprise and a challenge' to his colleagues.[3] In the first year of his presidency, the fellows gave up dressing for dinner in Hall on Sundays. When he discovered that many old members were having to go to the expense of hiring formal evening dress ('tails, white tie and waistcoat') for gaudies, he persuaded his colleagues to make it optional. He himself continued to wear 'the suit I'd had as an undergraduate. It had turned somewhat green with age, but this was not too obvious by artificial light, and was partly covered by a gown,' until the accidental destruction of his white waistcoat by the laundry. 'I had, not without some satisfaction, of necessity to appear in a dinner jacket. After that Tails became less and less favoured.'[4]

[1] TCA Lambert, 'Reminiscences on Presidential Elections'.

[2] *Report* (1970), 1–2. [3] 'A.G.O.', ibid. (1979), 5.

[4] 'The Presidency of Trinity', excerpt from Alexander George Ogston, 'Reminiscences 1911–1988', 9–10.

*13.1* Sir Arthur Norrington, President 1954–69, and Sandy Ogston, President 1969–78.

Ogston found the restrictions on women dining at Trinity particularly iniquitous. The College's first female lecturer, Dorothy Horgan, had been appointed in 1968, but for many years she did not enjoy the same dining rights as her male colleagues. The impetus for change was the election of a female fellow, Dorothy Osborn, to Trinity's sister college at Cambridge, Churchill, in 1972. In recognition of her automatic right to dine at Trinity, women were admitted to High Table every night except Friday, 'although there were some misgivings among my conservative colleagues,' admitted Ogston.[5]

[5] Ibid., 8–9.

Another ancient rule suddenly to disappear was the requirement to have a minimum of two fellows in residence during term. In 1973 James Holladay and his wife moved out of Kettell Hall, where they had lived since the building's refurbishment had been completed. The other fellow in residence, James Lambert, was on sabbatical leave. 'The College found itself unable to fulfil the provision of its Statutes,' wrote Ogston simply in the *College Report*, 'and has changed them.'[6]

## *From Servants to Staff*

In 1973 Robin Fletcher announced that he intended to give up the domestic bursarship. During his twenty-three years in office he had presided over the beginnings of an unstoppable change that has seen the traditional 'college servants' transformed into today's highly organized, specialized, and professional staff. From Philip Landon, Fletcher had inherited a loyal body of servants who spent their entire life in the service of the College, and who identified strongly with the College traditions and families. Many, Fletcher understood, had been trained in the 'great houses' of England. The smooth running of the college depended greatly on the relations of individual servants with the fellows and undergraduates. The most famous of all was Richard Cadman, who in 1968 retired after sixty-seven years, at the age of 94. He prided himself in his intimate knowledge of his 'three thousand sons' and he expected a particular code of behaviour to be followed by his charges.[7]

Cadman's six decades of service to Trinity College is a record unlikely ever to be broken. But, as Table 13.1 shows, many others were in the College's employ for forty or fifty years, and too many to enumerate for ten, twenty, or thirty. Perhaps the most famous of recent years was Albert Greenwood, who came as a scout's boy during the Second World War and retired as SCR butler in 2000. In 1997 he was awarded the MBE for services to the College. Another exceptional period of service is that of Malcolm Nolan, who reached his fortieth anniversary of employment during Trinity's 450th year.

The postwar years, however, saw many alternative careers for those who would once have been recruited by the College. In 1949 the newly appointed gardener Reg Carter showed surprising loyalty when

[6] *Report* (1973), 4–5.
[7] Richard Cadman speaking to Susan Cooper, *Sunday Times* (9 April 1961).

*13.2* President Weaver and the College servants, 1954. The two women are Miss Tuckey, the bursary typist, and Mrs Walker, wife of the retiring head porter.

*Table 13.1* Long-serving servants and staff of the twentieth century.

| *Name* | *Position* | *End of Service* | *Length of Service* |
|---|---|---|---|
| Barry Hayes | Wroxton bailiff | died 1911 | over 40 years |
| Henry Johnson | scout | retired 1914 | 50 years |
| Owen Charles Gillam | scout and porter | retired 1932 | 47 years |
| Reuben Harris | scout and common room man | retired 1933 | 46 years |
| Charles Lingfield | butler | died *c.*1944 | 46 years |
| Charles Honey | bursary clerk | died 1948 | 54 years |
| William Gynes | scout | died *c.*1948 | 48 years |
| Aubrey Walker | scout | died 1954 | 45 years |
| Charles Hastings | common room boy and scout | retired 1940 | approx. 45 years |
| Fred Williams | butler | retired 1954 | 50 years |
| W. T. Eley | scout | retired 1967 | 46 years |
| Harold Butterfield | assistant chef | | over 40 years |
| Harold Hemmings | clerk of the works | retired 1975 | 42 years |
| Jim Butterfield | chef | retired 1975 | 50 years |
| William Barson | scout and head porter | died 1976 | 42 years |
| Ivor James | scout | retired 1981 | 40 years |
| Ron Shelton | kitchen porter | retired 1989 | 47 years |
| Bill Sloper | scout and head scout | retired 1995 | 52 years |
| Albert Greenwood | scout and butler | retired 2000 | 47 years |

*Source*: *Reports*.

he approached President Weaver for a pay rise, 'though without any sort of complaint,' Weaver informed Landon. 'He says (a) that the new scale of Agricultural Wages places him in the *minimum* rate, (b) that he does find things difficult. After deduction for insurance etc he receives £14 4*s* 6*d* a week.' Landon wrote a note to Jack Honey, the bursary clerk. 'Will you add 10*s* a week to the wages of Carter . . . from Lady Day?'[8]

Jack Honey had grown up in a College house, 7 Parks Road, which was formerly the residence of the President's coachman. He had worked for Trinity as a boy, and in 1946 succeeded to his father's position as bursary clerk. But in December 1950 he left for a job at a school on the Isle of Man. In 1951 the word 'staff' first appeared on a bursary document.[9] By now Trinity had two female employees: Miss Tuckey, who worked in the bursary as a typist, and Nurse Kate Selvey,

[8] TCA Bursarial Committee Minutes, Weaver to Landon, Feb. 1949.

[9] TCA Bursarial Committee Minutes, 23 April 1951; TCA Honey Interview (26 July 1991).

who since 1948 had run a part-time sickbay in the cottages. Every student was charged 3*s* 6*d* termly for the right to consult her, and 3*s* 6*d* daily for morning and evening visits if they were ill.[10] When in 1954 both Weaver and Fred Walker, the head porter, were due to retire, a photograph was taken of the President and the College servants. Several of Trinity's employees were teenaged boys, who worked as staircase assistants, carrying fuel and water and performing the more arduous scouting chores. As the years passed it became harder and harder to recruit school-leavers, and it required higher and higher wages to persuade them to stay. During his domestic bursarship Fletcher worked hard to bring modern plumbing to all staircases, not only because it was expected in modern homes, but also because it considerably eased the workload for the domestic staff.

By 1966 Robin Fletcher was forced to admit that recently recruited scouts were failing to 'give the same degree of personal service' as their pre-war counterparts, or even to show 'a sense of loyalty towards the college'. Furthermore, he had come to question whether the College should expect them to. In a confidential paper to the Governing Body, he laid out some stark facts:

> It can no longer be claimed that the staircase servants have the same place in the Oxford College society as before. Most of them are incapable of accepting responsibility for their 'young men', while the undergraduates, unused to Servants, are unable to command them. A case might be made for the privileged of tomorrow learning something about staff relations, but having their shoes cleaned and their crockery washed for them may well be the worst possible introduction.

Besides the difficulties of recruitment, it was becoming too expensive to maintain an establishment where three meals a day were served by waiters (traditionally, the other duty of the scout). Fletcher proposed that breakfast and lunch should become self-service, and that 'room service' should be limited to 'cleaning', which in his opinion 'women tend to do . . . better than men,' and he envisaged that 'eventually the number of regular male staircase servants will decrease to half-a-dozen with a squad of women cleaners.' 'Special arrangements' would be required for 'bachelor Fellows', for whom he favoured the idea of 'a "bachelors' hostel" in the . . . Lodgings'.[11]

[10] TCA Bursary Files, 'College Nurse'.
[11] R. A. Fletcher, 'College Internal Arrangements', 5 Jan. 1966.

And so it came to pass. Breakfast and lunch became self-service, and students began to clean their own shoes, or not, as they pleased. Little did Fletcher imagine that within a decade, the JCR would be actively campaigning for cooking facilities for its members.

## Innovations

Robin Fletcher's replacement, at the end of 1974, was Richard Popplewell, already known to the College community as the chemistry lecturer during James Lambert's sabbatical leave. Popplewell was an enthusiastic modernizer, who worked closely with Ogston to bring about more innovations—or to bring down more cherished institutions—in the College. One significant aspect of all domestic changes at this time was the increasing involvement of students. In 1972 a Joint Disciplinary Committee was established, with a role that recognized the students' right of appeal against the dean. In 1973 Ogston invited student contributions to the *College Report*, and Alan Morgan (1970), JCR President, was the first to seize the opportunity. Of the Joint Disciplinary Committee he wrote:

> While the fact of this Committee's existence is important to the JCR, the theory behind its creation is of great significance: greater communication between senior and junior members will lead, one hopes, to understanding of the problems and resentments faced and felt by both—and that further evidence, contrary to the expectation of some, of the impartiality of the Governing Body on the one side, and of the responsibility of the Junior Members on the other, will inspire confidence and promote a harmonious progressive College atmosphere.

In 1972 the JCR campaigned (unsuccessfully) for the right to have overnight guests, and the right to control its own funds. But Morgan's vision was for the JCR to make a far wider impact on the College. 'For if we may . . . participate maturely on disciplinary matters,' he argued, 'there is no reason why we should not do so with equal success in all College matters which are of relevance to the JCR.'[12]

Morgan's successor, Peter Meredith (1971), sweetened his criticism of the Governing Body with some Lewis Carroll parody:

[12] A. W. Morgan, 'The JCR', *Report* (1972), 12–13.

> The JCR, eyes aflame with reform, tends to whiffle burblingly through tulgey woods, locked in grimatorial combat with a Governing Body whose blade is all too handily vorpal. It is galling that in a year which has seen the admission of the jabberwocky to the Governing Body meetings, uffish thought on the part of the tum-tum tree leaners still prevents the back gate remaining open after 7 p.m., and it is still impossible even to buy a mimsy postage stamp at the lodge. So often when the authorities' snicker-snack is heard the jabberwocky wonders what the slithy tove there was to argue about. A little more understanding and willingness to avoid unnecessary whiffling can lead only to a frabjous day for all.

There was no Commem Ball in 1973, owing to 'disagreement over conditions of use of the College'.[13] But regular victories were won. In 1974 weekend guests were permitted for an 'experimental' period. In 1976 cooking facilities were provided on some staircases. In 1977 'late-night' keys were issued 'without cash deposit' to all members of College. At the same time 'a new optional system of breakfast payments' was introduced (an obvious advantage to those who chose to stop out all night or stay in bed all morning).[14]

The main area of conflict between senior and junior members was over charges, which, in a period of high inflation, were rising steadily. In 1977 the JCR President noted with satisfaction that the increase in charges would be beneath the increase in the student grant, for the first time in three years.[15] The College authorities were as concerned as the students to reduce expenditure, and during 1974 both Ogston and Popplewell sat on an 'Economies Sub-Committee' of senior and junior members. For the year 1974–5, the College charge was £1.81 per day, or £103.17 for a fifty-seven-day term. Fees were £522 for undergraduates and £252 for postgraduates. The committee discussed such options as using student waiters at dinner, 'grading' room rents, reducing the quality and controlling the quantity of food served, and cleaning the windows twice instead of three times a year. In November the President summed up the committee's proposals. Lunch would be charged more realistically, with the cost of coffee and sandwiches more than doubling, from 3p and 5p to 7p and 11p.[16] He also estimated that a 2p increase in the price of chips would generate £400

[13] Peter Meredith, 'The JCR', ibid. (1973), 17–18.
[14] *Report* (1974), 13; (1976), 12; (1977), 11.
[15] A. J. de Mont 'Junior Common Room', ibid. (1977), 11.
[16] TCA Accounts, BF 3/9 'Magistratos', 28 May and 6 Nov. 1974.

a year.[17] At a further meeting, it was agreed 'in principle' to reduce still further the cleaning done by scouts: 'Daily service would be confined to waking in the morning. Occupants would be expected to make their own beds, do their own washing up, and to keep their rooms in reasonable order. It was agreed that there should be a system of penalties for "piggery".'[18]

The Governing Body also looked at ways to cut their own expenses: in 1973–4 the SCR Christmas Dinner cost £311, the Domus Dinner (instituted in 1955) £336, and the Trinity Monday Dinner £386. Another act of inclusivity of Ogston's presidency was the invitation of second-year undergraduates to the Trinity Monday Dinner, which had traditionally been enjoyed by the fellows and scholars alone.[19] In March 1975 the President pointed out to his colleagues how much was spent on daily dessert after dinner, and mooted the possibility of limiting to certain days this time-honoured custom (the fellows had been retiring to their Common Room for after-dinner refreshment for over 300 years).[20]

Ogston sat patiently through many a meeting to discuss economies and junior–senior relations. But he was less tolerant of academic failure, and determined to improve Trinity's results. In the 1972 *College Report* he launched a challenging attack on under-achievers. That year had seen six Firsts in finals and two in Mods, 'a respectable improvement on the figures (4 and 1) for 1971 and on those (1 and 1) for 1970'. 'May we dare look forward to still better results in 1973?' demanded the President:

> The only fly in the 1972 ointment was that the whole increase in Firsts was at the expense of Seconds, the number of Thirds remaining obstinately unchanged. Firsts are not everyone's to command; but it should be possible for almost everyone, with only reasonable efficiency, without loss of extra-academic enjoyment, and to his own advantage, to avoid a Third.[21]

Student life was also changed by the development of out-of-college accommodation, plans for which came slowly to fruition. Two houses on Rawlinson Road were purchased in 1973, and divided up into flats and bedsits for eighteen students. In 1979 work began on a new build-

[17] This would require consumption of 20,000 portions a year, which could be achieved by 200 individuals eating chips 100 times (approximately 4 times a week in term).

[18] TCA Accounts, BF 3/9, 'Magistratos', 14 Nov. 1974

[19] 'College Entertainments', n.d., ibid.

[20] TCA Bursarial Committee Minutes, 5 March 1975.

[21] *Report* (1972), 3.

ing in their garden, which would provide twelve 'units', each with two rooms, kitchen and bathroom, which from October 1980 were available to pairs of undergraduates, or to married graduate students.

Richard Popplewell meanwhile was striving to increase the efficiency of College administration. He disapproved of the Bursarial Committee's reactive approach to business—'discussing odd matters selected apparently at random'—and endeavoured to clarify policies and goals. He then launched a series of attacks on Trinity's traditional domestic arrangements. In January 1975 he found a way to increase the number of rooms by twelve, by converting sets on Staircases 5, 6, and 11 into 'bedsitters' (with 'combined wardrobes/vanitory units').[22] In June he reviewed the system for serving meals from the Hall passage, where 'the whole arrangement is extremely clumsy and makes it difficult to serve hot food.' A review of the washing up found it being done in three different places, with two members of staff operating the 'revolving brush machine' to clean plates ('better if it used hotter water'), another washing cutlery ('frequent complaints'), and two more washing glasses. Popplewell proposed a new dishwashing machine, and devised a new and open layout for all kitchen operations, which gave the chef better oversight of the staff. He was particularly concerned about 'portion control': 'I am sure that we are giving undergraduates a good deal more food than we or they can afford to pay for.' A servery was built to the west of the Hall, a doorway opened under the middle window, and the lunchtime queue first took the route that it follows today.[23] In 1977 Popplewell proposed gas fires to replace the electric fires, and in 1979 he had plans drawn up for a new 'laundrette' at the north end of the Jackson Building.[24]

Richard Popplewell was sometimes suspected of having too great an enthusiasm for modernization and, in particular, for gadgetry. He was gently satirized in the Michaelmas 1982 issue of the student magazine *Trinity Tales*:

> *A Life in the Week of a Domestic Bursar*
>
> *Monday:* Leaf through Machino-Mat catalogue. Hard to choose between a chip-frying machine and a shoe-cleaning bidet. Decide on chip machine as offering greatest scope for offending people—awful smell, useless product, need to clean, etc.

[22] TCA Accounts, Bursarial Committee Minutes, 13 January 1975; 'Undergraduate Rooms in College', 21 January 1975. [23] Ibid., 'Catering', 21 June 1975.
[24] Ibid., 2 May 1977; 'New Laundry', 23 May 1979.

In the afternoon count bricks beside the Danson Room. Convinced undergraduates are pilfering them. Can't think why. In the mood for counting things, so count bicycles as well. A colleague has suggested that 30 years ago there were more. I doubt it—but it needs a thorough enumeration. On the way fill stamp machine.

*Tuesday:* Chip machine arrives. Delighted. Send it away again at once in case people start using it. Have to refill stamp machine. Undergraduates are buying far too many stamps these days. Decide to discourage them by putting a 'Do Not Use' notice on the machine. Notice adjacent post-card machine and realise that the sale of one may have something to do with the sale of the other. Put 'Do Not Use' notice on the post-card machine as well.[25]

## *Presidents of the Late Twentieth Century*

On 1 August 1978 the presidency of Trinity passed to the distinguished Oxford philosopher and fellow of New College, Anthony Meredith Quinton (from 1982 Lord Quinton of Holywell). The fellows were looking for a head from outside the College, but not yet from outside Oxford. When Ogston handed on the baton to Quinton, he provided 'an invaluable loose-leaf volume containing a calendar of presidential activities and alphabetically arranged notes on every aspect of the task', and in 1987, Quinton passed an updated version to Sir John Burgh. Sir John was unique in Trinity's history for having not merely no formal connection with the College, but none with Oxford. He came to Trinity as the former Director General of the British Council, and his university experience—a graduate, and chairman of the governors, of the London School of Economics—was, as he admitted, 'no guide'. Previously accustomed to working with a team of professional administrators, now, he found, 'the Trinity dons do it themselves assisted by a small administrative staff.' John Burgh was the first Trinity President to respond to an advertisement for the position, and the first to be shown a job description, although as Robin Fletcher told him, he was really expected 'to do those chores we do not wish to do ourselves'.[26]

Trinity's twenty-sixth President, the Hon Michael J. Beloff, QC, was

[25] *Trinity Tales* (Michaelmas, 1982), 26. [26] Ibid. (1987–8), 1.

*13.3* Lord Quinton, President 1978–86, in his study.

elected in 1996. He was a graduate of Magdalen College, but also proud to be a Trinity old member, having spent 1965–6 as Trinity's law lecturer pending the arrival of Alan Milner. Called to the bar in 1967, and taking silk in 1981, Michael Beloff came to Trinity as joint head of 4/5 Gray's Inn Square and Justice of the Courts of Appeal of Jersey and Guernsey, specializing in human-rights law, and with the highest public profile of any President since Percival. In the *Chambers and Partners Directory* of 1996–7 he was named as 'one of the top three stars of the bar', and in *Legal Business* of 1999 as one of the legal 'faces of the decade'. A year after Beloff's election, a profile of 'Britain's Super Silks' in the *Evening Standard* described his style as

*13.4* Sir John Burgh, President 1986–96, and Anne, Lady Burgh.

'forensic and intellectual' and noted his propensity for working '15-hour days'.[27]

Presidential patronage has always played a part in student activities. In the 1950s Norrington associated himself with the Gryphon Club, to which he himself had belonged in 1920, and lent his enthusiastic support to the Trinity Players. Sandy Ogston encouraged the religious side of College life, inviting students to breakfast in the lodgings after Sunday morning Communion service, and 'on Ascension days, following an open-air Eucharist service in the garden, [to] a picnic breakfast in the Danson Room'. John Burgh took a particular interest in music, opening his drawing-room to concerts and establishing a link between the College and the Duke String Quartet. On at least one occasion, his strong commitment to the importance of senior–junior relationships led him and Lady Burgh to accept an invitation to dinner at a College flat.[28] Michael Beloff in his turn has been devoted to College sport, in particular athletics, and to the

[27] Chambers and Partners' Directory (1996–7), 1251; *Legal Business* (1999), 20; *Evening Standard* (16 July 1997).

[28] Ogston, *Reminiscences*, 28: 'Guy serves the chocolete mousse', photograph album of Ed. A. O'Reilly and Richard J. Newhouse (both 1989), TCA DD 110/155, 56

subject-based PPE and Law Societies. One feature of his presidency has been the inauguration of annual lectures: the Chatham Lecture (on public affairs) and the Margaret Howard Lecture (on law and literature), which are open to the University and have attracted famous speakers and large audiences.

## The Admission of Women

Trinity's most radical change in the late twentieth century was the admission of women. In the late 1970s there was a current joke—told by the women—that male colleges saw the admission of women entirely in terms of laundry provision:

> In another college, the Principal's secretary put it to the Governing Body that it might be appropriate to have a champagne reception to welcome the female students into the community. One dinosaur apparently spoke for them all when he replied, 'we've put an iron on their staircase, what more do they want?'

At Trinity it happened in the second year of Tony Quinton's presidency. In an interview for the undergraduate magazine *Trinity Tales*, he declared himself 'rather a strong defender' of co-residence, on the grounds that the men's colleges had a 'mass of advantages' and that 'it would be unfair not to let the women have a crack at it.'[29]

The feminization of Oxford's male colleges had been slow to begin, but the change, when it came, was rapid. The first serious discussions of how co-residence might be achieved began in December 1970, and in 1972 Congregation agreed that from 1974, 100 women should be admitted annually to five men's colleges, and the situation reviewed in 1977.[30] So successful did the experiment prove that the remaining colleges could hardly wait to follow suit. Of fourteen wishing to admit women at the earliest opportunity, eight, of which Trinity was one, were selected by ballot. Women were invited to apply for admission in October 1979.[31]

[29] Valerie Elson (née Hill), 'Women in Trinity', *Report* (1991–2), 61–2; *Trinity Tales* 4 (1978, December).

[30] Michael Brock, 'The University since 1970', *HUO* 8, 746–7.

[31] The ballot was ignored by the unsuccessful colleges, who, Ogston considered, behaved 'badly' in their unseemly rush (Ogston, *Reminiscences*, 12). By 1985 not one all-male college was left.

Trinity's first female intake comprised seventeen undergraduate and six postgraduate students. They were given rooms throughout the College, and, from the beginning, treated as an ordinary part of the community. The transition was entirely straightforward, involving nothing more exciting than the frequent setting off of the fire alarm on the first night: 'Never before had there been a demand for so many repeated viewings of such extensive yardage of Marks and Spencer brushed nylon' in the Garden Quadrangle, recalled Valerie Hill (1979). Louise Hebbourn (1979) struggled with the question 'what is it like to be a woman in Trinity?' for *Trinity Tales*. 'Being female in Trinity is extremely pleasant, but I do not think it is essentially very different from being a male in the college,' she concluded.[32] On their first day the female students were invited to a 'women-only drinks party' by the dean, Alan Milner. In Hall, Valerie Hill experienced mild prejudice against not her sex, but her Wigan home, as she 'exchanged pleasantries with a second year law student' who 'looked down at his plate and ventured that as I was from the North this was probably the first time that I had seen an avocado pear.'[33] The women entered into every aspect of College life, and Quinton wrote reassuringly in the *College Report*, 'at one stage our small population of first-year women had two boats on the river.' One female postgraduate, Lesley Smith (1979), was elected MCR Treasurer during her first year.[34] Despite the anxieties of some, the presence of women made little difference to the traditional quality of student life, as the cartoon 'Club JCR' drawn by David James (1983) for the magazine *Cloaca* reveals (Plate 13.5).

The proportion of women to men rose slowly but steadily. By 1989 it was 1:3, and Trinity had a female dining society, the Zuleika (its ten members chosen 'on the basis of contribution to college life') and a 'women's group'. Their first term card promised a varied range of meetings:

| | |
|---|---|
| 1st week | Chocolate Party |
| 2nd week | Introduction to Holistic Massage |
| 3rd week | 'Why would anyone want to be a nun?' with Sister Andrea |
| 4th week | Video: Victoria Wood live |

32 Louise Hebbourn, 'A Woman in Trinity!', *Trinity Tales* 8 (1980, March), 16.

33 Not all were experienced in male–female society. 'One boy', claimed Hill, 'confessed . . . I was only the third female he'd ever spoken to in his life—the other two being his mother and matron.' Elson, 'Women in Trinity', 61.

34 *Report* (1980), 1, 17.

*13.5* 'Club JCR', by David James.

| | |
|---|---|
| 5th week | Outing to the Body Shop |
| 6th week | Discussion |
| 7th week | 'Women in Academia' with Dinah Birch |
| 8th week | End of term Party.[35] |

Given that the female colleges had traditionally dominated the Norrington table, much interest was shown in the academic results of the newly mixed colleges. Trinity's results were already improving: 1981, the last year of all-male finalists, saw a record of fifteen Firsts and just six Thirds, achieved by the seventy-one finalists. The rise continued, as it did across the University. In 1999 twenty-one out of seventy-six finalists were awarded First Class degrees.

It would be wrong to blame the admission of women for the decline in the Trinity Boat Club or rugby team. Quinton put his finger on the real cause of the problem (if such it is) in his first 'President's Letter', as he described his initiation into presidential collections:

> An amazing and colourful panorama of activities was unrolled for me by the two hundred or so undergraduates who passed before my eyes. They told of the formation of a Morris dancing set, of a project to study longevity in a remote part of South America, of the fine achievement of victory in Drama Cuppers with a play about Sylvia Plath, of one or two eyes fixed on the 1980 Olympics, and . . . of a firm resolve to avenge defeat in the ballroom dancing Varsity Match.[36]

At the time, Trinity was still an all-male preserve. But it was, and had been for many years, a diverse society, in which rowing, ever popular as an Oxford pastime, had ceased to dominate. The Trinity Eight had been doing badly (in comparison to its pre-eminence in the 1930s and 1940s) for two decades. In 1964 there were five Trinity crews on the river—'nearly 25 per cent of the undergraduates rowing'—but the First Eight was bumped every night, and in 1965 found itself, for the first time in its history, in the Second Division. That year the crew fared even worse, 'going down six places in four nights (through a double over bump on the first . . .)'. In 1967, when the First Eight went up three places, and the second made five bumps, Norrington noted that only three men in the First Eight and two in the Second had any experience of rowing before they came up.[37]

[35] *Report* (1995), 87; 'Women's Group', JCR C/WG/1.
[36] *Report* (1979), 1. [37] Ibid. (1964), 15; (1965), 14; (1967), 16–17.

It would also be wrong to attribute the relative decline in Trinity's sporting excellence to the absence of Philip Landon, who retired from the bursarship in 1951 and from the law tutorship in 1955. At his funeral the Bishop of Exeter, who conducted the service, turned to Fletcher and asked, 'Where shall I get my Twickenham tickets now?'[38] Landon had encouraged oarsmen and rugby players to come to Trinity, but in doing so he was only fostering a dedication to the discipline and rigour of team sports that was created by the public-school system in the nineteenth century. Even before Landon's retirement, Oxford's—and, eventually, Trinity's—student population came from a widening range of schools, with an ever more serious attitude to individual academic work and a concomitant repositioning of college sport in their collective psyche. Even those from schools with the strongest sporting traditions are now more likely to have been coached in interview techniques than in rowing. In fact, today's Trinity women's crews seem to do better than their male counterparts, perhaps because very few women of any college have rowed before, and they compete on equal terms.

In recognition of a changing pattern of undergraduate sporting endeavour, 1979 saw the first holding of a Blues dinner, organized 'on the same lines' as the elusive bump supper. That year Trinity had thirteen Blues (one a double) who had completed in twelve Varsity events: soccer, athletics (3), cricket, fencing, the Isis eight, judo, racquets, rifle shooting, royal tennis, sailing, table-tennis, and water-polo. Quinton described the occasion as one 'in the highest traditions of Tudor festivity': 'The evening began with a fanfare provided by members of the Music Society and ended with a croquet match between Blues and Fellows which lasted well into the dark.'[39]

## A Changing Fellowship

The fellows' croquet lawn was yet another Trinity tradition to pass away during the closing decades of the twentieth century, a casualty of the changing character of the typical Trinity fellow. Quite likely to be married and with families, certain to have homes and extra-college social lives, and burdened with research commitments

[38] Lambert, 'Philip Landon', TCA DD 20 add 2. [39] *Report* (1979), 3, 18.

*13.6* The Governing Body, 1985.

(increasingly overseas), they found dinner in College—and after-dinner amusements—to be more and more of an irrelevance, or just simply impossible to fit in to their busy lives. The main corporate meal of the day is no longer High Table dinner, but SCR lunch. The main difference is not so much the change of time (Trinity has eaten a communal midday meal for much of its history) but of venue. Lunch is eaten in the seclusion of the Old Bursary, and the once important and inclusive daily ritual of the College dinner in Hall has virtually disappeared.

Planned social occasions began to replace the once informal relations between senior and junior members, with variable degrees of success. Note the names and titles in this description of a 1972 darts match: the championship was 'won by C. Douglas-Morris in a final against Bill Sloper [scout]. In a demonstration match afterwards, however, Professor Ogston, in a display which revealed what Darts is like at the top, beat the champion at a canter.' By 1980, 'efforts to provide more contact between Junior and Senior Members were not too successful,' reported the JCR President, David Richardson (1977): 'However, an SCR–JCR Darts match uncovered some hitherto hidden talents. Dr Martin showed with an uncannily brilliant display of "arrows" just how he had mis-spent his youth, and Mr Maclagan revealed his powers at the bar-football machine.'[40]

The Governing Body has continued to increase in size as new fellowships, both tutorial and professorial, have been added to its number. Science is more strongly represented, with additional fellows in mathematics, engineering science, materials science, and physics. Trinity's first fellow and tutor in management studies arrived in January 2003, almost exactly a century after the election of the first fellow and tutor in that new-fangled subject, English literature. Female elections to the fellowship have been slow to come (still in single figures by the end of the century), though this was to some extent inevitable given the slower turnover of personnel. Trinity's first woman fellow was Sue Kingsman, elected fellow and the College's first tutor in biochemistry in 1984; the second was Dorothy Horgan (1989), who had been lecturer in English since 1968. Between the election of Dinah Birch in 1990 and Dorothy Horgan's retirement in 1996, all of Trinity's English tuition was by women, and between 1996 and 2001 all of its law tuition. In the year 2000–1 Trinity's thirty-two-strong

[40] *Report* (1972), 12.

13.7 The Hon. Michael Beloff, QC, President 1996–, by Bob Tulloch.

Governing Body had four female members (compared to equal numbers of male and female students). Today's CUF (Central University Fund) appointments bring with them the complexity of University duties and an ever-increasing burden of paperwork.

## Benefactions

One aspect of Trinity that has changed remarkably little over the centuries is the College's dependence on benefactions. Major donors of the second half of the twentieth century included: Thomas J. L. Stirling-Boyd (1909); Liu Lit-Man; John H. Britton (1923 and honorary fellow 1979), who among many gifts gave a new Chapel organ; Gilbert Laithwaite (1912, honorary fellow 1955); Reginald H. Poole (1904); Miss Bertha Wiltshire; Wyatt Haskell (nephew of Wyatt Ruston (1916));

Robert and Julia Hunt-Grubbe; Michael Beloff; and Mrs Gillian Sutro, widow of John Sutro (1924).

When Sir John Burgh arrived at Trinity he found himself running a new College Appeal. It was launched in 1986, with objectives very similar to and just as pressing as those of 1969, but with a target now of £3.6m. First, there was the perennial need for more student accommodation. A site was purchased on the corner of Staverton and Woodstock Roads, and plans commissioned for a block of eighteen self-contained flats. The cost of the work was estimated at £1.6m in 1986, and at £2m in 1990. 'The flats are very nice indeed but bloody miles away,' says the JCR Freshers' Guide of 1995.[41] At the same time, an ingenious plan by Gray and Baynes had been drawn up for a twenty-four-room accommodation block in the Dolphin Yard, with rooms on three floors above a parking area and driveway beneath. The estimated cost for this was £0.6m. Sixty-three students could be housed at Staverton Road, and these gains put Trinity in a position to provide accommodation for 95 per cent of students. An additional need was the augmentation of the College's endowment. Over half of the income from the endowment was being spent on teaching and research, and for this to be maintained, the College needed further support from its old members. In honour of its benefactors, Trinity has the Danson Room, the Britton music room, the Stirling-Boyd fellowship in English, the Laithwaite fellowship in Modern History, the Wyatt Rushton fellowship in law, the Hunt-Grubbe fellowship in engineering, and the Sutro Arts Room.

Not every name given to a building will stick. Sandy Ogston was 'immensely flattered' by the choice of 'Ogston House' and by the decision 'to put the Ogston Arms in glass in the entrance', but 'Rawlinson Road' it remains.[42] The new building in the Dolphin Yard was called simply 'Staircase 18'. As part of the Trinity Society weekend, it was officially opened by the Chancellor, Lord Jenkins of Hillhead, on 4 October 1992. Four days later, its first residents were installed.

## *Professionalization*

The opening of Staircase 18 was managed by Michael Poyntz, domestic bursar 1987–2001. He came to Trinity not as an academic,

[41] TCA JCR D/9.5, 20. [42] Ogston, *Reminiscences*, 14.

but as a professional administrator with a background in catering, and during his term of office he oversaw a steady expansion and professionalization of the College staff. Almost every department of the College staff has grown considerably in the second half of the twentieth century, and the Burgh years saw a particularly rapid expansion, both in numbers and in specialization. Joan Barton had the Lodgings' basement almost to herself when she first worked for President Ogston (who was also Tutor for Admissions) in 1975. She recalled how he would 'sit down at the table and smoke his old pipe and tell me of the time when he first came to Oxford as a scholar of Balliol'. Her working environment was 'very old-fashioned, with a great big bookcase filled with old calf-bound College books, some beautifully illuminated, and a roll-top desk by the window. It was not until some years later that . . . Dr Popplewell bought us our first photocopier, then Mr Wright supplied us with a computer.' Joan Barton remembered a 'constant flow of typing' for the tutors, 'as they had not progressed to owning their own word-processors', and she and the fellows' secretary 'were kept very busy'.[43] The advent of PCs brought no diminution of the work load; rather it accelerated the increasing paper mountains being generated both in Colleges and in the University. In 1989 Joan Barton was succeeded by Katie Andrews, who in twelve years transformed the College office into a high-tech operational nub, herself into the Academic Administrator and the fellows' secretary into the administrative assistant. A new post was that of 'President's Secretary and Assistant Appeal Director', to which Marilyn Oakey was appointed in 1988.

Trinity was one of the first of Oxford's colleges to be computerized, largely thanks to the visionary interest of the bursar John Wright. A computer room was opened where fellows and students could avail themselves of the latest in dot matrix printers. Katie Andrews described the difference made by the appointment of a computing officer, Alastair Johnson, in 1997:

> Starting from small beginnings of 8 hours per week, which trebled in no time as students, fellows and staff all clamoured for his services, Alastair rushes around the College, sorting out hardware and software, troubleshooting in the student computer rooms, and helping anyone unfamiliar with the technology.[44]

[43] Joan Barton, 'A Few Thoughts on my Years as College Secretary', *Report* (1988–9), unpaginated.

[44] [Katie Andrews], 'Staff News in Brief', ibid. (1997), 16.

Besides Trinity's administrative offices, the Library has been transformed by computerization. It is an area of College unique for not having increased its staffing size since 1980, when Jan Martin was appointed (in the days when a job offer could be made by a fellow in a pub). In her early days she removed sleeping bags (and their occupants) from the Library, and disposed of runs of books that had stood undisturbed since 1928. Between 1992 and 1997 she oversaw the introduction of OLIS, Oxford's centralized cataloguing and ordering system, which required not merely extensive training and skilled operation, but, in a 'furious onslaught', the retrospective cataloguing of the library's 50,000 volumes. In 2000 Trinity installed the very first fully integrated circulatory system in any Oxford college. The problem of book loss—a gaudy in 1992 saw 'a small pile of long-since "missing" books heaped neatly, and anonymously outside the Library door' while an 'amnesty' in 1993 brought back '918 books (from a current annual loss of 1,091)'—was replaced overnight by the problem of where to put the books at the ends of terms. The solution, a new bay of shelves, and the ongoing acquisitions and donations have necessitated regular reorganization of the Library. The year 2004 saw the re-creation of the Chalmers Law Library, in a newly furbished room at the north end of the Library basement.[45]

The Bursary is another department to have seen tremendous growth. In the bursary the head clerk, Granville Ballinger, was succeeded in 1984 by Janet Underwood, who, during seventeen years in charge, evolved into the College accountant. The office of domestic bursar acquired first a secretary, then an assistant, then a housekeeper; today, Trinity runs its outside events through a full-time functions and conference administrator. The College kitchen is staffed year-round by a hierarchy of chefs of which any restaurant would be proud, and enjoys a reputation for the finest cuisine. The Lodge remains the first port of call for visitors to Trinity, but its team of porters presides over an ever-increasing complexity of security and communication systems, and, since 1994, 'custodians' have been employed to control the flow of tourists into Trinity. Individuals, and families, have spanned the changes in College employment. Valerie Parslow, the niece of Joyce (scout) and Allan Dinsdale (porter and head porter), came to Trinity as a seamstress in 1987 and left, in 2002, as accommodation manager. Her husband, Tony Parslow (clerk of works

[45] Jan Martin, 'Library Report', ibid. (1991–2), 66; (1993), 76; (1997), 61; (2000), 43–5.

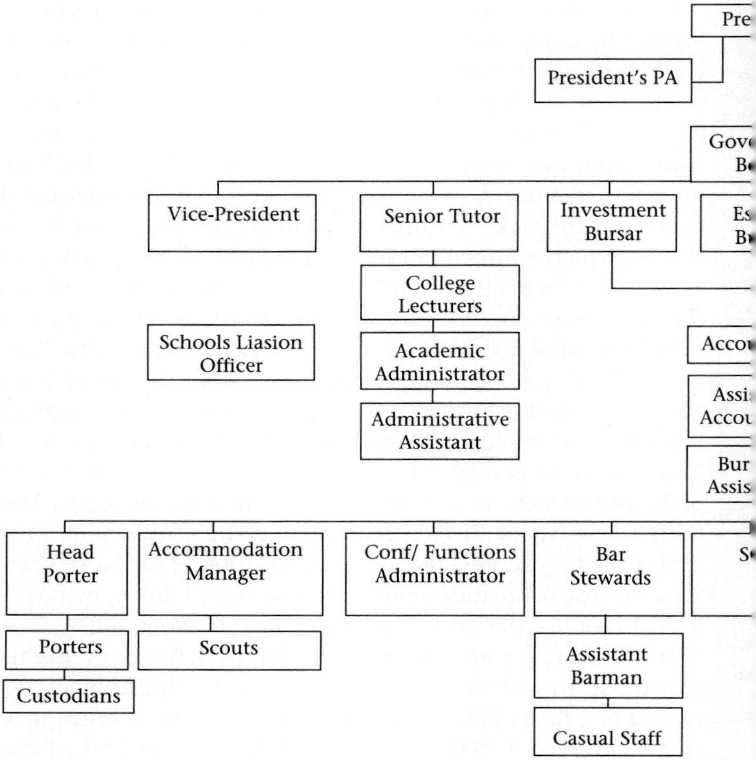


*Fig. 13.1* Trinity College organization chart 2005

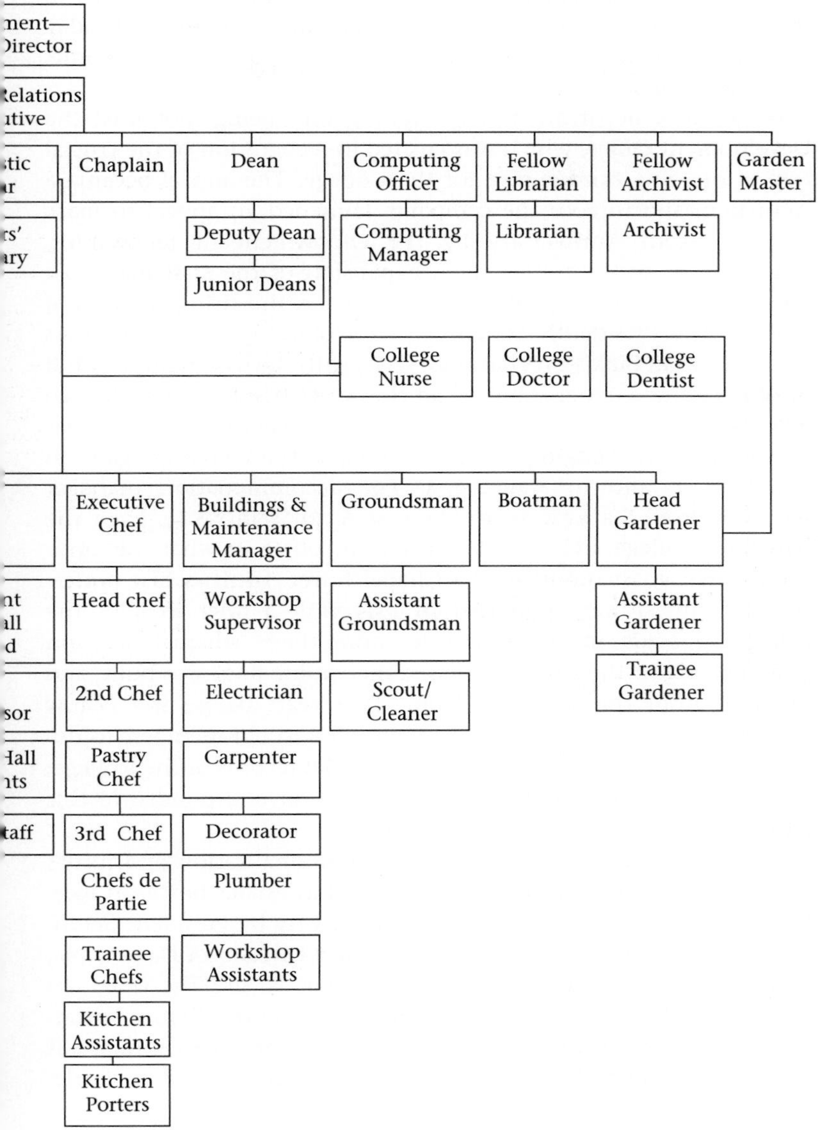
Chaplain
Dean
Deputy Dean
Junior Deans
Computing Officer
Computing Manager
Fellow Librarian
Librarian
Fellow Archivist
Archivist
Garden Master
College Nurse
College Doctor
College Dentist
Executive Chef
Head chef
2nd Chef
Pastry Chef
3rd Chef
Chefs de Partie
Trainee Chefs
Kitchen Assistants
Kitchen Porters
Buildings & Maintenance Manager
Workshop Supervisor
Electrician
Carpenter
Decorator
Plumber
Workshop Assistants
Groundsman
Assistant Groundsman
Scout/ Cleaner
Boatman
Head Gardener
Assistant Gardener
Trainee Gardener

1975–99), had presided over the growth of the workshop department (now under a maintenance manager and with its own foreman) to include electrician, carpenter, and painter and decorator, who today undertake the College's cycle of maintenance and improvements without recourse to outside contractors.

Whole new departments have sprung into being, not least the Development Office, which was created in recognition of the crucial role of ongoing fund-raising for the College. The appeal became a campaign, and in 2001 the campaign launched an appeal to mark Trinity's 450th Anniversary by the endowment of fellowships, scholarships, and bursaries. Such expansion of the staff makes an inevitable demand on College rooms, as has the rising number of fellows. The President's Lodgings is no longer quite the spacious house it was in Blakiston's bachelor days, with the basement now full of offices, and a spiral staircase on the western side leading to two fellows' rooms. In less than a decade, the Development Office has moved from the Lodgings, to Staircase 14, to the Lodgings again, to Kettell Hall, and to Staircase 8. The accommodation manager has gone from Staircase 11, to Staircase 8, to Staircase 14. Even the part-time College archivist clawed out an office in what was once the fellows' guest rooms in the Chapel tower. Trinity's first professional archivist was appointed in 1985 with a brief to 'put 'the college's records in order and to store them adequately . . . on new shelving in the tower'. In 1987 a mezzanine floor was built, and financed from the Blakiston Fund. Two years before the Fellow Archivist, Bryan Ward-Perkins, first appealed to old members to donate archival material to augment the official records of the College; in twenty years, just under 400 individuals have responded to this request.[46]

The last decade has seen a similar professionalization of Trinity's College officers. When John Wright retired as estates bursar in 1997, his replacement was headhunted from the City by President Beloff. John Martyn was the retiring Group Finance Director of Dalgety plc, and was a non-executive director of Littlewoods, and *The Times* ran a leader on the subject of his decision to take on the Trinity bursarship.[47] One significant change of the early twenty-first century was the introduction by John Martyn and the accountant, Robyn Searle,

[46] Bryan Ward-Perkins, 'The College Archive, A Planned Reorganisation and an Appeal for More Material', *Report* (1982–4), unpaginated. [47] *The Times* (25 May 1997).

of full management accounting, with every department receiving its own budget. This has been followed by the University-wide change from Franks to SORPS accounting, which Trinity was one of the first colleges to introduce. Michael Poyntz's successor as domestic bursar was David Mills, formerly the head of West Oxfordshire College in Witney. Domestic bursars of today are answerable not merely to their fellow fellows; they, and the College, are subject to a vast array of legislation, including the:

Disabled (Employment) Persons Act 1945 and 1960
Equal Pay Act 1970 (amended 1984)
Sex Discrimination Act 1975
Rehabilitation of Offenders Act 1974
Race Relations Act 1976
Disability Discrimination Act 1995
Asylum and Immigration Act 1996
Employment Rights Act 1996
Human Rights Act 1998
Data Protection Act 1998
Employment Relations Act 1999
Race Relations Amendment Act 2000
Freedom of Information Act 2000
Special Education Needs and Disability Act 2001.

There is also legislation concerning finance, building, planning, licensing, and the environment. Trinity's Governing Body is the most important of the many committees by which the College is run. These include the:

Bursarial Committee
2005 Campaign Committee
Cross College Administration Group
Equality Committee
Grants Committee
Health and Safety Committee
Joint Consultative Committee
Pastoral Committee
Tutorial Committee.

Health and safety alone encompasses the following:

Safety Representatives and Safety Committee Regulations 1977
The First Aid Regulations 1981
The Furniture and Furnishings (Fire) Safety Regulations 1988/1989
The Noise at Work Regulations 1989
The Electricity at Work Regulations 1989
The Workplace (Health, Safety and Welfare) Regulations 1992
The Manual Handling Operation Regulations 1992
The Health and Safety (Display Screen Equipment) Regulations 1992
The Personal Protective Equipment at Work Regulations 1992
Reporting of Injuries, Diseases and Dangerous Occurrences Regulations 1995
The Health and Safety (Consultation with Employees) Regulations 1996
Fire Precautions (Workplace) Regulations 1997
The Provision and Use of work Equipment Regulations 1998
The Working Time Regulations 1998 and 1999
The Management of Health and Safety at Work Regulations 1999
The Control of Substances Hazardous to Health Regulations 2002.

In 1988, Peter Hazzledine stood down after five years as senior tutor. He wrote,

> Trinity expects its senior tutor to be an amateur. It does not give him any dispensations and it pays him only enough, at tutorial rates, to cover two hours a week . . . It is only an overseeing role. The work is done by others, the administration by the college secretary . . . and the teaching arrangements by the Tutors.

He went on to describe the 10,000 letters he had written, the meetings, and the committees that the post in reality entailed.[48] In 2001 Trinity was one of the first colleges to relieve the fellows' burden of one of the most time-consuming College offices by the appointment of a full-time senior tutor. Trudy Watt (as an academic moving into administration) replaced the part-time officers of senior tutor, tutor for admissions, tutor for graduates, and tutor for undergraduates. The senior tutor convenes the tutorial committee, and sits on the pastoral, grants, disciplinary, and joint consultative committees, and represents the College in various inter-college and University matters.

The advent of professional administrators tied up in red tape and

[48] Peter Hazzledine, 'On being Senior Tutor', *Report* (1987–8), unpaginated.

weighed down by paperwork is just one of the changes that Trinity has seen over the last 450 years. The College has moved from the empty buildings of Durham College bought by Sir Thomas Pope to encourage Catholic learning, to its present-day role in a University that prides itself on being an international centre of education and research. Such a transformation was achieved by way of being, at different times, a bastion of Anglicanism, a finishing school for the English squirarchy, and a mainstay of Victorian educational reform. But one constant has remained: Trinity has always been a community working hard to achieve its aims, and to prosper the lives of its members.

Many have tried to express their love for Trinity College. Bathurst? His new buildings said it all. Newman? 'Trinity was never unkind to me,' he wrote in his *Apologia*.[49] Frank Douglas Mackinnon (1890) bequeathed to the College a silver cup, with the inscription 'Behold, how good and joyful a thing it is, Brethren, to dwell together in Trinity.' But let us give the last word to Dinah Birch, whose presence as a female fellow, and as a tutor in English, would have been unimaginable to the Founder. 'There's a domestic feeling about this college,' she said, 'and there seems to have been such a feeling about the place for a very long time.' Thomas Pope would have liked that. 'It is a place of hard learning and hard teaching,' she continued, 'and a place that sends its learning and teaching out into the world. That is its power, and that it why it matters.'[50] Thomas Pope would have liked that too.

[49] John H. Newman, *Apologia pro vita sua* (Oxford 1967), 213.
[50] TCA DD 375 Birch.

# Appendix 1.1

*Plan of Trinity College in 2005*

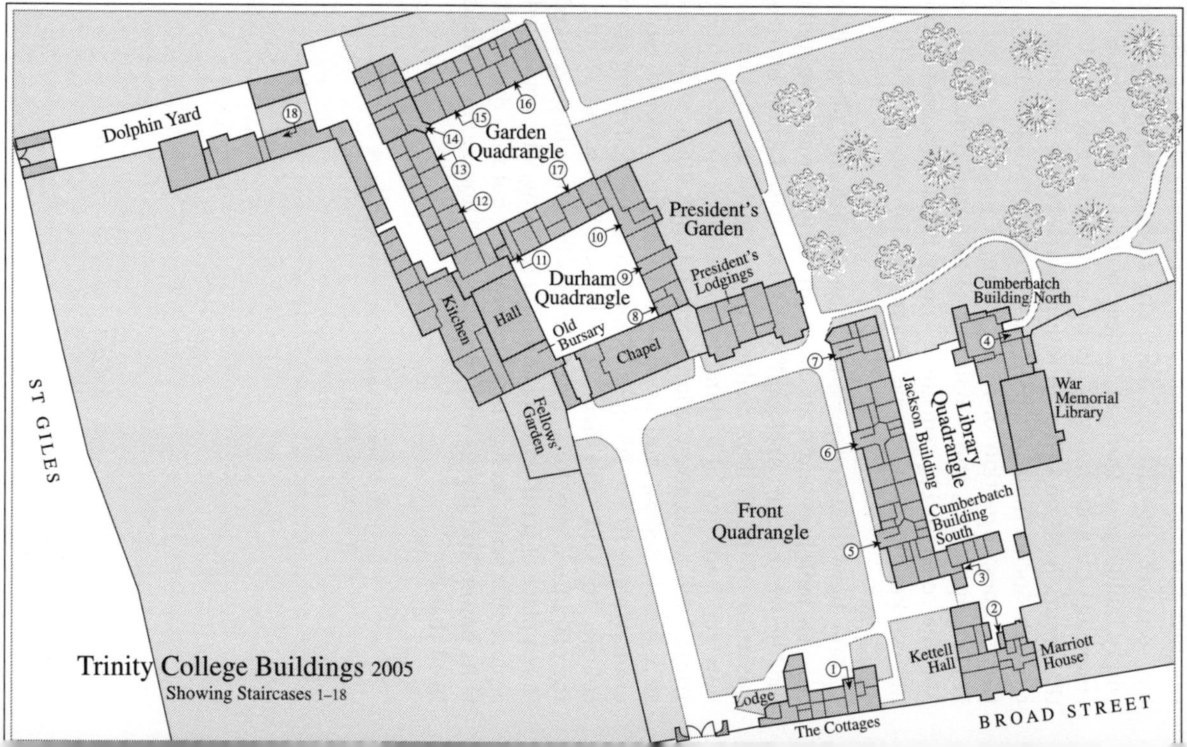

# *Appendix 1.2*

*Plans of the Dolphin Yard*

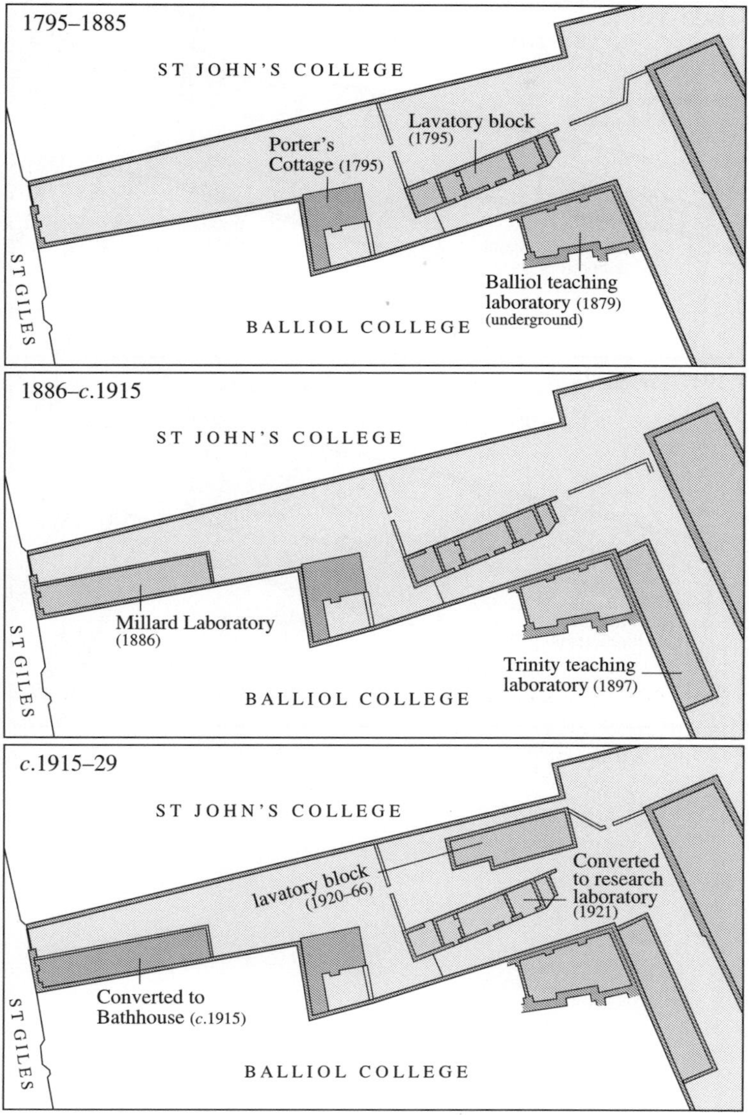

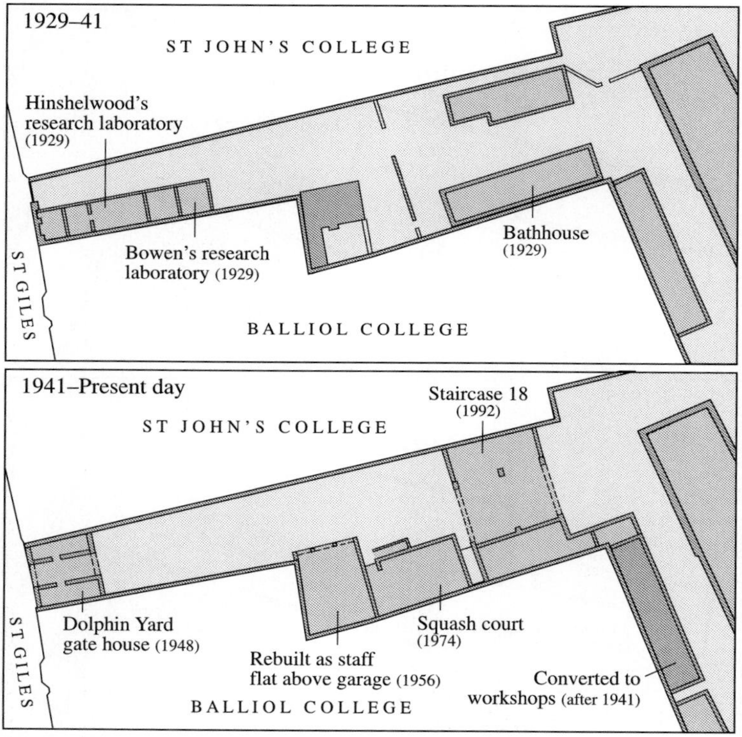
1929–41
ST JOHN'S COLLEGE
Hinshelwood's research laboratory (1929)
Bowen's research laboratory (1929)
Bathhouse (1929)
ST GILES
BALLIOL COLLEGE
1941–Present day
Staircase 18 (1992)
ST JOHN'S COLLEGE
Dolphin Yard gate house (1948)
Squash court (1974)
Rebuilt as staff flat above garage (1956)
Converted to workshops (after 1941)
ST GILES
BALLIOL COLLEGE

# Appendix II

## *Staircase Numbers*

| *Location* | *1754* | *1854* | *1899* | *1952* | *1965* | *1967* | *1992* |
|---|---|---|---|---|---|---|---|
| Chapel Tower | 1 | 1 | 7 | 8 | 8 | 8[1] | — |
| Above the kitchen | 2 | 3 | 10 | 10 | 10 | — | — |
| Garden Quad, north-west corner | 3 'Pump Court' | 7 'Old Back Buildings' | 14 | 14 | 14 | 14 | 14 |
| Above the Hall | 4 'Bell Staircase' | 4 | 11 | 11 | 11 | 11 | 11 |
| Garden Quad, west range, south staircase | 5 | 5 | 12 | 12 | 12 | 12 | 12 |
| Garden Quad, west range, north staircase | 6 | 6 | 13 | 13 | 13 | 13 | 13 |
| Garden Quad, north range, west staircase | 7 | 8 | 15 | 15 | 15 | 15 | 15 |
| Garden Quad, north range, east staircase | 8 'Fellows' Staircase' | 9 | 16 | 16 | 16 | 16 | 16 |
| Garden Quad, south range | 9 | 10 | 17 | 17 | 17 | 17 | 17 |
| Old Library | 10 | — | 9 | 9 | 9 | 9 | 9 |
| Bathurst's Building | 11 | 2 | — | — | — | — | — |
| Cottages | | | 1, 2, 3 | 1, 2, 3 | 1 | 1 | 1[2] |
| Jackson Building, nearest Broad Street | | | 4 'New Buildings' | 5 | 5 | 5 | 5 |
| Jackson Building, centre | | | 5 'New Buildings' | 6 | 6 | 6 | 6 |
| Jackson Building, JCR | | | 6 'undergraduate library'[3] | 7 | 7 | 7 | 7 |
| Durham Quad, President's Lodgings | | | — | — | — | 10 | 10 |
| Durham Quad, south-east staircase | | | 8 | — | — | 8 | 8 |
| Kettell Hall (and Marriott House)[4] | | | Kettell Hall | 4 | 2 | 2 | 2 |
| Cumberbatch Building South | | | | | 3 | 3 | 3 |
| Cumberbatch Building North | | | | | 4 | 4 | 4 |
| Dolphin Yard Building | | | | | | | 18 |

*Notes*:

1 The number 8 was relocated circa 1980.

2 The 'Lodge Annexe', formerly known as the 'Lodge Staircase', was occupied as a flat for the Head Porter between 1969 and 1999.

3 The undergraduate library became the JCR when the War Memorial Library was opened in 1928. The JCR was moved to the ground floor to increase access for disabled members, and the former Library became the 'Arts Room', reopened as the Sutro Room in 2005.

4 Marriott House was incorporated into Kettell Hall in 1968.

*Source*: TCA Room Registers and Lists.

# Appendix III

## Twentieth-century Fellows

| | | |
|---|---|---|
| Ashcroft, Fran M. | Research Fellow in physiology | 1992– |
| Ball, Sally A. | Law | 1998–2001 |
| Barber, Nick W. | Law | 2001– |
| Barnett, Frank J. | French | 1952–1986 |
| Birch, Dinah L. | English | 1990–2003 |
| Blakiston, Herbert E. D. | Classics | 1887–1907 |
| | President | 1907–1938 |
| Brierly, James L. | Law | 1913–1920 |
| Brown, Michael C. | Physiology | 1967–1996 |
| Brown, Peter G. McC. | Classics | 1968– |
| Buckler, Keith J. | Medicine | 2001– |
| Burden, Dennis H. | English | 1965–1989 |
| Burroughs, E. A. | Chaplain | 1920–1921 |
| Carey, Peter B. R. | Modern History | 1980– |
| Collin, Jack | University Reader in Surgery | 1980– |
| Cooper, John P. | Modern History | 1952–1978 |
| Coupland, Reginald | Ancient History | 1908–1914 |
| Crauford Smith, Rachel | Law | 1994–1998 |
| Crombie, Alistair C. | University Lecturer in the History of Science | 1970–1983 |
| Crosland, C. Anthony R. | Economics | 1947–1950 |
| Crouch, Colin J. | Politics and Sociology | 1986–1998 |
| Czernuszka, Jan T. | Materials Science | 1996– |
| Egdell, Russell G. | Inorganic Chemistry | 1990– |
| Ewert, Alfred | Professor of Romance Languages | 1930–1958 |
| Farrer, Austin M. | Chaplain | 1935–1960 |
| Fisher, Peter S. | Physics | 1964–1984 |
| Fisher, Stephen D. | Politics | 2002– |
| Fitzgerald, Patrick J. | Law | 1956–1960 |
| Fletcher, Robin A. | Fellow | 1950–1989 |
| | Domestic Bursar | 1951–1974 |
| Franzosi, Roberto | Politics | 1995–1999 |
| Furse, Michael B. | Chaplain | 1895–1903 |
| Geldart, William M. | Law | 1901–1909 |
| Ghosh, Kantik | English | 2002– |
| Good, Irving J. | Research | 1964–1967 |
| Green, Martin H. | Fellow under the old Statutes | 1872–1927 |
| Griffin, Clive H. | Spanish | 1975– |
| Hall, Robert L. | Economics | 1927–1950 |
| Hammersley, John M. | Research | 1960–1987 |
| Hancock, Gus | Physical Chemistry | 1976– |
| Harris, Roy | Professor of Romance Languages | 1976–1977 |
| Haskell, Francis J. H. | Professor of the History of Art | 1967–1995 |
| Hazzledine, Peter M. | Metallurgy | 1970–1991 |
| Higham, Thomas F. | Classics | 1914–1958 |

| | | |
|---|---|---|
| Hinshelwood, Cyril N. | Chemistry | 1921–1937 |
| Holladay, A. James | Ancient History | 1949–1982 |
| Horgan, Dorothy M. | English | 1989–1996 |
| Houlden, J. Leslie | Chaplain | 1960–1970 |
| Humphries, Simon N. | English | 2003– |
| Inwood, Michael J. | Philosophy | 1967– |
| Jones, Cyril A. | Spanish | 1963–1972 |
| Kelly, John M. | Law | 1960–1965 |
| Kemp, Martin J. | Professor of the History of Art | 1995– |
| Kingsman, Sue M. | Biochemistry | 1984–1997 |
| Kirchheim, Bernd | Mathematics | 2002– |
| Kirk, Kenneth E. | Chaplain | 1922–1933 |
| Knox, Ronald A. | Chaplain | 1910–1917 |
| Korsunsky, Alexander M. | Engineering | 1999– |
| Krebs, Hans A. | Whitley Professor of Biochemistry | 1954–1967 |
| Lack, David L. | Director of the Edward Grey Institute of Field Ornithology | 1963–1973 |
| Lambert, James D. | Chemistry | 1938–1976 |
| Landon, Philip A. | Law | 1920–1956 |
| | Domestic Bursar | 1921–1951 |
| Lemmon, Edward J. | Philosophy | 1957–1963 |
| Liddell, Edward G. T. | Research | 1921–1940 |
| Little, Ian D. M. | Economics | 1950–1952 |
| Lloyd, R. H. | Chaplain | 1903–1911 |
| Maclagan, Michael | Modern History | 1939–1981 |
| Mahadevan, Louis C. | Biochemistry | 1999– |
| Maiden, Martin D. | Professor of Romance Languages | 1996– |
| Mallinson, G. Jonathan | French | 1989– |
| Martin, Roderick | Politics and Sociology | 1969–1984 |
| Martyn, John R. | Estates Bursar | 1997–2002 |
| | Investment Bursar | 2002– |
| McMichael, Andrew J. | Professor of Immunology | 1982–2000 |
| McWatters, Sir Arthur | Extra-professorial | 1933–1946 |
| Mills, David | Domestic Bursar | 2001– |
| Milner, Alan | Law | 1965–1996 |
| Nagel, David H. | Chemistry | 1890–1920 |
| Norrington, Arthur L. P. | Extra-professorial | 1948–1954 |
| | President | 1954–1969 |
| Nowell-Smith, Patrick H. | Philosophy | 1945–1957 |
| Ogilvie, Frederick W. | Economics | 1920–1926 |
| Oppenheimer, David R. | Fellow by special election | 1975–1981 |
| Patterson, Melville W. | Modern History | 1897–1938 |
| Peck, Anthony | Philosophy | 1938–1946 |
| Pellew, Jill H. | Director of the University Development Office | 1994–1999 |
| Peters, Rudolph A. | Whitley Professor of Biochemistry | 1925–1954 |
| Phillips, Charles G. | Physiology | 1945–1966 |
| | Professor of Neurophysiology | 1966–1975 |
| Popplewell, Richard J. L. | Domestic Bursar | 1974–1986 |
| Porter, Rodney R. | Whitley Professor of Biochemistry | 1967–1985 |

| | | |
|---|---|---|
| Poyntz, J. Michael | Domestic Bursar | 1987–2001 |
| Price, Henry H. | Philosophy | 1924–1935 |
| Prichard, Harold A. | Philosophy | 1898–1924 |
| Prior, Chris R. | Mathematics | 1984– |
| Rae, Bill D. M. | Physics | 1987–1993 |
| Raper, Robert W. | Fellow under the old Statutes | 1871–1915 |
| Raven, David S. | Classics | 1958–1968 |
| Read, Peter L. | Physics | 1991– |
| Reid, Thomas B. R. | Professor of Romance Languages | 1958–1968 |
| Rundle, B. Bede | Philosophy | 1963–2004 |
| Salamon, Simon M. | Mathematics | 1984–1995 |
| Scott, Helen J. | Law | 2002– |
| Seidel, Victor F. P. | Management Studies | 2003– |
| Seymour, Jillaine K. | Law | 1996–2001 |
| Sheard, Steve J. | Engineering | 1988– |
| Smith, George, D. W. | Materials Science | 1991–1995 |
| | George Kelley Reader in Materials Science | 1995– |
| Southern, Ed M. | Whitley Professor of Biochemistry | 1986– |
| Stevens, Margaret J. | Economics | 1993–1997 |
| Stuart-Jones, Henry | Various | 1896–1919 |
| Studer, Paul | Professor of Romance Languages | 1926–1927 |
| Syme, Ronald | Ancient History | 1929–1949 |
| Thompson, Frank B. | Biological Science | 1987–1995 |
| | Agricultural Estates Bursar | 1995–2002 |
| Tiddy, Reginald J. E. | English | 1905–1916 |
| Ullmann, Stephen | Professor of Romance Languages | 1968–1975 |
| Wallace, Chris | Economics | 2000– |
| Ward-Perkins, Bryan R. | Modern History | 1981– |
| Wark, Justin S. | Physics | 1995– |
| | Estates Bursar | 2004– |
| Waters, Edwin G. R. | Professor of Romance Languages | 1927–1930 |
| Watt, Trudy A. | Senior Tutor | 2001– |
| Weaver, J. R. H. | Modern History | 1913–1938 |
| | President | 1938–1954 |
| Wernham, R. Bruce | Modern History | 1935–1951 |
| Whitehead, Henry | Fellow under the old Statutes | 1877–1903 |
| Wilkins, Robert J. | Medicine | 1998–2001 |
| Williams, Trevor S. M. | Theology and Chaplain | 1970– |
| Wind, Edgar | Professor of the History of Art | 1955–1967 |
| Woods Donald D. | Research | 1951–1955 |
| | Iveagh Professor of Microbiology | 1955–1964 |
| Wright, John F. | Economics | 1955–1990 |
| | Estates Bursar | 1955–1997 |

# *Appendix IV*

## *Trinity in the* Oxford Dictionary of National Biography

| *Name and title* | | *Life dates* | *Notable as* | *Date of admission to Trinity* |
|---|---|---|---|---|
| Addington | Anthony | 1713–1790 | Physician | 1733 |
| Alexander | Harold Rupert Leofric, 1st Earl Alexander of Tunis | 1891–1969 | Army officer | 1945 |
| Alford | Edward | 1566–1631/2 | Politician | 1581 |
| Alington | Cyril Argentine | 1872–1955 | Headmaster and Dean of Durham | 1891 |
| Allen | Sir Peter Christopher | 1905–1993 | Chemist and industrialist | 1925 |
| Allen | Thomas | 1540–1632 | Mathematician and antiquary | 1561 |
| Altham | Harry Surtees | 1888–1965 | Schoolmaster and cricket historian | 1908 |
| Anderson | Sir Alan Garrett | 1877–1952 | Public servant and shipowner | 1895 |
| Anderson | Sir Donald Forsyth | 1906–1973 | Shipowner | 1925 |
| Andrewes | John | b. 1582/3 | Poet [pseudonym I. A.] | 1601 |
| Apsley | Sir Allen | 1616–1683 | Royalist army officer and politician | 1631 |
| Archer | Thomas | 1669–1743 | Architect and courtier | 1686 |
| Ash | John | baptized 1722, d. 1798 | Physician | 1740 |
| Asplin | William | 1689–1758 | Church of England clergyman and writer | 1704 |
| Astbury | Sir John Meir | 1860–1939 | Judge | 1879 |
| Atkins | Sir Hedley John Barnard | 1905–1983 | Surgeon and medical administrator | 1925 |
| Atkins | Henry | 1555–1635 | Physician | 1574 |
| Aubrey | John | 1626–1697 | Antiquary and biographer | 1642 |
| Babington | Anthony | 1561–1586 | Conspirator | 1580 |
| Badeley | Henry John Fanshawe, Baron Badeley | 1874–1951 | Civil servant and engraver | 1893 |

| *Name and title* | | *Life dates* | *Notable as* | *Date of admission to Trinity* |
|---|---|---|---|---|
| Bagot | Sir Hervey Bagot, 1st baronet | 1591–1660 | Staffordshire gentry | 1608 |
| Balfour | Henry | 1863–1939 | Museum curator | 1881 |
| Bampton | John | 1689–1751 | Benefactor | 1706 |
| Barrowby | William | baptized 1682, d. 1758 | Physician | 1699 |
| Bateson | Sir Alexander Dingwall | 1866–1935 | Judge | 1885 |
| Bathurst | Allen, 1st Earl Bathurst | 1684–1775 | Politician | 1700 |
| Bathurst | Ralph | 1620–1704 | Dean of Wells and College head | 1634 |
| Beadon | Frederick | 1777–1879 | Church of England clergyman and centenarian | 1796 |
| Beauclerk | Topham | 1739–1780 | Book collector | 1757 |
| Benwell | William | baptized 1765, d. 1796 | Church of England clergyman and classical scholar | 1783 |
| Bernard | Montague | 1820–1882 | Jurist and international lawyer | 1838 |
| Bevan | Robert Cooper Lee | 1809–1890 | Banker | 1826 |
| Beyfus | Gilbert Hugh | 1885–1960 | Barrister | 1904 |
| Binyon | (Robert) Laurence | 1869–1943 | Poet and art historian | 1888 |
| Birkhead | Henry | 1617–1696 | Latin poet | 1633 |
| Blackwell | George | 1547–1613 | Archpriest | 1562 |
| Blakiston | Herbert Edward Douglas | 1862–1942 | College head | 1881 |
| Blount | Sir Henry | 1602–1682 | Traveller | 1615 |
| Blount | Richard | *c.*1565–1638 | Jesuit | 1583 |
| Blount | Sir Thomas Pope, 1st baronet | 1649–1697 | Politician and writer | 1674 |

| | | | | |
|---|---|---|---|---|
| Boldero | Sir Harold Esmond Arnison | 1889–1960 | Physician and medical administrator | 1908 |
| Boreham | Sir (Arthur) John | 1925–1994 | Statistician and civil servant | 1947 |
| Bosworth-Smith | Reginald | 1839–1908 | Schoolmaster and author | 1863 |
| Boutell | Charles | 1812–1877 | Writer on heraldry and antiquities | 1836 |
| Bowden | John William | 1798–1844 | Ecclesiastical writer | 1817 |
| Bowen | Sir George Ferguson | 1821–1899 | Colonial governor | 1840 |
| Bowles | William Lisle | 1762–1850 | Church of England clergyman and poet | 1781 |
| Brandram | Samuel | 1824–1892 | Reciter | 1842 |
| Bridge | Sir John | 1824–1900 | Police magistrate | 1842 |
| Bridges | John | baptized 1666, d. 1724 | County historian, Northamptonshire | 1683 |
| Brierly | James Leslie | 1881–1955 | International lawyer | 1913 |
| Brodribb | Charles William | 1878–1945 | Journalist and poet | 1897 |
| Bryce | James, Viscount Bryce | 1838–1922 | Jurist, historian, and politician | 1857 |
| Budden | John | 1566–1620 | Civil lawyer | 1582 |
| Budgell | Eustace | 1686–1737 | Writer | 1705 |
| Burrow | Edward John | 1785–1861 | Church of England clergyman and author | 1820 |
| Burton | Sir Richard Francis | 1821–1890 | Explorer and author | 1840 |
| Bury | Charles Rugeley | 1890–1968 | Chemist | 1908 |
| Butterworth | George Sainton Kaye | 1885–1916 | Composer and folk dancer | 1904 |
| Bysshe | Sir Edward | *c.*1610–1679 | Herald and politician | 1633 |
| Caccia | Harold Anthony, Baron Caccia | 1905–1990 | Diplomatist | 1925 |
| Cade | Salusbury | *c.*1660–1720 | Physician | 1678 |
| Calderon | George Leslie | 1868–1915 | Playwright | 1887 |
| Calvert | Cecil, 2nd Baron Baltimore | 1605–1675 | Colonial promoter | 1621 |
| Calvert | George, 1st Baron | 1580–1632 | Courtier and colonist in America | 1594 |
| Cannan | Charles | 1858–1919 | Aristotelian scholar and publisher | 1884 |

| *Name and title* | | *Life dates* | *Notable as* | *Date of admission to Trinity* |
|---|---|---|---|---|
| Carr | Sir Arthur Strettell Comyns | 1882–1956 | Barrister and politician | 1901 |
| Carter | Sir Lawrence | baptized 1668, d. 1745 | Judge | 1688 |
| Cary | (Arthur) Joyce Lunel | 1888–1957 | Writer | 1909 |
| Cary | Sir (Arthur Lucius) Michael | 1917–1976 | Civil servant | 1935 |
| Cecil [alias Snowden] | John | 1558–1626 | Roman Catholic priest and spy | 1573 |
| Chalmers | Sir Mackenzie Dalzell | 1847–1927 | Judge and civil servant | 1865 |
| Chamberlain | Bartholomew | baptized 1545, d. 1611? | Church of England clergyman | 1563 |
| Chamberlayne | John | 1669–1723 | Translator and literary editor | 1685 |
| Charles | Joseph | 1716–1786 | Church of England clergyman | 1734 |
| Charlett | Arthur | 1655–1722 | College head | 1669 |
| Charnock | John | 1756–1807 | Naval biographer | 1774 |
| Charnock | Robert | 1663–1696 | Jacobite conspirator | 1680 |
| Charteris | Hugo Francis Guy | 1922–1970 | Novelist | 1947 |
| Chavasse | Christopher Maude | 1884–1962 | Bishop of Rochester | 1905 |
| Chavasse | Noel Godfrey | 1884–1917 | Army medical officer and holder of two Victoria Crosses | 1905 |
| Chillingworth | William | 1602–1644 | Theologian | 1618 |
| Christie | John Traill | 1899–1980 | Headmaster and College head | 1919 |
| Clark | Kenneth Mackenzie, Baron Clark | 1903–1983 | Art patron and historian | 1922 |
| Claughton | Thomas Legh | 1808–1892 | Bishop of St Albans | 1826 |

| | | | | |
|---|---|---|---|---|
| Clerk | Sir George, of Penicuick, 6th baronet | 1787–1867 | Politician | 1806 |
| Clyde | James Latham McDiarmid, Lord Clyde | 1898–1975 | Judge | 1919 |
| Cobbe | Charles | 1687–1765 | Church of Ireland Archbishop of Dublin | 1705 |
| Cobden | Edward | 1683–1764 | Church of England clergyman and writer | 1702 |
| Coleridge | Bernard John Seymour, 2nd Baron Colderidge | 1851–1927 | Judge | 1871 |
| Coleridge | Henry James | 1822–1893 | Jesuit | 1840 |
| Compton | Spencer, Earl of Wilmington | *c.*1674–1743 | Prime Minister | 1690 |
| Constable | Henry, 1st Viscount Dunbar | 1588–1645 | Landowner and royalist army officer | 1596 |
| Copeland | William John | 1804–1885 | Historian and Church of England clergyman | 1824 |
| Coupland | Sir Reginald | 1884–1952 | Historian | 1908 |
| Cowley | Sir Arthur Ernest | 1861–1931 | Orientalist and librarian | 1879 |
| Cox | George William | 1827–1902 | Historian | 1845 |
| Coxter | Thomas | 1689–1747 | Literary scholar and editor | 1705 |
| Craven | William, Earl of Craven | baptized 1608, d. 1697 | Army officer and royal servant | 1623 |
| Crawley | Aidan Merivale | 1908–1993 | Politician and television executive | 1926 |
| Cripps | Arthur Shearley | 1869–1952 | Missionary and poet | 1887 |
| Cripps | Wilfred Joseph | 1841–1903 | Writer on silver | 1859 |
| Crosland | (Charles) Anthony Raven | 1918–1977 | Politician and writer | 1937 |
| Crozier | William Percival | 1879–1944 | Journalist | 1898 |
| Cuffe [Cuff] | Henry | 1563–1601 | Classical scholar and secretary to the Earl of Essex | 1578 |
| Cunningham | Sir Henry Stewart | 1832–1920 | Lawyer and novelist | 1851 |
| Curtis | Dunstan Michael Carr | 1910–1983 | Lawyer and civil servant in Europe | 1929 |
| Dallaway | James | 1763–1834 | Antiquary | 1778 |
| Davidson | Randall Thomas, Baron | 1848–1930 | Archbishop of Canterbury | 1867 |

| *Name and title* | | *Life dates* | *Notable as* | *Date of admission to Trinity* |
|---|---|---|---|---|
| Dawson | (Henry) Christopher | 1889–1970 | Cultural historian | 1908 |
| Delevingne | Sir Malcolm | 1868–1950 | Civil servant | 1887 |
| Denham | Sir John | 1615–1669 | Poet and courtier | 1631 |
| Derham | William | 1657–1735 | Church of England clergyman and natural philosopher | 1675 |
| Dicey | Albert Venn | 1835–1922 | Jurist | 1860 |
| Diodati | Charles | 1610–1638 | Friend of John Milton | 1621 or 1622 |
| Dodwell | William | 1709–1785 | Church of England clergyman and theologian | 1726 |
| Dornford | Josiah | 1763–1797 | Translator and writer | 1781 |
| Duckett | George | 1684–1732 | Author | 1700 |
| DuGard [Dugard] | Samuel | 1643–1697 | Church of England clergyman and author | 1661 |
| Duppa | Richard | baptized 1768, d. 1831 | Writer and draughtsman | 1807 |
| Eaton | John | 1575–1631 | Church of England clergyman | 1590 |
| Elderton | John | 1755–1832 | Antiquary and collector of documents | 1777 |
| Eliot | Sir Charles Norton | 1862–1931 | Diplomatist and university administrator | 1884 |
| Ellis | Robinson | 1834–1913 | Classical scholar | 1858 |
| Erle | Thomas | 1650–1720 | Army officer | 1667 |
| Evelyn | John [son of the diarist] | 1655–1699 | Translator and government official | 1667 |
| Eyre | James | 1748–1813 | Philologist | 1771 |
| Fagan | James Bernard | 1873–1933 | Actor, theatre manager, and playwright | 1892 |
| Farindon | Anthony | 1598–1658 | Church of England clergyman | 1612 |
| Farrer | Austin Marsden | 1904–1968 | Philosopher, theologian, and biblical scholar | 1935 |

| | | | | |
|---|---|---|---|---|
| Fforde | Sir Arthur Frederic Brownlow | 1900–1985 | Lawyer and headmaster | 1919 |
| Finer | Samuel Edward | 1915–1993 | Political scientist | 1934 |
| Fisher | Samuel | baptized 1604, d. 1665 | Quaker preacher and writer | 1623 |
| Fisher | Samuel | 1605 or 1606–1681 | Clergyman and ejected minister | 1623 |
| Flavell | John | 1596?–1617 | Writer on logic | 1611 |
| Flecker | (Herman) James Elroy | 1884–1915 | Poet and playwright | 1902 |
| Ford | Sir (Richard) Brinsley | 1908–1999 | Art connoisseur | 1927 |
| Ford | Sir Edward | baptized 1605, d. 1670 | Royalist army officer and inventor | 1621 |
| Ford | James | 1779–1850 | Antiquary and benefactor | 1797 |
| Ford | Richard | 1796–1858 | Art connoisseur and author | 1813 |
| Forde | Thomas | d. 1582 | Roman Catholic priest and martyr | 1560 |
| Fortescue | William | baptized 1687, d. 1749 | Judge | 1705 |
| Fraser | Alexander Garden | 1873–1962 | Educationalist and missionary | 1895 |
| Freeman | Edward Augustus | 1823–1892 | Historian | 1845 |
| Gairdner | William Henry Temple | 1873–1928 | Missionary | 1892 |
| Gaskin | George | 1751–1829 | Church of England clergyman and religious society administrator | 1771 |
| Gellibrand | Henry | 1597–1637 | Mathematician | 1616 |
| Gielgud | Val Henry | 1900–1981 | Radio executive and author | 1919 |
| Gil [Gill] | Alexander | 1597–1635 | Headmaster and poet | 1612 |
| Gilbert | John | 1693–1761 | Archbishop of York | 1713 |
| Gilbert | Thomas | baptized 1713, d. 1766 | Satirist and rake | 1729 |
| Gilkes | Christopher Herman | 1898–1953 | Headmaster | 1919 |

| *Name and title* | | *Life dates* | *Notable as* | *Date of admission to Trinity* |
|---|---|---|---|---|
| Glanvill | John | 1664–1735 | Poet and translator | 1678 |
| Glemham | Sir Thomas | 1595–1649 | Royalist army officer | 1610 |
| Goddard | Rayner, Baron Goddard | 1877–1971 | Judge | 1895 |
| Goodinge | Thomas | 1746–1816 | Church of England clergyman and headmaster | 1762 |
| Gore | Charles | 1853–1932 | Bishop of Oxford | 1875 |
| Greenhill | William Alexander | 1814–1894 | Physician and sanitary reformer | 1832 |
| Gregory | Edmund | b. 1615/16 | Author | 1634 |
| Haddan | Arthur West | 1816–1873 | Ecclesiastical historian | 1835 |
| Hale | Richard | 1670–1728 | Physician | 1689 |
| Hall | Robert Lowe, Baron Roberthall | 1901–1988 | Economist | 1927 |
| Hamilton | George Alexander | 1802–1871 | Politician | 1818 |
| Harpur | Joseph | 1733–1821 | Literary scholar | 1790 |
| Harrington | James | 1611–1677 | Political theorist | 1629 |
| Harris | John | 1666–1719 | Writer and lecturer on science | 1683 |
| Harris | Robert | 1581–1658 | College head | 1648 |
| Harris | Sir Ronald Montague Joseph | 1913–1995 | Civil servant | 1933 |
| Harwood | Basil | 1859–1949 | Organist and composer | 1876 |
| Haskell | Francis James Herbert | 1928–2000 | Art historian | 1967 |
| Hayter | Sir William Goodenough, 1st baronet | 1792–1878 | Politician and barrister | 1810 |
| Headley | Henry | 1765–1788 | Poet and writer on literature | 1782 |
| Herbert | Henry, 1st Baron Herbert of Cherbury | 1654–1709 | Politician | 1670 |

| | | | | |
|---|---|---|---|---|
| Hesketh-Fleetwood | Sir Peter, 1st baronet | 1801–1866 | Founder of the town of Fleetwood | 1819 |
| Hickes | Gaspar | 1605–1677 | Clergyman and ejected minister | 1621 |
| Highmore | Nathaniel | 1613–1685 | Chemical physician and anatomist | 1632 |
| Hill | James | 1697–1727 | Antiquary | 1713 |
| Hillary | Richard Hope | 1919–1943 | Air Force officer and author | 1937 |
| Hinshelwood | Sir Cyril Norman | 1897–1967 | Physical chemist | 1921 |
| Hobart | Vere Henry, Lord Hobart | 1818–1875 | Administrator in India | 1836 |
| Hoby | Sir Edward | 1560–1617 | Politician and diplomat | 1574 |
| Hodgson | Sir Robert MacLeod | 1874–1956 | Diplomatist | 1893 |
| Hooke [Hook] | William | 1601–1678 | Independent minister | 1620 |
| Hopkins | William | 1647–1700 | Church of England clergyman and antiquary | 1661 |
| How | Josiah | baptized 1612, d. 1701 | Church of England clergyman and poet | 1632 |
| Huddesford | George | baptized 1749, d. 1809 | Satiric poet | 1768 |
| Huddesford | William | baptized 1732, d. 1772 | Museum curator | 1750 |
| Hunt | William | 1842–1931 | Historian and biographer | 1861 |
| Hutchinson | Francis Ernest | 1871–1947 | Literary scholar and Church of England clergyman | 1890 |
| Ingram | Sir Bruce Stirling | 1877–1963 | Journalist and newspaper editor | 1894 |
| Ingram | James | 1774–1850 | Old English scholar and university teacher | 1793 |
| Ireton | Henry | baptized 1611, d. 1651 | Parliamentarian army officer and regicide | 1627 |
| Ironside | Gilbert | 1588–1671 | Bishop of Bristol | 1604 |
| Jekyll | Thomas | 1646–1698 | Church of England clergyman | 1663 |
| Jervis-Smith | Frederick John | 1848–1911 | Physicist | 1885 |
| Johnson | Charles | 1870–1961 | Archivist and historian | 1888 |

| *Name and title* | | *Life dates* | *Notable as* | *Date of admission to Trinity* |
|---|---|---|---|---|
| Jones | (William) Basil | 1822–1897 | Bishop of St David's | 1840 |
| Kennaway | James Peebles Ewing | 1928–1968 | Novelist and scriptwriter | 1948 |
| Kett | Henry | 1761–1825 | College teacher and writer | 1777 |
| Kettell | Ralph | 1563–1643 | College head | 1579 |
| Kinsey | William Morgan | 1788–1851 | Church of England clergyman and traveller | 1807 |
| Kirk | Kenneth Escott | 1886–1954 | Bishop of Oxford | 1904 |
| Kirk | Sir Peter Michael | 1928–1977 | Politician | 1946 |
| Knox | Ronald Arbuthnott | 1888–1957 | Roman Catholic priest and writer | 1910 |
| Knox | Wilfred Lawrence | 1886–1950 | Church of England clergyman and theologian | 1905 |
| Krebs | Sir Hans Adolf | 1900–1981 | Biochemist | 1954 |
| Lack | David Lambert | 1910–1973 | Ornithologist | 1963 |
| Laithwaite | Sir (John) Gilbert | 1894–1986 | Civil servant and diplomatist | 1912 |
| Lambert | Christopher Sebastian [Kit] | 1935–1981 | Popular music manager and producer | 1956 |
| Landor | Walter Savage | 1775–1864 | Poet and author | 1793 |
| Langton | Bennet | baptized 1736, d. 1801 | Friend of Samuel Johnson | 1757 |
| Lascelles | Sir Alan Frederick | 1887–1981 | Courtier | 1905 |
| Lawrence | Thomas | 1711–1783 | Physician | 1727 |
| Lawrence | William | c.1613–1682 | Lawyer | 1631 |
| Legge | William, 2nd Earl of Dartmouth | 1731–1801 | Politician | 1749 |
| Lethieullier | Smart | 1701–1760 | Antiquary | 1720 |
| Lewgar | John | d. 1665 | Colonial administrator and writer | 1616 |
| Lewin | Thomas | 1805–1877 | Legal writer and antiquary | 1825 |

| | | | | |
|---|---|---|---|---|
| Liddell | Edward George Tandy | 1895–1981 | Physiologist | 1914 |
| Lingen | Ralph Robert Wheeler, Baron Lingen | 1819–1905 | Civil servant | 1837 |
| Lloyd | Sir Nathaniel | 1669–1741 | College head | 1685 |
| Lodge | Thomas | 1558–1625 | Author and physician | 1574 |
| Lorimer | William Laughton | 1885–1967 | Classical scholar and translator | 1904 |
| Loveling | Benjamin | b. 1711 | Poet | 1728 |
| Lucy | William | 1594–1677 | Bishop of St David's | 1610 |
| Ludlow [Ludlowe] | Edmund | 1617–1692 | Army officer and regicide | 1634 |
| Luke | Sir Harry Charles | 1884–1969 | Colonial governor and writer | 1903 |
| Luyt | Sir Richard Edmonds | 1915–1994 | Colonial governor and educational administrator | 1937 |
| MacGillivray | Sir Donald Charles | 1906–1966 | Colonial administrator | 1925 |
| McGuinness | James Henry | 1912–1987 | Civil servant | 1932 |
| McKeown | Thomas | 1912–1988 | Medical historian and exponent of social medicine | 1935 |
| Mackinnon | Sir Frank Douglas | 1871–1946 | Judge and writer | 1890 |
| McWhirter | (Alan) Ross | 1925–1975 | Book editor and litigant | 1943 |
| Maitland | James, 8th Earl of Lauderdale | 1759–1839 | Politician and political economist | 1775 |
| Mansfield | Edward Dillon | 1845–1924 | Headmaster | 1864 |
| Mant | Richard | 1776–1848 | Bishop of Down, Connor, and Dromore | 1793 |
| Marriott | Wharton Booth | 1823–1871 | Schoolmaster | 1843 |
| Martin | John | 1619–1693 | Church of England clergyman | 1637 |
| Mason | Alfred Edward Woodley | 1865–1948 | Novelist | 1884 |
| Mathew | Theobald | 1866–1939 | Lawyer and wit | 1885 |
| Maxwell | Arthur Terence | 1905–1991 | Banker and company director | 1923 |
| Merivale | Herman | 1806–1874 | Civil servant and economist | 1825 |
| Merrick | James | 1720–1769 | Biblical and classical scholar and translator | 1736 |
| Meyrick | Frederick | 1827–1906 | Church of England clergyman and author | 1843 |

| *Name and title* | | *Life dates* | *Notable as* | *Date of admission to Trinity* |
|---|---|---|---|---|
| Micklem | Gerald Hugh | 1911–1988 | Golf administrator | 1930 |
| Miers | Sir Henry Alexander | 1858–1942 | Mineralogist and university administrator | 1877 |
| Mitchell | Sir Philip Euen | 1890–1964 | Colonial governor | 1909 |
| Molesworth | John Edward Nassau | 1790–1877 | Church of England clergyman | 1808 |
| Morgan | Hector Davies | 1785–1850 | Church of England clergyman | 1803 |
| Morris | Charles Richard, Baron, of Grasmere | 1898–1990 | University teacher and administrator | 1919 |
| Morris | Sir Philip Robert | 1901–1979 | Educationalist | 1920 |
| Morton | Sir William | baptized 1605, d. 1672 | Judge and politician | 1621 |
| Moseley | Henry Gwyn Jeffreys | 1887–1915 | Physicist | 1906 |
| Musgrave | Sir Philip, 2nd baronet | 1607–1678 | Royalist army officer and local politician | 1624 |
| Napier | Gerard | baptized 1606, d. 1673 | Politician | 1623 |
| Napier | Robert | 1611–1686 | Lawyer and office-holder | 1656 |
| Nelson | William | b. 1652/3 | Legal writer | 1669 |
| Newbery | Francis | 1743–1818 | Publisher | 1762 |
| Newdigate | John | 1600–1642 | Gentleman and diarist | 1618 |
| Newdigate | Sir Richard, 1st baronet | 1602–1678 | Lawyer and landowner | 1618 |
| Newman | Arthur | fl. 1607–1619 | Poet and essayist | 1617 |
| Newman | John Henry | 1801–1890 | Theologian and cardinal | 1816 |
| Newton | Thomas | 1545–1607 | Translator and Church of England clergyman | *c.*1560 |
| Nichols | Robert Malise Bowyer | 1893–1944 | Poet and playwright | 1913 |
| Nicholson | Edward Williams Byron | 1849–1912 | Librarian | 1867 |

| | | | | |
|---|---|---|---|---|
| Norrington | Sir Arthur Lionel Pugh | 1899–1982 | Publisher and university administrator | 1919 |
| North | Brownlow | 1741–1820 | Bishop of Winchester | 1760 |
| North | Francis, 1st Earl of Guildford | 1704–1790 | Politician | 1721 |
| North | Frederick, 2nd Earl of Guildford [Lord North] | 1732–1792 | Prime Minister | 1749 |
| Ogilvie | Sir Frederick Wolff | 1893–1949 | Economist and College head | 1920 |
| Ogle | James Adey | 1792–1857 | Physician | 1810 |
| Ogle | John William | 1824–1905 | Physician | 1844 |
| Oldham | Joseph Houldsworth | 1874–1969 | Missionary | 1892 |
| Oughton | Sir (James) Adolphus Dickenson | baptized 1710, d. 1780 | Army officer and antiquary | 1702 |
| Packer | John | 1572–1649 | Politician and landowner | 1590 |
| Paget | Thomas Catesby Uxbridge | 1689–1742 | Politician | 1707 |
| Palgrave | William Gifford | 1826–1888 | Traveller and diplomatist | 1843 |
| Palmer | Roundell, 1st Earl of Selborne | 1812–1895 | Lord Chancellor | 1830 |
| Palmes | Sir Brian | *c.*1599–1654 | Politician | 1615 |
| Parish | William Douglas | 1833–1904 | Writer on dialect | 1853 |
| Parker | Samuel | 1681–1730 | Nonjuror and theological writer | 1694 |
| Peel | Sidney Cornwallis, 1st baronet | 1870–1938 | Soldier and financier | 1893 |
| Peers [Piers] | Richard [Dic] | 1645–1690 | Translator and author | 1701 |
| Pelham | Henry Francis | 1846–1907 | Historian | 1865 |
| Pennington | Montagu | 1762–1849 | Writer and literary editor | 1777 |
| Percival | John | 1834–1918 | Headmaster and Bishop of Hereford | 1878 |
| Peters | Sir Rudolph Albert | 1889–1982 | Biochemist | 1925 |
| Phillips | Charles Garrett | 1916–1994 | Neurophysiologist | 1946 |
| Phipps | Henry, 1st Earl of Mulgrave | 1755–1831 | Diplomatist and politician | 1825 |

| *Name and title* | | *Life dates* | *Notable as* | *Date of admission to Trinity* |
|---|---|---|---|---|
| Pitt | William, 1st Earl of Chatham | 1708–1778 | Prime Minister | 1727 |
| Pittis | Thomas | baptized 1636, d. 1687 | Church of England clergyman | 1653 |
| Plummer | Alfred | 1841–1926 | Church of England clergyman and biblical scholar | 1865 |
| Pollen | Arthur Joseph Hungerford | 1866–1937 | Expert on gunnery and businessman | 1884 |
| Pope | Sir Thomas | *c.*1507–1559 | Founder of Trinity College, Oxford | |
| Porter | Rodney Ronald | 1917–1985 | Biochemist and immunologist | 1967 |
| Potter | Francis | 1594–1678 | Church of England clergyman, instrument maker, and experimentalist | 1609 |
| Potter | Hannibal | 1592–1664 | College head | 1607 |
| Price | Sir Charles, 1st baronet | 1708–1772 | Politician in Jamaica | 1724 |
| Price | Henry Habberley | 1899–1984 | Philosopher | 1924 |
| Pycroft | James | 1813–1895 | Writer on cricket | 1831 |
| Pycroft | Sir Thomas | 1807–1892 | East India Company servant | 1826 |
| Quiller-Couch | Sir Arthur Thomas | 1863–1944 | Writer and anthologist [pseudonym Q] | 1882 |
| Rampton | Sir Jack Leslie | 1920–1994 | Civil servant | 1939 |
| Randall | John | 1570–1622 | Church of England clergyman | 1583 |
| Raper | Robert William | 1842–1915 | College teacher and founder of University of Oxford careers service | 1861 |
| Rattigan | Sir Terence Mervyn | 1911–1977 | Playwright | 1930 |
| Rawlinson | George | 1812–1902 | Historian and Church of England clergyman | 1834 |
| Reeve | Richard [name in religion Wilfrid] | 1642–1693 | Benedictine monk | 1661 |

| | | | | |
|---|---|---|---|---|
| Reeve | Sir Thomas | 1673–1737 | Judge | 1688 |
| Richards | George | baptized 1767, d. 1837 | Poet and Church of England clergyman | 1785 |
| Richards | William | 1643–1705 | Church of England clergyman and author | 1659 |
| Rickards | Sir George Kettilby | 1812–1889 | Lawyer | 1829 |
| Ridley | Glocester | 1702–1774 | Writer | 1721 |
| Rivington | Septimus | 1846–1926 | Publisher | 1864 |
| Roberts | Francis | 1609–1675 | Church of England clergyman and author | 1625 |
| Robertson | Archibald | 1853–1931 | Bishop of Exeter | 1872 |
| Rodocanachi | Emmanuel Michael | 1855–1932 | Banker and financier | 1874 |
| Rogers | John | 1778–1856 | Church of England clergyman and biblical scholar | 1797 |
| Rogers | Thomas | 1660–1694 | Church of England clergyman | 1676 |
| Rous | Sir Edward, 2nd baronet | 1638–1677 | Worcestershire gentry | 1654 |
| Sadler | Sir Michael Ernest | 1861–1943 | Educationalist | 1880 |
| St John | John, 2nd Viscount Bolingbroke | 1746–1793 | Politician and fop | 1763 |
| St John | Oliver, 1st Viscount Grandison of Limerick | 1559–1630 | Lord Deputy of Ireland | 1577 |
| Salisbury [Salesbury] | Thomas | 1561–1586 | Conspirator | 1580 |
| Salmon | Thomas | baptized 1647, d. 1706 | Writer on music and Church of England clergyman | 1664 |
| Sanday | William | 1843–1920 | Biblical scholar | 1866 |
| Scholderer | (Julius) Victor | 1880–1971 | Bibliographer | 1899 |
| Settle | Elkanah | 1648–1724 | Playwright | 1666 |
| Shaw | Alexander, 2nd Baron Craigmyle | 1883–1944 | Politician | 1902 |
| Shaw | Joseph | 1671–1733 | Legal writer | 1687 |
| Sheepshanks | Sir Thomas Herbert | 1895–1964 | Civil servant | 1913 |

| *Name and title* | | *Life dates* | *Notable as* | *Date of admission to Trinity* |
|---|---|---|---|---|
| Sheldon | Gilbert | 1598–1677 | Archbishop of Canterbury | 1614 |
| Shirley | Sir Horatio | 1805–1879 | Army officer | 1823 |
| Shirley | John | baptized 1648, d. 1679 | Author | 1665 |
| Simpson | Nathaniel | 1599–1642 | Writer on arithmetic | 1616 |
| Sinclair | Sir John, 1st baronet | 1754–1835 | Agricultural improver, politician, and codifier of 'useful knowledge' | 1775 |
| Skinner | John | 1772–1839 | Diarist and antiquary | 1790 |
| Skinner | Robert | 1591–1670 | Bishop of Worcester | 1606 |
| Smalbroke | Richard | 1672–1749 | Bishop of Coventry and Lichfield | 1688 |
| Smith | Arthur Lionel | 1850–1924 | Historian and College head | 1874 |
| Smith | Isaac Gregory | 1826–1920 | Church of England clergyman | 1845 |
| Smith | Jeremiah | 1771–1854 | Headmaster | 1845 |
| Smith | Reginald Bosworth | 1839–1908 | Schoolmaster and author | 1863 |
| Smith | Richard | 1567–1655 | Vicar apostolic of the English Church | 1583 |
| Somers | John, Baron Somers | 1651–1716 | Lawyer and politician | 1667 |
| Somerset | Lord Charles Henry | 1767–1831 | Colonial governor | 1784 |
| Stanford | Henry | *c.*1552–1616 | Compiler of a manuscript miscellany | 1570 |
| Stanhope | James, 1st Earl Stanhope | 1673–1721 | Army officer, diplomat, and politician | 1688 |
| Stanton | Arthur Henry | 1839–1913 | Church of England clergyman | 1858 |
| Stewart | Desmond Stirling | 1924–1981 | Writer | 1942 |
| Stratford | Nicholas | baptized 1633, d. 1707 | Bishop of Chester | 1651 |
| Stuart-Jones | Sir Henry | 1867–1939 | Classical scholar and lexicographer | 1890 |

| | | | | |
|---|---|---|---|---|
| Stubbs | William | 1825–1901 | Historian and Bishop of Oxford | 1848 |
| Summers | (Augustus) Montague [name in religion Alphonsus Joseph-Mary] | 1880–1948 | Literary scholar, occultist, and eccentric | 1899 |
| Sutton | Sir Robert | 1672–1746 | Diplomatist and politician | 1688 |
| Syme | Sir Ronald | 1903–1989 | Roman historian | 1929 |
| Tate | Zouch | 1606–1650 | Politician | 1621 |
| Thomas | Ernest Chester | 1859–1892 | Bibliographer and lawyer | 1870 |
| Thompson | Sir Harold Warris | 1908–1983 | Physical chemist | 1925 |
| Thompson | Henry William [later Henry Byerley] | 1822–1867 | Judge in Ceylon | 1852 |
| Tiddy | Reginald John Elliott | 1880–1916 | Collector of folk plays | 1905 |
| Tindal | William | 1756–1804 | Antiquary | 1772 |
| Tindal-Atkinson | Sir Edward Hale | 1878–1957 | Lawyer | 1897 |
| Twistleton | Edward Turner Boyd | 1809–1874 | Civil servant | 1826 |
| Ullmann | Stephen | 1914–1976 | Linguist and university teacher | 1968 |
| Unwin | Rayner Stephens | 1925–2000 | Publisher and writer | 1944 |
| Vansittart | Robert | 1728–1789 | Jurist | 1745 |
| Verney | Sir Francis | 1584–1615 | Pirate | 1600 |
| Vigors | Nicholas Aylward | 1786–1840 | Zoological administrator and quinarian | 1803 |
| Wace | Henry | 1836–1924 | Dean of Canterbury | 1856 |
| Walmisley | Gilbert | baptized 1682, d. 1751 | Friend of Samuel Johnson | 1698 |
| Walter | John | 1776–1847 | Newspaper proprietor and politician | 1794 |
| Ward | Seth | 1617–1689 | Astronomer and Bishop of Exeter and Salisbury | 1659 |
| Warford | William | *c.*1560–1608 | Jesuit | 1574 |
| Warton | Thomas | 1728–1790 | Poet and historian | 1744 |
| Wentworth | Thomas, Earl of Cleveland | 1591–1667 | Royalist army officer | 1602 |
| Weston | Frank | 1871–1924 | Bishop of Zanzibar | 1890 |

| *Name and title* | | *Life dates* | *Notable as* | *Date of admission to Trinity* |
|---|---|---|---|---|
| Wharton | Edward Ross | 1844–1896 | Philologist and genealogist | 1862 |
| Whistler | Daniel | 1619–1684 | Physician | 1635 |
| Whitby | Daniel | 1638–1726 | Church of England clergyman and author | 1653 |
| Whitehead | Henry | 1853–1947 | Bishop of Madras | 1873 |
| Wildeblood | Peter | 1923–1999 | Journalist and campaigner for homosexual law reform | 1942 |
| Willes | Sir John | 1685–1761 | Judge and politician | 1700 |
| Williams | Isaac | 1802–1865 | Poet and theologian | 1821 |
| Williams | William Peere | 1665–1736 | Law reporter | 1679 |
| Wilmot | James | 1726–1807 | Literary scholar | 1742 |
| Wilson | Arthur | baptized 1595, d. 1652 | Historian | 1631 |
| Wilson | Herbert Wrigley | 1866–1940 | Writer and journalist | 1885 |
| Wind | Edgar Marcel | 1900–1971 | Philosopher and art historian | 1956 |
| Winnington | Sir Francis | 1634–1700 | Lawyer and politician | 1655 |
| Wise | Francis | 1695–1767 | Librarian and antiquary | 1711 |
| Wolseley | Robert | 1648/9–1697 | Eldest son of Sir Charles Wolseley | 1666 |
| Woodd | Basil | 1760–1831 | Hymn writer | 1778 |
| Woodford [Woodforde] | Samuel | 1636–1700 | Poet | 1653 |
| Woods | Donald Devereux | 1912–1964 | Microbiologist | 1951 |
| Wooldridge | Harry Ellis | 1845–1917 | Musician and artist | 1895 |
| Wright | Robert | 1560–1643 | Bishop of Coventry and Lichfield | 1574 |
| Wyllie | John William Shaw | 1835–1870 | Indian civil servant | 1854 |
| Yeldard | Arthur | *c.*1526–1599 | College head | 1555 |
| Young | Peter | 1915–1988 | Army officer and military historian | 1934 |

# Index

Italic type denotes plates. Where two names are identical, dates indicate years of admission to Trinity.

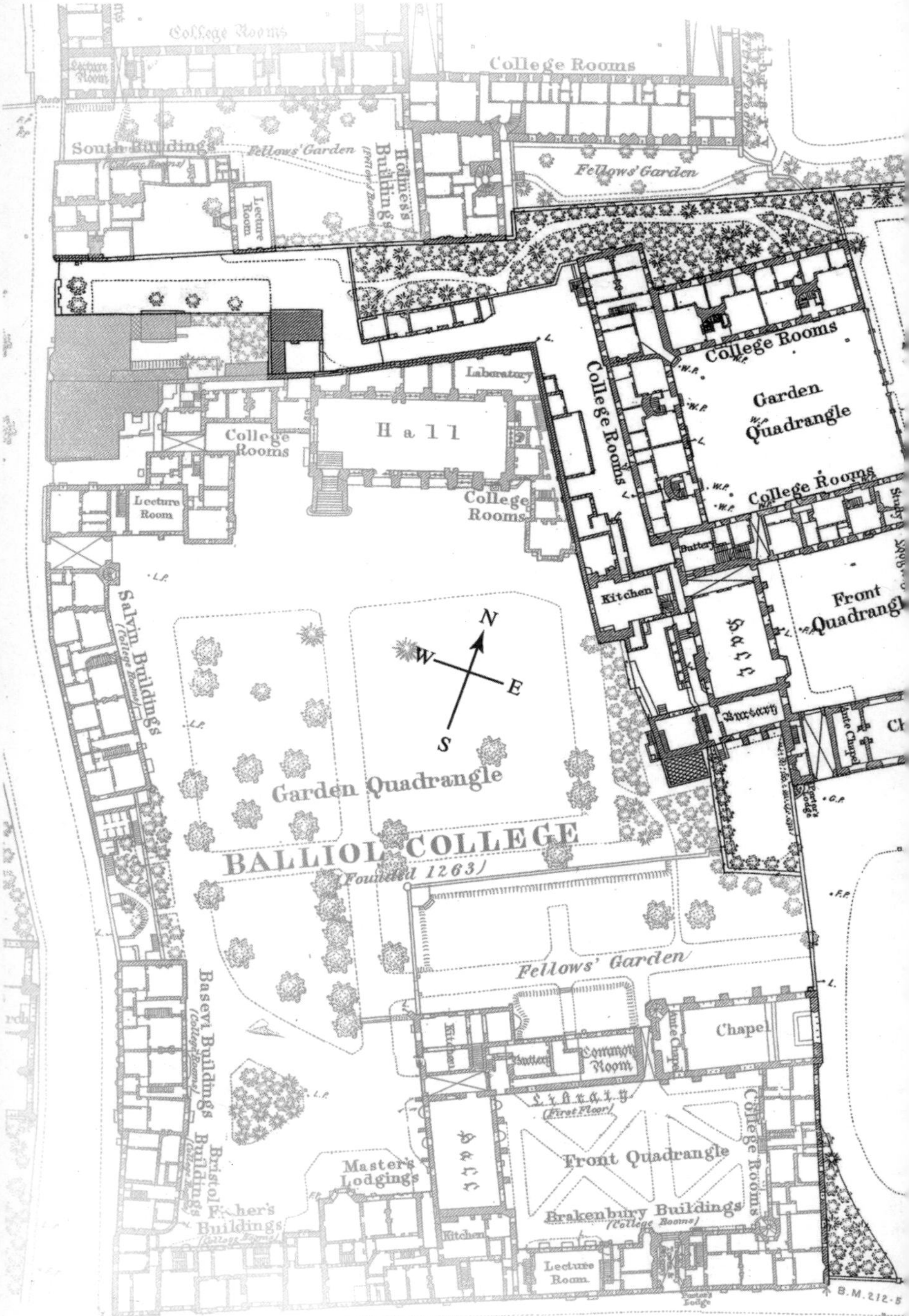

College Rooms
Lecture Room
South Buildings
Fellows' Garden
Holmess' Buildings
Lecture Room
Laboratory
College Rooms
Garden Quadrangle
Hall
College Rooms
Lecture Room
Kitchen
Buttery
Front Quadrangle
Salvin Buildings (College Rooms)
N
W
E
S
Garden Quadrangle
BALLIOL COLLEGE
(Founded 1263)
Fellows' Garden
Chapel
Ante Chapel
Kitchen
Buttery
Common Room
Library (First Floor)
Basevi Buildings (College Rooms)
Bristol Buildings
Fisher's Buildings
Master's Lodgings
Hall
Front Quadrangle
College Rooms
Brakenbury Buildings (College Rooms)
Kitchen
Lecture Room
Porter's Lodge
B.M. 212·5
Near this Cross, the Martyrs Latimer, Ridley & Cranmer
211
B R O A